Commodity Algorithms and Data Structures in C++

Simple and Useful

SECOND EDITION

Dmytro Kedyk

ISBN: 1519572646
ISBN-13: 978-1519572646

Library of Congress Control Number: 2014901334
CreateSpace Independent Publishing Platform: North Charleston, SC

Contents

Preface

This is an advanced book on algorithms and data structures. As such it includes topics that usually aren't covered in an algorithms class, and, for those that are, gives substantial extra material needed for implementation and complete understanding. **"Commodity"** means that, for an algorithm, every important design choice has been extensively researched and validated and is common knowledge. Many times, when considering specific problems, I couldn't find good algorithms for them in existing books, which eventually prompted me to write this one. E.g., how to implement a priority queue that allows keeping track of items for shortest path algorithms.

Every algorithm and data structure is presented mostly in the following format:

1. Description of the problem being solved
2. Description of the algorithm with illustrations of the main ideas
3. All relevant code
4. Performance analysis
5. Comments on methods
6. of optimization, extensions, comparison with other methods, and other interesting information

In some cases, known algorithms weren't good enough, so I developed my own. These aren't published in any other sources (to the best of my knowledge). Some are:

- Garbage-collected freelist (see the "Fundamental Algorithms" chapter)
- Sum heap (see the "Monte Carlo Algorithms" chapter)
- MCMC jump using grid search (see the "Monte Carlo Algorithms" chapter)
- Xorshift hash functions (see the "Hashing" chapter)
- Use of the sign test for decision and regression tree pruning (see the "Machine Learning—Classification" chapter)

The book tries to make clear decisions about which algorithms to use and not to use because I feel that this is very valuable to the reader. Unavoidably, many well-known algorithms are discarded. While such reasoning is often debatable, understanding it is more important than making the final decision about which algorithm to use.

Another controversial decision is using algorithms and data structures presented in the book, and not the ones provided by the C++ STL, as building blocks. Though this may cause some confusion, it allows better testing of the code and has certain usability advantages—e.g., checking bounds in `operator[]` of my own vector quickly caught many bugs that would otherwise take much longer to find. But for real-world development, the code, though reasonably tested, is merely a template for more robust implementations.

To keep things simple, the latest C++ features such as move semantics and lambdas are avoided. E.g., move semantics makes things faster when objects have efficient destructors, but otherwise compiler optimization is generally sufficient. Lambdas are useful, but not everyone is comfortable with them yet.

Though can use the book to learn basic algorithms, for self-study Heineman et al. (2015) is the easiest introduction, and this book is a good follow-up. All the code and some slides are available at https://github.com/dkedyk/CommodityADS2016Code. Feel free to download and play around with it.

Please don't hesitate to e-mail any feedback—I am eager to hear about both what you like about the book and what you feel needs to be added or improved. Enjoy reading, and **expect to learn something new in every chapter**!

References

Heineman, G. T., Pollice, G., & Selkow, S. (2016). *Algorithms in a Nutshell.* O'Reilly.

1 Background

1.1 Prerequisites

- C++, discrete mathematics, and probability theory—essential, for everything
- Computer architecture and operating systems—for some topics
- Statistics and stochastic processes—for more advanced topics, mainly concerning statistical computing
- Familiarity with mathematical proofs—for analysis of various algorithm properties

Specialized chapters such as the "Numerical algorithms" need specific math knowledge such as linear algebra and differential equations. Also, the book is meant to be read sequentially because some later chapters rely on some earlier ones.

1.2 Logics of Reasoning

A **logic** assumes **axioms** to decide truth of **statements** in a language. It's **complete** if every true statement is provable and **consistent** if false statements are unprovable. A statement true for all/some variable values is a **tautology/satisfiable**. It's possible to model many properties of algorithms using various logics, and this section, though not essential, intends to familiarize the reader with the most important ones.

Propositional logic has true/false variables and statements formed using Boolean operators *and* ("&"), *not* ("!"), *or* ("|"), *implies* ("→"), *xor* ("^"), *nand* ("#"), etc. A **truth table** evaluates a statement ∀ value assignment, showing if it's a tautology, satisfiable, or unsatisfiable. Each above operator is defined by a truth table of size 4 with all value assignments.

A **tableau system** is more efficient. Two **clauses** connected by an operator must evaluate to particular values for the operator to evaluate to a particular value. Let T(x)/F(x) mean that x is respectively true/false. Then T(x & y) ↔ Tx & Ty, F(x & y) ↔ Fx | Fy, T!x ↔ Fx, and F!x ↔ Tx. To prove x a tautology/unsatisfiable, disprove Fx/Tx. Applying the rules creates a tree with branches created by the *or* rules. A statement is false if !∃ contradiction-free path from the root to any leaf. Otherwise, values on such a path form a counter-example. E.g., to show that (x # x) # x is a tautology, from the definition of "#" deduce T(x # y) ↔ Fx | Fy and F(x # y) ↔ Tx & Ty. Then create the tree:

1. F((x # x) # x)
2. T(x # x)
3. Tx
4. Fx____Fx //from 2

Both branches contain Tx/Fx contradictions, so (x # x) # x is a tautology. To show that (x | y) & (!x | y) is satisfiable:

1. T((x | y) & (!x | y))
2. T(x | y)
3. T(!x | y)
4. Tx________________Ty //from 2
5. Fx____Ty //from 3   Fx____Ty //from 3

So satisfiable with Ty and either Tx or Fx.

A **reasoning rule** is a tautology of the form $A \to B$, e.g., (x & ($x \to y$)) $\to y$. A **fact** is any true statement. Can use both in tableau proofs, e.g., label T(x & !x) a contradiction without expanding it. Logic programming language Prolog automates such reasoning.

First-order logic is propositional logic with "∀" (for each/any) and "∃" (exists), which apply to each variable at most once. Let b be a bound variable ∉ tableau and f a free variable substitutable for any other variable. ∀ statement C containing variable x:

- $!\exists x C(x) \leftrightarrow \forall x !C(x)$
- $!\forall x C(x) \leftrightarrow \exists x !C(x)$

- $T\exists xC(x) \leftrightarrow TC(b)$
- $F\exists xC(x) \leftrightarrow FC(f)$
- $T\forall xC(x) \leftrightarrow TC(f)$
- $F\forall xC(x) \leftrightarrow FC(b)$

E.g., to prove $\exists y\forall xC(x,y) \rightarrow \forall x\exists yC(x,y)$:

1. $F(\exists y\forall xC(x,y) \rightarrow \forall x\exists yC(x,y))$
2. $T\exists y\forall xC(x,y)$
3. $F\forall x\exists yC(x,y)$
4. $T\forall xC(x, b_1)$ (from 2)
5. $TC(f_1, b_1)$ (from 4)
6. $F\exists yC(b_2, y)$ (from 3)
7. $FC(b_2, f_2)$ (from 6)
8. $TC(b_2, b_1)$ (from 5)
9. $FC(b_2, b_1)$)—contradiction (from 7)

Deciding values of free variables isn't mechanical. Trying each variable in the tableau proves every true statement, but ∀ unprovable one needn't terminate. For more on tableau proofs, see Smullyan (2014).

Second-order logic, which is the most natural logic, allows quantification over sets. It's incomplete because ∃ statements that lead to contradictions if provable. Need simpler logics.

Logic of knowledge is first order logic where agent *i* may know the truth of statement *x*. Additional axioms:

- $K_ix \rightarrow x$—if an agent knows something, it's true
- $K_ix \rightarrow K_iK_ix$—an agent is aware of what it knows
- $!K_ix \rightarrow K_i!K_ix$— an agent is aware of what it doesn't know
- $K_i(x \rightarrow y) \rightarrow (K_ix \rightarrow K_iy)$—allows an agent to deduce new knowledge

Note that $x \rightarrow K_ix$ is false.

Other logics are also useful for expressing various properties of algorithms:

- **Belief**—an agent may believe something false.
- **Temporal**—a statement's truth depends on discrete time and have additional operators *always* and *eventually*. E.g., *power failure & always traffic light isn't green on both sides* is a requirement for traffic lights.

1.3 Software Development

To create and maintain systems that solve problems of **economic value**, a team of developers usually:

- Identifies customer needs and specifies minimal functionality requirements. A **use case** is a complete user interaction scenario with the system.
- Designs high-level components to give each one distinct responsibility and maximize reuse. The resulting **system architecture** should have modular, extendable component structure to allow changes without needing substantial modification or increase in complexity. **Patterns** are documented, reusable good designs.
- Implements and tests the first version, developing algorithms and business logic ∀component and continuously revising requirements and component structure.
- Modifies the system for the rest of its deployment in response to enhancement requests, bug reports, and technology changes.

Experience shows that:

- Typical systems are large after years of development.
- Developer turnover, lack of documentation, and legacy technologies make parts of a system difficult to maintain. Systems with such characteristics and simple business logic are often completely rewritten.
- System rewrites can be problematic because **certain important use cases are expressed only in code** and invoked too rarely to be noticed. Migrating databases is particularly problematic because data can be modified or entered incorrectly, common-sense-encoded to bypass system constraints, not updated to reflect reality, or viewed through special, unknown error-correcting logic. **Automated regression** of all use cases is usually the only way to avoid mistakes, but not fool-proof

because rare or hard-to-test use cases can be missing.

- The only reliable documentation is the user manual and testing instructions or programs. Requirements and design decisions are often discussed informally and, even if recorded, are often invalidated by subsequent smaller changes. People who discussed them have vague memories and can switch departments or quit.
- Having standards for GUI design makes user experience consistent and more productive. Developers are naturally concerned with code and not GUI, but the system is what the user sees.
- Giving accurate estimates on how much time work will take is impossible due to unique aspects of each project, discovered only during design or implementation. To get a rough estimate, it's usually best to average the estimates of several informed developers (see bias-variance decomposition in the "General Machine Learning" chapter for a mathematical justification). To improve accuracy, they have a discussion to find out the reasons behind any differences.
- **Code reviews** and frequent testing of all functionality substantially reduce bugs.
- Releasing new functionality to users is the most critical activity in the development process and must be done right. Have all changes reviewed and tested, and make all stakeholders aware of the release.
- Useful development activities produce value. **Eliminate wasteful ones**. Usually these are easy to distinguish because the useful ones have been validated—e.g., testing, code reviews, documentation, automation tools, etc.
- Sometimes it's hard to tell if an activity is useful because this may be project-specific. So a development process should be **suggestive**, and not prescriptive, to allow developers to decide as needed.
- **Developers generally work on one small problem at a time** by understanding it, coming up with an initial solution, testing it on some input, and revising until correct. Also, instead of following a top-down or bottom-up process, they exploit mental "locality of reference" by solving one small subproblem at a time and moving on to a related subproblem.
- The most critical developer skill is the ability to model a problem abstractly.
- Automated tools such as IDEs, profilers, static analysis, version control, and debuggers bring substantial value.
- Developers do the best they can with what they have. High-quality libraries of supporting technologies are essential. Companies make low-level libraries open source to cut maintenance costs.
- Regardless of the developers' knowledge, almost any nontrivial project **needs learning** properties of considered technologies, users' needs, and properties of the deployment environment.

1.4 Patterns

Patterns are recipes for various system aspects (Buschmann et al. 2007).

Architectural—for organizing system components:

- **Layers**—assign levels to components and call lower or same-level functions from high-level functions. Used in every system where a high-level business logic component calls algorithm, network, screen, and other libraries.
- **Pipeline**—transform input by a sequence of components. Each performs specific work on its input and passes on the result. E.g., washer and dryer.
- **Model-view-controller** (MVC)—separate components handle data, how it's viewed, and user actions. The model contains data and a list of subscribed views, to which it sends updates. The controller manipulates views or changes data to process user requests. Organize views into a **transformation pipeline** and separate data from its presentation.
- **Blackboard**—several knowledge sources update data in a shared repository. E.g., several people solving a jigsaw puzzle. Used for problems that need a complex solution strategy, mostly for AI.
- **Reflection**—have a way to interact with components using a secondary interface, hidden from clients. Used to send configuration commands or collect statistics.
- **Declarative configuration**— use editable settings files to initialize components, making deployment more flexible.

- **Replicated components**—replicate very critical components, possibly using a different design. A manager component hides this from the caller, sending requests to all and returning the first or the majority answer. Allows parallel processing and taking components offline for maintenance.
- **Context object**—instead of maintaining state during component interaction, pass around an object with state. Allows to not store state.
- **Safe interface**—public/private methods trust nothing/everything. E.g., in case of concurrency, public methods ask for locks and private ones don't. For security, public methods check authorization and private ones don't.
- **Data normalization**—avoid redundancy in data as much as possible to avoid wrong and inconsistent data.

Design—for higher-level code issues:

- **Factory**—to create a complex object with desired properties, encapsulate creation in a separate function to isolate the complexity.
- **Builder**—if need several steps to construct an object, create, instead of a constructor with many parameters, an object that allows to construct its parts and retrieve the complete result.
- **Prototype**—to copy a complex object, create a cloning method that copies. C++ uses copy constructor and assignment operator.
- **Singleton**—to restrict the number of object instances to one, create a static function that returns the instance. It becomes available from any place in the code, but concurrent use needs a lock.
- **Command**—actions are objects with an `execute()` method. C++ uses `operator()`. Used to give actions state and make them generic.
- **Strategy**—to change behavior at runtime, assign a member object that causes the change. For behaviors determined statically, use a code, and for dynamically, a pointer to a command object.
- **Composite**—an object holds a list of several subobjects from which it's composed, and an operation on it applies to its own data and every subobject on the list. E.g., to `draw()` a complex object, `draw()` each subobject it contains.
- **Facade**—if several systems provide related functionality, create an interface to join them, possibly with a modified API. E.g., if must call several functions in specific order, create a single function with the fewest parameters that makes the calls.
- **Proxy**—represent an object by another object. E.g., `operator[]` for STL bitset returns a reference object that's constructible from and assignable to a Boolean.
- **Encapsulated implementation**—separate interface and implementation. Keeps API implementation secret and allows dynamically linked library updates without recompiling the caller. In C++, use the pointer to implementation idiom (PIMPL).
- **Iterator**—to go through all items in a data structure, create an iterator object that can efficiently access an item, go to the next one, and check if ∃ unvisited items.

Security:

- **Authorization**—pass an object holding access rights to functions that check authorization. E.g., if a user is logged in, the object contains login data.
- **Firewall**—check requests for safety by a firewall component before forwarding to applications. A firewall validates things not considered by an application's precondition checks. E.g., it can drop requests that come too often from a single client.
- **Role-based access**—create roles, each with only the needed privileges. Simplifies privilege management.

Concurrency and distribution:

- **Broker**—each component communicates to others through a proxy. E.g., applications needing network access use a router. Reduces the number of connections and decouples networking functionality.
- **Reactor**—a thread waits for and puts events into one of several queues, while other threads process events in each queue sequentially. Allows flexible concurrent event processing.
- **Proactor**—requests are asynchronous, with a handler waiting for the results, identified by unique completion tokens.

Resource management:

- **Resource acquisition is initialization** (RAII)—get resources in constructors and release in destructors. Ensures release in case of exceptions and multiple `return`s. In C++, use with `{}` for control.
- **Lookup**—a directory service tracks available services.
- **Resource pool**—keep a cache of resources, possibly leasing some if not using many.
- **Lazy acquisition**—get resources at the last moment and release as soon as possible. Maximizes resource availability to other applications.
- **Eager acquisition**—get all resources at start-up. Improves reliability.
- **Partial acquisition**—get resources in stages. E.g., online video buffers and plays before it's fully downloaded.
- **Leasing**—give resources for a limited time and take them back after it elapses. E.g., don't renew authorization for inactive users.
- **Reference counting**—∀ resource keep a count and release if count = 0. Useful if accessing a resource from several places and using dynamic memory.

1.5 Commodity Algorithms

An **algorithm** is a well-defined input-to-output transformation. A **data structure** allows efficient access and updates to stored data. To support software development effectively, both must be:

- **Correct** by providing a satisfactory solution to the exact problem. A formal proof, extensive testing, or intuition can deem an algorithm and its implementation correct. Can get only correctness with high certainty because formal proofs can be unobtainable, intuition wrong, and rarely invoked logic untested. Correctness can be randomized, so that an algorithm, wrong less often than the computer is hit by lightning, is effectively correct. An algorithm should verify its inputs when feasible and report failures such as the inability to allocate memory.
- **Extendable** by being applicable to general problems with only minor changes. Real-world problems have extra constraints that need augmenting existing algorithms. An algorithm that applies to a variety of problems is more valuable than a collection of top-performing custom algorithms ∀ problem. An implementation is extendable if the code applies to many problems unchanged.
- **Relatively simple** to understand, implement in different environments, and use as an abstract building block. Simplicity of understanding is measured by how long it takes to understand what the algorithm does in all cases, of implementation by the number of lines of properly structured code, and of use by how clean the API is in terms of the number of functions, their parameters, and presence of good defaults. An important part of simplicity of understanding is that everything useful about the algorithm is known, including theorems describing its behavior and details needed for a robust, efficient implementation.
- **Sufficiently efficient** in use of valuable resources, at least on practical problems. CPU time and memory are often the most important. Can't use more memory than time if accessing every used bit, but memory is more important because can wait for another hour but not another RAM chip, and, unlike time, memory accumulates. Other resources such as locks, file handles, network ports, requests to another process, and electrical energy also matter. Usually, paid development time and time waiting for the system to react are the most valuable. Humans don't differentiate between response times < 150 milliseconds, so no need to optimize response times below that.
- **Legal to use**. Many aspects of algorithms are intellectual property. Patents and trade secrets protect ideas, trademarks names, and copyrights code. Using protected software, including open source, requires a special contract called a license (see the "Introduction to Computer Law" chapter).

Correct, efficient, and legal algorithm is **useful**. Simplicity and extendability reduce development and maintenance time. A **commodity algorithm** is useful, simple, and extendable. In economics, a commodity is a cheaply available, highly used good or service. A system composed of commodity algorithms handles users' requests correctly and efficiently and allows quick feature addition and debugging.

Many useful algorithms giving solutions of substantial economic value aren't commodities, and domain experts design libraries of them for years. Such **algorithm engineering** produced impressive results in linear programming, finding shortest paths in continental road networks, computational geometry, etc. But can't fix library bugs yourself, and have no guarantee that the sublibraries are legal. Nevertheless, even for commodity algorithms, use the best available library and not something programmed yourself. Structure libraries in layers to maximize reuse and allow finding reusable components efficiently.

1.6 Proving Correctness

Input/output properties are **preconditions/postconditions**. They form an **algorithm's contract**, which is a guarantee that an input satisfying preconditions leads to an output satisfying postconditions. Correctness proofs show that, given precondition, postcondition holds and are feasible for many algorithms.

An **invariant** is a property that holds during a computation, particularly loops. Though not part of a contract, it helps to think about correctness after a particular stage of computation. E.g., consider trying to find the smallest and the second smallest elements in an integer array, returned by array indices, which may not be equal. This is a popular interview question, and a general solution is to keep two index variables and incrementally update them in a loop. But trying to solve this without an invariant usually leads to issues because it's hard to correct poor initialization in a loop. The simplest invariant is that after seeing k out of n elements, the minimum is correct and second minimum is −1 or correct. The clear, correct solution is then to initialize the minimum to 0, the second minimum to −1, and loop from index 1.

A function calling another assumes that the latter satisfies its contract. Preconditions of the callee propagate to the caller, and for a high-level function, the exact contract can be hard to find out. E.g., correct video streaming produces an error message if network data lookup fails.

1.7 Binary Polynomials

A bit string with bit i set represents a polynomial with binary coefficients, which has the term of degree i + 1. E.g., byte 00001101 represents $x^3 + x^2 + 1$. Multiword arithmetic with binary polynomials is more efficient than with numbers:

- $p + q = p - q$—p ^ q
- px—p << 1
- p/x—p >> 1 with remainder p & 1
- pq—term by term multiplication like with numbers
- pp—squaring each term because cross terms cancel out
- p/q and p % q—long division by repeatedly subtracting largest $qx^m < p$ from p

1.8 Error Management

A component goes into a **bad state** because of one or more of a:

- Bug
- Failure of a dependent component such as a database, a network connection, or a memory allocator
- Lag due to serving too many requests
- Model of computation error by memory corruption or loss of power

To avoid or limit loss of value for a **critical system**, consider:

- Limiting error impact
- Reporting errors to callers
- Trying to correct errors
- Trying to put the system into a good state

For critical components, develop management procedures ∀ likely error type. Solution patterns include (Buschmann et al. 2007):

- **Sanity checks**—check all preconditions, possibly invariants, and postconditions. Minimizes error effect on a component's state and helps catch bugs. Use assertions, exceptions, or error return codes. Exceptions and return codes don't force a crash, but for potentially unrecoverable conditions, such as out-of-bounds access, assertions are appropriate. For complex algorithms, sanity checks may be infeasible due to needing recomputation.
- **Execution trace**—all critical computations record a summary of inputs, invariants, and used resources. Allows to detect sources of errors and configure components dynamically. E.g., a manager component may restart a component that produced the trace for starting a computation but didn't produce the trace for finishing it after some time.

- **Known good state**—have a way to force the system into a known good state. A restart fixes most issues in most systems. Keep a previous version of the component ready to be deployed in case the new one fails.
- **Redundant data**—avoids model of computation errors with high probability. E.g., if a bank loses electricity after debiting a source account and before crediting the destination, without redundancy, the client would lose money.
- **Dedicated components**— $\exists$several component copies, each serving a specific part of the functionality. Then a copy's failure affects only its part of the functionality.
- **Multiple components**—maintains service if several components become unresponsive. The components should be separate processes at different computers and locations.
- **Replicated components pattern**—for avoiding random errors. Employed in systems that can't be wrong, such as airplane control. Using three independently developed components and picking the majority answer substantially reduces Pr(error).
- **Functionality reduction**—put an erring component in a reduced-functionality mode where it does only critical operations. Avoids future errors and is effective for performance issues.

A component is **robust** if it effectively handles precondition violations.

1.9 Asymptotic Notation

An algorithm working on an input of n items uses $r(n)$ resources, which for a large enough n, any constant b, and some constant c is:

- $O(f(n))$ iff $r(n)/f(n) \leq c$
- $o(f(n))$ iff $r(n)/f(n) < b$
- $\Theta(f(n))$ iff $r(n)/f(n) = c$
- $\omega(f(n))$ iff $r(n)/f(n) > b$
- $\Omega(f(n))$ iff $r(n)/f(n) \geq c$

Common $f(n)$ are 1, $\lg(n)$, $\sqrt{n}$, n, $n\lg(n)$, n^2, n^3, 2^n, and $n!$. Use the slowest growing $f(n)$ that applies. To check if a function grows faster than another, use the L'Hospital's rule. Superlinear memory and superquadratic runtime aren't scalable for typical tasks.

Asymptotic notation simplifies analysis by ignoring constant factors. Doing $O(f(n))$ computation $O(g(n))$ times is $O(f(n)g(n))$. E.g., if the body of a loop over the input takes $O(1)$ time, the runtime is $O(n)$.

1.10 Machine Models

A **machine model** is a set of operations with known contracts and efficiency. All programs consist of assembly language operations supported by the CPU and other hardware. The CPU operates on integer words of size $w = 32$ or 64, allowing 2^w memory locations. A `double` provides limited precision real arithmetic and has 1 bit for sign s, 52 for word w, and 11 for exponent e to represent $(-1)^s w2^e$. The CPU accesses caches, memory, disks, and other resources to get data and simultaneously executes many programs, which compete for resources. Simplified models assume different operation costs. For modern computers:

- Arithmetic, logical, and bit operations on `int`s and `double`s and function calls take $O(1)$ CPU cycles, with all except divisions taking about the same time and conditionals slowing CPU pipelining.
- Reading and writing from cache and memory take $O(1)$ cycles, but CPU registers are ≈ 100 times faster than memory and 10 than cache.
- Dynamic memory allocation and deallocation are done in software and take large $O(1)$ time even for large arrays, without the cost of constructors and destructors.
- Accessing devices such as disks, external drives, screens, and network routers takes thousands of cycles, though $O(1)$ if the exchanged data size is bounded.
- Waiting for a lock can take a long time, and managing it takes hundreds of cycles.

Models designed to simplify analysis ignore small constant factors and consider only particular bottleneck operations:

- **Word RAM**—all operations are on words of size $w > \lg$(input size) and take $O(1)$ time. Memory is unlimited. Don't have other resources. Most algorithms assume this.

- **Real RAM**—word RAM with infinite precision `double`. Avoids dealing with rounding errors.
- **Representative operations**—all operations except assumed bottlenecks cost 0. Helps to focus on the relevant operations.
- **I/O**—accessing various devices, particularly disks, takes large O(1) time when exchanged data size $\leq B$. Useful when device access is the bottleneck.
- **PRAM**—word RAM with ∞ parallel processors and shared memory; communication between processors costs 0. Shows limits of scalability.

Some models assume upper bounds instead of assigning costs and aren't machine models:

- **Real-time**—computing answers has deadlines, missing which is too costly.
- **Stream**—have O(1) memory, and inputs arrive continuously. Processing each may be real-time, e.g., for a network router. Generalization of the I/O model.
- **Massive data**—processing trillions of inputs stored on disk or streamed. Requires scalable processing times of maybe $O(n\lg(n))$.

1.11 Testing

Untested algorithms are usually wrong. Testing runs an algorithm with a subset of all possible inputs and checks if the outputs satisfy the contract. If the subset $\neq$ all possible inputs, testing can't prove absence of bugs, but increases confidence that none exist and checks performance problems.

Partition inputs into classes so that $\forall$contract condition $\exists$ a representative class and within a class pick inputs randomly. If such partitioning is difficult or inefficient, use random inputs to eventually test all cases; missing the rare ones during the finite testing time is okay.

Unit testing tests components individually, and **integration testing** tests the whole system. Theoretically, integration testing is enough, but unit testing discovers bugs faster because system test cases might miss a component's hard-to-invoke logic. **Automated regression** runs a system against many inputs.

Black box testing tests a system without knowledge of its implementation, and **white box testing** uses implementation knowledge to select inputs. For large systems, the latter is infeasible because a lot of complex code can implement simple business logic. For small algorithms, use white box testing to check border cases, such as the smallest and the largest inputs, which developers tend to neglect.

Testing can prove absence of bugs with very high certainty, though not 100%. If executing a use case gives loss 1 if anything fails and 0 otherwise, after n correct use cases, the chance of seeing a problem is $O(1/n)$ (by using the rule of three; see the "Monte Carlo Algorithms" chapter).

1.12 Randomized Algorithms

$\forall$ game $\exists$ an optimal randomized strategy even if $!\exists$ an optimal deterministic one. E.g., for rock-paper-scissors, the random choice draws on average, but a deterministic strategy is learnable. Randomization may allow processing inputs unpredictably with good expected performance when doing so deterministically is slow in the worst case. Randomized algorithms use a pseudorandom number generator such as `rand()` to make decisions and assume it's perfectly random.

A **Monte Carlo algorithm** gives wrong answers with some probability. A special case is a decision algorithm whose "yes" is correct and "no" wrong with probability p. Running it k times and getting "no" lowers failure probability to p^k.

A **Las Vegas algorithm** has expected efficiency. Repeating a Monte Carlo algorithm that has an answer verifier until the answer is correct creates a Las Vegas algorithm. If $!\exists$ a verifier, but can combine answers from different runs by a majority vote, repetition lowers failure probability.

Probability of a randomized algorithm's error or excessive inefficiency is often negligibly small. To analyze a Las Vegas algorithm consider its luck:

- Worst luck and input give the worst case
- Best luck and input give the best case
- Best luck and worst input give the lower bound

Randomized algorithms are often the most efficient ones, in particular for finding strings in a large text (see the "String Algorithms" chapter), testing if a number is prime (see the "Large Numbers" chapter), etc.

Perhaps the biggest problem in applying Las Vegas algorithms is their variance in metrics other than runtime. In some cases, this influences the results in an unpredictable way (e.g., with equal values, different random permutations result in different minimums). Also, for algorithms that approximate the answer, the quality of the result can differ from run to run.

1.13 Measuring Efficiency

∃ several ways of measuring resource use:

- Max/worst case—gives complete confidence, but can be much higher than expected average.
- Expected average over the algorithm's random choices or input randomness—with the former the result is input-independent, but sometimes only the latter is available.
- Pr(use > certain number)—acts as worst case for Las Vegas algorithms when negligibly small.
- **Amortized**—average worst case for a sequence of operations—allows occasionally expensive operations.
- **Competitive ratio**—max multiplicative factor by which a perfectly lucky algorithm beats an **online algorithm** when receiving inputs one by one and maintaining the best answer (e.g., LRU cache replacement is 2-competitive).
- **Smoothed**—expected average over the randomness of randomly perturbed worst case input. The middle between worst case and random by input, designed for algorithms with poor worst case and good practical performance (Müller-Hannemann & Schirra 2010).

Each can be:

- Exact—complexity has O(1) coefficients and relevant lower-order terms. Makes sense only if primitive operations have known exact costs.
- Asymptotic—asymptotically efficient solutions are timeless, machine-independent, and easy to compare, but allow hiding huge O(1) factors and justifying algorithms superior only for unrealistically large inputs.
- Experimental—average of running the algorithm on different problems many times.

Maximum, expected average, and amortized are more informative in this order when of the same complexity, though amortized is better than expected average in some cases. E.g., an algorithm calling O(lg(n)), amortized O(1), and expected O(1) algorithms is O(lg(n)) expected amortized. Worst case is propagated to the depending problems, but others aren't.

An algorithm's contract defines an information-theoretic lower bound on the efficiency of any algorithm for the task (e.g., any algorithm needs to at least read every input bit).

1.14 Data Types

A **data type** is a set of values. It's (Stepanov 2009):

- **Well-formable** if any bit sequence assigned to an object of its type represents a valid value. E.g., if a Boolean is a char with 1 = true and 0 = false, what is 2?
- **Partially formable** if the default constructor creates destructible objects that can be assigned to. Partially formable types can't have contracts if correctness needs construction from passed data.
- **Ambiguous** if the same bit sequence represents many logical values. E.g., dates with two-digit years don't distinguish centuries.
- **Uniquely represented** if every value corresponds to a unique bit sequence. E.g., for a Boolean represented by a byte, 0 is false, and anything else true.
- **Copyable** if it has a destructor, a copy constructor, and an assignment operator. This is the minimum requirement for placing objects into data structures.

The **value** of an object is what is obtainable from its public interface and is a subset of the object's state. A function is **regular** if replacing inputs with those of equal value doesn't change the output's value. E.g., random number generators, data readers, and timers aren't regular. Any function that uses properties of inputs not looked at by equality, such as memory addresses, isn't regular.

Representation of a type is one of a:

- Word
- Pointer to a type
- Array of types
- Structure of types

Functions defined on a type are its **computational basis**. A basis is:

- **Minimal** if using it can do all useful operations with negligible efficiency loss. For simplicity prefer smaller computational bases.
- **Expressive** if it includes convenience functions implemented in terms of the minimal basis.

In a large system, define classes with minimal bases and use nonmember functions or layers and facade patterns to give more functionality. For a complex type, a complete computational basis may be unknown, particularly when it's extended with augmentations, so libraries provide a reasonably complete set of operations to satisfy almost all users, while forcing some to implement customized data structures. This is much like abstract algebra, where the goal is to do computation with structures of limited ability. In C++, templates are also similar because can only rely on the subtypes and the functions defined within a type.

A type without pointers is **plain old data** (POD). A data structure provides **address persistence** if only deletions invalidate item addresses. A **concept** is a collection of data types with a common computational basis. E.g., copyable types define a containable item.

APIs must be designed as though they would become part of a language's standard library. In particular, avoid unjustified magic numbers as parameters.

1.15 Algorithm Experiments

To study performance of an algorithm to explain its behavior, or to compare performances with statistical significance:

1. Pick factors to study. A **factor** is any property, such as input size or a problem-specific input difficulty category, that influences the measurements. Pick input sizes by doubling to max values that patience allows. Algorithm and its configuration choices are also useful factors.
2. Pick metrics. Include resource use and operation counts for expensive or interesting operations and specialized metrics, such as solution quality for optimization problems. Operation counts is portable, but machine and compiler optimization differences affect resource use.
3. Pick inputs. Try to represent every factor value combination or at least each factor value. Common input types and their minor problems:
    - Real-world from industry—usually unavailable
    - From publicly available test libraries— needn't have unbiased samples
    - Randomly generated—may have special properties that make algorithms behave differently than with real-world inputs
4. Run tests in an unbiased environment with the same light system load where only the picked factors influence the results. Run deterministic algorithms on all inputs once. If the algorithms or the environment are random, run on the same input until know the averages of all measures with high accuracy.
5. Analyze the results using statistical techniques:
    - Linear regression (or lasso; see the "Machine Learning—Regression" chapter) on operation counts and resource use may predict the latter as a function of the former.
    - Regression with resource use or operation counts and inputs including 1, lg(n), $\sqrt{n}$, n, $n$lg(n), and n^2 may accurately show asymptotic performance.
    - If determined input size values by doubling, regression with lg of resource use or operation counts guesses a polynomial performance exponent.
    - For a given metric and factor combination, variance of the average shows the confidence with which it's known and may allow concluding that one algorithm is better than another. Beware of multiple comparison (see the "Monte Carlo Algorithms" chapter).
6. Optionally publish your results. They must be **newsworthy**, i.e., lead to valuable, new, and reproducible conclusions. Also publish unobtainable inputs and implementations. Many papers aren't newsworthy by reporting:
    - Already published conclusions. This is generally okay only if the latter aren't statistically significant, look at different factors, or use a different environment.
    - Nonportable metrics for specialized machines. Showing relative and not absolute values and reporting machine and compiler settings can sometimes fix this.
    - Results with no statistical significance.

- Results that don't lead to useful insight.

1.16 Memory Management

The operating system hands out memory in large byte arrays of size 512KB–4MB, called pages. Any executable uses at least one page. C++ `new` and `delete` partition pages into smaller blocks. An application needing more memory requests another page (or several if request > page size). Unused pages are returned.

On some machines, *x*-byte variables must be in an address divisible by *x*. The compiler does alignment unless variables are cast and reinterpreted. E.g., allocating `char x[8]`, placing a `double` there, and accessing it as a `double` may cause a hardware exception. For `struct Aligned{double d; char c;}` size is 16, and for `struct NotAligned{char c[9];}` 9.

A memory manager adds padding and bookkeeping to each allocated item. It satisfies alignment without knowing the type, and supports raw memory requests malloc and free used by constructor-based `new` and `delete`. ∃ theoretical limits on the worst case memory efficiency of any memory manager, but these don't occur in practice even in long-running systems. For well-implemented memory managers such as combinations of first fit and segregated lists (Bryant 2010):

- Operations take large O(1) time
- Wasted memory per allocation is 4–8 bytes
- Can't use a fraction of memory consisting of small disconnected chunks
- Most applications allocate many small items

1.17 Code Optimization

Make the code:

- Generic—express common functionality once and reuse it. Don't copy and paste or manually perform bloating optimizations such as inlining, loop unrolling, or replacing an expensive operation with a sequence of cheap ones. Don't overgeneralize by handling cases that won't be needed. Delete any unused code.
- Simple—short and self-documenting. Use consistent style, shortest descriptive names, and comment only high level actions.
- Efficient—the compiler's assembly output determines the ultimate efficiency. Unless you need debugging, enable the maximum optimization level that produces a portable executable and doesn't change semantics. The compiler can evaluate constant expressions, reorder instructions, inline a function by replacing its call with its body, etc. Assist it by writing the shortest code that is maximally restricted—use `const` when applicable, minimize variable scope, use minimal number of return statements, etc. Beware that aggressive optimization has been known to create bugs, though very rarely.

Efficiency should come from better algorithms and compiler optimizations. But sometimes manual optimizations help:

- Beware of machine-specific, undefined behavior. E.g., on mine −5 % 2 = −1.
- Profile the code to see where it spends most resources. Try to cut out that activity or optimize it by improving the logic.
- Using `void*` instead of templates prevents inlining and optimizations that use information about the function. Use `void*` only to hide implementation, compiling the cpp file as a library, with the header using a template wrapper around the `void*` for type safety.
- Disabling assertions by defining `NDEBUG` gains almost nothing but loses substantial debugging.
- Optimize alignment—the compiler inserts dummy bytes for alignment, and `sizeof`(structure) ≥ ∑`sizeof`(its elements). Variable order matters—e.g., `struct Wasteful{char a; double d; char b;}` has size 24, and `struct Smart{double d; char a; char b;}` 16. Declare bigger objects first; array size = its element size, and structure size = its `sizeof`.
- The compiler doesn't optimize floating point arithmetic or code that depends on its result because doing so usually changes semantics. E.g., addition isn't associative due to round-off, so it can't rearrange computations.

- The compiler converts a `switch` or an `if` sequence into one of an `if` sequence, a binary search, or an array of jump pointers indexed by case constants, so use whichever makes most sense.
- A loop evaluates its termination condition at every iteration, and the compiler moves it outside only if it can prove that doing so doesn't change semantics.
- Loading a large block of data from memory, processing it, and moving on to another one improves cache efficiency.
- Try making computations not depend on conditionals—the compiler guesses which instruction will go into the pipeline next, and, if wrong, the CPU redoes the computations.
- Return fat objects by reference to avoid extra copying unless the function interface becomes ugly or the compiler can optimize the copy.
- Don't use sentinels—many algorithms assume ∞ or null items to simplify presentation or avoid checks, but:
    - Branch prediction reduces the cost of saved comparisons
    - A general type doesn't have a logical ∞
    - A sentinel may need extra space that's unavailable
    - The computation is usually more difficult to understand
- Compute as much as possible at compile time, but don't use complicated techniques such as template meta-programming. Reduce the amount of code under a template. E.g., C++ pointer vectors have a `void*` specialization. If only a method of a class needs to be a template, don't make the class a template.
- Allocating memory in blocks of powers of two is efficient with all allocators. Beware that the OS doesn't allow arrays larger than some size.
- Don't use static and global variables because their total memory use could be large. Put variables on the stack with maximally restricted scope.
- Converting an array of Booleans to a bitset saves space but slows access.

1.18 Recursion

A recursive function puts local variables on the stack, calls itself, and waits for the return. For efficiency, put variables and parameters that don't change or appear before the recursive call inside `{}`, or make them class members.

Recursion depth is limited by the OS stack size. It also affects local variables and isn't portable (e.g., on my machine allocating an `int` array of size > 2^{19} crashes). Make any recursive algorithm that needs a large stack nonrecursive. This also optimizes function call overhead and enables inlining.

Tail recursion is when the recursive call is the function's last statement. To convert it to iteration:

1. Put a loop around the function call
2. Put any remembered variables outside the loop
3. At the loop's end, set values of the parameters passed to the recursive call and remove it

This simplifies the code unless it uses references. To remove general recursion, keep a stack of records to allow the algorithm to resume its work after a `return`, and put a loop around the recursive work that `break`s when the stack is empty. To ease thinking, formulate the algorithm nonrecursively by mentally executing it.

Can analyze many recursive algorithms using the **master theorem**: Let resource use $R(n) = f(n) + a(R(n/b)$ for $n >$ constant C and O(1) otherwise, and $k = \log_b(a)$. Then $R(n)$ is

- $\Theta(n^k)$ if $f(n) = \Theta(n^c)$ for $c < k$. The total work at the next level of recursion shrinks geometrically.
- $\Theta(n^c)\lg(n)^{j+1}$ if $f(n) = \Theta(n^c)\lg(n)^j$ for $c = k$. The total work on all $O(\lg(n))$ levels is the same.
- $\Theta(n^c)$ if $f(n) = \Theta(n^c)$ for $c > k$. The total work at the next level increases geometrically.

1.19 Choosing between Several Algorithms

Most algorithms are legal and correct, but differ in extendability, simplicity, and efficiency. Simplicity gain leads to economic gain, but efficiency gain does so only if the algorithm is on the critical path, and the extra efficiency matters to the user. **Choose the simplest reasonably efficient algorithm unless a slightly more complicated one is much more efficient**.

Implementing all algorithms where each is most efficient for a particular case and deciding among them at runtime is a maintenance nightmare that may cost more in development time than save in resource use, except when using a few simple algorithms.

Ideally want to avoid thinking and automate as much as possible. For things that can't be fully automated, it's important to clearly know what to think about and what not to.

1.20 Curriculum Recommendations for Students

Mathematics:

- Calculus—essential background
- Linear algebra—for numerical algorithms and prerequisite for high-level classes
- Probability—basis of randomized algorithms and much of mathematical modeling
- Mathematical statistics—probabilistic reasoning behind statistical inference

Optional:

- Stochastic processes—for simulation and understanding of some algorithms
- Abstract algebra—theoretical concepts relevant to design of many discrete systems
- Mathematical analysis—for algorithm analysis and general mathematical maturity
- Numerical methods—how computers solve equations, evaluate functions, etc.

Economics:

- Microeconomics—decisions for an individual, including utility theory and auctions
- Game theory—making decisions given information about other stakeholders

Optional:

- Macroeconomics—economy as a whole, useful for financial programmers, no connection to computer science
- Finance—topics for financial programmers, including valuing a cash flow, creating portfolios, behavioral finance, and news-based pricing

Computer science:

- Algorithms and data structures—the core of computing, take as many classes as you can
- Computability and complexity—limits of computation
- Computer architecture—how hardware works
- Operating systems—how the OS works, important for general understanding
- Networking—basic communication protocols
- Databases—storing data on disk and accessing it with SQL
- Artificial intelligence—solving games and puzzles, logic, and probabilistic computing
- Programming in a special environment—using various APIs to create real-world apps
- Machine learning—how computers do statistics

Optional:

- Cryptography—securing communications
- Computational geometry—useful for graphics programming
- Optimization—linear programming, approximation algorithms, and metaheuristics
- String algorithms—text computation, including searching, automata, biological sequences, and data compression
- Compilers and programming languages—how compilers work and which language is useful for which task

The math classes are the most useful because the topics are much harder to learn on your own and give intuitive insight into various computations.

1.21 Interviews

An interview aims to distinguish a suitable candidate from an unsuitable one and sell the position. Interviewers consider technical competence, motivation, and communication. Competence questions test critical thinking and basic knowledge.

Typically an interview starts with a discussion of the candidate's experience or education. For experienced candidates, the focus is on the former and, for recent graduates, on the latter. For recent graduates, it helps to have had an internship because it gives something to discuss during the interview and may prepare for questions that concern group software development practices. The candidate must clearly communicate any previous experience on the resume. It's okay to not know some things, but the candidate must be able to explain everything. Remember that communication is about ability to explain things to another person in a logical way, and not perfect language mastery.

A popular experience-question technique is **STAR**—describe a situation or a task, the taken actions, and the results. The candidate should understand and have used the solution technology at least as a black box. To make the answer more useful, the question could ask to describe something challenging and how the candidate handled it. Candidates must remember to be careful to not disclose proprietary aspects of such projects because doing so is illegal and gives the impression of carelessness. For experienced candidates, this part of the interview will take more time.

Some basic knowledge questions may follow. These are typically reasonable and depend on what the candidate claims to know explicitly or implicitly. E.g., everyone can be asked about stack vs. heap memory allocation. Those who took operating systems or have experience with multithreaded programming can be asked about deadlocks.

Most companies prefer strong critical thinking and basic knowledge over extensive knowledge and medium critical thinking because software development needs constant learning of proprietary technologies. So the main part of the interview concentrates on technical questions. Main question types:

- Coding—implement a simple algorithm. A correct answer demonstrates coding and basic problem-solving abilities.
- Puzzles—good ones are purely mathematical and not outside-the-box ones. These test more complicated problem solving.
- System design—given simple requirements, think about how to design the system. This typically doesn't require coding, as the intention is to test problem solving and communication. Experienced candidates should expect more of these.

The communication aspect is much more important than it seems for all questions. Interviewers look for the ability to discuss the problem and ask clarifying questions, sometimes even deliberately omitting crucial details. Many candidates make the mistake of immediately jumping into solving the problem without understanding exactly what is wanted. It's crucial to fully load the problem in your mind and not jump to an ad hoc solution. Pay attention to all mentioned information because usually need all of it to solve the problem. Being able to work with new information is often a part of many questions.

All it takes to solve most questions is to have a clear invariant $\forall$part of the solution. During coding, it's critical to check over the code and mentally test it with a few use cases. Don't present rough draft code as a finished solution without making an effort to check it. Also, pay attention to the API, and try to handle corner cases. If this is problematic, ask the interviewer about what they want instead of ignoring the issue.

Interviewers reuse questions or take them from various compilations. Study such sources to know what to expect. Most candidates don't prepare, and those who do get the full score. Practice is always useful, and interview preparation is like SAT preparation in high school—it helps to get a better score.

Effective questions have decision power like statistical tests, i.e., with high probability a bad/good response should respectively mean unsuitable/suitable. Some effective questions from my experience:

- Basic knowledge—to test understanding of CS fundamentals:
  - Discuss some strategies for avoiding deadlocks
  - Compare any balanced tree and any hash table from a user's point of view
  - Describe what happens when running a recursive function that allocates an integer on the heap and calls itself with no base case
- Simpler type—to test basic coding ability:
  - Reverse a string where consecutive numbers represent single "logical" characters
  - Nonrecursively calculate the nth Fibonacci number
  - Find the smallest and the second smallest item indices in an array, which are different even in the presence of equal values
  - Implement a queue using two stacks and analyze its performance
  - Describe how to find the intersection of two arrays and analyze the solution's performance
- More complex—to test the ability to use CS knowledge:
  - Describe how to find the approximate area of a collection of possibly overlapping circles

specified by centers and radii (hint—use Monte Carlo or count pixels in an image)

- Describe how to implement an LRU cache
- Given a marathon track with n runners and m sensors that report passing runners, design a data structure to keep track of leading $k \leq n$ runners
- Describe how to maintain 5th and 95th order statistics (hint—use two priority queues and don't forget about edge cases)

Interviewers are usually working programmers, so their ultimate impression of a candidate is about whether they want him/her on their team. Accordingly, candidates should approach problems as they would if such problems were to be encountered during work. In particular, if you are stuck on a problem, make an effort to solve it and, if still stuck after a short while, ask for a hint. Another strategy is to first try a simple, inefficient solution, and then make it better. This at least confirms a basic understanding of the problem. Present yourself as a confident, motivated problem solver who can be independent but collaborates.

1.22 References

Bryant, R., & David Richard, O. H. (2010). *Computer Systems: a Programmer's Perspective*. Addison-Wesley.

Buschmann, F., Henney, K., & Schimdt, D. (2007). *Pattern-oriented Software Architecture: On Patterns and Pattern Language* (Vol. 5). Wiley.

Müller-Hannemann, M., & Schirra, S. (Eds.). (2010). *Algorithm Engineering: Bridging the Gap between Algorithm Theory and Practice* (Vol. 5971). Springer.

Smullyan, R. M. (2014). *A Beginner's Guide to Mathematical Logic*. Dover.

Stepanov, A. A., & MacJones, P. R. (2009). *Elements of Programming*. Addison-Wesley.

Wikipedia (2013). Master theorem. https://en.wikipedia.org/wiki/Master_theorem. Accessed July 30, 2013.

2 Introduction to Computer Law

Law is a huge subject and is different in other countries despite ongoing standardization though various treaties. This chapter summarizes useful general information about the US law, which continually changes. **To get a legal opinion, talk to a lawyer about a particular issue in detail**.

2.1 Intellectual Property

Knowledge is costly to create and most beneficial when secret. To encourage sharing, the law makes some shared knowledge property. Legally, a **property** is a set of owner's rights and using it in any infringing way without permission is illegal. For intellectual property, the permission is a **license**. ∃several types of intellectual property:

Property	Owned through	Software example
Idea	**Patent or trade secret**	Algorithm
Expression	**Copyright**	Source code
Association	**Trademark**	Program name

2.2 Patents

A patent:

- Covers "**new and useful**" processes, machines, manufactures, and compositions, which respectively are a sequence of steps to transform some physical object, a device, items made by a human or a device, and a chemical formula.
- Gives exclusive right to make, use, or sell the invention or anything containing it for a limited time, usually 20 years.
- Goes into the public domain after expiration.
- Can be unknowingly infringed. You are liable if using someone's infringing software, even if can't check for infringement.

Almost anything is *useful* as long as a person with "ordinary skill in the art" can recreate it without unreasonable effort. *New* means not obvious to someone with ordinary skill in the art at time of publication and not published more than a year before the patent application. For less, special rules apply. Generally, disclosing the invention means publishing it unless the disclosee signs a nondisclosure agreement.

Can't patent things that are:

- Naturally occurring—discoveries aren't inventions
- Purely abstract—an idea isn't a tangible invention, but might bypass this by making the idea part of a machine that creates some product and listing it in the claims of the patent for the machine
- Not new functionally—e.g., something artistic

Applying for a patent is simple in concept, but complicated in details, and costly (approximately $10,000 to apply and $20,000 over the life of the patent). An examiner does research and accepts the application or returns it for revision if rejecting some claimed novelties. Can appeal a rejection. At first, most patents are overly broad and get revised until less broad claims are accepted.

A granted patent contains most importantly:

- A list of inventions and inventors for each. Each independently owns the inventions for which they are listed unless all assigned their rights to someone else, in which case that entity is the owner.
- Dates— the **issue date** is when the patent becomes enforceable, the **application date** when it's applied for, and the **priority date** when the invention is deemed to be conceived. Complex rules determine from which date to calculate the twenty-year expiration, but the result is always between the priority and the application dates. Internationally, the application date is the invention date, and the twenty years is counted from it.

- Written description of one or more examples and illustrative drawings. These must be enough to allow reproducing the invention, or the patent is invalid. The application may not withhold important details.
- **Claims** to what is the inventive part—what the patent protects needs to be written broadly to avoid minor changes that produce logical noninfringements. It's an infringement to produce "essentially equivalent" functionality, but this may be hard to prove.

Damages for patent infringement may include:

- Lost profits
- Reasonable royalty
- Injunction against further use of the invention if not against public interest

If you find out that an algorithm is patented, even if it's obvious, use another.

2.3 Trade Secrets

A trade secret:

- Covers information that isn't publicly known, not illegal, derives part of its value from being secret, is kept reasonably secret, and not acquired by fraud. Companies strengthen that definition in employment contracts by considering anything inside the company a trade secret unless it's necessary to share it with outsiders.
- Protects against disclosure by improper means or breach of confidential relationship. **Improper means** is any fraud, such as an employee bribe. You can't disclose anything learned by accident if have a good reason to suspect it's secret unless the disclosure makes it publicly known. Using a trade secret needs explicit or implied permission.
- A **confidential relationship** arises between parties doing business with each other and is breached if one party reveals another's secrets. So many businesses don't view sealed offers that don't state that nothing contained is secret.
- Doesn't protect against independent invention and reverse engineering.
- Loses protection if it becomes publicly known, i.e., by sufficiently many people. If an employee publishes a secret online, it stops being secret, though the company can sue the employee.
- Needn't be uniquely owned. Several companies can own a secret to the same idea, but, if any discloses it, all lose it. In case of an infringement, only the owner from whom it was stolen is entitled to damages.

2.4 Copyrights

A copyright protects the exact expression of original works of authorship fixed in any tangible medium, in particular the rights to make copies, distribute them, and make derived works.

- Any record suffices. E.g., writing a poem on a napkin or a computer both qualify.
- Ideas and facts aren't protected. An expression isn't protected when needed to state an idea. A collection of facts isn't copyrightable unless the selection is creative; only a particular arrangement or presentation is copyrightable if creative.
- Need very little originality. A combination of several elements is treated as a combination and not a whole if the combining is functional and not creative. E.g., dividing a GUI into components and giving protection only to components protected individually determines the look and feel protection.
- Owned by multiple parties if each created the expression without copying. E.g., for reverse engineering, a development team gets complete functional specifications of the product but isn't allowed to see it.
- Automatic and needn't be registered. "This material is copyright" isn't necessary in the U.S. but internationally is enough to own a copyright.
- Generally valid for the lifetime of the author + 70 years. For works before 1978 or **work for hire**, expiration is usually 95 years after publication. Anything before 1923 is in the public domain, but beware of copyright renewals.
- The artist is the owner and not the machine used for creation or its owner. If a tourist asks you to

take a picture with his camera, you own the copyright. But need permission for any copyrighted work used by the machine.

- If you produce copyrighted content as part of working for someone, they likely own it as work for hire. Because of exceptions, you usually sign an agreement to transfer all rights.
- Joint work by several authors is owned entirely by each author if they intended to combine their individual contributions. Derivative work isn't joint even if permitted.
- Owner's rights are very broad. E.g., downloading an illegal copy violates the owner's right to distribution because of the copy in the download.
- The **fair use doctrine** allows copying all or parts of a work in some cases, particularly small amounts for education or critique. E.g., taking a few pixels from an image or copying a legally acquired CD for personal use isn't infringement.
- The **first-sale doctrine** allows a purchaser of a copyrighted work to resell it, with exceptions. Almost all software disallows resale in its license, which is usually binding.
- Substantial assistance of infringement leads to liability as does the combination of knowing of the infringement, having a financial gain from it, and being able to control it. That's why Kazaa is out of business. It's illegal to try or help break copyright protection by creating or selling devices for doing so. Content providers such as YouTube aren't liable for users' infringements if they quickly remove infringing material when given notice.

2.5 Trademarks

A trademark is any symbol used commercially to identify goods. A **service mark** does that for services. Also, ∃ **certification** and **collective marks**. Need to register a trademark to sue for infringement and should do so to avoid disputes when many parties want it. “<Trademark>®” denotes a registered trademark and “<Trademark>™” or “<Servicemark>℠” an unregistered one.

Only its owner can use a trademark to mark goods or services so that consumers associate the mark with the producer's reputation. Intending to or causing a reasonable confusion or dilution infringes (e.g., "Yihaa" search engine or "micro-soft" underwear). An exception is artistic work, particularly parody, if it's clear that the trademark owner didn't produce it.

A trademark symbol can't be:

- Functional—useful information, such as a direction sign, can't be a trademark.
- Offensive, generic, or misleading—a random symbol is the strongest possible trademark; e.g., "Igmdk" works, but "Joe's Pizza" is generic. To pass a generic trademark, can make a distinctive spelling alteration; e.g., "Joe's ZzaPi".
- Variation of an existing trademark—to prevent consumer confusion. ∃ exceptions for different industries and locations.

A trademark never expires but can be revoked if becomes too common or isn't used commercially for three years and !∃ intent to resume use. E.g., "zipper" and "escalator" became too common. Using a trademark means displaying it, so that it's associated with goods or services, and actively defending it by suing all infringers. Registering a domain name is nonuse because only registration isn't commercial use.

If several parties claim ownership, the one with earliest use wins unless one party has registered and used a trademark for five years, in which case it's incontestable.

2.6 Intellectual Property Management

Patents and trade secrets are mutually exclusive. But some trade secrets can become patents, and both work well with trademarks because after patent expiry or secret discovery consumers used to the product usually don't switch.

A **standard** may be created to combine several intellectual properties to promote commerce. It's guaranteed to be free of intellectual property claims, but some royalties are usually paid to the standards body.

2.7 Contracts

A contract is an agreement among several parties to have each do something specific. For it to be legally enforceable:

- An **offer** is made and, until rejected or expired, accepted by a reasonable means of communication such as mail, e-mail, or as specified by the offer. Negotiation of terms is a counteroffer and an implicit rejection. Simply asking questions about the offer isn't negotiation.
- !∃ illegal activity. If a contract was made with intent of fraud or a party was forced to sign, it's void.
- All parties must get something in return (**consideration**) that isn't already owed to them. E.g., if you pay someone part of owed money, a promise that they won't seek the rest is void.
- Parties must be competent. A contract made with a minor or someone incapacitated is generally void. For a contract with a corporation, the individual making the contract on its behalf must have enough authority.
- All parties must fully understand all the **material terms**. E.g., "you hereby assign me the rights to your house" in small print isn't binding unless you are aware of it. Common contracts such as leasing tend to be standardized, and all parties are assumed to know the common provisions; the uncommon ones need specific mention. So it's safe to sign without reading the small print.
- It must be in writing in cases such as buying real estate. For provability, most contracts of nonnegligible value are in writing, but most oral contracts are valid. An electronic contract with click acceptance is as valid as a written one.

A party's performance is **complete** if everything promised is done with changes that aren't material, i.e., other parties can't reasonably expect them to be essential, and the contract doesn't forbid them. If a party fails to perform, other parties can sue but not force performance. The court may award damages or force performance if it's irreplaceable (e.g., sale of unique items) and not too damaging to the performing party.

In some cases, a contract is automatic to avoid injustice or unjust enrichment. E.g., can't refuse to pay a reasonable price after eating in a restaurant because you didn't explicitly agree to it before ordering food.

2.8 Licenses

For software, a license is a contract between you and the owner. Without a license, you most likely can't use the property at all.

∃ much freedom in what the owner gets. An author's pride in someone's using his software qualifies. The six pack license asks for beer. An open-source license may ask you to make your code available upon request if you use anything covered by it as a component. Another license may ask to show some notice. Most licenses ask for payment and specify that you can't resell or share the software. A combined license is possible, e.g., allowing personal and educational use under one license and commercial under another.

Licensing isn't a sale, and the first-sale doctrine doesn't apply. When a "license inside" label is present, in some cases acceptance of some terms happens at the purchase and not the "I agree" click during installation. It's legal to reverse-engineer even if the license forbids it if you're not bypassing copyright protection. A license also contains:

- Payment terms.
- Quality guarantees and litigation control. Usually, a company mandates litigation in jurisdiction favorable to it and disclaims all liability in case of improper operation, intellectual property, and other claims by other parties.
- How to update and ask for tech support. New version updates may be mandated.
- Use conditions. An **exclusive license** means the owner may not license the property to anyone else. With a low fee, it can make intellectual property almost useless. Open source licenses may require making any derivatives public.

To license your property, use the existing popular licenses and not your own because you can incorrectly specify too many things.

2.9 Employment Agreements

When you get a programming job, you usually sign a contract with terms of employment, such as duties and compensation, and a **nondisclosure agreement** (NDA). The contract ensures that you don't reveal any proprietary information and don't claim anything produced for the company as your own. Usually, any such intellectual property is work for hire, but ∃ exceptions. In particular, you may not be allowed to own any work not produced for the company but related to its business, regardless of whether you produce it during company hours or on your own time and whether you use company resources.

If you are working during your off hours on a project covered by the agreement, get a written permission from the company's legal department before starting. Also, periodically show them what you have so far and get a written statement that they don't have claims to it. Many companies have established workflows for this.

An NDA also forbids disclosing the employer's secrets, even after employment termination. The agreement usually extends the definition of a secret.

A less common part of an NDA is a **noncompete agreement**, which disallows working for a competitor or a specific industry for some time. In most cases, it's at best enforceable only if reasonable.

2.10 Privacy

People have a right to privacy, in particular, electronic privacy. Libel laws prevent disclosure of information, even if it's true, if it's both:

- Highly offensive to a reasonable person
- Not of a legitimate concern to the public

∃ legal liability if stolen information wasn't properly protected.

You get privacy when can reasonably expect it. If you find a coworker watching adult material, and he gets fired, he can't complain. But searching his/her bag is illegal.

A program may not spy on your actions unless you allowed it. Software must respect users' tracking and data collection preferences. It's illegal to collect data of children of age 13 and younger without specific permission.

2.11 Computer Crime

An e-mail solicitor must allow unsubscribing, and a registration form must allow opting out of receiving advertising.

Unauthorized use of a system and identity theft are illegal. This includes using someone's password to break in. When assessing unauthorized use, intent and caused damage matter.

2.12 References

Landy, G. K. (2008). *The IT/Digital Legal Companion: A Comprehensive Business Guide to Software, Internet, and IP Law.* Syngress.

Lindberg, Van (2008). *Intellectual Property and Open Source—A Practical Guide to Protecting Code.* O'Reilly.

3 Fundamental Data Structures

3.1 Utility Functions

C++ has no macro to print a variable's name and value. Its implementation in `<Debug.h>` illustrates good file design.

```
#ifndef DEBUG_H
#define DEBUG_H
#include <iostream>
using namespace std;
namespace igmdk{

#define DEBUG(var) cout << #var " "<< (var) << endl;

}//end namespace
#endif
```

In particular, for efficient **large scale code management**:

- Headers have **include guards**, include everything needed, and contain only reusable code
- All functionality ∈ `namespace`
- Neither `using` a namespace nor implementing functionality in a header is recommended, but both are convenient, and the latter is compatible with templates

Some useful functionality that's not in C++ libraries:

- Ceiling of integer division
- Wrappers around placement `new` and `delete`
- A generic assignment operator—destroys the target and copies the value into it using placement `new`
- A key-value pair

```
template<typename ITEM> ITEM* rawMemory(int n)
    {return (ITEM*)::operator new(sizeof(ITEM) * n);}
void rawDelete(void* array){::operator delete(array);}
template<typename ITEM> void rawDestruct(ITEM* array, int size)
{
    for(int i = 0; i < size; ++i) array[i].~ITEM();
    rawDelete(array);
}
long long ceiling(unsigned long long n, long long divisor)
    {return n/divisor + bool(n % divisor);}
template<typename TYPE> TYPE& genericAssign(TYPE& to, TYPE const& rhs)
{
    if(&to != &rhs)
    {
        to.~TYPE();
        new(&to)TYPE(rhs);
    }
    return to;
}
template<typename KEY, typename VALUE> struct KVPair
{
    KEY key;
    VALUE value;
    KVPair(KEY const& theKey = KEY(), VALUE const& theValue = VALUE()):
```

```
        key(theKey), value(theValue) {}
};
```

Comparators are useful for many algorithms. For efficiency, provide both "<" and "=" comparisons. Can implement the latter in terms of the former because $x = y \leftrightarrow\ !(x < y)\ \&\&\ !(y < x)$, but the latter needs two comparisons.

```
template<typename ITEM>bool operator<=(ITEM const& lhs, ITEM const& rhs)
    {return !(rhs < lhs);}
template<typename ITEM>bool operator>(ITEM const& lhs, ITEM const& rhs)
    {return rhs < lhs;}
template<typename ITEM>bool operator>=(ITEM const& lhs, ITEM const& rhs)
    {return !(lhs < rhs);}
template<typename ITEM>bool operator==(ITEM const& lhs, ITEM const& rhs)
    {return lhs <= rhs && lhs >= rhs;}
template<typename ITEM>bool operator!=(ITEM const& lhs, ITEM const& rhs)
    {return !(lhs == rhs);}
template<typename ITEM> struct DefaultComparator
{
    bool isLess(ITEM const& lhs, ITEM const& rhs)const{return lhs < rhs;}
    bool isEqual(ITEM const& lhs, ITEM const& rhs)const{return lhs == rhs;}
};
template<typename ITEM> struct ReverseComparator
{
    bool isLess(ITEM const& lhs, ITEM const& rhs)const{return rhs < lhs;}
    bool isEqual(ITEM const& lhs, ITEM const& rhs)const{return lhs == rhs;}
};
template<typename ITEM> struct PointerComparator
{
    bool isLess(ITEM const& lhs, ITEM const& rhs)const{return *lhs < *rhs;}
    bool isEqual(ITEM const& lhs, ITEM const& rhs)const{return *lhs == *rhs;}
};
template<typename ITEM> struct IndexComparator
{
    ITEM* array;
    IndexComparator(ITEM* theArray): array(theArray){}
    bool isLess(int lhs, int rhs)const{return array[lhs] < array[rhs];}
    bool isEqual(int lhs, int rhs)const{return array[lhs] == array[rhs];}
};
template<typename KEY, typename VALUE, typename COMPARATOR =
    DefaultComparator<KEY> > struct KVComparator
{
    COMPARATOR comparator;
    KVComparator(COMPARATOR const& theComparator = COMPARATOR()):
        comparator(theComparator) {}
    bool isLess(KVPair<KEY, VALUE> const& lhs, KVPair<KEY, VALUE>const& rhs)
        const{return comparator.isLess(lhs.key, rhs.key);}
    bool isEqual(KVPair<KEY, VALUE> const& lhs, KVPair<KEY, VALUE>const& rhs)
        const{return comparator.isEqual(lhs.key, rhs.key);}
};
```

Variable-length arrays are usually compared **lexicographically**, i.e., using the dictionary order (e.g., "cat" < "mouse"). `LexicographicComparator` works for types supporting `operator[]` and `getSize`. The items past the last are implicitly null with null = null. For arrays of length k, comparisons take $O(k)$ time but less on average, depending on how long is the common prefix.

```
template<typename VECTOR> struct LexicographicComparator
{
    bool isLess(VECTOR const& lhs, VECTOR const& rhs, int i)
    {
        return i < lhs.getSize() ? i < rhs.getSize() && lhs[i] < rhs[i] :
            i < rhs.getSize();
```

```
    }
    bool isEqual(VECTOR const& lhs, VECTOR const& rhs, int i)
    {
        return i < lhs.getSize() ? i < rhs.getSize() && lhs[i] == rhs[i] :
            i >= rhs.getSize();
    }
    bool isEqual(VECTOR const& lhs, VECTOR const& rhs)
    {
        for(int i = 0; i < min(lhs.getSize(), rhs.getSize()); ++i)
            if(lhs[i] != rhs[i]) return false;
        return lhs.getSize() == rhs.getSize();
    }
    bool isLess(VECTOR const& lhs, VECTOR const& rhs)
    {
        for(int i = 0; i < min(lhs.getSize(), rhs.getSize()); ++i)
        {
            if(lhs[i] < rhs[i]) return true;
            if(rhs[i] < lhs[i]) return false;
        }
        return lhs.getSize() < rhs.getSize();
    }
    int getSize(VECTOR const& value){return value.getSize();}
};
```

Another frequently used operation is finding the minimum or the maximum in an array, possibly relative to a comparator or a function that evaluates the items:

```
template<typename ITEM, typename COMPARATOR> int argMin(ITEM* array,
    int size, COMPARATOR const& c)
{
    assert(size > 0);
    int best = 0;
    for(int i = 1; i < size; ++i)
        if(c.isLess(array[i], array[best])) best = i;
    return best;
}
template<typename ITEM> int argMin(ITEM* array, int size)
    {return argMin(array, size, DefaultComparator<ITEM>());}
template<typename ITEM> int argMax(ITEM* array, int size)
    {return argMin(array, size, ReverseComparator<ITEM>());}
template<typename ITEM> int valMin(ITEM* array, int size)
{
    int index = argMin(array, size);
    assert(index > -1);
    return array[index];
}
template<typename ITEM> int valMax(ITEM* array, int size)
{
    int index = argMax(array, size);
    assert(index > -1);
    return array[index];
}
template<typename ITEM, typename FUNCTION> int argMinFunc(ITEM* array,
    int size, FUNCTION const& f)
{
    assert(size > 0);
    int best = -1;
    double bestScore;
    for(int i = 0; i < size; ++i)
    {
```

```
        double score = f(array[i]);
        if(best == -1 || score < bestScore)
        {
            best = i;
            bestScore = score;
        }
    }
    return best;
}
template<typename ITEM, typename FUNCTION> ITEM valMinFunc(ITEM* array,
    int size, FUNCTION const& f)
{
    int index = argMinFunc(array, size, f);
    assert(index > -1);
    return array[index];
}
```

3.2 Vector

A vector implements an array of dynamic size. The initial and min sizes are small powers of two to cut the number of memory manager calls and not use excessive memory. In a dynamically allocated array of size `capacity`, the first `size` items are constructed:

```
1: Vector0to4
  capacity = 8
  size     = 5
  items    = 0x60003a4c0
.items[0]@8 → 0|1|2|3|4|...|...|...
```

```
template<typename ITEM> class Vector
{
    enum{MIN_CAPACITY = 8};
    int capacity, size;
    ITEM* items;
public:
    ITEM* getArray(){return items;}
    ITEM* const getArray()const{return items;}
    int getSize()const{return size;}
    ITEM& operator[](int i)
    {
        assert(i >= 0 && i < size);
        return items[i];
    }
    ITEM const& operator[](int i)const
    {
        assert(i >= 0 && i < size);
        return items[i];
    }
};
```

Constructors create a vector of certain capacity and either construct some items from a template item or don't need the items' default constructor.

```
    Vector(ITEM* const array = 0, int theSize = 0): capacity(max(theSize,
        int(MIN_CAPACITY))), size(theSize), items(rawMemory<ITEM>(capacity))
    {
        assert(size >= 0);
        for(int i = 0; i < size; ++i) new(&items[i])ITEM(array[i]);
    }
    explicit Vector(int initialSize, int nContstruct = 0, ITEM const& value =
        ITEM()): size(0), capacity(max(initialSize, int(MIN_CAPACITY))),
```

```
        items(rawMemory<ITEM>(capacity))
        {for(int i = 0; i < nContstruct; ++i) append(value);}
    Vector(Vector const& rhs): capacity(rhs.capacity), size(rhs.size),
        items(rawMemory<ITEM>(capacity))
        {for(int i = 0; i < size; ++i) new(&items[i])ITEM(rhs.items[i]);}
    Vector& operator=(Vector const& rhs){return genericAssign(*this, rhs);}
    ~Vector(){rawDestruct(items, size);}
```

The main modification operation is **appending** items to the end. A vector uses **array doubling** (also see the "Algorithmic Techniques" chapter) to create space for extra items when needed:

1. **Allocate a new array of capacity = 2 × the size**
2. **Copy all the items into it**
3. **Deallocate the old array**

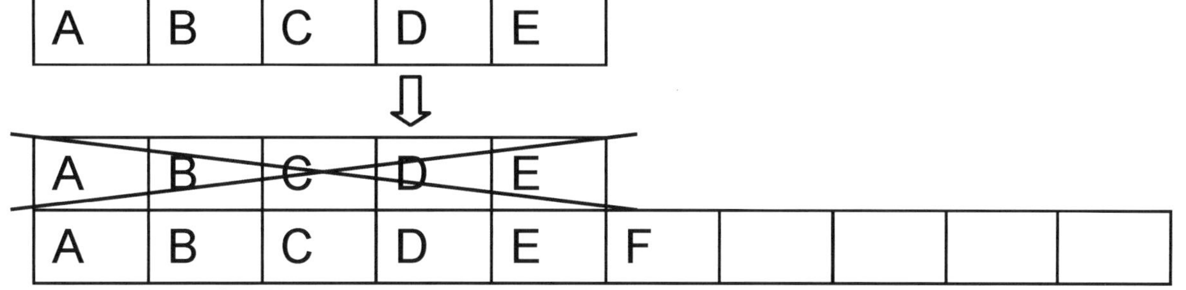

This makes O(lg(n)) memory manager calls for n appends. Appending is O(n) and amortized O(1) because n/2 items must have been inserted since the last resizing.

Deletion of the last item resizes if `size` < ¼ × `capacity` to 2 × `size`:

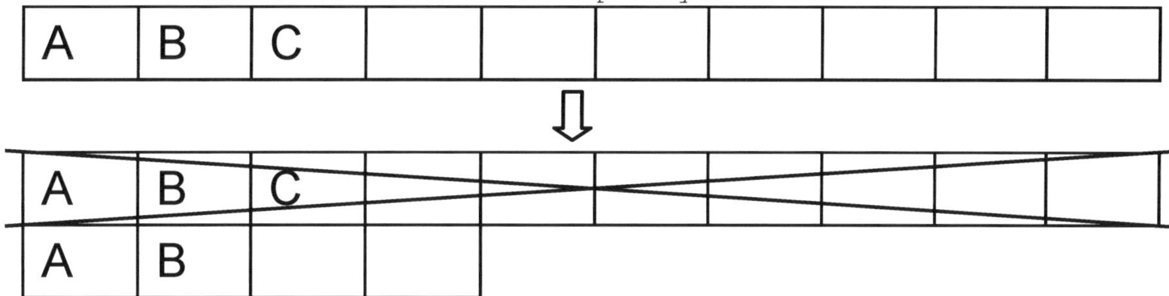

Using ¼ or other values < ½, insertion and deletion are amortized O(1).

```
    void resize()
    {
        ITEM* oldItems = items;
        capacity = max(2 * size, int(MIN_CAPACITY));
        items = rawMemory<ITEM>(capacity);
        for(int i = 0; i < size; ++i) new(&items[i])ITEM(oldItems[i]);
        rawDestruct(oldItems, size);
    }
    void append(ITEM const& item)
    {
        if(size >= capacity) resize();
        new(&items[size++])ITEM(item);
    }
    void removeLast()
    {
        assert(size > 0);
        items[--size].~ITEM();
        if(capacity > MIN_CAPACITY && size * 4 < capacity) resize();
    }
    void swapWith(Vector& other)
    {
        swap(items, other.items);
        swap(size, other.size);
```

```
        swap(capacity, other.capacity);
    }
```

Advantages of vector over other dynamic array data structures:

- Fastest possible random access
- Cache-efficient iteration
- Can pass as a single contiguous array to a C API

Disadvantages:

- O(n) insertion, most felt by expensive-to-copy items
- After doubling, ½ of the new array is unused
- Can fail to allocate a very large array
- Reallocation invalidates item references

The STL vector doesn't shrink on deletion. To do so, swap it with a temporary empty vector, and assign the temporary to the vector. To pass to a C API, use `&vector[0]`. This is wrong when size = 0, but `getArray()` is always correct.

For convenience, a vector supports working with the last item, arithmetic operations, and appending vectors:

```
    ITEM const& lastItem()const{return items[size - 1];}
    ITEM& lastItem(){return items[size - 1];}
    void reverse(int left, int right)
        {while(left < right) swap(items[left++], items[right--]);}
    void reverse(){reverse(0, size - 1);}
    void appendVector(Vector const& rhs)
        {for(int i = 0; i < rhs.getSize(); ++i) append(rhs[i]);}
    Vector& operator+=(Vector const& rhs)
    {
        assert(size == rhs.size);
        for(int i = 0; i < size; ++i) items[i] += rhs.items[i];
        return *this;
    }
    Vector& operator-=(Vector const& rhs)
    {
        assert(size == rhs.size);
        for(int i = 0; i < size; ++i) items[i] -= rhs.items[i];
        return *this;
    }
    template<typename SCALAR> Vector& operator*=(SCALAR const& scalar)
    {
        for(int i = 0; i < size; ++i) items[i] *= scalar;
        return *this;
    }
    friend Vector operator+(Vector const& a, Vector const& b)
    {
        Vector result(a);
        return result += b;
    }
    friend Vector operator-(Vector const& a, Vector const& b)
    {
        Vector result(a);
        return result -= b;
    }
    friend Vector operator*(Vector const& a, ITEM const& scalar)
    {
        Vector result(a);
        return result *= scalar;
    }
    friend ITEM operator*(Vector const& a, Vector const& b)
    {
```

```
        assert(a.size == b.size);
        ITEM result(0);
        for(int i = 0; i < a.size; ++i) result += a[i] * b[i];
        return result;
    }
    Vector operator-(){return *this * -1;}
    bool operator==(Vector const& rhs)const
    {
        if(size == rhs.size)
        {
            for(int i = 0; i < size; ++i)
                if(items[i] != rhs[i]) return false;
            return true;
        }
        return false;
    }
```

3.3 Block Array

A block array contains many arrays of fixed size k, indexed by a vector of pointers:

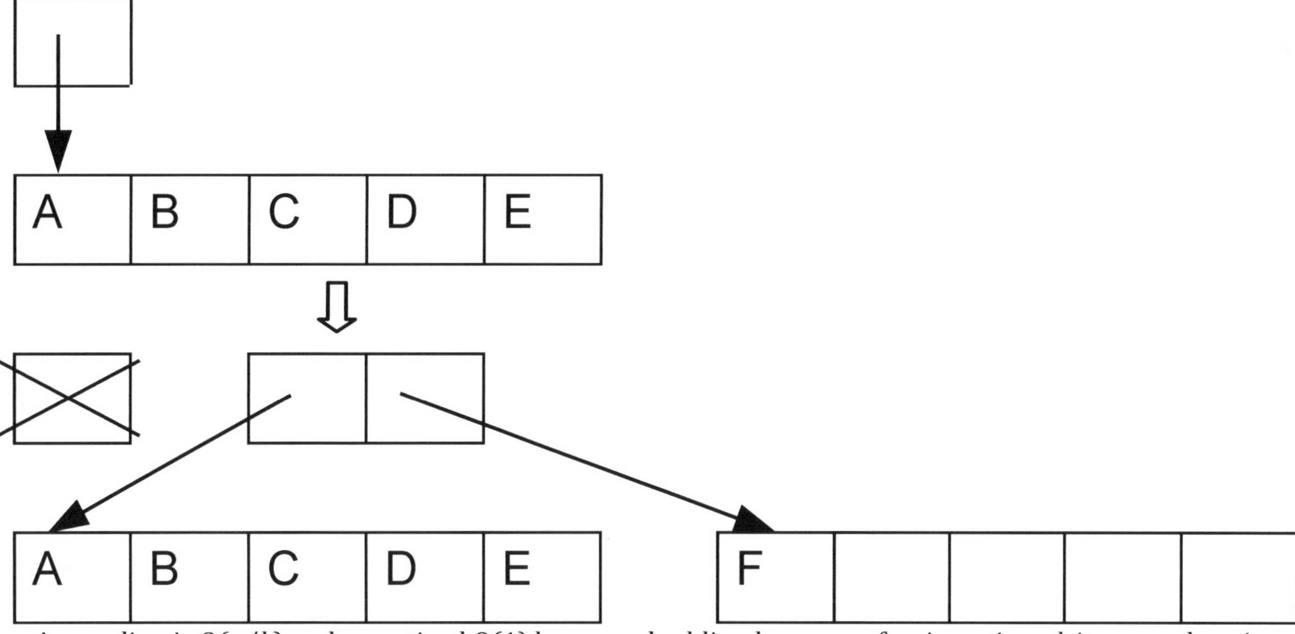

Appending is $O(n/k)$ and amortized $O(1)$ because doubling happens after inserting nk items and copies n/k pointers. The ith item = vector[i/k][i % k] and k is 64, 128, or another not too large/small value.
Advantages:

- Wasted space after a resizing is negligible $O(n/k + k)$
- Don't need very large arrays
- Items aren't copied
- Iteration is still cache-efficient
- Item references are valid after reallocation

Disadvantages:

- Slow random access
- Can't pass to a C API
- Insertion and deletion are $O(n/k)$

Prefer vector due to faster random access and the ability to pass to a C API. Consider a block array for compressed representation where arrays containing 0's aren't allocated or when need a very large vector.

Complex methods using blocks of variable sizes have optimal $O(1)$ random access, append, and remove last operations and $O(\sqrt{n})$ wasted space. Experimentally, among several dynamic array structures, vector performs best and block array second best, and block array is best when vector approaches the memory limit (Joannou & Raman 2011).

3.4 Linked List

A linked list is a sequence of items linked by pointers:

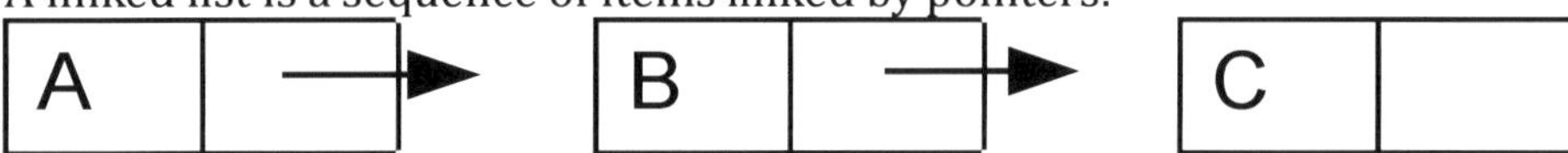

It can be **doubly-linked**, with bidirectional pointers, and **circular**, with the last item pointing to the first. A list supports O(1) node movement, but:

- Doesn't support random access unless store node pointers externally, and to access the ith item need O(i) time
- Wastes space on navigation pointers and freelist bookkeeping
- Iteration isn't cache-inefficient because of pointer jumping

With few items, when don't need random access, a list is better than a vector. Such implementations for efficiency usually use own linked lists and don't reuse a generic one. Also, can implement data structures consisting of nodes linked by pointers on top of an array where each array item is a node. This avoids dynamic memory allocation but removes most advantages of a list.

A simple doubly-linked list implementation allows appending, **prepending** (adding to front), and **cutting** nodes. Such operations are useful for some other data structures, covered later. Must relink pointers correctly for the affected node, the previous node, and the next node.

*((),last)
4: List0to2
root = 0x60004a560
last = 0x60003a4b0
*((),root)
item = 0
next = 0x60004a540
prev = 0x0
*((),next)
*((),prev)
item = 1
next = 0x60003a4b0
prev = 0x60004a560
*((),next)
*((),prev)
item = 2
next = 0x0
prev = 0x60004a540

```
template<typename ITEM> struct SimpleDoublyLinkedList
{
    struct Node
    {
        ITEM item;
        Node *next, *prev;
        template<typename ARGUMENT>
        Node(ARGUMENT const& argument, Node* theNext): item(argument),
            next(theNext), prev(0) {}
    } *root, *last;
    SimpleDoublyLinkedList(): root(0), last(0){}
    void prepend(Node* node)
    {
        assert(node);
        node->next = root;
        if(root) root->prev = node;
        node->prev = 0;
        root = node;
        if(!last) last = node;
    }
    void cut(Node* node)
    {
        assert(node);
        (node == last ? last : node->next->prev) = node->prev;
        (node == root ? root : node->prev->next) = node->next;
    }
    bool isEmpty(){return !root;}
    ~SimpleDoublyLinkedList()
    {
        while(root)
        {
            Node* toBeDeleted = root;
            root = root->next;
```

```
            delete toBeDeleted;
        }
    }
};
```

3.5 Garbage-collecting Freelist

A **freelist** is a collection of blocks of memory, allocated once and cut into smaller objects. Freelists avoid allocating many small objects one by one, but this isn't a problem with modern memory manager implementations. A freelist can collect garbage for a data structure, but deallocated memory isn't available to other parts of the program, and can't merge or swap data structures faster than by making a complete copy.

A freelist gives back `ITEM*` on allocation and takes `ITEM*` on deallocation. `ITEM*` is a cast `Item*`, where Item is a structure containing a raw memory `ITEM` as the first member and some bookkeeping. This is safe because the address of the first member of a `struct` = its address.

A freelist without garbage collection is a linked list of blocks consisting of memory for k `Items` and a `next` link. An `Item` consists of an `isDestructed` Boolean and a `union` of an `ITEM`, a returned pointer, and an alignment `double`. Have pointers to the next `Item` of last allocated block and the head of the returned list. The latter is defined implicitly by the returned pointers.

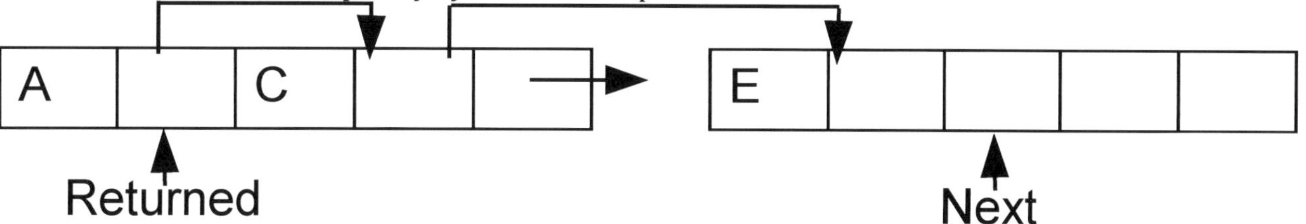

Allocation:

1. **If the returned list isn't empty, use its first node**
2. **Else if last block is full, allocate another block**
3. **Use the next item of the last block to allocate the item**

The cost is O(constructor call + memory manager call). The latter is amortized due to allocation in blocks. Deallocation:

1. **Destruct the item**
2. **Mark it destructed**
3. **Prepend it to the returned list**

Space use is O(max number of items allocated at any time). The destructor goes through the list of blocks and deallocates each, which is correct if all allocated items were returned.

For garbage collection, need a doubly-linked list of static one-block freelists and items to know from which block they came. Two lists index the blocks: `full` has blocks that have no more space, and `next` blocks that do:

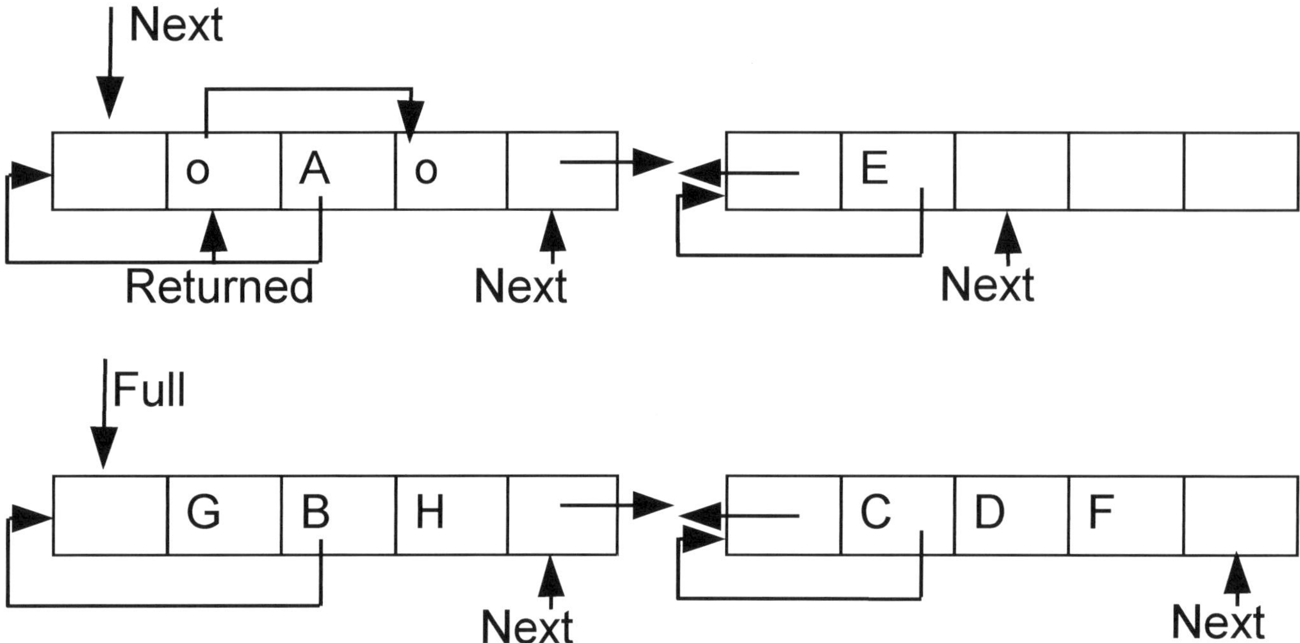

Allocation:

1. **Use the next block off *next*, creating one if needed**
2. **Take the space for the item from there**
3. **If the block becomes full, move it to *full***

Deallocation:

1. **Return the item to the block from which it came**
2. **If the block was full, move it to *next***
3. **Else if it became empty, deallocate it**

For garbage collection, each block has the list of returned pointers and the maximum allocated address. The index of an item to destruct = its address − the array's address. This allows iterating over all items and collecting the unreturned ones. The cost is O(the number of live items × the destructor cost + total size of the remaining blocks).

The blocks are in sizes increasing by a factor of 2, from 32 to 8192, to be efficient and useful for small sizes. The unlikely worst case space use O(min(max number of items allocated at any time × (`sizeof(ITEM)` + `sizeof`(pointer)), the number of allocated items × size of a block)) occurs when each block has a single item.

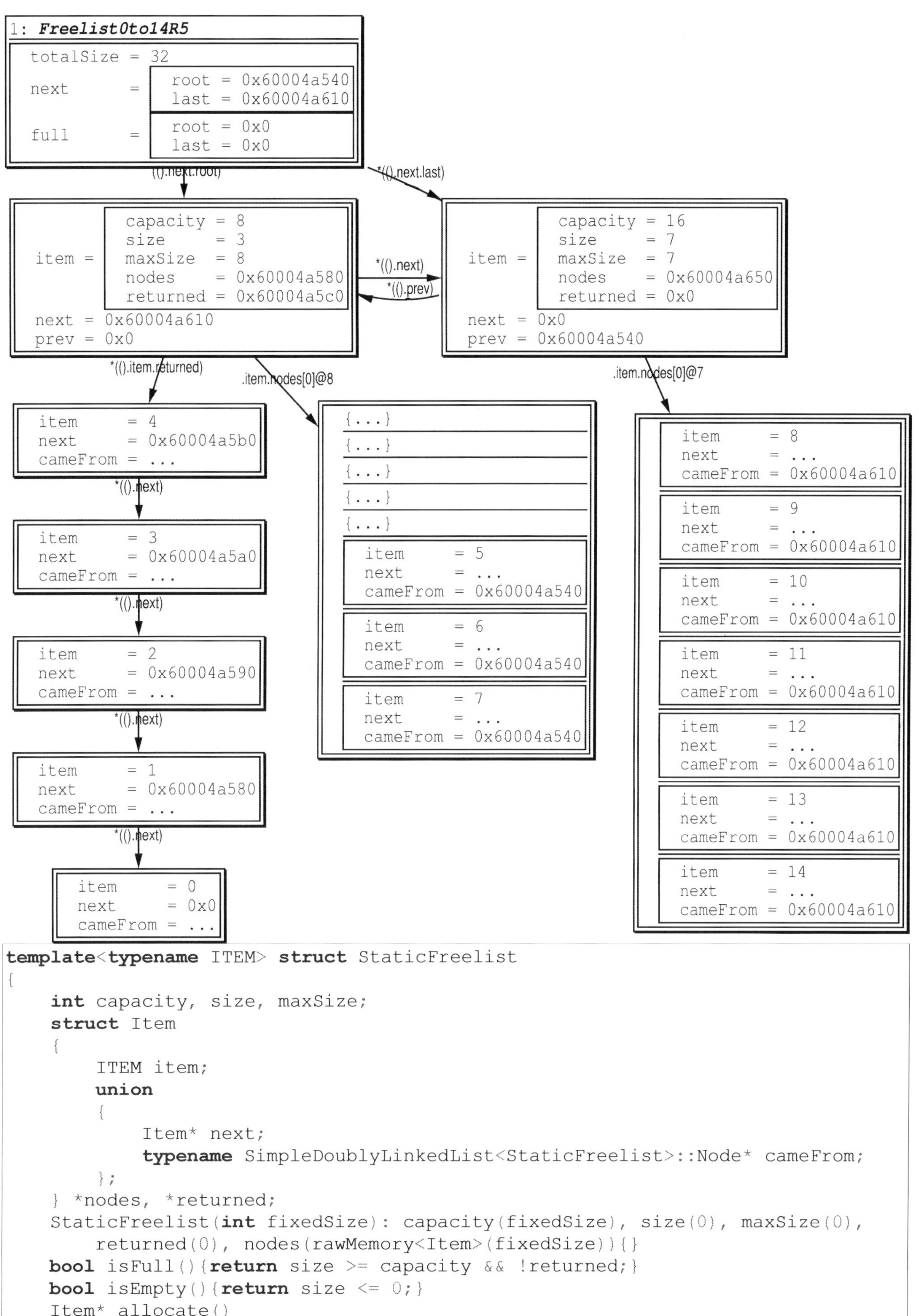


```
template<typename ITEM> struct StaticFreelist
{
    int capacity, size, maxSize;
    struct Item
    {
        ITEM item;
        union
        {
            Item* next;
            typename SimpleDoublyLinkedList<StaticFreelist>::Node* cameFrom;
        };
    } *nodes, *returned;
    StaticFreelist(int fixedSize): capacity(fixedSize), size(0), maxSize(0),
        returned(0), nodes(rawMemory<Item>(fixedSize)){}
    bool isFull(){return size >= capacity && !returned;}
    bool isEmpty(){return size <= 0;}
    Item* allocate()
```

```
    {
        Item* result = returned;
        if(result) returned = returned->next;
        else result = &nodes[maxSize++];
        ++size;
        return result;
    }
    void remove(Item* item)
    {
        item->item.~ITEM();
        item->next = returned;
        returned = item;
        --size;
    }
    ~StaticFreelist()
    {//O(1) if all items are returned, O(maxSize) otherwise
        if(!isEmpty())
        {//mark allocated nodes, unmark returned ones, destruct marked ones
            bool* toDelete = new bool[maxSize];
            for(int i = 0; i < maxSize; ++i) toDelete[i] = true;
            while(returned)
            {//nodes must come from this list for this to work
                toDelete[returned - nodes] = false;
                returned = returned->next;
            }
            for(int i = 0; i < maxSize; ++i)
                if(toDelete[i])nodes[i].item.~ITEM();
            delete[] toDelete;
        }
        rawDelete(nodes);
    }
};
template<typename ITEM> class Freelist
{
    enum{MAX_BLOCK_SIZE = 8192, MIN_BLOCK_SIZE = 8, DEFAULT_SIZE = 32};
    int totalSize;
    typedef SimpleDoublyLinkedList<StaticFreelist<ITEM> > ListType;
    typedef typename StaticFreelist<ITEM>::Item Item;
    typedef typename ListType::Node NodeType;
    ListType next, full;
    Freelist(Freelist const&);
    Freelist& operator=(Freelist const&);
public:
    Freelist(int initialSize = DEFAULT_SIZE): totalSize(max<int>(
        MIN_BLOCK_SIZE, min<int>(initialSize, MAX_BLOCK_SIZE))) {}
    ITEM* allocate()
    {
        if(next.isEmpty())
        {
            next.prepend(new NodeType(totalSize, 0));
            totalSize = min<int>(totalSize * 2, MAX_BLOCK_SIZE);
        }
        NodeType* root = next.root;
        Item* result = root->item.allocate();
        result->cameFrom = root;
        if(root->item.isFull())
        {
            next.cut(root);
            full.prepend(root);
```

```
        }
        return (ITEM*)result;
    }
    void remove(ITEM* item)
    {
        if(!item) return;
        Item* node = (Item*)(item);
        NodeType* cameFrom = node->cameFrom;
        StaticFreelist<ITEM>& bucket = cameFrom->item;
        bool wasFull = bucket.isFull();
        bucket.remove(node);
        if(bucket.isEmpty())//if 1 item buckets were allowed this would fail
        {//as item would be in full, not next
            totalSize -= bucket.capacity;
            next.cut(cameFrom);
            delete cameFrom;
        }
        else if(wasFull)
        {
            full.cut(cameFrom);
            next.prepend(cameFrom);
        }
    }
};
```

3.6 Stack

A stack implements a **first-in-last-out** sequence where can only **push** (add) items to the **top** and access/**pop** (remove) the top item.

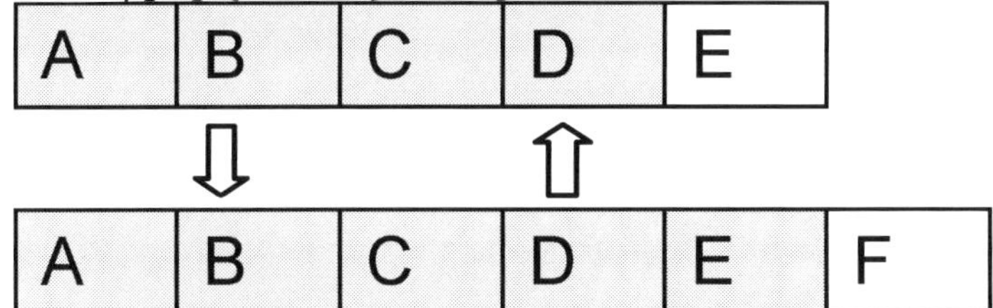

To implement, can use one of a:

- Array with a top counter, if the size is O(1) and the items have a default constructor—fastest and simplest
- Vector—fast, takes little code, and results in few memory allocations if the stack reaches a stable size
- Block array—same code as for vector and efficient for very large sizes or items, but a repetitive push/pop sequence on the block boundary causes repetitive allocation/deallocation
- Linked list—not competitive because allocating single nodes is inefficient
- Linked list of blocks of sizes possibly increasing up to some bound—similar to the block array, but needs extra code and is slightly faster

The vector/block array implementations have amortized O(1) push/pop due to resizing.

```
1: Stack0to4
storage = capacity = 8
          size     = 5
          items    = 0x60003a4c0
.storage.items[0]@5 -> 0|1|2|3|4
```

```
template<typename ITEM, typename VECTOR = Vector<ITEM> > struct Stack
{
    VECTOR storage;
    void push(ITEM const& item){storage.append(item);}
```

```
    ITEM pop()
    {
        assert(!isEmpty());
        ITEM result = storage.lastItem();
        storage.removeLast();
        return result;
    }
    ITEM& getTop()
    {
        assert(!isEmpty());
        return storage.lastItem();
    }
    bool isEmpty(){return !storage.getSize();}
};
```

It's unlikely that stack operations are the bottleneck, and developers should treat stack as an abstract concept with a single implementation.

3.7 Queue

A queue implements a **first-in-first-out** sequence allowing **enqueuing** (adding) items to the back and accessing or **dequeuing** (removing) them from the front:

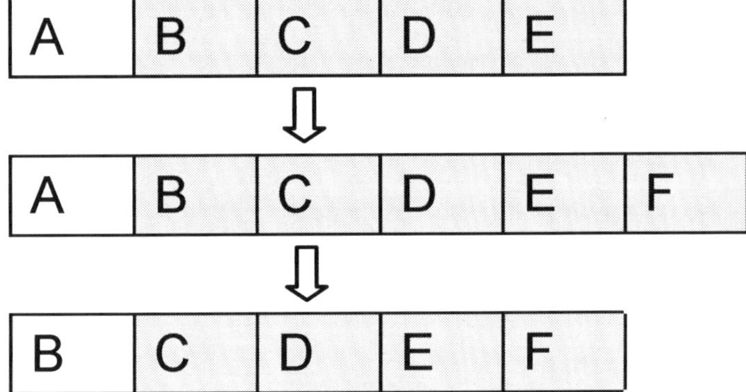

To implement, can use one of a:

- Linked list
- Linked list of blocks of sizes possibly increasing up to some bound
- Circular queue with doubling—the simplest reasonably efficient choice
- Array with extra space at both ends, doubling it when either runs out—O(1) amortized push/pop, but too clumsy
- Block array where the index array is handled as above

Can extend these to a **double-ended queue**, where can enqueue/dequeue from both ends.

A circular queue with doubling uses a dynamic array, like vector, but, to allow efficient operations at the beginning, doesn't allocate items starting at index 0. Items start at index *front*, so that index(*i*) = (*front* + *i*) % *capacity* and *back* = index(the size − 1). Push and pop at both ends resize as for vector; their runtime is amortized O(1).

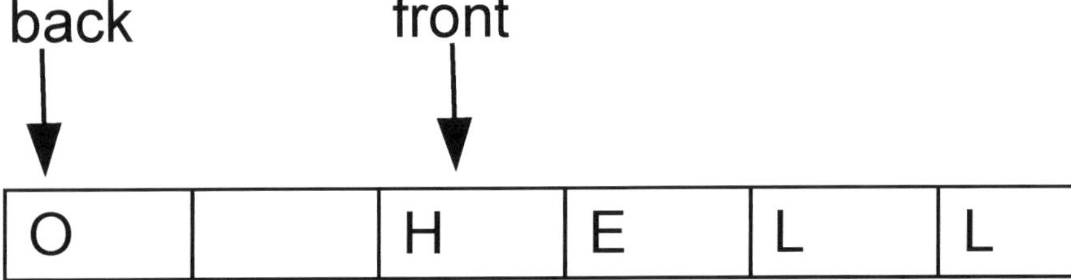

For simplicity the implementation only supports a regular queue.

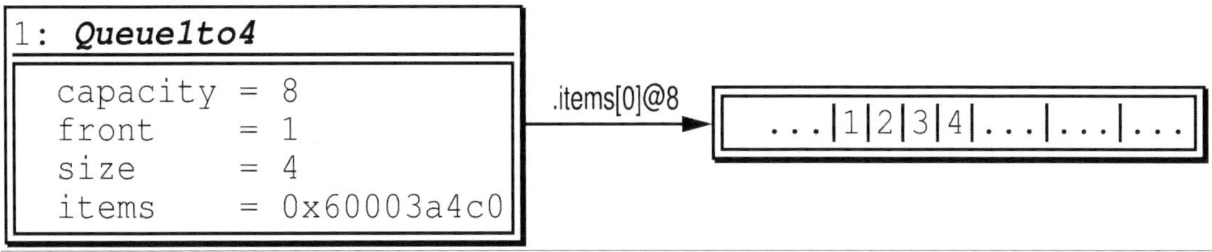

```
1: Queue1to4
  capacity = 8
  front    = 1
  size     = 4
  items    = 0x60003a4c0
```

.items[0]@8 → ...|1|2|3|4|...|...|...

```
template<typename ITEM> class Queue
{
    enum{MIN_CAPACITY = 8};
    int capacity, front, size;
    ITEM* items;
    int offset(int i){return (front + i) % capacity;}
    void resize()
    {
        ITEM* oldArray = items;
        int newCapacity = max(int(MIN_CAPACITY), size * 2);
        items = rawMemory<ITEM>(newCapacity);
        for(int i = 0; i < size; ++i)new(&items[i])ITEM(oldArray[offset(i)]);
        deleteArray(oldArray);
        front = 0;
        capacity = newCapacity;
    }
    void deleteArray(ITEM* array)
    {
        for(int i = 0; i < size; ++i) array[offset(i)].~ITEM();
        rawDelete(array);
    }
public:
    bool isEmpty()const{return size == 0;}
    Queue(int theSize = MIN_CAPACITY): capacity(max(int(MIN_CAPACITY),
        theSize)), front(0), size(0), items(rawMemory<ITEM>(capacity)) {}
    Queue(Queue const& rhs): capacity(rhs.capacity), size(rhs.size),
        front(rhs.front), items(rawMemory<ITEM>(capacity))
    {
        for(int i = 0; i < size; ++i)
            new(&items[i])ITEM(rhs.items[offset(i)]);
    }
    Queue& operator=(Queue const& rhs){return genericAssign(*this, rhs);}
    ~Queue(){deleteArray(items);}
    void push(ITEM const& item)
    {
        if(size == capacity) resize();
        new(&items[offset(size++)])ITEM(item);
    }
    ITEM pop()
    {
        assert(!isEmpty());
        ITEM result = items[front];
        items[front].~ITEM();
        front = offset(1);
        if(capacity > 4 * --size && capacity > MIN_CAPACITY) resize();
        return result;
    }
    ITEM& top()const
    {
        assert(!isEmpty());
        return items[front];
    }
```

```
};
```

The circular queue has a simple implementation and is extendable by supporting random access and simplification to a fixed size circular buffer. The clumsier linked list of blocks might be faster and use less memory, but queue operations usually aren't the bottleneck.

3.8 Trees

A **tree** is similar to a linked list, but a node has pointers to all its **children**. A node that doesn't have any children is **external/leaf** and **internal** otherwise. A tree with n nodes has $n - 1$ pointers. A tree is **binary** if each node has at most two children. Binary trees are easy to represent and form many data structures.

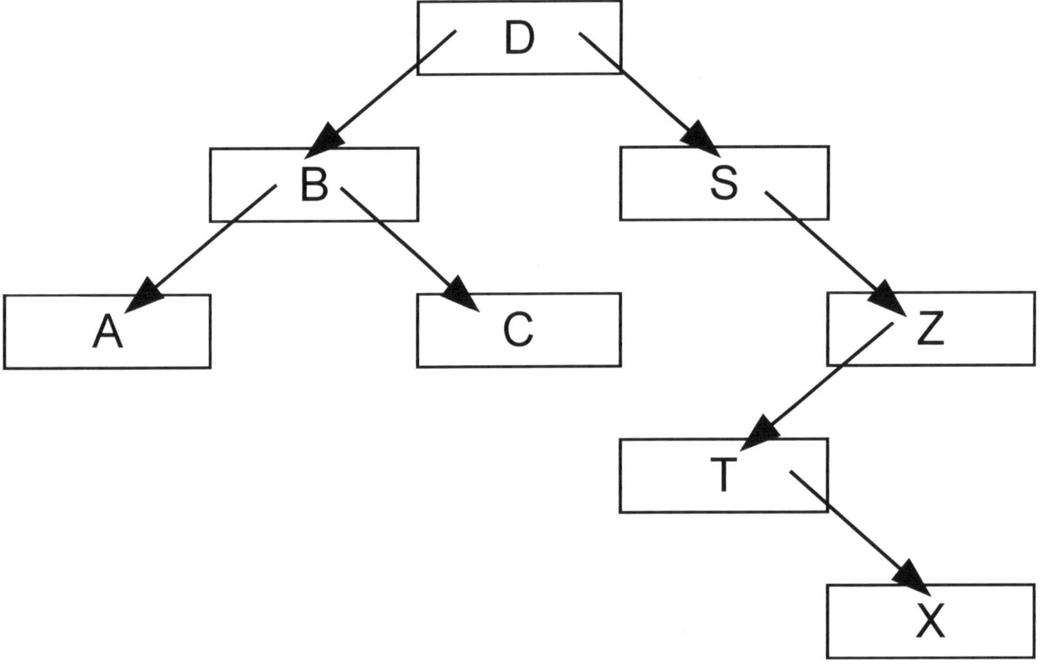

A non-binary tree is isomorphic to a binary tree using (first child, next sibling)↔(left child, right child). A node may have a pointer to its parent. For **ordered trees**, the data in a left node < the data in the parent node ≤ the data in the right node.

3.9 Bit Algorithms

C++ doesn't have instructions for lg, **pop count** (the number of set bits in a word) and many other operations doable in O(1) time in assembly. Remember:

- Shifts by < 0 or ≥ the number of bits in a word are undefined.
- Signed word right shift fills up with *1* and not *0*.
- `numeric_limits<WORD>::digits` is 1 less for signed words.
- 1 = `sizeof(char)` ≤ `sizeof(short)` ≤ `sizeof(int)` ≤ `sizeof(long)` ≤ `sizeof(long long)` and `unsigned long long` has ≥ 64 bits. E.g., `int` can have 32 or 64 bits, `long long` 64 or 128, and pointer or `int` has more bits than the other. When relying on word sizes, use portable fixed types.
- `<cstdint>` defines `intX_t` and `uintX_t` for `X` = 8, 16, 32, 64, but an implementation may omit `X` for which !∃word type.
- `<cstdint>` defines `int_leastX_t` and `uint_leastX_t` for *X* = 8, 16, 32, 64. These have at least the specified number of bits. Use them with `0xFF...ull` masks to simulate unavailable fixed-width types.

Bit operations allow working efficiently with powers of two for positive integers:

- $\lfloor \lg(x) \rfloor$ = the position of the highest set bit.
- If x is a power of two, then $x - 1$ has all lower bits = 1. This is an example of **bit-parallelism**, i.e., working on several bits at once with a single word operation.

```
unsigned long long twoPower(int x){return 1ull << x;}
```

```
//careful: returns true for 0
bool isPowerOfTwo(unsigned long long x){return !(x & (x - 1));}
int lgFloor(unsigned long long x)
{
    assert(x);//log of 0 is undefined
    int result = 0;
    while(x >>= 1) ++result;
    return result;
}
int lgCeiling(unsigned long long x){return lgFloor(x) + !isPowerOfTwo(x);}
unsigned long long nextPowerOfTwo(unsigned long long x)
    {return isPowerOfTwo(x) ? x : twoPower(lgFloor(x) + 1);}
```

A **bit mask** is a word such that applying a bit operation to it and *x* gives the wanted result. To work with a single bit at position *i*, the mask for the ith bit is 2^i. Some operations for manipulating bits in word *x*:

- `getValue` produces the word formed by the *n* bits starting from position *i* of *x*
- `setValue` sets the *n* bits of *x* starting from position *i* to the first *n* bits of word `value`
- `isSubset` checks if `subset` represents a subset of `word`, where i^{th} bit determines the item membership
- Masking bit ranges

The main work for these is in computing the mask.

```
namespace Bits
{
unsigned long long const ZERO = 0, ONE = 1, FULL = ~ZERO;
bool get(unsigned long long x, int i){return x & twoPower(i);}
bool flip(unsigned long long x, int i){return x ^ twoPower(i);}
template<typename WORD> void set(WORD& x, int i, bool value)
{
    if(value) x |= twoPower(i);
    else x &= ~twoPower(i);
}
unsigned long long upperMask(int n){return FULL << n;}//11110000
unsigned long long lowerMask(int n){return ~upperMask(n);}//00001111
unsigned long long middleMask(int i, int n)
    {return lowerMask(n)<<i;}//00111000
unsigned long long sideMask(int i, int n)
    {return ~middleMask(i, n);}//11000111
bool isSubset(unsigned long long subset, unsigned long long set)
    {return subset == subset & set;}
template<typename WORD>
unsigned long long rotateLeft(unsigned long long x, int i)
    {return (x << i) || (x >> numeric_limits<unsigned long long>::digits);}
unsigned long long getValue(unsigned long long x, int i, int n)
    {return (x >> i) & lowerMask(n);}
template<typename WORD>
void setValue(WORD& x, unsigned long long value, int i, int n)
{
    WORD mask = middleMask(i, n);
    x &= ~mask;
    x |= mask & (value << i);
}
}//end namespace
```

To compute pop count, i.e., the number of set bits in a word, break it up into bytes, and use a table of precomputed bit counts ∀ byte. On some hardware, if the table isn't in the cache, simple shifting and counting could be faster despite using many more instructions.

```
static char popCount8[] = {
0,1,1,2,1,2,2,3,1,2,2,3,2,3,3,4,1,2,2,3,2,3,3,4,2,3,3,4,3,4,4,5,
1,2,2,3,2,3,3,4,2,3,3,4,3,4,4,5,2,3,3,4,3,4,4,5,3,4,4,5,4,5,5,6,
```

```
1,2,2,3,2,3,3,4,2,3,3,4,3,4,4,5,2,3,3,4,3,4,4,5,3,4,4,5,4,5,5,6,
2,3,3,4,3,4,4,5,3,4,4,5,4,5,5,6,3,4,4,5,4,5,5,6,4,5,5,6,5,6,6,7,
1,2,2,3,2,3,3,4,2,3,3,4,3,4,4,5,2,3,3,4,3,4,4,5,3,4,4,5,4,5,5,6,
2,3,3,4,3,4,4,5,3,4,4,5,4,5,5,6,3,4,4,5,4,5,5,6,4,5,5,6,5,6,6,7,
2,3,3,4,3,4,4,5,3,4,4,5,4,5,5,6,3,4,4,5,4,5,5,6,4,5,5,6,5,6,6,7,
3,4,4,5,4,5,5,6,4,5,5,6,5,6,6,7,4,5,5,6,5,6,6,7,5,6,6,7,6,7,7,8};
int popCount(unsigned long long x)
{
    int result = 0;
    for(; x; x >>= 8) result += popCount8[x & 0xff];
    return result;
}
```

Mixing arithmetic and bit operations enables efficient manipulation of right bits. E.g., to count rightmost *0*'s before the first *1* in a word, change the word so that they become *1* and the other bits *0*, and count the *1*'s:

```
int rightmost0Count(unsigned long long x)
    {return popCount(~x & (x - 1));}
```

Using a table is also a fast, simple method to reverse rightmost bits, which is used in FFT (see the "Large Numbers" chapter):

```
unsigned char reverseBits8[] =
{
0x00, 0x80, 0x40, 0xc0, 0x20, 0xa0, 0x60, 0xe0,
0x10, 0x90, 0x50, 0xd0, 0x30, 0xb0, 0x70, 0xf0,
0x08, 0x88, 0x48, 0xc8, 0x28, 0xa8, 0x68, 0xe8,
0x18, 0x98, 0x58, 0xd8, 0x38, 0xb8, 0x78, 0xf8,
0x04, 0x84, 0x44, 0xc4, 0x24, 0xa4, 0x64, 0xe4,
0x14, 0x94, 0x54, 0xd4, 0x34, 0xb4, 0x74, 0xf4,
0x0c, 0x8c, 0x4c, 0xcc, 0x2c, 0xac, 0x6c, 0xec,
0x1c, 0x9c, 0x5c, 0xdc, 0x3c, 0xbc, 0x7c, 0xfc,
0x02, 0x82, 0x42, 0xc2, 0x22, 0xa2, 0x62, 0xe2,
0x12, 0x92, 0x52, 0xd2, 0x32, 0xb2, 0x72, 0xf2,
0x0a, 0x8a, 0x4a, 0xca, 0x2a, 0xaa, 0x6a, 0xea,
0x1a, 0x9a, 0x5a, 0xda, 0x3a, 0xba, 0x7a, 0xfa,
0x06, 0x86, 0x46, 0xc6, 0x26, 0xa6, 0x66, 0xe6,
0x16, 0x96, 0x56, 0xd6, 0x36, 0xb6, 0x76, 0xf6,
0x0e, 0x8e, 0x4e, 0xce, 0x2e, 0xae, 0x6e, 0xee,
0x1e, 0x9e, 0x5e, 0xde, 0x3e, 0xbe, 0x7e, 0xfe,
0x01, 0x81, 0x41, 0xc1, 0x21, 0xa1, 0x61, 0xe1,
0x11, 0x91, 0x51, 0xd1, 0x31, 0xb1, 0x71, 0xf1,
0x09, 0x89, 0x49, 0xc9, 0x29, 0xa9, 0x69, 0xe9,
0x19, 0x99, 0x59, 0xd9, 0x39, 0xb9, 0x79, 0xf9,
0x05, 0x85, 0x45, 0xc5, 0x25, 0xa5, 0x65, 0xe5,
0x15, 0x95, 0x55, 0xd5, 0x35, 0xb5, 0x75, 0xf5,
0x0d, 0x8d, 0x4d, 0xcd, 0x2d, 0xad, 0x6d, 0xed,
0x1d, 0x9d, 0x5d, 0xdd, 0x3d, 0xbd, 0x7d, 0xfd,
0x03, 0x83, 0x43, 0xc3, 0x23, 0xa3, 0x63, 0xe3,
0x13, 0x93, 0x53, 0xd3, 0x33, 0xb3, 0x73, 0xf3,
0x0b, 0x8b, 0x4b, 0xcb, 0x2b, 0xab, 0x6b, 0xeb,
0x1b, 0x9b, 0x5b, 0xdb, 0x3b, 0xbb, 0x7b, 0xfb,
0x07, 0x87, 0x47, 0xc7, 0x27, 0xa7, 0x67, 0xe7,
0x17, 0x97, 0x57, 0xd7, 0x37, 0xb7, 0x77, 0xf7,
0x0f, 0x8f, 0x4f, 0xcf, 0x2f, 0xaf, 0x6f, 0xef,
0x1f, 0x9f, 0x5f, 0xdf, 0x3f, 0xbf, 0x7f, 0xff
};
template<typename WORD> WORD reverseBits(WORD x)
{
    WORD result = 0;
    for(int i = sizeof(x) - 1; i >= 0; --i)
```

```
    {
        result = (result << 8) + reverseBits8[x & 0xff];
        x >>= 8;
    }
    return result;
}
template<typename WORD> WORD reverseBits(WORD x, int n)
{
    int shift = sizeof(x) * 8 - n;
    assert(n > 0 && shift > n);
    return reverseBits(x) >> shift;
}
```

3.10 Bitset

A bitset behaves like a vector of Booleans, each of which `operator[]` returns by value and not by reference because each is represented by a bit in a vector of words.

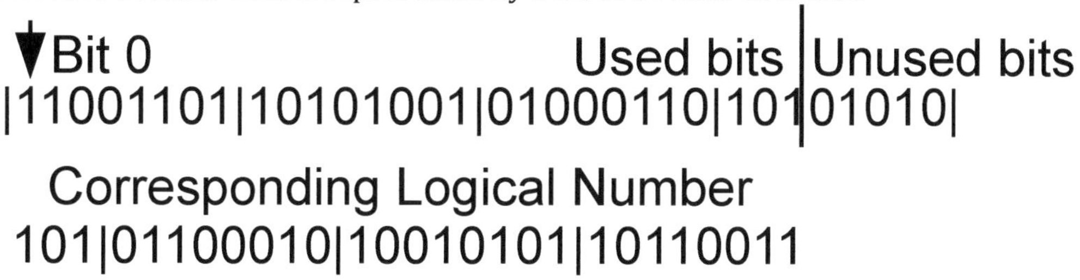

```
Bit 0                              Used bits | Unused bits
|11001101|10101001|01000110|101|01010|

 Corresponding Logical Number
101|01100010|10010101|10110011
```

A bitset supports set operators "&", "|", "^", and "~", which behave as if it were an integer with the least significant bit at 0. For efficiency, bit operations try to use word operations and words of largest possible size, so `unsigned long long` is the default, though on 32-bit machines `unsigned int` may be faster. For portable storage, `unsigned char` avoids endianness incompatibility.

The extra bits in the last word are garbage and zeroed out when needed—simpler than keeping them 0. Let B be the number of bits in the word. The bits are in little-endian order and the logical bit i corresponds to the bit $B - 1 - i \% B$ in the word i/B. Get/set find the word and the bit and apply the corresponding bit operations. Due to using vector, the cost of append is amortized O(1).

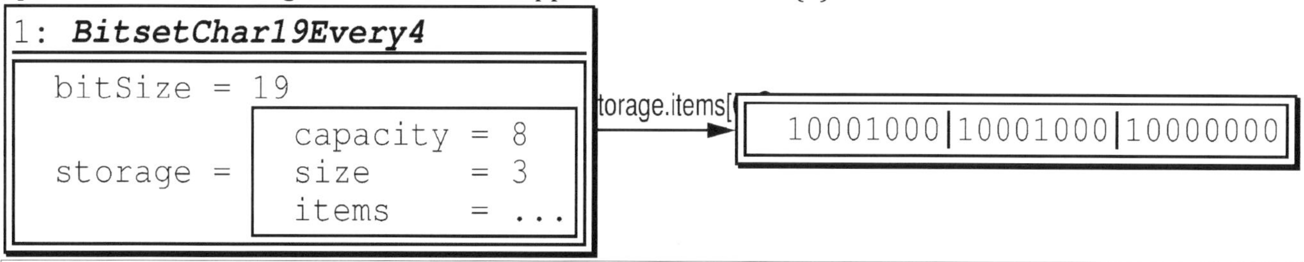

```
1: BitsetChar19Every4
   bitSize = 19
   storage = | capacity = 8
             | size     = 3
             | items    = ...   --storage.items[--> 10001000|10001000|10000000
```

```
template<typename WORD = unsigned long long> class Bitset
{
    enum{B = numeric_limits<WORD>::digits, SHIFT = B - 1};
    unsigned long long bitSize;
    Vector<WORD> storage;
    void zeroOutRemainder()
        {storage.lastItem() &= Bits::upperMask(B - lastWordBits());}
    bool get(int i)const
    {
        assert(i >= 0 && i < bitSize);
        return Bits::get(storage[i/B], SHIFT - i % B);
    }
    unsigned long long wordsNeeded()const{return ceiling(bitSize, B);}
public:
    Bitset(unsigned long long initialSize = 0):
        bitSize(initialSize), storage(wordsNeeded(), wordsNeeded(), 0){}
    Bitset(Vector<WORD> const& vector):
```

```
        storage(vector), bitSize(B * vector.getSize()){}
    int lastWordBits()const
    {
        assert(bitSize > 0);
        int result = bitSize % B;
        if(result == 0) result = B;
        return result;
    }
    int garbageBits()const{return B - lastWordBits();}
    Vector<WORD>& getStorage(){return storage;}
    unsigned long long getSize()const{return bitSize;}
    unsigned long long wordSize()const{return storage.getSize();}
    bool operator[](int i)const{return get(i);}
    void append(bool value)
    {
        ++bitSize;
        if(wordSize() < wordsNeeded()) storage.append(0);
        set(bitSize - 1, value);
    }
    void set(int i, bool value)
    {
        assert(i >= 0 && i < bitSize);
        Bits::set(storage[i/B], SHIFT - i % B, value);
    }
    void removeLast()
    {
        assert(bitSize > 0);
        if(lastWordBits() == 1) storage.removeLast();
        --bitSize;
    }
    bool operator==(Bitset const& rhs)const{return storage == rhs.storage;}
    Bitset& operator&=(Bitset const& rhs)
    {
        for(int i = 0; i < min(wordSize(), rhs.wordSize()); ++i)
            storage[i] &= rhs.storage[i];
        return *this;
    }
    void flip()
        {for(int i = 0; i < wordSize(); ++i) storage[i] = ~storage[i];}
};
```

Replacing `&=` with `|=` or `^=` gives code for these operations. Can implement other set operations efficiently on top of the above.

Shifts ensure that the shift amount > 0 and mod `bitSize`, split it into word and bit shifts, and apply each separately. The word shift part moves the words and fills up the end with 0's. The bit shift part keeps track of carries to split and recombine words correctly. The left shift makes the logical number larger and the right smaller, even though the bits move in the other direction. Both take $O(n/B)$ time.

```
    Bitset& operator>>=(int shift)
    {
        if(shift < 0) return operator<<=(-shift);
        int normalShift = shift % bitSize, wordShift = normalShift/B,
            bitShift = normalShift % B;
        if(wordShift > 0)//shift words
            for(int i = 0; i + wordShift < wordSize(); ++i)
            {
                storage[i] = storage[i + wordShift];
                storage[i + wordShift] = 0;
            }
        if(bitShift > 0)//shift bits
```

```
        {//little endian shift 00000101|00111000 >>= 4 -> 01010011|10000000
            WORD carry = 0;
            zeroOutRemainder();
            for(int i = wordSize() - 1 - wordShift; i >= 0; --i)
            {
                WORD tempCarry = storage[i] >> (SHIFT - bitShift);
                storage[i] <<= bitShift;
                storage[i] |= carry;
                carry = tempCarry;
            }
        }
        return *this;
    }
    Bitset& operator<<=(int shift)
    {
        if(shift < 0) return operator>>=(-shift);
        int normalShift = shift % bitSize, wordShift = normalShift/B,
            bitShift = normalShift % B;
        if(wordShift > 0)//shift words
            for(int i = wordSize() - 1; i - wordShift >= 0; --i)
            {
                storage[i] = storage[i - wordShift];
                storage[i - wordShift] = 0;
            }
        if(bitShift > 0)//shift bits
        {////little endian shift 01010011|10000000 <<= 4 -> 00000101|00111000
            WORD carry = 0;
            for(int i = wordShift; i < wordSize(); ++i)
            {
                WORD tempCarry = storage[i] << (SHIFT - bitShift);
                storage[i] >>= bitShift;
                storage[i] |= carry;
                carry = tempCarry;
            }
        }
        return *this;
    }
```

To check if all bits = 0 or set all bits, for efficiency work with words and not bits:

```
    void setAll(bool value = true)
    {
        for(int i = 0; i < wordSize(); ++i)
            storage[i] = value ? Bits::FULL : Bits::ZERO;
    }
    bool isZero()
    {
        zeroOutRemainder();
        for(int i = 0; i < wordSize(); ++i) if(storage[i])return false;
        return true;
    }
```

To manipulate the bit sequences of size *n* at position *i*, find the affected words and work with their affected bits. In case of several words, the affected bits will be the right ones for the first word, all for the middle words, and the left ones for the last word, i.e., given *xxxxyyyy|yyyyyyyy|yyxxxxxx*, *y* are the affected bits. The cost is O(the number of affected words).

```
    unsigned long long getValue(int i, int n)const
    {
        assert(n <= numeric_limits<unsigned long long>::digits
            && i >= 0 && i + n <= bitSize);
        unsigned long long result = 0;
```

```
        for(int j = 0; j < n; ++j) Bits::set(result, n - 1 - j, get(i + j));
        return result;
    }
    unsigned long long getBitReversedValue(int i, int n)const
    {
        assert(n <= numeric_limits<unsigned long long>::digits && i >= 0 &&
            i + n <= bitSize && n > 0);
        i += n - 1;
        int index = i/B, right = SHIFT - i % B;
        unsigned long long result = Bits::getValue(storage[index], right, n);
        for(int m = B - right; m < n; m += B)
            result |= Bits::getValue(storage[--index], 0, n - m) << m;
        return result;
    }
    void setValue(unsigned long long value, int i, int n)
    {
        assert(n <= numeric_limits<unsigned long long>::digits && i >= 0 &&
            i + n <= bitSize && n > 0);
        for(int j = 0; j < n; ++j) set(i + j, Bits::get(value, n - 1 - j));
    }
    void setBitReversedValue(unsigned long long value, int i, int n)
    {
        assert(n <= numeric_limits<unsigned long long>::digits && i >= 0 &&
            i + n <= bitSize && n > 0);
        i += n - 1;
        int index = i/B, right = SHIFT - i % B;
        assert(index >= 0 && index < storage.getSize());
        Bits::setValue(storage[index], value, right, n);
        for(int m = B - right; m < n; m += B)
        {
            --index;
            assert(index >= 0);
            Bits::setValue(storage[index], value >> m, 0, n - m);
        }
    }
```

The append operations are implemented in terms of `setValue` by increasing capacity if needed and setting the last bits to the wanted value:

```
    void appendValue(unsigned long long value, int n,
        bool reverseBits = false)
    {
        int start = bitSize;
        bitSize += n;
        int k = wordsNeeded() - wordSize();
        for(int i = 0; i < k; ++i) storage.append(0);
        if(reverseBits) setBitReversedValue(value, start, n);
        else setValue(value, start, n);
    }
    void appendBitset(Bitset const& rhs)
    {
        for(int i = 0; i < rhs.wordSize(); ++i)
            appendValue(rhs.storage[i], B, true);
        bitSize -= B - rhs.lastWordBits();
        if(wordSize() > wordsNeeded()) storage.removeLast();
    }
```

Reversing the bits is like that of vector but uses value-based swap because !∃references to single bits. Pop count = ∑pop counts of individual words.

```
    void reverse()
    {
```

```
        for(int i = 0; i < bitSize/2; ++i)
        {
            bool temp = get(i);
            set(i, get(bitSize - 1 - i));
            set(bitSize - 1 - i, temp);
        }
    }
    int popCount()
    {
        zeroOutRemainder();
        int sum = 0;
        for(int i = 0; i < wordSize(); ++i) sum += popCount(storage[i]);
        return sum;
    }
```

3.11 *k*-Bit Word Vector

To save space for representing sequences of enumerations such as DNA, use a vector of k-bit integers representing values $\in [0, 2^k - 1]$. It's a facade implemented on top of bitset. Random access is O(1), and append amortized O(1).

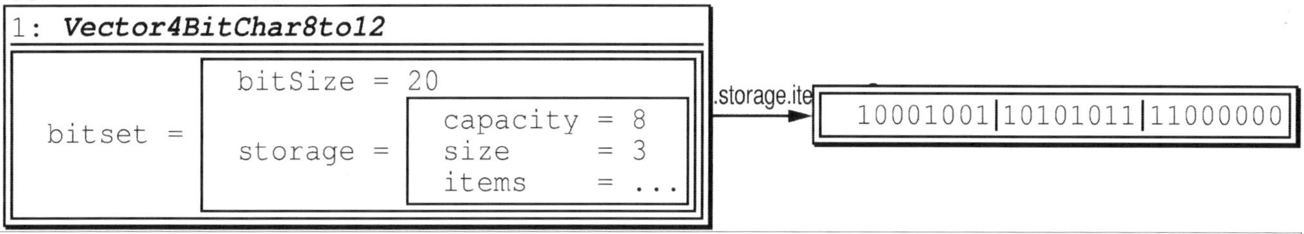

```
1: Vector4BitChar8to12
bitset =   bitSize = 20
           storage =   capacity = 8
                       size     = 3
                       items    = ...   .storage.ite → 10001001|10101011|11000000
```

```
template<int N, typename WORD = unsigned long long> class KBitVector
{
    Bitset<WORD> bitset;
public:
    WORD operator[](unsigned long long i){return bitset.getValue(i * N, N);}
    void set(WORD value, unsigned long long i)
        {bitset.setValue(value, i * N, N);}
    void append(WORD value){bitset.appendValue(value, N);}
    unsigned long long getSize(){return bitset.getSize()/N;}
};
```

3.12 Union-Find

Union-find solves the **disjoint set problem** of maintaining an equivalence relation on subsets of items. Supported operations:

- Increase the set's size
- **Join** two subsets
- Check if two items are in the same subset
- Get the size of the subset containing an item

Without loss of generality, consecutive positive integers represent all items. The data structure is a vector of integers, initially set to −1, with vector[i] representing the node i. The integers represent negative subset sizes for root nodes and parent indices otherwise. Two items are in the same subset if their root indices are equal. To join two roots:

1. **Make one child of the other**
2. **Change its integer to the index of the other**
3. **Set the integer of the other to −total size**

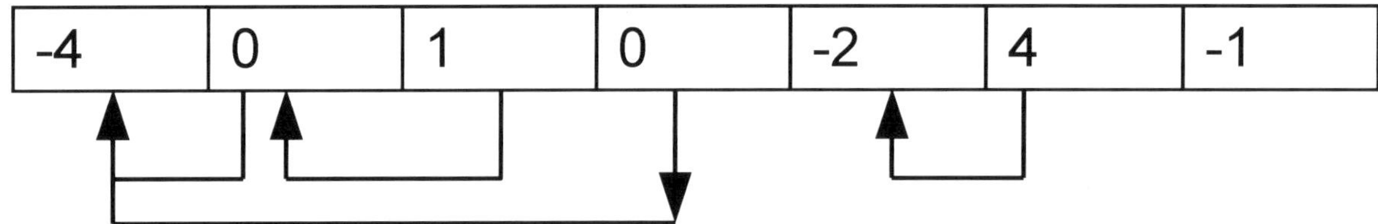

Finding a root follows the chain of parent pointers to it, compresses the path by setting the parent of every visited node to the root, and returns its index. Getting the subset size returns −the value at `findRoot`. Join makes the root of the smaller subset a child of the root of the larger one.

```
class UnionFind
{
    Vector<int> parent;//parent or negated size of the tree
public:
    UnionFind(int size): parent(size, size, -1){}
    int find(int n)
        {return parent[n] < 0 ? n : (parent[n] = find(parent[n]));}
    void join(int i, int j)
    {
        int parentI = find(i), parentJ = find(j);
        if(parentI != parentJ)
        {//parent[parentI] and parent[parentJ] are negative sizes
            if(parent[parentI] > parent[parentJ]) swap(parentI, parentJ);
            parent[parentI] += parent[parentJ];
            parent[parentJ] = parentI;
        }
    }
    bool areEquivalent(int i, int j){find(i) == find(j);}
    int subsetSize(int i){return -parent[find(i)];}
    void increaseSize(int newSize)
        {while(parent.getSize() < newSize) parent.append(-1);}
};
```

Find and join are O(lg(n)) and amortized O(1) ∀ practical n. A slightly faster algorithm (Patwary et al. 2010) is more complicated and doesn't allow checking subset sizes.

3.13 References

Joannou, S., & Raman, R. (2011). An empirical evaluation of extendible arrays. In *Experimental Algorithms* (pp. 447–458). Springer.

Patwary, M. M. A., Blair, J., & Manne, F. (2010). Experiments on union-find algorithms for the disjoint-set data structure. In *Experimental Algorithms* (pp. 411–423). Springer.

Warren, H. S. (2012). *Hacker's Delight*. Addison-Wesley.

4 Monte Carlo Methods

4.1 A Quick Review of Probability

Probability measures likelihood of events E_i, which are subsets of a sample space S. E.g., S can be the real numbers and E_i intervals. Mathematically, probability is defined by the **Kolmogorov axioms**:

- $\Pr(E_i) \geq 0$
- $\Pr(S) = 1$
- For disjoint events, $\Pr(\cup E_i) = \sum E_i$

A **probability distribution** uses a **probability density function** (PDF) f to assign values to $x \in S$ such that $\forall E \Pr(E) = \int_{x \in E} f(x)$. The **cumulative distribution function** (CDF) $F(x) = \int_{\infty < t \leq x} f(t)$ is often more convenient to work with. Some important distributions with their PDFs and CDFs:

- **Normal**(μ, σ)—μ is the mean and σ the standard deviation. It models many events and is heavily used. E.g., normal(0, 1):

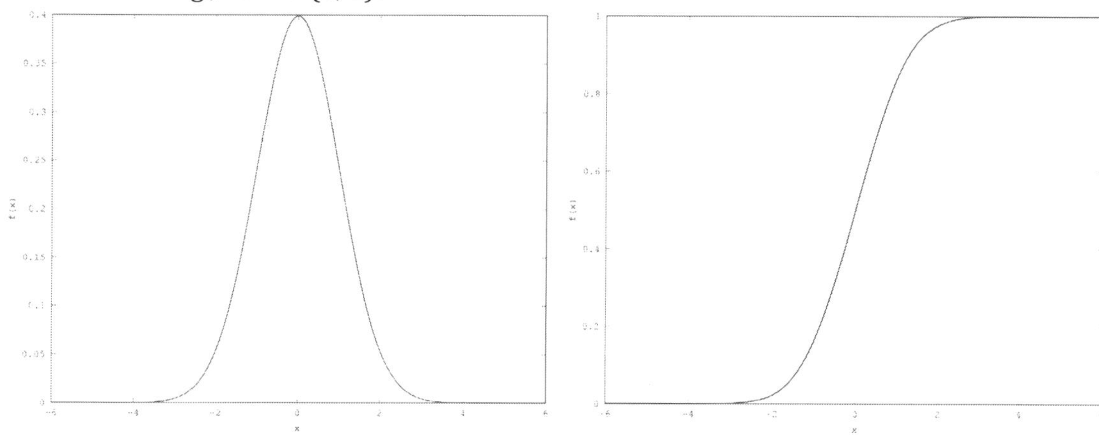

- **Geometric**(p)—$f(x) = (1 - p)^{x-1}p$—for discrete x. E.g., geometric(0.5):

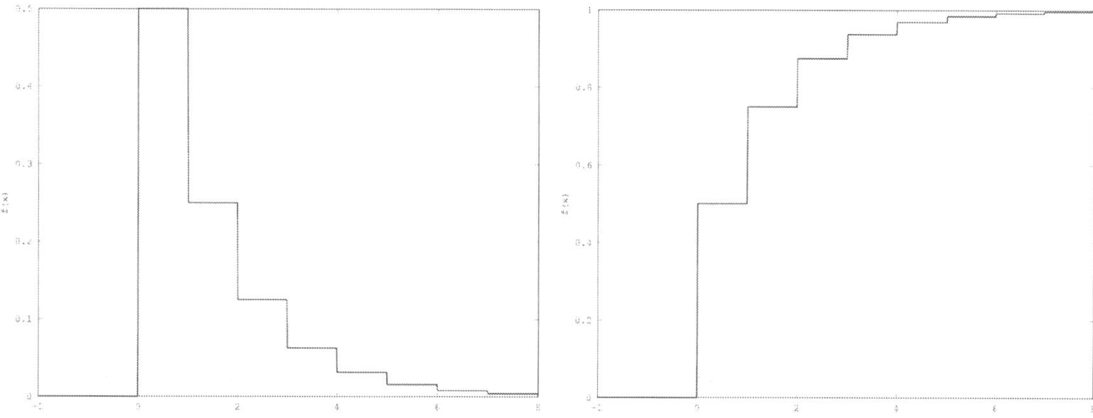

Certain naturally occurring events don't have known probabilities, and distributions are often used to assign probabilities approximately. Because many events follow the normal distribution, many others are incorrectly considered normally distributed when they aren't. Every distribution is a good approximate model for some events and a bad one for others. E.g., the normal is a bad model for a flying bird's avoiding a pole because the bird will swerve left or right, producing a two-peaked distribution:

In many cases, the needed information about the data isn't the full probability distribution but a summary statistic such as **expected value** $\mu = \int_{x \in S} x f(x)$ or **variance** $\sigma^2 = E[(x - \mu)^2]$.

4.2 Pseudorandom Number Generation

Games, randomized algorithms, and simulations use random numbers, from which can create more complex random objects. A number sequence is random if observing its past outputs doesn't help predict the next one.

Uniformly distributed physical phenomena such as atmospheric noise or radioactive decay give such random numbers and should be used in lotteries or jury selection, where need high quality randomness. E.g., see www.random.org. Also, special generator devices are available, and operating systems have a random stream generated from the CPU or hard drive activity. These are used for cryptographic algorithms but are slow and unportable. If a binary source generates heads with probability $p \neq 0.5$, can get unbiased bits:

1. **Flip twice until get HT or TH**
2. **If HT return H**
3. **Else return T**

This way heads and tails occur with equal probability. E[number of flips] = $1/(p(1 - p))$, and technically have no finite worst case bound.

```
template<typename BIASED_COIN> class FairCoin
{
    BIASED_COIN biasedCoin;
    FairCoin(BIASED_COIN const& theBiasedCoin = BIASED_COIN()):
        biasedCoin(theBiasedCoin){}
    bool flip()
    {//HT is 1, TH is 0, ignore HH and TT
        bool flip1;
        do{flip1 = biasedCoin.flip();} while(flip1 == biasedCoin.flip());
        return flip1;
    }
};
```

Fast **pseudo-random generators** generate a random sequence starting from some **initial state**. The output and the next state are respectively output and **transition** functions of the current state. Usually, need O(1) time for both and O(1) space for state.

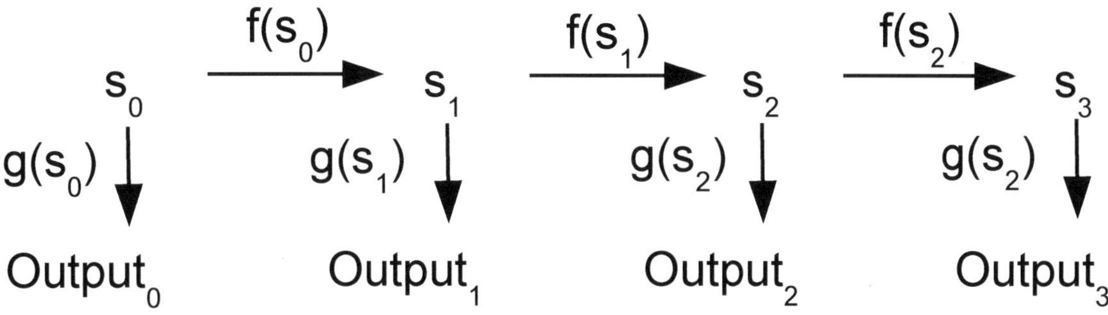

The initial state can be a function of the system time and a password, for simplicity and portability. Use other sources if need more random bits. For a complete independence of generator runs, save its state to a file, and restore for the next simulation.

Generators differ only in state representation and transition and output functions. The simplest generators use a single word state and the identity output function. Output usually has 32 or 64 bits. Combine consecutive 32-bit outputs to get 64-bit outputs if needed. Good generators:

- Pass most tests of extensive statistical suites, such as TestU01 (L'Ecuyer & Simard 2007), that try to reject the hypothesis that the sequence is random and have **period** (after how many transitions the state = the initial state) $\geq 2^{64}$ and high **equidistribution** (max k for which a sequence of k outputs can be any sequence).
- Are efficient, simple, portable, and easy to initialize.
- Return a random `double` $u \in (0, 1)$, and not $[0, 1]$, to avoid undefined results for transformations such as $\log(u)$. No generator produces 2^w, so normalization constant $\geq 2^w$ takes care of the 1. Some generators also don't produce 0, which takes care of the 0. If a generator produces 0, use $\max(1, u)$ or generate until $u \neq 0$.
- Optionally generate **independent streams** for parallel computations. This implies very long period and the ability to skip forward efficiently.

Historically popular **linear congruential generator** with single-word state s transition $s = (as + c)$ % m (e.g., with $a = 69069$, $c = 1234567$, and $m = 2^{32}$), has poor quality:

- The period of the lower k bits = 2^k
- It fails many tests
- To avoid overflow, the multiplication needs double-word precision or breaking up into parts

The C++ `rand()` is based on a LCG.

4.3 Xorshift

The transition multiplies the bit vector represented by *state* by a sparse Boolean matrix and is implemented by a sequence of shifts and xors. The sequence used here has good test suite results; mathematical justification of Xorshift properties is complicated (Press et al. 2007).

```
class Xorshift
{
    unsigned int state;
    enum{PASSWORD = 19870804};
public:
    Xorshift(unsigned int seed = time(0) ^ PASSWORD)
    {
        assert(numeric_limits<unsigned int>::digits == 32);
        state = seed ? seed : PASSWORD;
    }
    static unsigned int transform(unsigned int x)
    {
        x ^= x << 13;
        x ^= x >> 17;
        x ^= x << 5;
        return x;
```

```
    }
    unsigned int next(){return state = transform(state);}
    double uniform01(){return 2.32830643653869629E-10 * next();}
};
```

The period is only $2^{32} - 1$ (0 is never generated), and the bits of successive numbers have some correlation due to linearity of matrix multiplication. So, for 32 bits, **ImprovedXorshift** outputs Xorshift + the LCG from the previous section example. This improves correlation and increases the period of the higher-order bits.

```
class ImprovedXorshift
{
    unsigned int state1, state2;
    enum{PASSWORD = 19870804};
public:
    ImprovedXorshift(unsigned int seed = time(0) ^ PASSWORD)
    {
        assert(numeric_limits<unsigned int>::digits == 32);
        state1 = seed ? seed : PASSWORD;
        state2 = state1;
    }
    unsigned int next()
    {
        state1 ^= state1 << 13;
        state1 ^= state1 >> 17;
        state1 ^= state1 << 5;
        state2 = state2 * 69069U + 1234567U;
        return state1 + state2;
    }//may return 0
    double uniform01(){return 2.32830643653869629E-10 * max(1u, next());}
};
```

For the 64-bit versions, which use different shifts, reducing correlation is more important than increasing the period, so **QualityXorshift64** outputs the LCG successor of the result:

```
class QualityXorshift64
{
    unsigned long long state;
    enum{PASSWORD = 19870804};
public:
    QualityXorshift64(unsigned long long seed = time(0) ^ PASSWORD)
    {
        assert(numeric_limits<unsigned long long>::digits == 64);
        state = seed ? seed : PASSWORD;
    }
    static unsigned long long transform(unsigned long long x)
    {
        x ^= x << 21;
        x ^= x >> 35;
        x ^= x << 4;
        return x * 2685821657736338717ull;
    }
    unsigned long long next(){return state = transform(state);}
    double uniform01(){return 5.42101086242752217E-20 * next();}
};
```

It doesn't generate 0 because the multiplication constant is prime, and for a prime p $0 = xp \% 2^{64} \rightarrow xp = c2^{64}$. Because $c > p$, c divides p, implying a contradiction that $x = (p/c)2^{64}$, while x is less. The Xorshift transitions are one-to-one and the LCG ones aren't.

4.4 MRG32k3a

Multiple recursive generator (MRG) generalizes LCG by being a linear combination of several last states mod m. MRG32k3a combines output of two three-state generators, which use the transition $s_{i,\text{next}} = c_i = s_i T_i \% m_i$, with suitably chosen transition matrices T_i and moduli m_i. Both parameters were picked by an exhaustive search, and the suggested matrices are sparse for efficiency (L'Ecuyer 1999). The output is a combination of the c_i. Efficient stream skipping is supported because can skip using efficient exponentiation mod m (see the "Large Numbers" chapter) on the matrix, and multiply the result by the state vector. The recommended jump size = 2^{76}, and the resulting matrices are already computed (L'Ecuyer et al. 2002).

```
struct MRG32k3a
{
    enum{PASSWORD = 19870804};
    static long long const m1 = 4294967087ll, m2 = 4294944443ll;
    long long s10, s11, s12, s20, s21, s22;
    void reduceAndUpdate(long long c1, long long c2)
    {
        if(c1 < 0) c1 = m1 - (-c1 % m1);
        else c1 %= m1;
        if(c2 < 0) c2 = m2 - (-c2 % m2);
        else c2 %= m2;
        s10 = s11; s11 = s12; s12 = c1;
        s20 = s21; s21 = s22; s22 = c2;
    }
public:
    unsigned int next()
    {
        long long c1 = (1403580 * s11 - 810728 * s10),
            c2 = (527612 * s22 - 1370589 * s20);
        reduceAndUpdate(c1, c2);
        return (c1 <= c2 ? m1 : 0) + c1 - c2;
    }
    //s1(0-2) and s2(0-2) must be respectively < m1 and m2 and not all 0
    MRG32k3a(): s10(max(time(0) ^ PASSWORD, 1l) % m2), s11(0), s12(0),
        s20(s10), s21(0), s22(0){}
    double uniform01(){return next()/(m1 + 1.0);}
    void jumpAhead()
    {
        const long long A1p76[3][3] = {
            {  82758667u, 1871391091u, 4127413238u},//for s10
            {3672831523u,   69195019u, 1871391091u},//for s11
            {3672091415u, 3528743235u,   69195019u}},//for s12
            A2p76[3][3] = {
                {1511326704u, 3759209742u, 1610795712u},//for s20
                {4292754251u, 1511326704u, 3889917532u},//for s21
                {3859662829u, 4292754251u, 3708466080u}};//for s22
        long long s1[3] = {s10, s11, s12}, s2[3] = {s20, s21, s22};
        for(int i = 0; i < 3; ++i)
        {
            long long c1 = 0, c2 = 0;
            for(int j = 0; j < 3; ++j)
            {
                c1 += s1[j] * A1p76[i][j];
                c2 += s2[j] * A2p76[i][j];
            }
            reduceAndUpdate(c1, c2);
        }
    }
};
```

4.5 RC4

Cryptographically secure random output isn't predicable by any efficient method whose result is more than negligibly better than a guess. RC4 securely generates a byte at a time from a random enough initial key. To avoid known attacks, it drops the first 1024 bytes. "RC4" is trademarked and implementations call it "**ARC4**", though the trademark is probably lost due to nondefense. The logic behind the algorithm is complicated, and its security is still not well-understood (Wikipedia 2013). Intuitively, it tries to generate and maintain something like a random permutation.

```
struct ARC4
{
    unsigned char sBox[256], i, j;
    enum{PASSWORD = 19870804};
    void construct(unsigned char* seed, int length)
    {
        j = 0;
        for(int k = 0; k < 256; ++k) sBox[k] = k;
        for(int k = 0; k < 256; ++k)
        {//different from the random permutation algorithm
            j += sBox[k] + seed[k % length];
            swap(sBox[k], sBox[j]);
        }
        i = j = 0;
        for(int dropN = 1024; dropN > 0; dropN--) nextByte();
    }
    ARC4(unsigned long long seed = time(0) ^ PASSWORD)
        {construct((unsigned char*)&seed, sizeof(seed));}
    //for crytographic initialization from a long seed
    ARC4(unsigned char* seed, int length){construct(seed, length);}
    unsigned char nextByte()
    {
        j += sBox[++i];
        swap(sBox[i], sBox[j]);
        return sBox[(sBox[i] + sBox[j]) % 256];
    }
    unsigned long long next()
    {
        unsigned long long result = 0;
        for(int k = 0; k < sizeof(result); ++k)
            result |= ((unsigned long long)nextByte()) << (8 * k);
        return result;
    }
    double uniform01(){return 5.42101086242752217E-20 * max(1ull, next());}
};
```

It still uses O(1) time and space due to 256's being a constant.

4.6 Picking a Generator

Generator	Period, Memory for state	Number of TestU01 failures	Seconds for 2^{30} `next()` calls	Special considerations
Xorshift	$2^{32}-1$, 4 bytes	> 65	3	Simplest, fastest, good as a 32-bit hash function
ImprovedXorshift	$2^{64}-1$, 8 bytes	8	4.2	May return 0, useful only if 64-bit arithmetic isn't available
Xorshift64	$2^{64}-1$, 8 bytes	16, with different shifts	6.3	Useful only as a building block

QualityXorshift64	$2^{64} - 1$, 8 bytes	0 for smaller suite Diehard	6.6	Simple, good as a 64-bit hash function
MGR32k3a	$\approx 2^{182}$, 24 bytes	0	25.6	Supports skipping
RC4	Huge, 256 bytes	0	47.8	Cryptographic

Simulations aim to not lose significance due to nonrandomness, and randomized algorithms to be efficient overall. All generators are fast enough to make use of the result the bottleneck in most cases. Use QualityXorshift64 as default. For simulations, use MGR32k3a due to its very high quality and independent stream support. For cryptography, use RC4.

A global object does generation. It also generates numbers mod n and $\in [a, b]$, and most random object generators are its members. Random objects, such as permutations and samples from probability distributions, are heavily used by various randomized algorithms and calculation methods.

```
template<typename GENERATOR = QualityXorshift64> struct Random
{
    GENERATOR random;
    unsigned long long next(){return random.next();}
    unsigned long long mod(unsigned long long n)
    {
        assert(n > 0);
        return next() % n;
    }
    long long inRange(long long a, long long b){return a + mod(b - a + 1);}
    double uniform01(){return random.uniform01();}
};
```

4.7 Generating Samples from Distributions

Most generation algorithms use u generated by uniform(0, 1). Several general methods work for continuous distributions:

- **Inverse**—a cumulative probability distribution F is a function $x \to [0, 1]$, so $F^{-1}(u)$ is a random variate. E.g., see the exponential distribution in the next section. This works well when F^{-1} is easy to calculate; otherwise, numerically solving $F(x) = u$ works but is slow. For the latter, find a range containing the x corresponding to u, using exponential search starting from $x = 0$ in the "+" or the "−" direction depending on whether $F(0) < u$, and apply bisection (see the "Numerical Algorithms" chapter). This also works for discrete distributions but not for multidimensional ones. MCMC methods (discussed later in this chapter) are usually more efficient.

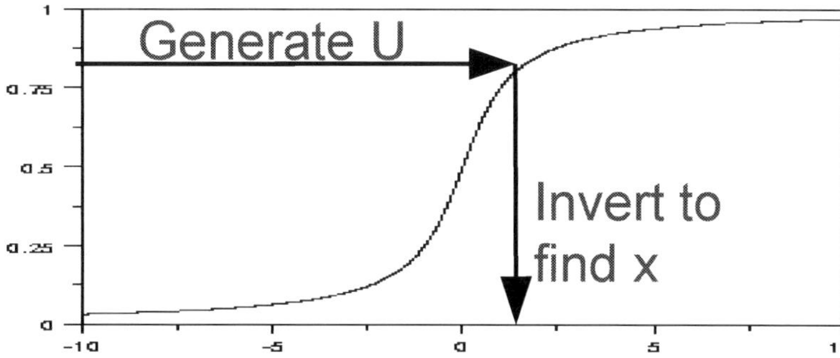

- **Accept/reject**—If $x \in A$ is uniformly distributed in A, $B \subseteq A$, and $x \in B$, then x is uniformly distributed in B. Let f, g be PDFs such that for some constant $c > 0$ $\forall x \in \mathbb{R}^D$ $f(x) < cg(x)$. If x is generated from g and u from uniform(0, $cg(x)$) and $u \leq f(x)$, then x is distributed according to f (Devroye 1986). So generate x and u until $u \leq f(x)$ and return x. This works for discrete and multidimensional distributions, but for large D is inefficient because E[the number of rejections] is exponential in D. Need only an inside/outside membership tester, and can speed up generation by checking if a sample is inside a fast-to-test-membership **squeeze function** contained by f (e.g., see the gamma generator later in this chapter). A technical issue is that the number of generations is $O(\infty)$, even though it's exponentially unlikely to be large.

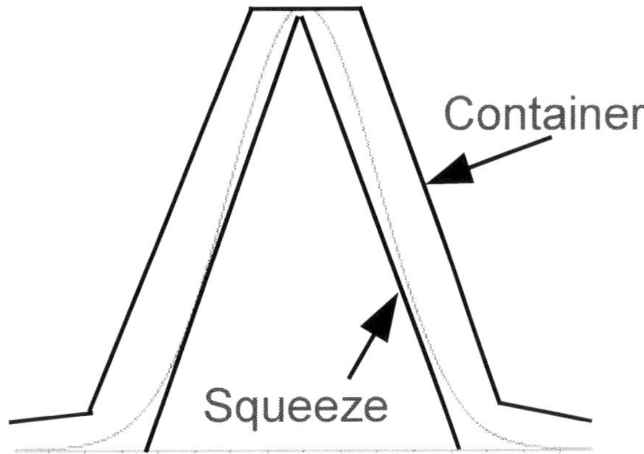

- Relationships among distributions—can use variates from some distributions, particularly normal and gamma, to generate from related distributions.
- **Composition method**—can partition a density defined on (a, b) into two densities defined on (a, c) and (c, b), and generate from each using different method. This is most convenient for distribution parameters—e.g., the gamma generator uses different strategies depending on whether the shape parameter < 1.

4.8 Generating Samples from Discrete Distributions

For an arbitrary bounded discrete distribution represented as an array p of n probabilities, if need to generate only O(1) values, the simplest and fastest method is to generate u and do a linear search to find the first index i such that $\sum p_i \geq u$.

For many values, the **alias method** uses $O(n)$ memory and supports O(1) generation. With equal probabilities, each is $1/n$. In general, some probabilities will have more (**rich**) and others less (**poor**), but the average is still $1/n$. So can pair up every poor with a single rich that gives it probability. A rich can get poor by giving too much and will be paired with another rich. Then $\forall i$ $1/n = p_i$ + the net taken and given amount. An alias is the index of the donor. To sample:

1. Generate uniformly random *i*
2. If *i* has no donor, return *i*
3. Else generate uniform(0, $1/n$), and return *i* or its donor, with probability proportional to the taken amount

All probability is accounted for. To simplify, instead of the probabilities use wealth$_i$ = np_i. The pairing is greedy:

1. Put every index *i* in the poor list if its wealth < 1, and the rich list otherwise
2. Until either list is empty
3. Pick a poor and a rich, take from the rich as much as the poor needs
4. Move the rich to the poor list if it becomes poor

Can use any type of list, but a stack is simple and common. Both lists should become empty at the same time, but not always due to round-off. The total shrinks even if a rich becomes poor, so have $O(n)$ runtime.

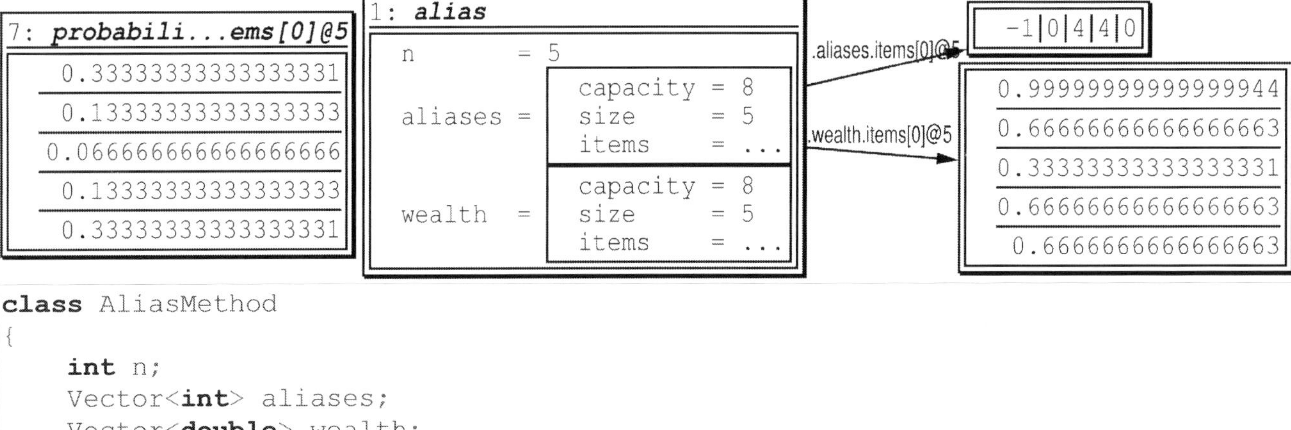


```
class AliasMethod
{
    int n;
    Vector<int> aliases;
    Vector<double> wealth;
public:
```

```
    AliasMethod(Vector<double> const& probabilities):
        n(probabilities.getSize()), aliases(n, -1), wealth(n, 0)
    {
        Stack<int> smaller, greater;
        for(int i = 0; i < n; ++i)
        {//separate into poor and rich
            (wealth[i] = n * probabilities[i]) < 1 ?
                smaller.push(i) : greater.push(i);
        }
        while(!smaller.isEmpty() && !greater.isEmpty())
        {//reassign wealth until no poor remain
            int rich = greater.getTop(), poor = smaller.pop();
            aliases[poor] = rich;
            wealth[rich] -= 1 - wealth[poor];
            if(wealth[rich] < 1) smaller.push(greater.pop());
        }
    }
    int next()
    {//-1 check handles wealth round-off accumulation
        int x = GlobalRNG.mod(n);
        return GlobalRNG.uniform01() < wealth[x] || aliases[x] == -1 ?
            x : aliases[x];
    }
};
```

Sum heap uses no extra space and allows efficient generation, updates, retrieval, and cumulative probability retrieval. It's a tree where the value of parent = ∑the values of its children and itself:

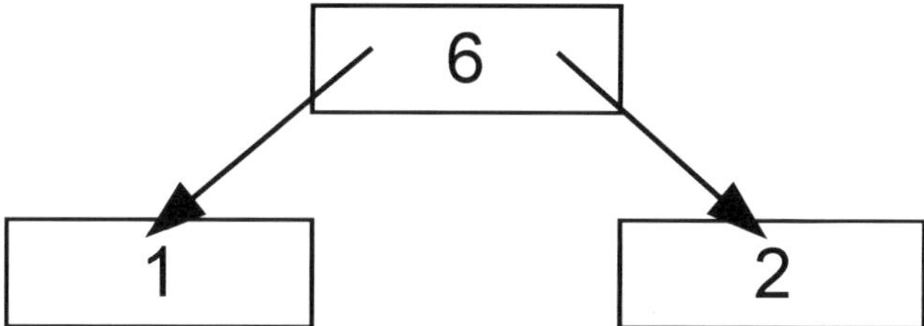

For a probability distribution, the root's value = 1, unless the distribution isn't normalized and the root's value is the normalization constant. The heap represents [0, 1] recursively by [left CDF] ∪ [right CDF] ∪ [parent PDF], where value of parent PDF = parent – left – right. It initializes every value to 0. Most operations take O(lg(n)) time with low constant factors. Values are set using incremental updates. An update adds the increment amount to the node and its every ancestor. As for binary heap (see the "Priority Queues" chapter), the implementation uses a vector for storage.

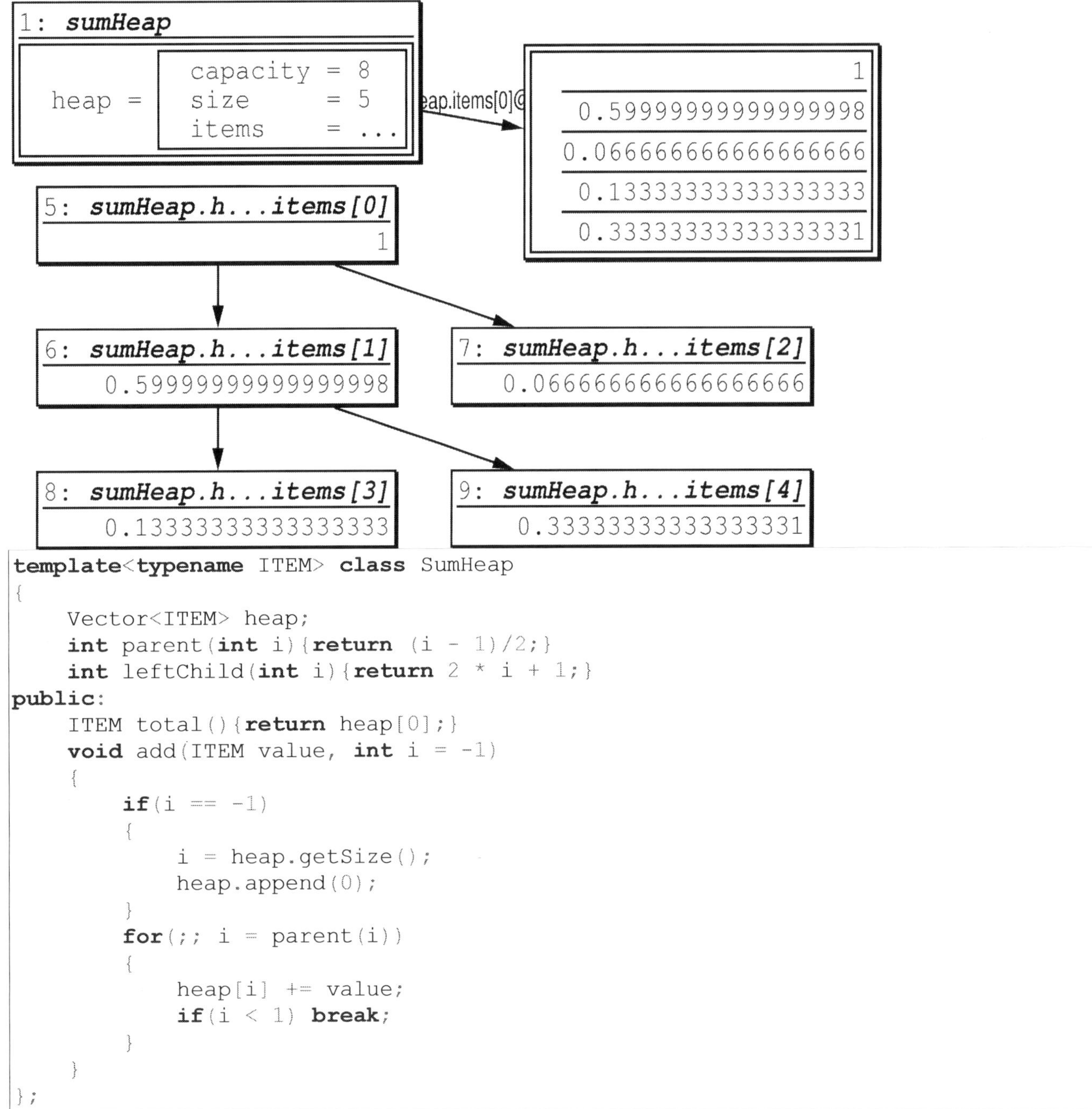


```
template<typename ITEM> class SumHeap
{
    Vector<ITEM> heap;
    int parent(int i){return (i - 1)/2;}
    int leftChild(int i){return 2 * i + 1;}
public:
    ITEM total(){return heap[0];}
    void add(ITEM value, int i = -1)
    {
        if(i == -1)
        {
            i = heap.getSize();
            heap.append(0);
        }
        for(;; i = parent(i))
        {
            heap[i] += value;
            if(i < 1) break;
        }
    }
};
```

Generation uses the interval relationship. Given a value ∈ [0, the root's value], find the corresponding node by checking where it lands in the interval of the current node and returning it or continuing to one of its children:

```
    int find(ITEM value)
    {//boundary goes to index with smaller cumulative
        assert(0 <= value && value <= total());
        ITEM left = 0;
        for(int i = 0, c;; i = c)
        {
            c = leftChild(i);
            if(c >= heap.getSize()) return i;
            if(value > left + heap[c])
            {
                left += heap[c++];
                if(c >= heap.getSize() || value > left + heap[c]) return i;
            }
        }
```

```
    }
    int next(){return find(GlobalRNG.uniform01() * total());}
```

CDF of a node = its value + ∑the values of all its left siblings on the path to the root.

```
    ITEM cumulative(int i)
    {
        ITEM sum = heap[i];
        while(i > 0)
        {
            int last = i;
            i = parent(i);
            int l = leftChild(i);
            if(l != last) sum += heap[l];
        }
        return sum;
    }
    ITEM get(int i)
    {
        ITEM result = heap[i];
        int c = leftChild(i);
        if(c < heap.getSize())
        {
            result -= heap[c];
            if(++c < heap.getSize()) result -= heap[c];
        }
        return result;
    }
```

4.9 Generating Samples from Specific Distributions

The mathematics behind many generation algorithms is complicated and discussed in the references. Important continuous distributions:

- **Uniform(*a*, *b*)** with $a < b$. $f(x) = 1/(b - a)$ if $a \leq x \leq b$ and 0 otherwise. $F(x) = 0$ if $x < a$, $(x - a)/(b - a)$ if $a \leq x \leq b$, and 1 if $x > b$. The generator scales u:

```
    double uniform(double a, double b){return a + (b - a) * uniform01();}
```

- **Exponential(*a*)** models times between independent events, such as times between traffic accidents for a particular driver. $f(x) = ae^{-ax}$ and $F(x) = 1 - e^{-ax}$. To use the inverse method, let $F(x) = u$, and solve for x to get $x = -\ln(1 - u)/a$, which simplifies to $-\ln(u)/a$ because u and $1 - u$ have the same distribution (don't forget that in `<cmath>` `log` uses base e):

```
    double exponential(double a){return -log(uniform01())/a;}
```

- **Cauchy(*μ*, *σ*)**—very fat tails and undefined expectation. Intuitively, the latter because a single observation can account for > 99% of the sample variance. $f(x) = 1/(\pi + ((x - \mu)/\sigma)^2)$ and $F(x) = \arctan((x - \mu)/\sigma)/\pi + 0.5$. Generation uses the inverse method by solving this:

```
    static double PI(){return 3.1415926535897932384626433832795;}
    double cauchy(double m, double q)
        {return (tan((uniform01() - 0.5) * PI()) + m) * q;}
```

- **Normal(*μ*, *σ*)**—widely used and needed by other generators. $f(x) = \exp(-((x - \mu)\sigma)^2/2)/(\sigma\sqrt{2\pi})$ and $F(x) = (1 + erf((x - \mu)/(\sigma\sqrt{2})))/2$, where *erf* is the error function. Generation uses the **polar method**, specific to the normal distribution, whose mechanics and proof are complicated (Press et al. 2007). E[the runtime] = O(1).

```
    double normal01()
    {
        for(;;)
        {
            double a = 2 * uniform01() - 1, b = 2 * uniform01() - 1,
                c = a * a + b * b;
            if(c < 1)
```

```
            {
                double temp = sqrt(-2 * log(c)/c);
                return a * temp;//can return b * temp as 2nd iid sample
            }
        }
    }
    double normal(double m, double q){return m + q * normal01();}
```

- **Gamma(1, *b*)**—used by other generators. The generator mechanics are complicated, but the basic idea is to accept/reject with a fast polynomial squeeze function (Marsaglia & Tsang 2000). E[the runtime] = O(1).

```
double gamma1(double b)
{
    if(b >= 1)
    {
        for(double third = 1.0/3, d = b - third, x, v, u, xs;;)
        {
            do
            {
                x = normal01();
                v = 1 + x * third/sqrt(d);
            }while(v <= 0);
            v *= v * v; u = uniform01(), xs = x * x;
            if(u > 0.0331 * xs * xs || log(u) < xs/2 +
                d * (1 - v + log(v))) return d * v;
        }
    }
    else
    {
        assert(b > 0);
        return pow(uniform01(), 1/b) * gamma1(b + 1);
    }
}
```

- Derived from gamma using relationships between distributions:

```
double erlang(double m, int k){return gamma1(k) * m/k;}
double chiSquared(int k){return 2 * gamma1(k/2.0);}
double t(int v){return sqrt(v/chiSquared(v)) * normal01();}
double beta(double p, double q)
{
    double G1 = gamma1(p);
    return G1/(G1 + gamma1(q));
}
double F(int v1, int v2)
    {return v2 * chiSquared(v1)/(v1 * chiSquared(v2));}
```

- **Triangular(*middle*)**—PDF is the triangle formed by the points (0,0), (*middle*, 1), and (1, 0). Generator is obtained by integrating to get CDF and using the inverse method (Wikipedia 2015d):

```
double triangular01(double middle)
{
    double u = uniform01();
    return sqrt(u <= middle ? middle * u : (1 - middle) * (1 - u));
}
```

For discrete distributions using relationships between distributions often gives good generators.

- **Bernoulli(*p*)**—1 with probability p and 0 with $1 - p$:

```
bool bernoulli(double p){return uniform01() <= p;}
```

- **Binomial(*p*, *n*)**—a sum of n Bernoulli(p). The runtime is O(n).

```
int binomial(double p, int n)
{
```

```
    int result = 0;
    for(int i = 0; i < n; ++i) result += bernoulli(p);
    return result;
}
```

- **Geometric(p)**—the number of times Bernoulli(p) = 0 before it's 1. E[the runtime] = O($1/p$).

```
int geometric(double p)
{
    assert(p > 0);
    int result = 0;
    while(!bernoulli(p)) ++result;
    return result;
}
```

- **Poisson(l)**—the number of independent events in a given time interval with l average. Intervals between events are exponentially distributed, so generate intervals between events and count how many fit into the l interval. To avoid logs in exponential generator, work with the exponentiated values directly. The runtime is O(l).

```
int poisson(double l)
{
    assert(l > 0);
    int result = -1;
    for(double p = 1; p > exp(-l); p *= uniform01()) ++result;
    return result;
}
```

```
GlobalRNG.uniform01() 0.904229
GlobalRNG.uniform(10, 20) 10.2389
GlobalRNG.normal01() 0.508248
GlobalRNG.normal(10, 20) -8.47315
GlobalRNG.exponential01() 1.42522
GlobalRNG.gamma1(0.5) 0.00646845
GlobalRNG.gamma1(1.5) 0.355508
GlobalRNG.weibull1(20) 0.894177
GlobalRNG.erlang(10, 2) 13.6015
GlobalRNG.chiSquared(10) 10.7126
GlobalRNG.t(10) 0.492003
GlobalRNG.logNormal(10, 20) 5.51916e+010
GlobalRNG.beta(0.5, 0.5) 0.205863
GlobalRNG.F(10 ,20) 2.49824
GlobalRNG.cauchy01() 0.585426
GlobalRNG.binomial(0.7, 20) 14
GlobalRNG.geometric(0.7) 0
GlobalRNG.poisson(0.7) 2
```

4.10 Generating Random Objects

Can't generate some objects because the number of bits needed to specify an object > that in the generator state, but in practice this isn't a problem.

To **randomly permute** n items, swap the first with a random one, and randomly permute the remaining $n - 1$:

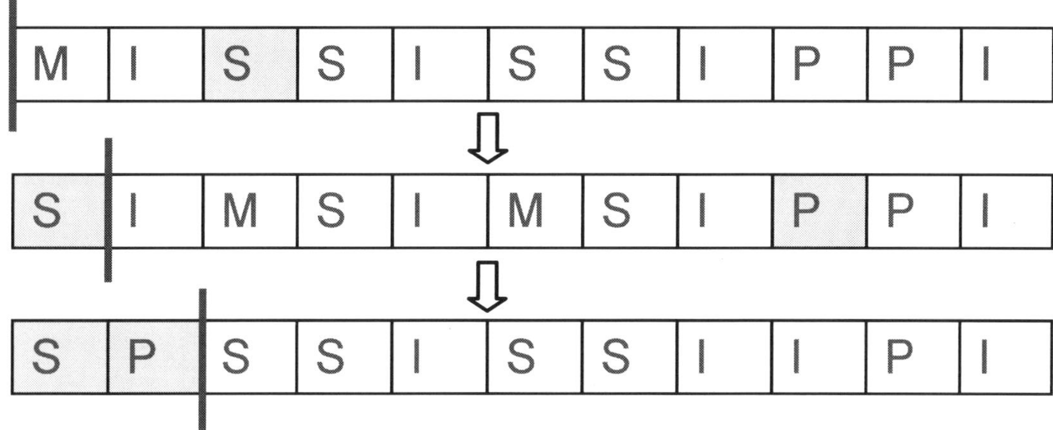

```
template<typename ITEM>void randomPermutation(ITEM* numbers, int size)
{
    for(int i = 0; i < size; ++i)
        swap(numbers[i], numbers[inRange(i, size - 1)]);
}
```

The runtime is O(n), which is faster than using the more obvious sorting with random number priorities. But the latter is faster for external memory (see the "External Memory Algorithms" chapter).

To generate an **ordered sample** of k integers ∈ [0, n – 1], select each with probability (k – *nSelected*)/(n – *nConsidered*). E.g., 0 is included with probability k/n and 1 with probability $(k - 1)/(n - 1)$ if 0 is selected, and $k/(n - 1)$ if not, with total probability $(k - 1)/(n - 1)k/n + (k/(n - 1))(1 - k/n) = k/n$. Each item is selected with probability k/n, and k items are selected because if `selected` = k, probability = 0 and, if probability = 1, all subsequent items are selected.

```
Vector<int> sortedSample(int k, int n)
{
    Vector<int> result;
    for(int considered = 0, selected = 0; selected < k; ++considered)
        if(bernoulli(double(k - selected)/(n - considered)))
        {
            result.append(considered);
            ++selected;
        }
    return result;
}
```

The runtime is O(n), and this is more efficient than generating random integers and sorting them with the O(n) counting sort. The algorithm can produce samples online.

Reservoir sampling finds a sample of size k from a stream of unknown size in one pass with O(1) work per item:

1. **Select the first k items**
2. **For $n > k$, when the nth item arrives, let r = random number % count**
3. **If $r < k$, replace the rth item with the new item, otherwise discard it**

```
template<typename ITEM> struct ReservoirSampler
{
    int k, nProcessed;
    Vector<ITEM> selected;
    void processItem(ITEM const& item)
    {
        ++nProcessed;
        if(selected.getSize() < k) append(item);
        else
        {
            int kickedOut = GlobalRNG.mod(nProcessed);
            if(kickedOut < k) selected[kickedOut] = item;
        }
    }
    ReservoirSampler(int wantedSize): k(wantedSize), nProcessed(0){}
};
```

Sorting (or multiple-selecting; see the "Sorting" chapter) n random variates from a given distribution gives **order statistics**. For only an ith order statistic out of n, where possible, it's usually more efficient to generate a uniform i^{th} (starting from 1) order statistic, distributed as beta(i, $n - i + 1$) (Devroye 1986), and apply the inverse method to it.

```
double uniformOrderStatistic(int i, int n){return beta(i, n - i + 1);}
```

4.11 Generating Samples from Multidimensional Distributions

Accept/reject and transformations between distributions work for $D > 1$, but the inverse method doesn't. But for accept/reject the probability of acceptance shrinks exponentially in D, making the method ineffective for large D. The remaining effective general methods are distribution-specific generators and transformations.

For multidimensional normal with mean μ and covariance matrix Σ, generate vector V of normal(0, 1) variates and return $\mu + L \times V$, where L is computed by Cholesky factorization of Σ (see the "Numerical Algorithms" chapter). This works because resulting the variate has mean μ and variance $LL^T = \Sigma$.

```
class MultivariateNormal
{
    Vector<double> means;
    Choletsky<double> cho;
public:
    MultivariateNormal(Vector<double> const& theMeans,
        DenseMatrix<double> const& covariances): means(theMeans),
        cho(covariances){assert(!cho.failed);}
    Vector<double> next()const
    {
        Vector<double> normals;
        for(int i = 0 ; i < means.getSize(); ++i)
            normals.append(GlobalRNG.normal01());
        return means + cho.l * normals;
    }
};
```

4.12 Markov Chain Monte Carlo

For distributions without known generators, feasible and sometimes the only available generation methods use the **Markov chain Monte Carlo** (MCMC) techniques. They produce dependent and identically distributed samples, which is the next best thing when **independent and identically distributed** (iid) samples are unavailable.

Random walk Metropolis algorithm (RWM) requires PDF f of the distribution, specified upto a normalization constant, from which want samples:

1. **Start from an initial sample x_0 such that $f(x_0) \neq 0$**
2. **Use user-provided symmetric proposal sampling function p to generate a sample, given x**
3. **$x_{new} = x +$ the sample**
4. **Set $x \leftarrow x_{new}$ if uniform(0, 1) $\leq f(x_{new})/f(x)$**

E.g., possible p are uniform and normal with mean 0 or Cauchy with 0 median.

The x_i form a Markov chain, whose eventual distribution is f if $p > 0$ everywhere. This is because the Markov chain is **ergodic** if this holds, and it satisfies the **detailed balance** condition by construction. These ensure convergence to the correct distribution $\forall\ x_0$ and p (Krose et al. 2011). Technically, the convergence is immediate because x_0 might have been a random sample from the correct distribution. But it may be very unlikely according to f, and using it for a finite simulation may introduce noticeable bias. The rule of thumb is to discard some number, usually 1000, of the first x_i. Though it's almost never an issue, technically the chain is never ergodic because numerical error causes p values to become 0 in the tails, particularly if p has thin tails.

Theoretical guidance on picking the variance of p is limited, but it should be such that the acceptance rate is far from both 0 and 1. Problems with using RWM as a black box are that it's hard to pick the correct p and the samples are correlated. A simple way to remove correlation and use the samples as though they are independent, is to discard some after the last used sample, but it's unclear how many.

A simple heuristic to solve these problems is to let the chain find the correct distribution using grid search. To generate a new sample, first sample from a uniform distribution with very small variance, and gradually increase it to very large. Small variance proposals are mostly accepted but make no difference, and large variance proposals are mostly rejected. So the algorithm only uses correct magnitude variances and takes several steps to reduce correlation of the resulting samples. The number of calls to f is still O(1).

```
template<typename PDF> class GridRWM
{
    PDF f;
    double x, fx, aFrom, aTo;
```

```
    int from, to;
    double sampleHelper(double a)
    {
        double xNew = x + GlobalRNG.uniform(-a, a), fxNew = f(xNew);
        if(fx * GlobalRNG.uniform01() <= fxNew)
        {
            x = xNew;
            fx = fxNew;
        }
        return x;
    }
public:
    GridRWM(double x0 = 0, PDF const& theF = PDF(), int from = -10,
        int to = 20): x(x0), f(theF), fx(f(x)), aFrom(pow(2, from)),
        aTo(pow(2, to)) {}
    double sample()
    {
        for(double a = aFrom; a < aTo; a *= 2) sampleHelper(a);
        return x;
    }
};
```

For $D > 1$, generate a multidimensional uniform sample, but, because the chance of a rejection increases with D, use the multiplicative factor $2^{1/D}$ for the grid. Due to $O(D)$ runtime, this scales to large D.

```
template<typename PDF> class MultidimGridRWM
{
    PDF f;
    Vector<double> x;
    double fx, aFrom, aTo, factor;
    Vector<double> sampleHelper(double a)
    {
        Vector<double> xNew = x;
        for(int i = 0; i < xNew.getSize(); ++i)
            xNew[i] += GlobalRNG.uniform(-a, a);
        double fxNew = f(xNew);
        if(fx * GlobalRNG.uniform01() <= fxNew)
        {
            x = xNew;
            fx = fxNew;
        }
        return x;
    }
public:
    MultidimGridRWM(Vector<double> const& x0, PDF const& theF = PDF(),
        int from = -10, int to = 20): x(x0), f(theF), fx(f(x)), aFrom(pow(2,
        from)), aTo(pow(2, to)), factor(pow(2, 1.0/x.getSize())) {}
    Vector<double> sample()
    {
        for(double a = aFrom; a < aTo; a *= factor) sampleHelper(a);
        return x;
    }
};
```

Shrinking the range of the grid, using information from the initial simulations, may improve the performance by a large constant factor by not sampling from too small/large variances. For high-dimensional distributions, grid search may be too slow or not give sufficiently independent samples, so it's best to verify its outputs. Reducing the multiplication factor is one way to reduce correlation. Though ergodicity doesn't hold with a uniform p, which is cut at the tails, this doesn't affect the algorithm if the large variances are large enough.

4.13 Approximating the Normal CDF

For statistical inference, often need to evaluate the normal CDF. Because can't evaluate *erf* exactly, need a fast numerical approximation. Suitable for most statistical inference, $erf(x) = 1 - (1 + \sum_{0 \le i < 6} a_i x)^{-16}$, where a_i are special constants, has maximum error 3×10^{-7} for $0 \le x \le \infty$ (Wikipedia 2014d). The runtime is O(1).

```
double approxErf(double x)
{//for 0 <= x < inf, max error = 3e-7
    double a[6] = {0.0705230784, 0.0422820123, 0.0092705272, 0.0001520143,
        0.0002765672, 0.0000430638}, poly = 1, xPower = x;
    for(int i = 0; i < 6; ++i)
    {
        poly += a[i] * xPower;
        xPower *= x;
    }
    for(int i = 0; i < 4; ++i) poly *= poly;
    return 1 - 1/poly;
}
double approxNormalCDF(double x){return 0.5 + approxErf(x/sqrt(2))/2;}
double approxNormal2SidedConf(double x){return 2 * approxNormalCDF(x) - 1;}
```

4.14 Monte Carlo Method

The **law of large numbers** (LLN): Given n iid samples x_i such that $E[x_i] = \mu$, $(\sum x_i)/n \to \mu$ for $n \to \infty$. E.g., the **sample mean** $m = (\sum x_i)/n \to \mu$ and the **sample variance** $s^2 = (\sum(x_i - m)^2)/(n - 1) \to \sigma^2$. Use $n - 1$ instead of n because variance $= E[x_j - (\sum_{i \ne j} x_i)/n] = E[(x_j - m)n/(n - 1)]$. Intuitively, $E[(x_j - m)]$ doesn't work, because the x_j affect m. This generalizes into **degrees of freedom** logic, where $n - k$ samples estimate k^{th} independent parameter.

The **central limit theorem** (CLT): Given n iid samples x_i from a distribution with finite σ^2, for $n \to \infty$ m is distributed as normal(μ, σ^2/n). The LLN and Slutsky's theorem (Wikipedia 2014e) allow using s^2 instead of σ^2. So m estimates μ with error s^2/n. Some of these converge in probability, and others with probability 1. In practice, there is little difference between them, but intuitively the former means convergence in mean, and the latter in tails.

Many natural events are normally distributed because they are an aggregation of many random interactions, which is normal by the CLT. **Monte Carlo method** applies the CLT to compute a quantity of interest μ if:

- ∃ an event generator function f producing iid events with value x_i such that $E[x_i] = \mu$
- Important events are generated often enough to ensure that μ exists and n needn't be too large for the CLT to kick in

1. Come up with μ and f
2. Until out of patience or n is large enough and error small enough
3. $x_i \leftarrow f()$
4. Incrementally update m and s^2 with x_i
5. Return $\mu \leftarrow m$, which is within error $3s/\sqrt{n}$ with 99.73% probability asymptotically

Assuming event generation takes O(1) time and space, a simulation needs O(n) time and O(1) space due to not needing to store the x_i. The error calculation follows from the CLT.

E.g., consider computing π. The area of a circle with radius r is πr^2 and of its enclosing square $4r^2$, so let $\mu = \pi/4$ = (area of the circle)/(area of the square). Let f generate a random point $p \in (-1, 1) \times (-1, 1)$ and return x_i = 1 if distance(p, (0, 0)) ≤ 1, and 0 otherwise. Both $x_i = 1$ and $x_i = 0$ should happen often, so small n should be enough.

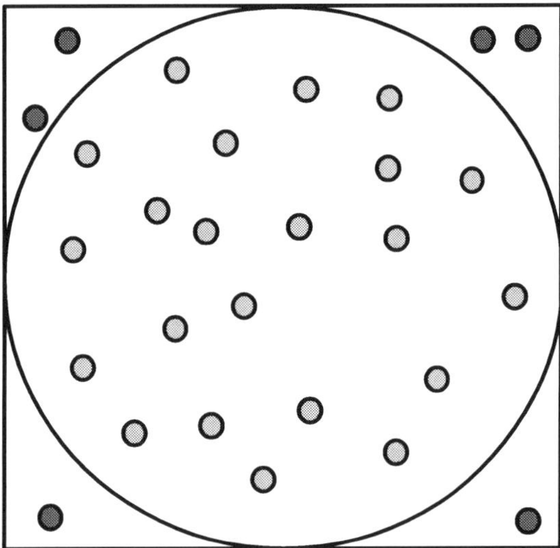

$\pi \approx 4 \times 22/(22 + 6) \approx 3.142$

Experimentally, after 10^8 variates $\pi = 3.14182 \pm 0.000493$.

Some tasks for which Monte Carlo fails:

- Estimating μ of samples from a Cauchy distribution—it doesn't exist
- Estimating the average income of the county in which a billionaire lives—the result is very different, depending on whether he/she is included in the sample

Can extend Monte Carlo in several ways:

- For error calculation needn't use multiplier 3 with 99.73% probability; can use the standard 95% confidence with 1.96 multiplier, or others. Have the value tables in many references. Also, given a multiplier, can evaluate the normal CDF to get the associated confidence. $\Pr(|\text{error}| < \epsilon) = 2 \times F((\epsilon - m)/s) - 1$, where F is the normal CDF. Use ϵ = multiplier × s.
- A simulated event can produce k values. This effectively performs k related simulations at the cost of one. The simulation would run until all k errors are small enough or the computational budget is exceeded.

The implementation uses $s^2 = (\sum x_i^2 - (\sum x_i)^2/n)/(n - 1)$, which is less numerically stable due to possible cancellation in subtraction of large numbers, but allows incrementally updating $\sum x_i$ and $\sum x_i^2$. Cancellation isn't a problem with double-word precision unless the error is already extremely small. So it's safe to assume that the error is 0 in case of cancellation.

To monitor error and at the end of the simulation, a normal distribution summary data structure is computed and holds the mean and the variance of the mean. The normal distribution allows adding and subtracting independent normal distributions and scaling by a constant. Scaling by 2 is different from adding to itself because addition only applies to independent distributions. Also, can create the data structure from a binomial distribution, which is useful for working with count data.

```
struct NormalSummary
{
    double mean, variance;
    double stddev()const{return sqrt(variance);}
    double error9973()const{return 3 * stddev();}
    explicit NormalSummary(double theMean = 0, double theVariance = 0):
        mean(theMean), variance(theVariance){}
    NormalSummary operator-(NormalSummary const& b)const
        {return NormalSummary(mean - b.mean, variance + b.variance);}
    NormalSummary operator+=(NormalSummary const& b)
    {
        mean += b.mean;
        variance += b.variance;
        return *this;
    }
    NormalSummary operator*=(double a)
```

```
    {
        mean *= a;
        variance *= a * a;//change f code and description
        return *this;
    }
};
struct IncrementalStatistics
{
    double sum, squaredSum, minimum, maximum;
    long long n;
    IncrementalStatistics(): n(0), sum(0), squaredSum(0),
        minimum(numeric_limits<double>::max()), maximum(-minimum){}
    double getMean(){return sum/n;}
    double getVariance(){return n < 2 ? 0 :
        max(0.0, (squaredSum - sum * getMean())/(n - 1.0));}
    void addValue(double x)
    {
        ++n;
        maximum = max(maximum, x);
        minimum = min(minimum, x);
        sum += x;
        squaredSum += x * x;
    }
    NormalSummary getSummary()
        {return NormalSummary(getMean(), getVariance()/n);}
    double error9973(){return getSummary().error9973();}
};
```

A tail inequality shows that the probability of the error being very large is exponentially small—let $z = (x - m)/s$; then $\Pr(Z > z) < f(z)/z$, where f is the normal PDF (StackExchange 2014).

Can use Monte Carlo to find E[the resource use] of a randomized algorithm if the randomness in its performance is iid. For speed testing:

```
template<typename FUNCTION> struct SpeedTester
{
    FUNCTION f;
    SpeedTester(FUNCTION const& theFunction=FUNCTION()): f(theFunction){}
    int operator()()const
    {
        int now = clock();
        f();
        return clock() - now;
    }
};
```

An important property of the normal distribution is that normal(a, b) – normal(c, d) = normal($a - c$, $b + d$). This allows using Monte Carlo to compare performance of randomized algorithms because can conclude with 99.73% probability that $a > c$ if $0 \notin [a - c \pm 3\sqrt{b + d}]$. Problems with Monte Carlo:

- In theory, need complete independence of events. In practice, these may be correlated or form correlated sequences. A general technique to handle correlation is to average correlated subsequences and assume that the resulting **batch averages** are independent.
- Convergence is too slow because the error bound is $O(1/\sqrt{n})$.
- For very rare events, n needs to be arbitrarily large for the CLT to kick in. E.g., an event that needs a simulated fair coin be tails 100 times in row won't happen.

Variance reduction techniques speed up error reduction. **Common random numbers** fixes everything that isn't simulated. E.g., when simulating performance of a randomized algorithm, run all simulations on the same input, not different ones. To test on various inputs use each several times. When comparing performance, run each algorithm on each input to reduce variance due to input difficulty differences. But inappropriate use can introduce bias due to nonrandomness, possibly resulting in wrong conclusions.

To simulate a system, use a priority queue (see the "Priority Queues" chapter) of events scheduled for some absolute or relative times. Until it's empty, dequeue an event, execute it, and possibly enqueue some others.

4.15 Finite Sample Bounds

The CLT is asymptotic, and, even without rare events, convergence to a normal can take a while. If the range of f is bounded to [0, 1], have bounds on μ that hold $\forall n$. More generally, for $x_i \in [a, b]$, map x_i into [0, 1], compute the bound, and map that to $[a, b]$, which works by the linearity of expectation.

Let $\epsilon(p) = \sqrt{\ln(1/p)/(2n)}$ for the **Hoeffding inequality**, $\sqrt{2V\ln(1/p)/n} + \ln(1/p)/(3n)$ for the **Bernstein inequality**, and $\sqrt{2s\ln(2/p)/n} + 7\ln(2/p)/(3n)$ for the **empirical Bernstein inequality** (Gao & Zhou 2012). Then with probability $\geq 1 - p$ have any one of:

- Upper bound: $\mu \leq m + \epsilon$
- Lower bound: $\mu \geq m - \epsilon$
- Confidence interval: $\mu \in m \pm \epsilon(p/2)$

The confidence interval follows from the union bound (a version of Bonferroni inequality). The lower bound follows from the upper bound using the transformation $\mu = 1 - \mu$. Hoeffding is usually better for large s, and Bernstein for small. Unlike for Hoeffding and Bernstein, the union bound doesn't give the best known confidence interval for the empirical Bernstein, which is (Audibert et al. 2009): $\mu \in m \pm (\sqrt{2(n-1)s\ln(3/p)} + 3\ln(3/p))/n$.

Bernstein needs knowing σ^2. But for $\mu \in [0, 1]$, $\sigma^2 \leq \mu(1 - \mu)$, which is exact for Bernoulli distribution and approximate for others (Anguita et al. 2013). So can substitute this for σ^2 and get two-sided version get $|\mu - m| \leq \sqrt{2\mu(1-\mu)t} + t/3$, where $t = \ln(2/p)/n$. Solving, have $\mu \in [\mu_{min}, \mu_{max}]$ where $\mu_{bound} = (x + 2y + \text{sign} \times \sqrt{x(x + 4y(1-y))})/(2(1+x))$ for $x = 2t$, $y = m - t/3$ for μ_{min} and $m + t/3$ for μ_{max}, and sign = −1 for μ_{min} and 1 for μ_{max}. If $y > 1$, have no solution and the bound is 0 for μ_{min} and 1 for μ_{max}. A member function of `IncrementalStatistics` computes this **approximate Bernstein** bound:

```
static double bernHelper(double x, double y, double sign)
{
    return (x + 2 * y + sign * sqrt(x * (x + 4 * y * (1 - y))))/2/
        (1 + x);
}
pair<double, double> bernBounds(double confidence = 0.9973)
{
    assert(n > 1 && confidence > 0 && confidence < 1);
    double p = 1 - confidence, t = log(2/p)/n, yMin = getMean() - t/3,
    yMax = getMean() + t/3;
    return make_pair(yMin > 1 ? 0 : bernHelper(2 * t, yMin, -1),
        yMax > 1 ? 1 : bernHelper(2 * t, yMax, 1));
}
```

Can combine symmetric Hoeffding and empirical Bernstein:

```
double finiteSamplePlusMinusError01(double confidence = 0.9973)
{//combined Hoeffding and empirical Bernstein
    assert(n > 1 && confidence > 0 && confidence < 1);
    double p = 1 - confidence, tempB = log(3/p);
    return min(sqrt(log(2/p)/2/n), (sqrt(2 * (n - 1) * getVariance() *
        tempB) + 3 * tempB)/n);
}
```

Can combine the result and approximate Bernstein. The latter is exact and always better than the other two for Bernoulli, but not for the uniform and other distributions, where the σ^2 bound is weak.

```
pair<double, double> combinedBounds(double confidence = 0.9973)
{
    pair<double, double> result = bernBounds(confidence);
    double symBound = finiteSamplePlusMinusError01(confidence);
    result.first = max(result.first, getMean() - symBound);
    result.second = min(result.second, getMean() + symBound);
    return result;
}
```

Finite sample bounds are the best that can be hoped for, but don't have them without assumptions such as bounded range, because otherwise very rarely a huge value such as 10^9 can occur.

4.16 Sobol Sequence

Might get better variance reduction using a fixed number of random variates per run, e.g., for multidimensional integral evaluation. Want samples that cover the multidimensional volume maximally uniformly. Theoretically, the best sample sequences give $O(\lg(n)^D/n)$ error for n samples, which, despite asymptotics, exceeds Monte Carlo's $O(1/\sqrt{n})$ for typical n and not too small D, but in practice is much less even for large D and n.

The Sobol sequence has the theoretical performance, beats it in practice, and is fast to evaluate (Bratley & Fox 1988). ∀ dimension precompute initialization data:

1. **Pick a not yet picked primitive binary polynomial $x^D + a_1x^{D-1} + \ldots + a_{D-1}x + 1$ of smallest degree**
2. **Let precision of a `double` be B bits. $\forall j \in [0, B-1]$ compute $v_j = (2j+1)/2^{B-1-j}$ for $j < D$, and v_{j-D} ^ $v_{j-D}/2^D$ ^ $a_{D-1}v_{j-1}$ ^ ... ^ a_1v_{j-D} otherwise**
3. **Set the count $k = 1$ and initial variate $x = 0$**
4. **To generate: $x = x$ ^ v_c, where c is the position of the rightmost 1 bit of k**

The implementation uses a large enough fixed number of polynomials, found in Press et al. (2007) or online. Very long simulations might need to check that $k < 2^B$. Values of v are binary fractions represented as integers with the normalizing factor 2^{-B}.

```
unsigned char const SobolPolys[] = {0,1,1,2,1,4,2,4,7,11,13,14,1,13,16,19,22,
25,1,4,7,8,14,19,21,28,31,32,37,41,42,50,55,56,59,62,14,21,22,38,47,49,50,52,
56,67,70,84,97,103,115,122};
unsigned char const SobolDegs[] = {1,2,3,3,4,4,5,5,5,5,5,5,6,6,6,6,6,6,7,7,7,
7,7,7,7,7,7,7,7,7,7,7,7,7,7,7,7,8,8,8,8,8,8,8,8,8,8,8,8,8,8,8,8};
class Sobol
{//SobolPolys don't represent highest and lowest 1s
    enum{B = numeric_limits<double>::digits};
    unsigned long long k;
    Vector<unsigned long long> x, v;
    double factor;
    int index(int d, int b){return d * B + b;}
public:
    bool reachedLimit(){return k >= twoPower(B);}
    static int maxD(){return sizeof(SobolDegs);}
    Sobol(int d): factor(1.0/twoPower(B)), v(d * B, 0), x(d, 0), k(1)
    {
        assert(d <= maxD());
        for(int i = 0; i < d; ++i)
            for(int j = 0; j < B; ++j)
            {
                unsigned long long value;
                int l = j - SobolDegs[i];
                if(l < 0) value = (2 * j + 1) * twoPower(B - j - 1);
                else
                {
                    value = v[index(i, l)];
                    value ^= value/twoPower(SobolDegs[i]);
                    for(int k = 1; k < SobolDegs[i]; ++k)
                        if(Bits::get(SobolPolys[i], k - 1))
                            value ^= v[index(i, l + k)];
                }
                v[index(i, j)] = value;
            }
        next();
    }
```

```
    void next()
    {
        assert(!reachedLimit());
        for(int i = 0, c = rightmost0Count(k++); i < x.getSize(); ++i)
            x[i] ^= v[index(i, c)];
    }
    double getValue(int i){return x[i] * factor;}
};
```

4.17 Bootstrap Method

Consider estimating $E_s[f(S)]$, where f is some function and S an iid sample of size n from some distribution T. An estimator Q of this quantity, computed from S, is **consistent** if $Q \to E_S[f(S)]$ as $n \to \infty$ and **unbiased** if $E[Q] = E_S[f(S)]$. If f = the mean and can sample from T, by the CLT Monte Carlo produces unbiased and consistent Q. Good Q have been discovered for many common f. E.g., the t-test is appropriate for small samples from the normal distribution. But for an arbitrarily f, producing a good Q may need substantial mathematical work or research. E.g., what's a good Q for f = median? For arbitrary f, the obvious $Q = f$(sample) may be biased and inconsistent.

The bootstrap method generalizes Monte Carlo by allowing $f \neq$ mean and a fixed S. Let f not depend on the order of the S_i. Then $f(S_0, \ldots, S_{n-1})$ is a sample from some functional value distribution D. E.g., if f = mean, D is normal by the CLT, but for other f such as the median it needn't be. Using f and S, bootstrap creates samples f_i from a distribution that is close to D, treats them as iid from D, and uses them to find Q:

1. b times
2. Pick n random items from S with replacement
3. $f_i \leftarrow f$(the resample)
4. Calculate Q and its confidence interval from b f_i values

Usually b = 10000 or as much as feasible. Since D needn't be normal, compute a nonparametric confidence interval by sorting and finding f_i that enclose the confidence level % of the data c. The implementation uses two heaps of size $t \approx b \times (1 - c)/2$ to save space by storing only the tails with smallest and largest values. The resource use is $O(fb\ln(t))$ time and $O(t)$ space.

E.g., on single run on a sample of 1000 uniform01 values, with f = mean Monte Carlo gave $Q = 0.509 \pm 0.027$, and bootstrap with b = 10000 gave $Q = 0.500$ $-0.027/+0.028$ and $f(S) = 0.500$, with confidence 99.73% for both. Bootstrap gave correct confidence intervals without any knowledge of the normal distribution. With f = median and the same parameters, bootstrap gave $Q = 0.480$ $-0.045/+0.043$ and $f(S) = 0.479$.

Optimal b is hard to find; can double b until doing so doesn't improve the confidence interval by enough. Because confidences are computed by ranking the f_i, b should be large enough to give sufficient confidence resolution. E.g., with b = 100, it's pointless to ask for a 99.5% confidence interval. Also, computation with b > number of distinct resamples causes no improvement in accuracy. The latter = Choose($2n - 1$, n) > Choose($2n$, n)/$n \approx 4^n/(n\sqrt{\pi n})$ by the Stirling's approximation, and usually exceeds any practical choice of b. Because $b \to \infty$ gains nothing, n limits the accuracy.

No known theorem gives useful general conditions under which Q is unbiased and consistent and the confidence interval is correct, but in practice both are usually true (Wikipedia 2014a). Resampling produces iid samples from the empirical distribution $F(x) = \sum_i(x > S_i)/n$. **Dvoretzky-Kiefer-Wolfowitz inequality**: $\Pr(\max_x(|T(x) - F(x)| > \epsilon)) < 2 \times \exp(-2n\epsilon^2)$ for error $\epsilon > 0$, i.e., $F \to T$ exponentially fast as $n \to \infty$. So if f is such that increasing n doesn't magnify the error of sampling from F instead of D faster than DKW reduces it, heuristically bootstrap is arbitrarily accurate as $n \to \infty$. E.g., for the mean it works well because the computation cancels and not magnifies errors. Contradictory to this reasoning, bootstrap may produce better confidence intervals for small samples than analytical statistics (Wikipedia 2014a). E.g., can use bootstrap instead of the t-test. In a way, bootstrap gets all information from a sample, so the bigger it is, the more informative the result is.

As μ estimates, both $f(S)$ and the bootstrap mean are useful. The latter is also an estimator with bias and variance. When getting bootstrap confidence intervals, want to use it's mean for safety, but the mean should agree with $f(S)$, and disagreement is usually a red flag.

Can extend bootstrap to deal with multisample functionals. E.g., to compute a confidence interval for the difference of medians of two samples, bootstrap resamples from both, and output the difference of the resample medians.

Bootstrap fails for some practically unlikely cases, e.g., for f = max of n iid uniform(0, 1) variates (Andrews 2000). Also, T may not allow confidence intervals (e.g., if variance = ∞). Finally, n or b can be too small. !∃proven method to reliably detect when bootstrap produces wrong Q or confidence intervals. Some red flags:

- $f(S)$ is very different from Q
- Obtained confidence interval is too small/large
- Q is outside the confidence interval
- Repeating gives substantially different results—increase b

4.18 Statistical Tests

Want to see if a yes/no claim is supported by data. The **null hypotheses** is that the claim is false and the **alternative** is that it's true. Generic hypothesis test:

1. **Pick a statistic**
2. **Define its distribution when calculated on sample, assuming the null is true**
3. **Calculate *p*-value = Pr(can have a more in-the-tail value than the sample statistic)**
4. **If it's small enough (usually 0.05), reject the null and assume the alternative is true**
5. **Else not enough evidence to reject the null, so assume the alternative is false**

This is similar to arguing by contradiction—if the null poorly explains the data, it can't be true so the alternative must be. A test can make mistakes:

- **Type I**—falsely rejecting the null—e.g., jailing the innocent
- **Type II**—falsely failing to reject the null—e.g., freeing the guilty

The type I error is more important, and most tests try to control it explicitly, i.e., not have higher error than promised. The ability to control type II error is **power of a test**. Given two tests for the same scenario that control type I error, want a more powerful one. Tests usually have the runtime = $O(n)$.

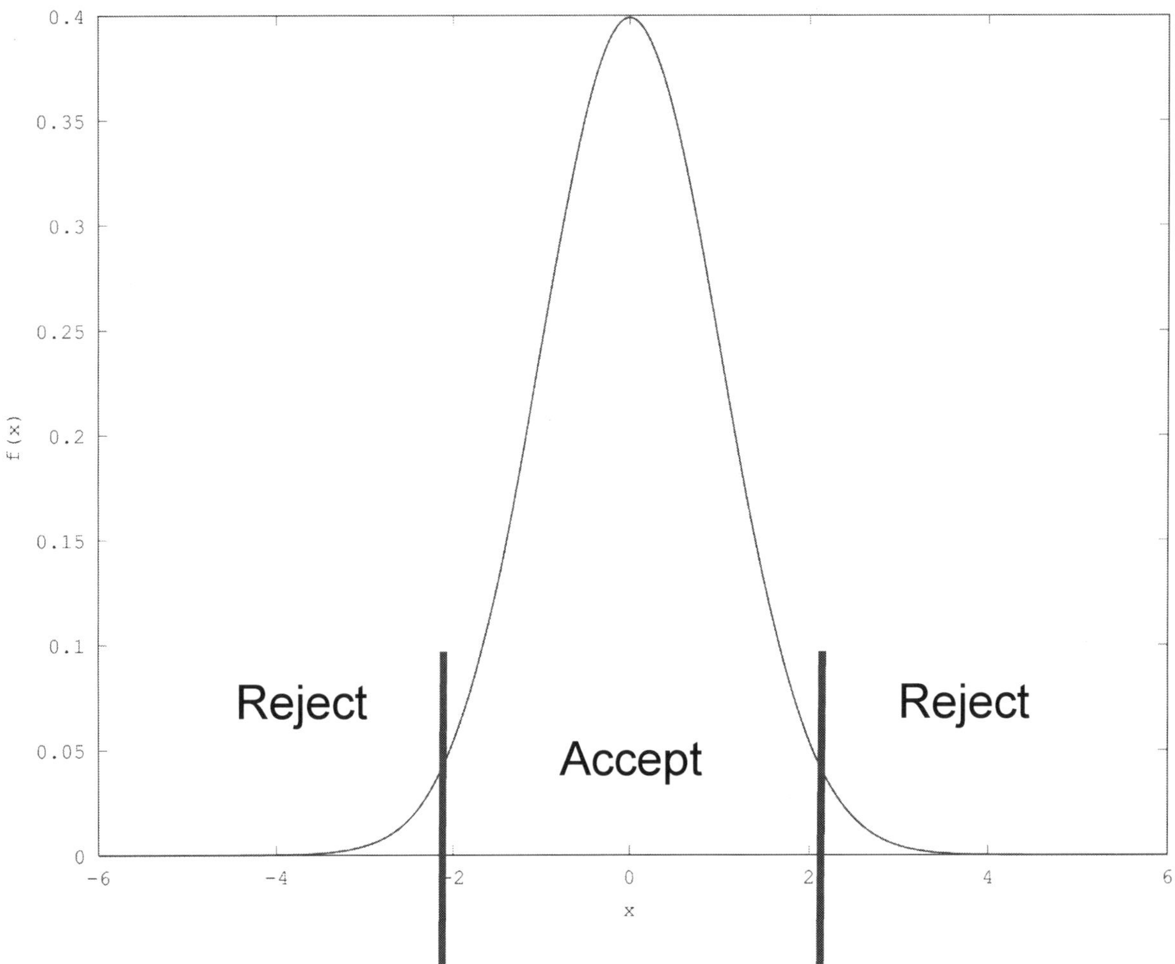

Beware that tests always have less information than the data. If it doesn't have enough information to conclude something, neither do the tests. Many tests are technically not needed because can use bootstrap instead. But bootstrap is less computationally efficient, it doesn't explicitly control the type I error, and its assumptions may not work for some problems. On the other hand, most tests tend to make assumptions which are hard to verify and thus ignored in practice. This is wrong use of tests because many of their properties such as type I error control are invalidated. So strict control of type I error is less important than it seems, though is still wanted.

Pr(the null is true) ≠ p-value, unlike often assumed. This causes certain philosophical criticism of hypothesis testing. But a small p-value does mean that the null is unlikely to be true, but without putting a probability on the conclusion. Beware that a test tests exactly what is asked and not necessary what users wants. E.g., can conclude with significance that one alternative is better than another, even if the difference is too tiny to matter. If have a large enough sample, can make such difference significant—e.g., have 0.1% when the user thinks only 2% is significant. Usually, a good performance metric is how often archive sufficient performance, and not % of best.

4.19 Comparing Matched Pairs

A **matched pairs design** is when have not iid, but paired observations (e.g., performances of two algorithms on a set of benchmark tasks). Want to discover if the better one, if any, is significantly so.

The **sign test** assumes that the observations come from a continuous distribution. But continuity is a weak assumption because can make a discrete distribution continuous by adding a bit of PDF to make connections. So effectively make the **general position assumption** that observations don't follow any exact pattern. Theoretically, adding a bit of noise to each observation will satisfy this in all cases, so the sign test is truly distribution-free. Of course, this is only a conceptual solution because usually avoid modifying data.

The idea is that given equal performance on n "games", the distribution of who "won" is binomial(n/2, n), and a significant deviation rejects this. Count ties as draws, but technically for the discreteness of the binomial, with an odd number of ties must drop one observation, reducing the power of the test. But because typically use the normal approximation binomial($n/2$, n) = normal($n/2$, $n/4$), draws don't cause issues. Then use the z-score test.

```
bool signTestAreEqual(double winCount1, double winCount2, double z = 3)
{
    double nGames = winCount1 + winCount2;
    return abs(winCount1 - nGames/2)/sqrt(nGames/4) < z;
}
```

Wilcoxon signed rank test assumes observations:

- Are symmetrically distributed around the median
- Come from a continuous distribution

Then, when observations are joined and converted to ranks, calculate the mean and the variance of the **signed rank** sum distribution, approximate it as normal, and use the z-score test. Signed rank = rank of abs(paired observation difference) × the sign, where the sign = 1 if the first group observation > the second group one, and −1 otherwise.

Ranks of tied observations are averaged. A good way to handle 0 differences is distribute them evenly and drop one if the number is odd, though in theory don't have ties due to the continuity assumption. Given n remaining observations, under the null, the mean = $n(n + 1)/4$, and the variance = the mean × $(2n + 1)/6$ (Hollander et al. 2013). With some equal ranks, the variance is actually a bit less, and can adjust it to gain a bit of power, but doing so is slightly complicated and unnecessary because still control type I error.

```
struct SignedRankComparator
{
    typedef pair<double, double> P;
    int sign(P const& p)const{return p.first - p.second > 0 ? 1 : -1;}
    double diff(P const& p)const{return abs(p.first - p.second);}
    bool isLess(P const& lhs, P const& rhs)const
        {return diff(lhs) < diff(rhs);}
    bool isEqual(P const& lhs, P const& rhs)const
        {return diff(lhs) == diff(rhs);}
};
bool signedRankAreEqual(Vector<pair<double, double> > a, double z = 3)
{
    SignedRankComparator c;
    quickSort(a.getArray(), 0, a.getSize() - 1, c);
    int nP = a.getSize(), i = 0;
    //if odd number of 0's, drop first, distribute rest evenly
    while(i < a.getSize() && c.diff(a[i]) == 0) ++i;
    if(i % 2) --nP;
    double signedRankSum = 0, mean = nP * (nP + 1)/4;
    for(i = i % 2; i < a.getSize(); ++i)
    {//rank lookahead to scan for ties, then sum computation
        int j = i;
        while(i + 1 < a.getSize() && c.isEqual(a[i], a[i + 1])) ++i;
        double rank = (i + j)/2.0 + 1 + nP - a.getSize();
        while(j <= i) signedRankSum += c.sign(a[j++]) * rank;
    }
    return nP == 0 || (abs(signedRankSum) - mean)/
        sqrt(mean * (2 * nP + 1)/6) < z;
}
```

If observations are normally distributed, asymptotically the signed rank test has 95% of the power of the t-test, and the sign test has 50% of the power of the signed rank test (Conover 1999). So in practice it's always better to use the signed rank test, and not the t-test, because it assumes less. The t-test is actually robust to deviations from the normal in terms of type I error, but not robust in terms of power, and can be arbitrarily less powerfull than Wilcoxon.

4.20 Comparing Matched Tuples

With tuples, have $k > 2$ alternatives. A basic question is if all alternatives are same vs if some are different, without pointing out the different ones.

Friedman test—generalization of the sign test, assumes observations come from a continuous distribution (Wikipedia 2015c). First convert observations to ranks in each domain. Ranks are unique with a continuous distribution, but in practice this isn't always true. Handle ties by averaging tied ranks. Calculate:

- $\forall_j\, r_{\text{ave},j}$ = the average ranks ∀ alternative
- r_{ave} = the domain rank = the average rank over all alternatives
- Ss_t—the sum of squared domain rank differences to the average rank
- Ss_e—the sum of squared individual ranks differences to the average rank

SS_t/SS_e is distributed as chi-squared with $k - 1$ degrees of freedom under the null equality.

```
Vector<double> convertToRanks(Vector<double> a)
{//create index array, sort it, and convert indices into ranks
    int n = a.getSize();
    Vector<int> indices(n);
    for(int i = 0; i < n; ++i) indices[i] = i;
    IndexComparator<double> c(a.getArray());
    quickSort(indices.getArray(), 0, n - 1, c);
    for(int i = 0; i < n; ++i)
    {//rank lookahead to scan for ties, then change a entries
        int j = i;
        while(i + 1 < n && c.isEqual(i, i + 1)) ++i;
        double rank = (i + j)/2.0 + 1;
        for(; j <= i; ++j) a[indices[j]] = rank;
    }
    return a;
}
bool FriedmanAreAllEqual(Vector<Vector<double> > const& a,
    double conf = 0.95)
{//a[i] is vector of responses on domain i
    assert(a.getSize() > 0 && a[0].getSize() > 1);
    int n = a.getSize(), k = a[0].getSize();
    double totalRank = 0, sst = 0, sse = 0;
    Vector<double> optionTotalRanks(k);
    for(int i = 0; i < n; ++i)//calculate total and alternative rank sums
    {
        Vector<double> ri = convertToRanks(a[i]);
        for(int j = 0; j < k; ++j)
        {
            totalRank += ri[j];
            optionTotalRanks[j] += ri[j];
        }
    }
    totalRank /= n * k;
    optionTotalRanks *= 1.0/k/n;
    for(int i = 0; i < n; ++i)//calculate sums of squared ranks
    {
        sst += (optionTotalRanks[i] - totalRank) *
            (optionTotalRanks[i] - totalRank);
        Vector<double> ri = convertToRanks(a[i]);
        for(int j = 0; j < k; ++j)
            sse += (ri[j] - totalRank) * (ri[j] - totalRank);
    }
    sst *= n;
    sst /= n * (k - 1);
    return evaluateChiSquaredCdf(sst/sse, k - 1) > conf;
}
```

If Friedman detects differences, can apply **Nemenyi test** for pairs of differences or **Holm procedure** for best subset (Hollander et al. 2013) to try to detect exact places of difference. But bootstrap is usually more statistically powerful because the tests apply Bonferroni correction (discussed in the next section), which is too loose. Friedman is first because it's more powerful—can show a difference that follow-up tests can't detect. Also, the tests aren't designed for finding a best subset or a subset with particular performance.

Multiple comparison is a common statistical fallacy that happens due to not using adjustment such as Bonferroni correction. E.g., consider sending buy/sell investment advice to 1024 people for 10 days, so that after each day the wrong prediction half is dropped. In the end, to a single person it will seem that the predictor is always right.

4.21 Multiple Comparison for Simulated Alternatives

With $k = 2$, to decide if one alternative is statistically better, simulate each many times, compute the normal difference, and check if the confidence interval for the mean difference excludes 0.

But this doesn't generalize to $k > 2$ because even if one is better than every other with confidence, it's not the best with the same confidence. E.g., given many distributions with similar μ, the chance that the one with the lowest μ will produce the lowest E[x] on a small sample is tiny.

So pick an alternative with the smallest sample average m_0, and derive confidence intervals on the joint probability distribution of all k alternatives that the pick is the best one, as $\Pr(m_0 < m_1 \cap \ldots \cap m_0 < m_{k-1})$. This is usually impossible to compute. Applying **Bonferroni inequality** (also called **Bonferroni correction**, **union bound**, or **Boole inequality**, upto the trivial difference of subtracting both sides from 1), $\Pr(m_0 < m_1 \cap \ldots \cap m_0 < m_{k-1}) \geq 1 - \sum_{i>0}(1 - \Pr(m_0 < m_i))$. When the m_i are normally distributed, e.g., in case of simulation with many enough samples, can deduce $\Pr(m_0 < m_i)$ from the normal difference between alternatives 0 and i, as for $k = 2$. For normal distributions, experimentally, the Bonferroni confidence < the real confidence, but usually not by much (Chen & Lee 2010). Intuitively, the normal tails drop exponentially fast, so getting adjusted probability even with many alternatives only needs, e.g., maybe 3.5 instead of 3 standard deviations.

Can extend the difference to be significant given a precision, so that for means differing by no more than that it doesn't matter which one is picked.

```
bool multipleComparison(Vector<NormalSummary>const& data,
    double meanPrecision = 0, double confidence = 0.9973)
{//smallest is best with precision meanPrecision
    assert(data.getSize() > 1);
    double probability = 1;
    for(int i = 1; i < data.getSize(); ++i)
    {
        NormalSummary diff = data[i] - data[0];
        probability -= (1 - approxNormalCDF(
            (diff.mean + meanPrecision)/sqrt(diff.variance)));
    }
    return probability >= confidence;
}
```

If the m_i aren't normally distributed, e.g., obtained from small samples and can't simulate more, can use multisample bootstrap by taking a random resample from each sample, and counting how often a resample from sample 0 has the smallest value. After doing this b times, E[the count/b] = $\Pr(m_0 < m_1 \cap \ldots \cap m_0 < m_{k-1})$. Even if the m_i are normally distributed, for large enough b, the bootstrap confidence > the Bonferroni confidence if the empirical distribution isn't too different from the real one.

Using this method, a simple heuristic to check if a group of k alternatives are best is to discard the top $k - 1$ and check if k^{th} is better than the rest. But in this case using bootstrap instead of Bonferroni will probably give better results.

Another goal may be to find an alternative with a particular property (e.g., simplest), whose performance isn't much worse than that of the best alternative or a set of alternatives. A general heuristic for this is the **one standard error rule**—pick an alternative with the desired property, whose performance ≥ performance of the best model – standard error of its performance estimate. This works with all kinds of estimators. Another possibility is picking an alternative whose performance isn't worse than the best by maybe 5% of the its performance.

4.22 Comparing Alternatives via Simulation

The m_i are normally distributed by the CLT with enough simulations. A naive approach to decide which alternative has the smallest E[x] is to simulate each once until Bonferroni confidence is large enough to declare the smallest m_i alternative as the best. It wastes simulations by giving them to alternatives with small variances and uncompetitive means.

∃ several more efficient strategies. At best they will do k times fewer simulations if using the same termination criteria. The **OCBA heuristic** is simple and one of the most efficient (Chen & Lee 2010). OCBA theorem: If, as a result of initial simulations, the m_i are normally distributed with variances s_i^2, the number of additional simulations T needed to reach Bonferroni confidence p is minimized as $p \to 1$ when the relative allocation ratios are given by:

- $R_i = s_i^2/(m_i - m_0)^2$ for i > 0
- $R_0 = (s_0^2 \sum_{i>0} R_i^2/s_i^2)^{1/2}$

Because $T \to \infty$ as $p \to 1$, the theorem doesn't lead to an algorithm directly but heuristically gives the next simulation to the alternative with the highest ratio. E.g., if currently have normal(1, 0.1), normal(2, 0.2), normal(3, 0.3), then $R_1 = 0.2$, $R_2 = 0.075$, and $R_0 \approx 0.15$, so choose alternative 1.

1. **Simulate each alternative n_0 times to get initial m_i and s_i**
2. **Until satisfy the Bonferroni confidence**
3. **Simulate the alternative with the highest R_i**

n_0 should be ≥ 30 to allow use of the normal distribution, for the CLT to take effect, and to avoid premature convergence. For applications where simulations are very expensive, use $n_0 \geq 5$ (Chen & Lee 2010). If simulations are cheap, use $n_0 = 1000$. If several best alternatives have the same E[x], OCBA will exceed max allowed T trying to distinguish between them. To handle this, introduce a mean indifference parameter ϵ, such that the user doesn't care if the picked alternative is worse than the best by ϵ. OCBA handles this using $m_0 - \epsilon$ instead of m_0 when computing R_i. The number of needed simulations is unknown, but in the worst case, when all alternatives have the same E[x] and large s_i^2, should need $O(\sum s_i^2 \epsilon^{-2})$ simulations, based on how the Monte Carlo confidence is calculated.

```
template<typename MULTI_FUNCTION> pair<Vector<IncrementalStatistics>, int>
    OCBA(MULTI_FUNCTION& f, int initialSims, int maxSims = 100000,
    double meanPrecision = 0, double confidence = 0.9973)
{
    int k = f.getSize(), winner = -1;
    assert(k > 1 && initialSims > 1 && maxSims > initialSims * k);
    Vector<IncrementalStatistics> data(k);
    for(int i = 0; i < k; ++i)
        for(int j = 0; j < initialSims; ++j) data[i].addValue(f(i));
    for(int j = initialSims * k; j < maxSims; ++j)
    {//put current best alternative in index 0
        Vector<NormalSummary> s;
        for(int i = 0; i < k; ++i) s.append(data[i].getSummary());
        int bestI = 0, bestRatioI = -1;
        double bestMean = s[0].mean, ratioSum = 0, bestRatio;
        for(int i = 1; i < k; ++i)
            if(s[i].mean < bestMean) bestMean = s[bestI = i].mean;
        swap(s[0], s[bestI]);
        //check if Bonferroni confidence is satisfied
        if(multipleComparison(s, meanPrecision, confidence))
        {
            winner = bestI;
            break;
        }
        //compute largest OCBA ratio
        for(int i = 1; i < k; ++i)
        {
            double meanDiff = s[i].mean - bestMean - meanPrecision, ratio =
                s[i].variance/(meanDiff * meanDiff);
            ratioSum += ratio * ratio/s[i].variance;
```

```
            if(bestRatioI == -1 || ratio > bestRatio)
            {
                bestRatio = ratio;
                bestRatioI = i;
            }
        }
        double ratioBest = sqrt(ratioSum * s[0].variance);
        if(ratioBest > bestRatio) bestRatioI = bestI;
        else if(bestRatioI == bestI) bestRatioI = 0;
        //simulate alterative with largest ratio
        data[bestRatioI].addValue(f(bestRatioI));
    }
    return make_pair(data, winner);
}
```

E.g., given 6 alternatives, let the true performance of alternative i be given by normal($0.1i$, $10 - i$). OCBA and the naive approach respectively took 402669 and 810786 simulations to find the best with 0.9973 confidence, using $n_0 = 1000$ and $\epsilon = 0$. From run to run, alternative 0 is always correctly selected, but the number of simulations for both approaches vary substantially. If the results are suspect, run with higher n_0. Can extend the code to start from the vector of incremental statistics computed in the previous runs. The runtime per iteration is $O(k)$.

4.23 Multiple Comparison on Multiple Domains

Previous methods compare alternatives on a single domain. Comparison on multiple unrelated domains is harder because it usually makes no sense to aggregate over all domains using functions such as the average. E.g., even if ∀ domain and alternative performance scores are normally distributed, an average over the domains will weigh larger-value domains more. ∃ several good ways to transform domain-specific scores so that aggregating them is meaningful:

- Divide scores by the mean or the median. These represent the scale well, unless the top performers are much better than the rest. Scores must be all positive/negative for this to work.
- Transform scores into ranks. E.g., if on domain 0 alternatives 0, 1, and 2 respectively got scores 95, 90, and 70, these would be converted into 1, 2, and 3. To handle tie-breaks, assign same or averaged rank to any equal score alternatives. Though rank conversion loses information, aggregating ranks doesn't create problems and ranks are robust. The main issue is that negligible score differences result in noticeable rank differences—e.g., 1 vs 2 seems different from 98 vs 95. In particular, given 10 alternatives with similar performances, their "rank grades" 1 – (rank – 1)/10 are 1, 0.9, 0.8, 0.7, etc., which are significant differences. But with many domains, using ranks results in almost no loss of information because small random differences on one domain are usually canceled out by small random differences on another.
- Map scores from [min, max] to [0, 1]. This preserves information better than the ranks, but also runs into trouble when performances are very similar. E.g., students with grades 99 and 98 would respectively get adjusted grades 100 and 0.
- For percentage scores and when larger values are better, map [0, max] into [0, 1]. This avoids the problem of magnifying differences between close scores.
- When min is better, map absolute scores into relative ones by dividing by the performance of a baseline alternative, which is usually the worst-performing method. E.g., this is useful for comparing runtimes.

Which is best depends on application. If aggregation uses the average, each option allows using the CLT to describe the aggregate score, reducing the problem to multiple comparison of normals. Even for ranks and few domains, normality may be reasonable because assuming normal ranks overestimates confidence and Bonferroni underestimates it, which cancel out somewhat. But each domain may behave differently, so summing up the normals may not be justified as some will have more weight in the sum.

Some options give better normality. In particular, if domain-specific scores are normal, the rank transformation loses this information, but other options don't because averaging and scaling preserve normality. Beware that scaling isn't by a constant, but by using data-dependent max and min values, which are random, so technically scaling doesn't preserve normality. But usually max and min values vary little and are effectively constant, so assuming normality preservation isn't a problem.

Sometimes assuming normality of aggregate scores is unjustified. A more correct but much less efficient technique applies if domain-specific scores have known distributions. The idea is to use bootstrap:

1. ∀ resample of domain, sample performance ∀ alternative
2. ∀ alternative calculate new average aggregate scores
3. Rank the alternatives using the scores
4. ∀ score get confidence estimates

With large *b*, using ranks is probably the best way to aggregate regardless of the aggregation method used for the non-bootstrap part. One reason is that the results are also intuitively meaningful because can see the percentages of times where each alternative took the ith place (Caruana & Niculescu-Mizil 2006). Can also do this analysis if can't sample each metric, by resampling the domains, but the results would be less accurate. Bootstrap tells accurate average rank of each alternative along with a confidence interval and can be used to estimate the best performers directly along with corresponding confidence bounds.

The average isn't the only way to aggregate; in fact, for ranks !∃ a perfect combination rule (Wikipedia 2014f). **Arrow's impossibility theorem**: Given three or more alternatives and their rankings by various voters, can't have all of:

- Absence of dictatorship—no single voter controls the result
- Unanimity—if all voters prefer A over B, so does the group
- **Independence of irrelevant alternatives** (IIA)—the group's preference of A vs B must depend only on voters' preferences of the two and not on the other alternatives

Most rank combination systems sacrifice IIA, which isn't necessarily a bad thing in statistics despite being so in elections. Intuitively, the fundamental dilemma is that prefer both an alternative that performs better on more domains (or with more voters) as well as one that doesn't perform very poorly on some domains. These can conflict, resulting in an unusual event. In particular, adding a noncompetitive alternative can give a different best performer because the existing best is worse than that alternative on one domain, but usually this isn't a problem. E.g., given choice among two good students, one of whom got an F on a single exam, adding more C students will lower the rank of the unlucky student's performance on that test, perhaps enough to let another good student win by average rank.

A special case of IAA is **Condorcet criterion**—no other candidate may be preferred by the majority over the winner. The Bush-Gore-Nader election is the classic violation because without Nader Gore would have won. A Condorset winner doesn't exist under transitive preferences, but in practice this occurs rarely. Similar issues apply to curved grade methods, because IIA can give unfair advantage to some alternatives by doing superbly on tasks where competition does well.

Also, at first can consider subgroups of alternatives for comparison, but the winners from each must be compared against all alternatives to avoid multiple testing in the final choice.

Often want to answer different questions:

- Is the wanted solution significantly worse than the best one?
- Given current solution, can picking another one give a significantly better result?
- What can be concluded if some data (usually of poor quality) is discarded, but testing on it introduced multiple testing?

For many of these don't have statistical tests, but can use bootstrap in some cases. Beware that poor alternatives may do well if the problem is too easy. For the comparison result to be meaningful, need a baseline expert method to outperform a baseline poor method.

4.24 Permutation Tests

Permutation (or **randomization**) tests are usually the most assumption-free where they apply, though computationally expensive. They are fundamentally different from the usual parametric and nonparametric tests in formulation of the null hypotheses. Suppose compare two groups for equality and have iid, unpaired observations. The null is that **compared distributions are equal**; other tests assume equality of particular statistics. This leads to **exchangeability**—e.g., given two treatments, under the null the observations from one might as well have appeared in the other. Since a particular observation appeared where it did, this could be by chance or because the null is false. To test, pick a statistics, and check its value ∀ assignment of observations to groups.

The tested statistic can be anything, usually pick the mean or whatever else makes most sense for the problem. An important computational trick is, like in bootstrap, don't check all possible assignments, but sample some number of them, maybe 10000 (to get reasonable Monte Carlo–estimated *p*-value precision). Because a single simulation produces a yes/no event, the estimated *p*-value has a binomial distribution, and should use 1-sided 95% Bernstein confidence interval to compute it. Taking the lower bound of this interval makes a reasonable attempt to control type I error and encourages doing more simulations (to get a smaller confidence interval).

Identifying exchangeability is sometimes tricky and may have to be heuristic. Not everything is exchangeable—e.g., given patients and treatments, treatments are exchangeable, but patients aren't. In case of such paired observations, previously handled by the sign and signed rank tests, all assignments are generated by considering treatment swaps for a patient. Then, over all possible swaps calculate distribution of difference in means, and check if the difference on the sample is too large.

General procedure:

1. Identify an exchangeability and choose a statistic *f*
2. *b* times (for *b* = 10000 or so)
3. Generate a random assignment ("permutation") within the exchangeability
4. Calculate *f*(assignment)
5. Check if *f*(the sample) ∉ the chosen confidence interval
6. Calculate the lower bound *p*-value
7. Accept/reject accordingly

This is similar to bootstrap—if the value of the statistic on the sample ∉ 95% or so confidence interval formed by all assignment statistics, the null is rejected. In comparison, bootstraps resamples empirical distributions, whereas permutation tests resample possible value assignments. Permutation tests are more reliable than bootstrap tests due to explicit type I error control but, unlike bootstrap, don't apply to estimation problems and don't work for problems without sufficient exchangeability.

Permutation tests are very reliable where they apply. Fisher, who invented them, actually used them to check *t*-test accuracy (Edgington & Onghena 2007). In practice, when efficiency isn't a concern and a permutation test applies, should always use it instead of the equivalent parametric or rank-based nonparametric test. See Edgington & Onghena (2007) for many permutation tests.

Multiple testing still applies, and, though can use a permutation test instead of Friedman's, need to apply Bonferroni to compare individual alternatives.

4.25 Working with Count Data

Often can model count data using binomial(k, n) distribution, which can convert to normal with little loss of accuracy if k isn't close to 0 or n. The count approximation has mean k and variance $k(n - k)$, so the rate approximation has mean $p = k/n$ and variance $p(1 - p)/n$.

```
NormalSummary binomialRate(int k, int n)
{
    double p = 1.0 * k/n;
    return NormalSummary(p, p * (1 - p)/n);
}
NormalSummary binomialCount(int k, int n)
    {return NormalSummary(k, k * (1 - 1.0 * k/n));}
```

For small or large p this is very inaccurate; consider using Bernstein inequality instead. In particular, to test the difference of p from 0 at certain a z-score, the null equality is rejected if $p \geq 1/(1 + n/z^2)$, which means almost always. E.g., after seeing n *yes* samples Pr(*no*) = 0 by the normal approximation.

A classical statistical solution to this 0 problem is the "**rule of three**" (Wikipedia 2015a). If only *yes* events were observed, p must be small. Pr(n *yes* events) = $(1 - p)^n$. 95% confidence means that $(1 - p)^n \geq 0.05$ for this to have happened. Solving this, that lg(0.05) ≈ 3, and that $\lg(1 - p) \approx p$ for very small p, lead to $p \leq 3/n$. I.e., with 95% confidence $p \in [0, 3/n]$ and can't shrink this further. Though the proportion of *no* events shrinks with n at a fixed confidence, can't eliminate their existence. In software development terms, testing doesn't prove absence of buggy use cases but reduces the chance of discovering one.

A similar issue is the **black swan problem**, i.e., find Pr(!∃ a black swan after seeing n white ones). Fundamentally, a black swan event isn't predictable because the distribution needn't be binomial (blank swans were eventually discovered in Australia and !∃ any in other continents). Similarity, for thousands of years Europeans believed that the coast of Portugal was as west as possible because no explorer discovered otherwise:

An interesting warning of "black swan" logic is that many models can be useless. The idea is that "things are the way they are because they got this way", and a few extreme, unpredictable events tend to account for most of the "got"; thus assuming some average tendency based on historical data is deceptive. E.g., consider a sum of Cauchy random variates—most of its value is usually attributed to several samples.

4.26 Testing Distribution Differences

Want to check similarity of:

- Two continuous distributions
- A continuous distribution to a normal
- Two discrete distributions

For discrete, the main tool is the **chi-squared test**. It needs to evaluate the chi-squared CDF, but exact evaluation is slow and has to deal with many cases (Temme 1994), so evaluate approximately. Chi-squared is very similar to normal, but need a transformation to improve approximation quality. In particular (Canal 2005), if X is distributed as ChiCDF(n), $x = (X/n)^{1/6} - (X/n)^{1/3}/2 + (X/n)^{1/2}/3$ is distributed as Normal01CDF($(x - \mu)/\sigma$), where μ and σ^2 are $\sum a_i/x_i$, with respective $a_i = \{5/6, -1/9, -7/648, 25/2187\}$ and $\{0, 1/18, 1/162, -37/11664\}$. This has the worst case $O(10^{-2})$ and typical $O(10^{-5})$ errors, becoming more accurate with larger n.

```
double evaluateChiSquaredCdf(double chi, int n)
{
    assert(chi >= 0 && n > 0);
    double m = 5.0/6 - 1.0/9/n - 7.0/648/n/n + 25.0/2187/n/n/n,
        q2 = 1.0/18/n + 1.0/162/n/n - 37.0/11664/n/n/n, temp = chi/n,
        x = pow(temp, 1.0/6) - pow(temp, 1.0/3)/2 + pow(temp, 1.0/2)/3;
    return approxNormalCDF((x - m)/sqrt(q2));
}
double chiSquaredP(Vector<int> const& counts,
    Vector<double> const& means, int degreesOfFreedom)
{
    double chiStat = 0;
    for(int i = 0; i < counts.getSize(); ++i)
        if(means[i] > 0 && counts[i] > 0) chiStat +=
            (counts[i] - means[i]) * (counts[i] - means[i])/means[i];
    return evaluateChiSquaredCdf(chiStat, degreesOfFreedom);
}
```

For continuous distributions, a more complicated **Kolmogorov-Smirnov test** is a good option, though for testing normality have slightly more efficient tests (Wikipedia 2015b).

4.27 Testing Variance Differences

Often need to evaluate the F distribution CDF. Exact evaluation is problematic, but the **Paulson approximation** (Ferreira 2011) gives accurate results, up to 0.01 error for small v_1 and v_2, and < 0.001 for large. Here $F(x, v_1, v_2) \approx$ Normal01CDF(z) for $z = \frac{(1-t_2)x^{1/3} - 1 + t_1}{\sqrt{t_2 x^{2/3} + t_1}}$ with $t_i = 2/(9v_i)$.

```
double evalFCdf(double x, int v1, int v2)
{//Paulson approximation
    assert(x >= 0 && v1 > 0 && v2 > 0);
    double temp1 = 2.0/v1/9, temp2 = 2.0/v2/9;
    return approxNormalCDF(((1 - temp2) * pow(x, 1.0/3) - 1 + temp1)/
        sqrt(temp2 * pow(x, 2.0/3) + temp1));
}
```

4.28 Correlation Analysis

Correlation analysis detects monotonic relationships. **Pearson correlation** detects linear relationships using correlation = $(\sum(x_i - m_x)(y_i - m_y))/(s_x s_y)$. The answer $\in [-1, 1]$, with 1 meaning perfect linear relationship and −1 perfect negated linear one. Values with absolute value away from 1 mean lack of a linear relationship, but not of any relationship. E.g., for samples from $y = x^2$, correlation = 0. |correlation| ≥ 0.95 is considered strong.

```
double PearsonCorrelation(Vector<pair<double, double> > const& a)
{
    IncrementalStatistics x, y;
    for(int i = 0; i < a.getSize(); ++i)
    {
        x.addValue(a[i].first);
        y.addValue(a[i].second);
    }
    double covSum = 0;
    for(int i = 0; i < a.getSize(); ++i)
        covSum += (a[i].first - x.getMean()) * (a[i].second - y.getMean());
    return covSum/sqrt(x.getVariance() * y.getVariance());
}
```

Because variables may be related monotonically but not linearly, **Spearman correlation** first transforms the variables into ranks and then calculates Pearson correlation between them.

```
double SpearmanCorrelation(Vector<pair<double, double> > a)
{
    Vector<double> x, y;
    for(int i = 0; i < a.getSize(); ++i)
    {
        x.append(a[i].first);
        y.append(a[i].second);
    }
    x = convertToRanks(x), y = convertToRanks(x);
    for(int i = 0; i < a.getSize(); ++i)
    {
        a[i].first = x[i];
        a[i].second = y[i];
    }
    return PearsonCorrelation(a);
}
```

This code isn't the most efficient but is the simplest. Can calculate rank mean and variance more directly, but this gets complicated when have ties.

A different question is whether a correlation coefficient is significant, that is truly larger than a certain value. This is best computed by a specialized permutation test (Edgington & Onghena 2007) or bootstrap.

4.29 Ill-posed Problems

Many problems are perceived intuitively as well-defined but, when specified mathematically, have no best sensible solution. Such problems are **ill-posed**, meaning don't have some necessary info.

Ill-posed problems concern statistical algorithms because in some cases don't have sufficient data. E.g., consider estimating s^2 from a single example.

The main approach to solving such problem is assuming something that should hold naturally, but isn't part of the problem specification. Such assumptions can make a problem solvable but conceivably result in solving a somewhat different problem.

4.30 Comments

!∃ use cases for other pseudorandom generators, including **Mersenne Twister**, which is as fast as QualityXorshift64 and of very high quality but more complex and uses an array of 623 integers as state.

Other methods for Monte Carlo variance reduction, including **antithetic variates**, **control variates**, or **importance sampling**, aren't useful because they need some knowledge about the system and give only O(1) error reduction, while simulation is most useful when know nothing.

Empirical Bernstein is very recent; subsequent research may improve the constants. Slightly better finite sample bounds are available from the original Hoeffding or exact Clopper-Pearson bounds, but need numeric evaluation (Anguita et al. 2013).

For Wilcoxon, an alternative for handling 0 differences is to drop all of them, as suggested in various sources, but this fails when have $n \to \infty$ 0's, $m \to \infty$ nonzeros, and $n/m \to \infty$ because can conclude difference when !∃ one.

For testing equality of several alternatives, a classic parametric test is **ANOVA**. Despite wide use, it needs many assumptions and is only slightly more powerful than Friedman's when these are met. Likewise, **Tukey's test** is an alternative to Nemenyi's.

Both frequentist and Bayesian methods have pluses and minuses. Depending on the problem, either can be simpler or give better solution properties. E.g., certain events, such as who will win a particular presidential election, don't have associated probability distribution from a frequentist viewpoint because they occur only once, but Bayesian method model beliefs, and this causes no conceptual flaw.

General **multiple hypothesis testing** considers having k dependent or independent hypotheses and needing to decide which are true at some significance (Westfall et al. 2011). Finding the best alternative is a special case of this. Though Bonferroni is the only known method for simultaneous confidence intervals, committing to particular p-values allows more efficient testing. A typical goal is to minimize one of:

- **Family-wise error rate** (FWER)—Pr(one or more false hypotheses is found significant). This is natural, but with large k far too many true hypotheses can be deemed insignificant.
- **False discovery rate** (FDR)—Pr(more than some proportion of false hypotheses is found significant). This seems unscientific by allowing errors, but in exploratory analysis is very useful due to dramatically cutting down false rejections. Can use independent data for subsequent validation.

It would be interesting to develop a two-sided finite sample bound OCBA, which doesn't assume normality. This is tricky because the calculations break down, and need to use another criteria to pick the next simulation.

Test power calculation is generally possible only when assume enough about the data to be able to simulate it and calculate power using Monte Carlo, which is essentially when the data is assumed to follow a known distribution. Though parametric tests shine in cases for which they were designed, for some bad case distributions they have low power, unlike the corresponding nonparametric equivalents (Conover 1999).

When don't know the data distribution, power calculation is impossible because don't have enough information. In many areas of statistics, unknowns lead to ill-posed problems (such as finding test power or a best test). Bayesian methods, which allow assuming any unknowns, might handle such cases well.

In manufacturing, the basic idea of **statistical quality control** is to monitor variance and intervene if it becomes high enough to cause defects.

In many applications of statistics, generic models will do fine. But for best results need to research specialized literature that makes use of domain-specific knowledge. E.g., the significance of a fingerprint match strongly depends on prior knowledge about fingerprints, and "reasonable" domain-agnostic guesses are useless.

General techniques fail for applications like extreme value estimation (Coles 2003). A typical example is estimating water dam height that is enough to prevent floods for several centuries with high probability, given measurements of several years of water levels. Simulation/resampling fails because an extreme future value will surely exceed anything observed. A reasonable approach is to assume that water levels follow a normal or some other distribution, estimate its parameters, simulate several centuries of samples, and take the 99% or so order statistic of the results. Though the particular distribution assumption is ad hoc, the result is better than guessing without any method.

4.31 References

Andrews, D. W. (2000). Inconsistency of the bootstrap when a parameter is on the boundary of the parameter space. *Econometrica, 68*(2), 399–405.

Anguita, D., Ghelardoni, L., Ghio, A., & Ridella, S. (2013). A survey of old and new results for the test error estimation of a classifier. *Journal of Artificial Intelligence and Soft Computing Research, 3*(4), 229–242.

Audibert, J. Y., Munos, R., & Szepesvári, C. (2009). Exploration–exploitation tradeoff using variance estimates in multi-armed bandits. *Theoretical Computer Science, 410*(19), 1876–1902.

Bratley, P., & Fox, B. L. (1988). Algorithm 659: implementing Sobol's quasirandom sequence generator. *ACM Transactions on Mathematical Software (TOMS), 14*(1), 88–100.

Canal, L. (2005). A normal approximation for the chi-square distribution. *Computational Statistics & Data Analysis, 48*(4), 803–808.

Caruana, R., & Niculescu-Mizil, A. (2006). An empirical comparison of supervised learning algorithms. In *Proceedings of the 23rd International Conference on Machine learning* (pp. 161–168). ACM.

Chen, C. H., Lee L.H. (2010). *Stochastic Simulation Optimization: an Optimal Computing Budget Allocation* (Vol. 1). World Scientific.

Coles, S. (2001). *An Introduction to Statistical Modeling of Extreme Values*. Springer.

Conover, W. J. (1999). Practical Nonparametric Statistics. Wiley.

Devroye, L. (1986). *Non-uniform Random Variate Generation.* Springer.

Edgington, E., & Onghena, P. (2007). *Randomization tests.* CRC Press.

Ferreira, D. F. (2011). A normal approximation to the F distribution. *Rev. Bras. Biom. Sao Paulo, 29*(2), 222–228.

Gao, W., & Zhou, Z. H. (2013). On the doubt about margin explanation of boosting. *Artificial Intelligence, 203*, 1–18.

Hollander, M., Wolfe, D. A., & Chicken, E. (2013). *Nonparametric Statistical Methods.* Wiley.

L'Ecuyer, P.(1999). Good parameters and implementations for combined multiple recursive random number generators. *Operations Research 47*: 159–164.

———, & Simard, R. (2007). TestU01: a C library for empirical testing of random number generators. *ACM Transactions on Mathematical Software (TOMS), 33*(4), 22.

———, Simard, R., Chen, E. J., & Kelton, W. D. (2002). An object-oriented random number package with many long streams and substreams. *Operations Research, 50*(6), 1073–1075.

Kroese, D. P., Taimre, T., & Botev, Z. I. (2011). *Handbook of Monte Carlo Methods.* Wiley.

Marsaglia, G., & Tsang, W. W. (2000). A simple method for generating gamma variables. *ACM Transactions on Mathematical Software (TOMS), 26*(3), 363–372.

Press, W.H. et al. (2007). *Numerical Recipes: The Art of Scientific Computing*, 3rd ed. Cambridge University Press.

Spall, J. C. (2003). *Introduction to Stochastic Search and Optimization: Estimation, Simulation, and Control.* Wiley.

StackExchange (2014). Proof of upper-tail inequality for standard normal distribution. Accessed June 25, 14.

Temme, N. M. (1994). A set of algorithms for the incomplete gamma functions. *Probability in the Engineering and Informational Sciences, 8*(02), 291–307.

Westfall, P. H., Tobias, R. D., & Wolfinger, R. D. (2011). *Multiple Comparisons and Multiple Tests Using SAS.* SAS Institute.

Wikipedia (2013). RC4. http://en.wikipedia.org/wiki/RC4. Accessed May 12, 2013.

——— (2014a). Bootstrapping. http://en.wikipedia.org/wiki/Bootstrapping_(statistics). Accessed June 25, 2014.

——— (2014b). Consistent estimator. http://en.wikipedia.org/wiki/Consistent_estimator. Accessed June 25, 2014.

——— (2014c). Dvoretzky-Kiefer-Wolfowitz inequality. http://en.wikipedia.org/wiki/Dvoretzky–Kiefer–Wolfowitz_inequality. Accessed June 25, 2014.

——— (2014d). Error function. http://en.wikipedia.org/wiki/Error_function. Accessed June 25, 2014.

——— (2014e). Slutsky's theorem. http://en.wikipedia.org/wiki/Slutsky's_theorem. Accessed June 25, 2014.

——— (2014f). Arrow's impossibility theorem. http://en.wikipedia.org/wiki/Arrow's_impossibility_theorem. Accessed November 23, 2014.

——— (2015a). Rule of three. https://en.wikipedia.org/wiki/Rule_of_three_(statistics). Accessed December 31, 2015.

——— (2015b). Kolmogorov-Smirnov test. https://en.wikipedia.org/wiki/Kolmogorov-Smirnov_test. Accessed November 18, 2015.

——— (2015c). Friedman test. https://en.wikipedia.org/wiki/Friedman_test. Accessed November 18, 2015.

——— (2015d). Triangular distribution. https://en.wikipedia.org/wiki/Triangular_distribution. Accessed November 1, 2015.

5 Sorting

A collection of items satisfying a **weak order relation** "<" is sorted. Don't use "≤" because it's not weak. For n items, ∃ n! orders, and k binary comparisons decide between at most 2^k of them, so to sort $k = \Theta(n\lg(n))$. Sorting is **stable** if equal items keep their original relative order. Using item location as **secondary key** ensures stability but is slow. Item sorting analysis assumes O(1) time comparisons. For expensive-to-copy items, sort an array of pointers to them.

5.1 Insertion Sort

For small arrays, insertion sort is stable and the fastest. It mimics sorting a hand of cards. Given a sorted array, initially with the first item, iteratively insert the next one into the correct place.

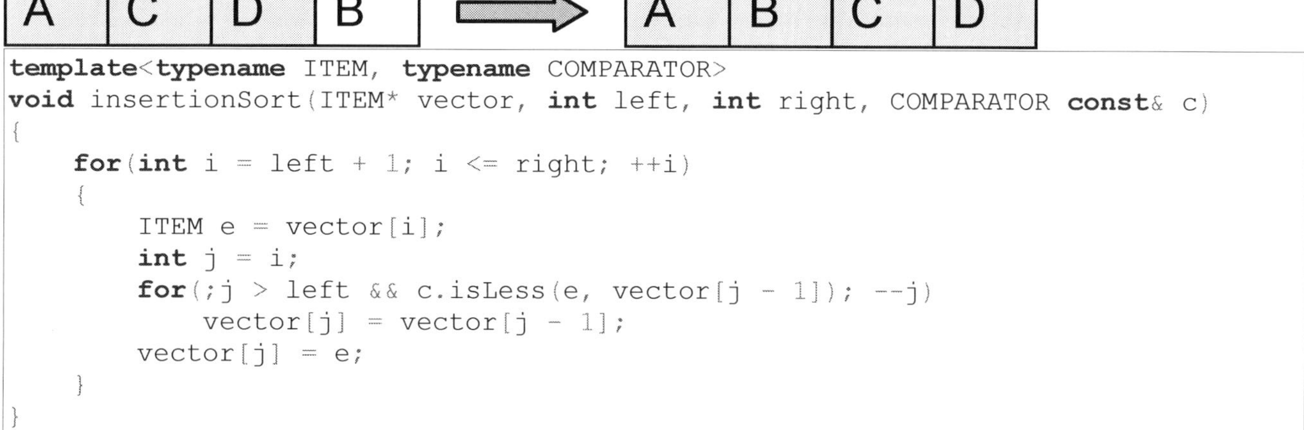


```
template<typename ITEM, typename COMPARATOR>
void insertionSort(ITEM* vector, int left, int right, COMPARATOR const& c)
{
    for(int i = left + 1; i <= right; ++i)
    {
        ITEM e = vector[i];
        int j = i;
        for(;j > left && c.isLess(e, vector[j - 1]); --j)
            vector[j] = vector[j - 1];
        vector[j] = e;
    }
}
```

The runtime is $O(n^2)$, with very low constant factors, and O(the number of reversed pairs called **inversions**) = $O(n)$ for almost sorted input.

5.2 Quicksort

If don't need stability, quicksort is the fastest. The basic version:

1. **Pick a pivot item**
2. **Partition the array so that items ≤/≥ the pivot are on the left/right**
3. **Sort the two halves recursively**

The order of items within each subarray after a partition doesn't matter:

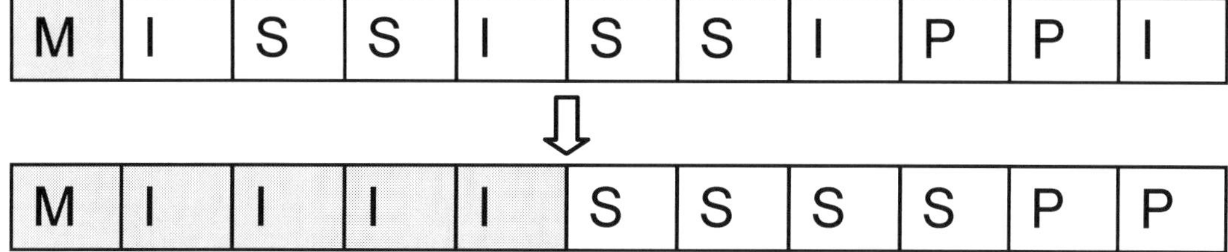

The most practical pivot is the **median of three** random items:

- Deterministic picks may give $O(n^2)$ runtime
- A single random pivot is slightly slower
- Using five or more pivots is negligibly faster but more complex

```
template<typename ITEM, typename COMPARATOR>
int pickPivot(ITEM* vector, int left, int right, COMPARATOR comparator)
{
    int i = GlobalRNG.inRange(left, right), j =
        GlobalRNG.inRange(left, right), k = GlobalRNG.inRange(left, right);
```

```
    if(comparator.isLess(vector[j], vector[i])) swap(i, j);
    //i <= j, decide where k goes
    return comparator.isLess(vector[k], vector[i]) ?
        i : comparator.isLess(vector[k], vector[j]) ? k : j;
}
```

Partitioning divides items into < pivot, = pivot, and > pivot, moving equal items to the sides:

=	<	?	>	=

Use left and right pointers to scan the array from both directions at the same time. If a scanned item doesn't belong to corresponding "<" or ">" section, it's marked for swapping. The process stops when the pointers cross.

```
template<typename ITEM, typename COMPARATOR> void partition3(ITEM* vector,
    int left, int right, int& i, int& j, COMPARATOR comparator)
{
    ITEM p = vector[pickPivot(vector, left, right, comparator)];
    int lastLeftEqual = i = left - 1, firstRightEqual = j = right + 1;
    for(;;)//the pivot is the sentinel for the first pass
    {//after one swap swapped items act as sentinels
        while(comparator.isLess(vector[++i], p));
        while(comparator.isLess(p, vector[--j]));
        if(i >= j) break;
        swap(vector[i], vector[j]);
        //swap equal items to the sides
        if(comparator.isEqual(vector[i], p))
            swap(vector[++lastLeftEqual], vector[i]);
        if(comparator.isEqual(vector[j], p))
            swap(vector[--firstRightEqual], vector[j]);
    }
    //invariant: i == j if they stop at an item = pivot
    //and this can happen at both left and right item
    //or they cross over and i = j + 1
    if(i == j){++i; --j;}
    //swap side items to the middle
    for(int k = left; k <= lastLeftEqual; ++k) swap(vector[k], vector[j--]);
    for(int k = right; k >= firstRightEqual; --k)
        swap(vector[k], vector[i++]);
}
```

Either *i* or *j* may be out of bounds. The postcondition:

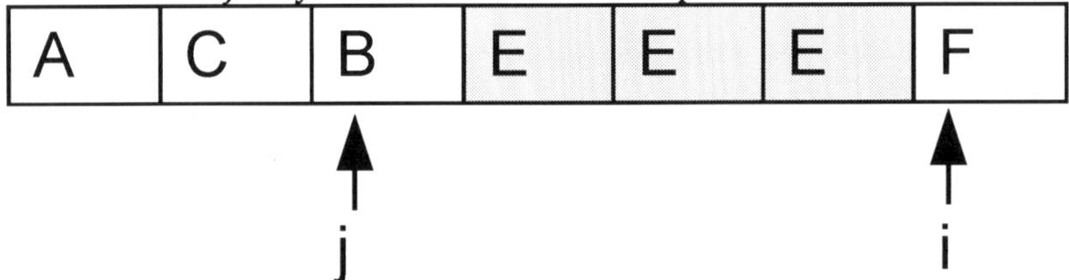

The extra work and complexity are small relative to the basic partitioning (that pays no special attention to equal items). Also, it's faster for many equal items and used for vector sorting. Optimizations:

- Sorting smaller subarrays first ensures O(lg(n)) extra memory, which practically guarantees that the recursion stack won't run out.
- Use insertion sort for small subarrays of size 5–25. Due to caching, recursing to insertion sort is faster than a single insertion sort over the whole array in the end, despite using more instructions.
- Remove the tail recursion. Removing the other one complicates the algorithm.

```
template<typename ITEM> void quickSort(ITEM* vector, int left, int right)
    {quickSort(vector, left, right, DefaultComparator<ITEM>());}
template<typename ITEM, typename COMPARATOR>
void quickSort(ITEM* vector, int left, int right, COMPARATOR comparator)
{
```

```
    while(right - left > 16)
    {
        int i, j;
        partition3(vector, left, right, i, j, comparator);
        if(j - left < right - i)//smaller first
        {
            quickSort(vector, left, j, comparator);
            left = i;
        }
        else
        {
            quickSort(vector, i, right, comparator);
            right = j;
        }
    }
    insertionSort(vector, left, right, comparator);
}
```

E[the runtime] = O($n$lg(n)). Suppose the pivot is random and all items are unique. Let X_{ij} be the number of times that the item at i was compared to the item at j in the sorted array with $j > i$. E[X_{ij}] = Pr(i or j was a pivot) because i and j were compared at most once and only if one of them was a pivot in a subarray containing the other. Else, if an item at $> j$ or $< i$ was a pivot, i and j go into the same subarray, else into separate ones. Because $\exists\, j - i + 1$ separating pivots, Pr(i or j was a pivot) = $2/(j - i + 1)$, and the E[the total number of comparisons] = $E(\sum_{0 \le i < n}\sum_{i+1 \le j < n} X_{ij}) < 2\sum_{0 \le i < n}\sum_{1 \le k < n} 1/k < 2n\lg(n)$. The unlikely worst case is O(n^2).

5.3 Mergesort

Mergesort is the most efficient stable sort:

1. **Split the array into equal halves**
2. **Mergesort each recursively**
3. **Merge the halves in O(n) time**

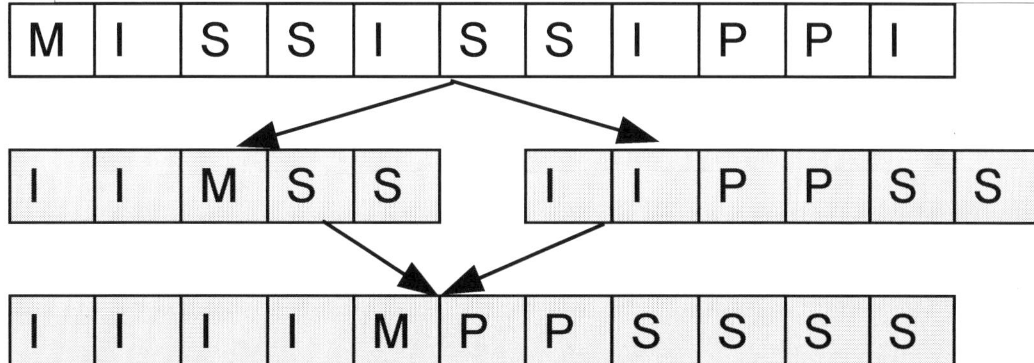

Optimizations:

- Alternate the data and the temporary storage arrays to avoid unnecessary copies
- Use insertion sort for small arrays

Merging iteratively moves the smallest leftmost item of both arrays to the result array. The rightmost index of the left array is `middle`.

```
template<typename ITEM, typename COMPARATOR> void merge(ITEM* vector,
    int left, int middle, int right, COMPARATOR const& c, ITEM* storage)
{
    for(int i = left, j = middle + 1; left <= right; ++left)
    {
        bool useRight = i > middle || (j <= right &&
            c.isLess(storage[j], storage[i]));
        vector[left] = storage[(useRight ? j : i)++];
    }
```

```
}
template<typename ITEM, typename COMPARATOR> void mergeSortHelper(
    ITEM* vector, int left, int right, COMPARATOR const& c, ITEM* storage)
{
    if(right - left > 16)
    {//sort storage using vector as storage
        int middle = (right + left)/2;
        mergeSortHelper(storage, left, middle, c, vector);
        mergeSortHelper(storage, middle + 1, right, c, vector);
        merge(vector, left, middle, right, c, storage);
    }
    else insertionSort(vector, left, right, c);
}
template<typename ITEM, typename COMPARATOR>
void mergeSort(ITEM* vector, int n, COMPARATOR const& c)
{
    if(n <= 1) return;
    Vector<ITEM> storage(vector, n);
    mergeSortHelper(vector, 0, n - 1, c, storage.getArray());
}
template<typename ITEM> void mergeSort(ITEM* vector, int n)
    {mergeSort(vector, n, DefaultComparator<ITEM>());}
```

The runtime $R(n) = O(n) + 2R(n/2)$. By the master theorem, $R(n) = O(n\lg(n))$.

5.4 Integer Sorting

Can sort integers in $O(n)$ time by not using "<". For integers mod N, **counting sort** counts how many times each occurs and creates a sorted array from the counts in $O(n + N)$ time. It's stable.

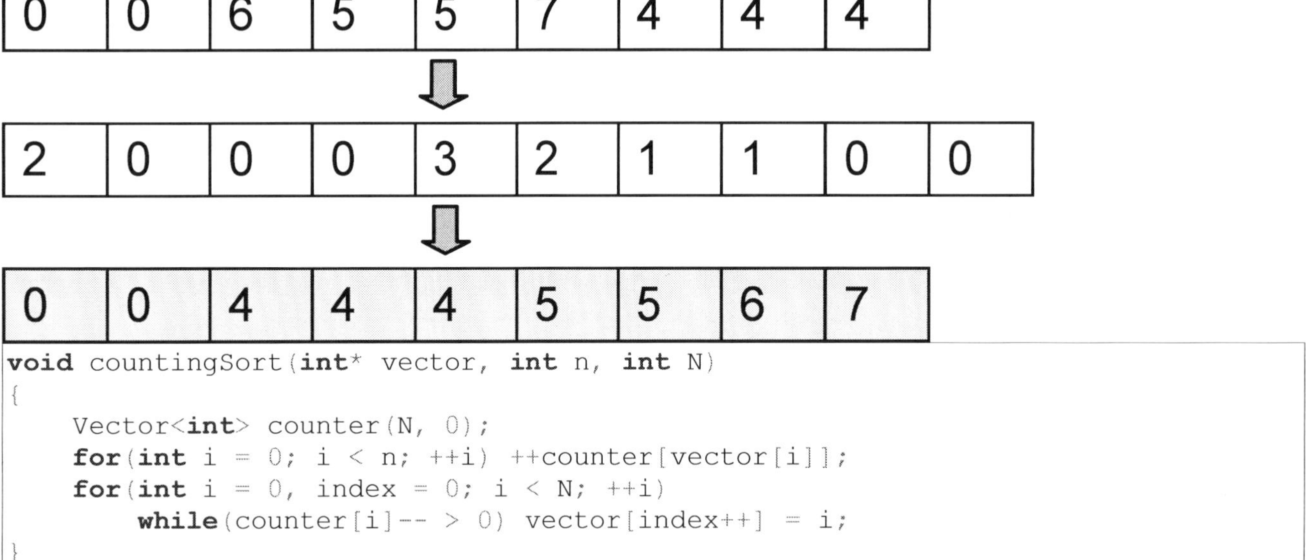


```
void countingSort(int* vector, int n, int N)
{
    Vector<int> counter(N, 0);
    for(int i = 0; i < n; ++i) ++counter[vector[i]];
    for(int i = 0, index = 0; i < N; ++i)
        while(counter[i]-- > 0) vector[index++] = i;
}
```

For items with integer mod N keys, **key-indexed counting sort** (KSort) counts how many have a particular key, uses the cumulative counts to create a temporary sorted array, and copies it into the original. The implementation needs a functor `ORDERED_HASH` that extracts items' keys.

```
template<typename ITEM, typename ORDERED_HASH> void KSort(ITEM* a, int n,
    int N, ORDERED_HASH const& h)
{
    ITEM* temp = rawMemory<ITEM>(n);
    Vector<int> count(N + 1, 0);
    for(int i = 0; i < n; ++i) ++count[h(a[i]) + 1];
    for(int i = 0; i < N; ++i) count[i + 1] += count[i];//accumulate counts
    //rearrange items
```

```
    for(int i = 0; i < n; ++i) new(&temp[count[h(a[i])]++])ITEM(a[i]);
    for(int i = 0; i < n; ++i) a[i] = temp[i];
    rawDelete(temp);
}
```

It's stable and takes $O(n + N)$ time.

5.5 Vector Sorting

Sorting n vectors of size k as items takes $O(kn\lg(n))$ time. For quicksort on n vectors of length ∞, E[the runtime] = $O(n\lg(n)^2)$ (Vallee et al. 2009). This is intuitive because for two random sequences in a collection of n with items from an alphabet of size A, E[**lcp** (least common prefix)] = $\log_A(n)$, requiring that time for a comparison.

Multikey quicksort three-partitions on the first letter and recurses on each subarray, going to the next letter for the equal part:

Sort Left on 0			Sort Middle on 1			Sort right on 0
A	C	B	E	E	E	F
D	A	A	A	E	A	O
	T	T	R	L	R	R
			L			D

The comparator keeps track of current depth, starting with 0, which allows sorting arbitrary tuples.

```
template<typename VECTOR, typename COMPARATOR> void multikeyQuicksort(VECTOR*
    vector, int left, int right, COMPARATOR comparator)
{
    if(right - left < 1) return;
    int i, j;
    partition3(vector, left, right, i, j, comparator);
    ++comparator.depth;
    multikeyQuicksort(vector, j + 1, i - 1, comparator);
    --comparator.depth;
    multikeyQuicksort(vector, left, j, comparator);
    multikeyQuicksort(vector, i, right, comparator);
}
```

Remove the recursion to not run out of stack for long vectors with high lcp. The depth parameter allows computing suffix arrays (see the “String Algorithms” chapter).

```
template<typename VECTOR, typename COMPARATOR> void multikeyQuicksortNR(
    VECTOR* vector, int left, int right, COMPARATOR comparator,
    int maxDepth = numeric_limits<int>::max())
{
    Stack<int> stack;
    stack.push(left);
    stack.push(right);
    stack.push(0);
    while(!stack.isEmpty())
    {
        comparator.depth = stack.pop();
        right = stack.pop();
        left = stack.pop();
        if(right - left > 0 && comparator.depth < maxDepth)
        {
            int i, j;
```

```
            partition3(vector, left, right, i, j, comparator);
            //left
            stack.push(left);
            stack.push(j);
            stack.push(comparator.depth);
            //right
            stack.push(i);
            stack.push(right);
            stack.push(comparator.depth);
            //middle
            stack.push(j + 1);
            stack.push(i - 1);
            stack.push(comparator.depth + 1);
        }
    }
}
```

E[the runtime] = O($n$lg(n)), and the runtime with respect to the length is the optimal O(n(the length + lg(n))) (Sedgewick 1999). The unlikely worst case is O(n(length + n)). For arrays of large items, use pointers to avoid copying because otherwise vector sorting gains nothing.

If items are vectors of small integers of fixed length k, **LSD sort** is stable and the most efficient. It sorts k times using vector[$k - i$] as the key to KSort in pass i, with the overall runtime O(nk). This works because KSort is stable.

5.6 Permutation Sort

To sort according to a permutation defined by an array of sorted indices, can copy the items to a temporary array and populate the original from it according to the permutation. But, can avoid the temporary because a permutation is a product of disjoint cycles. Think of f = permutation[i] as specifying from where to take the item for position i. Mark permutation[i] as processed by setting it to i, and process permutation[f] from which took the item. Need to remember only the first item in the cycle, which is immediately replaced, and a loop over the array gets all cycles in O(n) time.

```
template<typename ITEM>void permutationSort(ITEM* a, int* permutation, int n)
{
    for(int i = 0; i < n; ++i) if(permutation[i] != i)
    {
        ITEM temp = a[i];
        int from = i, to;
        for(;;)
        {
            from = permutation[to = from];
            permutation[to] = to;//mark processed
            if(from == i) break;
            a[to] = a[from];
        }
        a[to] = temp;//complete cycle
    }
}
```

E.g., consider the permutation 3210 applied to *abcd*. Start with 0. Remember v[0] = a, from position p[0] = 3 take d, and put it into position 0. Check p[3] = 0 to discover the end of cycle due to p[0] = 0, and put stored a into position 3. Move to position 1. The same logic swaps b and c. After this, all positions are marked identity, and moving to 2 and 3 changes nothing.

5.7 Selection

Want to arrange array items so that the specified item is in the correct place, e.g., to find the median. **Quickselect** is like quicksort but doesn't sort the subarray that can't contain the item. It iteratively shrinks the interval containing the item.

```
template<typename ITEM, typename COMPARATOR> ITEM quickSelect(ITEM* vector,
    int left, int right, int k, COMPARATOR comparator)
{
    assert(k >= left && k <= right);
    for(int i, j; left < right;)
    {
        partition3(vector, left, right, i, j, comparator);
        if(k >= i) left = i;
        else if(k <= j) right = j;
        else break;
    }
    return vector[k];
}
```

E[the runtime] = O(n). The unlikely worst case is O(n^2). For vectors, somewhat unintuitively also E[the runtime] = O(n) (Vallee et al. 2009), but can extend multikey quicksort to **multikey quickselect**. Same for partial sort and multiple select (covered later in the chapter).

```
template<typename VECTOR, typename COMPARATOR> void multikeyQuickselect(
    VECTOR* vector, int left, int right, int k, COMPARATOR comparator)
{
    assert(k >= left && k <= right);
    for(int d = 0, i, j; right - left >= 1;)
    {
        partition3(vector, left, right, i, j, comparator);
        if(k <= j) right = j;
        else if (k < i)
        {
            left = j + 1;
            right = i - 1;
            ++comparator.depth;
        }
        else left = i;
    }
}
```

5.8 Partial Sort

To sort only the first k items, an optimal O(n + $k$lg(k)) solution is to run quicksort(0, k – 1) on the result of quickselect(k).

To sort incrementally, sorting another item only if needed, select it but reuse the right bound values from the previous calls, stored on a stack. This uses the optimal expected O(n + $k$lg(k)) time after selecting k items (Paredes & Navarro 2006) and works because selection is from left to right, so quickselect always executes `right = j`. Before the first call, the stack needs to contain the array's rightmost index, and after each call pop it to ensure `left` + 1 ≤ `right` for the next call. The array is sorted when the stack is empty, and `left` ≥ `right`. Can't modify the stack and the vector between calls.

```
template<typename ITEM, typename COMPARATOR> ITEM incrementalQuickSelect(
    ITEM* vector, int left, Stack<int>& s, COMPARATOR comparator)
{
    for(int right, i, j; left < (right = s.getTop()); s.push(j))
        partition3(vector, left, right, i, j, comparator);
    s.pop();
    return vector[left];
}
```

The unlikely worst case is O(n^2). To sort completely using partial sort:

```
template<typename ITEM, typename COMPARATOR> void incrementalSort(
    ITEM* vector, int n, COMPARATOR const& c)
{
    Stack<int> s;
```

```
    s.push(n - 1);
    for(int i = 0; i < n; ++i) incrementalQuickSelect(vector, i, s, c);
}
```

5.9 Multiple Selection

To output an array with only the specified items in correct places, specify them with a Boolean array, and have quicksort not recurse into subarrays without any selected items. E.g., can compute quartiles or quantiles for statistics this way.

```
template<typename ITEM, typename COMPARATOR> void multipleQuickSelect(ITEM*
    vector, bool* selected, int left, int right, COMPARATOR comparator)
{
    while(right - left > 16)
    {
        int i, j;
        for(i = left; i <= right && !selected[i]; ++i);
        if(i == right + 1) return;//none are selected
        partition3(vector, left, right, i, j, comparator);
        if(j - left < right - i)//smaller first
        {
            multipleQuickSelect(vector, selected, left, j, comparator);
            left = i;
        }
        else
        {
            multipleQuickSelect(vector, selected, i, right, comparator);
            right = j;
        }
    }
    insertionSort(vector, left, right, comparator);
}
```

∀ selection E[the runtime] is optimal, but depends on the number and the positions of the specified items (Kaligosi et al. 2005). The unlikely worst case is $O(n^2)$.

5.10 Searching

Sequential search is the fastest for few items despite the $O(n)$ runtime and the only choice if items aren't sorted. For sorted data, **binary search** is worst-case optimal, taking $O(\lg(n))$ time. It starts in the middle, and if query ≠ item, goes left if query < item and right otherwise.

```
template<typename ITEM, typename COMPARATOR> int binarySearch(ITEM const*
    vector, int left, int right, ITEM const& key, COMPARATOR comparator)
{
    while(left <= right)
    {
        int middle = (left + right)/2;
        if(comparator.isEqual(key, vector[middle])) return middle;
        comparator.isLess(key, vector[middle]) ?
            right = middle - 1 : left = middle + 1;
    }
    return -1;
}
```

Exponential search is useful when the "array" upper bound is unknown. It assumes that it's 1, then 2, 4, 8, etc., and, after it's found, does binary search between bound/2 and bound. It's not useful for arrays, which know their bounds, but very useful if a function implicitly represents the search range. E.g., can guess a positive number that someone thinks of but discloses only comparison results of it to other numbers. The runtime is O(lg(the upper bound)).

5.11 Comments

Some slower $O(n^2)$ sorts:

- **Selection sort**—swap the minimum item with the first item, then repeat this for the rest of the array—makes the minimal possible number of item moves
- **Bubble sort**—exchange adjacent items until every item is in correct order—how people in a group sort themselves by height

Three-partitioning is a solution to the **Dutch national flag problem**. The classic algorithm for it by Dijkstra uses fewer instructions and is a bit simpler but has higher constant factors with few equal items, which is often the case for sorting (Sedgewick 1999). Must be very careful with partitioning code because it's easy to get it wrong, particularly with sentinels for the `while` loops.

An interesting idea is using several pivots, resulting, in particular, in **dual-pivot quicksort**. It's slightly faster than regular quicksort, but needs twice more code and is more complicated. The analysis is still ongoing, but currently the conclusion is that have fewer cache misses, which more than compensates for more instructions (Kushagra et al. 2013).

The STL uses quicksort with deterministic median-of-three pivot but switches to a slower, safer heapsort (see the "Priority Queues" chapter) on reaching a high enough depth. Though this strategy ensures $O(n\lg(n))$ runtime, it too benefits from using random pivots. Due to E[the runtime] guarantees, the switch seems unnecessary and doesn't generalize to other situations such as vector sorting. **Shellsort** is suboptimal but empirically slightly faster than heapsort (Sedgewick 1999); despite that it has no use case.

An interesting search algorithm for sorted numeric items is **interpolation search** (Wikipedia 2015). It's like binary search but, instead of using the average index, uses the index based on the item values. E[the runtime for uniformly distributed items] = $O(\ln(\ln(n))$, but such use case is very limited and any gain over binary search is negligible.

An interesting problem is sorting a linked list. Because a list doesn't support random access, the only goal is traversing in sorted order. Can adapt mergesort to sort without using extra memory (Roura 1999).

5.12 References

Kaligosi, K., Mehlhorn, K., Munro, J. I., & Sanders, P. (2005). Towards optimal multiple selection. In *Automata, Languages, and Programming* (pp. 103–114). Springer.

Kushagra, S., López-Ortiz, A., Munro, J. I., & Qiao, A. (2013). Multi-pivot Quicksort: theory and experiments. In *Proc. 16th Workshop on Algorithm Engineering and Experiments (ALENEX)*. SIAM.

Paredes, R., & Navarro, G. (2006). Optimal incremental sorting. In *Proc. 8th Workshop on Algorithm Engineering and Experiments and 3rd Workshop on Analytic Algorithmics and Combinatorics (ALENEX-ANALCO'06)* (pp. 171–182). SIAM.

Mehlhorn, K., & Sanders, P. (2008). *Algorithms and Data Structures: The Basic Toolbox*. Springer.

Roura, S. (1999). Improving mergesort for linked lists. In *Algorithms-ESA'99* (pp. 267–276). Springer.

Sedgewick, R. (1999). *Algorithms in C++, Parts 1–4* (Vol. 1). Addison-Wesley.

Vallée, B., Clément, J., Fill, J. A., & Flajolet, P. (2009). The number of symbol comparisons in Quicksort and Quickselect. In *Automata, Languages, and Programming* (pp. 750–763). Springer.

Wikipedia (2015). Interpolation search. https://en.wikipedia.org/wiki/Interpolation_search. Accessed November 3, 2015.

6 Dynamic Sorted Sequences

A **dynamic sorted sequence** maintains a collection of items in sorted order. For key x, it efficiently supports:

- **Map** operations **find**, **insert**, and **remove**.
- Max and min.
- **In-order iteration** between any two elements.
- **Predecessor** and **successor**, which respectively are the previous max item $< x$ and the next min item $> x$. Iteration and predecessor give find and successor. Combining these with iteration enables efficient **range search**.
- **Join** of two sequences such that keys in one < keys in the other.
- **Split** of a sequence such that the first has items $\leq x$, and the second $> x$.
- Various augmentations can support other operations, such as finding the kth element. Join and split of two sequences are rarely useful and not efficiently supported by a freelist-based implementation.

Map operations, min, max, predecessor, and successor usually take the same worst case and/or expected time $O(\lg(n))$, where n = the number of currently maintained items. Iteration over all items usually needs $O(n)$ time and is faster than finding them one by one. Unlike for sorting, items with nonunique keys aren't supported by most data structures and must be handled by augmenting keys with tiebreak information.

6.1 Skip List

A **skip list** is a collection of linked lists in sorted order, where list i has each item with probability p^i for a constant p. The bottom list has all the items, and higher level lists outline lower level ones for efficient operations.

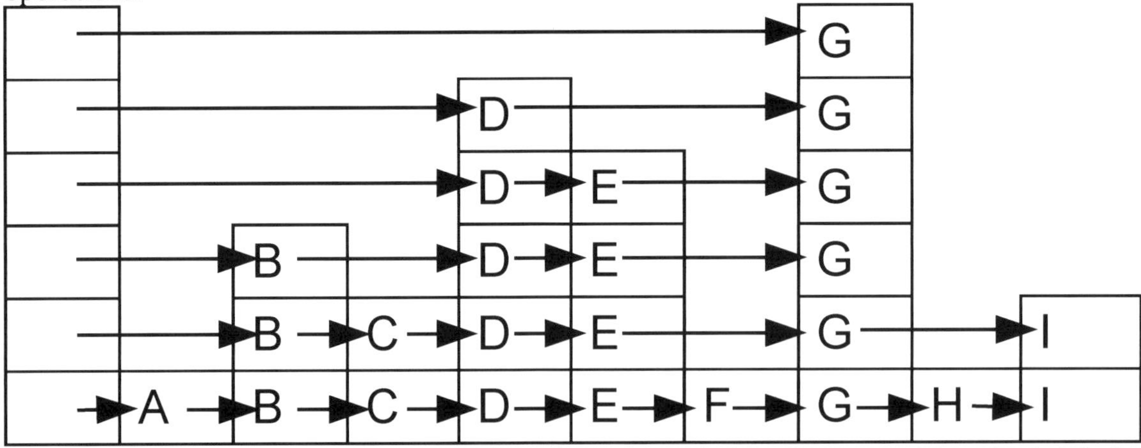

The number of levels should be $\approx \lg(n)$, and in practice $\lg(n) < 32$, so use 32 as the height bound for simplicity. Most operations support items with nonunique keys.

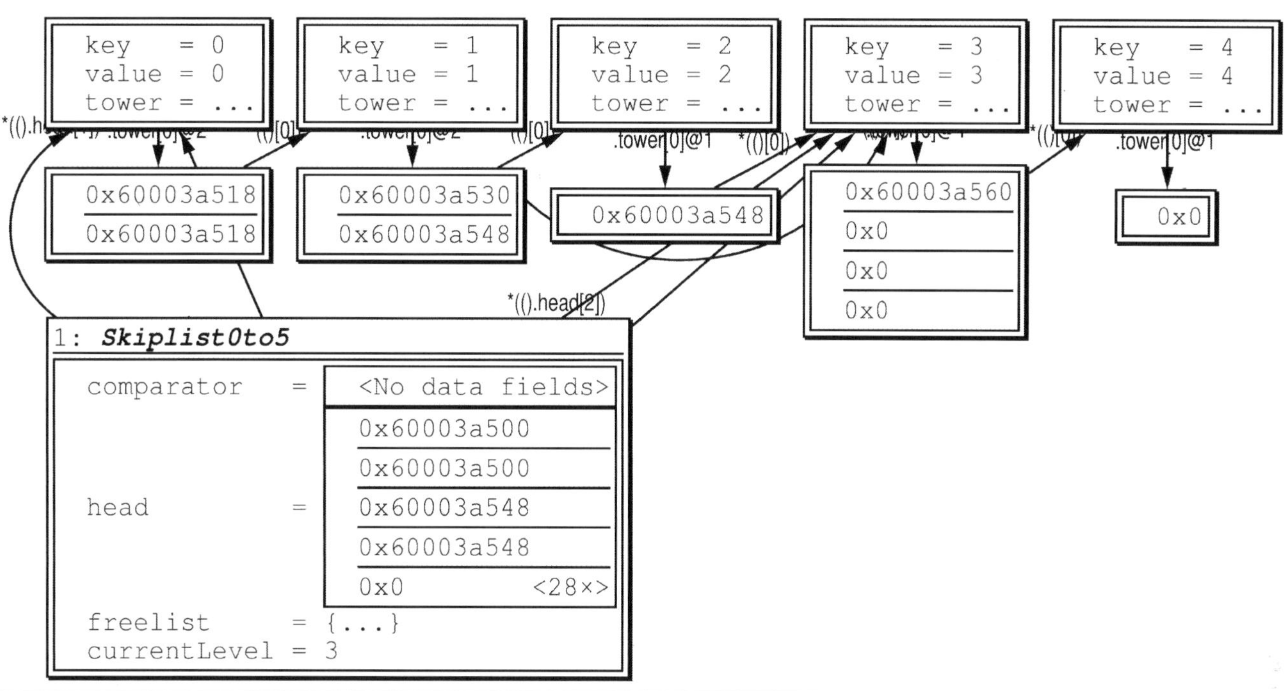


```
template<typename KEY, typename VALUE, typename COMPARATOR =
    DefaultComparator<VALUE> > class SkipList
{
    COMPARATOR comparator;
    enum{MAX_HEIGHT = 32};
    struct Node
    {
        KEY key;
        VALUE value;
        Node** tower;
        Node(KEY const& theKey, VALUE const& theValue, int height):
            key(theKey), value(theValue), tower(new Node*[height]) {}
        ~Node(){delete[] tower;}
    }* head[MAX_HEIGHT];
    Freelist<Node> freelist;
    int currentLevel;
public:
    typedef Node NodeType;
    SkipList(COMPARATOR const& theComparator = COMPARATOR()):
        currentLevel(0), comparator(theComparator)
        {for(int i = 0; i < MAX_HEIGHT; ++i) head[i] = 0;}
    SkipList(SkipList const& rhs): currentLevel(0),
        comparator(rhs.comparator)
    {//order of items with nonunique keys in copy is reversed
        for(int i = 0; i < MAX_HEIGHT; ++i) head[i] = 0;
        for(Node* node = rhs.head[0]; node; node = node->tower[0])
            insert(node->key, node->value, false);
    }
    SkipList& operator=(SkipList const&rhs){return genericAssign(*this,rhs);}
};
```

Search:

1. **Start with the highest nonempty list**
2. **Follow the links until reach list 0, going one list down when the next item > query**
3. **Linearly search list 0**

This allows efficient predecessor operation, in terms of which some others are implemented.

```
    NodeType* predecessor(KEY const& key)
```

```
{
    Node **tower = head, *pred = 0;
    for(int level = currentLevel; level >= 0; --level)
        for(Node* node; (node = tower[level]) &&  comparator.isLess(
            node->key, key); tower = node->tower) pred = node;
    return pred;
}
NodeType* inclusiveSuccessor(KEY const& key)
{
    Node* pred = predecessor(key);
    return pred? pred->tower[0] : findMin();
}
NodeType* findNode(KEY const& key)
{
    Node* node = inclusiveSuccessor(key);
    return node && !comparator.isLess(node->key, key) ? node : 0;
}
NodeType* successor(KEY const& key)
{//is inclusiveSuccessor with nonunique keys
    Node* node = inclusiveSuccessor(key);
    if(node && !comparator.isLess(node->key, key)) node = node->tower[0];
    return node;
}
VALUE* find(KEY const& key)
{
    Node* result = findNode(key);
    return result ? &result->value : 0;
}
```

Insert relies on that the higher lists have fewer nodes than the lower ones:

1. Generate item height as 1 + geometric(1 – p)
2. Start at the highest level
3. ∀level
4. Find the place to insert the node so that have sorted order
5. Link the previous node to the inserted node and it to the next node
6. Move one list down
7. For convenience, return a handle to the inserted node

E[the number of pointers per node] = $1/(1 - p)$, and E[the number of comparisons] $\leq \log_{1/p}(n)/p + 1(1 - p) + 1$, which for large n is minimized when $p = 1/e$ (Pugh 1990).

```
Node* insert(KEY const& key, VALUE const& value, bool unique = true)
{
    if(unique)
    {
        Node* result = findNode(key);
        if(result)
        {
            result->value = value;
            return result;
        }
    }
    int newLevel = min(MAX_HEIGHT - 1, GlobalRNG.geometric(0.632));
    Node* newNode = new(freelist.allocate())Node(key, value,
        newLevel + 1);
    if(currentLevel < newLevel) currentLevel = newLevel;
    Node** tower = head;
    for(int level = currentLevel; level >= 0; --level)
    {
        for(Node* node; (node = tower[level]) &&
            comparator.isLess(node->key, key); tower = node->tower);
```

```
            if(level <= newLevel)
            {
                newNode->tower[level] = tower[level];
                tower[level] = newNode;
            }
        }
        return newNode;
    }
```

Remove removes the item from every list it's in, using the same first-down-then-right search.

```
    void remove(KEY const& key)
    {
        Node **tower = head, *result = 0;
        for(int level = currentLevel; level >= 0; --level)
            for(Node* node; (node = tower[level]) &&
                !comparator.isLess(key, node->key); tower = node->tower)
                if((result && result == node) ||
                    (!result && !comparator.isLess(node->key, key)))
                {//can simplify the "if" if don't allow nonunique keys
                    tower[level] = node->tower[level];
                    if(!head[currentLevel]) --currentLevel;
                    result = node;
                    break;
                }
        if(result) freelist.remove(result);
    }
```

Min is the first element and needs O(1) time to get. Max is at the list's end.

```
    NodeType* findMin(){return head[0];}
    NodeType* findMax()
    {
        Node *result = 0, **tower = head;
        for(int level = currentLevel; level >= 0; --level)
            for(Node* node; node = tower[level]; tower = node->tower)
                result = node;
        return result;
    }
```

The bottom list is easy to iterate due to being a linked list:

```
    class Iterator
    {
        Node* current;
    public:
        Iterator(Node* node): current(node){}
        Iterator& operator++()
        {
            assert(current);
            current = current->tower[0];
            return *this;
        }
        NodeType& operator*()
        {
            assert(current);
            return *current;
        }
        NodeType* operator->()
        {
            assert(current);
            return current;
        }
        bool operator==(Iterator const& rhs){return current == rhs.current;}
```

```
        bool operator!=(Iterator const& rhs){return current != rhs.current;}
    };
    Iterator begin(){return Iterator(findMin());}
    Iterator end(){return Iterator(0);}
```

E[the runtime] = $O(\lg(n) + k)$ for range search returning k items, and E[the runtime for other operations] = $O(\lg(n))$. A skip list is a bit less efficient than a tree-based dynamic sorted sequence, because of variable length nodes and larger constant factors, but is more extendable by:

- Having items in sorted order at the bottom level
- Supporting nonunique items, which allows it to be a multimap or a priority queue as is
- Supporting many augmentations

The worst case highly unlikely runtime for operations is $O(n)$.

6.2 Treap

Tree height = the max number of ancestors of any node. An ordered binary tree with height h implements dynamic sorted sequence operations in $O(h)$ time. The first item becomes a single node tree. The next replaces the current if =, is inserted into the left child if <, and into the right child if >. When items are inserted in sorted/random order, h is respectively $n/O(\lg(n))$ (Seidel & Aragon 1996). A tree is **balanced** if $h = O(\lg(n))$, which automatically ensures $O(\lg(n))$ runtimes.

The treap is the simplest balanced binary tree. At insertion, a newly created node gets a random priority. The tree is structured so that the node's priority ≤ its parent's priority. This is **heap order**.

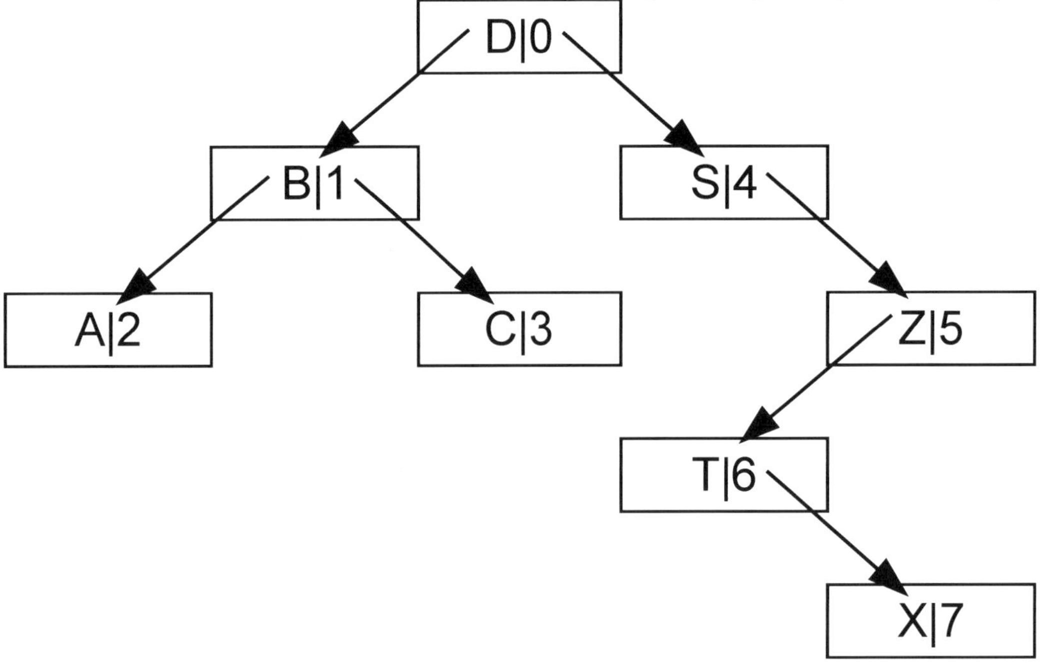

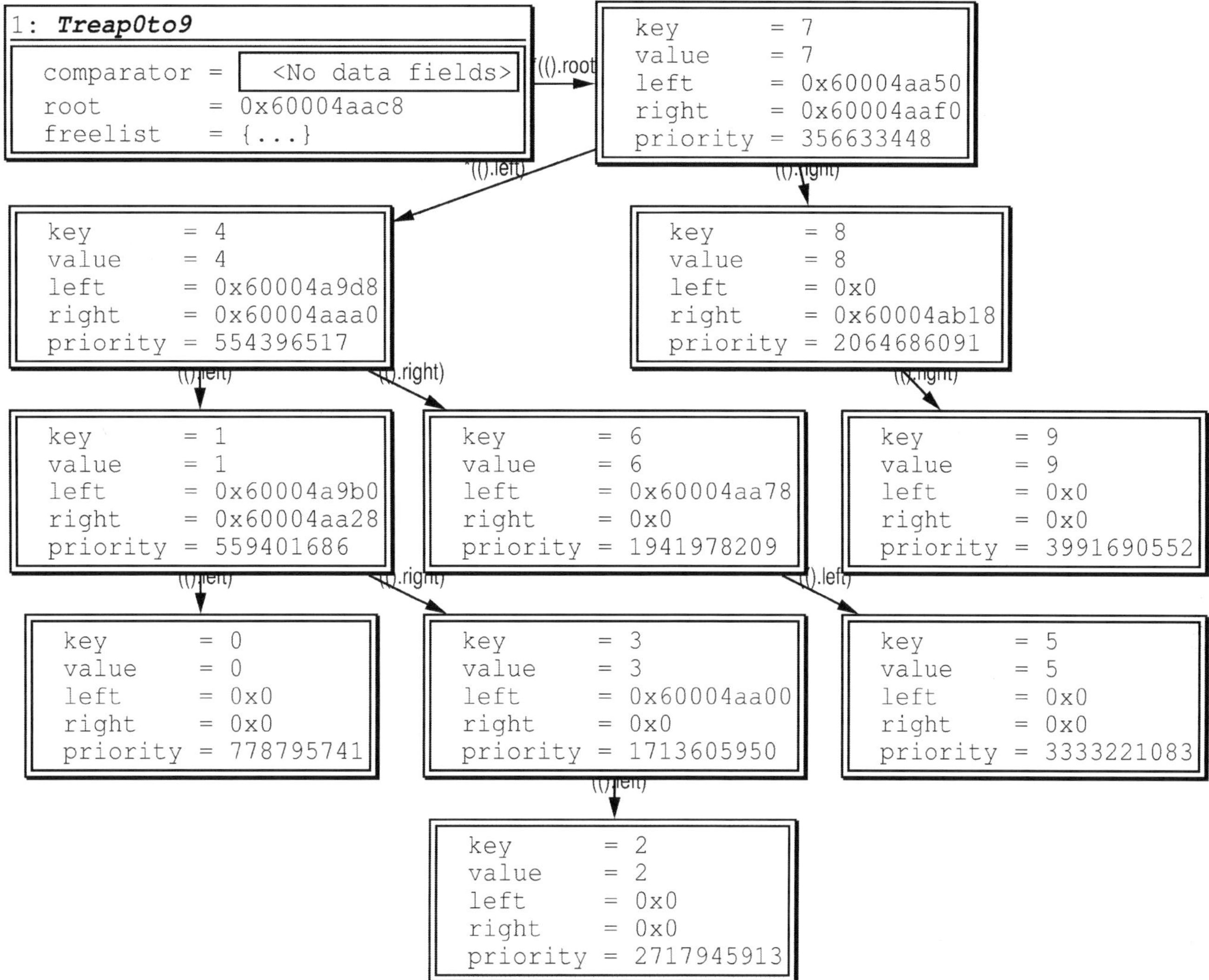

The copy constructor is recursive, copying the root and then each child, in overall $O(n)$ time. This is a general pattern ∀ tree implementation.

```
template<typename KEY, typename VALUE, typename COMPARATOR =
    DefaultComparator<KEY> > class Treap
{
    COMPARATOR comparator;
    struct Node
    {
        KEY key;
        VALUE value;
        Node *left, *right;
        unsigned int priority;
        Node(KEY const& theKey, VALUE const& theValue): key(theKey),
            value(theValue), left(0), right(0), priority(GlobalRNG.next()){}
    }* root;
    Freelist<Node> freelist;
    Node* constructFrom(Node* node)
    {
        Node* tree = 0;
        if(node)
        {
            tree = new(freelist.allocate())Node(node->key, node->value);
            tree->priority = node->priority;
            tree->left = constructFrom(node->left);
            tree->right = constructFrom(node->right);
```

```
        }
        return tree;
    }
public:
    typedef Node NodeType;
    bool isEmpty(){return !root;}
    Treap(COMPARATOR const& theComparator = COMPARATOR()):
        root(0), comparator(theComparator){}
    Treap(Treap const& other): comparator(other.comparator)
        {root = constructFrom(other.root);}
    Treap& operator=(Treap const& rhs){return genericAssign(*this, rhs);}
};
```

Find:

1. **Start at the root**
2. **Until reach the sought or a null node**
3. **Go left or right, depending on the value of the current node key**
4. **Return a pointer to the pointer to the node containing the item**

The pointer to pointer is reused for remove.

```
    Node** findPointer(KEY const& key)
    {
        Node *node, **pointer = &root;
        while((node = *pointer) && !comparator.isEqual(key, node->key))
            pointer = &(comparator.isLess(key, node->key) ?
                node->left : node->right);
        return pointer;
    }
    NodeType* findNode(KEY const& key){return *findPointer(key);}
    VALUE* find(KEY const& key)
    {
        Node* node = findNode(key);
        return node ? &node->value : 0;
    }
```

Rotations transform the tree while preserving the sorted order. The right rotation:

1. **The new root = the subtree's root's left child**
2. **The new root's right child = the root**
3. **The new root's left child = the left child's right child**

The left rotation is symmetric. Both need O(1) time. A balanced tree can't have nonunique keys because rotations break “<”.

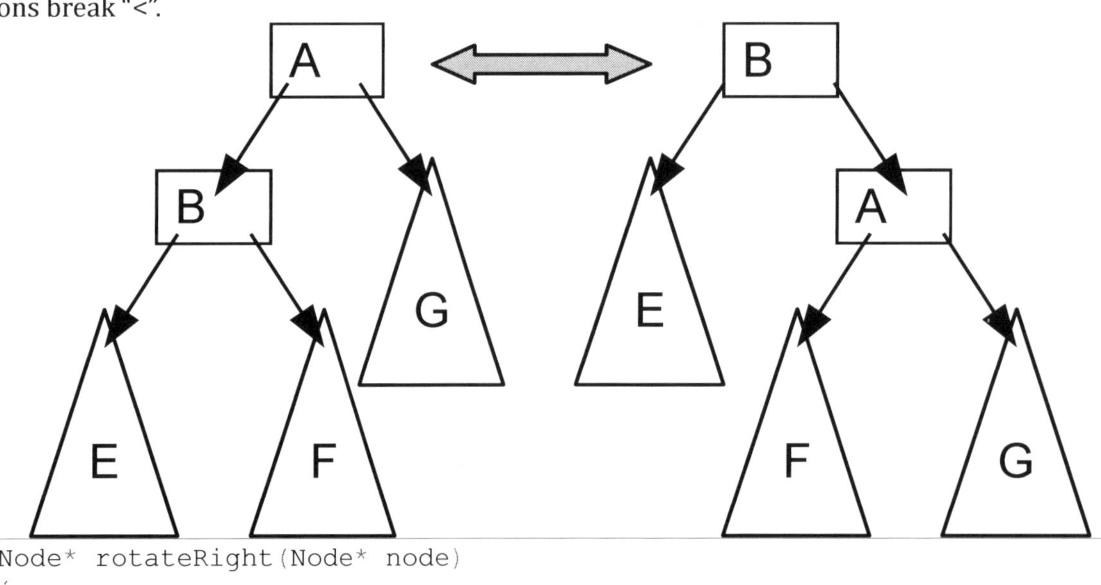


```
    Node* rotateRight(Node* node)
    {
        Node* goingUp = node->left;
```

```
        node->left = goingUp->right;
        goingUp->right = node;
        return goingUp;
    }
    Node* rotateLeft(Node* node)
    {
        Node* goingUp = node->right;
        node->right = goingUp->left;
        goingUp->left = node;
        return goingUp;
    }
```

A node is first inserted as though the tree is unbalanced, taking left or right branches until hitting a leaf and becoming its child. Then it's rotated up until its priority satisfies heap order. Rotations preserve heap order of other items.

```
    Node* insertInto(KEY const& key, VALUE const& value, Node* node)
    {
        if(!node) return new(freelist.allocate())Node(key, value);
        if(comparator.isEqual(key, node->key)) node->value = value;
        else
        {
            bool goLeft = comparator.isLess(key, node->key);
            Node*& chosenChild = goLeft ? node->left : node->right;
            chosenChild = insertInto(key, value, chosenChild);
            if(chosenChild->priority < node->priority)
                node = goLeft ? rotateRight(node) : rotateLeft(node);
        }
        return node;
    }
    void insert(KEY const& key, VALUE const& value)
        {root = insertInto(key, value, root);}
```

It's clumsy to return a pointer to the new node, so this isn't done. The resulting tree is unique if the priorities are unique. Using random priorities is equivalent to inserting items into an unbalanced tree in random order, so E[h] = O(lg(n)), regardless of the past insert/delete sequence. For a small constant c, Pr(h > 1+ 2$c$ln(n)) < 2(n/e)$^{-c\ln(c/e)}$, effectively making runtimes O(lg(n)) for not too small n. The worst case highly unlikely h = O(n). E[the number of rotations for insert] = O(1) (Seidel & Aragon 1996).

Join makes the smaller priority child the subtree root and recursively joins the other child with the appropriate child of the chosen root:

```
    Node* join(Node* left, Node* right)
    {
        if(!left) return right;
        if(!right) return left;
        if(left->priority < right->priority)
        {
            left->right = join(left->right, right);
            return left;
        }
        else
        {
            right->left = join(left, right->left);
            return right;
        }
    }
```

It also takes O(h) time. Remove:

1. **Find the node corresponding to *x***
2. **Remove it**
3. **Join the children**
4. **Attach the result to the parent**

```
    void remove(KEY const& key)
    {
        Node **pointer = findPointer(key), *node = *pointer;
        if(node)
        {
            *pointer = join(node->left, node->right);
            freelist.remove(node);
        }
    }
```

Alternatively, can remove by rotating the node to make it a leaf, or replacing it with a successor from its subtree and deleting the successor. Rotation to leaf is simpler with augmentations (discussed later in this chapter). Min is the leftmost node and max the rightmost:

```
    NodeType* findMin()
    {
        Node* node = root;
        if(node) while(node->left) node = node->left;
        return node;
    }
    NodeType* findMax()
    {
        Node* node = root;
        if(node) while(node->right) node = node->right;
        return node;
    }
```

Successor and predecessor are similar to find and have symmetric logic. For predecessor, get as close as possible to x from the left:

1. While not at a leaf
2.   If node ≥ x go left
3.   Else if have a right child, go there
4.   Else stop

```
    NodeType* predecessor(KEY const& key)
    {
        for(Node* node = root; node;)
        {
            if(!comparator.isLess(node->key, key)) node = node->left;
            else if(!node->right) return node;
            else node = node->right;
        }
        return 0;
    }
    NodeType* successor(KEY const& key)
    {
        for(Node* node = root; node;)
        {
            if(!comparator.isLess(key, node->key)) node = node->right;
            else if(!node->left) return node;
            else node = node->left;
        }
        return 0;
    }
    NodeType* inclusiveSuccessor(KEY const& key)
    {
        Node* node = findNode(key);
        return node ? node : successor(key);
    }
```

6.3 Tree Iterators

Can iterate in several ways:

- Use **parent pointers**, i.e., with children pointing to their parents—makes iterator operations simple, but needs an extra pointer per node and updating it during insertions and deletions. Allows all operations to return and accept iterators, which is convenient for users but doesn't generalize to structures that don't have iterators, such as *k*-d tree (see the "Computation Geometry" chapter). STL does this and gives bidirectional iterators.
- Keep the path to the current node on a stack. Avoids parent pointers, but finding iterators to items needs creating stacks. Adding a function to build an iterator corresponding to a particular key allows the same operations as parent pointers, but without the consistency of using iterators for all operations.
- Pass a functor to a range search. When, e.g., summing all values, the functor has a pointer to the current sum and updates it. This is the most efficient solution and generalizes to *k*-d tree, but creating a functor is clumsy for users.
- Do range search as above, with a predefined functor that creates a vector of found items—more convenient for users, but needs memory for the vector.

The stack-based iterator, when incremented with the right child = null, goes up until returning from a left child:

```
template<typename NODE> class TreeIterator
{
    NODE* current;
public:
    Stack<NODE*> ancestors;
    TreeIterator(NODE* root){current = root;}
    TreeIterator& operator++()
    {
        assert(current);
        if(current->right)
        {
            ancestors.push(current);
            current = current->right;
            for(; current; current = current->left) ancestors.push(current);
            current = ancestors.pop();
        }
        else if(!ancestors.isEmpty())
        {
            NODE* parent = ancestors.pop();
            while(parent->right == current && !ancestors.isEmpty())
            {
                current = parent;
                parent = ancestors.pop();
            }
            current = parent->right == current ? 0 : parent;
        }
        else current = 0;
        return *this;
    }
    NODE& operator*()
    {
        assert(current);
        return *current;
    }
    NODE* operator->()
    {
        assert(current);
        return current;
```

```
    }
    bool operator!=(TreeIterator const& rhs){return current != rhs.current;}
};
```

The parent pointer logic is less clumsy but very similar. The treap iterator uses a generic binary tree iterator and gives a builder function for convenience, using the same process as find to create the stack:

```
    typedef TreeIterator<Node> Iterator;
    Iterator end(){return Iterator(0);}
    Iterator begin(){return buildIterator(findMin());}
    Iterator buildIterator(Node* theNode)
    {
        if(!theNode) return end();
        Iterator i(theNode);
        Node* node = root;
        while(node && !comparator.isEqual(theNode->key, node->key))
        {
            i.ancestors.push(node);
            node = comparator.isLess(theNode->key, node->key) ?
                node->left : node->right;
        }
        return i;
    }
```

6.4 Augmentations and API Variants

Can implement **inclusive successor** and **inclusive predecessor** using their noninclusive versions, find, and range search by iterating from the inclusive successor of the min key to the successor of the max key, or a null iterator if latter doesn't exist.

Common augmentations for trees:

- Store the number of nodes in each subtree—allows selecting the kth item and finding rank of x
- Store the parent pointer in each node—allows iteration without a stack

A dynamic sorted sequence API can be a:

- Map—implement other variants in terms of it
- **Multimap**, allowing equal items—a map where the item type is a vector of items
- **Set**, with keys but not values—a map where the item type is ignored Boolean
- **Multiset**, where keys aren't unique—a map where the item is a vector of keys

Skip list supports the multi variants directly. The STL implements maps in terms of sets using key-item pairs as set items, but items need a default constructor because find constructs a key-item pair. Other then using a vector of keys, can keep a global insertion count, and use it as a secondary priority. This is simpler when maintain rank information.

6.5 Vector Keys

When keys are variable-length arrays of objects comparable in O(1) time, assuming length k, comparisons take O(k) time, giving O($k$lg(n)) operations. On average, this isn't an issue because E[lcp of two random strings over an alphabet of size a out of a collection of n] = $\log_a(n)$. Additional operations:

- **Prefix search**—given a length, find all items with lcp(x, item's key) ≥ length. Iteration from the inclusive predecessor of the prefix gives the result.
- **Longest match**—find the item maximizing lcp(x, item's key). The predecessor or its successor is the result.

To improve efficiency, the idea is finding the lcp and comparing key[lcp]. Lcp of any key with $-\infty$ or ∞ is 0. $\forall\ x \leq y \leq z$:

- lcp(x, y) ≥ lcp(x, z) with equality only if $y = z$
- lcp(x, z) = min(lcp(x, y), lcp(y, z))

6.6 LCP Augmentation for Trees

Store in each node the lcps between it and both its predecessor and successor among the nodes on its search path (Grossi & Italiano 1999; Crescenzi et al. 2003). `unsigned short` is used to save space. The lcps are 0 for the root, relative to the imaginary ∞ keys.

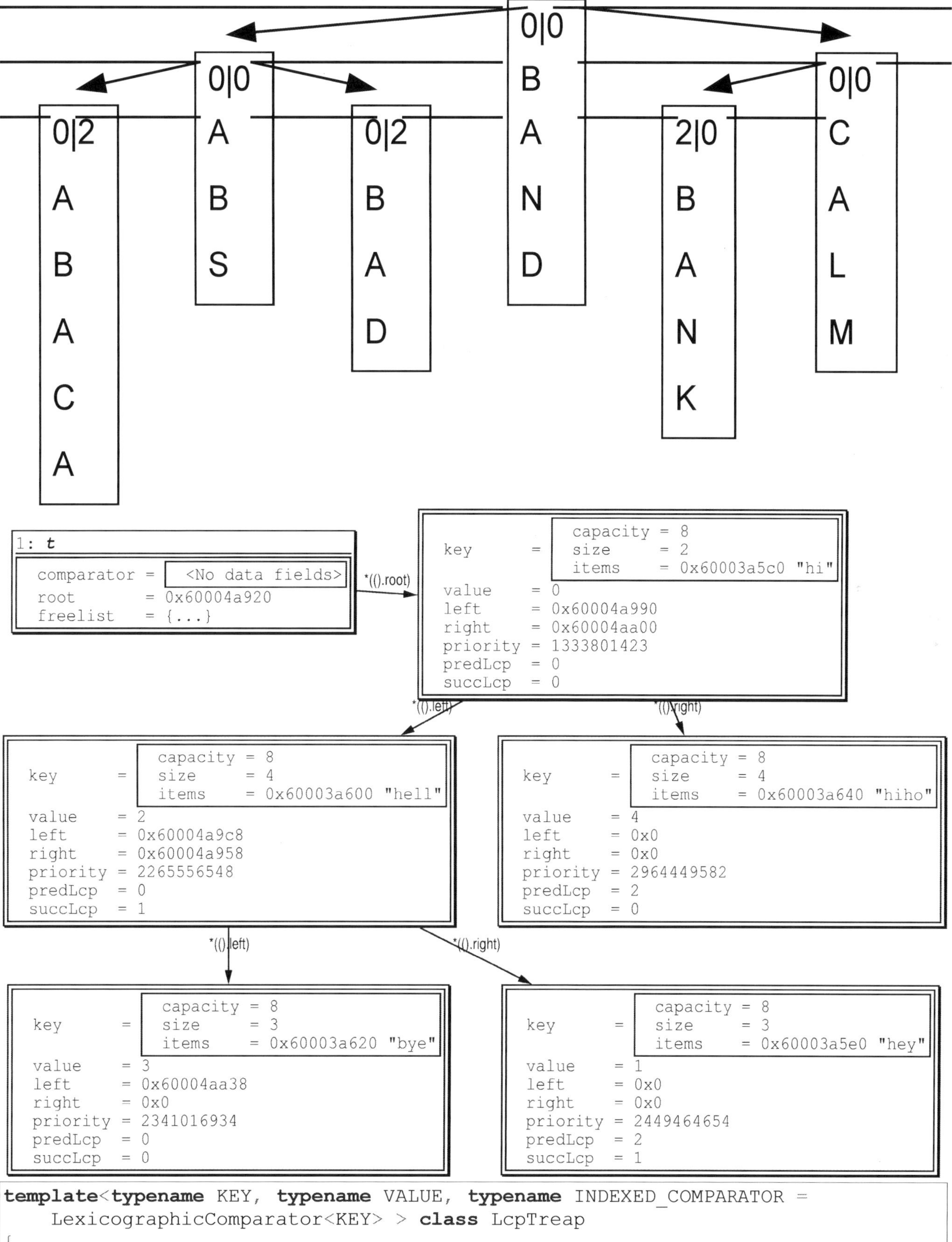


```
template<typename KEY, typename VALUE, typename INDEXED_COMPARATOR =
    LexicographicComparator<KEY> > class LcpTreap
{
```

```
    INDEXED_COMPARATOR comparator;
    struct Node
    {
        KEY key;
        VALUE value;
        Node *left, *right;
        unsigned int priority;
        unsigned short predLcp, succLcp;
        Node(KEY const& theKey, VALUE const& theValue): key(theKey),
            value(theValue), left(0), right(0), priority(GlobalRNG.next()),
            predLcp(0), succLcp(0) {}
    }* root;
    Freelist<Node> freelist;
    Node* constructFrom(Node* node)
    {
        Node* tree = 0;
        if(node)
        {
            tree = new(freelist.allocate())Node(node->key, node->value);
            tree->priority = node->priority;
            tree->predLcp = node->predLcp;
            tree->succLcp = node->succLcp;
            tree->left = constructFrom(node->left);
            tree->right = constructFrom(node->right);
        }
        return tree;
    }
public:
    typedef Node NodeType;
    LcpTreap(INDEXED_COMPARATOR theComparator = INDEXED_COMPARATOR()):
        root(0), comparator(theComparator) {}
    LcpTreap(LcpTreap const& other): comparator(other.comparator)
        {root = constructFrom(other.root);}
    LcpTreap& operator=(LcpTreap const& rhs)
        {return genericAssign(*this, rhs);}
};
```

When compare x with the current node c with ancestor predecessor p and successor s:

- $p < x < s$, and let $\max(\text{lcp}(p, x), \text{lcp}(s, x)) = m$
- $p < c < s$, and let $\text{lcp}(p, c) = l$ and $\text{lcp}(s,c) = r$

If $\text{lcp}(p, x) = m$

- If $l < m$, $c[l] > x[l]$ because $p[l] < c[l]$ and $p[l] = x[l]$, and $\text{lcp}(c, x) = l$ because it can't be greater or smaller
- Else $\text{lcp}(c, x) \geq m$ because c and p are the same up to position l

If $\text{lcp}(r, x) = m$

- If $r < m$, $c[r] < x[r]$ because $c[r] < s[r]$ and $s[r] = x[r]$, and $\text{lcp}(c, x) = r$ because it can't be greater or smaller
- Else $\text{lcp}(c, x) \geq m$ because c and p are the same up to position r

To decide whether m is from p or s, keep $\text{lcp}(p, x)$ in `predM`; `findLcp` calculates $\text{lcp}(c, x)$ and updates m.

```
    int findLCP(KEY const& key, Node* node, int predM, int& m)
    {
        int lcp = predM == m ? node->predLcp : node->succLcp;
        if(m <= lcp)
        {
            while(m < comparator.getSize(key) &&
               comparator.isEqual(key, node->key, m)) ++m;
            lcp = m;
        }
```

```
        return lcp;
    }
```

If $c \neq x$, lcp(c, x) is the first index at which $c \neq x$, so operations look only at one item when comparing. If both have the same length = lcp, then $c = x$. m is never decreased because search moves to closer nodes and $\leq k$, so map operations cost O(k + lg(n)). When going right, set `predM` to lcp(c, x) because c becomes p.

```
    Node** findPointer(KEY const& key)
    {
        Node** pointer = &root, *node;
        int m = 0, predM = 0;
        while(node = *pointer)
        {
            int lcp = findLCP(key, node, predM, m);
            if(comparator.getSize(key) == lcp &&
                comparator.getSize(node->key) == lcp) break;
            if(comparator.isLess(key, node->key, lcp)) pointer = &node->left;
            else
            {
                pointer = &node->right;
                predM = lcp;
            }
        }
        return pointer;
    }
    Node* findNode(KEY const& key){return *findPointer(key);}
    VALUE* find(KEY const& key)
    {
        Node* node = findNode(key);
        return node ? &node->value : 0;
    }
```

Rotations maintain the lcp information. For left rotation, the node's right child becomes its ancestor successor, so `succLcp` is set to `predLcp` of the right child because the node is the right child's ancestor predecessor. The right child loses its ancestor predecessor, so its `predLcp` becomes lcp(it, the ancestor predecessor of the node) = the min of the two `predLcp` values by the triangle equality. Right rotation is symmetric and the runtime of both is O(1).

```
    Node* rotateRight(Node* node)
    {
        Node* goingUp = node->left;
        node->predLcp = goingUp->succLcp;
        goingUp->succLcp = min(node->succLcp, goingUp->succLcp);
        node->left = goingUp->right;
        goingUp->right = node;
        return goingUp;
    }
    Node* rotateLeft(Node* node)
    {
        Node* goingUp = node->right;
        node->succLcp = goingUp->predLcp;
        goingUp->predLcp = min(node->predLcp, goingUp->predLcp);
        node->right = goingUp->left;
        goingUp->left = node;
        return goingUp;
    }
```

Insert is a hybrid of find and the treap insert. It creates the node and updates its `predLcp` and `succLcp` when going left or right. During insertion, `predLcp` = `predM`.

```
    Node* insertNode(Node* newNode, Node* node, int m)
    {
        if(!node) return newNode;
```

```
        int lcp = findLCP(newNode->key, node, newNode->predLcp, m);
        if(comparator.getSize(node->key) == lcp &&
           comparator.getSize(newNode->key) == lcp)
        {
            node->value = newNode->value;
            freelist.remove(newNode);
        }
        else
        {
            bool goLeft = comparator.isLess(newNode->key, node->key, lcp);
            (goLeft ? newNode->succLcp : newNode->predLcp) = lcp;
            Node*& chosenChild = goLeft ? node->left : node->right;
            chosenChild = insertNode(newNode, chosenChild, m);
            if(chosenChild->priority < node->priority)
                node = goLeft ? rotateRight(node) : rotateLeft(node);
        }
        return node;
    }
    void insert(KEY const& key, VALUE const& value)
    {
        root = insertNode(new(freelist.allocate())Node(key, value), root, 0);
    }
```

Deletion uses rotation to leaf because join needs to maintain the lcp information.

```
    Node* removeFound(Node* node)
    {
        Node *left = node->left, *right = node->right;
        if(left && right)
        {
            bool goRight = left->priority < right->priority;
            node = goRight ? rotateRight(node) : rotateLeft(node);
            Node*& child = goRight ? node->right : node->left;
            child = removeFound(child);
        }
        else
        {
            freelist.remove(node);
            node = left ? left : right;
        }
        return node;
    }
    void remove(KEY const& key)
    {
        Node** node = findPointer(key);
        if(node) *node = removeFound(*node);
    }
```

Min, max, and inclusive successor are identical to those of treap. Successor and predecessor differ only in that they find lcp and compare key[lcp]:

```
    NodeType* predecessor(KEY const& key)
    {
        int m = 0, predM = 0;
        for(Node* node = root; node;)
        {
            int lcp = findLCP(key, node, predM, m);
            if(!comparator.isLess(node->key, key, lcp)) node = node->left;
            else
            {
                if(!node->right) return node;
                node = node->right;
```

```
                predM = lcp;
            }
        }
        return 0;
    }
    NodeType* successor(KEY const& key)
    {
        int m = 0, predM = 0;
        for(Node* node = root; node;)
        {
            int lcp = findLCP(key, node, predM, m);
            if(!comparator.isLess(key, node->key, lcp))
            {
                node = node->right;
                predM = lcp;
            }
            else if(!node->left) return node;
            else node = node->left;
        }
        return 0;
    }
```

The runtime is the same as for map operations. **Prefix successor** is similar to successor, but skips over items > the prefix that have it:

```
    NodeType* prefixSuccessor(KEY const& key)
    {
        int m = 0, predM = 0;
        for(Node* node = root; node;)
        {
            int lcp = findLCP(key, node, predM, m);
            if(comparator.getSize(key) == lcp ||
                !comparator.isLess(key, node->key, lcp))
            {
                node = node->right;
                predM = lcp;
            }
            else if(!node->left) return node;
            else node = node->left;
        }
        return 0;
    }
```

The runtime is the same as for the map operations. Building an iterator is based on find, as for treap:

```
    typedef TreeIterator<Node> Iterator;
    Iterator end(){return Iterator(0);}
    Iterator buildIterator(Node* theNode)
    {
        if(!theNode) return end();
        Iterator i(theNode);
        int m = 0, predM = 0;
        for(Node* node = root; node && node != theNode;)
        {
            i.ancestors.push(node);
            int lcp = findLCP(theNode->key, node, predM, m);
            if(comparator.isLess(theNode->key, node->key, lcp))
                node = node->left;
            else
            {
                node = node->right;
                predM = lcp;
```

```
            }
        }
        return i;
    }
    Iterator begin(){return Iterator(root);}
```

While the lcp augmentation is useful, can avoid it in many cases for efficiency:

- Implement a map with integer pair keys by encoding pairs into `long long` and using it as key with a treap or a skip list
- For longest match on bit sequences ≤ word size, e.g., in network routers, use a treap with the longest match implemented as predecessor

6.7 Tries

A trie is a map where keys are variable-length arrays of objects comparable in O(1) time. Conceptually, it's a document filing system with many folders named by a letter, with each folder containing subfolders and documents. Supposing that vectors are strings, a trie is a tree where each node has a pointer to a string, consisting of the i characters that lead to the node, and a map from the next letter to the corresponding node. The root branches on letter 0 and points to the item represented by the empty string. A child of a node checking letter i checks letter $i + 1$. Find starts at the root and follows pointers until characters or nodes run out, taking $O(hM)$ time, where M the time to look up the next node.

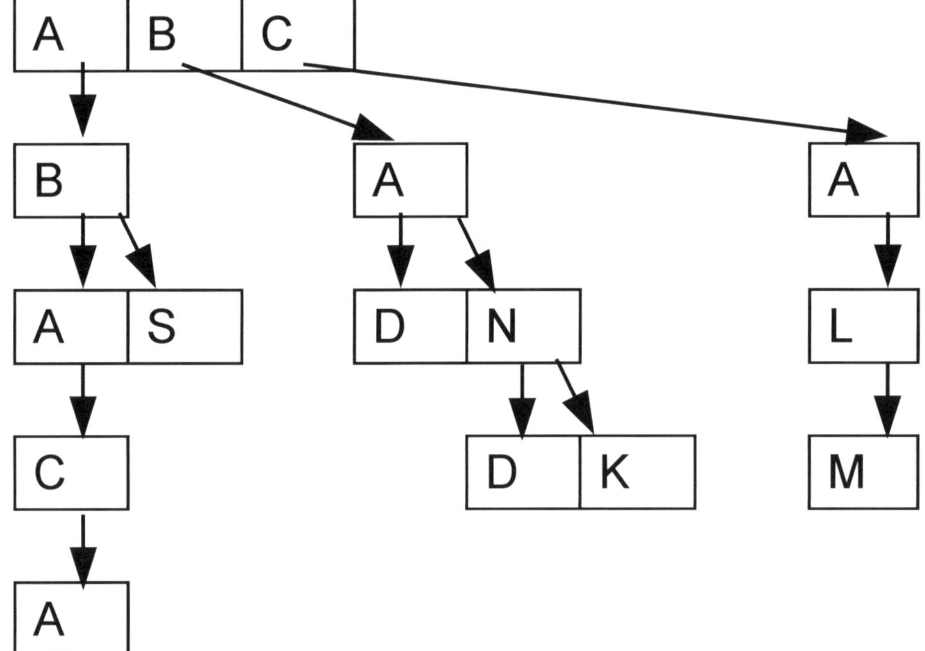

Can implement the map in many ways, most importantly as an array or a dynamic sorted sequence. For array, $M = O(1)$, but use too much space and have inefficient in-order iteration. For dynamic sorted sequence, $M = O(\lg(\text{the alphabet size}))$. A trie additionally supports:

- **Incremental search**—e.g., searching consecutively for *h*, *he*, *hel*, *hell*, and *hello* takes $O(h)$ time
- Suffix augmentations—keys reachable from a node of height i share a prefix of length i

!∃other good reasons to use a trie due to efficiency. A trie with any map implementation usually uses more memory than LCPTreap and doesn't represent keys as single objects, making iteration that needs key values difficult. The map is one reason for high memory use, and **suffix expansion** is another. After some depth, a prefix of a key uniquely identifies it, but a trie uses a node per key object instead of a single node with the suffix. So it's a bad choice for long strings with small average lcp.

6.8 Ternary Treap Trie

A ternary treap trie (TTT) efficiently implements the dynamic sorted sequence node map. It mimics multikey quicksort and uses left, down, and right pointers with a pivot character. Find goes down if the ith character = the node's pivot, left if <, and right if >. Items are stored at nodes where the last character = the pivot. Treap priorities decide tree structure of nodes checking the ith character. The operations use the asymptotically optimal space and expected time for any comparable objects. The latter is O(lg(n) + the average key length). Don't support the key of length 0, but can handle it externally.

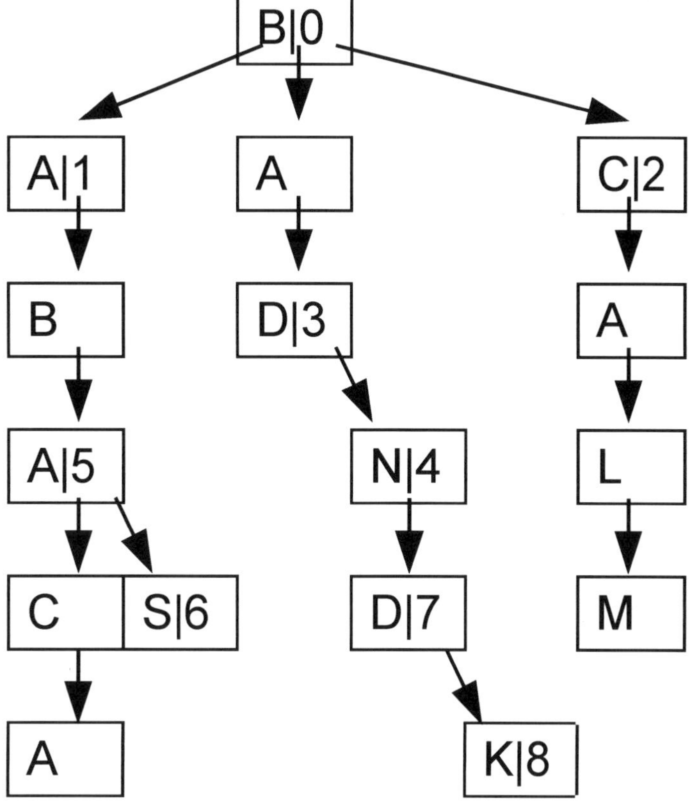

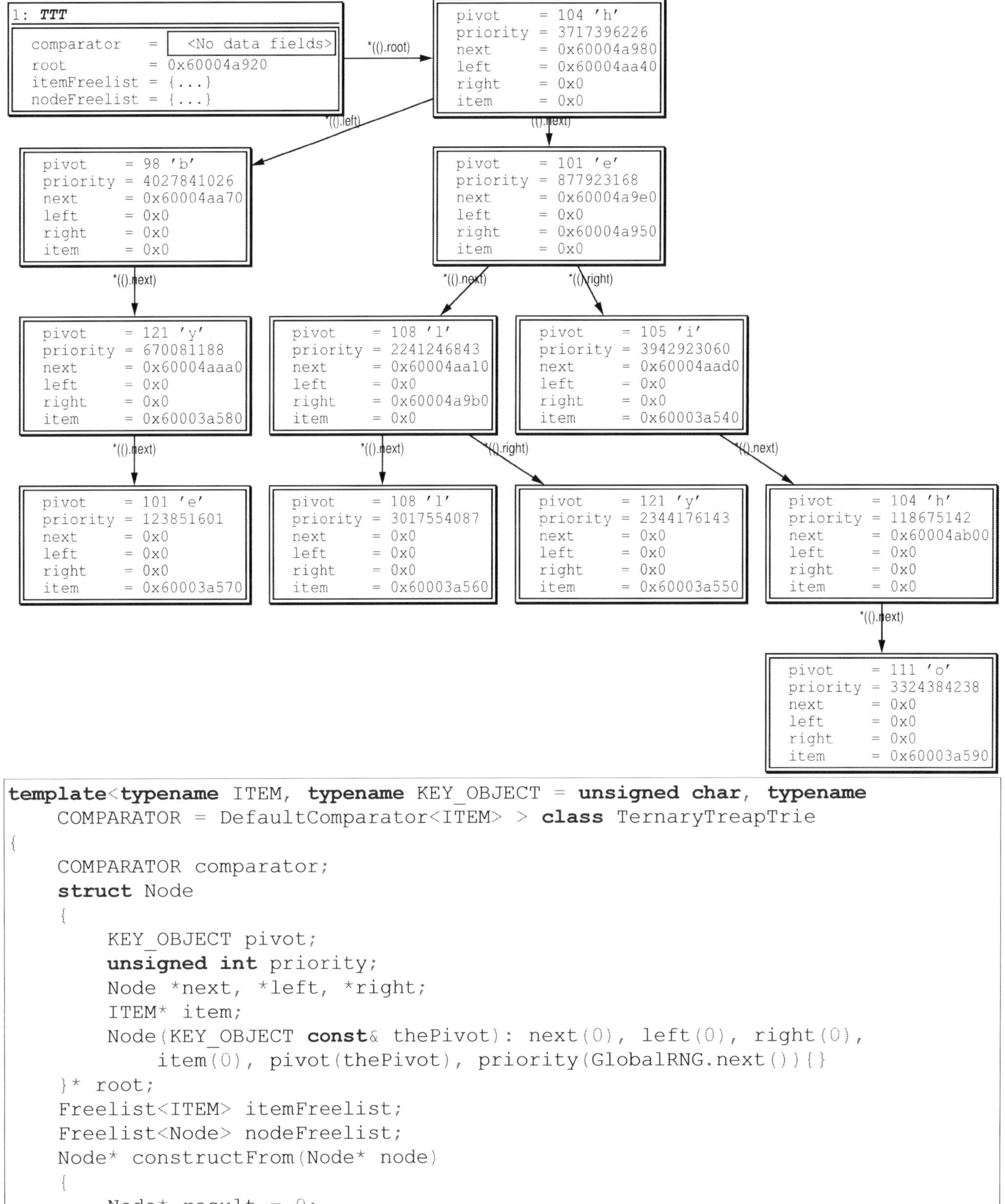


```
template<typename ITEM, typename KEY_OBJECT = unsigned char, typename
    COMPARATOR = DefaultComparator<ITEM> > class TernaryTreapTrie
{
    COMPARATOR comparator;
    struct Node
    {
        KEY_OBJECT pivot;
        unsigned int priority;
        Node *next, *left, *right;
        ITEM* item;
        Node(KEY_OBJECT const& thePivot): next(0), left(0), right(0),
            item(0), pivot(thePivot), priority(GlobalRNG.next()){}
    }* root;
    Freelist<ITEM> itemFreelist;
    Freelist<Node> nodeFreelist;
    Node* constructFrom(Node* node)
    {
        Node* result = 0;
        if(node)
        {
            result = new(nodeFreelist.allocate())Node(node->pivot);
            result->priority = node->priority;
            if(node->item)
                result->item = new(itemFreelist.allocate())ITEM(node->item);
            result->left = constructFrom(node->left);
            result->next = constructFrom(node->next);
            result->right = constructFrom(node->right);
```

```
        }
        return result;
    }
public:
    TernaryTreapTrie(COMPARATOR const& theComparator = COMPARATOR()):
        root(0), comparator(theComparator){}
    TernaryTreapTrie(TernaryTreapTrie const& other):
        comparator(other.comparator){root = constructFrom(other.root);}
    TernaryTreapTrie& operator=(TernaryTreapTrie const& rhs)
        {return genericAssign(*this, rhs);}
};
```

The memory overhead is five words per key object, leading to costly suffix expansion, but many nodes are shared if the items have high average lcp. In comparison, LCPTreap has five words of overhead per key.

Find is implemented in terms of incremental find that manages a handle to the current node. The idea of incremental find is to start not from the root but from an existing node, which is known to be a prefix of the sought key. The handle object encapsulates this for user's convenience.

```
    struct Handle
    {
        Node* node;
        int i;
        Handle(): node(0), i(0){}
    };
    Node* findNodeIncremental(KEY_OBJECT* key, int keySize, Node*& node,
        int& i)
    {
        while(node && i < keySize)
        {
            if(comparator.isEqual(key[i], node->pivot))
            {
                if(i == keySize - 1) return node;
                else{node = node->next; ++i;}
            }
            else if(comparator.isLess(key[i], node->pivot))node = node->left;
            else node = node->right;
        }
        i = 0;
        node = 0;
        return 0;
    }
    ITEM* findIncremental(KEY_OBJECT* key, int keySize, Handle& h)
    {
        if(!h.node) h.node = root;
        Node* result = findNodeIncremental(key, keySize, h.node, h.i);
        return result ? result->item : 0;
    }
    Node* findNode(KEY_OBJECT* key, int keySize)
    {
        Node* temp = root;
        int i = 0;
        return findNodeIncremental(key, keySize, temp, i);
    }
    ITEM* find(KEY_OBJECT* key, int keySize)
    {
        Node* result = findNode(key, keySize);
        return result ? result->item : 0;
    }
```

The runtime of incremental find is same as that for regular find, but n is size of the starting node subtree, and key length is reduced by the passed prefix. Rotations and join are same as for treap. Insert moves as find but adds new nodes when existing ones run out and, as for treap, rotates the non-down links on the way up to restore heap order.

```
Node* insertNode(Node* node, KEY_OBJECT* key, int keySize,
    ITEM const& item, int i)
{
    if(!node) node = new(nodeFreelist.allocate())Node(key[i]);
    if(comparator.isEqual(key[i], node->pivot))
        if(i == keySize - 1)
        {
            if(node->item) *node->item = item;
            else node->item = new(itemFreelist.allocate())ITEM(item);
        }
        else node->next = insertNode(node->next, key, keySize, item,
            i + 1);
    else
    {
        bool goLeft = comparator.isLess(key[i], node->pivot);
        Node*& chosenChild = goLeft ? node->left : node->right;
        chosenChild = insertNode(chosenChild, key, keySize, item, i);
        if(chosenChild->priority < node->priority)
            node = goLeft ? rotateRight(node) : rotateLeft(node);
    }
    return node;
}
void insert(unsigned char* key, int keySize, ITEM const& item)
{
    assert(keySize > 0);
    root = insertNode(root, key, keySize, item, 0);
}
```

Remove finds the item and removes nodes on the path to it that have no item or down pointer:

```
Node* removeR(Node* node, KEY_OBJECT* key, int keySize, int i)
{
    if(node)
    {
        bool isEqual = comparator.isEqual(key[i], node->pivot);
        if(isEqual && i == keySize - 1)
        {//remove found item
            if(!node->item) return node;
            itemFreelist.remove(node->item);
            node->item = 0;
        }
        else
        {//go to next node
            Node** child;
            if(isEqual){child = &node->next; ++i;}
            else if(comparator.isLess(key[i], node->pivot))
                child = &node->left;
            else child = &node->right;
            *child = removeR(*child, key, keySize, i);
        }
        if(!node->item && !node->next)
        {//remove empty node
            Node* left = node->left, *right = node->right;
            nodeFreelist.remove(node);
            node = (left || right) ? join(left, right) : 0;
        }
    }
    return node;
}
```

```
void remove(KEY_OBJECT* key, int keySize)
{
    assert(keySize > 0);
    root = removeR(root, key, keySize, 0);
}
```

Longest match finds the item with the greatest lcp with *x*. This is particularly fast for tries in general.

```
ITEM* longestMatch(KEY_OBJECT* key, int keySize)
{
    Node* node = root, *result = 0;
    for(int i = 0; node && i < keySize;)
        if(comparator.isEqual(key[i], node->pivot))
        {
            result = node;
            if(i == keySize - 1) break;
            else {node = node->next; ++i;}
        }
        else if(comparator.isLess(key[i], node->pivot))
            node = node->left;
        else node = node->right;
    return result ? result->item : 0;
}
```

The runtime is O(lg(n) + lcp). For-each iterates over nodes in-order and executes a user-specified functor on each. E.g., a useful functor copies all items to a vector. Using these, can find all nodes whose keys share a prefix:

```
template<typename ACTION> void forEachNode(Node* node, ACTION& action)
{
    if(node)
    {
        action(node);
        forEachNode(node->left);
        forEachNode(node->next);
        forEachNode(node->right);
    }
}
struct CopyAction
{
    Vector<ITEM*>& result;
    CopyAction(Vector<ITEM*>& theResult): result(theResult){}
    void operator()(Node* node)
        {if(node->item) result.append(node->item);}
};
Vector<ITEM*> prefixFind(KEY_OBJECT* key, int lcp)
{
    Vector<ITEM*> result;
    CopyAction action(result);
    forEachNode(findNode(key, lcp), action);
    return result;
}
```

The runtime is O(prefix find + the number of nodes in the found subtree).

6.9 Comments

Simplicity of skip list makes it the choice for a general dynamic sorted sequence implementation. For only map operations, hash tables (see the "Hashing" chapter) are faster. Use treap when its augmentations are more convenient or need successor or predecessor but not iteration.

∃ many different balanced trees with some giving O(lg(n)) map operations and/or other nice properties, but none are as simple as treap and outperform it on average. Many libraries implement **red-black tree** (Cormen et al. 2009). It gives O(lg(n)) map operations but is more complicated than treap or skip list, and its balancing doesn't work for ternary trie. Also, want amortized O(1) rotations per insertion, which is important for augmentations. For map operations, experimentally, treap is faster than red-black tree, which is faster than skip list (Heger 2004). **Left-learning red-black tree** (Sedgewick & Wayne 2011; Sedgewick 1998) is a simpler version, but seems to lose the O(1) amortized rotation due to being isomorphic to older **2-3 tree**. B-tree (see the "External Memory Algorithms" chapter) with $B = 2$ is **2-3-4 tree** (Mehlhorn & Sanders 2008), isomorphic to red-black tree, and enjoys the same properties. The latter was derived from the former to save space on empty nodes.

Splay tree (Brass 2008) has impractical constant factors but is theoretically interesting because it doesn't use extra space for balancing, and every sequence of m map operations on k elements takes $O(m\lg(k))$ amortized time. **AVL tree** (Brass 2008) balances using rotations to maintain fixed height differences. Compared to red-black tree, it's slightly more balanced, giving slightly faster search, but insertions are slower and don't have the O(1) amortized rotation. So despite AVL tree's being simpler, libraries implement red-black trees. **Weight-balanced tree** (Brass 2008) is similar to AVL tree but balances weight, i.e., the number of nodes in each subtree. This has the advantage of getting the node size augmentation at no extra memory cost but is slower for both find and insert. Same for **randomized tree** (Sedgewick 1999) that adjusts itself to be random after every operation, using node count proportions. See Mehta & Sahni (2004) for a discussion of balancing in general.

For lcp augmentation of skip list attach lcp to each tower pointer (Ciriani et al. 2007).

Using treap priorities seems to be one of the few ways to balance a ternary trie. Don't have a worst case balancing strategy, because the usual height or weight balancing doesn't work (Badr & Oommen 2005). ∃ many trie varieties, but all have problems:

- Array map trie with key object = 4 bits of key—makes map sizes seem reasonable, but still suffers from high memory use, loses generality and simple prefix operations, and becomes a bad hash table.
- Bucket trie—works with any node map, the idea is to put items that share common prefix into a single linearly-searchable small bucket to reduce memory due to suffix expansion. While applicable to any trie, including TTT, this makes operations clumsy and inefficient due to needing to keep track of several node types and occasionally convert between them on insertion and deletion.
- **Digital search tree** (DST) (Sedgewick 1999)—like a tree but uses bits of keys to branch instead of comparisons. I.e., at level i, if the ith bit is 0, go left, else right. So $h \leq$ key size in bits. This may look appealing but works with bit sequences only, is inefficient for sequences with high bit lcp, and supports other operations such as predecessor only if lexicographic bit order leads to correct comparisons. The last one isn't even universally true for integers due to big- and little-endian architectures. So DST is at best a bad hash table.
- **Patricia trie** (Sedgewick 1999; Mehta & Sahni 2004)—improves DST by jumping directly to bits that differ. This results in recommendation of this data structure for longest bit sequence matching for network routers. But can do the same with any dynamic sorted sequence using predecessor, as discussed before, and the slowness of testing one bit at a time and applicability to only bit sequences remain. Can branch on several bits at a time for more efficient operation with high lcp long keys (this make deletions difficult though), but the lcp augmentation does this much better.

6.10 References

Cormen, T. H., Leiserson, C. E., Rivest, R. L., & Stein, C. (2009). *Introduction to Algorithms*. MIT Press.

Badr, G. H., & Oommen, B. J. (2005). Self-adjusting of ternary search tries using conditional rotations and randomized heuristics. *The Computer Journal*, *48*(2), 200–219.

Brass, P. (2008). *Advanced Data Structures*. Cambridge University Press.

Ciriani, V., Ferragina, P., Luccio, F., & Muthukrishnan, S. (2007). A data structure for a sequence of string accesses in external memory. *ACM Transactions on Algorithms (TALG)*, *3*(1), 6.

Crescenzi, P., Grossi, R., & Italiano, G. F. (2003). Search data structures for skewed strings. In *Experimental and Efficient Algorithms* (pp. 81–96). Springer.

Grossi, R., & Italiano, G. F. (1999). Efficient techniques for maintaining multidimensional keys in linked data structures. In *Automata, Languages, and Programming* (pp. 372–381). Springer.

Heger, D. A. (2004). A disquisition on the performance behavior of binary search tree data structures. *European Journal for the Informatics Professional*, *5*(5), 67–75.

Mehlhorn, K., & Sanders, P. (2008). *Algorithms and Data Structures: The Basic Toolbox*. Springer.

Mehta, D. P., & Sahni, S. (Eds.). (2004). *Handbook of Data Structures and Applications*. CRC Press.
Pugh, W. (1990). Skip lists: a probabilistic alternative to balanced trees. *Communications of the ACM, 33*(6), 668–676.
Sedgwick, R. (1999). *Algorithms in C++*. Parts 1–4. Addison-Wesley.
———. (2008). Left-leaning red-black trees. In *Dagstuhl Workshop on Data Structures*.
———, & Wayne, K. (2011). *Algorithms*. Addison-Wesley.
Seidel, R., & Aragon, C. R. (1996). Randomized search trees. *Algorithmica, 16*(4–5), 464–497.

7 Hashing

7.1 Hash Functions

A **hash function** h maps objects x to integers mod m for some m; h must be regular (see the "Background" chapter) and should have few **collisions**, where for $x \neq y$, $h(x) = h(y)$. Theoretically, need h only for variable length byte arrays because can interpret any object as such, but for specific data types have more efficient h. Hash other types such as `double` by converting them into an efficiently hashable type.

For a set of objects of size $n > m$, all h hash at least n/m of them to the same value. So every h hashes all inputs to the same value in the worst case. To be useful, h must evaluate in O(1) time with respect to n. In particular, for an object of size s want O(s) time. Also want to avoid collisions on average, so a **random** h is theoretically ideal due to not having any biases. A practical h is:

- **Universal** if it's initialized with random seed a, calculates $h(x) = f(x, a)$ and $\forall\, x \neq y$, $\Pr(h(x) = h(y)) <$ constant/m. So for integer k and any item, $\Pr(h(x) = k) <$ constant/m. A random seed doesn't break regularity because it's stored and reused. As discussed later, this is as close as can get in practice to random.
- **Fair** if, when hashing all possible items, every value is about as likely as any other. These are fastest acceptable quality h, taking O(1) time even for large s.
- **Rolling** if, when adding or removing vector items, can compute their hash from the previous hash in o(s) time.
- **Portable** if it produces the same value $\forall$ architecture and word size.

Most hash functions have the form $h(x)$ % m for some m, and some applications don't need the % m or can replace it by the faster &(m − 1) when $m = 2^b$.

```
template<typename HASHER = PrimeHash> class MHash
{
    unsigned int m;
    HASHER h;
public:
    MHash(unsigned int theM = 1ull << 31): m(theM){}
    template<typename POD> unsigned int hash(POD const& x)
        {return h.hash(x) % m;}
    template<typename NUMBER> unsigned int hash(NUMBER* array, int size)
        {return h.hash(array, size) % m;}
};
template<typename HASHER = PrimeHash> class BHash
{
    unsigned int mask;
    HASHER h;
public:
    BHash(unsigned int b = 31): mask(Bits::lowerMask(b)){}
    template<typename POD> unsigned int hash(POD const& x)
        {return h.hash(x) & mask;}
    template<typename POD> unsigned int hash(POD* array, int size)
        {return h.hash(array, size) & mask;}
};
```

Another wrapper makes basic h efficiently applicable to many data types. To hash a POD, interpret it as an array of words, possibly switching to a smaller word type to get an array of the same byte size. To hash a `float`, union-cast it to an `int`, which is reasonable default behavior for applications that need to hash `float`s. A `double` is handled by the POD hash.

```
template<typename HASHER = PrimeHash> struct EHash32
{
```

```
    HASHER h;
    Ehash32() {}
    EHash32(unsigned long long data): h(data) {}
    typedef unsigned int WORD;
    WORD hash(WORD x){return h.hash(x);}
    WORD hash(int x){return h.hash((WORD)x);}
    WORD hash(short x){return h.hash((WORD)x);}
    WORD hash(unsigned short x){return h.hash((WORD)x);}
    template<typename POD> WORD hash(POD x)
    {
        int rem = sizeof(x) % sizeof(WORD);
        if(rem == 0) return hash((WORD*)&x, sizeof(x)/sizeof(WORD));
        else if(rem == 2) return hash((unsigned short*)&x,
            sizeof(x)/sizeof(unsigned short));
        else return hash((unsigned char*)&x, sizeof(x));
    }
    WORD hash(float x)
    {
        union{float a; WORD b;} c;
        c.a = x;
        return h.hash(c.b);
    }
    template<typename NUMBER> unsigned int hash(NUMBER* array, int size)
        {return h.hash(array, size);}
};
```

7.2 Universal Hash Functions

Theorem A: If h is universal with constant c and hash n items, E[the number of items hashing to the same value] < cn/m. Proof: Let $X_i = 1$ if $h(x_i) = k$ and 0 otherwise. E[the number of items hashing to k] = $E[\sum X_i] = \sum \Pr(h(x_i) = k) < \sum c/m = cn/m$.

Lagrange's theorem: a polynomial % p of degree k, where p is prime, has $\leq k$ solutions mod p if one or more coefficients aren't divisible by p and $k < p$. It doesn't matter if some coefficients are negative because % p makes them positive.

Theorem B: For a variable-length array of numbers x, prime p, $m \leq p$, and random seed $a \in [0, p - 1]$, $h(x) = (\sum x_i a^i)$ % p % m is universal with $c = 2k$, where k is the length of the longest hashed vector. Indexing of x is one-based. Proof: Let $x \neq y$ be variable-length arrays of length $\leq k$. Then $h(x) = h(y) \leftrightarrow (\sum x_i a^i)$ % p % m = $(\sum y_i a^i)$ % p % $m + qm$, for $qm \in (-p, p) \leftrightarrow (\sum(x_i - y_i)a^i) + qm)$ % $p = 0$, with any x_i or y_i that don't exist due to length difference set to 0. This is a polynomial % p with coefficients $(x_i - y_i)$ and qm. By Lagrange's theorem, because qm isn't divisible by p, $\forall q\ \exists\ k$ or fewer seed choices that cause equality. Because $\exists$ fewer than $2p/m$ values of q, the chance of finding such seed $\leq (2kp/m)/p = 2k/m$.

- The proof holds only if the calculations don't overflow. Use 64 bits with $x_i, p \leq 32$ bits, and compute a^i incrementally mod p.
- If $m = p$, don't need the "% m", and h is rolling because can add or subtract $x_i a^i$ terms in O(lg(i)) time, computing a^i using efficient modular exponentiation (see the "Large Numbers" chapter).
- $k = 1$ leads to a universal h for integers with $c = 2$.
- c is large for long strings.
- Can use h for error detection because only need the seed to rehash. CRC (see the "Miscellaneous Algorithms" chapter) has larger error detection probability, but using several hashes makes it arbitrary close to 1.

```
class PrimeHash2
{
    static unsigned int const PRIME = (1ull << 32) - 5;
    unsigned long long seed;//could be > PRIME but that's ok
public:
    PrimeHash2(): seed(GlobalRNG.next() % PRIME) {}
    unsigned int hash(unsigned int x){return seed * x % PRIME;}
```

```
    template<typename NUMBER> unsigned int hash(NUMBER* array, int size)
    {//numbers in the array must fit into unsigned int
        unsigned long long sum = 0;
        for(int i = 0; i < size; ++i) sum = (sum + seed * array[i]) % PRIME;
        return sum;
    }
};
```

Theorem C: For a variable-length array of numbers x, a prime p, $m \leq p$, and k random seeds $a_i \in [0, p - 1]$, where k is the length of the longest hashed vector, $h(x) = (\sum a_i x_i) \% p \% m$ is universal with $c = 2$. Proof: Let $x \neq y$; $h(x) = h(y) \leftrightarrow (\sum a_i x_i) \% p = (\sum a_i y_i) \% p + qm$, for $qm \in (-p, p) \leftrightarrow (a_j(y_j - x_j) - \sum_{i \neq j} a_i(x_i - y_i) + qm \% p) \% p = 0$, where j is such that $(y_j - x_j) \neq 0$. Think of a_i for $i \neq j$ as constants, so the resulting polynomial has at most one solution for a_j. $\exists$ fewer than $2p/m$ values of q and p^{k-1} values of a_i with $i \neq j$ that cause equality, so Pr(equality) $< (2p/m)p^{k-1}/p^k = 2/m$.

- The proof holds only if the calculations don't overflow. In practice, 64 bits are used with x_i and $p < 2^{32}/k$
- If $m = p$, don't need the "% m"
- $k = 1$ leads to a universal h for integers with $c = 2$

Using $a = pg$ for constant g reduces c only by a factor of g.

```
class PrimeHash
{
    static unsigned int const PRIME = (1ull << 32) - 5;
    unsigned long long seed;//could be > PRIME but that's ok
public:
    PrimeHash(): seed(GlobalRNG.next()) {}
    unsigned int hash(unsigned int x){return seed * x % PRIME;}
    template<typename NUMBER> unsigned int hash(NUMBER* array, int size)
    {//numbers in the array must fit into unsigned int
        unsigned long long sum = 0, a = seed;
        for(int i = 0; i < size; ++i)
        {
            sum += a * array[i];
            a = Xorshift::transform(a);
        }//possible overflow but that's ok
        return sum % PRIME;
    }
};
```

Theorem D: For w-bit integers, $m = 2^b$, and odd random $a \in [0, 2^w - 1]$, $h(x) = (xa \% 2^w)/2^{w-b}$ is universal even if xa overflows (Ditzfelbinger et al. 1997). Beware that small a hash small x to 0. Combining the h from theorems C and D gives a very efficient combined universal h for $m = 2^b$:

```
class BUHash
{
    unsigned int a, wLessB;
    BHash<PrimeHash> h;
public:
    BUHash(unsigned int b = 31): a(GlobalRNG.next() | 1),
        wLessB(numeric_limits<unsigned int>::digits - b), h(b) {}
    unsigned int hash(unsigned int x){return (a * x) >> wLessB;}
    template<typename POD> unsigned int hash(POD* array, int size)
        {return h.hash(array, size);}
};
```

7.3 Fair Hash Functions

For random x, use the fastest fair h because, if hash(x) = $h(x)$ % m and $x \neq y$, $\Pr(h(x) = h(y)) = 1/m$. For integers use $h(x) = x$ and, for byte arrays $h(x)$ = word formed by any 4 bytes. For the latter, not looking at all bytes can save much runtime.

```
struct FairHash
```

```
{
    unsigned int hash(unsigned int x){return x;}
    unsigned int hash(unsigned char* array, int size)
    {
        unsigned int result = 0;
        for(int i = 0; i < min(size, 4); ++i)
            result = (result << 8) | array[i];
        return result;
    }
    template<typename NUMBER> unsigned int hash(NUMBER* array, int size)
        {return hash((unsigned char*)array, size * sizeof(NUMBER));}
};
```

7.4 Nonuniversal Hash Functions

Sometimes h must always give the same result for the same object and can't be universal. E.g., in Java, every object's `hashCode` gives the same 32-bit hash. High-quality h do well on (Henke et al. 2008; 2009):

- **Avalanche**—changing any input bit changes each h bit with 50% probability
- Bias—inputs of any length and value hash equally likely into any range
- Collisions—E[the number] = that of a random h

For high-quality **FNV hash function** for variable length byte arrays, $hC(x, i) = (hC(x, i - 1)b) \wedge x[i]$ with $hC(x, -1) = a$, where a, b = 2166136261, 16777619 for 32 bits and 14695981039346656037, 1099511628211 for 64. The values of b are special primes and of a arbitrary.

```
struct FNVHash
{
    template<typename POD> unsigned int hash(POD const& x)
        {return hash((unsigned char*)&x, sizeof(x));}
    unsigned int hash(unsigned char* array, int size)
    {
        unsigned int sum = 2166136261u;
        for(int i = 0; i < size; ++i) sum = (sum * 16777619) ^ array[i];
        return sum;
    }
    template<typename NUMBER> unsigned int hash(NUMBER* array, int size)
        {return hash((unsigned char*)array, size * sizeof(NUMBER));}
};
```

A variable-length-array and computable incrementally h must have the form $h_i(x) = f(\text{combine}(h_{i-1}(x), x[i]))$, with $h_{-1}(x) = 0$ or some seed. Prefer this form over $\text{combine}(f(h_{i-1}(x)), x[i])$ because for simple combiners the last byte doesn't affect all bits of h. Obvious f are random generator transitions and obvious combiners operators "+" and "^". A combiner should be different from f. For efficiency, h should hash arrays of integers, and not byte by byte.

Xorshift hash function uses Xorshift transitions and combiner operator "+". When the initial sum is random, it's similar to a universal h. For 64 bits use the QualityXorshift64 transition.

```
class Xorshift32Hash
{
    unsigned int seed;
public:
    Xorshift32Hash(): seed(GlobalRNG.next()) {}
    unsigned int hash(unsigned int x){return Xorshift::transform(seed + x);}
    template<typename NUMBER> unsigned int hash(NUMBER* array, int size)
    {
        unsigned int sum = seed;
        for(int i = 0; i < size; ++i)
            sum = Xorshift::transform(sum + array[i]);
        return sum;
    }
};
```

LCG hash function uses combiner "+" and an LCG with prime multiplier 1099087573, which is good for 32-bit words (L'Ecuyer 2007). It's rolling by being equivalent to a linear combination. E.g., the hash of a two-character string has the form $a^2c_0 + ac_1$. Using only operators "+" and "×" makes it useful for script languages with a limited set of operations.

```
struct LCGHash
{
    unsigned int hash(unsigned int x){return 1099087573u * x;}
    template<typename NUMBER> unsigned int hash(NUMBER* array, int size)
    {
        unsigned int sum = 0;
        for(int i = 0; i < size; ++i) sum = 1099087573u * (sum + array[i]);
        return sum;
    }
};
```

7.5 Rolling Hash Functions

The fastest and most convenient rolling *h* is **table hashing**, also called **Zobrist hashing**: interpret *x* as a variable-length byte array. Then $h(x) = \text{XOR}\sum table[x_i]$, where *table* has size 256 and holds random numbers. Rolling uses hash ^= *table*[old] ^ *table*[new] and needs O(1) time. All byte permutations of *x* hash to the same number, making *h* unsuitable for general use.

```
class TableHash
{
    unsigned int table[256];
public:
    TableHash(){for(int i = 0; i < 256; ++i) table[i] = GlobalRNG.next();}
    unsigned int hash(unsigned char* array, int size)
    {
        unsigned int result = 0;
        for(int i = 0; i < size; ++i) result ^= table[array[i]];
        return result;
    }
    template<typename NUMBER>unsigned long long hash(NUMBER* array, int size)
        {return hash((unsigned char*)array, size * sizeof(NUMBER));}
    template<typename POD> unsigned int hash(POD const& x)
        {return hash((unsigned char*)&x, sizeof(x));}
    unsigned int update(unsigned int currentHash, unsigned char byte)
        {return currentHash ^ table[byte];}//for both additions and removals
};
```

Board games, a major application, hash piece-square pairs. A board generally consists of squares with at most one piece each. E.g., chess has 64 × (2 × 6 + 1) = 832 possible piece-squares. Can represent each with two bytes, but it's more efficient and higher quality to use *table* of size 832. If ∃many piece-squares, avoid *table* by picking a hash function *g* and using $h(x) = \text{XOR}\sum g(x_i)$.

7.6 Collection of Hash Functions

If need *k* hash functions, e.g., for Bloom filter (discussed later in this chapter), for $k > 2$, $h_i = h_1 + ih_2$ gives sufficiently random results and is more efficient than hashing *k* times (Kirsch & Mitzenmacher 2006).

7.7 Hash Tables

A hash table efficiently supports map operations by placing objects *x* into an array of size *m* at location *h*(*x*). With *n* items, *m*/*n* is the **load factor**. Hash tables differ by when to resize and how to resolve collisions. For most implementations, E[the runtime of a map operation] = O(1). It's impossible to have a map of size O(*n*) with both amortized O(1) find and insert (Ditzfelbinger et al. 1994). Beware that if using *h* with a random seed, ∀seed the iteration order of items is different, which causes problems when computing order-sensitive functions such as max.

Due to more efficient *h*, table sizes are powers of two. The discussed *h* don't work directly with non-POD types and aren't efficient for some POD types due to working on one byte at a time. In both cases use custom *h*, such as the below for a vector of integral types and string:

```
template<typename HASHER = EHash32<BUHash> > struct DataHash
{
    HASHER h;
    unsigned int hash(string const& item)
        {return h.hash(item.c_str(), item.size());}
    template<typename VECTOR> unsigned int hash(VECTOR const& item)
        {return h.hash(item.getArray(), item.getSize());}
};
```

7.8 Chaining

Each array cell has a linked list with items that hashed to the corresponding index:

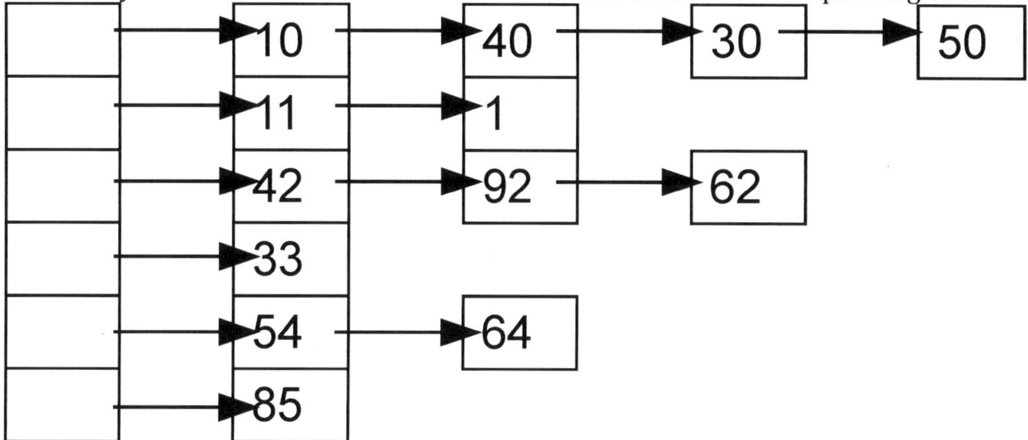

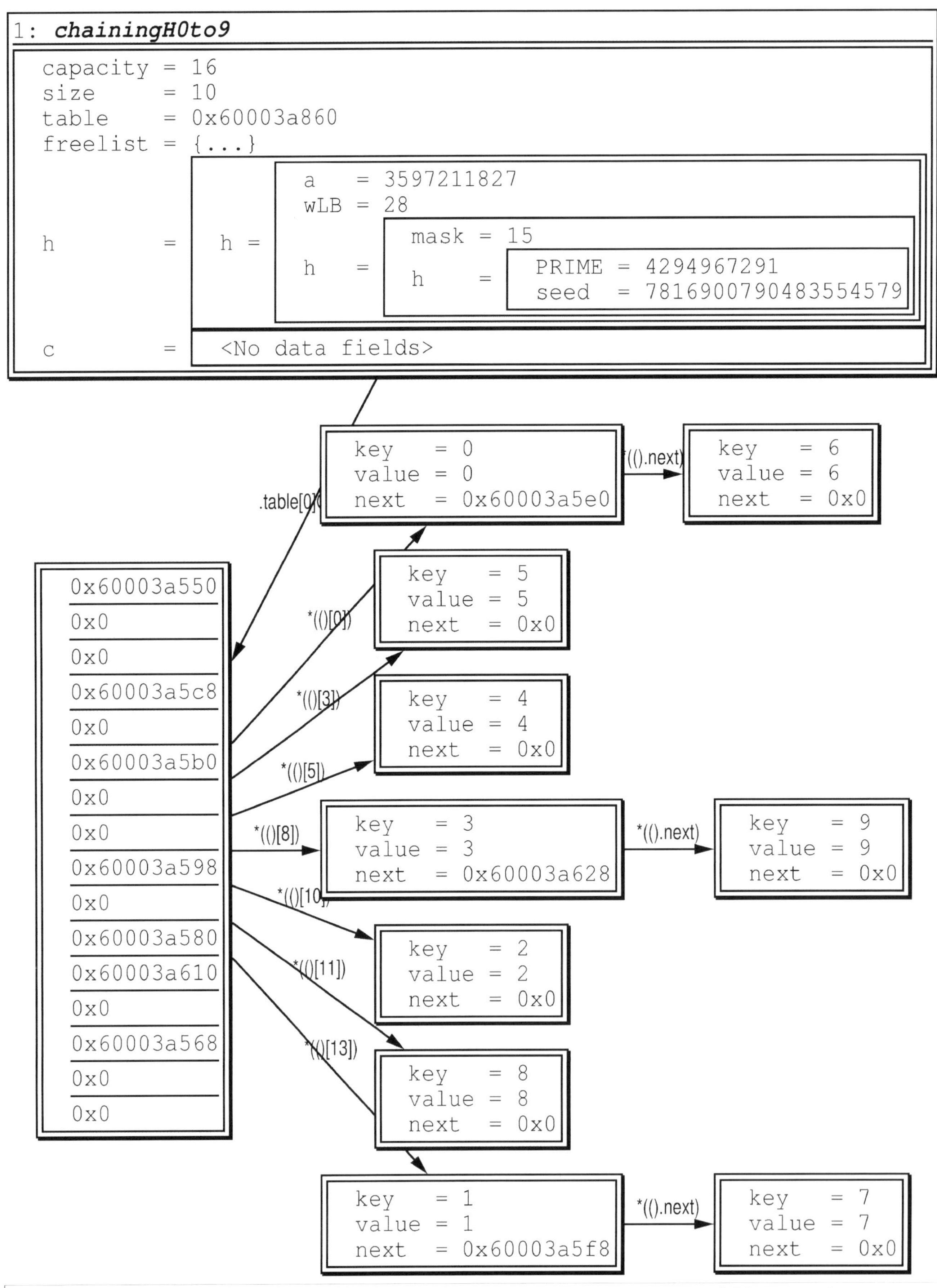


```
template<typename KEY, typename VALUE, typename HASHER = EHash32<BUHash>,
    typename COMPARATOR = DefaultComparator<KEY> >class ChainingHashTable
{
```

```
    int capacity, size;
    struct Node
    {
        KEY key;
        VALUE value;
        Node* next;
        Node(KEY const& theKey, VALUE const& theValue): key(theKey),
            value(theValue), next(0) {}
    }** table;
    Freelist<Node> freelist;
    HASHER h;
    COMPARATOR c;
    void allocateTable(int requestedSize)
    {
        int bits = lgCeiling(max(requestedSize, 8));
        capacity = twoPower(bits);
        h = HASHER(bits);
        size = 0;
        table = new Node*[capacity];
        for(int i = 0; i < capacity; ++i) table[i] = 0;
    }
    void resize()
    {
        int oldCapacity = capacity;
        Node** oldTable = table;
        allocateTable(size * 2);
        for(int i = 0; i < oldCapacity; ++i)
            for(Node* j = oldTable[i], *tail; j; j = tail)
            {
                tail = j->next;
                j->next = 0;
                insertNode(j);
            }
        delete[] oldTable;
    }
public:
    typedef Node NodeType;
    void getSize(){return size;}
    ChainingHashTable(int initialCapacity = 8, COMPARATOR const&
        theComparator = COMPARATOR()): c(theComparator)
        {allocateTable(initialCapacity);}
    ChainingHashTable(ChainingHashTable const& rhs): capacity(rhs.capacity),
        size(rhs.size), h(rhs.h), table(new Node*[capacity]), c(rhs.c)
    {
        for(int i = 0; i < capacity; ++i)
        {
            table[i] = 0;
            Node** target = &table[i];
            for(Node* j = rhs.table[i]; j; j = j->next)
            {
                *target = new(freelist.allocate())Node(*j);
                target = &(*target)->next;
            }
        }
    }
    ChainingHashTable& operator=(ChainingHashTable const& rhs)
        {return genericAssign(*this, rhs);}
    ~ChainingHashTable(){delete[] table;}
};
```

Map operations hash the key, linearly search the list for the item with the key, and update the list if inserting/removing.

```
Node** findPointer(KEY const& key)
{
    Node** pointer = &table[h.hash(key)];
    for(;*pointer && !c.isEqual((*pointer)->key, key);
        pointer = &(*pointer)->next);
    return pointer;
}
Node* findNode(KEY const& key){return *findPointer(key);}
VALUE* find(KEY const& key)
{
    Node* next = findNode(key);
    return next ? &next->value : 0;
}
```

Insert updates the value if found and appends to the list otherwise, doubling if the load factor ≥ 1. If h is universal, by theorem A with O(1) load factor E[list size] = O(1), so E[the runtime of a map operation] = O(1).

```
Node* insertNode(Node* node)
{
    Node** pointer = findPointer(node->key);
    if(*pointer)
    {
        (*pointer)->value = node->value;
        freelist.remove(node);
        node = *pointer;
    }
    else
    {
        *pointer = node;
        if(++size >= capacity) resize();//not > where will have x4 size
    }
    return node;
}
Node* insert(KEY const& key, VALUE const& value)
    {return insertNode(new(freelist.allocate())Node(key, value));}
```

Resize iterates over the old table and copies all nodes into the new one. E[the runtime] = O(n), and this happens at most every O(n) insertions, giving amortized expected O(1) insertion. After a resize, the load factor = 0.5 and item pointers don't change.

```
void resize()
{
    int oldCapacity = capacity;
    Node** oldTable = table;
    allocateTable(size * 2);
    for(int i = 0; i < oldCapacity; ++i)
        for(Node* j = oldTable[i], *tail; j; j = tail)
        {
            tail = j->next;
            j->next = 0;
            insertNode(j);
        }
    delete[] oldTable;
}
```

Remove cuts out the found node and resizes if the load factor < 0.1, which seems to be a reasonable balance between space use and frequency of resizing:

```
void remove(KEY const& key)
{
```

```
        Node** pointer = findPointer(key);
        Node* i = *pointer;
        if(i)
        {
            *pointer = i->next;
            freelist.remove(i);
            if(--size < capacity * 0.1) resize();
        }
    }
```

The runtime is also amortized expected O(1). Iteration loops over the array, going into and looping over each cell's list. Going though all items takes $O(n)$ time.

```
    struct Iterator
    {
        int i;
        Node* nextLink;
        ChainingHashTable& t;
        void advance(){while(i < t.capacity && !(nextLink = t.table[i++]));}
    public:
        Iterator(ChainingHashTable& theHashTable): i(0), nextLink(0),
            t(theHashTable) {advance();}
        Iterator& operator++()
        {
            if(nextLink) nextLink = nextLink->next;
            else ++i;
            advance();
            return *this;
        }
        NodeType& operator*(){assert(nextLink); return *nextLink;}
        NodeType* operator->(){assert(nextLink); return nextLink;}
        bool operator!=(Iterator const& rhs)
            {return nextLink != rhs.nextLink;}
    };
    Iterator begin(){return Iterator(*this);}
    Iterator end()
    {
        Iterator result(*this);
        result.i = capacity;
        result.nextLink = 0;
        return result;
    }
```

With random h, Pr(an item lands in a given cell) = $1/m$. x = the number of items in a given cell after inserting n items = the number of coins landing on heads with probability $p = 1/m$ after n throws, modeled as binomial(x, p, n) ≈ Poisson(x, a) = $a^x/(x!e^a)$. So:

- E[list size] = a
- E[% of cells with k items] = Poisson(k, a), which for $a = 1$ is ≈ 0.37 for $k = 0$ and 1, 0.18 for 2, 0.06 for 3, etc.
- Pr(list size ≥ k) = $\sum_{k \leq x \leq \infty}$Poisson($x$,$a$) = $\sum_{k \leq x \leq \infty} a^x/x!e^a \leq a^k/(k!e^a)\sum_{0 \leq x \leq \infty} a^x/x!$ = Poisson(k, a)e^a, which $< 10^{-12}$ for $x = 15$ and $a = 1$

7.9 Linear Probing

Disadvantages of chaining are space for links, use of freelist, and clumsy iteration. Linear probing avoids these by using an array of items and an array of Booleans that mark occupied cells. Collided items go to the next free cell, like books in library shelves. The probing sequence is cache-oblivious (see the "External Memory Algorithms" chapter) and allows deletions.

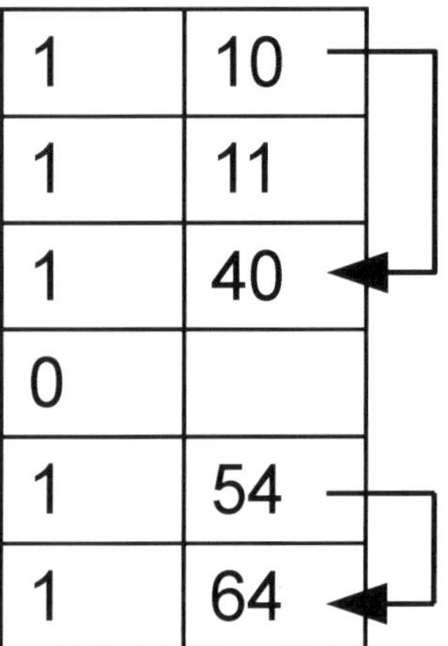

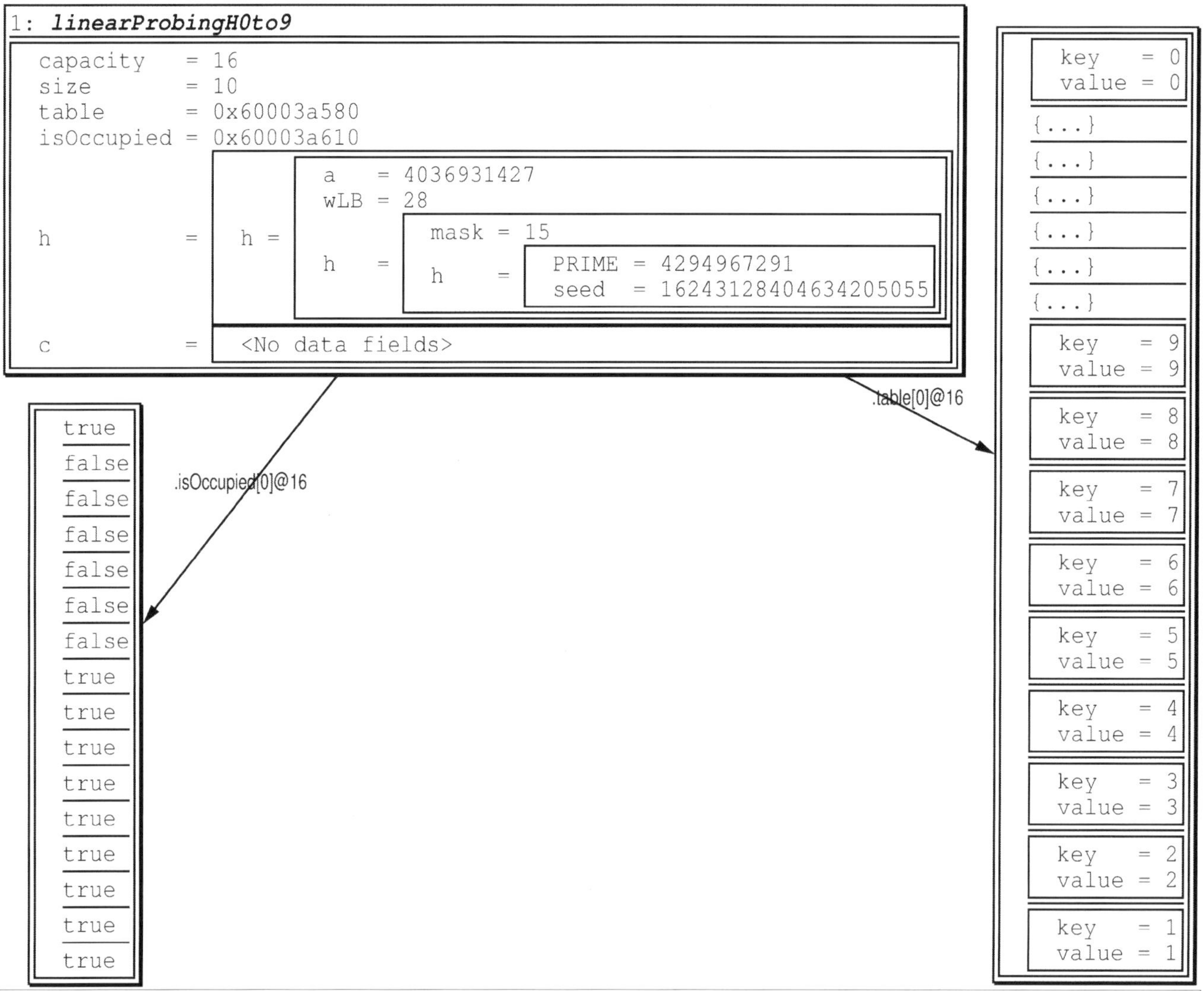

```
1: linearProbingH0to9
   capacity   = 16
   size       = 10
   table      = 0x60003a580
   isOccupied = 0x60003a610
                      a   = 4036931427
                      wLB = 28
   h          = h =         mask = 15
                      h   = h    = PRIME = 4294967291
                                   seed  = 16243128404634205055
   c          = <No data fields>
```

.isOccupied[0]@16

```
true
false
false
false
false
false
false
true
true
true
true
true
true
true
true
true
```

.table[0]@16

```
key   = 0
value = 0
{...}
{...}
{...}
{...}
{...}
{...}
key   = 9
value = 9
key   = 8
value = 8
key   = 7
value = 7
key   = 6
value = 6
key   = 5
value = 5
key   = 4
value = 4
key   = 3
value = 3
key   = 2
value = 2
key   = 1
value = 1
```

```
template<typename KEY, typename VALUE, typename HASHER = EHash32<BUHash>,
typename COMPARATOR = DefaultComparator<KEY> > class LinearProbingHashTable
{
    int capacity, size;
    typedef KVPair<KEY, VALUE> Node;
    Node* table;
    bool* isOccupied;
    HASHER h;
    COMPARATOR c;
    void allocateTable(int requestedSize)
    {
```

```
        int bits = lgCeiling(max(requestedSize, 8));
        capacity = twoPower(bits);
        h = HASHER(bits);
        size = 0;
        table = rawMemory<Node>(capacity);
        isOccupied = new bool[capacity];
        for(int i = 0; i < capacity; ++i) isOccupied[i] = false;
    }
    static void cleanUp(Node* theTable, int theCapacity, bool* isOccupied)
    {
        for(int i = 0; i < theCapacity; ++i)
            if(isOccupied[i]) theTable[i].~Node();
        rawDelete(theTable);
        delete[] isOccupied;
    }
    void resize()
    {
        int oldCapacity = capacity;
        Node* oldTable = table;
        bool* oldIsOccupied = isOccupied;
        allocateTable(2 * size);
        for(int i = 0; i < oldCapacity; ++i)
            if(oldIsOccupied[i]) insert(oldTable[i].key, oldTable[i].value);
        cleanUp(oldTable, oldCapacity, oldIsOccupied);
    }
public:
    typedef Node NodeType;
    void getSize(){return size;}
    LinearProbingHashTable(int initialCapacity = 8,
        COMPARATOR const& theComparator = COMPARATOR()): c(theComparator)
        {allocateTable(initialCapacity);}
    LinearProbingHashTable(LinearProbingHashTable const& rhs):
        capacity(rhs.capacity), h(rhs.h), size(rhs.size), c(rhs.c),
        isOccupied(new bool[capacity]), table(rawMemory<Node>(capacity))
    {
        for(int i = 0; i < capacity; ++i)
            if(isOccupied[i] = rhs.isOccupied[i]) table[i] = rhs.table[i];
    }
    LinearProbingHashTable& operator=(LinearProbingHashTable const& rhs)
        {return genericAssign(*this, rhs);}
    ~LinearProbingHashTable(){cleanUp(table, capacity, isOccupied);}
};
```

Map operations find index i of the cell where the item should be. If a different item is there, go to cell $(i + 1)$ % m, until find an empty one.

```
    int findNode(KEY const& key)
    {
        int cell = h.hash(key);
        for(;isOccupied[cell] && !c.isEqual(key, table[cell].key);
            cell = (cell + 1) % capacity);
        return cell;
    }
    VALUE* find(KEY const& key)
    {
        int cell = findNode(key);
        return isOccupied[cell] ? &table[cell].value : 0;
    }
```

Insert puts the item in the next available cell or updates the value of the item with an equal key. With random h, E[the number of probes for a successful find] = $(1 - 1/(1 - a))/2$, and for an unsuccessful find or insert it's $(1 - 1/(1 - a)^2)/2$ (Cormen et al. 2009), which, respectively, = 3 and 13 for $a = 0.8$.

```
    void insert(KEY const& key, VALUE const& value)
    {
        int cell = findNode(key);
        if(isOccupied[cell]) table[cell].value = value;
        else
        {
            new(&table[cell])Node(key, value);
            isOccupied[cell] = true;
            if(++size > capacity * 0.8) resize();
        }
    }
```

Due to resizing, the runtime of insert and delete are amortized expected O(1). Resize changes the load factor to 0.5:

```
    void resize()
    {
        int oldCapacity = capacity;
        Node* oldTable = table;
        bool* oldIsOccupied = isOccupied;
        allocateTable(2 * size);
        for(int i = 0; i < oldCapacity; ++i)
            if(oldIsOccupied[i]) insert(oldTable[i].key, oldTable[i].value);
        cleanUp(oldTable, oldCapacity, oldIsOccupied);
    }
```

Remove removes the found item and, because this may break probing for the next items, deletes and reinserts them, resizing if the load factor < 0.1:

```
    void destroy(int cell)
    {
        table[cell].~Node();
        isOccupied[cell] = false;
        --size;
    }
    void remove(KEY const& key)
    {
        int cell = findNode(key);
        if(isOccupied[cell])
        {//reinsert subsequent nodes in the found value's chain
            destroy(cell);
            while(isOccupied[cell = (cell + 1) % capacity])
            {
                Node temp = table[cell];
                destroy(cell);
                insert(temp.key, temp.value);
            }
            if(size < capacity * 0.1) resize();
        }
    }
```

The runtime is still expected O(1) because E[chain length] is. Going though all items takes $O(n)$ time and is cache-efficient.

```
    struct Iterator
    {
        int i;
        LinearProbingHashTable& t;
        void advance(){while(i < t.capacity && !t.isOccupied[i]) ++i;}
    public:
        Iterator(LinearProbingHashTable& theHashTable): i(0),
            t(theHashTable) {advance();}
        Iterator& operator++()
```

```
        {
            ++i;
            advance();
            return *this;
        }
        NodeType& operator*(){assert(i < t.capacity); return t.table[i];}
        NodeType* operator->(){assert(i < t.capacity); return &t.table[i];}
        bool operator!=(Iterator const& rhs){return i != rhs.i;}
    };
    Iterator begin(){return Iterator(*this);}
    Iterator end()
    {
        Iterator result(*this);
        result.i = capacity;
        return result;
    }
```

A universal *h* doesn't guarantee E[the runtime of a map operation] = O(1) because lists of items hashing to the same cell aren't independent. But joint randomness of a universal *h* and structure of data usually give performance of a random *h* (Mitzenmacher & Vadhan 2008). Can replace the Boolean array by a slower bit vector. If the key and the item take 8 bytes, this saves ≈ 10% memory for ≈ 50% slowdown.

7.10 Timings

My machine is 32-bit and the timings are in seconds for 1.5×10^6 and 1.5×10^5 insertions for, respectively, `int`s and `Fat2` objects of 10 ints, and 100 times more finds. A 64-bit machine would favor 64-bit *h*. Tests with universal *h* ran 100 times.

Hash function	Hash 1.5×10^9 `ints`	Hash 1.5×10^8 `Fat2`	Linear probing, `int`	Linear probing, `Fat2`	Chaining, `int`	Chaining, `Fat2`
E-BU	0.89	3.45	3.53 ± 0.6 (min 2.03, max 15.86)	Same as E-*b*-Prime	2.71 ± 0.93 (min 1.22, max 32.1)	Same as E-*b*-Prime
E-*b*-Prime	10.2	3.57	10.81 ± 13.3 (min 2.89, max 44.81)	1.67 ± 0.96 (min 1.17, max 3.7)	4.83 ± 0.58 (min 2.76, max 21.56)	1.04 ± 0.26 (min 0.95, max 1.47)
E-*b*-Prime2	Same as E-*b*-Prime	16.83	Same as E-B-Prime	4.40 ± 0.23 (min 4.00, max 11.53)	Same as E-B-Prime	4.04 ± 0.40 (min 3.90, max 4.68)
E-*b*-X32	2.1	3.58	2.52	1.79	2.19	1.23
E-*b*-X64	9.95	12.96	3.88	3.54	3.41	2.79
E-*b*-LCG	1.16	5.44	2.54	1.73	1.75	1.58
b-FNV	5.87	12.34	5.49	3.42	4.06	3.08
m-FNV	10.51	13.35	5.95	3.78	4.39	3.19
E-*b*-Fair	1.18	0.46	0.25	Too long	0.3	276
b-Table	2.46	4.52	16.88	2.07	6.39	1.45

Based on the timings, use E-BU as default. The *m*-hashes are slower, particularly for integers. E-*b*-X32 is faster than FNV due to working on words. Fair *h* are faster for the right data. Chaining vs linear probing:

- Chaining has item persistence
- Linear probing uses less memory for small items
- Chaining is more robust and has expected O(1) guarantee with a universal *h*
- Memory allocator quality and use of freelist affect chaining speed

- Linear probing has faster iteration

Use chaining as default and linear probing for small items to cut memory use. For static maps, use a sorted array.

7.11 Bloom Filter

A Bloom filter supports only `isInserted` and insert and has a fixed size, but uses much less space. It consists of a bitset of size *m* and *k* hash functions. To insert *x*, set each $h_i(x)$ bit. If all the $h_i(x)$ bits are set, *x* was inserted with high probability, and not inserted otherwise. Delete and rebuild aren't supported.

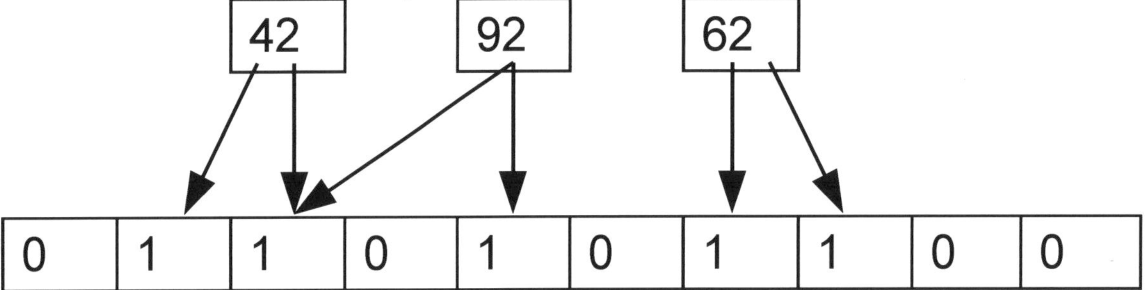


```
template<typename ITEM, typename HASHER = EHash32<MHash<PrimeHash> > >
class BloomFilter
{
    Bitset<unsigned char> items;
    HASHER h1, h2;
    int nHashes;
    int hash(int hash1, int hash2, int i)
    {
        if(i == 0) return hash1;
        if(i == 1) return hash2;
        return (hash1 + i * hash2) % items.getSize();
    }
public:
    BloomFilter(int size, int theNHashes = 7): nHashes(theNHashes), items(
        size), h1(size), h2(size) {assert(size > 0 && nHashFunctions > 0);}
    void insert(ITEM const& item)
    {
        int hash1 = h1.hash(item), hash2 = h2.hash(item);
        for(int i = 0; i < nHashes; ++i) items.set(hash(hash1, hash2, i));
    }
    bool isInserted(ITEM const& item)
    {
        int hash1 = h1.hash(item), hash2 = h2.hash(item);
        for(int i = 0; i < nHashes; ++i)
            if(!items[hash(hash1, hash2, i)]) return false;
        return true;
    }
};
```

As with chaining, Pr[*x* items are in a particular cell] = Poisson(*x*, *ka*). For $x = 0$, this = e^{-ka} = Pr(a given bit remains 0). So Pr(`isInserted` is wrong) = p = Pr[*k* given bits are 1] = $(1 - e^{-ka})^k$; $k = \ln(2)/a = 0.69/a$ minimizes *p*, so, neglecting that *k* is integer, $p = 0.5^{\ln(2)/a} = e^{-0.48/a}$, and $m = -n\ln(p)/0.48$. Given application-specific *n* and *p*, solve for *m*, then for *k*.

7.12 Comments

Many hash functions are criticized by Valloud (2008). Can turn any pseudorandom generator into a hash function by interpreting a key as the seed (though need their sizes to match).

Linear probing is a special case of more general **open addressing**. Another popular variant is **double hashing**. The idea is to improve collision resolution of linear probing by jumping to a random cell using another *h*, instead of to the next cell. This reduces the expected insertion time but doesn't improve performance (Heileman & Luo 2005) and is a bad choice because:

- Lose cache-efficiency
- Need to evaluate another *h* and the caller to specify one
- Lose deletions and can only do weak ones (see the "Algorithmic Techniques" chapter)

Quadratic probing (Cormen et al. 2009) simplifies double hashing by using deterministic step sizes to remove the cost of another *h*. But this increases the expected insertion time and needs load factor < 0.5.

Cuckoo hashing allows O(1) find and remove by hashing an item in one of only two possible locations, chosen by two independent *h*. But insertion, despite being expected O(1) for hash functions with certain theoretical guarantees (stronger than universal; Mitzenmacher 2009), has no worst case bound and may need to rebuild the table. This makes cuckoo dangerous and clumsy in practice because the caller might not give *h*s with the wanted properties, or give ones with a flawed random number generator, etc.

Perfect hashing (Cormen et al. 2009) makes collision-free two-level hash tables for fixed *n*. But it's advantage over chaining and linear probing is unclear, and bad case memory use and construction time are problematic.

Can try to improve Bloom filter in several ways, but at most get slightly better efficiency with much more complicated implementation (Putze et al. 2009).

7.13 References

Cormen, T. H., Leiserson, C. E., Rivest, R. L., & Stein, C. (2009). *Introduction to Algorithms*. MIT Press.

Dietzfelbinger, M., Karlin, A., Mehlhorn, K., Meyer auf der Heide, F., Rohnert, H., & Tarjan, R. E. (1994). Dynamic perfect hashing: upper and lower bounds. *SIAM Journal on Computing*, *23*(4), 738–761.

Dietzfelbinger, M., Hagerup, T., Katajainen, J., & Penttonen, M. (1997). A reliable randomized algorithm for the closest-pair problem. *Journal of Algorithms*, *25*(1), 19–51.

Heileman, G. L., & Luo, W. (2005). How caching affects hashing. In *ALENEX/ANALCO* (pp. 141–154). SIAM.

Henke, C., Schmoll, C., & Zseby, T. (2008). Empirical evaluation of hash functions for multipoint measurements. *ACM SIGCOMM Computer Communication Review*, *38*(3), 39–50.

———. (2009). Empirical evaluation of hash functions for packetid generation in sampled multipoint measurements. In *Passive and Active Network Measurement* (pp. 197–206). Springer.

Kirsch, A., & Mitzenmacher, M. (2006). Less hashing, same performance: building a better Bloom filter. In *Algorithms–ESA 2006* (pp. 456–467). Springer.

L'Ecuyer, P., & Simard, R. (2007). TestU01: A C library for empirical testing of random number generators. *ACM Transactions on Mathematical Software (TOMS)*, *33*(4), 22.

Mitzenmacher, M. (2009). Some open questions related to cuckoo hashing. In *Algorithms-ESA 2009* (pp. 1–10). Springer.

———, & Vadhan, S. (2008). Why simple hash functions work: exploiting the entropy in a data stream. In *Proceedings of the Nineteenth Annual ACM–SIAM Symposium on Discrete Algorithms* (pp. 746–755). SIAM.

Putze, F., Sanders, P., & Singler, J. (2009). Cache-, hash-, and space-efficient Bloom filters. *Journal of Experimental Algorithmics (JEA)*, *14*, 4.

Tarkoma, S., Rothenberg, C. E., & Lagerspetz, E. (2012). Theory and practice of Bloom filters for distributed systems. *Communications Surveys & Tutorials, IEEE*, *14*(1), 131–155.

Valloud, A. (2008). *Hashing in Smalltalk: Theory and Practice*.

Wikipedia (2013). Universal hashing. https://en.wikipedia.org/wiki/Universal_hashing. Accessed May 18, 2013.

8 Priority Queues

A **priority queue** can:

- Insert an item with a given priority
- Find the smallest priority item
- Remove the smallest priority item

Additional operations:

- Change an item's priority
- Remove an item
- Merge two priority queues

The functionality limitation allows a more efficient implementation, than by a dynamic sorted sequence. Because a priority queue can sort, delete min or insert takes ≥ amortized O(lg(n)) time.

8.1 Binary Heap

A binary heap is a vector representing a binary tree where for the node at index i:

- Parent = $(i - 1)/2$
- Left child = $2i + 1$
- Right child = $2i + 2$

The item in any node < the items in its children.

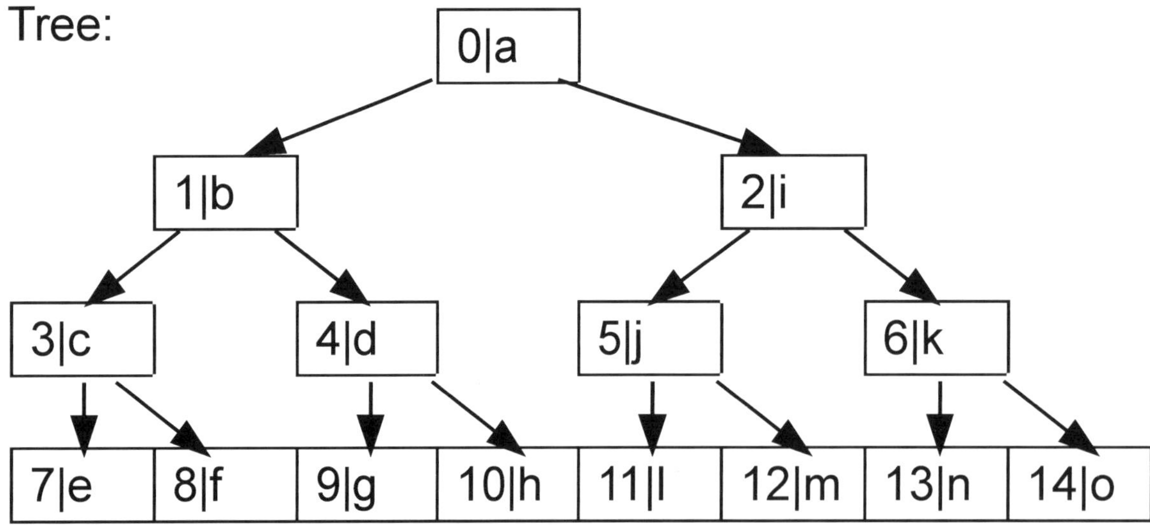

Item movement is optionally reported to the caller for indexing, as discussed later.

```
template<typename ITEM, typename COMPARATOR = DefaultComparator<ITEM>,
    typename REPORTER = ReportDefault<ITEM> > class Heap
{
    REPORTER r;
    int getParent(int i){return (i - 1)/2;}
    int getLeftChild(int i){return 2 * i + 1;}
public:
    COMPARATOR c;
    Vector<ITEM> items;
    Heap(COMPARATOR const& theComparator = COMPARATOR(), REPORTER const&
        theReporter = REPORTER()): r(theReporter), c(theComparator){}
    bool isEmpty(){return items.getSize() <= 0;}
```

```
  int getSize(){return items.getSize();}
  ITEM const& getMin()
  {
      assert(!isEmpty());
      return items[0];
  }
```

Move up exchanges the item with its parent while parent < item:

```
  void moveUp(int i)
  {
      ITEM temp = items[i];
      for(int parent; i > 0 && c.isLess(temp, items[parent =
          getParent(i)]); i = parent) r(items[i] = items[parent], i);
      r(items[i] = temp, i);
  }
```

Move down exchanges the item with its smallest child while it has one:

```
  void moveDown(int i)
  {
      ITEM temp = items[i];
      for(int child; (child = getLeftChild(i)) < items.getSize();
          i = child)
      {//find smaller child
          int rightChild = child + 1;
          if(rightChild < items.getSize() && c.isLess(items
              [rightChild], items[child])) child = rightChild;
          //replace with the smaller child if any
          if(!c.isLess(items[child], temp)) break;
          r(items[i] = items[child], i);
      }
      r(items[i] = temp, i);
  }
```

Insert appends the item and moves it up:

```
  void insert(ITEM const& item)
  {
      items.append(item);
      moveUp(items.getSize() - 1);
  }
```

To remove item *i*:

1. **Replace the item with a copy of the last item**
2. **Move it down**
3. **Remove the last item**

Reporting −1 signals that the item is deleted.

```
  ITEM deleteMin(){return remove(0);}
  ITEM remove(int i)
  {
      assert(i >= 0 && i <= items.getSize());
      ITEM result = items[i];
      r(result, -1);
      if(items.getSize() > i)
      {
          items[i] = items.lastItem();
          report(items[i], i);
          moveDown(i);
      }
      items.removeLast();
      return result;
  }
```

Change key of item *i* makes the change and moves it up if the new key < the old key, and down otherwise. To replace the minimum, use `changeKey(0)`.

```
    void changeKey(int i, ITEM const& item)
    {
        assert(i >= 0 && i <= items.getSize());
        bool decrease = c.isLess(item, items[i]);
        items[i] = item;
        decrease ? moveUp(i) : moveDown(i);
    }
```

All operations take O(the height) = O(lg(n)) time, but insert and remove are amortized due to vector doubling. To merge several heaps, insert into one all items from the rest. If all items will eventually be removed, the cost is amortized O(lg(n)).

Heapsort is using a heap to sort by inserting items into it and getting them out in sorted order using delete min. Can run a heap directly on the unsorted array of items and use faster bulk insertion, called the **heapify** operation. This takes O($n$lg(n)) time, but with larger constant than other efficient sorts.

8.2 Addressable Binary Heap

An **indexed heap** uses an address-persistent chaining hash table to associate items with caller-provided handles. The heap item consists of the real item and the pointer to the map node containing the handle. The heap reporter uses the pointers to update item indices. The binary heap's amortized O(lg(n)) and the hash table's expected O(1) lead to expected amortized O(lg(n)) operations. The implementation assumes a hashable-by-default handle type for simplicity but is easily extended. E.g., for random priorities and counter handles, have:

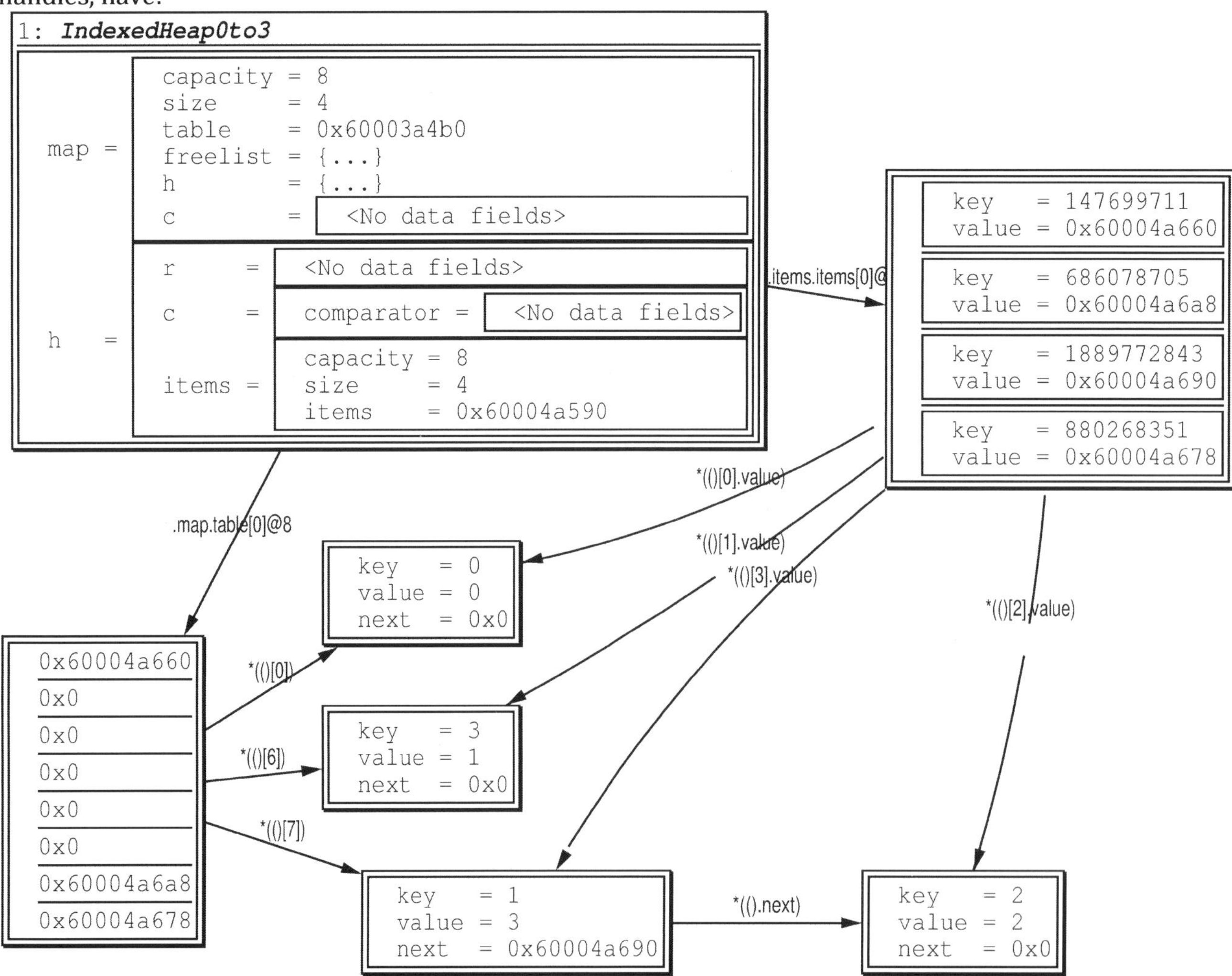

The operations reduce to calling the corresponding heap operations and updating the map in cases where the reporter can't do so completely on its own.

```
template<typename ITEM, typename COMPARATOR = DefaultComparator<ITEM>,
```

```
    typename Handle = int> class IndexedHeap
{
    ChainingHashTable<Handle, int> map;
    typedef typename ChainingHashTable<int, int>::NodeType* POINTER;
    typedef KVPair<ITEM, POINTER> Item;
    typedef KVComparator<ITEM, POINTER, COMPARATOR> Comparator;
    struct Reporter
        {void operator()(Item& item, int i){item.value->value = i;}};
    Heap<Item, Comparator, Reporter> h;
public:
    IndexedHeap(COMPARATOR const& theComparator = COMPARATOR()):
        h(Comparator(theComparator)) {}
    int getSize(){return h.getSize();}
    ITEM* find(Handle handle)
    {
        int* pointer = map.find(handle);
        return pointer ? &h.items[*pointer].key : 0;
    }
    bool isEmpty(){return h.isEmpty();}
    void insert(ITEM const& item, Handle handle)
    {
        POINTER p = map.insert(handle, h.getSize());
        h.insert(Item(item, p));
    }
    ITEM const& getMin(){return h.getMin().key;}
    ITEM deleteMin()
    {
        Item result = h.deleteMin();
        map.remove(result.value->key);
        return result.key;
    }
    void changeKey(ITEM const& item, Handle handle)
    {
        POINTER p = map.findNode(handle);
        if(p) h.changeKey(p->value, Item(item, p));
        else insert(item, handle);
    }
    void deleteKey(Handle handle)
    {
        assert(find(handle));
        h.remove(*map.find(handle));
        map.remove(handle);
    }
};
```

Using a vector as the map is more efficient for small-integer handles. Its size is dynamically increased to the maximum handle value.

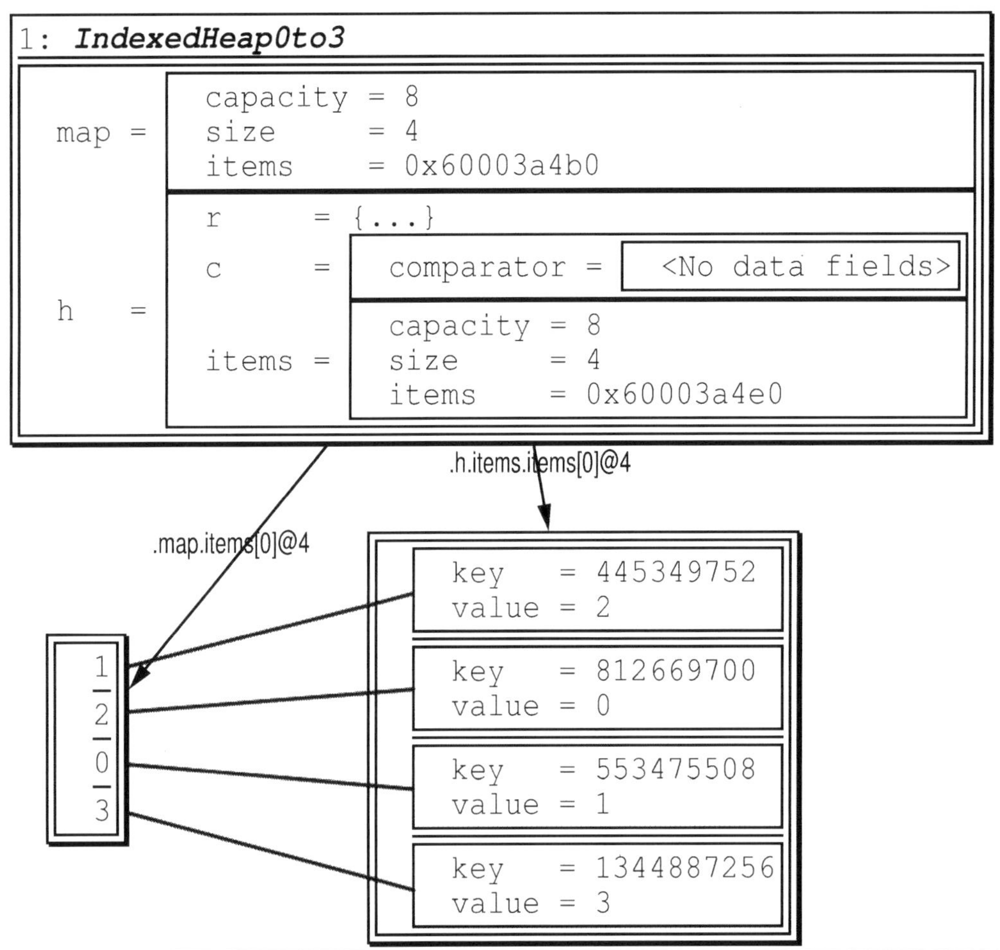


```
template<typename ITEM, typename COMPARATOR = DefaultComparator<ITEM> >
class IndexedArrayHeap
{
    Vector<int> map;
    typedef KVPair<ITEM, int> Item;
    typedef KVComparator<ITEM, int, COMPARATOR> Comparator;
    struct Reporter
    {
        Vector<int>& pmap;
        Reporter(Vector<int>& theMap): pmap(theMap) {}
        void operator()(Item& item, int i){pmap[item.value] = i;}
    };
    Heap<Item, Comparator, Reporter> h;
public:
    IndexedArrayHeap(COMPARATOR const& theComparator = COMPARATOR()):
        h(Comparator(theComparator), Reporter(map)) {}
    ITEM* find(int handle)
    {
        int pointer = map[handle];
        return pointer != -1 ? &h.items[pointer].key : 0;
    }
    bool isEmpty(){return h.isEmpty();}
    void insert(ITEM const& item, int handle)
    {
        if(handle >= map.getSize())
            for(int i = map.getSize(); i <= handle; ++i) map.append(-1);
        h.insert(Item(item, handle));
    }
    ITEM const& getMin(){return h.getMin().key;}
```

```
    ITEM deleteMin()
    {
        Item result = h.deleteMin();
        map[result.value] = -1;
        return result.key;
    }
    void changeKey(ITEM const& item, int handle)
    {
        int p = map[handle];
        if(p != -1) h.changeKey(p, Item(item, handle));
        else insert(item, handle);
    }
    void deleteKey(int handle)
    {
        h.remove(map[handle]);
        map[handle] = -1;
    }
};
```

8.3 Comments

∃ many priority queues with various properties. None are useful because binary heap is simpler, performs competitively in all cases, and uses less memory. Major alternatives:

- **Bucket queue**— for items with priorities ∈ [0, *N* – 1], it's an array of *N* linked lists, with list *i* containing the items with priority *i*, and an integer containing the smallest index of a nonempty list. E.g., can schedule tasks by giving them priorities ∈ [1, 10]. For small *N*, it's faster than a binary heap but uses much more memory.
- **Pairing heap**—uses a collection of heap-ordered pointer-based trees. Decrease key and merge take O(1) time. The problems are clumsy implementation, much higher memory use, and larger constant factors. Even more so for the better-known **Fibonacci heap** and other complex pointer-based heaps. Traditionally, these were designed as indexed heaps due to the ease of change key, but !∃ a practical need.

For a **double-ended heap** supporting insertion and deletion of both max and min, use a skip list with nonunique items. Min-max heap (Mehta & Sahni 2004) is specially designed for this and may be a little more efficient, but have the cost of implementing and maintaining it. A further generalization is a **multidimensional heap**, with items ranked by each dimension (Brass 2008). Can implement it using an indexed heap ∀coordinate, putting every item in every heap and using the indices to delete from other heaps after a delete in a particular heap.

8.4 References

Brass, P. (2008). *Advanced Data Structures*. Cambridge University Press.
Mehta, D. P. & Sahni, S. (Eds.). (2004). *Handbook of Data Structures and Applications*. CRC Press.
Mehlhorn, K. & Sanders, P. (2008). *Algorithms and Data Structures: The Basic Toolbox*. Springer.

9 Graph Algorithms

A **graph** consists of V **vertices** connected by E **edges** such that ∃ at most one edge between any two vertices, and no vertex has an edge to itself. A sequence of edges is a **path**. A graph is:

- **Sparse** if it has < $V^2/2$ edges, and **dense** otherwise. For most useful graphs, $E = O(V)$.
- **Undirected** if edges are bidirectional, and **directed** otherwise.
- **Strongly connected** if directed and ∀ vertex ∃ path to any other vertex.
- **Connected** if undirected and strongly connected. A disconnected graph consists of several connected components.
- **Acyclic** if directed and ∀ vertex !∃ a path to itself.
- A **tree** if acyclic and each vertex has at most one incoming edge.
- **Bipartite** if vertices form two groups, and !∃ edges between same-group vertices.
- **Implicit** if not represented by a data structure, and some function determines vertices, edges and data.

The below graph is directed, cyclic, not strongly connected, and sparse:

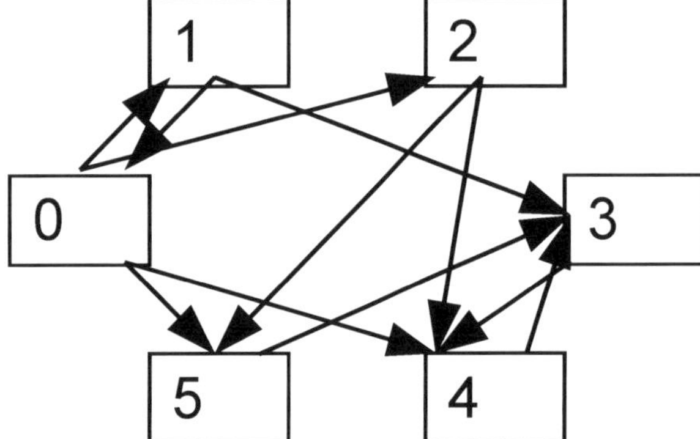

The below graph is undirected, sparse, connected, and the edge data is an implicit Euclidean distance between vertex coordinates:

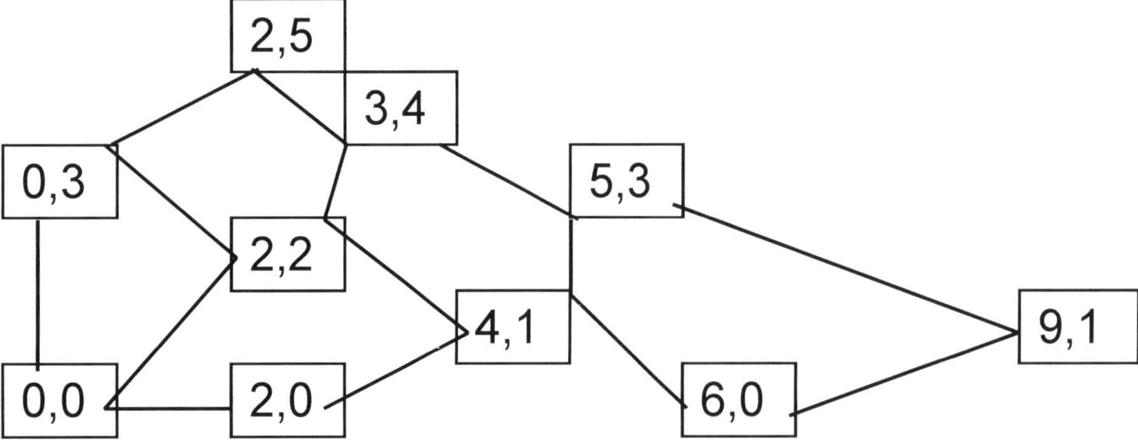

9.1 Graph Representation

A graph supports:

- Construction
- Iteration over vertices
- Iteration over edges of a vertex

Some algorithms need map operations with edges or vertices, particularly finding outgoing edges of a vertex. Any representation takes $O(V + E)$ space, unless part of the graph is implicit. A dense graph needs $O(V^2)$ bits. Undirected graphs are represented as directed, but with both edges present. Vertex data is more efficiently represented by the caller and edge data by the graph, because many graphs don't have vertex data.

A dynamic sorted sequence of vertices, each of which has its number, and a dynamic sorted sequence of outgoing vertex numbers and corresponding edge data form a data structure that efficiently supports all operations. But vector of vectors (**adjacency array**) representation has less overhead, supports incremental construction and iteration, and most algorithms use it.

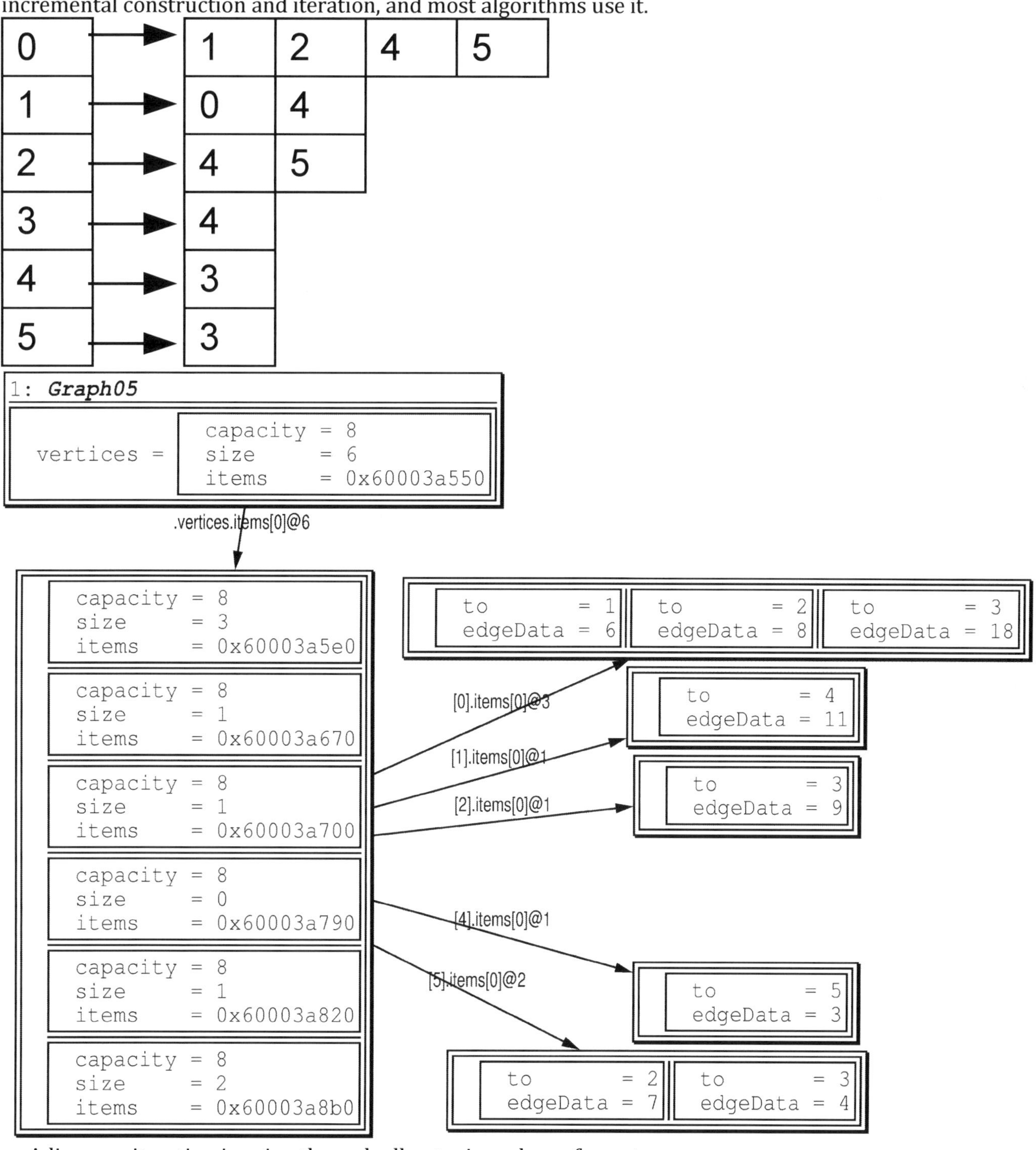

Adjacency iteration is going through all outgoing edges of a vertex.

```
template<typename EDGE_DATA> class GraphAA
{
    struct Edge
    {
        int to;
        EDGE_DATA edgeData;
        Edge(int theTo, EDGE_DATA const& theEdgeData): to(theTo),
```

```
            edgeData(theEdgeData) {}
    };
    Vector<Vector<Edge> > vertices;
public:
    GraphAA(int initialSize = 0): vertices(initialSize) {}
    int nVertices()const{return vertices.getSize();}
    int nEdges(int v)const{return vertices[v].getSize();}
    class AdjacencyIterator
    {
        Vector<Edge> const* edges;
        int j;
    public:
        AdjacencyIterator(GraphAA const& g, int v, int theJ):
            edges(&g.vertices[v]), j(theJ){}
        AdjacencyIterator& operator++()
        {
            ++j;
            return *this;
        }
        int to(){return (*edges)[j].to;}
        EDGE_DATA const& data(){return (*edges)[j].edgeData;}
        bool operator!=(AdjacencyIterator const& rhs){return j != rhs.j;}
    };
    AdjacencyIterator begin(int v)const
        {return AdjacencyIterator(*this, v, 0);}
    AdjacencyIterator end(int v)const
        {return AdjacencyIterator(*this, v, nEdges(v));}
    void addVertex(){vertices.append(Vector<Edge>());}
    void addEdge(int from, int to, EDGE_DATA const& edgeData = EDGE_DATA())
    {
        assert(to >= 0 && to < vertices.getSize());
        vertices[from].append(Edge(to, edgeData));
    }
    void addUndirectedEdge(int from, int to,
        EDGE_DATA const& edgeData = EDGE_DATA())
    {
        addEdge(from, to, edgeData);
        addEdge(to, from, edgeData);
    }
};
```

For static graphs, a more compact representation is to merge all edge arrays. It has all edges from vertex 0, then 1, etc., and the vertex array indexes into the edge array. Byte code or some other mechanism (see the "Compression" chapter) can compress this further. The vector of edges representation is useful only for storing graphs.

9.2 Search

Vertex and edge iterators allow graph traversal, but orders such as the one generated by **depth-first search** (DFS) have useful properties. Called on a source vertex, DFS iterates over its edges, recursively calling itself on every unvisited destination vertex. The traversal forms a tree with edges classified as:

- **Tree**—when visiting an unvisited vertex
- **Backward**—when backtracking from a tree edge
- **Forward**—when jumping to a visited descendant of the current vertex
- **Cross**—when jumping to a visited nondescendant of the current vertex

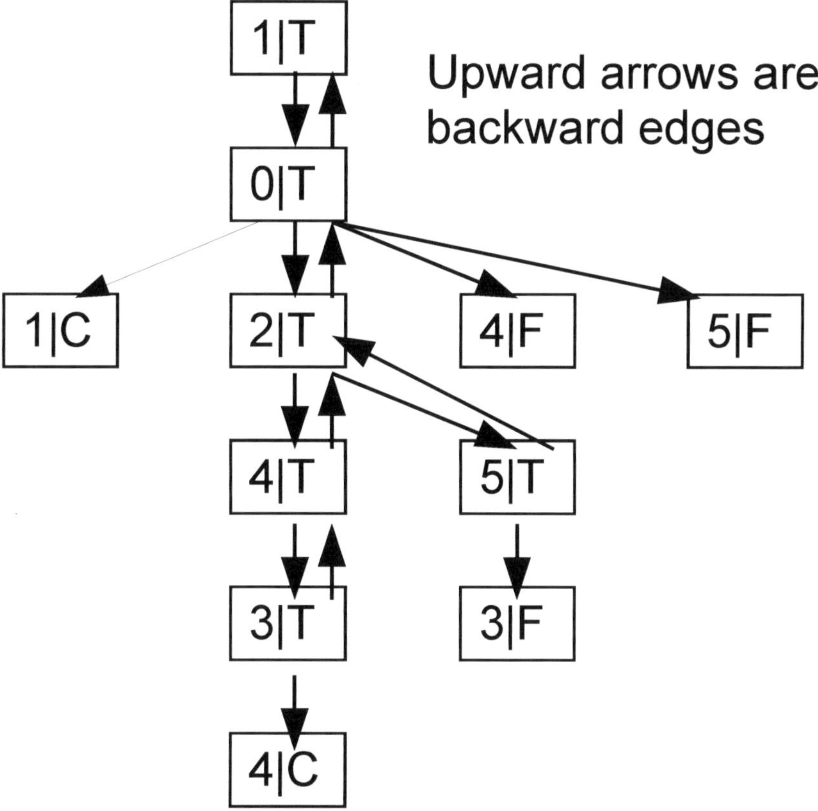

To not run out of memory for large graphs, DFS uses a stack. It pushes the current vertex and the next child to be visited and pops when taking a backward edge, calling an event point action functor when entering source or taking a tree, forward, cross, or backward edge.

```
template<typename GRAPH, typename ACTION> void DFSComponent(GRAPH const& g,
    int source, Vector<bool>& visited, ACTION& a = ACTION())
{
    Stack<int> vertexStack;
    typedef typename GRAPH::AdjacencyIterator ITER;
    Stack<ITER> nextStack;
    vertexStack.push(source);
    nextStack.push(g.begin(source));
    while(!vertexStack.isEmpty())
    {
        int v = vertexStack.getTop();
        ITER& j = nextStack.getTop();
        if(j != g.end(v))
        {
            if(visited[j.to()]) a.nonTreeEdge(j.to());
            else
            {
                a.treeEdge(j.to());
                visited[j.to()] = true;
                vertexStack.push(j.to());
                nextStack.push(g.begin(j.to()));
            }
            ++j;
        }
        else
        {
            vertexStack.pop();
            nextStack.pop();
            if(!vertexStack.isEmpty())
                a.backwardEdge(vertexStack.getTop());
```

```
        }
    }
}
```

Because a graph may be disconnected, DFS is called on each vertex. This doesn't affect correctness and the asymptotic runtime because vertices are marked visited, and a nontree action isn't called when entering the source.

```
template<typename GRAPH, typename ACTION> void DFS(GRAPH const& g,
    ACTION& a = ACTION())
{
    Vector<bool> visited(g.nVertices(), g.nVertices(), false);
    for(int i = 0; i < g.nVertices(); ++i) if(!visited[i])
    {
        a.source(i);
        visited[i] = true;
        DFSComponent(g, i, visited, a);
    }
}
```

Breadth-first search (BFS):

```
1. Enqueue the source vertex
2. Until the queue is empty
3.      Dequeue a vertex
4.      Iterate over its edges, enqueuing each
```

!∃event points because essentially the only result of BFS is the number of edges taken to reach each vertex from the source. BFS visits vertices in order of this distance from the source and sets distances when enqueuing vertices that aren't enqueued, which ensures correctness.

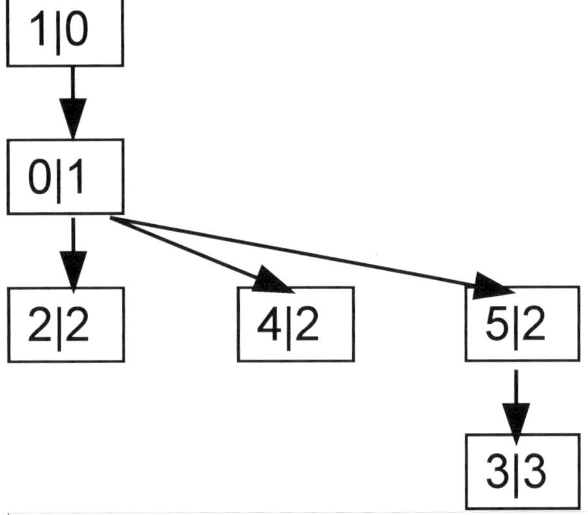


```
template<typename GRAPH> Vector<int> BFS(GRAPH& g, int source)
{
    Vector<int> distances(g.nVertices(), g.nVertices(), -1);
    Queue<int> q(g.nVertices());
    distances[source] = 0;
    q.push(source);
    while(!q.isEmpty())
    {
        int i = q.pop();
        for(typename GRAPH::AdjacencyIterator j = g.begin(i); j != g.end(i);
            ++j) if(distances[j.to()] == -1)
            {
                distances[j.to()] = distances[i] + 1;
                q.push(j.to());
            }
    }
```

```
    return distances;
}
```

BFS is useful only for exploring a single component. DFS walks a continuous path, and BFS jumps across vertices. Both take $O(V+E)$ time, assuming actions take $O(1)$ time.

9.3 Applications of Search

DFS finds **connected components** of a graph when called with a functor which adds a new component when entering source and adds any newly visited vertex to the current component.

```
struct ConnectedComponentAction
{
    Vector<Vector<int> > components;
    void source(int v)
    {
        components.append(Vector<int>());
        treeEdge(v);
    }
    void treeEdge(int v){components.lastItem().append(v);}
    void nonTreeEdge(int v){}
    void backwardEdge(int v){}
};
template<typename GRAPH>
Vector<Vector<int> > connectedComponents(GRAPH const& g)
{
    ConnectedComponentAction a;
    DFS(g, a);
    return a.components;
}
```

Topological sort of a directed acyclic graph is such that ∀vertex !∃ a path to any previous vertex. When DFS returns to a vertex and goes into its next outgoing edge, can visit the vertices on the returned path last in topological order, so assigning ranks, starting from $V-1$, to vertices when taking backward edges finds a topological sort.

A graph with a cross edge has a **cycle**. E.g., in the DFS tree drawing, the cross edges (0,1) and (3,4) correspond to cycles. If they are removed, when DFS returns to 2 from 3 and goes into 5, it assigns rank 5 to 3 and 4 to 4. Then when returning from 5 to 1, it assigns 3 to 5, 2 to 2, 1 to 0, and 0 to 1.

```
struct TopologicalSortAction
{
    int k, last;
    Vector<int> ranks;
    bool hasCycle;
    TopologicalSortAction(int nVertices): k(nVertices), last(-1),
        ranks(k, k, -1), hasCycle(false) {}
    void source(int v){treeEdge(v);}
    void treeEdge(int v){last = v;}
    void nonTreeEdge(int v){if(ranks[v] == -1) hasCycle = true;}
    void backwardEdge(int v)
    {
        if(last != -1)
        {
            ranks[last] = --k;
            last = -1;
        }
        ranks[v] = --k;
    }
};
template<typename GRAPH> Vector<int> topologicalSort(GRAPH const& g)
{//empty result means presence of cycle
    TopologicalSortAction a(g.nVertices());
```

```
    DFS(g, a);
    if(a.hasCycle) a.ranks = Vector<int>();
    return a.ranks;
}
```

DFS can generate a random maze:

1. **Start with a rectangular grid of unit-size cells with walls between any two neighboring cells and a bounding box around all cells**
2. **Represent the grid as a graph, with vertices corresponding to cells and edges to walls**
3. **Randomly permute each edge array**
4. **Starting from any vertex, run DFS that ∀tree edge erases the corresponding wall**
5. **Pick any starting and ending square, and erase the corresponding bounding box walls**

9.4 Minimum Spanning Tree

When edges hold distances between vertices they connect, a minimum spanning tree (MST) connects all vertices with $V - 1$ edges such that $\sum$edge distance is minimal.

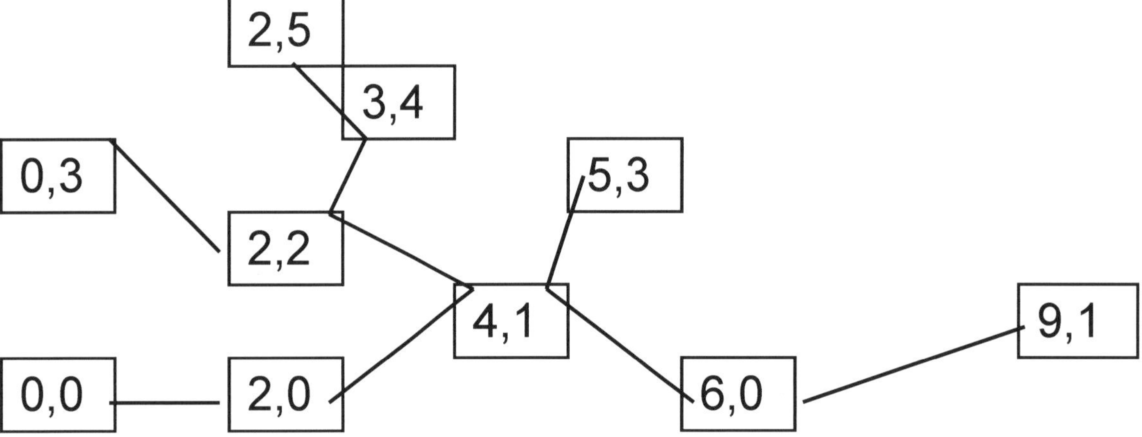

Prim's algorithm iteratively adds the vertex whose edge cost from any vertex already in the tree is minimal:

1. **Create an indexed priority queue that orders by distance from any vertex in the tree**
2. **Enqueue all vertices with priority ∞**
3. **Until the queue is empty**
4. **Dequeue a vertex**
5. **Decrease known distances to its children**

The implementation represents the result by storing the parent vertex of each vertex, with the parent of the root = −1.

```
template<typename GRAPH> Vector<int> MST(GRAPH& g)
{
    Vector<int> mst(g.nVertices(), -1);
    typedef KVPair<double, int> QNode;
    IndexedArrayHeap<QNode, KVComparator<double, int> > pQ;
    for(int i = 0; i < g.nVertices(); ++i)
        pQ.insert(QNode(numeric_limits<double>::max(), i), i);
    while(!pQ.isEmpty())
    {
        int i = pQ.deleteMin().value;
        for(typename GRAPH::AdjacencyIterator j = g.begin(i); j != g.end(i);
            ++j)
        {
            QNode* current = pQ.find(j.to());
            if(current && j.data() < current->key)
            {
                pQ.changeKey(QNode(j.data(), j.to()), j.to());
                mst[j.to()] = i;
```

```
            }
        }
    }
    return mst;
}
```

The memory use is O(V), and the runtime O(Eln(V)) due to O(E) change key operations.

9.5 Shortest Paths

When edges have associated distances between the vertices, ∃a shortest path from any vertex to any other. The distance of any vertex to itself = 0.

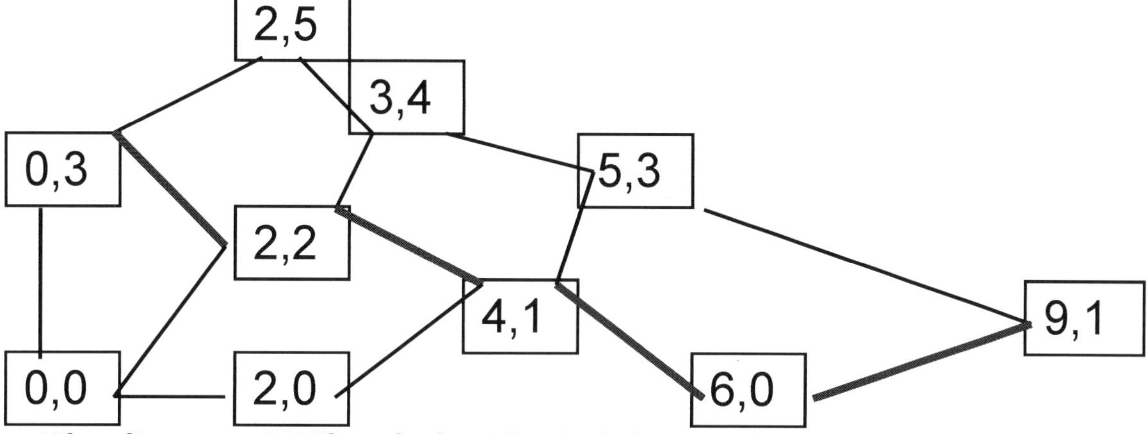

When distances ≥ 0, **Dijkstra's algorithm** finds distances from a source vertex to all others and can stop when the distance to a destination vertex is found:

1. **Create an indexed priority queue that orders by distance from the source**
2. **Put all vertices with distance ∞ and the source with distance 0**
3. **Until the queue is empty**
4. **Dequeue the next vertex**
5. **∀unprocessed destination vertex**
6. **Distance = distance to the vertex + distance(the vertex, destination) if shorter**

The result gives ∀ vertex the next vertex on the path to the source.

```
template<typename GRAPH>
Vector<int> ShortestPath(GRAPH& g, int from, int dest = -1)
{
    assert(from >= 0 && from < g.nVertices());
    Vector<int> pred(g.nVertices(), -1);
    typedef KVPair<double, int> QNode;
    IndexedArrayHeap<QNode, KVComparator<double, int> > pQ;
    for(int i = 0; i < g.nVertices(); ++i) pQ.insert(
        QNode(i == from ? 0 : numeric_limits<double>::max(), i), i);
    while(!pQ.isEmpty() && pQ.getMin().value != dest)
    {
        int i = pQ.getMin().value;
        double dj = pQ.deleteMin().key;
        for(typename GRAPH::AdjacencyIterator j = g.begin(i); j != g.end(i);
            ++j)
        {
            double newDistance = dj + j.data();
            QNode* current = pQ.find(j.to());
            if(current && newDistance < current->key)
            {
                pQ.changeKey(QNode(newDistance, j.to()), j.to());
                pred[j.to()] = i;
            }
        }
```

```
    }
    return pred;
}
```

The memory use is O(V), and the runtime O(Eln(V)) due to O(E) change key operations.

When some distances < 0, can have **negative cycles** of distance < 0, traversing which makes the total distance arbitrarily small. This happens, e.g., if ∃an arbitrage opportunity in a currency market, with possible exchanges modeled as edges. If ∃a negative cycle, shortest paths are undefined.

With distances < 0, Dijkstra's algorithm is wrong and unable to detect negative cycles. **Bellman-Ford algorithm** doesn't assume that the best distance to a vertex is known once it's processed:

```
1. Set known distances to all vertices to ∞
2. Enqueue the source vertex with distance 0
3. Until the queue is empty or a negative cycle is found
4.     Dequeue a vertex
5.     ∀destination vertex
6.         Enqueue it
7.         Distance = distance to the vertex + distance(the vertex, destination) if shorter
```

The result gives ∀ vertex the next vertex on the path to the source.

```
template<typename GRAPH> struct BellmanFord
{
    int v;
    Vector<double> distances;
    Vector<int> pred;
    bool hasNegativeCycle;
    bool findNegativeCycle()
    {
        UnionFind uf(v);
        for(int i = 0; i < v; ++i)
        {
            int p = pred[i];
            if(p != -1)
            {
                if(uf.areEquivalent(i, p)) return true;
                uf.join(i, p);
            }
        }
        return false;
    }
    BellmanFord(GRAPH& g, int from): v(g.nVertices()), pred(v, -1),
        distances(v, v, numeric_limits<double>::max()), hasNegativeCycle(false)
    {
        assert(from >= 0 && from < v);
        Vector<bool> onQ(v, 0);
        Queue<int> queue;
        int cost = 0;
        distances[from] = 0;
        onQ[from] = true;
        queue.push(from);
        do
        {
            int i = queue.pop();
            onQ[i] = false;
            for(typename GRAPH::AdjacencyIterator j = g.begin(i);
                j != g.end(i); ++j)
            {
                double newDistance = distances[i] + j.data();
                if(newDistance < distances[j.to()])
                {
```

```
                        distances[j.to()] = newDistance;
                        pred[j.to()] = i;
                        if(!onQ[j.to()])
                        {
                            queue.push(j.to());
                            onQ[j.to()] = true;
                        }
                    }
                    if(++cost % v == 0) hasNegativeCycle = findNegativeCycle();
                }
            }while(!queue.isEmpty() && !hasNegativeCycle);
    }
};
```

The negative cycle check makes sure that no vertex is its own ancestor and occurs every *V* distance updates. Using union-find, it joins each vertex with its parent. !∃a cycle if no vertex is in the same subset as its parent before they are joined because otherwise the join completes the cycle.

```
    bool findNegativeCycle()
    {
        UnionFind uf(v);
        for(int i = 0; i < v; ++i)
        {
            int p = pred[i];
            if(p != -1)
            {
                if(uf.areEquivalent(i, p)) return true;
                uf.join(i, p);
            }
        }
        return false;
    }
```

The runtime is $O(VE)$ because each edge is enqueued at most *V* times if !∃ a negative cycle, otherwise it's detected in this time (Ahuja et al. 1993). In practice, the algorithm is much faster.

9.6 Flow Algorithms

Flow is a general model of distribution and delivery of goods. Given a connected directed graph with source and sink vertices, need to find an assignment of flows to edges such that:

- Except for the source and the sink, ∑flow into a vertex = ∑flow out of it
- ∀ vertex, flow out > 0

The **max flow** problem gives each edge a capacity ≥ the flow assignment and asks to find a flow assignment maximizing ∑flow out of the source.

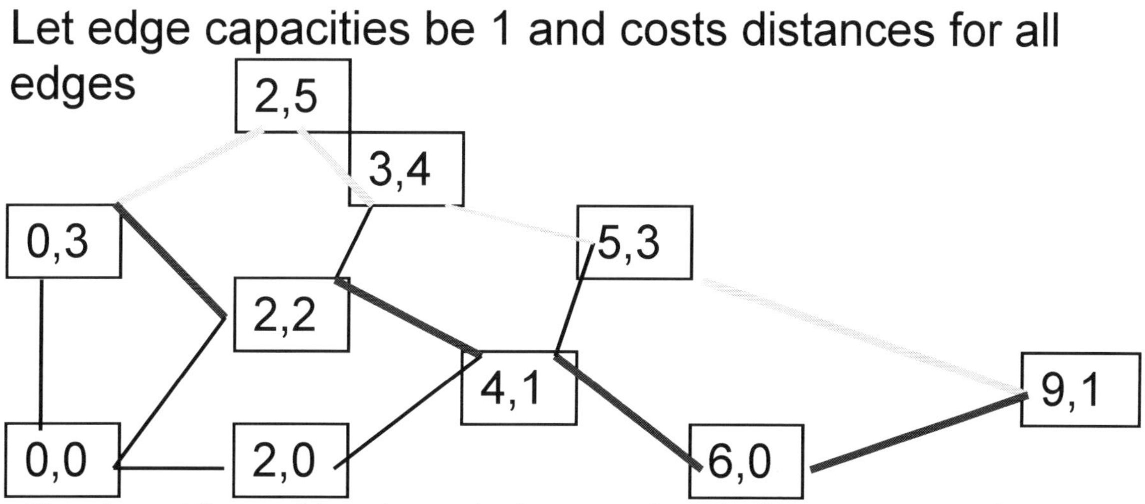

Let edge capacities be 1 and costs distances for all edges

The **min cost flow** problem gives each edge a capacity ≥ the flow assignment and a cost and asks to find max flow ≥ needed amount, such that ∑flow costs is minimal.

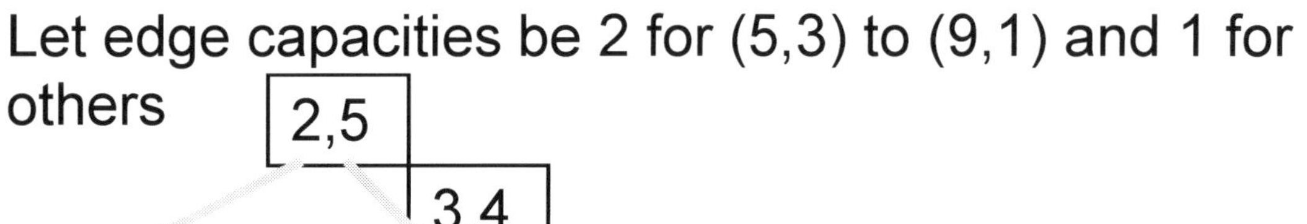

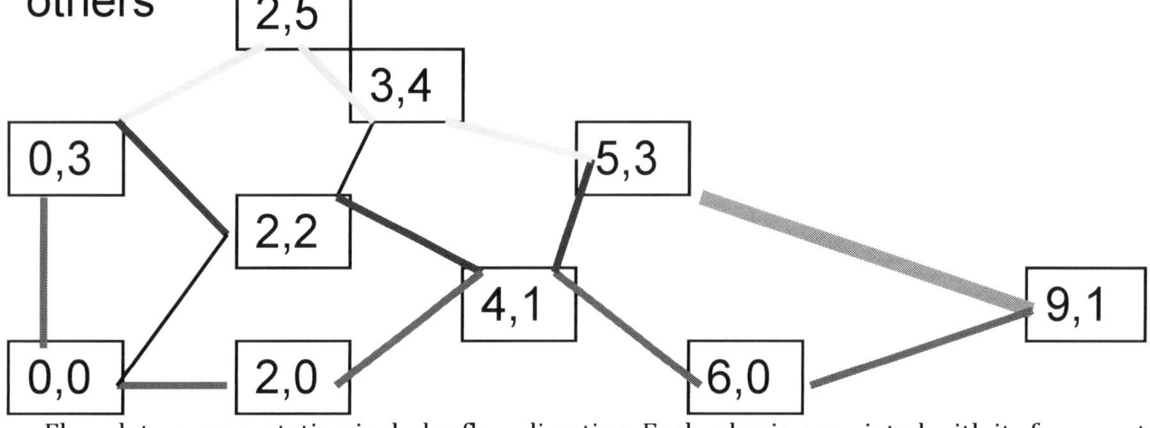

Flow data representation includes flow direction. Each edge is associated with its from-vertex. Can increase or decrease flow along an edge.

```
struct FlowData
{
    int from;
    double flow, capacity, cost;//cost used only for min flow
    FlowData(int theFrom, double theCapacity, double theCost = 0):
        from(theFrom), capacity(theCapacity), flow(0), cost(theCost) {}
    double capacityTo(int v){return v == from ? flow : capacity - flow;}
    void addFlowTo(int v, double change)
        {flow += change * (v == from ? -1 : 1);}
};
```

The **augmenting path algorithm** for max flow:

1. **Find a path from the source to the sink, using which can send flow > 0**
2. **If not found, stop**
3. **Send through the path max amount**
4. **Go to (1)**

This works for both max and min cost flow, depending on how the paths are found. The implementation sets `neededFlow` to 0 for max flow. Data structures *pred* and *path* store the edge sequence and indices of flow edges.

```
template<typename GRAPH> class ShortestAugmentingPath
{
    int v;
    Vector<int> path, pred;
public:
    double total, neededFlow;
    ShortestAugmentingPath(GRAPH& g, Vector<FlowData>& fedges, int from,
        int to, double theNeededFlow = 0): v(g.nVertices()), total(0),
        path(v, -1), pred(v, -1), neededFlow(theNeededFlow)
    {
        assert(from >= 0 && from < v && to >= 0 && to < v);
        while(neededFlow > 0 ? hasMinCostAugmentingPath(g, fedges, from, to)
            : hasAugmentingPath(g, fedges, from, to))
        {
            double increment = numeric_limits<double>::max();
            for(int j = to; j != from; j = pred[j])
                increment = min(increment, fedges[path[j]].capacityTo(j));
            if(neededFlow > 0)increment = min(increment, neededFlow - total);
            for(int j = to; j != from; j = pred[j])
                fedges[path[j]].addFlowTo(j, increment);
```

```
            total += increment;
        }
    }
};
```

Finding a path for max flow uses BFS augmented to ignore edges filled to capacity:

```
    bool hasAugmentingPath(GRAPH& g, Vector<FlowData>& fedges, int from,
        int to)
    {
        for(int i = 0; i < v; ++i) pred[i] = -1;
        Queue<int> queue;
        queue.push(pred[from] = from);
        while(!queue.isEmpty())
        {
            int i = queue.pop();
            for(typename GRAPH::AdjacencyIterator j = g.begin(i);
                j != g.end(i); ++j)
                if(pred[j.to()] == -1 &&
                    fedges[j.data()].capacityTo(j.to()) > 0)
                {
                    path[j.to()] = j.data();
                    pred[j.to()] = i;
                    queue.push(j.to());
                }
        }
        return pred[to] != -1;
    }
```

The runtime is $O(VE^2)$ because can have $O(VE)$ augmentations with BFS (Ahuja et al. 1993). In practice, the algorithm is much faster.

For min cost flow, the algorithm finds the shortest path with respect to cost and ignores full edges. The implementation builds another graph to reuse shortest path algorithms. Replace Dijkstra with Bellman-Ford if can have negative costs.

```
    bool hasMinCostAugmentingPath(GRAPH& g, Vector<FlowData>& fedges,
        int from, int to)
    {
        if(total >= neededFlow) return false;
        GraphAA<double> costGraph(v);
        for(int i = 0; i < v; ++i)
            for(typename GRAPH::AdjacencyIterator j = g.begin(i);
                j != g.end(i); ++j)
                if(fedges[j.data()].capacityTo(j.to()) > 0)
                    costGraph.addEdge(i, j.to(), fedges[j.data()].cost);
        pred = ShortestPath(costGraph, from, to);
        for(int i = to; pred[i] != -1; i = pred[i])
            for(typename GRAPH::AdjacencyIterator j = g.begin(pred[i]);
                j != g.end(pred[i]); ++j)
                if(j.to() == i) path[j.to()] = j.data();
        return pred[to] != -1;
    }
```

The algorithm is fast in practice but finds shortest paths $O(VU)$ time, where $U \geq$ any vertex outflow (Ahuja et al. 1993).

9.7 Bipartite Matching

Given two groups of vertices and a set of allowed edges, want to find a subset of the latter such that as many as possible vertices have only one edge. The matching is **perfect** if all vertices get an edge.

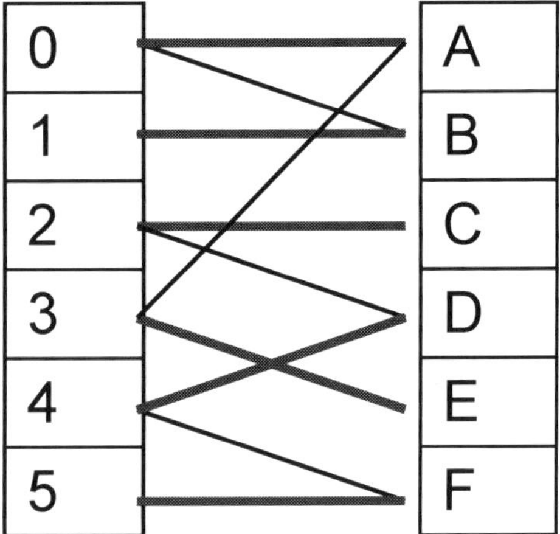

The simplest solution is reduction to max flow. Attach a source to all vertices in group one, a sink to all in group two, and give all edges capacity 1. The runtime is O(VE) (Ahuja et al. 1993).

```
Vector<pair<int, int> > bipartiteMatching(int n, int m,
    Vector<pair<int, int> > const& allowedMatches)
{//v = n + m + 2, e = n + m + allowedMatches.getSize(), time is O(ve)
    GraphAA<int> sp(n + m + 2);
    Vector<FlowData> data;
    for(int i = 0; i < allowedMatches.getSize(); ++i)
    {
        data.append(FlowData(allowedMatches[i].first, 1));
        sp.addUndirectedEdge(allowedMatches[i].first,
            allowedMatches[i].second, i);
    }
    int source = n + m, sink = source + 1;
    for(int i = 0; i < source; ++i)
    {
        int from = i, to = sink;
        if(i < n)
        {
            from = source;
            to = i;
        }
        data.append(FlowData(from, 1));
        sp.addUndirectedEdge(from, to, i + allowedMatches.getSize());
    }
    ShortestAugmentingPath<GraphAA<int> > dk(sp, data, source, sink);
    Vector<pair<int, int> > result;
    for(int i = 0; i < allowedMatches.getSize(); ++i)
        if(data[i].flow > 0) result.append(allowedMatches[i]);
    return result;
}
```

9.8 Stable Matching

When each of m "men" and n "women" has preferences, a matching is stable if no two pairs can break up because a man in one pair and a woman in the other prefer each other to their current partners. If $n \leq m$, men are choosing women, otherwise women are choosing men. Without loss of generality, $n \leq m$. Preferences for a man are an ordered list of women, and for a women equivalent ranks of men.

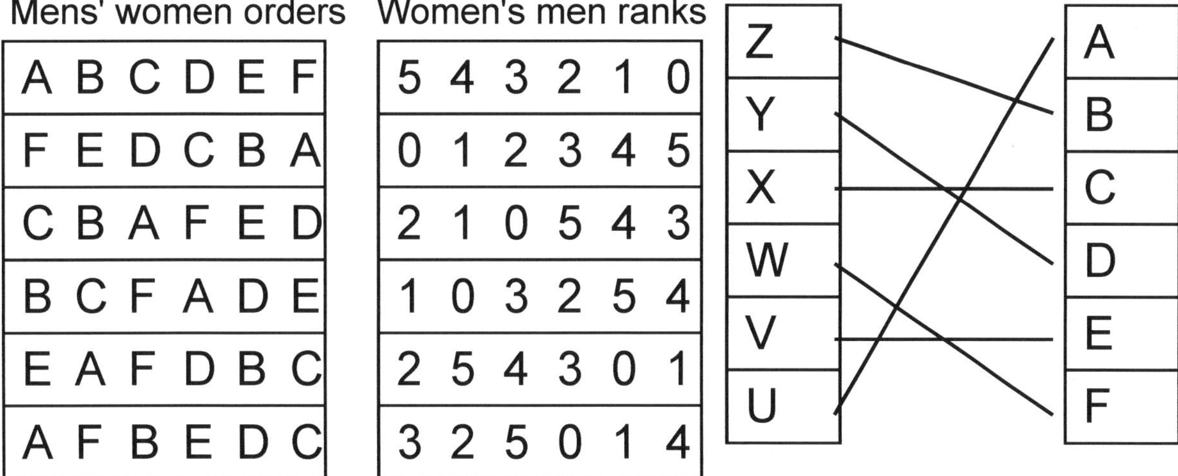

Gale-Shapley algorithm computes a stable matching iteratively:

1. **Initially, all are unassigned**
2. **Until all men are assigned**
3. **Any unassigned man proposes to the best woman to whom he hasn't proposed**
4. **She accepts him if he > her current partner and rejects otherwise**

```
Vector<int> stableMatching(Vector<Vector<int> > const& womenOrders,
    Vector<Vector<int> > const& menScores)
{
    int n = womenOrders.getSize(), m = menScores.getSize();
    assert(n <= m);
    Stack<int> unassigned;//any list type will do
    for(int i = 0; i < n; ++i) unassigned.push(i);
    Vector<int> currentMan(m, -1), nextWoman(n, 0);
    while(!unassigned.isEmpty())
    {
        int man = unassigned.pop(), woman, current;
        do//man finds best woman that prefers him to her current partner
        {
            woman = nextWoman[man]++;
            current = currentMan[woman];
        }while(current != -1 &&
            menScores[woman][man] <= menScores[woman][current]);
        if(current != -1) unassigned.push(current);
        currentMan[woman] = man;
    }
    return currentMan;
}
```

If preferences of each woman are the same, the algorithm runs fastest when men are in order of descending rank, in which case no woman chooses a different partner. Because each woman and man are paired at most once, the runtime is O(nm).

9.9 Assignment Problem

Similar to bipartite matching, but with edges having weights, and need to find a matching that minimizes $\sum$edge costs.

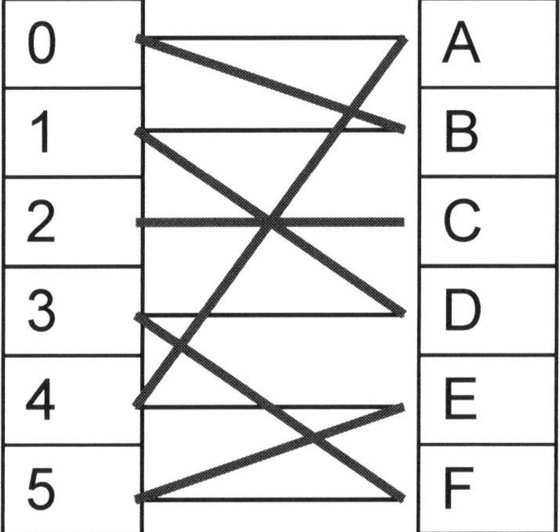

A simple solution is reduction to min cost flow. It's the same as for bipartite matching, except using weights $\neq 1$.

```
Vector<pair<int, int> > assignmentProblem(int n, int m,
    Vector<pair<pair<int, int>, double> > const& allowedMatches)
{//v = n + m + 2, e = n + m + allowedMatches.getSize()
    GraphAA<int> sp(n + m + 2);
    Vector<FlowData> data;
    for(int i = 0; i < allowedMatches.getSize(); ++i)
    {
        data.append(FlowData(allowedMatches[i].first.first, 1,
            allowedMatches[i].second));
        sp.addUndirectedEdge(allowedMatches[i].first.first,
            allowedMatches[i].first.second, i);
    }
    int source = n + m, sink = source + 1;
    for(int i = 0; i < source; ++i)
    {
        int from = i, to = sink;
        if(i < n)
        {
            from = source;
            to = i;
        }
        data.append(FlowData(from, 1, 0));
        sp.addUndirectedEdge(from, to, i + allowedMatches.getSize());
    }
    ShortestAugmentingPath<GraphAA<int> > dummy(sp, data, source, sink,
        min(n, m));
    Vector<pair<int, int> > result;
    for(int i = 0; i < allowedMatches.getSize(); ++i)
        if(data[i].flow > 0) result.append(allowedMatches[i].first);
    return result;
}
```

When using the shortest augmenting path method, the runtime is $O(V^2E)$ with Bellman-Ford (Ahuja et al. 1993).

9.10 Generating Random Graphs

Proper testing of graph algorithms needs large graphs. A generated graph should be sparse and may need to satisfy other algorithm-specific requirements.

A simple method is to create an edge between two vertices with probability p. But E[the space use of the result] = $O(pV^2)$. A useful model is to have a directed graph with k outgoing edges per vertex:

```
template<typename GRAPH>
GRAPH randomDirectedGraph(int vertices, int edgesPerVertex)
{
    assert(edgesPerVertex <= vertices);
    GRAPH g(vertices);
    for(int i = 0; i < vertices; ++i)
    {
        Vector<int> edges = GlobalRNG.sortedSample(edgesPerVertex, vertices);
        for(int j = 0; j < edgesPerVertex; ++j) g.addEdge(i, edges[i]);
    }
    return g;
}
```

Another useful model is generating n points in the unit square and creating a graph that connects each vertex to its k nearest neighbors or to all points within some distance, but these are less efficient. Batagelj & Brandes (2005) give efficient generators for various models.

9.11 Comments

For finding an MST, **Kruskal's algorithm** sorts edges by distance and iteratively adds the next shortest edge that connects two not-yet-connected components, found using union-find. But it needs $O(E)$ memory and doesn't work directly with adjacency array.

Dijkstra's algorithm can also find a shortest path with the shortest longest edge by using max(distance to the vertex, distance(the vertex, child)) instead of distance to the vertex + distance(the vertex, child).

For finding shortest paths in very large graphs, preprocessing gives huge speedups for queries. Google **contraction hierarchies** if curious. A different model is finding several shortest paths of good quality, so that users can pick the best according to their needs. Finding several different shortest paths isn't useful because they tend to be very similar. A useful model sets required edge alternatives or defines several distance functions using, e.g., travel time, fuel costs, number of transfers, etc., solving for each.

Fastest known flow algorithms use more complicated optimized **push-relabel** techniques (Ahuja et al. 1993).

9.12 References

Ahuja, R. K., Magnanti, T. L., & Orlin, J. B. (1993). *Network Flows: Theory, Algorithms, and Applications*. MIT Press.
Batagelj, V., & Brandes, U. (2005). Efficient generation of large random networks. *Physical Review E*, *71*(3), 036113.
Heineman, G. T., Pollice, G., & Selkow, S. (2016). *Algorithms in a Nutshell*. O'Reilly.
Mehlhorn, K., & Sanders, P. (2008). *Algorithms and Data Structures: The Basic Toolbox*. Springer.
Sedgewick, R., & Wayne, K. (2011). *Algorithms*. Addison-Wesley.

10 External Memory Algorithms

10.1 Disks and Files

A **disk drive** is a slow-to-access persistent memory. Technologies differ, but in all cases:

- Random access called **seek** is supported
- Writing is negligibly or substantially slower than reading
- Reading and writing contiguous bytes is orders of magnitude faster than accessing one byte at a time
- Both seeking and **data transfer** are costly, and data transfer is costlier
- Need to read data into internal memory to work on it

Logically, a **file** is an array of bytes. In C++, a file is a dynamic array that remembers the last accessed index and increments it after an I/O. The OS handles the dynamic aspect. The implementation uses a subset of the C++ file API that implements such abstraction:

```
class File
{
    fstream file;
    void goToEnd(){file.seekg(0, ios::end);}
    void create(const char* filename){ofstream dummy(filename, ios::trunc);}
public:
    static bool exists(const char* filename){return ifstream(filename);}
    static int remove(const char* filename){return std::remove(filename);}
    File(const char* filename, bool truncate)
    {
        if(truncate || !exists(filename)) create(filename);
        file.open(filename, ios::binary | ios::in | ios::out);
        assert(file);
    }
    long long getPosition(){return file.tellg();}
    long long getSize()
    {
        long long current = getPosition();
        goToEnd();
        long long length = getPosition();
        file.seekg(current);
        return length;
    }
    long long bytesLeft(){return getSize() - getPosition();}
    void setPosition(long long position)
    {
        assert(0 <= position && position <= getSize());
        file.seekg(position);
    }
    void read(char* buffer, long long size)
    {
        assert(size <= bytesLeft());
        file.read(buffer, size);
    }
    void write(char* buffer, long long size)
    {
        file.write(buffer, size);
        file.flush();
```

```
    }
    void append(char* buffer, long long size)
    {
        goToEnd();
        write(buffer, size);
    }
};
```

Beware:

- The OS limits the number of files open by a single executable, so close unneeded files.
- C++ `fstream` fails to open a file for writing if its permissions don't allow writes.
- The random access pointer of the read stream is a get pointer, and of the write stream a put pointer. In `fstream`, they are the same because a single buffer is used, and can use either set of accessors. But must flush after every write if both reading and writing because otherwise the behavior of a read after a write is undefined.

Using external memory gives:

- **Persistence**—any external memory data structure is stored on disk after the computation
- Increased memory—for applications working with massive data, !∃enough internal memory

External memory algorithms are all about efficiency because not working with contiguous data gives orders-of-magnitude slowdowns. The most common use case of reading a file, doing the computation in memory, and writing the result to another file is the most efficient way to process a file. But in many cases, e.g., for databases, need to work on only a small part of a huge file.

10.2 File Layout

Serialization is converting a data structure into a byte sequence. Assuming a single file holds the entire data structure, the following layout patterns can represent every data structure:

- Integers representing offsets from the beginning of a file act as pointers.
- Items and arrays have known fixed or stored variable length.
- Split a file into a variable-length part and a fixed-length item array part to ensure fast contiguous operations.
- Use a fixed-length header to specify file format, check sums, permissions, and other useful data.
- Use JSON- or XML-like encoding to make complex data structure representation human-readable. Binary and text files are equivalent when using only printable characters.
- To avoid issues with portability due to existence of big- and little-endian systems, each of which views bytes of an integer in different order, represent integers using byte or reinterpret code (see the "Compression" chapter). When designing a file format, specify each byte logically. The algorithms in this chapter ignore this for simplicity.

E.g., might have *|HEADER|LENGTH|{JSON_VAR: VAL1, JSON_ARR: [VAL2, VAL3]}|*.

10.3 I/O Model

The I/O model models speedups of accessing contiguous data. This is similar to transporting a shopping cart of food from the supermarket to your fridge, instead of item by item.

- Seek times cost 0 because they are done only before the slower data transfer.
- The read cost = the write cost. This is true for magnetic disks but not for flash or SSD.
- Data is transferred in blocks of size ≤ B, with B picked so that increasing it gives no further speedup. Each transfer is an I/O.
- Disk size is unlimited, and memory size is M, which is much larger than B.
- Internal memory operations cost 0 because I/Os are orders of magnitude slower.

The model also holds when disk is memory and memory cache, except for the constant factors and that can't ignore operations inside the cache. The assumptions lead to the number of I/Os lower bounds for several important tasks (Dementiev 2008):

- Scanning—$O(n/B)$
- Map operations—$O(\log_B(n))$

- Sorting—$O((n/B)\log_{M/B}(n/B))$
- Priority queue—amortized $O(\log_{M/B}(n/B))$ per insert/delete

Though the I/O model is generally accurate:

- Disks have large fast caches.
- Seeks can dominate the runtime if doing many more seeks than I/Os.
- The OS may allocate large files in blocks of size < B. The size can be as small as 512 bytes, and adjacent blocks needn't be contiguous, which effectively reduces B to the block size, so many databases use raw file systems. The minimum file system chunk size is the smallest possible file size. Increasing it speeds up access but wastes space because most files are tiny. In C++, the block size is `BUFSIZ` from `<cstdio>`. It's also the size of a single-character text file.
- Internal memory computation can be the bottleneck.

Absent other information, set B to 2048 or 4096. Many algorithms such as B-tree (covered later in this chapter) need $O(B)$ internal memory work, so B can't be too large. A file layout that supports the I/O model is a variable-length vector of blocks of large fixed size. Data structures using it encode any configuration data into some items or use a separate variable-length file.

```
class BlockFile
{
    File file;
    int blockSize, size;
    void setBlock(long long blockId){file.setPosition(blockId * blockSize);}
public:
    long long getBlockSize(){return blockSize;}
    BlockFile(string const& filename, int theBlockSize):
        file(filename.c_str(), false), blockSize(theBlockSize),
        size(file.getSize()/blockSize) {}
    void appendEmptyBlock()
    {
        ++size;
        Vector<char> block(blockSize, 0);
        file.append(block.getArray(), blockSize);
    }
    void writeBlock(long long blockId, Vector<char>const& block)
    {
        assert(0 <= blockId && blockId < getSize() &&
            block.getSize() == blockSize);
        setBlock(blockId);
        file.write(block.getArray(), blockSize);
    }
    long long getSize(){return size;}
    void readBlock(long long blockId, Vector<char>& block)
    {
        assert(0 <= blockId && blockId < getSize() &&
            block.getSize() == blockSize);
        setBlock(blockId);
        file.read(block.getArray(), blockSize);
    }
};
```

To use D concurrently accessible disks, make a superblock of size DB, and work with D subblocks in parallel. Usually, some controller or indirection layer handles this **RAID0** configuration and appears as a single disk to the application. Particular algorithms may be more efficient accessing all disks directly, but the speedup is usually minor and not worth the complexity increase.

When B is unknown, the I/O model is the **cache-oblivious model**. An algorithm is cache-oblivious if it has an $O(1)$ factor slowdown relative to an optimal algorithm that knows B. For this to work, the model assumes that the OS transfers data in optimal-size blocks. Major building blocks:

- Scanning an array sequentially takes the optimal n/B I/Os.
- Divide and conquer splitting eventually gets down to a block size < B. E.g., mergesort and quicksort

are cache-oblivious, taking $O((n/B)\lg(n/B))$ I/Os.

Though cache-friendliness is important, cache-oblivious algorithms aren't worth implementing:

- Constant factors lost due to not knowing B are large
- When disk is memory, the gains are minor because caches are large, constant factor differences small, and the OS task scheduler evicts cached data
- They are usually complicated

10.4 Internal Memory Caches

Any operation that must read data makes ≥ 1 I/O, so it's important to use internal memory effectively without using too much of it. For a block file, the simplest cache strategy is to keep the current block in memory:

```
class SingleBlockBuffer
{
    BlockFile& blockFile;
    Vector<char> block;
    long long loadedBlock;
    bool changed;
    void flush()
    {
        if(changed) blockFile.writeBlock(loadedBlock, block);
        changed = false;
    }
    void loadBlock(long long blockId)
    {
        if(blockId != loadedBlock)
        {
            flush();
            blockFile.readBlock(blockId, block);
            loadedBlock = blockId;
        }
    }
public:
    SingleBlockBuffer(BlockFile& theBlockFile): changed(false),
        loadedBlock(-1), blockFile(theBlockFile),
        block(blockFile.getBlockSize(), 0) {}
    ~SingleBlockBuffer(){flush();}
    void get(char* data, long long blockId, int start, int n)
    {
        loadBlock(blockId);
        for(int i = 0; i < n; ++i) data[i] = block[start + i];
    }
    void set(char* data, long long blockId, int start, int n)
    {
        loadBlock(blockId);
        for(int i = 0; i < n; ++i) block[start + i] = data[i];
        changed = true;
    }
};
```

An asymptotically optimal strategy keeps a buffer of several least recently used blocks using a LRU cache (see the "Miscellaneous Algorithms" chapter). Need to check if any evicted block has changes and flush it to the disk.

```
class LRUBlockBuffer
{
    typedef pair<Vector<char>, bool> ITEM;//bool is changed flag
    BlockFile& blockFile;
    LRUCache<ITEM, long long> blocks;
    ITEM* loadBlock(long long blockId)
```

```
    {
        ITEM* item = blocks.read(blockId);
        if(!item)
        {
            long long* evictee = blocks.evicteeOnWrite(blockId);
            if(evictee)
            {
                ITEM* evicteeItem = blocks.read(*evictee);
                if(evicteeItem->second) flushWork(evicteeItem, *evictee);
            }
            Vector<char> block(blockFile.getBlockSize(), 0);
            blockFile.readBlock(blockId, block);
            blocks.write(blockId, make_pair(block, false));
            item = blocks.read(blockId);
        }
        return item;
    }
    void flushWork(ITEM* item, long long blockId)
    {
        if(item->second)
        {
            blockFile.writeBlock(blockId, item->first);
            item->second = false;
        }
    }
public:
    LRUBlockBuffer(BlockFile& theBlockFile, int cacheSize = 5):
        blocks(cacheSize), blockFile(theBlockFile) {}
    ~LRUBlockBuffer()
    {
        for(LRUCache<ITEM, long long>::Iterator i = blocks.begin();
            i != blocks.end(); ++i) flushWork(&i->value, i->key);
    }
    void get(char* data, long long blockId, int start, int n)
    {
        ITEM* item = loadBlock(blockId);
        for(int i = 0; i < n; ++i) data[i] = item->first[start + i];
    }
    void set(char* data, long long blockId, int start, int n)
    {
        ITEM* item = loadBlock(blockId);
        for(int i = 0; i < n; ++i) item->first[start + i] = data[i];
        item->second = true;
    }
};
```

Both strategies need ≤ 1 I/O per operation. Beware:

- External memory data structures can contain only POD items without constructors or destructors.
- Cache item references invalidate when the corresponding blocks are replaced, which can happen in the same line of code. E.g., for an external memory vector *v* with a single block buffer, `v[i] = v[j]` assigns to a dead reference if `v[i]` gets it, and `v[j]` causes block replacement. So accessors can't safely return items by reference. This can also happen in recursion, with child calls invalidating references of the parent calls.

10.5 External Memory Vector

Want to implement vector operations, but with data stored on the disk. For efficiency, partition items in blocks and load an entire block to memory when needed, using user-specified buffer strategy. To handle blocks at the end of the file that aren't full, return the number of extra items that can fit without increasing the file length, and write it to a separate configuration file, or store the size externally. Some differences from in-memory vector:

- Append doesn't double but allocates another block when needed because the I/O cost is same.
- Have get and set methods because can't return by reference.
- Remove only decreases internal size without reducing memory use due to lack of API support for that. Users can do so on their own by rebuilding.
- Need a file name to work with; this allows persistence.

E.g., with B = 16 bytes (4 `int`s), after inserting integers 0 to 9, the last two (8 and 9) will be part of the last block, and its other items will be garbage:

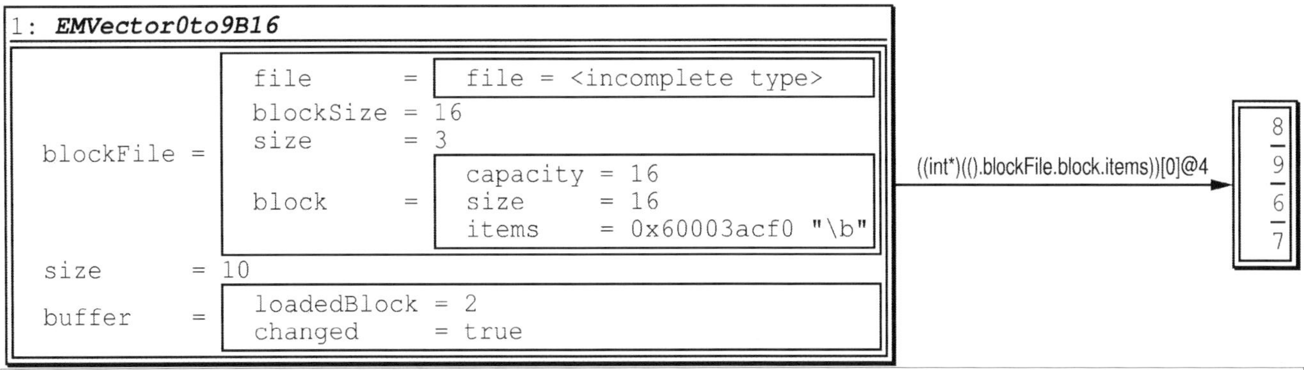

```
1: EMVector0to9B16
blockFile = file      = file = <incomplete type>
            blockSize = 16
            size      = 3
            block     = capacity = 16
                        size     = 16
                        items    = 0x60003acf0 "\b"
size      = 10
buffer    = loadedBlock = 2
            changed     = true

((int*)(().blockFile.block.items))[0]@4 -> 8 | 9 | 6 | 7
```

```
template<typename POD, typename BUFFER = SingleBlockBuffer> class EMVector
{
    BlockFile blockFile;
    long long size;
    int itemsPerBlock(){return blockFile.getBlockSize()/sizeof(POD);}
    long long block(long long i){return i/itemsPerBlock();}
    long long index(long long i){return i % itemsPerBlock();}
    BUFFER buffer;
public:
    long long getSize(){return size;}
    EMVector(string const&filename, int blockSize = 2048, int extraItems = 0)
        : buffer(blockFile), blockFile(filename, blockSize),
        size(blockFile.getSize() * itemsPerBlock() - extraItems)
        {assert(blockSize % sizeof(POD) == 0);}
    long long extraItems()
        {return blockFile.getSize() * itemsPerBlock() - size;}
    void append(POD const& item)
    {
        ++size;
        if(extraItems() < 0) blockFile.appendEmptyBlock();
        set(item, size - 1);
    }
    void set(POD const& item, long long i)
    {
        assert(i >= 0 && i < size);
        char* data = (char*)&item;
        buffer.set(data, block(i), index(i) * sizeof(POD), sizeof(POD));
    }
    POD operator[](long long i)
    {
        assert(i >= 0 && i < size);
        POD result;
        char* data = (char*)&result;
        buffer.get(data, block(i), index(i) * sizeof(POD), sizeof(POD));
        return result;
    }
    void removeLast()
```

```
    {
        assert(size > 0);
        --size;
    }
};
```

Due to caching, random access takes $1/B$ and 1 I/Os for respectively contiguous and random locations.

10.6 Sorting

A simple way to sort efficiently:

1. **Divide the vector into Q chunks of C items each, except for the last one**
2. **Sort each in internal memory, and write the result to a temporary file**
3. **Create Q buffers of size B and a priority queue containing the smallest item from each chunk and the chunk's number**
4. **While the queue isn't empty**
5. **Write the dequeued item to the vector**
6. **Put the smallest remaining item from the written item's buffer into the queue, refilling the buffer if it's empty, and the chunk has more items**

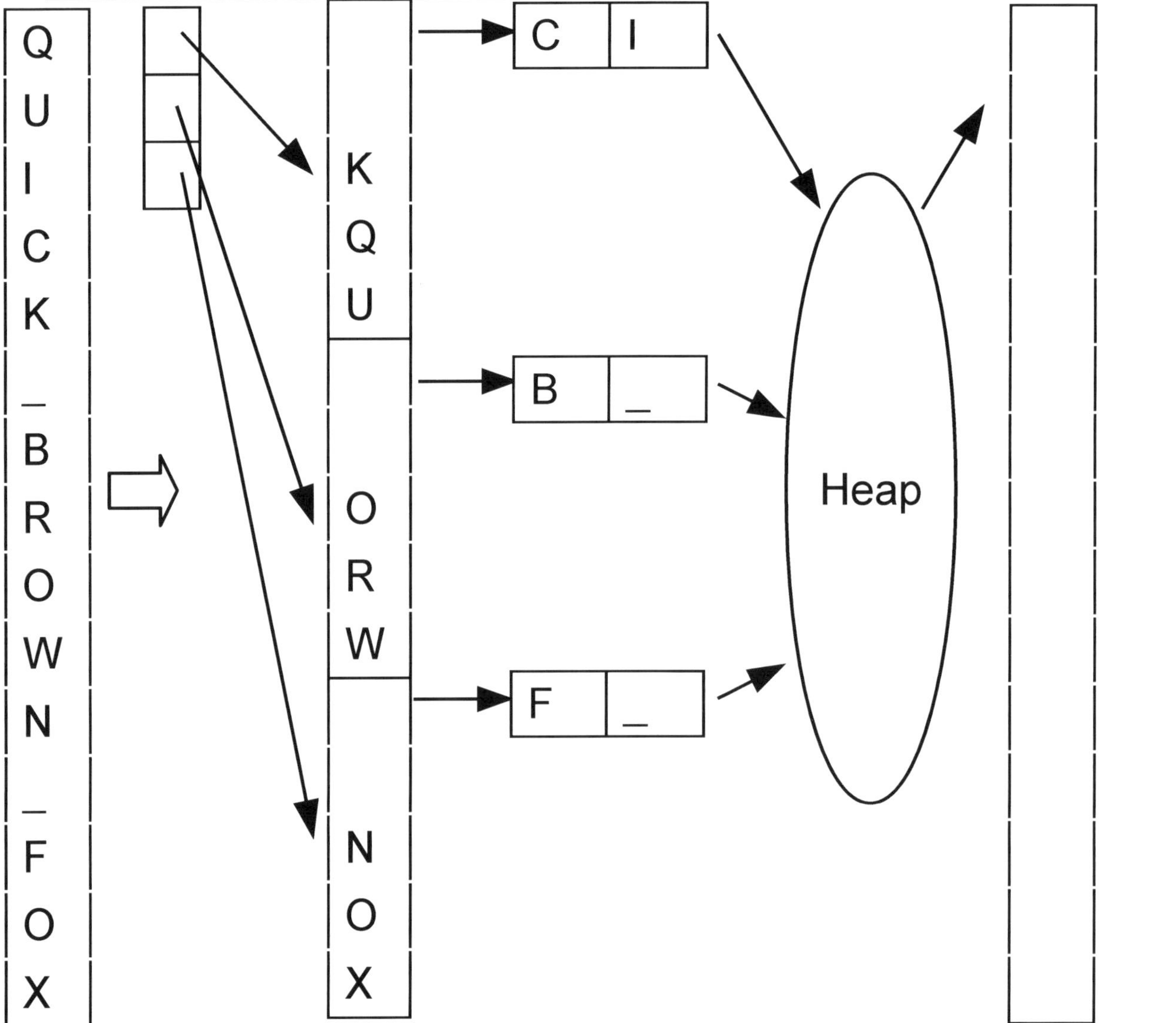

With p items per block, must have enough internal memory for C items during sorting and pQ items during merging. So $C = \sqrt{np}$, and $Q = n/C$ minimizes internal memory use.

```
    friend void IOSort(EMVector& vector)
    {
        {
```

```
        long long C = sqrt(vector.getSize() * vector.itemsPerBlock()),
            Q = vector.getSize()/C, lastQSize = vector.getSize() % C;
        EMVector temp("IOSortTempFile.igmdk");
        typedef KVPair<POD, long long> HeapItem;
        Heap<HeapItem, KVComparator<POD, long long> > merger;
        Vector<pair<Queue<POD>, long long> > buffers(Q + 1);
        for(long long i = 0, k = 0; i < Q + 1; ++i)
        {
            long long n = i == Q ? lastQSize : C;
            if(n > 0)
            {//sort each block and write the result to a temp vector
                Vector<POD> buffer;
                for(long long j = 0; j < n; ++j)
                    buffer.append(vector[k++]);
                quickSort(buffer.getArray(), 0, buffer.getSize() - 1);
                for(long long j = 0; j < n; ++j) temp.append(buffer[j]);
                //record number of unmerged items in the block
                buffers[i].second = n - 1;
                //put smallest item of each block on the heap
                merger.insert(HeapItem(temp[i * n], i));
            }
        }
        for(long long i = 0; i < vector.getSize(); ++i)
        {//merge
            long long q = merger.getMin().value;
            vector.set(merger.deleteMin().key, i);
            bool bufferIsEmpty = buffers[q].first.isEmpty();
            if(!bufferIsEmpty || buffers[q].second > 0)
            {
                if(bufferIsEmpty)
                {//refill
                    long long j = 0, next = q * C +
                        (q == Q ? lastQSize : C) - buffers[q].second;
                    while(j < vector.itemsPerBlock() &&
                        buffers[q].second-- > 0)
                        buffers[q].first.push(temp[next + j++]);
                }
                merger.insert(HeapItem(buffers[q].first.pop(), q));
            }
        }
    }
    File::remove("IOSortTempFile.igmdk");
}
```

The algorithm needs $O(n/B)$ I/Os. If don't have enough internal memory, merge the sorted chunks with each other in a mergesort-like process until Q is small enough to begin the heap merge.

10.7 Vector-based Data Structures

Many data structures are implemented I/O-optimally using vector:

- Stack—beware that a push/pop sequence on a block boundary causes 1 I/O per operation. Using size 2 LRU buffer leads to the optimal amortized $1/B$ I/Os per operation.
- Free list—one vector contains the nodes and another indices of returned nodes.
- Queue—use doubling on a circular queue, avoiding temporaries after doubling by copying the first half into the second.

10.8 B+ Tree

A B+ tree is a dynamic sorted sequence where the leaves hold values and the internal nodes keys. For many database uses, keys are small and values huge, so the separation improves efficiency and allows linking leaves for iteration. Keys for some nodes appear in the tree several times, but in total the internal nodes have fewer keys than external nodes.

An internal node has a size and M (key, I/O pointer) pairs. M is even, ≥ 4, and such that its byte size $\approx B$. A node of size k generalizes binary tree node and has k pointers and $k - 1$ keys, where pointer$_i$ points to the node with keys < key$_i$, and pointer$_{i+1}$ to the node with keys $\geq$ key$_i$. The pair $k - 1$ only has a pointer. Search inside an internal node finds the pointer to the next node according to this definition. A leaf has a sorted array of items of size L. L is such that the node's byte size $\approx B$, ≥ 2, and even.

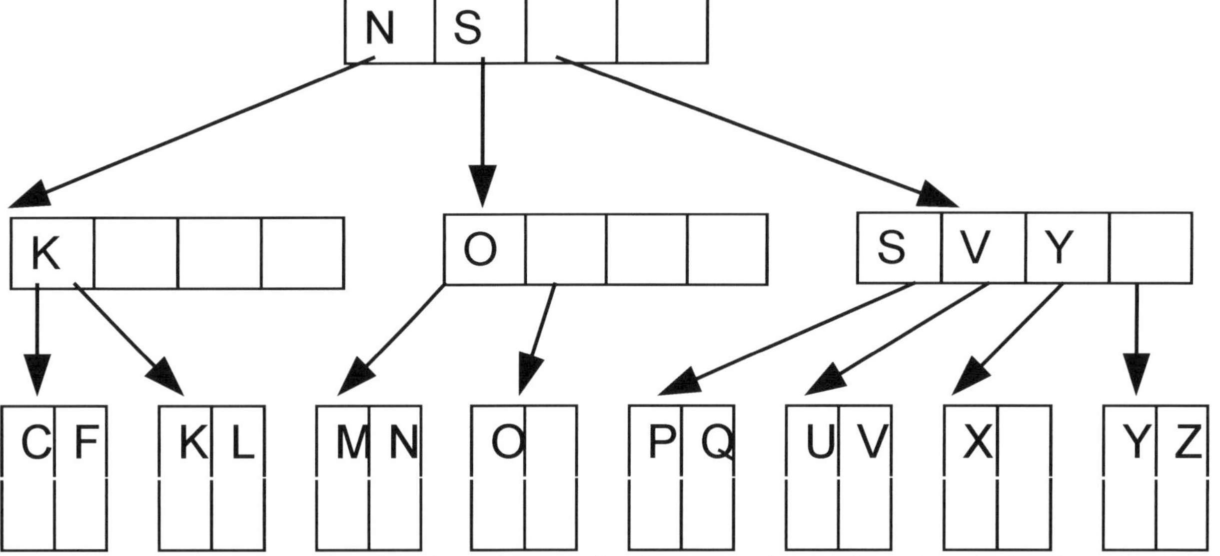

To save space, use a convention that −1 is a null pointer, numbers ≥ 0 are internal node pointers, and numbers < −1 leaf pointers. The leaves supports inclusive successor of a key, and internal nodes finding index of a key. Use linear search for both.

```
template<typename KEY, typename ITEM> class EMBPlusTree
{
    enum{NULL_IO_POINTER = -1};
    typedef KVPair<KEY, long long> Key;
    typedef KVPair<KEY, ITEM> Record;
    enum{B = 2048, M = 2 * (2 + B/2/sizeof(Key)),
        L = 2 * (1 + B/2/sizeof(Record))};
    struct Node
    {//last item contains only a pointer, the first M - 1 items contain data
        int size;
        Key next[M];
        Node(): size(1) {next[0].value = NULL_IO_POINTER;}
        int findChild(KEY const& key)
        {
            int i = 0;
            while(i < size - 1 && key >= next[i].key) ++i;
            return i;
        }
    };
    struct Leaf
    {
        int size;
        long long next;
        Record records[L];
        Leaf(): size(0), next(NULL_IO_POINTER) {}
        int inclusiveSuccessorRecord(KEY const& key)
        {
            int i = 0;
            while(i < size && key > records[i].key) ++i;
```

```
            return i;
        }
    };
    long long leafIndex(long long index){return -(index + 2);}
    long long root;
    EMVector<Node> nodes;
    EMVector<Leaf> leaves;
    void splitInternal(long long index, int child)
    {
        Node parent = nodes[index];
        long long childIndex = parent.next[child].value;
        Node left = nodes[childIndex], right;
        //copy middle item key into parent
        for(int i = parent.size++; i > child; --i)
            parent.next[i] = parent.next[i - 1];
        parent.next[child].key = left.next[M/2 - 1].key;
        parent.next[child + 1].value = nodes.getSize();
        //move items starting from middle into right
        right.size = M/2 + 1;
        for(int i = 0; i < right.size; ++i)
            right.next[i] = left.next[i + M/2 - 1];
        left.size = M/2;
        nodes.append(right);
        nodes.set(left, childIndex);
        nodes.set(parent, index);
    }
    void splitLeaf(long long index, int child)
    {
        Node parent = nodes[index];
        long long childIndex = parent.next[child].value;
        Leaf left = leaves[leafIndex(childIndex)], right;
        //copy middle item key into parent
        for(int i = parent.size++; i > child; --i)
            parent.next[i] = parent.next[i - 1];
        parent.next[child].key = left.records[L/2].key;
        parent.next[child + 1].value = leafIndex(leaves.getSize());
        //move items starting from middle into right
        left.size = right.size = L/2;
        for(int i = 0; i < right.size; ++i)
            right.records[i] = left.records[i + L/2];
        right.next = left.next;
        left.next = leaves.getSize();
        leaves.append(right);
        leaves.set(left, leafIndex(childIndex));
        nodes.set(parent, index);
    }
public:
    EMBPlusTree(string const& keyFilename, string const& recordFilename,
        long long storedRoot = NULL_IO_POINTER, int extraItemsKey = 0,
        int extraItemsRecord = 0): root(storedRoot),
        nodes(keyFilename, sizeof(Node), extraItemsKey),
        leaves(recordFilename, sizeof(Leaf), extraItemsRecord) {}
    long long getRoot(){return root;}
};
```

Find uses the internal node invariant to find the leaf containing the value and searches it:

```
    long long findLeaf(KEY const& key)
    {
        long long current = root;
        while(current >= 0)
```

```
        {
            Node node = nodes[current];
            current = node.next[node.findChild(key)].value;
        }
        return current;
    }
    ITEM find(KEY const& key, bool& status)
    {
        status = true;
        long long current = findLeaf(key);
        if(current != NULL_IO_POINTER)
        {
            Leaf leaf = leaves[leafIndex(current)];
            int i = leaf.inclusiveSuccessorRecord(key);
            if(i < leaf.size && key == leaf.records[i].key)
                return leaf.records[i].value;
        }
        status = false;
    }
```

Insert balances using splits. When a node is full, and its parent isn't:

1. **Put the right half of the keys in the node in a new node**
2. **Insert a pointer to the new node into the parent after the pointer to the node**
3. **Copy the middle key to the parent, and move it to the new node**

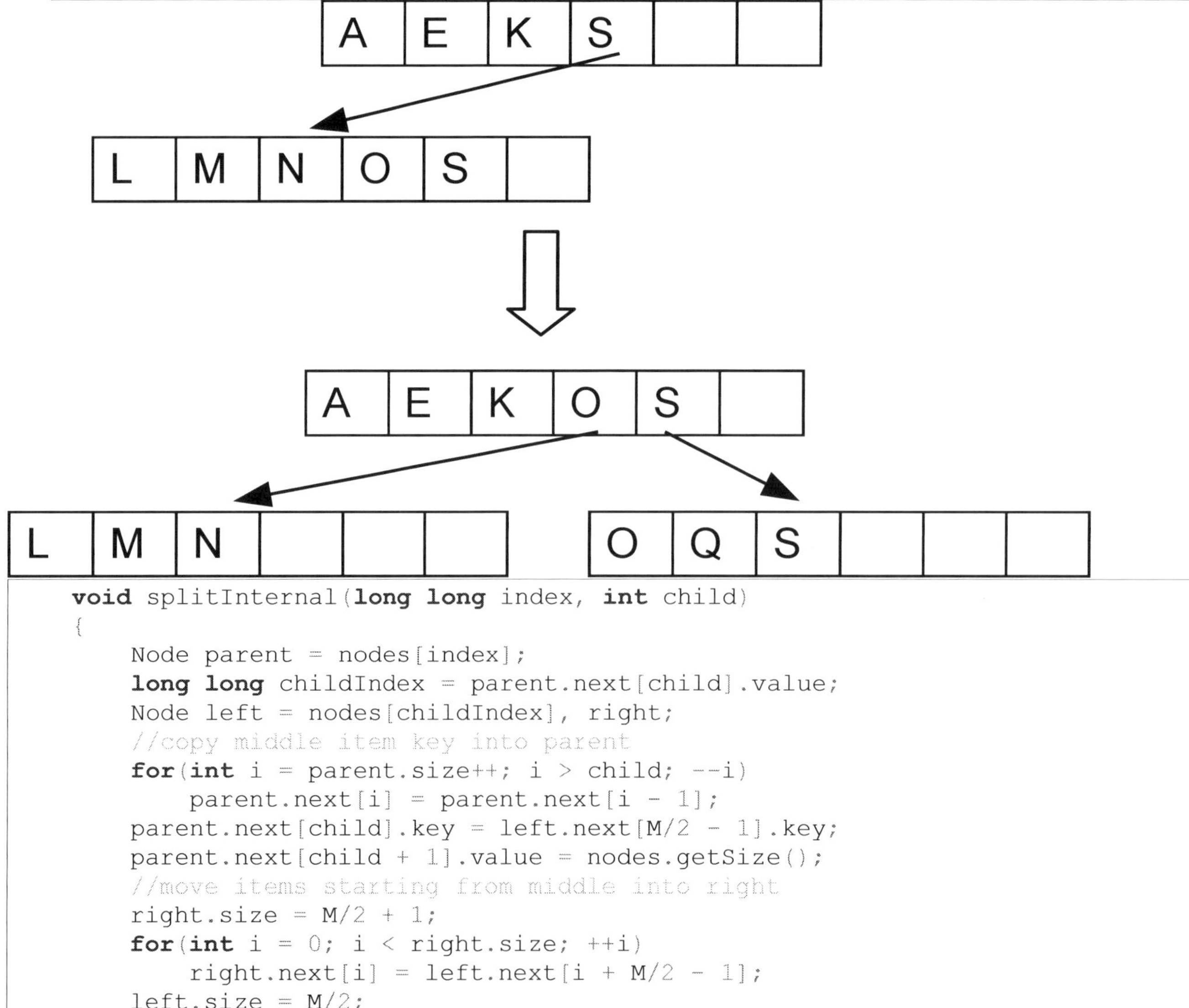


```
    void splitInternal(long long index, int child)
    {
        Node parent = nodes[index];
        long long childIndex = parent.next[child].value;
        Node left = nodes[childIndex], right;
        //copy middle item key into parent
        for(int i = parent.size++; i > child; --i)
            parent.next[i] = parent.next[i - 1];
        parent.next[child].key = left.next[M/2 - 1].key;
        parent.next[child + 1].value = nodes.getSize();
        //move items starting from middle into right
        right.size = M/2 + 1;
        for(int i = 0; i < right.size; ++i)
            right.next[i] = left.next[i + M/2 - 1];
        left.size = M/2;
```

```
        nodes.append(right);
        nodes.set(left, childIndex);
        nodes.set(parent, index);
    }
```

Splitting a leaf is slightly different because it contains no dummy keys, maintains the pointer to the next leaf, and the items are stored differently:

```
    void splitLeaf(long long index, int child)
    {
        Node parent = nodes[index];
        long long childIndex = parent.next[child].value;
        Leaf left = leaves[leafIndex(childIndex)], right;
        //copy middle item key into parent
        for(int i = parent.size++; i > child; --i)
            parent.next[i] = parent.next[i - 1];
        parent.next[child].key = left.records[L/2].key;
        parent.next[child + 1].value = leafIndex(leaves.getSize());
        //move items starting from middle into right
        left.size = right.size = L/2;
        for(int i = 0; i < right.size; ++i)
            right.records[i] = left.records[i + L/2];
        right.next = left.next;
        left.next = leaves.getSize();
        leaves.append(right);
        leaves.set(left, leafIndex(childIndex));
        nodes.set(parent, index);
    }
```

To insert:

1. **Create the root if it's missing, and split if full**
2. **Find the wanted leaf in the same way as find, inserting the key into each node, and splitting full nodes on the way down**
3. **Insert the item into the appropriate leaf**

```
    bool shouldSplit(long long node)
    {
        return node < NULL_IO_POINTER ?
            leaves[leafIndex(node)].size == L : nodes[node].size == M;
    }
    void insert(KEY const& key, ITEM const& value)
    {
        if(root == NULL_IO_POINTER)
        {
            root = leafIndex(leaves.getSize());
            leaves.append(Leaf());
        }
        else if(shouldSplit(root))
        {//check if need to split the root
            Node newRoot;
            newRoot.next[0].value = root;
            bool wasLeaf = root < NULL_IO_POINTER;
            root = nodes.getSize();
            nodes.append(newRoot);
            wasLeaf ? splitLeaf(root, 0) : splitInternal(root, 0);
        }
        long long index = root;
        while(index > NULL_IO_POINTER)
        {
            Node node = nodes[index];
            int childI = node.findChild(key),child = node.next[childI].value;
            if(shouldSplit(child))
```

```
            {//split children on they way down if needed
                child < NULL_IO_POINTER ? splitLeaf(index, childI) :
                    splitInternal(index, childI);
                if(key > nodes[index].next[childI].key)
                    child = nodes[index].next[childI + 1].value;
            }
            index = child;
        }
        //insert the item into the leaf
        Leaf leaf = leaves[leafIndex(index)];
        int i = leaf.inclusiveSuccessorRecord(key);
        if(i < leaf.size && key == leaf.records[i].key)
            leaf.records[i].value = value;
        else
        {
            for(int j = leaf.size++; j > i; --j)
                leaf.records[j] = leaf.records[j - 1];
            leaf.records[i] = Record(key, value);
        }
        leaves.set(leaf, leafIndex(index));
    }
```

A concurrent implementation would lock a node when an operation looks at it and unlock when done. The top-down nature of all operations makes this correct. Remove removes the node from the leaf without merging any nodes. Databases use this simple strategy because it's efficient for concurrency. Also, real-world databases are rebuilt occasionally, particularly when adding new data fields, which takes care of the merging. With substantial extra logic, can merge nodes < ½ full in a process opposite of splitting.

```
    void remove(KEY const& key)
    {
        long long current = findLeaf(key);
        if(current != NULL_IO_POINTER)
        {
            Leaf leaf = leaves[leafIndex(current)];
            int i = leaf.inclusiveSuccessorRecord(key);
            if(i < leaf.size && key == leaf.records[i].key)
            {
                --leaf.size;
                for(int j = i; j < leaf.size; ++j)
                    leaf.records[j] = leaf.records[j + 1];
            }
            leaves.set(leaf, leafIndex(leafIndex(current)));
        }
    }
```

B+ tree is I/O-optimal for dynamic sorted sequence operations. Without deletions, each node ≥ ½ full, so with n items the height is $O(\log_B(n))$, which < 4 in practice. Retrieving a large record takes the optimal O(the height + reading the record) time. Caching the root and LRU nodes improves performance.

For cases such as adding a field to a database, need to rebuild the tree. To construct a B+ tree bottom-up from a sorted file:

1. **Sort**
2. **Copy every B^{th} node to the next level**
3. **Recurse (2) on the *B*-separators until all fit in one block, which becomes the root**

This costs O(sort) < O(n insertions).

10.9 Comments

Many algorithms are difficult or impossible to make I/O-efficient. E.g., for graph algorithms DFS's jumping causes 1 I/O per vertex.

For a **B-tree**, keys and items aren't separated, leading to worse runtime. For simplicity, it's common to call B+ tree *B-tree*.

For map operations, can use slightly faster hash tables such as linear probing or **linear hashing**. But hash tables don't support ordered operations, can't be efficiently rebuilt from sorted data, and have problematic worst cases (Dementiev 2007).

10.10 References

Cormen, T. H., Leiserson, C. E., Rivest, R. L., & Stein, C. (2009). *Introduction to Algorithms*. MIT Press.

Folk, M. Zoellick, B. and Riccardi G. (1998). *File Structures: An Object-Oriented Approach with C++*. Addison-Wesley.

Dementiev, R. (2007). *Algorithm Engineering for Large Data Sets*. Springer.

Meyer, U., Sanders, P., and Sibeyn, J. (2003). *Algorithms for Memory Hierarchies: Advanced Lectures*. Springer.

11 Algorithmic Techniques

11.1 Computation Strategies

Several strategies can solve many problems:

- **Divide and conquer**—divide the input into parts, and combine answers from each. E.g., quicksort and mergesort split an array and work on each part separately.
- **Greedy**—at every step take the most promising action. E.g., Prim's algorithm iteratively adds the smallest-cost vertex to the current MST.
- **Dynamic programming**—when the solution is a sequence of n actions and E[the total cost] = $\sum$E[cost of each action], to find the best action at step i, pick the best actions for steps 0 to $i - 1$ and then the best action for step i. E.g., a path from A to B passing through C is optimal if the paths from A to C and C to B are optimal, so from B find the best path to each nearby C, and check which leads to the best overall path. Dynamic programming generally applies when can solve the problem by recursion much less efficiently. E.g., when calculating the nth Fibonacci number, recursion recalculates subresults such as the $(n - 2)^{\text{th}}$ number, which dynamic programming calculates only once.
- **Algorithm mixing**—if two algorithms are best in different cases, run each when it's best. E.g., STL sort uses deterministic median-of-3-pivot quicksort, and switches to heapsort if the stack is too deep, giving fast average runtime and the $O(n\lg(n))$ guarantee.

11.2 Making Static Data Structures Dynamic

A data structure is **dynamic** if it supports updates, **semi-dynamic** if it doesn't support deletions, and **static** if it doesn't support updates. If parameters determined at construction prevent growing, **rebuilding** applies if the data structure has enough information. E.g., it applies to vector but not to Bloom filter.

Partial rebuilding rebuilds part of a data structure after a sequence of updates or an event. E.g., to balance a tree without rotating, randomized rebuilding keeps the tree random by giving every node in every subtree an equal chance of being its root. Nodes keep node count, and insertion into a subtree with n nodes rebuilds it with probability $1/n$, using incremental construction that processes the new node and then the nodes in the existing subtree, rooting the subtree with the new node. With probability $(n - 1)/n$, insertion proceeds as unbalanced tree insertion. Because for a random tree Pr(height > $c\lg(n)$ for $c > 2$) is exponentially small, assume that any node has ≤ factor $1/b$ more descendants relative to its sibling, for $0.5 < b < 1$. If rebuilding costs $n\lg(n)$, E[the cost of insertion] = $C(n) = (1/n)n\lg(n) + ((n - 1)/n)C(nb) < \lg(n) + C(nb)$. Using the master theorem, $C(n) = O(\lg(n)^2)$.

Another way to maintain $0.5 < b < 1$ is creating a perfectly balanced subtree out of the highest subtree made unbalanced by insertion. The amortized cost of insertion is $O(\lg(n)^2)$ if rebuilding takes $O(n\lg(n))$ time, though on average it's smaller. Weight balance guarantees $O(\lg(n))$ height (Overmars 1983).

Total rebuilding rebuilds the whole data structure. **Array doubling** does this for vector. Updates are **weak** if after $O(n)$ updates the resource use of operations increases by $O(1)$. In this case, rebuilding after every $O(n)$ updates cuts the amortized cost of rebuilding by a factor of $O(n)$.

The ability to rebuild and weakly delete enables making any semi-dynamic data structure dynamic. When deleting an item, mark it with a Boolean **tombstone**. After deleting enough items, rebuild to remove them. The cost of a weak deletion is amortized O(rebuild/the number of deleted items). Rebuilding for deletions must be rarer than for insertions, so that a sequence of insertions and deletions doesn't cause frequent rebuilds.

Making array doubling worst-case-efficient is clumsy but useful in some real-time systems. When the array is ½ full, create another of twice its capacity. On append, append the item to both, and copy a different item from the old array to the new one. So when the old array is full, the new one has all items and is ½ full. Delete the old array, and repeat the process.

A problem is **order-decomposable** if can derive the result of a query on a data set by combining results of queries on any of the set's partitions. Order-decomposability allows representing a data structure by a collection of blocks. In particular, for a data structure with n items, blocks have sizes 2^i for $0 \leq i \leq \lg(n)$, $\sum$sizes $\geq n$, and each i is unique; have $\leq \lg(n)$ blocks. Insertion builds a structure of size 1 and, if have one already, rebuilds both into a structure of size 2, etc. This is like maintaining a binary counter and enables amortized $O(\lg(n))$ insertion when rebuilding is $O(n)$. Deletions are weak.

If blocks support insertion before they are full, inserting into the largest block until it's full and allocating another block of twice the size is more efficient. Garbage-collecting freelist uses this with blocks connected by a linked list.

11.3 Making Data Structures Persistent

After every update, a data structure as a whole is different, but may want to record its past versions. E.g., an svn code commit creates a new version of the repository. A data structure is **partially persistent** when each version is accessible, and updates affect only the latest version. Cloning the data structure on every update does this.

The **fat node method** is more efficient. When the data structure is a collection of linked nodes, replace each node pointer with a vector of (version number, pointer) pairs, and keep a data structure version number. During an update, copy and update every affected node, append (the new version number, the new pointer) to every affected vector, and increment the version number. The extra cost of an update is the time to copy the affected nodes. To access the latest version, use the last pair in each vector, and, to access a version k versions ago in extra $O(\lg(k))$ time, use binary search.

A persistent node can be the whole data structure, a single bit, or something in-between such as a memory location and unrelated to the specifics of the data structure. For efficiency, chose nodes so that an update touches few of them. E.g., for a treap make each node persistent, and copy if item or child pointers change:

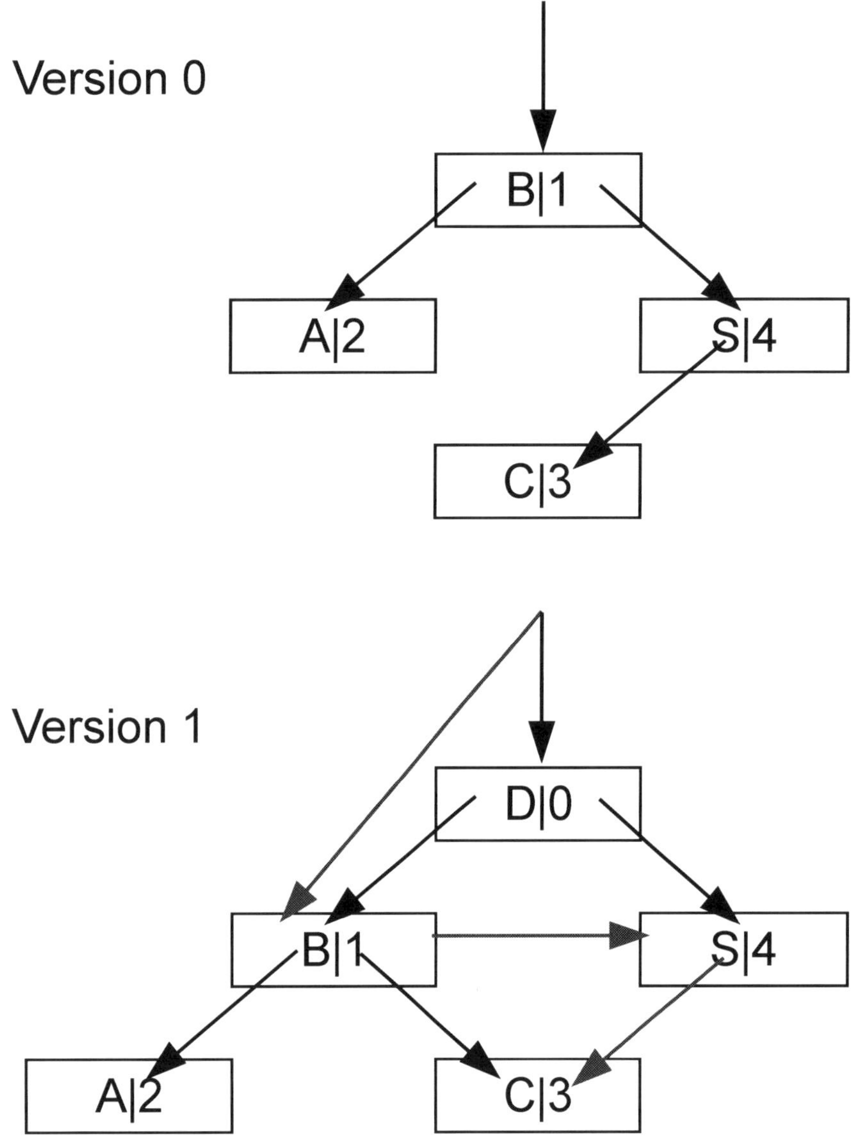

11.4 Making Algorithms Parallel

Concurrency is useful when the application computes something that takes too long or interacts with several resources. E.g., many computations use clusters of computers, and a browser displays part of a web page before waiting for it to download fully. Scalable computations that don't use IO don't need concurrency. Decompose a problem by:

- Input—each processor handles a part. Applies to divide-and-conquer algorithms, randomized algorithms rerun with many random seeds, and systems that process independent events. E.g., in the PRAM model, unsorted array search takes $O(n)$ time and $O(\lg(n))$ parallel time by recursively giving each subarray half to a separate processor.
- Functionality—each processor handles a particular transformation (e.g., washer and dryer).

Can implement concurrency by:

- Separate processes—communication uses **message passing**, either directly or through a router. The processes can run on different machines. Message costs follow the IO model, and the OS need extra resources $\forall$process.
- Separate threads—a threads costs < a process and uses shared memory, as assumed by PRAM. Locks ensure correct concurrent access. Programming with locks is difficult and inefficient if many threads wait for a lock.

If locking public methods, a data structure is atomic but not completely safe. E.g., a **race condition** occurs when two threads try to check if a stack is empty and pop, even when these methods are locked. Can lock, in order of increasing complexity and performance but decreasing applicability:

1. The code range containing calls to the data structure
2. Public methods of the data structure
3. To allow a single writer or unlimited number of readers
4. Parts of the data structure accessed at the moment

Another issue is **deadlocks**. If two threads are waiting for two locks, and each gets a different one, none will make progress. A deadlock is impossible if all threads get locks in the same order.

11.5 Complexity Theory

All problems have intrinsic difficulty. The most important difficulty classes:

- **Easy/tractable**— can solve in polynomial time $O(n^k)$, for some constant k
- **Hard/intractable**—need more than polynomial resources
- **Undecidable**—can't solve by any algorithm

Can't solve tasks for which !∃information such as predicting the future, but ∃ unsolvable tasks with complete information. E.g., the **halting problem**: ∀program *X*, does *X* go into an infinite loop for some input? If ∃ program *A*(source of *X*, input) that computes *terminates/loops*, make program *B*(source of *X*) that calls *A*(source of *X*, source of *X*), and if the answer is *terminates*, enters an infinite loop. Call *B*(source of *B*). If *A*(source of *B*, source of *B*) called by *B* returned *terminates*, *B*(source of *B*) goes into a loop, and if *loops*, *B*(source of *B*) terminates, contradicting *A*'s answer in both cases. The main characteristic of an undecidable problem is going into a loop and not knowing when to exit. Technically, !∃undecidability on finite-memory computers because any program whose memory state repeats is in an infinite loop, but this makes no practical difference.

A problem ∈ **NP** if it has a *yes/no* answer and ∃ a polynomial-time algorithm that can verify its correctness. A computation is easy with respect to class *C* if performing it takes less resources than solving the most difficult problem ∈ *C*. E.g., a polynomial-time algorithm is easy with respect to NP. A problem *X* is ***C*-hard** if can use it as a black-box solver ∀ problem *A* ∈ *C*, after reducing an instance of *A* to an instance of *X* by an easy-with-respect-to-*C* algorithm. A problem is ***C*-complete** if it's C-hard and ∈ *C*.

Many NP-complete problems ask for minimum-cost solutions. They are equivalent to **decision problems** that ask if ∃ a solution of a specific cost because using exponential search on cost with a black-box decision solver solves optimization.

Problems ∈ **PSPACE** need polynomial space and are harder than NP-complete, e.g., multiplayer games. Think about how prove checkmate in *n* moves in chess, no matter what the opponent does.

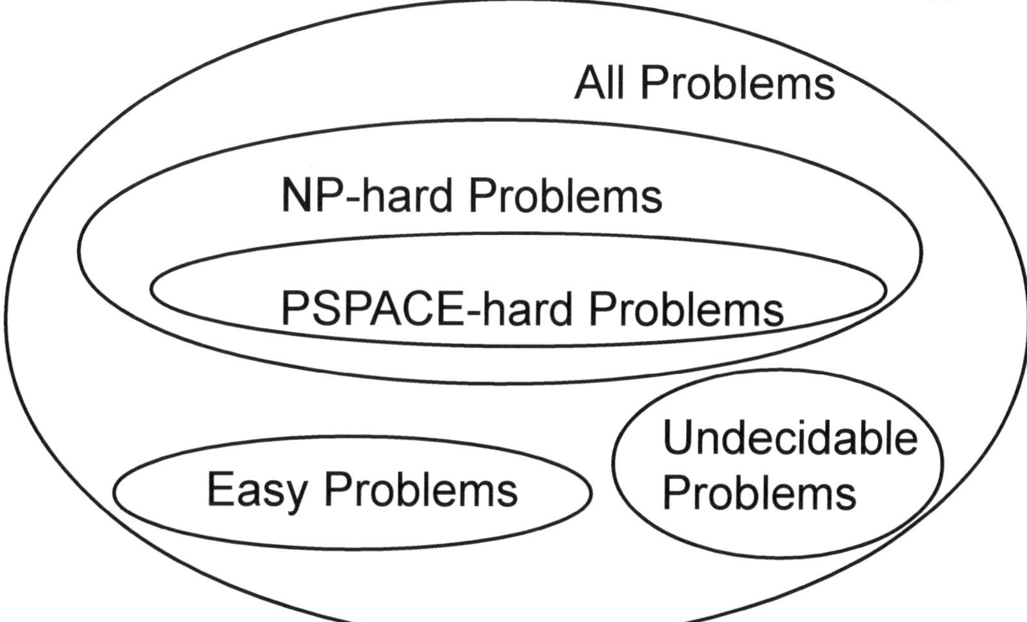

An algorithm trying to solve a hard problem must give up one of:

- Worst case polynomial time—try to be fast on average
- Exact answer—get a close-enough approximation
- Working ∀case—only solve problems with a specific structure that allows efficient solution

11.6 References

Overmars, M. H. (1983). *The Design of Dynamic Data Structures*. Springer.
Brass, P. (2008). *Advanced Data Structures*. Cambridge University Press.
Herlihy, M., & Shavit, N. (2012). *The Art of Multiprocessor Programming, Revised Reprint*. Elsevier.
Sipser, M. (2005). *Introduction to the Theory of Computation*. Course Technology.

12 String Algorithms

A **string** is a vector of characters from some alphabet. Character comparisons are assumed to take O(1) time. An **alphabet** is:

- **Indexed** if every character corresponds to a number
- **Bounded** if the number of possible characters is bounded
- **Ordered** if it supports comparisons
- **General** if it supports equality testing

Important substrings (also called **factors**):

- ***q*-gram**—has size q
- **Prefix**— starts at the beginning
- **Suffix**—ends at the end

12.1 Single-pattern Search

The task is finding all occurrences of a pattern string of length m in a larger text string of length n. For the obvious brute force algorithm and a general alphabet, the runtime = $O(mn)$ and E[the runtime] = $O(n)$ (Crochemore et al. 2007). Lower bounds for the number of character comparisons:

- Worst case $O(n)$
- Expected $O(n\log_a(m)/m)$ for random strings over a bounded alphabet of size a

Fast algorithms work with small indexed alphabets, e.g., bytes:

```
enum{ALPHABET_SIZE = 1 << numeric_limits<unsigned char>::digits};
```

Checking occurrence at a given position of the text assumes that the text has enough characters and compares them one by one with the pattern ones:

```
template<typename VECTOR> bool matchesAt(int position, VECTOR text,
    VECTOR pattern, int patternSize)
{
    int i = 0;
    while(i < patternSize && pattern[i] == text[i + position]) ++i;
    return i == patternSize;
}
```

Horspool algorithm shifts the pattern from left to right. E.g., given pattern *apple* and text *there_is_a_particularly_healthy_fruit_called_apple*, compare *apple* with *there*, *here_*, *ere_i*, etc. Instead of shifting by 1, it pre-processes the pattern to compute ∀ character the max possible shift = m − the last position of the character − 1, with positions of characters ∉ pattern = −1. Using this information, the last character of the current text factor determines the shift. E.g., after comparing *apple* with *there*, shift by 5 to align with *_is_a* because *apple* has no other *e*'s. Then by 4 to align with *a_par* because *apple* starts with *a*. Then by 5 until aligned with *_appl*, and by 1 to find a match.

```
class Horspool
{
    int shift[ALPHABET_SIZE], position, textSize, patternSize;
    unsigned char *text, *pattern;
public:
    Horspool(unsigned char* theText, int theTextSize,
        unsigned char* thePattern, int thePatternSize): position(0),
        textSize(theTextSize), text(theText),
        patternSize(thePatternSize), pattern(thePattern)
    {
        for(int i = 0; i < ALPHABET_SIZE; ++i) shift[i] = patternSize;
        for(int i = 0; i < patternSize - 1; ++i)
            shift[pattern[i]] = patternSize - 1 - i;
```

```
    }
    int findNext()
    {
        while(position + patternSize <= textSize)
        {
            int result = position;
            position += shift[text[position + patternSize - 1]];
            if(matchesAt(result, text, pattern, patternSize)) return result;
        }
        return -1;
    }
};
```

For random strings, E[the runtime] = O(n/min(m, a) + the number of matches) (Navarro & Raffinot 2002). **HashQ** has the optimal expected runtime (Lecroq 2007) and is practically faster for small alphabets or very long patterns. Both are O(mn). HashQ calculates the shifts using q-grams for $q > 1$, which requires $m \geq q$; $q = 2\log_a(m)$ is optimal (Baeza-Yates & Ribeiro-Neto 2011). Because q-grams need a large shift table, it uses a hash table of size m/q and resolves collisions by giving preference to smaller shifts. To find the shift amount during matching, lookup the last q-gram of the current text factor. For simplicity, the implementation uses $q = 3$ and a fast, lower-quality h.

```
struct Q3Hash
{
    int size;
    int operator()(unsigned char* substring, int position)
    {//assumes q = 3;
        substring += position;
        unsigned char result = substring[0];
        result += substring[1] << 1;
        result += substring[2] << 2;
        return result % size;
    }
};
```

For small alphabets, specialized h are more efficient. E.g., for DNA use $q = 4$ with h = concatenation of all bits. For $q = 1$, identity h, and table size a, the algorithm is equivalent to Horspool.

```
template<typename VECTOR, typename HASH> class HashQ
{
    int position, textSize, patternSize, q;
    Vector<int> shift;
    VECTOR const &text, &pattern;
    HASH h;
public:
    HashQ(VECTOR const& theText, int theTextSize, VECTOR const& thePattern,
        int thePatternSize, int theQ = 3, HASH theHash = HASH()):
        position(0), textSize(theTextSize), text(theText), q(theQ),
        pattern(thePattern), patternSize(thePatternSize),
        shift(patternSize/q), h(theHash)
    {
        h.size = shift.getSize();
        assert(patternSize >= q);
        int temp = patternSize - q;
        for(int i = 0; i < shift.getSize(); ++i) shift[i] = temp + 1;
        for(int i = 0; i < temp; ++i) shift[h(pattern, i)] = temp - i;
    }
    int findNext()
    {
        while(position + patternSize <= textSize)
        {
            int result = position;
            position += shift[h(text, position + patternSize - q)];
```

```
            if(matchesAt(result, text, pattern, patternSize))return result;
        }
        return -1;
    }
};
```

12.2 Multiple Patterns

Can match k patterns of different lengths one by one, but **Wu-Manber algorithm** is more efficient. It's a generalization of HashQ with E[the runtime] = $O(n\log_a(mk)/m)$, $q = \log_a(mk)$, and table size mk/q, with m the average length. Match any patterns of length < q separately, by Wu-Manber with $q = 1$ or one by one. The algorithm hashes each pattern's suffix q-gram and ∀ hash value creates a list of patterns that hash to it. Hash of the last q-gram of the current text factor determines the shift = the min possible shift ∀pattern and possible match, which are checked by brute force.

```
template<typename HASH = Q3Hash> class WuManber
{
    unsigned char* text;
    Vector<pair<unsigned char*, int> >const& patterns;
    int shift[ALPHABET_SIZE], position, q, minPatternSize, textSize;
    Vector<int> candidates[ALPHABET_SIZE];
    HASH hash;
    void findMatches(int h, Vector<int>& matches)
    {
        for(int i = 0; i < candidates[h].getSize(); ++i)
        {
            int j = candidates[h][i], patternISize = patterns[j].second;
            if(position + patternISize <= textSize && matchesAt(position,
                text, patterns[j].first, patternISize))  matches.append(j);
        }
    }
public:
    WuManber(unsigned char* theText, int theTextSize,
        Vector<pair<unsigned char*, int> >const& thePatterns,
        HASH theHash =  HASH()): text(theText),
        patterns(thePatterns), position(0),  hash(theHash), q(3),
        textSize(theTextSize), minPatternSize(numeric_limits<int>::max())
    {
        hash.size = ALPHABET_SIZE;
        for(int i = 0; i < patterns.getSize(); ++i)
            minPatternSize = min(patterns[i].second, minPatternSize);
        assert(minPatternSize >= q);
        int temp = minPatternSize - q;
        for(int i = 0; i < ALPHABET_SIZE; ++i) shift[i] = temp + 1;
        for(int j = 0; j < patterns.getSize(); ++j)
            for(int i = 0; i < temp + 1; ++i)
            {
                int h = hash(patterns[j].first, i);
                if(i == temp) candidates[h].append(j);
                else shift[h] = min(temp - i, shift[h]);
            }
    }
    int findNext(Vector<int>& matches)
    {
        while(position + minPatternSize <= textSize)
        {
            int h = hash(text, position + minPatternSize - q),
                result = position;
            findMatches(h, matches);
```

```
            position += shift[h];
            if(matches.getSize() > 0) return result;
        }
        return -1;
    }
};
```

12.3 Regular Expressions

A **regular expression** matches text specified by rules. It's formed by applying operators "*"(left may occur zero or more times), "|" (left or right), and "&" (left concatenated with right) to clauses, in this precedence order. A **clause** is any parenthesized subexpression, including a single character with implicit parenthesis. "&" isn't explicitly written. Use escape character "/" if operators occur as characters. E.g., */(xxx/)xxxx-xxx* for $0 \leq x \leq 9$ matches phone numbers. Can represent other operators such as jokers and character classes in terms of these. To find if the text contains a pattern matched by *expression*, use **expression**.

Glushkov algorithm converts the expression to a nondeterministic finite automaton, where the epsilon transitions don't consume characters. The implementation assumes no escape characters for simplicity. Parsing an expression of *m* characters creates a graph with a vertex for the final state, a vertex ∀state before reading a character, and an edge ∀ epsilon transition, which is added:

- To the next state for "*", "(", and ")"
- Between a clause start and the next state if it's "*"
- For "|" from before the left start to the right start and from before the right start to the clause end

E.g., boring C++ file *zzzzzz.cpp* and its variants match:

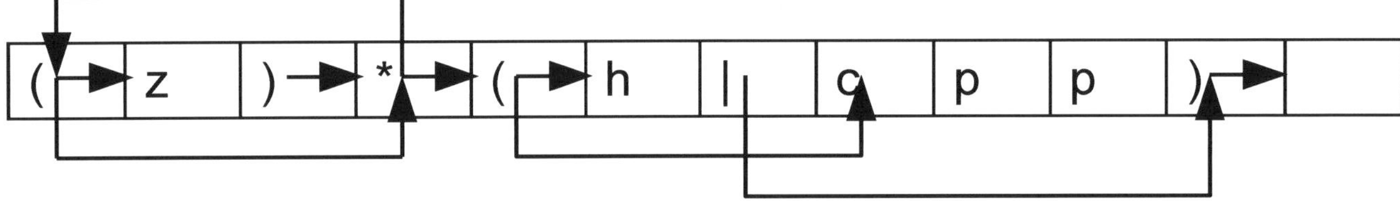

A stack holds open clauses so that "(" opens a clause, "|" is inside a clause, and ")" closes it. For simplicity, assume "|" only inside parenthesis and no escape characters.

```
struct RegularExpressionMatcher
{
    string re;
    int m;
    GraphAA<bool> g;
    RegularExpressionMatcher(string const& theRe): re(theRe), m(re.length()),
        g(m + 1)
    {
        Stack<int> clauses;
        for(int i = 0; i < m; ++i)
        {
            int clauseStart = i;
            if(re[i] == '(' || re[i] == '|') clauses.push(i);
            else if(re[i] == ')')
            {
                int clauseOp = clauses.pop();
                if(re[clauseOp] == '|')
                {
                    clauseStart = clauses.pop();
                    g.addEdge(clauseStart, clauseOp+1);
                    g.addEdge(clauseOp, i);
                }
                else clauseStart = clauseOp;
            }
            if(i < m - 1 && re[i + 1] == '*')
                g.addUndirectedEdge(clauseStart, i + 1);
```

```
            if(re[i] == '(' || re[i] == '*' || re[i] == ')')
                g.addEdge(i, i + 1);
        }
    }
};
```

Active states initially consist of state 0. DFS computes all states reachable from them by taking epsilon transitions. Taking the read character transitions from the result gives the next set of active states. The text matches if the final state *m* is active after reading all characters.

```
    struct VisitedAction
    {
        Vector<bool> visited;
        VisitedAction(int nVertices): visited(nVertices, false) {}
        void treeEdge(int v){}
        void nonTreeEdge(int v){}
        void backwardEdge(int v){}
    };
    Vector<int> findActiveStates(Vector<int> sources = Vector<int>())
    {
        VisitedAction a(g.nVertices());
        if(sources.getSize() == 0) DFSComponent(g, 0, a.visited, a);
        else for(int i = 0; i < sources.getSize(); ++i)
                if(!a.visited[sources[i]])
                {
                    a.visited[sources[i]] = true;
                    DFSComponent(g, sources[i], a.visited, a);
                }
        Vector<int> activeStates;
        for(int i = 0; i < a.visited.getSize(); ++i)
            if(a.visited[i]) activeStates.append(i);
        return activeStates;
    }
    bool matches(string const& text)
    {
        Vector<int> activeStates = findActiveStates();
        for(int i = 0; i < text.length(); ++i)
        {
            Vector<int> match;
            for(int j = 0; j < activeStates.getSize(); ++j)
                if(activeStates[j] < m && re[activeStates[j]] == text[i])
                    match.append(activeStates[j] + 1);
            activeStates = findActiveStates(match);
        }
        for(int j = 0; j < activeStates.getSize(); ++j)
            if(activeStates[j] == m) return true;
        return false;
    }
```

The runtime is $O(nm)$ due to needing to update active states after every character of text.

12.4 Extended Patterns

An **extended pattern** is a regular expression that uses "*" and "|" on only single characters, allowing faster search. The simplest solution is to extend single pattern search algorithm **shift-and**. For a substring pattern of length *m*, it maintains state bit string *s* of *m* bits, such that bit *i* is on if the last $i + 1$ characters of the text matched the pattern prefix of length $i + 1$. A match occurs if bit $m - 1$ is on. ∀ possible character, precompute bit string *c* of size *m*, with bits set at the positions where the character occurs in the pattern. Initially $s = 0$. After reading text character $t[j]$, set *s* to `(s << 1 | 1) & c[t[j]]`. A set bit remain set in the shifted position if the corresponding character matched. If reading character *j* results in a match, $j - (m - 1)$ is its start. The implementation assumes that $m <$ word size *w*. If not, use a bitset. Reporting all matches takes $O(nm/w)$ time.

```
class ShiftAnd
{
    unsigned char *pattern, *text;
    int textSize, patternSize, position;
    unsigned long long charPos[ALPHABET_SIZE], state;
public:
    ShiftAnd(unsigned char* theText, int theTextSize,
        unsigned char*  thePattern, int thePatternSize): position(0),
        textSize(theTextSize), text(theText), patternSize(thePatternSize),
        pattern(thePattern), state(0)
    {
        assert(patternSize <= numeric_limits<unsigned long long>::digits);
        for(int i = 0; i < ALPHABET_SIZE; ++i) charPos[i] = 0;
        for(int i = 0; i < patternSize; ++i)
            charPos[pattern[i]] |= 1ull << i;
    }
    int findNext()
    {
        unsigned long long limit = 1ull << (patternSize - 1);
        while(position < textSize)
        {
            state = ((state << 1) | 1) & charPos[text[position++]];
            if(state & limit) return position - patternSize;
        }
        return -1;
    }
};
```

To extend for:

- **Joker characters** matching any character and "|" of several characters, set the corresponding *c* bits of every matching character.
- Repeatable characters corresponding to regular expression *xx**, remember their matching pre-shift positions in *s* after shifting. If bit string *R* marks the positions, use ((*s* << 1 | 1) | (*s* & *R*)) & *c*.
- Possibly consecutive optional characters that may be omitted, let bit string *O* indicate their positions. After reading a character, ∀ set bit in *s*, if the next *k* positions are optional, set the next *k* bits. The preprocessing calculates *L* and *P*—respectively the last and the preceding positions of blocks of consecutive set bits in *O*. E.g., if *O* = 01010110, and *s* = 00100001, *s* becomes 01100111, *F* 01010100, and *P* 00101001. The calculation of *P* assumes no optional characters in bit 0, corresponding to pattern start, which isn't a problem because can omit optional characters at the beginning and the end of the pattern. After a character update, set *s* to *s* | (*L* ^ ~(*L* − (*s* & *P*)). The effect is to add extra states to *s*. ∀ block of consecutive set bits in *O*, *L* − (*s* & *P*) gives *O* >> 1 if the bits need to be set, and *L* if not because the subtraction flips the bits in the first case. Then ∀ block *L* ^~result gives *O* | (*O* >> 1) for the first case and 0 for the second.

"*x**" is equivalent to making *x* optional and repeatable. The implementation assumes the caller sets up `charPos` mask to allow "|" of characters.

```
class ShiftAndExtended
{
    unsigned char *pattern, *text;
    int textSize, patternSize, position;
    unsigned long long *charPos, P, L, S, state;
public:
    ShiftAndExtended(unsigned char* theText, int theTextSize,
        int thePatternSize, unsigned long long* theCharPos,
        unsigned long long optionalPos, unsigned long long repeatedPos):
        position(0), textSize(theTextSize), text(theText),
        patternSize(thePatternSize), S(repeatedPos), state(0)
    {
```

```
        assert(patternSize <= numeric_limits<unsigned long long>::digits);
        unsigned long long sides = optionalPos ^ (optionalPos >> 1);
        P = (optionalPos >> 1) & sides;
        L = optionalPos & sides;
    }
    int findNext()
    {
        unsigned long long limit = 1ull << (patternSize - 1);
        while(position < textSize)
        {
            state = (((state << 1) | 1) | (state & S)) &
                charPos[text[position++]];
            state |= L ^ ~(L - (state & P));
            if(state & limit) return position - patternSize;
        }
        return -1;
    }
};
```

The runtime is the same as for regular shift-and.

12.5 String Distance Algorithms

∃several distances between strings, based on the number of operations to edit one string into another, which allow characters to be:

- **Hamming**—replaced
- **Indel**—inserted/deleted
- **Lewenstein**—inserted/deleted/replaced
- **Transpose**—inserted/deleted/replaced/transposed

The first three are metric with unit costs ∀operation. Common use is computing a **difference between two strings**, which uses the indel distance to create an edit script that changes string a into string b by a sequence of commands:

- Insert i—insert $b[i]$ into position i of a
- Delete i—delete $a[i]$

To apply the script to a without knowing b, store inserted $b[i]$ in a vector c so that the jth insertion to position i inserts $c[j]$ into position i of a. This is useful, e.g., for svn, where text files are strings of line "characters" and all past versions of a file are stored as differences between consecutive versions.

```
1: SinkIntoThink
  capacity = 8
  size     = 3
  items    = 0x60003a900
items[0]@3 →
  | prev     = ...  | prev     = ...  | prev     = ...   |
  | position = 0    | position = 1    | position = 2     |
  | isInsert = true | isInsert = true | isInsert = false |
```

```
struct Edit
{
    Edit* prev;
    int position;
    bool isInsert;
};
```

Let prefix(s, j) be the first j letters of s. Then distance(a, b) =

- Distance(prefix(a, $m-1$), prefix(b, $n-1$) if $a[m-1] = b[n-1]$
- Min(distance(a, prefix(b, $n-1$), distance(prefix(a, $m-1$), b) +1 otherwise

As a base case, distance("", a string of size n) = n. The corresponding dynamic programming uses $O(nm)$ time and space but is extendable to other distances and nonunit costs.

WMMM algorithm is more efficient. Let x correspond to prefix(b, $x+1$), and y to prefix(a, $y+1$). Then x and y define a set of diagonals with constant $x-y$. Diagonal $m+1$ has $(-1, -1)$, and diagonal $n+1$ $(n-1, m-1)$. If need p deletions, the dynamic programming relation can reach base case $(-1, -1)$ from $(n-1, m-1)$ by computing within diagonals $m+1-p$ to $n+1-p$, and the script consists of p deletions and $n-m$ insertions, leading to edit distance $n-m+p$. The solution is a shortest path from $(-1, -1)$ to $(n-1, m-1)$, where can move to $(x + 1, y + 1)$ at 0 cost if $a[y] = b[x]$. Otherwise, a move to $(x + 1, y)$ costs an insertion and to $(x, y + 1)$ a deletion.

5	6	7	8	9	10	11			
4			-1	0	1	2	3	4	
3				t	h	i	n	k	
2	-1		0	1	2	3	4	5	
1	0	s	1	2	3	4	5	6	
0	1	i	2	3	4	3	4	5	
	2	n	3	4	5	4	3	4	
	3	k	4	5	6	5	4	3	

The shortest path logic maintains ∀ diagonal its current x and the sequence of edits that lead to (x, y), calculating $y = x - (\text{diagonal} - 1 - m)$. The x are stored as a ***frontier*** vector, initialized to −2 for the base cases. Because don't know p, it's initially 0 and iteratively incremented, extending all diagonals until reaching $(n - 1, m - 1)$. Need $\leq n + m + 3$ diagonals. Extending border diagonal first leads to $O(np)$ and expected $O(n + dp)$ time and space use, where d is the edit distance (Wu et al. 1989). The implementation assumes $m \leq n$.

```
template<typename CHAR>
Vector<Edit> DiffInternal(Vector<CHAR>const& a, Vector<CHAR>const& b)
{
    int M = a.getSize(), N = b.getSize(), size = M + N + 3, d = N + 1;
    assert(M <= N);//a must be shorter then b
    Vector<int> frontierX(size, -2);
    Vector<Edit*> edits(size, 0);
    Freelist<Edit> freelist;
    int p = 0;
    for(; frontierX[d] < N - 1; ++p)
    {
        for(int diagonal = M + 1 - p; diagonal < d; ++diagonal)
            extendDiagonal<CHAR>(diagonal, frontierX, edits, a, b, freelist);
        for(int diagonal = d + p; diagonal >= d; --diagonal)
            extendDiagonal<CHAR>(diagonal, frontierX, edits, a, b, freelist);
    }
    Vector<Edit> result;
    for(Edit* link = edits[d]; link; link = link->prev) result.append(*link);
    result.reverse();
    //distance is N - M + 2 * (p - 1) with p - 1 deletions
    assert(result.getSize() == N - M + 2 * (p - 1));
    return result;
}
```

The algorithm extends a diagonal by allowing one more edit operation. Because a deletion from the *frontier* point on diagonal $i + 1$ or an insertion from the one on diagonal $i - 1$ lead to the furthest point on diagonal i, can compute $x = \max(frontier[i - 1] + 1, frontier[i + 1])$. This costs an edits, except when jumping into $(-1, -1)$. Then can extend the computed furthest point at no edit cost by incrementing x while $a[y + 1] = b[x + 1]$.

```
template<typename CHAR> void extendDiagonal(int diagonal,
    Vector<int>& frontierX, Vector<Edit*>& edits, Vector<CHAR>const& a,
    Vector<CHAR>const& b, Freelist<Edit>& freelist)
{
    int x = max(frontierX[diagonal - 1] + 1, frontierX[diagonal + 1]),
        y = x - (diagonal - 1 - a.getSize());
    if(x != -1 || y != -1)
    {
        bool isInsert = x != frontierX[diagonal + 1];
        edits[diagonal] = new(freelist.allocate())Edit();
        edits[diagonal]->isInsert = isInsert;
        edits[diagonal]->prev = edits[diagonal + (isInsert ? -1 : 1)];
        edits[diagonal]->position = isInsert ? x : y;
    }
    while(y + 1 < a.getSize() && x + 1 < b.getSize() && a[y + 1] == b[x + 1])
    {
        ++y;
        ++x;
    }
    frontierX[diagonal] = x;
}
```

Editing a into b is the same as b into a with *insert* and *delete* swapped, so $m \le n$ isn't a problem. Need to add to the deletion positions the number of insertions − the number of deletions because each edit shifts the remaining character positions. Insertions aren't affected because each character of b inserted into a is in the same position in both.

```
template<typename CHAR>
Vector<Edit> Diff(Vector<CHAR>const& a, Vector<CHAR>const& b)
{//edits needed to get a into b
    bool change = a.getSize() > b.getSize();
    Vector<Edit> result = change ? DiffInternal(b, a) : DiffInternal(a, b);
    for(int i = 0, offset = 0; i < result.getSize(); ++i)
    {
        if(change) result[i].isInsert = !result[i].isInsert;
        if(result[i].isInsert) ++offset;
        else result[i].position += offset--;
    }
    return result;
}
```

12.6 Inverted Index

An inverted index maps a term to the list of all documents that contain it and supports the Boolean query *contains(term)*. E.g., a book index is an inverted index, where the map is a sorted vector of words. To create an index, run a document-specific parser on each document and insert its id into the list of every term found by the parser. This works when words have separators such as spaces and punctuation marks. Can define many types of queries, in particular Boolean formulas such as *contains(inverted) & contains(index)*.

For very large indices stored on disk, such as the ones managed by search engines, the map is a B-tree and the lists are compressed by sorting them and storing the first number in byte code (see the "Compression" chapter) and any other number as byte-encoded difference to the previous number. To make the index parallel, use a hash table and dedicate each server to a particular range of the hash function's output.

12.7 Suffix Index

A **suffix array** of a string of size n is an array of positions of the string's suffixes in lexicographic order. Multikey quicksort computes it in $O(n^2\lg(n))$ and expected $O(n\lg(n))$ time.

mississippi

10	i
7	ippi
4	issippi
1	ississippi
0	mississippi
9	pi
8	ppi
6	sippi
3	sissippi
5	ssippi
2	ssissippi

An asymptotically optimal algorithm for a general alphabet uses the **doubling lemma**: Let $r(i, k)$ be the rank of the suffix at position i in the list of suffixes sorted on the first k letters, defined by how many suffixes, distinct on the first k letters, < a given suffix. E.g., for *aba*, $r(0, 1) = 0$, $r(1, 1) = 1$, and $r(2, 1) = 0$. Then $r(i, 2k)$ is the rank of $(r(i, k), r(i + k, k))$ in a lexicographically sorted list of all such pairs.

Rank for positions $\geq n$ is -1 for suffix array and position % n for Burrows-Wheeler transform (see the "Compression" chapter).

```
struct SARank
{
    int* ranks;
    int n, k;
    int operator()(int i)const{i += k; return i < n ? ranks[i] + 1 : 0;}
};
struct BWTRank
{
    int* ranks;
    int n, k;
    int operator()(int i)const{return ranks[(i + k) % n];}
};
```

Compute the suffix array by sorting all characters to get ranks with $k = 1$ and doubling k until $k \geq n$, or all ranks are unique. The algorithm maps ranks from $[-1, n - 1]$ to $[0, n]$ and sorts rank pairs with KSort in $O(n)$ time, giving $O(n\lg(n))$ runtime and $3n$-word working space. It updates and returns the current permutation of suffixes.

```
template<typename RANKER, typename ITEM>
Vector<int> suffixArray(ITEM* const vector, int n)
{
    Vector<int> ranks(n, 0), p(n, 0);
    for(int i = 0; i < n; ++i) p[i] = i;
    quickSort(p.getArray(), 0, n - 1, IndexComparator<ITEM>(vector));
```

```
    ranks[p[0]] = 0;//set ranks based on first char
    for(int i = 1, r = 0; i < n; ++i)
    {
        if(vector[p[i]] != vector[p[i - 1]]) ++r;
        ranks[p[i]] = r;
    }
    for(int k = 1; k < n; k *= 2)
    {
        RANKER r1 = {ranks.getArray(), n, k}, r2 = {ranks.getArray(), n, 0};
        KSort(p.getArray(), n, n + 1, r1);
        KSort(p.getArray(), n, n + 1, r2);
        if(k * 2 < n)
        {//set ranks based on the tuples
            Vector<int> ranks2(n, 0);
            ranks2[p[0]] = 0;
            for(int i = 1, r = 0; i < n; ++i)
            {
                if(r1(p[i]) != r1(p[i - 1]) || r2(p[i]) != r2(p[i - 1])) ++r;
                ranks2[p[i]] = r;
                if(r == n - 1) return p;//ranks already unique
            }
            ranks2.swapWith(ranks);
        }
    }
    return p;
}
```

An **lcp array** stores lcps between adjacent suffixes in the suffix array; $lcp[i] = \text{lcp}(sa[i-1], sa[i])$. Its computation uses the permuted lcp array, defined by $PLCP[sa[i]] = lcp[i]$, and temporary array *pred*, defined by $pred[i] = sa[i-1]$, with *pred*[*0*] logically undefined but $= sa[size-1]$ for simplicity. $PLCP[i] = \text{lcp}(i, pred[i])$. For $i > 0$, $PLCP[i] \geq PLCP[i-1] - 1$ (Karkkainen et al. 2009). So compute *PLCP* by a linear scan of *pred* and, for $i > 0$, not looking at the first $PLCP[i-1] - 1$ characters. Because $\sum$differences between consecutive *PLCP* values = $O(n)$, the runtime is $O(n)$.

```
template<typename ITEM> Vector<int> LCPArray(ITEM* text, int size, int* sa)
{
    Vector<int> pred(size, 0), PLCP(pred);
    for(int i = 0; i < size; ++i) pred[sa[i]] = sa[(i ? i : size) - 1];
    for(int i = 0, p = 0; i < size; ++i)
    {
        while(text[i + p] == text[pred[i] + p]) ++p;
        PLCP[i] = p;
        p = max(p - 1, 0);
    }//pred becomes the LCP array now
    for(int i = 0; i < size; ++i) pred[i] = PLCP[sa[i]];
    return pred;
}
```

Suffix and lcp arrays form a suffix index, efficient for many pattern matching tasks. Finding all pattern occurrences takes $O(m\lg(n))$ time with two binary searches, by computing an interval where all suffixes are prefixes of the pattern. The number of matches = `right - left` + 1.

```
1: Mississippi
text = capacity = 11
       size     = 11
       items    = 0x60003a4c0 "mississippi\200\001"
sa   = capacity = 11
       size     = 11
       items    = 0x60003a550
lcpa = capacity = 11
       size     = 11
       items    = 0x60003a510
.sa.items[0]@11                .lcpa.items[0]@11
10|7|4|1|0|9|8|6|3|5|2         0|1|1|4|0|0|1|0|2|1|3
```

```
template<typename ITEM> struct SuffixIndex
{
    Vector<ITEM> text;
    Vector<int> sa, lcpa;
    SuffixIndex(Vector<ITEM> const& theText): text(theText),
        sa(suffixArray<SARank>(text.getArray(), text.getSize())),
        lcpa(LCPArray(text.getArray(), text.getSize(), sa.getArray())) {}
    bool isKLess(ITEM* a, int aSize, ITEM* b, int bSize, int k)
    {
        for(int i = 0; i < min(aSize, bSize); ++i)
            if(a[i] > b[i]) return false;
        return max(aSize, bSize) < k;
    }
    pair<int, int> interval(ITEM* pattern, int size)
    {
        int left = 0, right = sa.getSize();
        while(left < right)
        {
            int i = (left + right)/2;
            if(isKLess(&text[sa[i]], sa.getSize() - sa[i], pattern, size,
                size)) left = i + 1;
            else right = i - 1;
        }
        int left2 = left - 1, right2 = sa.getSize() - 1;
        while(left2 < right2)
        {
            int i = (left2 + right2)/2;
            if(isKLess(pattern, size, &text[sa[i]], sa.getSize() - sa[i],
                size)) right2 = i - 1;
            else left2 = i + 1;
        }
        return make_pair(left, right2);
    }
};
```

Can find the longest repeated substring in O(n) time by checking which two suffixes have the largest lcp.

12.8 Syntax Tree

In a **syntax tree**, each node has value that is a constant or a function of its children. The root's value = the value of its functional expression. A function can represent any relationship of its node's children.

A syntax tree is usually a result of converting text commands. E.g., *5 + 4* corresponds to the array [(+, 1, 2), (5, -1, -1), (4, -1, -1)], that represents its syntax tree. Lexical analysis partitions character sequences into symbols and uses specific grammar rules, such as precedence order, to convert them into the tree.

For readable and editable specification of something, formats such as XML and JSON usually give enough functionality.

12.9 Comments

Far too many algorithms for string search have been proposed and compared (Faro & Lecroq 2010). Horspool and HashQ are among the simplest ones and perform competitively in almost all cases.

Many algorithms have been proposed for finding string difference, but in the typical case of relatively few differences, the WMMM algorithm is the most efficient. Unix diff command uses its older, less efficient version (Hunt et al. 1998).

A major area of research in string algorithms is compressed indices such as the FM index (Adjeroh et al. 2008). A suffix array takes a lot of space to compute and represent, so want to compress it as much as possible using bit algorithms, though at the cost of a slowdown. The idea is that for applications such as DNA sequencing, this constant-factor memory reduction can make a difference between solvable and unsolvable. But with 64-bit architectures and growing memory sizes, this is questionable.

12.10 References

Adjeroh, D., Bell, T. C., & Mukherjee, A. (2008). *The Burrows-Wheeler Transform: Data Compression, Suffix Arrays, and Pattern Matching*. Springer.

Crochemore, M., Hancart, C., & Lecroq, T. (2007). *Algorithms on Strings*. Cambridge University Press.

Faro, S., & Lecroq, T. (2010). The exact string matching problem: a comprehensive experimental evaluation. *arXiv preprint arXiv:1012.2547*.

Hunt, J. J., Vo, K. P., & Tichy, W. F. (1998). Delta algorithms: an empirical analysis. *ACM Transactions on Software Engineering and Methodology (TOSEM)*, *7*(2), 192–214.

Kärkkäinen, J., Manzini, G., & Puglisi, S. J. (2009). Permuted longest-common-prefix array. In *Combinatorial Pattern Matching* (pp. 181–192). Springer.

Lecroq, T. (2007). Fast exact string matching algorithms. *Information Processing Letters*, *102*(6), 229–235.

Navarro, G., & Raffinot, M. (2002). *Flexible Pattern Matching in Strings: Practical On-line Search Algorithms for Texts and Biological Sequences*. Cambridge University Press.

Baeza-Yates, R., & Ribeiro-Neto, B. (2011). *Modern Information Retrieval*. Addison-Wesley.

Sedgewick, R., & Wayne, K. (2011). *Algorithms*. Addison-Wesley.

Wu, S., Manber, U., Myers, G., & Miller, W. (1990). An O(NP) sequence comparison algorithm. *Information Processing Letters*, *35*(6), 317–323.

13 Compression

13.1 Fundamental Limits

Compression saves space by converting a bit string, representing maybe a large image file, into a shorter bit string, which can be converted back to the original. No algorithm can shrink every bit string, otherwise applying it repeatedly shrinks the size to 0. Compression and decompression are one-to-one functions, and ∃ more sequences of length $n + 1$ than n, so every algorithm that shortens some bit strings lengthens others. Lengthened bit strings can have only 1 extra bit—e.g., output shorter(the original, the compressed) and a bit to show which.

Can highly compress certain bit strings. E.g., *million 0's* compresses a bit string consisting of a million *0*'s. The shortest description of a bit string is its **Kolmogorov complexity**, computing which is undecidable because a seemingly incompressible, long bit string could be generated by a clever pseudorandom generator and be representable as the seed and generator's code. Technically, Kolmogorov complexity is defined with respect to a universal machine, but this is irrelevant because the idea only has conceptual value.

13.2 Entropy

A practical measure of compressibility of a sequence of symbols from an alphabet of size k, occurring with probabilities given by distribution X, is **first order entropy** $\mathrm{H}(X) = -\sum\Pr(\text{symbol})\lg(\Pr(\text{symbol})))$. When each symbol is a **supersymbol** made of k symbols (e.g., a `short` is made of two `char`s), entropy is first order entropy for $k \to \infty$. The length of an optimal codeword for a symbol $\approx -\lg(\Pr(\text{symbol})))$.

Creating a superalphabet doesn't change entropy if symbols are independent, e.g., using byte and bit symbols gets the same result if the bits are independent. Otherwise, creating supersymbols reduces entropy, and $\mathrm{H}(X) \geq \mathrm{H}(X^k)/k$. E.g., entropy of an ASCII text is lower using letters and not bits because most 8-bit values never occur, and e is more likely than z.

Entropy is min E[the number of bits per symbol] to communicate a supersymbol sequence, meaning it's the limit of compressibility without other information. A sequence's representation's size − its entropy ≥ max compression gain. E.g., entropy of English > 1 bit per letter, and some algorithms compress a variety of ASCII texts to < 2 bits per letter (Sayood 2002).

13.3 Bit Stream

A bit stream can read and write bits and is a wrapper around bitset. Its interface is an abstraction and can be implemented as an external memory or a byte stream. For efficiency, writing a value reverses its bits, which assumes every value is written and read as a value, and not bit by bit.

```
struct Stream
{
    unsigned long long position;
    Stream(): position(0) {}
};
struct BitStream : public Stream
{
    Bitset<unsigned char> bitset;//unsigned char for portability
    enum{B = 8};
    BitStream() {}
    BitStream(Bitset<unsigned char> const& aBitset): bitset(aBitset) {}
    BitStream(Vector<unsigned char> const& vector): bitset(vector) {}
    void writeBit(bool value){bitset.append(value);}
    bool readBit()
    {
```

```
        assert(bitsLeft());
        return bitset[position++];
    }
    void writeByte(unsigned char byte){writeValue(byte, B);}
    unsigned char readByte(){return readValue(B);}
    void writeValue(unsigned long long value, int bits)
        {bitset.appendValue(value, bits, true);}
    unsigned long long readValue(int bits)
    {
        assert(bits <= bitsLeft());
        position += bits;
        return bitset.getBitReversedValue(position - bits, bits);
    }
    unsigned long long bitsLeft()const{return bitset.getSize() - position;}
    unsigned long long bytesLeft()const{return bitsLeft()/B;}
};
```

The stream acts as a builder for a bitset. To convert a bitset to a byte vector, encode the number of bits in the last byte of the bitset storage into the last byte of the vector:

```
Vector<unsigned char> ExtraBitsCompress(Bitset<unsigned char> bitset)
{
    bitset.getStorage().append(bitset.garbageBits());
    return bitset.getStorage();
}
Bitset<unsigned char> ExtraBitsUncompress(Vector<unsigned char> byteArray)
{
    int garbageBits = byteArray.lastItem();
    byteArray.removeLast();
    Bitset<unsigned char> result(byteArray);
    while(garbageBits--) result.removeLast();
    return result;
}
```

Both take $O(n)$ time.

13.4 Codes

A code assigns a bit sequence ∀ symbol ∈ alphabet. Assume that symbols are integers because can map other objects to integers. Compression methods **model**, transforming the input sequence into a compressed or easier-to-compress sequence, and **code**, encoding the input into a bit string.

Prefix-free codes, where no codeword is a prefix of another, are uniquely decodable. They satisfy **Kraft's inequality**: $\sum 2^{-\text{length(codeword } i)} \leq 1$, which is stronger than the entropy bound because can't use fractional bits. A codeword consists of a value and a **length indication**. The latter is one of:

- A **terminating character** such as a space
- Encoded length preceding the value
- Length convention, e.g., `int` has 32 bits

In terms of bit error robustness, preceding length < terminating character < length convention. The input alphabet is usually a code with fixed length convention, such as ASCII.

13.5 Static Codes

A static code assigns the same bit sequence to the same symbol. E.g., binary code uses 8 bits for `char` and 32 for `int`. It's almost perfect when know how many bits to use. E.g., for DNA, $(A, C, G, T) \rightarrow (00, 01, 10, 11)$.

Unary code outputs value-many *1*'s and *0* for termination. E.g., $5 \rightarrow 111110$. A b-bit number needs $O(2^b)$ bits, so the code is useful only as a building block. Other efficient codes are between binary and unary and need $O(b)$ time and codeword space.

```
void UnaryEncode(int n, BitStream& result)
{
    while(n--) result.writeBit(true);
```

```
    result.writeBit(false);
}
int UnaryDecode(BitStream& code)
{
    int n = 0;
    while(code.readBit()) ++n;
    return n;
}
```

Gamma code expresses the number as $2^x + y$ for largest possible x and writes x in unary and y in binary using x bits, e.g., $5 \to$ *11001* because $5 = 2^2 + 1$; $\approx 2\lg(n)$ bits represent n, which makes the code asymptotically optimal, because $\lg(n)$ is the minimum. $!\exists$code for 0, but $1 \to$ *1*.

```
void GammaEncode(unsigned long long n, BitStream& result)
{
    assert(n > 0);
    int N = lgFloor(n);
    UnaryEncode(N, result);
    if(N > 0) result.writeValue(n - twoPower(N), N);
}
unsigned long long GammaDecode(BitStream& code)
{
    int N = UnaryDecode(code);
    return twoPower(N) + (N > 0 ? code.readValue(N) : 0);
}
```

Codes correspond to strategies for finding an unknown positive number using comparisons. Unary code is similar to linear search and gamma to exponential.

Any n is uniquely represented as $\sum$some of the Fibonacci numbers $\leq n$. So no two consecutive Fibonacci numbers appear in the sum (otherwise they would be replaced by their sum). **Fibonacci code**:

1. **Find the numbers representing the sum**
2. **$\forall$number, from smallest to largest, put *1* if included and *0* if not**
3. **Put terminator *1***

Two consecutive *1*'s signal termination. E.g., $7 \to$ *01011* because $7 = 0 \times 1 + 1 \times 2 + 0 \times 3 + 1 \times 5$. Because the ith Fibonacci number $\approx G^i$, where G is the golden ratio, and $i + 1$ bits represent n, $G^i \leq n < G^{i+1}$, and $\approx \lg(n)/\lg(G) + 1 \approx 1.44\lg(n) + 1$ bits represent n.

```
void advanceFib(unsigned long long& f1, unsigned long long& f2)
{
    unsigned long long temp = f2;
    f2 += f1;
    f1 = temp;
}
void FibonacciEncode(unsigned long long n, BitStream& result)
{
    assert(n > 0);
    //find largest fib number f1 <= n
    unsigned long long f1 = 1, f2 = 2;
    while(f2 <= n) advanceFib(f1, f2);
    //mark the numbers from highest to lowest
    Bitset<unsigned char> reverse;
    while(f2 > 1)
    {
        reverse.append(n >= f1);
        if(n >= f1) n -= f1;
        unsigned long long temp = f1;
        f1 = f2 - f1;
        f2 = temp;
    }//change order to lowest to highest and add terminator
    reverse.reverse();
    result.bitset.appendBitset(reverse);
```

```
    result.writeBit(true);
}
unsigned long long FibonacciDecode(BitStream& code)
{
    unsigned long long n = 0, f1 = 1, f2 = 2;
    for(bool prevBit = false;; advanceFib(f1, f2))
    {//add on the next Fibonacci number until see 11
        bool bit = code.readBit();
        if(bit)
        {
            if(prevBit) break;
            n += f1;
        }
        prevBit = bit;
    }
    return n;
}
```

Byte code represents numbers in base 128 by a little-endian sequence of bytes, where the highest bit signals the last character, with *0* meaning last. E.g., $128^2 \rightarrow$ 10000000|10000000|00000001. Byte code is fast due to not needing bit manipulations, efficient, using ceiling($\log_{128}(n)$) bytes = $\Theta(1.14\lg(n))$ bits, and usually the method of choice for data structure compression. UTF8 uses byte code for Unicode characters.

```
void byteEncode(unsigned long long n, BitStream& result)
{
    do
    {
        unsigned char r = n % 128;
        n /= 128;
        if(n) r += 128;
        result.writeByte(r);
    }while(n);
}
unsigned long long byteDecode(BitStream& stream)
{
    unsigned long long n = 0, base = 1;
    for(;; base *= 128)
    {
        unsigned char code = stream.readByte(), value = code % 128;
        n += base * value;
        if(value == code) break;
    }
    return n;
}
```

For portability, can transform a number into a sequence of bytes:

```
Vector<unsigned char> ReinterpretEncode(unsigned long long n, int size)
{
    Vector<unsigned char> result;
    while(size-- > 0)
    {
        result.append(n % 256);
        n /= 256;
    }
    return result;
}
unsigned long long ReinterpretDecode(Vector<unsigned char> const& code)
{
    unsigned long long n = 0, base = 1;
    for(int i = 0; i < code.getSize(); ++i)
    {
```

```
        n += base * (code[i] % 256);
        base *= 256;
    }
    return n;
}
```

Best code for values ∈ [1, 7] is gamma, ∈ [4, 33] ∪ [128, 1596] Fibonacci, and ∈ [21, 127] ∪ [987, ∞) byte.

Value	Unary	Gamma	Fibonacci	Byte
0	0	N/A	N/A	'00000000
1	10	1	'11	'00000001
2	110	100	'011	'00000010
3	1110	101	'0011	'00000011
4	11110	11000	'1011	'00000100
5	111110	11001	'00011	'00000101
6	1111110	11010	'10011	0'0000110
7	11111110	11011	'01011	'00000111
8	111111110	1110000	'000011	'00001000
16	Too long	111100000	'0010011	'00010000
32		11111000000	'00101011	'00100000
64		1111110000000	'1000100011	'01000000
128		111111100000000	'100010001011	'1000000000000001
256		'11111111000000000	'0100001000011	'1000000000000010
512		'1111111110000000000	'10101001010011	'1000000000000100
1024		'111111111100000000000	'0010000100000011	'1000000000000100

13.6 Huffman Codes

Huffman codes are optimal ∀ particular empirical distribution of observed symbols. The algorithm gathers probabilities in the first pass over the data and uses them to calculate the codes in the second. Binary trees with a leaf ∀symbol represent all prefix-free codes for a bounded alphabet. Walking to a symbol's leaf and outputting *0* for going left and *1* for right gives its codeword.

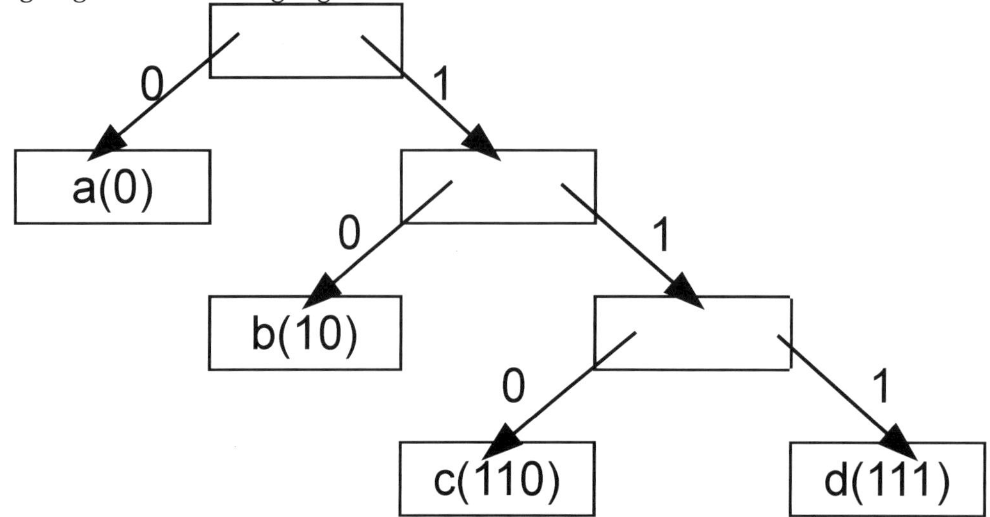

E.g., given *a*, *b*, *c*, *d*, codeword sets include (*00*, *01*, *10*, *11*) and (*0*, *10*, *110*, *111*). If the letters occur with probability ¼, E[the codeword length] = 2 for the first set and 2.25 for the second, but for probabilities ½, ¼, ⅛, and ⅛, for the second set E[the length] = 1.75. Want to find for a given distribution a tree that minimizes E[the length].

Huffman coding provably computes an optimal tree. It builds it bottom-up:

```
1. Create a forest with a symbol in each leaf
2. Until have a single tree
3.      Merge two trees with smallest symbol occurrence counts
```

So every node has 0 or 2 children, and to decide if it's a leaf only check if the left child is null.

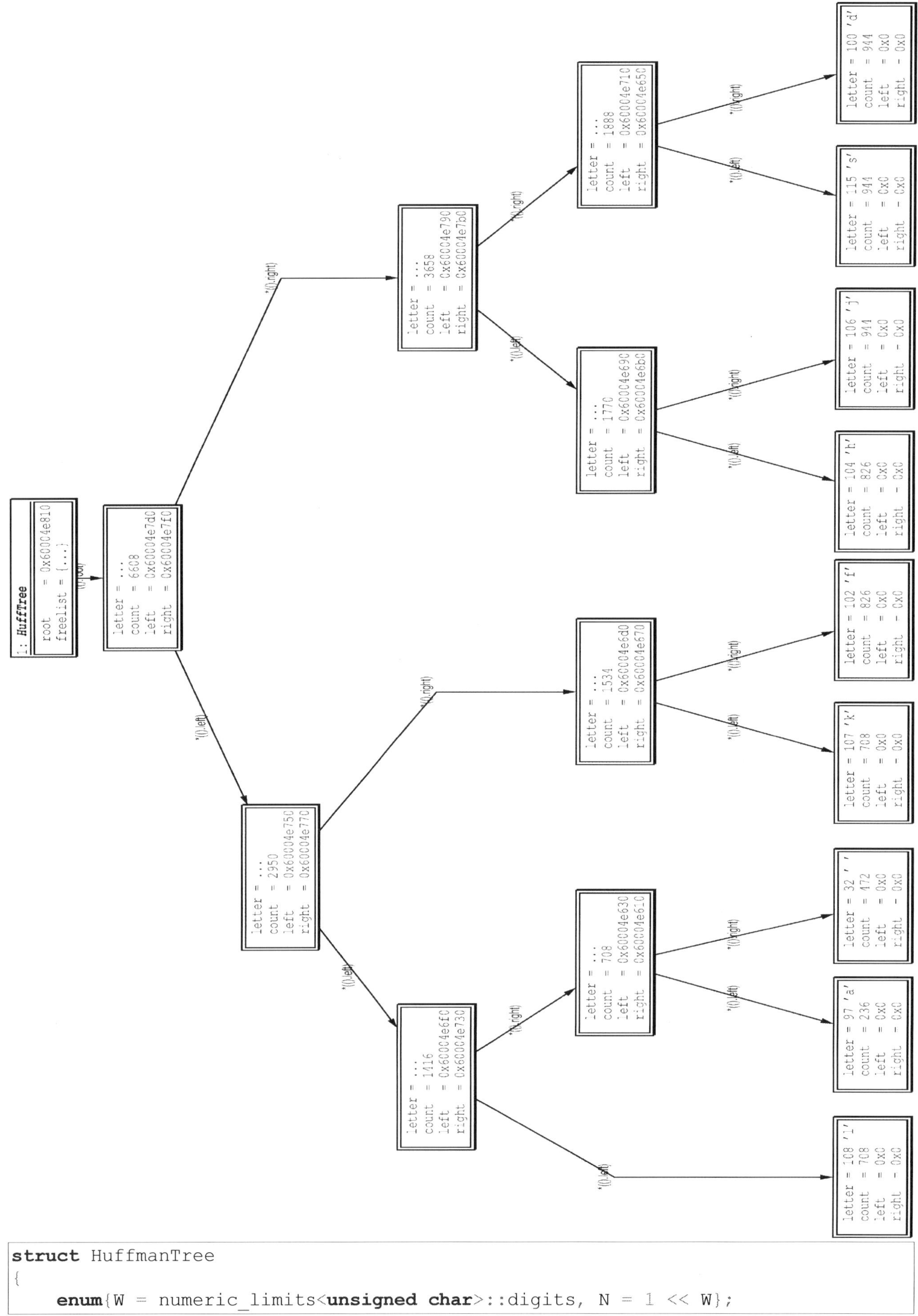


```
struct HuffmanTree
{
    enum{W = numeric_limits<unsigned char>::digits, N = 1 << W};
```

```
    struct Node
    {
        unsigned char letter;
        int count;
        Node *left, *right;
        Node(int theCount, Node* theLeft, Node* theRight,
             unsigned char theLetter): left(theLeft), right(theRight),
             count(theCount), letter(theLetter) {}
        bool operator<(Node const& rhs)const{return count < rhs.count;}
    }* root;
    Freelist<Node> freelist;
    HuffmanTree(Vector<unsigned char> const& byteArray)
    {//calculate frequencies
        int counts[N];
        for(int i = 0; i < N; ++i) counts[i] = 0;
        for(int i = 0; i < byteArray.getSize(); ++i) ++counts[byteArray[i]];
        //create leaf nodes
        Heap<Node*, PointerComparator<Node*> > queue;
        for(int i = 0; i < N; ++i)
            if(counts[i] > 0) queue.insert(new(freelist.allocate())
                Node(counts[i], 0, 0, i));
        //merge leaf nodes to create the tree
        while(queue.getSize() > 1)
        {
            Node *first = queue.deleteMin(), *second = queue.deleteMin();
            queue.insert(new(freelist.allocate())
                Node(first->count + second->count, first, second, 0));
        }
        root = queue.getMin();
    }
};
```

Traversing the tree, implemented as a member function of *Node*, creates a **codebook** that maps each symbol to a code.

```
        void traverse(Bitset<unsigned char>* codebook,
            Bitset<unsigned char>& currentCode)
        {
            if(left)
            {
                currentCode.append(false);
                left->traverse(codebook, currentCode);
                currentCode.removeLast();
                currentCode.append(true);
                right->traverse(codebook, currentCode);
                currentCode.removeLast();
            }
            else codebook[letter] = currentCode;
        }
```

Encoding writes the codebook and the codeword ∀symbol to a byte vector with the extra bits encoding.

```
Vector<unsigned char> HuffmanCompress(Vector<unsigned char>const& byteArray)
{
    HuffmanTree tree(byteArray);
    Bitset<unsigned char> codebook[HuffmanTree::N], result;
    tree.populateCodebook(codebook);
    tree.writeTree(result);
    for(int i = 0; i < byteArray.getSize(); ++i)
        result.appendBitset(codebook[byteArray[i]]);
    return ExtraBitsCompress(result);
}
```

To write the codebook, by preorder traversal of the tree, for a non-leaf write *0*, and recurse on both children, and for a leaf write *1* and the 8-bit symbol. E.g., for the tree in the drawing have *01a01b01c1d*, with the characters replaced by the corresponding bit sequences.

```
        void append(Bitset<unsigned char>& result)
        {
            result.append(!left);
            if(left)
            {
                left->append(result);
                right->append(result);
            }
            else result.appendValue(letter, W);
        }
    void writeTree(Bitset<unsigned char>& result){root->append(result);}
    void populateCodebook(Bitset<unsigned char>* codebook)
    {
        Bitset<unsigned char> temp;
        root->traverse(codebook, temp);
    }
```

Decoding reads the tree and uses it to decode each symbol:

```
Vector<unsigned char> HuffmanUncompress(
    Vector<unsigned char>const& byteArray)
{
    BitStream text(ExtraBitsUncompress(byteArray));
    HuffmanTree tree(text);
    Vector<unsigned char> result;
    tree.decode(text, result);
    return result;
}
    Node* readHuffmanTree(BitStream& text)
    {
        Node *left = 0, *right = 0;
        unsigned char letter;
        if(text.readBit()) letter = text.readValue(W);
        else
        {
            left = readHuffmanTree(text);
            right = readHuffmanTree(text);
        }
        return new(freelist.allocate())Node(0, left, right, letter);
    }
    HuffmanTree(BitStream& text){root = readHuffmanTree(text);}
    void decode(BitStream& text, Vector<unsigned char>& result)
    {
        for(Node* current = root;;
            current = text.readBit() ? current->right : current->left)
        {
            if(!current->left)
            {
                result.append(current->letter);
                current = root;
            }
            if(!text.bitsLeft()) break;
        }
    }
```

For a text of length n and alphabet A with $n > |A|$, need $O(n\lg(|A|))$ time to encode and $O(n)$ to decode. E[the code length] − $H(X) < 1$ (Salomon & Motta 2010). So for binary alphabet have no compression, and, for a model with k joined symbols, E[the code length] − $H(X) < 1/k$. E.g., for 8-bit symbols, bit redundancy ≤

12.5%. For small alphabets, use supersymbols for efficiency. For a very large file, can also divide it into blocks for convenience, and compress each independently with minimal efficiency loss. Huffman works with a general alphabet when using a hash table to hold the codebook.

13.7 Dictionary Compression

The idea is to encode a word by its position in the list of all words. **LZW** is the simplest dictionary method. Encoding and decoding start with a dictionary containing all single bytes and maintain the same dictionary of size n, so that dictionary of the encoder before/after writing word j = dictionary of the decoder respectively before/after reading word $j + 1$.

Encoding:

```
Initialize the dictionary with all single-symbol words
The current word = blank
Until EOF
    Append the read byte to the last word
    If the result ∉ dictionary
        Output the index of the current word
        Add the result to the dictionary
        Set the current word to the read byte
Output the index of the current word
```

The dictionary has size $\leq 2^{maxBits}$ and is a ternary treap trie for incremental search. Indices are encoded in binary using $\lceil \lg(n) \rceil$ bits, which is the number of bits needed to read any previous word. E.g., to encode *abhababa*:

Read Letter	Current Word	In the Dictionary?	Next Index	Output
a	a	yes	256	none
b	ab	no	256	97(a), 8 bits
h	bh	no	257	98(b), 9 bits
a	ha	no	258	104(h), 9 bits
b	ab	yes	258	none
a	aba	no	259	256(ab), 9 bits
b	ab	yes	259	none
a	aba	yes	259	none
				259(aba), 9 bits

```
void LZWCompress(BitStream& in, int maxBits, BitStream& out)
{
    if(!in.bytesLeft()) return;
    Vector<unsigned char> word(1);
    TernaryTreapTrie<int> dictionary;
    TernaryTreapTrie<int>::Handle h;
    int n = 0;
    while(n < 256)
    {
        word[0] = n;
        dictionary.insert(word.getArray(), 1, n++);
    }
    word = Vector<unsigned char>();
    do
    {
        unsigned char c = in.readByte();
        word.append(c);
        if(!dictionary.findIncremental(word.getArray(), word.getSize(), h))
```

```
        {
            out.writeValue(*dictionary.find(word.getArray(),
                word.getSize() - 1), lgCeiling(n));
            if(n < twoPower(maxBits))
                dictionary.insert(word.getArray(), word.getSize(), n++);
            word = Vector<unsigned char>();
            word.append(c);
        }
    }while(in.bytesLeft());
    out.writeValue(*dictionary.find(word.getArray(), word.getSize()),
        lgCeiling(n));
}
```

E[the runtime] = $O(n \times maxBits)$ due to incremental search, but can be smaller, depending on the text. Decoding builds an array dictionary from indices to words. When reading an index not-for-the-first time, it inserts the new word = the word corresponding to the last index + the first character of the word corresponding to the index. The latter ∈ dictionary unless it = the word added to the dictionary after outputting the last word. This can only happen if it = the last word + its first character. E.g., if *ababa* is decoded when *ab* ∈ dictionary, *aba* is added to the dictionary and immediately used to decode the *aba* suffix. The first word is read using 8 bits because it's not added to the dictionary, and ∀ other word the number of bits of the next possible index = $\min(maxBits, \lceil \lg(n + 1) \rceil)$. For a given word, the number of index bits is the same after/before respectively the encoder/decode adds it. To decode the encoding example output:

Next Index	Last Word	Read Index	Is in the dictionary	Added word
256	none	97(a), 8 bits	yes	none
256	97(a)	98(b), 9 bits	yes	ab
257	98(b)	104(h), 9 bits	yes	bh
258	104(h)	257(ab), 9 bits	yes	ha
259	257(ab)	259(aba), 9 bits	no	aba

```
void LZWUncompress(BitStream& in, int maxBits, BitStream& out)
{
    int size = twoPower(maxBits), n = 0, lastIndex = -1;
    Vector<Vector<unsigned char> > dictionary(size);
    for(; n < 256; ++n) dictionary[n].append(n);
    while(in.bitsLeft())
    {
        int index = in.readValue(lastIndex == -1 ? 8 :
            min(maxBits, lgCeiling(n + 1)));
        if(lastIndex != -1 && n < size)
        {
            Vector<unsigned char> word = dictionary[lastIndex];
            word.append((index == n ? word : dictionary[index])[0]);
            dictionary[n++] = word;
        }
        for(int i = 0; i < dictionary[index].getSize(); ++i)
            out.writeByte(dictionary[index][i]);
        lastIndex = index;
    }
}
```

The runtime is $O(n + 2^{maxBits})$.

13.8 Run Length Encoding

The idea is to count repeating bytes and output bytes and counts, which compresses when many bytes are repeated and is efficient because of working with bytes. One way to set this up is to reserve escape symbols $a = 255$ and $b = 254$, and ∀character c output:

- *cak* if the count of the remaining same symbols $k > 1$, or $c = a$ and $k = 1$
- *ab* if $c = a$ and $k = 0$
- c otherwise

Counts ≤ 253 fit into a byte and don't collide with the escape symbols. E.g., the byte sequence 0,0,0,0,0,127,127,255,254,255,255 → 0,255,4,127,127,255,254,254,255,255,1.

```
enum {RLE_E1 = 255, RLE_E2 = 254};
Vector<unsigned char> RLECompress(Vector<unsigned char>const& byteArray)
{
    Vector<unsigned char> result;
    for(int i = 0; i < byteArray.getSize();)
    {
        unsigned char letter = byteArray[i++];
        result.append(letter);
        int count = 0;
        while(count < RLE_E2 - 1 && i + count < byteArray.getSize() &&
            byteArray[i + count] == letter) ++count;
        if(count > 1 || (letter == RLE_E1 && count == 1))
        {
            result.append(RLE_E1);
            result.append(count);
            i += count;
        }
        else if(letter == RLE_E1) result.append(RLE_E2);
    }
    return result;
}
```

Only compression is possible if a is never present. After reading e, the next byte is a count unless it's a or b. If a the next byte is a count, and, if b, decode a single a.

```
Vector<unsigned char> RLEUncompress(Vector<unsigned char>const& byteArray)
{
    Vector<unsigned char> result;
    for(int i = 0; i < byteArray.getSize();)
    {
        unsigned char letter = byteArray[i++];
        if(letter == RLE_E1 && byteArray[i] != RLE_E1)
        {
            unsigned char count = byteArray[i++];
            if(count == RLE_E2) count = 1;
            else letter = result.lastItem();//need temp if vector reallocates
            while(count--) result.append(letter);
        }
        else result.append(letter);
    }
    return result;
}
```

The runtime for both is O(n).

13.9 Move-to-front Transform

MTF puts all symbols ∈ alphabet into a list in known order, e.g., by increasing numeric values, and ∀ input symbol outputs its rank and moves it to the front of the list. This transforms frequent numbers into small ranks, leading to compression during coding. E.g., repeating symbols lead to sequences of *0*'s.

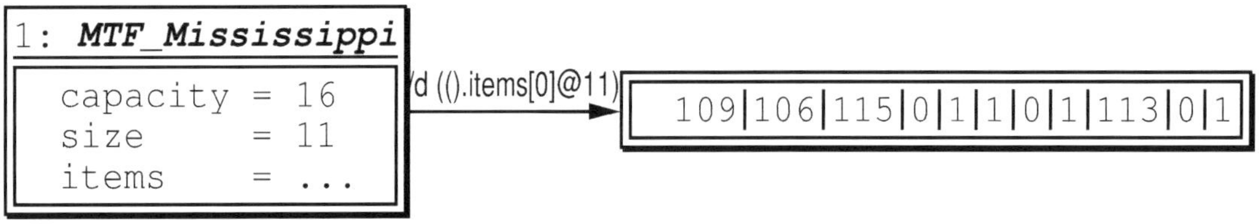

```
1: MTF_Mississippi
  capacity = 16
  size     = 11
  items    = ...
d (().items[0]@11) → 109|106|115|0|1|1|0|1|113|0|1
```

Decoding keeps a list of ranks, and ∀ rank outputs the symbol in that position and moves the rank to the front.

```
Vector<unsigned char> MoveToFrontTransform(bool compress,
    Vector<unsigned char>const& byteArray)
{
    unsigned char list[256], j, letter;
    for(int i = 0; i < sizeof(list); ++i) list[i] = i;
    Vector<unsigned char> resultArray;
    for(int i = 0; i < byteArray.getSize(); ++i)
    {
        if(compress)
        {
            j = 0;
            letter = byteArray[i];
            while(list[j] != letter) ++j;
            resultArray.append(j);
        }
        else
        {
            j = byteArray[i];
            letter = list[j];
            resultArray.append(letter);
        }
        for(; j > 0; --j) list[j] = list[j - 1];
        list[0] = letter;
    }
    return resultArray;
}
```

The runtime is $O(n|A|)$ for an alphabet A for encoding and decoding, but with small constant factors and cache-friendliness.

13.10 Burrows-Wheeler Transform

BWT of a string consists of the last column of the character matrix, formed by the sorted list of the string's rotations, and the index of the original rotation. E.g., *click* has rotations:

- *ckcli*
- *click*
- *ickcl*
- *kclic*
- *lickc*

The original rotation is in row 1, and the last column is *iklcc*. BWT creates easier-to-compress output because every section tends to use few distinct characters.

The suffix array algorithm computes BWT using the BWT rank functor to sort the rotations. Let t be the last column, corresponding to the transformed string. Because each row is a rotation, its rightmost character precedes the leftmost, so $t[i]$ = string[(BWT[i] – 1) % n], and the index of the original rotation is that of the rotation with the suffix at index 0.

```
Vector<unsigned char> BurrowsWheelerTransform(
    Vector<unsigned char>const& byteArray)
{
    int original = 0, size = byteArray.getSize();
    Vector<int> BTWArray = suffixArray<BWTRank>(byteArray.getArray(), size);
```

```
    Vector<unsigned char> result;
    for(int i = 0; i < size; ++i)
    {
        int index = BTWArray[i];
        if(index == 0)
        {
            original = i;
            index = size;
        }
        result.append(byteArray[index - 1]);
    }//make portability assumption that 4 bytes is enough
    Vector<unsigned char> code = ReinterpretEncode(original, 4);
    for(int i = 0; i < code.getSize(); ++i) result.append(code[i]);
    return result;
}
```

The runtime is O($n$lg(n)). The reverse transformation is O(n). It uses character counts to create arrays:

- **Ranks**—how many same characters in *t* precede the character at a given position. The left column ranks = the right column ranks because ∀ rows *xc* and *yc*, ending with same character *c*, *cx* and *cy* are their right rotations, and if *xc* < *yc* then *cx* < *cy*.
- **First positions**—the first positions of characters in the left column, computable because these are sorted and ∈ [0, 255]. If extending the algorithm to work with a different range, extract the sorted list of unique characters from *t*.

Can traverse the original rotation in reverse order because *t*[the original index] is the last character of the string, and ∀ other character *c* = *t*[*j*], the previous text character = *t*[*firstPositions*[*c*] + *ranks*[*j*]] because it's the position of the rotation with *c* in the first column and the wanted next character in the last. Intuitively, *firstPositions* finds all rotations that begin with *c*, and *ranks* tells which one corresponds to the right column character because ranks in both columns are the same. E.g., for *iklcc* with original position 1, the ranks are 00001 and first positions for *cikl* are 0234. The rotation sequence is 1 → *k*, 3 + 0 = 3 → *c*, 0 + 0 = 0 → *i*, 2 + 0 = 2 → *l*, 4 + 0 = 4 → *c*, the reverse of which is *click*.

```
Vector<unsigned char> BurrowsWheelerReverseTransform(
     Vector<unsigned char> const& byteArray)
{
    int counts[256], firstPositions[256], textSize = byteArray.getSize() - 4;
    for(int i = 0; i < 256; ++i) counts[i] = 0;
    Vector<int> ranks(textSize);
    for(int i = 0; i < textSize; ++i) ranks[i] = counts[byteArray[i]]++;
    firstPositions[0] = 0;
    for(int i = 0; i < 255; ++i)
        firstPositions[i + 1] = firstPositions[i] + counts[i];
    Vector<unsigned char> index, result(textSize);
    for(int i = 0; i < 4; ++i) index.append(byteArray[i + textSize]);
    for(int i = textSize - 1, ix = ReinterpretDecode(index); i >= 0; --i)
        ix = ranks[ix] + firstPositions[result[i] = byteArray[ix]];
    return result;
}
```

The compression system Huffman(RLE(MTF(BWT(input)))), implemented by **BZIP2**, is fast and effective. MTF exploits symbol grouping of BWT, producing small numbers. RLE compresses runs of *0*'s, *1*'s, and *2*'s, and its a = 255 is unlikely to appear in MFT output.

```
Vector<unsigned char> BWTCompress(Vector<unsigned char>const& byteArray)
{
    return HuffmanCompress(RLECompress(MoveToFrontTransform(true,
        BurrowsWheelerTransform(byteArray))));
}
Vector<unsigned char> BWTUncompress(Vector<unsigned char>const& byteArray)
{
    return BurrowsWheelerReverseTransform(MoveToFrontTransform(false,
       RLEUncompress(HuffmanUncompress(byteArray))));
```

```
}
```

13.11 Comments

∃many other static codes. **Turnstall code** uses binary code and, when alphabet size ≠ a power of two, assigns the remaining values to pairs of symbols. E.g., with alphabet *a*, *b*, *c*, *ab* → 3. But it's hard to decide which pairs are most likely. Some codes are optimal for specific data distributions, e.g., **Golomb** for geometric, and **Vigna** for power law, but more complex and do poorly for different distributions.

Some data structures such as splay tree can make MTF optimally asymptotically efficient, but are complicated and have high constant factors. MTF is usually far from being the compression pipeline's performance bottleneck, so no point using those.

For BWT, ∃complicated O(n) algorithms and new ones are still being proposed.

BZIP2 is the best general compressor. If efficiency is critical, prefer faster dictionary methods such as **GZIP**. Slightly more effective but much slower are variants of **PPM** (Salomon & Motta 2010).

Decompression speed is usually more important than compression speed because a file is often compressed once and decompressed many times, e.g., when it's uploaded to a server and downloaded many times. For applications such as file backups, compression speed is more important because most files are never accessed.

Compression is **lossy** when decompressed data closely resembles the original. This is useful for media and implemented by standards such as MP3 and MPEG. The idea is to reduce quality, but so that humans don't notice any difference, and apply lossless methods. Quality reduction is media-dependent, but often use a Fourier transform, and discard higher frequencies.

13.12 References

Adjeroh, D., Bell, T. C., & Mukherjee, A. (2008). *The Burrows-Wheeler Transform: Data Compression, Suffix Arrays, and Pattern Matching*. Springer.
Salomon, D. & Motta, G. (2010). *Handbook of Data Compression*. Springer.
Sayood, K. (2002). *Lossless Compression Handbook*. Academic Press.
Sedgewick, R., & Wayne, K. (2011). *Algorithms*. Addison-Wesley.

14 Miscellaneous Algorithms

14.1 Generating the First *N* Primes

Sieve of Eratosthenes keeps a list of first n numbers and ∀ prime $\leq \sqrt{n}$ removes its multiples. The list correctly tells which numbers are prime when going through it and removing in increasing order. For efficiency, the list is a bitset representing odd numbers ≥ 3.

```
class PrimeTable
{
    long long maxN;
    Bitset<> table;//marks odd numbers starting from 3
    long long nToI(long long n){return (n - 3)/2;}
public:
    PrimeTable(long long primesUpto): maxN(primesUpto - 1),
        table(nToI(maxN) + 1)
    {
        assert(primesUpto > 1);
        table.setAll(true);
        for(long long i = 3; i <= sqrt(maxN); i += 2)
            if(isPrime(i))//remove every odd multiple i <= k <= maxN/i
                for(long long k = i; i * k <= maxN; k += 2)
                    table.set(nToI(i * k), false);
    }
    bool isPrime(long long n)
    {
        assert(n <= maxN);
        return n == 2 || (n > 2 && n % 2 && table[nToI(n)]);
    }
};
```

The algorithm needs $O(n)$ time and $\approx n/16$ bytes of space.

14.2 Maintaining a Cache

Size and replacement policy define cache behavior. For a fixed size, an ideal policy caches resources to optimize their future access. The **least recently used** (LRU) policy has competitive ratio 2 (Wikipedia 2013). When the cache is full, and a resource ∉ cache is accessed, it evicts the oldest accessed resource. The optimal implementation is using a linked list, indexed by a hash table:

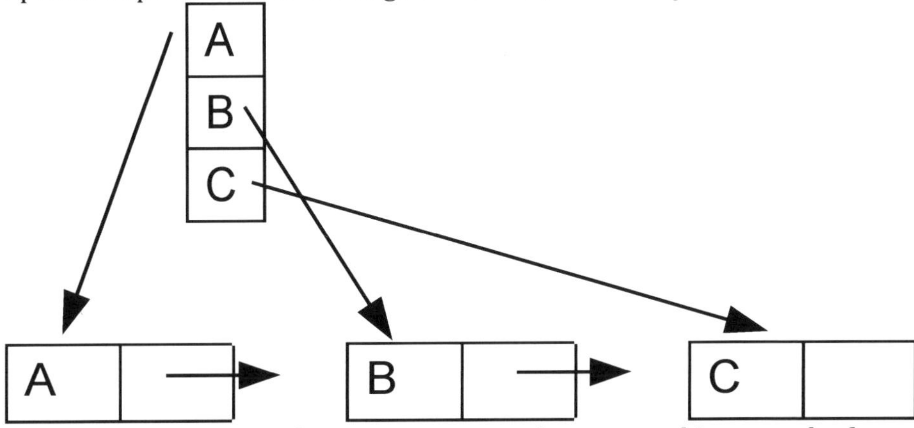

The list orders items by access time, moving accessed items to the front, and the hash table allows efficient search, so that operations take O(hash table) time.

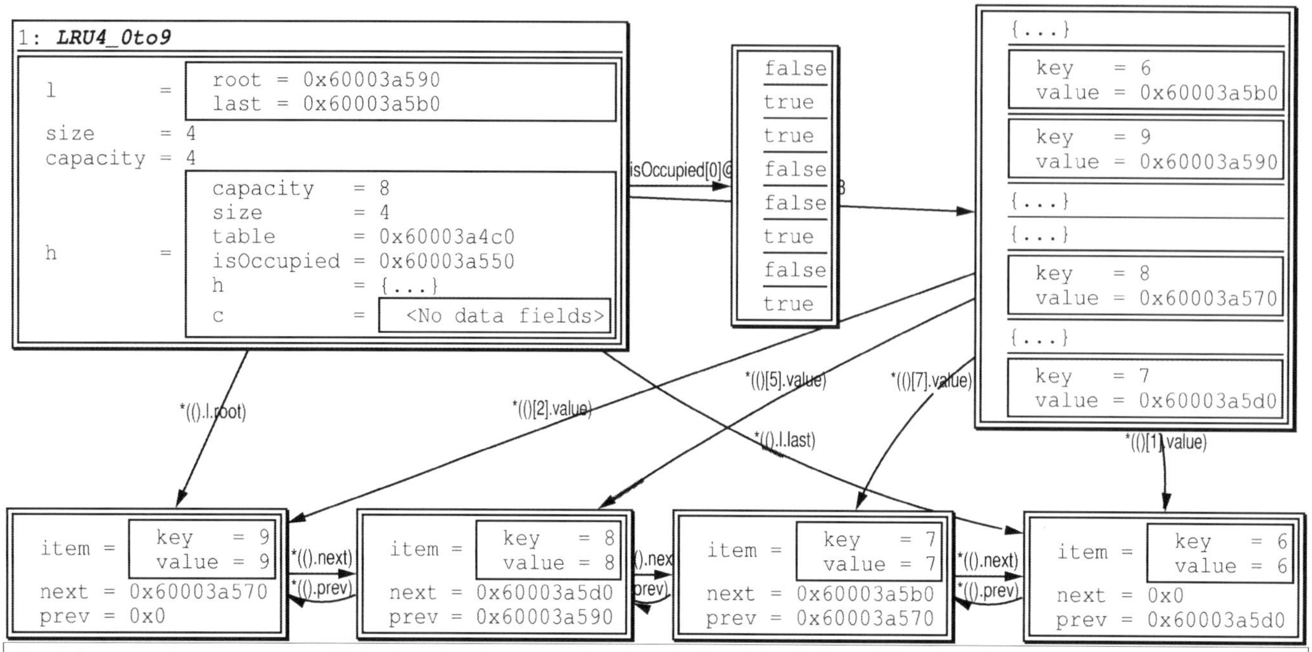

```
template<typename VALUE, typename KEY = int,
    typename HASHER = EHash32<BUHash> > class LRUCache
{
    typedef KVPair<KEY, VALUE> ITEM;
    typedef SimpleDoublyLinkedList<ITEM> LIST;
    typedef typename LIST::Node NODE;
    LIST l;
    int size, capacity;
    LinearProbingHashTable<KEY, NODE*, HASHER> h;
public:
    LRUCache(int theCapacity): size(0), capacity(theCapacity)
        {assert(capacity > 0);}
    struct Iterator
    {
        NODE* current;
        Iterator(NODE* node): current(node){}
        Iterator& operator++()
        {
            assert(current);
            current = current->next;
            return *this;
        };
        ITEM& operator*()const{assert(current); return current->item;}
        ITEM* operator->()const{assert(current); return &current->item;}
        bool operator!=(Iterator const& rhs)const
            {return current != rhs.current;}
    };
    VALUE* read(KEY const& k)
    {
        NODE** n = h.find(k);
        if(n)
        {
            assert(*n);
            l.cut(*n);
            l.prepend(*n);
            return &(*n)->item.value;
        }
        return 0;
    }
```

```
    KEY* evicteeOnWrite(KEY const& k)
    {
        if(size == capacity) return &l.last->item.key;
        return 0;
    }
    void write(KEY const& k, VALUE const& v)
    {
        KEY* evictee = evicteeOnWrite(k);
        NODE* n = l.last;
        if(evictee)
        {
            h.remove(*evictee);
            l.cut(n);
            n->item.key = k;
            n->item.value = v;
        }
        else
        {
            ++size;
            n = new NODE(ITEM(k, v), 0);
        }
        l.prepend(n);
        h.insert(k, l.root);
    }
    Iterator begin(){return Iterator(l.root);}
    Iterator end(){return Iterator(l.last);}
};
```

Can use this to implement a facade over various resources, so that API users are unaware that a cache is used, e.g., as is usually the case for disk access. The main difference between the various facades is whether need to write, and if yes, whether commit a write immediately or as late as possible.

```
template<typename KEY, typename VALUE, typename HASHER, typename RESOURCE>
class ReadLRUCache
{
    RESOURCE const& r;
    LRUCache<KEY, VALUE, HASHER> c;
public:
    ReadLRUCache(RESOURCE const& theR, HASHER const& h, int capacity):
        r(theR), c(h, capacity) {}
    static VALUE* readWork(KEY const& k, LRUCache<KEY, VALUE, HASHER>& c,
        RESOURCE const& r)
    {
        VALUE* v = c.read(k);
        if(!v)
        {
            v = r.read(k);
            if(v) c.write(k, *v);
        }
        return v;
    }
    VALUE* read(KEY const& k){return readWork(k, c, r);}
};
template<typename KEY, typename VALUE, typename HASHER, typename RESOURCE>
class InstantCommitLRUCache
{
    RESOURCE & r;
    LRUCache<KEY, VALUE, HASHER> c;
public:
    InstantCommitLRUCache(RESOURCE& theR, HASHER const& h, int capacity):
```

```
        r(theR), c(h, capacity) {}
    VALUE* read(KEY const& k)
    {
        return ReadLRUCache<KEY, VALUE, HASHER, RESOURCE>::readWork(k, c, r);
    }
    void write(KEY const& k, VALUE const& v)
    {
        c.write(k, v);
        r.write(k, v);
    }
};
template<typename KEY, typename VALUE, typename HASHER, typename RESOURCE>
class DelayedCommitLRUCache
{
    typedef pair<VALUE, bool> MARKED_VALUE;
    RESOURCE & r;
    LRUCache<KEY, MARKED_VALUE, HASHER> c;
public:
    DelayedCommitLRUCache(RESOURCE& theR, HASHER const& h, int capacity):
        r(theR), c(h, capacity) {}
    VALUE* read(KEY const& k)
    {
        MARKED_VALUE* mv = ReadLRUCache<KEY, MARKED_VALUE, HASHER,
            RESOURCE>::readWork(k, c, r);
        return mv ? &mv->first : 0;
    }
    void write(KEY const& k, VALUE const& v)
    {
        MARKED_VALUE* mv = c.evicteeOnWrite(k);
        if(mv && mv->second) r.write(k, mv->first);
        c.write(k, MARKED_VALUE(v, true));
    }
    ~DelayedCommitLRUCache()
    {
        typedef typename LRUCache<KEY, MARKED_VALUE, HASHER>::Iterator I;
        for(I i = c.begin(); i != c.end(); ++i)
            if(i->second) r.write(i->first.key, i->first.value);
    }
};
```

14.3 Generating All Permutations

To compute the **lexicographic successor** of a permutation:

1. **Find the last element < the next element**
2. **Swap it with its successor from the elements to its right**
3. **Reverse the latter**

This works because the elements to the right are in decreasing order after the swap. E.g., for 045837621, swap 3 with 6, and reverse to produce 045861237.

To skip a class of permutations, sort the remaining elements in decreasing order, and go to the next permutation. E.g., if don't need permutations beginning with 04586, skip them by producing 045867321 and going to 045871236.

```
struct Permutator
{
    Vector<int> p;
    Permutator(int size){for(int i = 0; i < size; ++i) p.append(i);}
    bool next()
    {//find largest i such that p[i] < p[i + 1]
        int j = p.getSize() - 1, i = j - 1;
```

```
        while(i >= 0 && p[i] >= p[i + 1]) --i;
        bool backToIdentity = i == -1;
        if(!backToIdentity)
        {//find j such that p[j] is next largest element after p[i]
            while(i < j && p[i] >= p[j]) --j;
            swap(p[i], p[j]);
        }
        p.reverse(i + 1, p.getSize() - 1);
        return backToIdentity;//true if returned to smallest permutation
    }
    bool advance(int i)
    {
        assert(i >= 0 && i < p.getSize());
        quickSort(p.getArray(), i + 1, p.getSize() - 1,
            ReverseComparator<int>());
        return next();
    }
};
```

Going to the next permutation takes O(n) and amortized O(1) time for a permutation of n elements because $(n - m)!$ out of $n!$ permutations need reversing m elements, and the total average work = $\sum_{0 \leq m < n} m(n - m)!)/n! = O(1)$. Visiting all permutations takes O($nn!$) time and is the bottleneck. The algorithm also works with repeated elements and can be templatized to work on any copyable and comparable elements.

14.4 Generating All Combinations

To compute the lexicographic successor of a combination c of m out of n numbers ∈ [0, n – 1]:

1. **Find the last index *i* at which *c*[*i*] < *n* – *m* + *i***
2. **Increment *c*[*i*]**
3. **∀*j* > *i* reset *c*[*j*] to *c*[*j* – 1] + 1**

E.g., for a (4, 6) combination 0145, i = 1, and the next combination is 0234. Skipping at i resets at i. The algorithm takes O(m) time per combination.

```
struct Combinator
{
    int n;
    Vector<int> c;
    Combinator(int m, int theN): n(theN), c(m, -1)
    {
        assert(m <= n && m > 0);
        skipAfter(0);
    }
    void skipAfter(int i)
    {//increment c[i] and reset all c[j] for j > i
        assert(i >= 0 && i < c.getSize());
        ++c[i];
        for(int j = i + 1; j < c.getSize(); ++j) c[j] = c[j - 1] + 1;
    }
    bool next()
    {//find rightmost c[i] which can be increased
        int i = c.getSize() - 1;
        while(i >= 0 && c[i] == n - c.getSize() + i) --i;
        bool finished = i == -1;
        if(!finished) skipAfter(i);
        return finished;
    }
};
```

14.5 Generating All Subsets

A subset of a set of size *m* is most economically represented as a bit string of size *m* with present items marked with 1 bits. To generate all subsets in lexicographic order, set the bit string to $2^n - 1$, and decrement until 0. To skip, zero out the wanted lower bits. The operations take O(1) time if use a single word as bit string.

This method is an application of general **ranking/unranking** technique. The idea is to define a mapping from the objects of interest to integers. Then can generate all objects by counting and unranking the current integer.

14.6 Generating All Partitions

A **partition** is an equivalence relation, where each item belongs to a group. For *n* items, the most economical representation is an array of group numbers starting from 0. Because putting every item in group 0 = putting every item in group 1, the max allowable value of $p[i]$, m_i, is $\max(m_{i-1}, p[i-1]+1)$ for $i > 0$ and 0 for $i = 0$. To generate the lexicographic successor, increase the rightmost increasable element, and set the rest to 0. E.g., for 010123, the second 0 is the rightmost increasable element and the next partition is 011000. To skip at *i*, make the values to its right the largest possible, and generate the successor. The algorithm takes O(*m*) time per partition.

```
struct Partitioner
{
    Vector<int> p;
    Partitioner(int n): p(n, 0) {assert(n > 0);}
    bool skipAfter(int k)
    {//set trailing elements to maximum values and call next
        assert(k >= 0 && k < p.getSize());
        for(int i = k; i < p.getSize(); ++i) p[i] = i;
        return next();
    }
    bool next()
    {//find rightmost p[j] which can be increased
        int m = 0, j = -1;
        for(int i = 0; i < p.getSize(); ++i)
        {
            if(p[i] < m) j = i;
            m = max(m, p[i] + 1);
        }
        bool finished = j == -1;
        if(!finished)
        {//increase it and reset the tail
            ++p[j];
            for(int i = j + 1; i < p.getSize(); ++i) p[i] = 0;
        }
        return finished;
    }
};
```

14.7 Generating All Constrained Objects

E.g., want to generate all syntax trees for a function of five variables using only three levels of operators "+" and "*". For generating all values of any type:

- Check if the type is isomorphic to an easily generatable type
- Find the most economical representation
- Use lexicographic order
- Avoid storing state

If all else fails, generate a less constrained class of objects, and accept/reject each, ultimately generating all binary sequences of some large length and outputting those that represent valid objects.

14.8 Error Detection

Sending data over a network can flip a few bits. Adding k bits of redundancy to a message allows to detect an error with probability $1 - 2^{-k}$ because a random message produces random bits. Interpreting the message as a large number, and finding the remainder of dividing it by a k-bit prime gives almost this probability, but is inefficient.

The **CRC** algorithm appends to the message k *0*'s, and returns the k-bit modulus of the result's binary polynomial division by a picked $(k + 1)$-bit polynomial. The implementation ignores its $(k + 1)^{\text{th}}$ bit = 1 and uses p = its k lower bits. Given a k-bit memory word w, divide:

1. **Append *k 0*'s to the message**
2. ***w* = *k* msd bits of the message**
3. **While the message has more bits**
4. ***w* = (*w* << 1) ^ the next bit of the message**
5. **If the msd bit of the previous *w* == 1, *w* ^= *p***
6. **Return word**

Since the last k bits = 0, the message bits affect w only as **control bits** for the xor-with-p-or-not decisions. So need to load the message only in the control bits, not in w. This eliminates needing to augment with k *0*'s:

1. ***w* = 0**
2. **While the message has more bits**
3. ***w* = (*w* << 1)**
4. **If (the msd bit of the previous *w* ^ the next bit of message == 1), *w* ^= *p***
5. **Return *w***

It's more efficient to process bytes. The next 8 control bits and p decide the next 8 xor-with-p-or-not decisions. Because xor is cumulative, for a given p and every possible byte, precompute the xors into a single constant, and use control bytes:

1. **Compute the constants**
2. ***w* = 0**
3. **While the message has more bytes**
4. ***w* = *w* << 8**
5. ***w* ^= constant[the msd byte of the previous *w* ^ the next byte of the message]**
6. **Return *w***

The 32-bit implementation can use any p to get Pr(can detect) = $1 - 2^{-k}$, but 0xFA567D89 is good at detecting all errors with a particular Hamming distance (Koopman 2002). The calculation can be online, with $O(n)$ total runtime.

```
class CRC32
{
    unsigned int polynomial, constant[256];
public:
    CRC32(unsigned int thePolynomial = 0xFA567D89u):polynomial(thePolynomial)
    {
        for(int i = 0; i < 256; ++i)
        {
            constant[i] = i << 24;
            for(int j = 0; j < 8; ++j) constant[i] =
                (constant[i] << 1) ^ (constant[i] >> 31 ? polynomial : 0);
        }
    }
    unsigned int hash(unsigned char* array, int size, unsigned int crc = 0)
    {
        for(int i = 0; i < size; ++i)
            crc = (crc << 8) ^ constant[(crc >> 24) ^ array[i]];
        return crc;
    }
};
```

14.9 Error Correction

A **binary symmetric channel** (BSC) flips each message bit with probability p. If $p \neq ½$, the channel gives random bits, and $p > ½$ is equivalent to $p < ½$, with all bits flipped. Can correct some errors using redundancy. A **(*n*, *k*) code** has 2^k n-bit codewords with $n \geq k$, and Hamming distance between any two codewords $\geq d$ for some d. Any received word becomes the nearest codeword in terms of Hamming distance, so can correct $\geq (d - 1)/2$ errors, and Pr(can't correct) = $O(p^{(d-1)/2})$. A code's **rate** $R = k/n$.

The **singleton bound**: the distance between codewords of an (n, k) code satisfies $d \leq n - k + 1$. This is because two (k, k) codewords are different in ≥ 1 bit, and adding another $n - k$ bits makes $d \leq n - k + 1$. The **channel capacity theorem**: By definition, capacity of a BSC channel = $1 - H(p) = 1 - (p\lg(p) + (1 - p)\lg(1 - p))$. In the worst case, $p = ½$, $H(p) = 0$, and communication is impossible. $\forall R < H(p)$ $\exists$ a finite-length code that makes Pr(can't correct) arbitrarily small.

The simplest way to correct errors is to detect them using CRC, and resend corrupt messages. This works well only for high-capacity channels with tiny p, so that E[the number of resent messages] is small. But e.g., DVD surface scratches introduce errors, which resending can't fix. For storage applications and lower capacity channels, **low density linear parity** (LDPC) code is a good solution.

A (n, k) code is **linear** if encoding is equivalent to interpreting a message m of size k as a bit vector and multiplying it by a code matrix C of size $k \times n$, using binary arithmetic. A code is **systematic** if the first $k \times k$ submatrix of $C = I$. Code matrices transformed by column permutations or elementary row operations produce the same codewords up to a bit permutation, and only need to store the $(n - k) \times k$ nonidentity part. Each redundancy bit corresponds to a parity bit of a subset of bits of m.

Every C corresponds to a **parity check matrix** P of size $n \times k$, such that $CP = 0$. A received word w is a codeword if $wP = 0$. When $C = [I|X]$, $P = [I|X]^T$. A code with parity check matrix P has d = the min number of linearly dependent columns of any column. LDPC code has very sparse P, allowing efficient decoding, but the implementation is complicated (Moon 2005).

An effective way to use an error-correcting code is **refreshing**—periodically decode and encode the data. This corrects bit errors after they are introduced, but before $\exists$too many to correct.

14.10 References

Koopman, P. (2002). 32-bit cyclic redundancy codes for internet applications. *International Conference on Dependable Systems and Networks* (pp. 459–468). IEEE.

Nayak, A., & Stojmenovic, I. (Eds.). (2007). *Handbook of Applied Algorithms: Solving Scientific, Engineering, and Practical Problems*. Wiley-IEEE Press.

Moon, T. K. (2005). *Error Correction Coding: Mathematical Methods and Algorithms*. Wiley.

Williams, R. (1993). A painless guide to CRC error detection algorithms. http://www.repairfaq.org/filipg/LINK/F_crc_v3.html. Accessed 5/18/2013.

Wikipedia (2013). Cache algorithms. http://en.wikipedia.org/wiki/Cache_algorithms. Accessed May 18, 2013.

15 Optimization

Want to find the best choice among possibly uncountably many, using some quality score. Solution algorithms look for the minimum, because the maximum is the minimum over the negated values. Conceptually, the value of a choice is its **economic utility**, which is happiness derived from the results of making the choice. E.g., empirical utility for human happiness as a function of wealth is believed to be O(lg(wealth)). Usually utilities are mathematically inconvenient or unknown, so use the identity function utility.

Checking each choice is too inefficient, but for some problems smart brute force is feasible for moderately large instances. Most useful optimization problems are NP-hard.

15.1 Typical Problems

The **traveling salesman problem** (TSP) gives a collection of points and distances between every pair and asks for a permutation of points such that visiting them in its order minimizes $\sum$traveled distance. Can include or exclude coming back from the last point to the first. The distances are usually Euclidean.

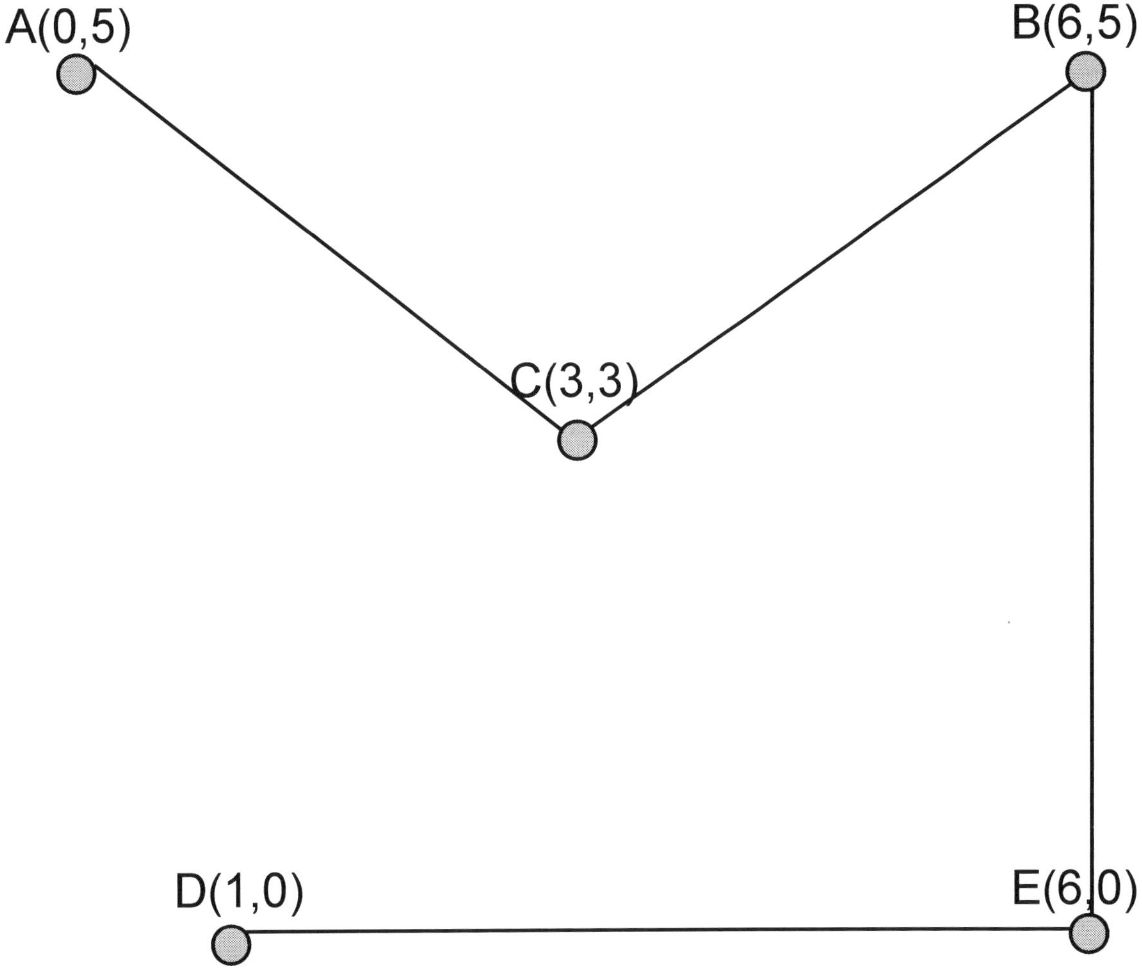

The TSP is the benchmark for new optimization algorithms, and much is known about it (Applegate et al. 2011). For random points $\in [0, 1]^2$, E[the best tour cost] = $\sqrt{n/2}$. For Euclidean distance, the best solution visits convex hull vertices in convex hull order (see the "Computation Geometry" chapter).

The **knapsack problem** gives max weight and a set of items with profits and weights and asks for a subset of items that maximizes $\sum$profits such that $\sum$weights $\leq$ max weight.

The **bin packing problem** gives a set of items with weights and ∞-many bins of capacity > the max weight and asks to partition the items, so that $\forall$subset $\sum$weights $\leq$ the bin capacity, and the number of subsets is minimal.

The **satisfiability problem** (SAT) gives n Boolean variables and a formula that is an *and* of many clauses, each of which is an *or* of several variables, and asks for a subset of true variables, such that when the rest are false the formula is true, or to declare the problem unsatisfiable.

The **integer programming problem** is the linear programming problem (see the "Numerical Algorithms" chapter), where every solution variable is discrete. **Rounding down** the corresponding linear program solution variables gives a suboptimal solution because an optimal one rounds down only some of them. Can model many problems as integer programming.

These problems are NP-complete and involve finding some combinatorial object, including a permutation, a subset, or a partition, that gives the best solution.

15.2 Approximation Algorithms

An approximation algorithm gives in polynomial time a solution that is suboptimal by at most a factor of C. Efficient approximation algorithms are usually greedy heuristics. E.g., for bin packing, the **next fit** strategy is 2-approximate (Vazirani 2004). It closes a bin when an item doesn't fit and opens another one.

Approximation algorithms are useful only when fast and simple. Unfortunately:

- Need to develop one, and prove it C-approximate $\forall$problem
- For many problems, useful approximation algorithms provably don't exist
- Many approximation algorithms have high-order polynomial runtimes
- Solutions found by heuristics are usually better

15.3 Greedy Construction Heuristics

For many hard problems, can get a good enough solution by constructing it using a greedy criteria. Some of these are approximation algorithms. E.g., for knapsack, picking items by decreasing profit/cost until before exceeding the max weight usually gives good results, though it's not an approximation algorithm. But **greedy algorithms are usually scalable to at least medium problem sizes and are often the method of choice**.

15.4 Branch and Bound

For some problems with incrementally constructable solutions, can compute a **lower bound** on the rest of the solution. E.g., for the TSP, the cost of visiting the remaining cities ≥ the cost of their MST + a cost of shortest edge from the last visited city to any unvisited one. B&B starts with a global lower bound ∞ and recursively enumerates all solutions by specifying one component at a time. Lower bounds allow to:

- Try the most promising component next
- Not consider a component further when the cost so far + the lower bound $\geq$ the global lower bound

For the TSP example:

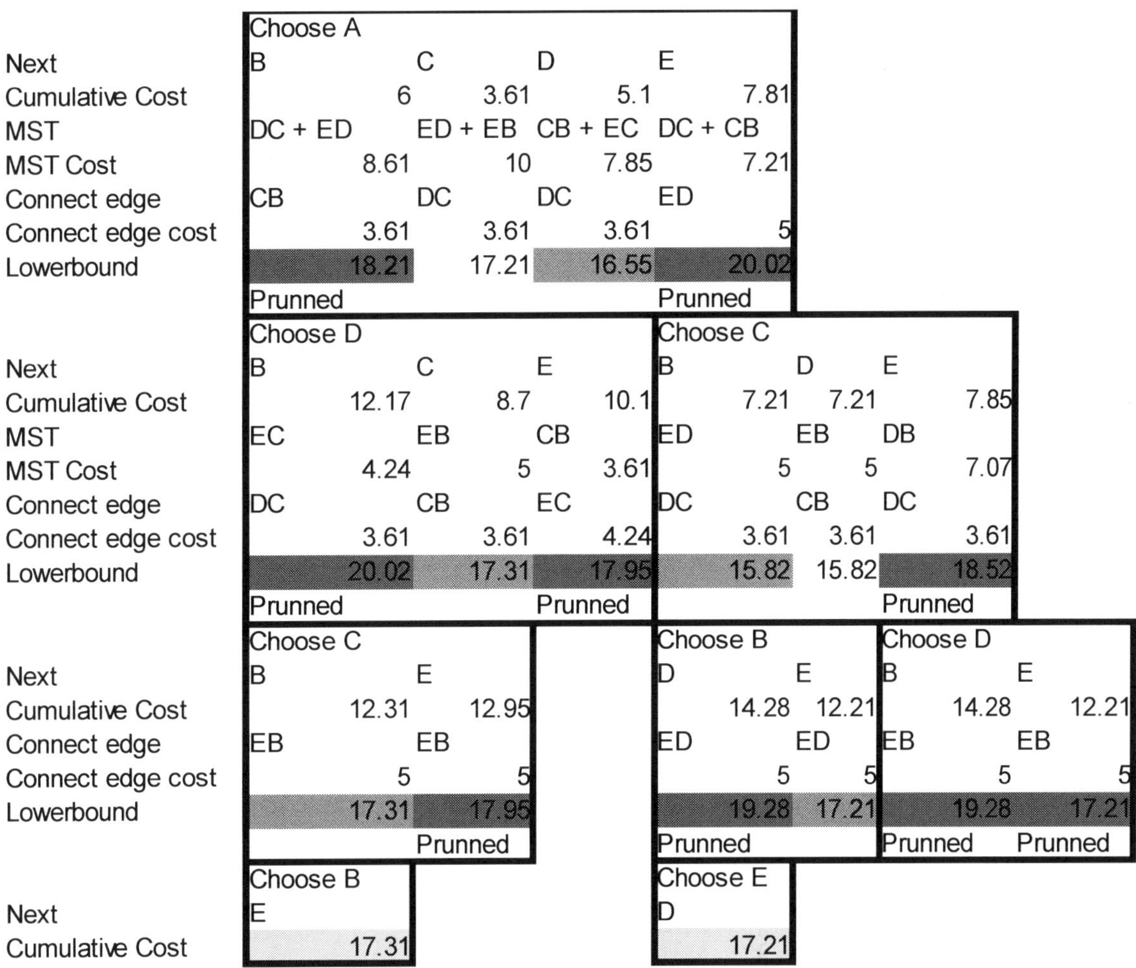

With tight enough lower bounds, it prunes many suboptimal solutions early and finds the optimum relatively quickly. B&B is an **anytime algorithm**, meaning stopping when time runs out gives the best answer found so far. To make the implementation generic, the problem data structure keeps track of lower bounds and decides if to prune.

```
template<typename PROBLEM> void branchAndBound(PROBLEM& p)
{
    if(!p.processSolution())
    {
        Vector<KVPair<double, typename PROBLEM::Move> > moves =
            p.generateMoves();
        quickSort(moves.getArray(), 0, moves.getSize() - 1,
            KVComparator<double, typename PROBLEM::Move>());
        for(int i = 0; i < moves.getSize(); ++i)
        {
            p.move(moves[i].value);
            branchAndBound(p);
            p.undoMove(moves[i].value);
        }
    }
}
```

E.g., B&B improves the greedy knapsack construction using lower bound = the solution where, using fraction items, fill the remaining capacity with the best profit/cost items. The runtime strongly depends on the quality of the lower bounds and can be exponential in the worst case.

15.5 State Space Shortest Path Search with Lower bounds

A **state space** is a huge implicit graph, with possible problem states as vertices and actions to transition from one state to another as edges. Each edge cost ≥ 0. A shortest path from the start to the goal states forms the solution. **A*** is a generalization of Dijkstra's algorithm that prioritizes vertices by the known cost to them + the lower bound on the rest of the path but doesn't consider all vertices in the graph from the start. Lower bounds and goal checks depend only on the current state and the path to it. The **open set** holds considered nodes with the best known lower bounds, and the **closed set** fully visited nodes with exactly known distances.

1. **Put the start node into the open set**
2. **Until the open set is empty**
3. **Take off the best-lower-bound node**
4. **Update it with the exact distance, and put it in the closed set**
5. **If it's the goal, return the solution path**
6. **Put its children in the open set; if already present, update the lower bound if lower**
7. **Report no solution**

For the open set use an indexed heap, and for the closed set a hash table to allow reconstruction of the solution path. The implementation assumes that states have unique ids, and the caller maps between them and its own state representation. E.g., to solve the TSP, the graph is a tree where any node has an edge to each untried city:

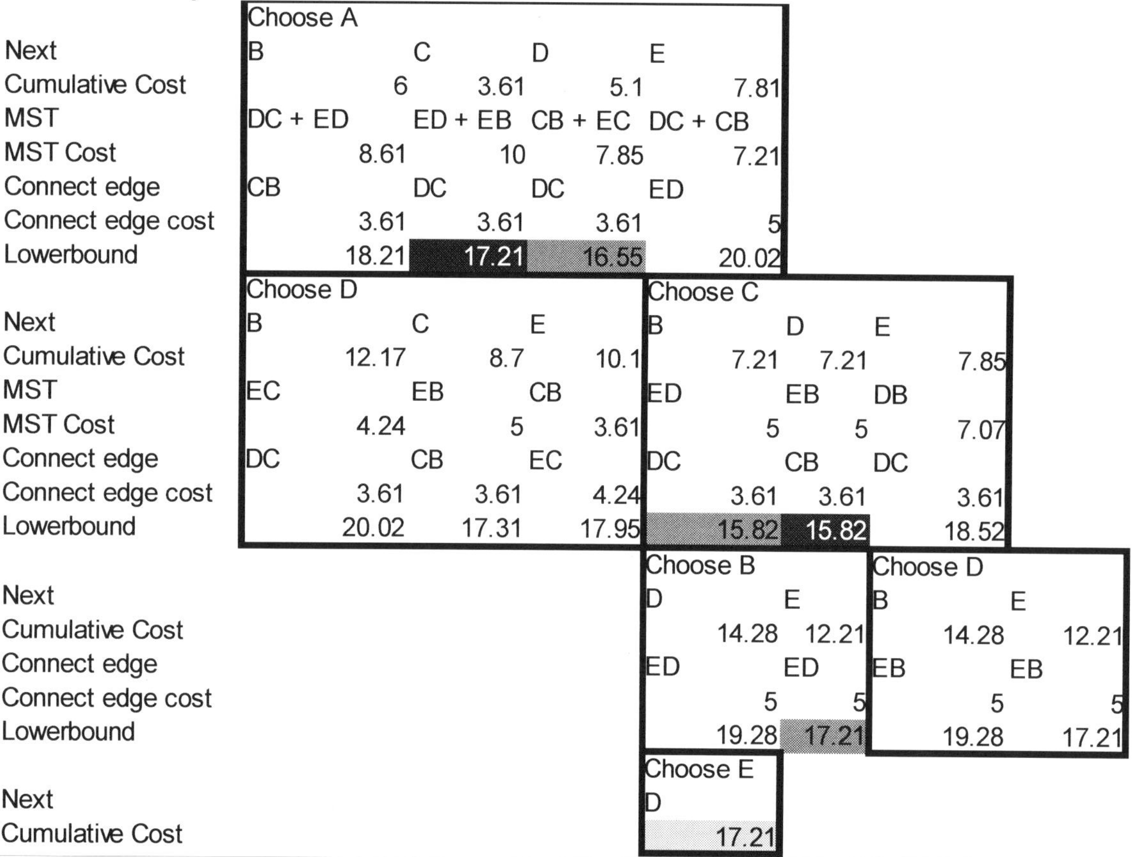

Choose A
Next: B, C, D, E
Cumulative Cost: 6, 3.61, 5.1, 7.81
MST: DC + ED, ED + EB, CB + EC, DC + CB
MST Cost: 8.61, 10, 7.85, 7.21
Connect edge: CB, DC, DC, ED
Connect edge cost: 3.61, 3.61, 3.61, 5
Lowerbound: 18.21, 17.21, 16.55, 20.02
Choose D
Next: B, C, E
Cumulative Cost: 12.17, 8.7, 10.1
MST: EC, EB, CB
MST Cost: 4.24, 5, 3.61
Connect edge: DC, CB, EC
Connect edge cost: 3.61, 3.61, 4.24
Lowerbound: 20.02, 17.31, 17.95
Choose C
Next: B, D, E
Cumulative Cost: 7.21, 7.21, 7.85
MST: ED, EB, DB
MST Cost: 5, 5, 7.07
Connect edge: DC, CB, DC
Connect edge cost: 3.61, 3.61, 3.61
Lowerbound: 15.82, 15.82, 18.52
Choose B
Next: D, E
Cumulative Cost: 14.28, 12.21
Connect edge: ED, ED
Connect edge cost: 5, 5
Lowerbound: 19.28, 17.21
Choose D
Next: B, E
Cumulative Cost: 14.28, 12.21
Connect edge: EB, EB
Connect edge cost: 5, 5
Lowerbound: 19.28, 17.21
Choose E
Next: D
Cumulative Cost: 17.21


```
template<typename PROBLEM, typename STATE_ID = unsigned long long>
struct AStar
{
    LinearProbingHashTable<STATE_ID, STATE_ID> pred;
    AStar(PROBLEM& p)
    {
        typedef KVPair<double, STATE_ID> QNode;
        IndexedHeap<QNode, KVComparator<double, STATE_ID> > pQ;
        STATE_ID j = p.start();
        pred.insert(j, -1);
        pQ.insert(QNode(p.lowerbound(j, pred), j), j);
        while(!pQ.isEmpty() && !p.isGoal(j = pQ.getMin().value, pred))
        {
            double dj = pQ.deleteMin().key - p.lowerbound(j, pred);
```

```
            Vector<STATE_ID> next = p.nextStates(j, pred);
            for(int i = 0; i < next.getSize(); ++i)
            {
                STATE_ID to = next[i];
                if(!pred.find(to)) pred.insert(to, j);
                double newDistance = dj + p.distance(to, j) +
                    p.lowerbound(to, pred);
                QNode* current = pQ.find(to);
                if(!current || newDistance < current->key)
                {
                    pQ.changeKey(QNode(newDistance, to), to);
                    pred.insert(to, j);
                }
            }
        }
    }
};
```

A* is optimal for a given lower bound function in the number of considered states, on which the runtime depends (Russell & Norvig 2010). But the open/closed state data structures can get too large. A* considers fewer states than B&B because it expands the node with the best global lower bound, and not the best child of current node. But the states need to remember the path to themselves, while B&B needs O(the path length) memory. For problems where paths represents states, B&B is usually more efficient.

Recursive best-first search (RBFS) uses O(the path length) space but revisits some states by storing in each node the best known value of the best alternative subtree that is accessible from any ancestor node and forgetting its non-root nodes.

1. ∀node the value = 0, and the alternative = ∞
2. The current node = the root
3. Until the stack has the path to a goal, or the root's value = ∞ when a solution doesn't exist and the stack is empty
4. Sort the current node's children by priority. If have none, and the node isn't a goal, the lowest priority = ∞
5. If the lowest priority ≥ the alternative, the current node's value = the lowest priority, and the current node = the parent
6. Else the current node = the lowest priority child, and the alternative = min(the second best child's priority, the current node's alternative)

	Choose A			
Next	B	C	D	E
Cumulative Cost	6	3.61	5.1	7.81
MST	DC + ED	ED + EB	CB + EC	DC + CB
MST Cost	8.61	10	7.85	7.21
Connect edge	CB	DC	DC	ED
Connect edge cost	3.61	3.61	3.61	5
Lowerbound	18.21	17.21	16.55	20.02
Updated LB			17.31	

	Choose D			Choose C		
Next	B	C	E	B	D	E
Cumulative Cost	12.17	8.7	10.1	7.21	7.21	7.85
MST	EC	EB	CB	ED	EB	DB
MST Cost	4.24	5	3.61	5	5	7.07
Connect edge	DC	CB	EC	DC	CB	DC
Connect edge cost	3.61	3.61	4.24	3.61	3.61	3.61
Lowerbound	20.02	17.31	17.95	15.82	15.82	18.52
Updated LB				17.21		

	Choose B		Choose D	
Next	D	E	B	E
Cumulative Cost	14.28	12.21	14.28	12.21
Connect edge	ED	ED	EB	EB
Connect edge cost	5	5	5	5
Lowerbound	19.28	17.21	19.28	17.21

	Choose E
Next	B
Cumulative Cost	17.21

```
template<typename PROBLEM, typename STATE_ID = unsigned long long>
struct RecursiveBestFirstSearch
{
    Stack<STATE_ID> pred;
    PROBLEM& p;
    enum{SUCCESS = -1};
    typedef KVPair<double, STATE_ID> INFO;
    double work(INFO state, double alternative, double pathCost)
    {
        if(p.isGoal(state.value, pred)) return SUCCESS;
        Vector<STATE_ID> next = p.nextStates(state.value, pred);
        if(next.getSize() == 0) return numeric_limits<double>::max();
        Heap<INFO, KVComparator<double, STATE_ID> > children;
        for(int i = 0; i < next.getSize(); ++i)
            children.insert(INFO(max(state.key, pathCost +
                p.distance(state.value, next[i]) +
                p.lowerbound(next[i], pred)), next[i]));
        for(;;)
        {
            INFO best = children.deleteMin();
            if(best.key > alternative) return best.key;
            pred.push(best.value);
            best.key = work(best, children.isEmpty() ?
                alternative : min(children.getMin().key, alternative),
                pathCost + p.distance(state.value, best.value));
            if(best.key == SUCCESS) return SUCCESS;
            children.insert(best);
            pred.pop();
        }
```

```
    }
    RecursiveBestFirstSearch(PROBLEM& theProblem): p(theProblem)
    {
        pred.push(p.start());
        work(KVPair<double, int>(0.0, p.start()),
            numeric_limits<double>::max(), 0);
    }
};
```

RBFS uses too little memory. The runtime should be similar to A* but is hard to analyze because much depends on the greedy choice success. To improve it, store the values of the forgotten subtrees in a hash table, and clear some of it on reaching the memory limit, but this is complicated to implement.

15.6 Local Search

Similar solutions for most problems are of similar quality. So local search starts with an initial solution (constructed randomly, by a heuristic, an approximation algorithm, or other means) and makes small improving changes until reaching a **local optimum**, like climbing a hill step by step. The **steps** can be:

- First found improving—usually not useful
- Best—most useful if efficiently computable (not by checking all steps)
- Random improving—simple and efficient, but to detect a local optimum check if the last k steps weren't improving, e.g., for $k = 100$

∃general step functions for common solution representations (the complexities are for random steps and a problem of size n):

- Permutation:
    - Remove an element and insert it between two others—$O(n)$
    - Swap two possibly adjacent elements—$O(1)$
    - Reverse a part of the permutation array—$O(n)$
- Subset:
    - Select i, and deselect j items—$O(i + j)$
- Partition:
    - Move i items from partition A to partition B and j items from B to A—$O(i + j)$

E.g., for the TSP, starting with a random solution and reversing random parts of the permutation usually leads to good solutions.

In many cases, step functions use **incremental evaluation**, i.e., compute a candidate solution's quality from the current solution's quality and step properties in $o(n)$ time, even if the solution representation space and the stepping runtime are $O(n)$. This makes random nonimproving steps cheap to reject. The implementation allows all step types and incremental evaluation. With best step, use max stall = 1.

```
template<typename SOLUTION> void localSearch(SOLUTION& s, long long maxMoves,
    int maxStall)
{
    for(int i = 0; maxMoves-- && i < maxStall; ++i)
        if(s.proposeMove() >= 0)
        {
            i = -1;
            s.applyMove();
        }
}
```

A step function forms a graph with vertices corresponding to solutions and having outgoing edges to vertices reachable by allowable steps. The number of iterations of local search ≤ the size of the longest improving path and is O(exponential in n), so limit the number of iterations. A step function is **complete** if the graph is strongly connected. Completeness allows visiting every solution. Visually, the graph is a mountainous terrain, with floor heights corresponding to solution qualities.

The **global optimum** is the best solution. Local search may get stuck in lower-quality local optima. Difficult landscape features:

- **Plateau**—a flat area where solutions have about the same quality

- **Golf hole**—a local optimum that is much better than all nearby solutions

A solution's **neighborhood** is the set of all solutions reachable from it by a single step. Its size is the number of allowable steps. A neighborhood **contains** another if it contains its every solution. Local optimum in one neighborhood needn't be so in another not contained by it. Local search can use several neighborhoods that don't contain each other and switch when the current one gets stuck, or use an expensive step function in a large neighborhood when a cheap one gets stuck in a contained neighborhood.

15.7 Simulated Annealing

Simulated annealing allows local search to escape local optima. It works with random steps and accepts worsening steps with probability that starts high and decreases until becoming too small and making the process equivalent to local search. The random motion gets the search into the landscape part with the global optimum, and the eventual local search finds it.

Quality change and "**temperature**" T determine Pr(accept a bad move) as accept if $e^{\text{change}/T} > uniform01$ or the equivalent change > $-T \times exponential01$. Every iteration multiplies T by a "**cooling factor**".

```
template<typename SOLUTION> void simulatedAnnealing(SOLUTION& s, double T,
    double coolingFactor, long long maxMoves)
{
    while(maxMoves--)
    {
        double change = s.proposeMove();
        if(change > -T * GlobalRNG.exponential01()) s.applyMove();
        T *= coolingFactor;
    }
}
```

!∃universal choices of parameters, but for the first attempt try:

- T_0 = 10000. Initially accept most moves to explore. If the starting solution is already of high quality, use T_0 = −the allowed initial change/ln(the desired initial acceptance probability).
- Cooling factor = 0.9999. Beware that a typical cooling factor makes $T < 1$ in relatively few iterations, and the random move stage may be too short.
- Max iterations = 10000. This controls the runtime. Usually need many iterations to find the global optimum, so pick as many as patience allows, and set the cooling factor so that later iterations aren't doing only local search.

Storing the best solution found so far has negligible quality benefit and might dominate the runtime. Simulated annealing eventually finds the global optimum with probability 1.

15.8 Iterated Local Search

Simulated annealing is most suited for random steps, and iterated local search for best or first improving steps. Starting from an initial solution, it iteratively finds a local minimum and jumps far in the landscape, storing the best found solution. The jump should be irreversible by local search. A **partial restart solution** doesn't lose all current solution components and is usually better than a random restart solution, which tends to be of average quality by the CLT. This phenomenon is called the **central limit catastrophe**.

For the first try, set max iterations to 10000 and subsequently to as many as patience allows.

```
template<typename SOLUTION>
void iteratedLocalSearch(SOLUTION& s, long long maxBigMoves)
{
    while(maxBigMoves--)
    {
        s.localSearchBest();
        s.updateBest();
        s.bigMove();
    }
}
```

15.9 Problem-specific Preprocessing

For some types of problems, can analyze a particular problem and reduce its size by using various properties, e.g., symmetries. This needs insight and can't be done automatically. E.g., for **train scheduling**, merging common routes, stations, and using other problem-specific information reduced the problem size enough to use brute force (Weihe 2001).

15.10 Multiobjective Optimization

Want to find a solution that optimizes several objectives. A decision maker may want to see all possibilities instead of optimizing some function of the objectives.

Any solution not worse than any other in all objectives is optimal. Optimal solutions form a possibly-infinitely-large **Pareto-optimal front**. It's harder to manage than a single solution, so it's best to optimize some utility function, such as a linear combination of the desired parameters, with logical weights that consider one attribute at a time, weigh all attributes equally, or require certain attributes to have values from some range, etc.

15.11 Constraint Processing

For some optimization problems, solutions consist of variables with values ∈ some integral domain. A **constraint** is a set of disallowed value tuples. E.g., a Sudoku solution consists of 81 variables ∈ [1, 9], and each box, row, and column must contain all numbers. A constraint problem solution consists of value assignments that don't violate the constraints. If !∃ a solution, the problem is **unsatisfiable**. Constraints that involve two variables are **binary**, the most efficient to represent, and work with.

The simplest way to represent variables and allowed values is a vector of bitsets where each variable is associated with a bitset of size = its domain, and bit i is set if the ith value in the domain is allowed. The simplest way to represent binary constraints is a graph with vertices corresponding to variables and edges to constraints between the involved vertices. Edge data has a constraint functor that checks if a value is allowed.

```
template<typename CONSTRAINT> struct ConstraintGraph
{
    typedef GraphAA<CONSTRAINT> GRAPH;
    GRAPH g;
    Vector<Bitset<> > variables;
    void addVariable(int domain)
    {
        g.addVertex();
        variables.append(Bitset<>(domain));
    }
    void addConstraint(int v1, int v2, CONSTRAINT const& constraint)
    {
        assert(v1 != v2);
        g.addUndirectedEdge(v1, v2, constraint);
    }
    void disallow(int variable, int value)
        {variables[variable].set(value, false);}
    bool hasSolution(int variable){return !variables[variable].isZero();}
};
```

A value is allowed if any other variable can take on one or more values such that the pair of values doesn't violate the constraint between them:

```
    bool isAllowed(int variable, int value, int otherVariable,
        CONSTRAINT const& constraint)
    {
        for(int i = 0; i < variables[otherVariable].getSize(); ++i)
            if(variables[otherVariable][i] && constraint.isAllowed(variable,
                value, otherVariable, i)) return true;
        return false;
    }
```

To check a variable against another and **revise** its domain by removing values that aren't allowed, check every set value:

```
bool revise(int variable1, int variable2, CONSTRAINT const& constraint)
{
    bool changed = false;
    for(int i = 0; i < variables[variable1].getSize(); ++i)
        if(variables[variable1][i] &&
            !isAllowed(variable1, i, variable2, constraint))
        {
            disallow(variable1, i);
            changed = true;
        }
    return changed;
}
```

Revising every variable using every variable with which it has a constraint while ∃ one gives a correct solution. **Simplified AC3** makes this more efficient because after the first revision a variable isn't revisable until its neighbors are revised:

```
Revise every variable with respect to its every neighbor, and enqueue it
Until the queue is empty
    Dequeue a variable
    ∀neighbor variable
        Revise it with respect to the variable
        Enqueue if successfully revised
```

Can use any list data structure instead of a queue.

```
bool AC3Helper(int v, Queue<int>& q, Vector<bool>& onQ, bool isFirstPass)
{
    onQ[v] = false;
    for(typename GRAPH::AdjacencyIterator i = graph.begin(v);
        i != graph.end(v); ++i)
    {
        int revisee = i.to(), against = v;
        if(isFirstPass) swap(revisee, against);
        if(revise(revisee, against, i.data()))
        {
            if(!hasSolution(revisee)) return false;
            if(!onQ[revisee]) q.push(revisee);
            onQ[revisee] = true;
        }
    }
    return true;
}
bool AC3()
{
    Queue<int> q;
    Vector<bool> onQ(graph.nVertices(), true);
    for(int j = 0; j < graph.nVertices(); ++j)
        if(!AC3Helper(j, q, onQ, true)) return false;
    while(!q.isEmpty())if(!AC3Helper(q.pop(), q, onQ, false))
        return false;
    return true;
}
```

Let d = max domain size, and c = the number of constraints. `revise` enqueues each vertex $v_i \le |\text{domain}(v_i)|$ times and is called $\le cd$ times, with each call taking $O(d^2)$ time. AC3 needn't work on problems where values satisfy pair but not higher-order-tuple constraints.

Many constraint problems are efficiently solvable using a B&B that uses AC3 to check the current value assignment and reduce domains of not-yet-selected variables and selects the next variable as the one with the smallest domain to maximize pruning.

The **AllDifferent constraint** requires a subset of variables to take on different values. It allows, e.g., to model Sudoku as a binary constraint problem:

```
struct AllDifferent
{
    LinearProbingHashTable<int, bool> variables;
    void addVariable(int variable){variables.insert(variable, true);}
    struct Handle
    {
        LinearProbingHashTable<int, bool>& variables;
        bool isAllowed(int variable, int value, int variable2, int value2)
            const
        {
            if(variables.find(variable) && variables.find(variable2))
                return value != value2;
            return true;
        }
        Handle(LinearProbingHashTable<int, bool>& theVariables):
            variables(theVariables) {}
    } handle;
    AllDifferent(): handle(variables) {}
};
```

15.12 Stochastic problems

For problems where the objective function is noisy and want to find an instance with the best E[quality], sample average/path approximation methods (see the "Numerical Algorithms" chapter) are effective.

The presented algorithms aren't designed to handle noise, though some do so well. E.g., for simulated annealing, deciding if the generated solution is better using a single comparison is invalid because of the noise, but can still use it as is for small levels of noise.

15.13 General Advice

The **no free lunch theorem** (NFL) states that over all possible problem instances no algorithm does better than random search, ending discussion about which particular method is best in all cases. The main idea is that over all problems local information is ineffective because it's helpful for some problems and harmful for others. I.e., knowing local information is equality likely to be helpful or misleading over all problems (same for the NFL for learning; see the "General Machine Learning" chapter). But in practice rarely solve problems where local information is harmful. Still, it's likely to be only a little useful. Though don't want to solve every possible problem, ∀ problem some algorithms exploit problem-specific info better than others, and vice versa for other problems.

No algorithm is effective where all solutions except the best have similar quality. Conclusions of the NFL and general experience:

- Use problem-specific information. Better lower bounds and step functions are what makes an algorithm efficient by allowing it to not consider low-quality solutions. Must use useful local search or bound information to solve a problem in a reasonable time. Not having such structure means that can't solve the problem. Incremental evaluation and efficient problem representation also make a big difference.
- Efficient algorithms have low modeling overhead. E.g., for the TSP, B&B is better than A*.
- Well-designed algorithms eventually find the solution with probability 1.
- Metaheuristics may not work well for constrained problems, and even a feasible starting solution may be hard to find.
- For very large instances, only greedy algorithms and sometimes local search are feasible.
- Many problems have **phase transitions**, where instances randomly generated with certain parameters are easy, but adjusting the parameters beyond some thresholds creates practically unsolvable problems with ineffective problem-specific information.
- Many well-studied problems have complicated solution methods that outperform generic ones like

local search.

15.14 Comments

Another solution approach is expressing a problem in terms of integer programming, for which well-engineered solvers handle problems of small to medium size. Algebraic modeling languages are more expressive but less efficient, e.g., **ZIMPL**.

15.15 References

Applegate, D. L., Bixby, R. E., Chvatal, V., & Cook, W. J. (2011). *The Traveling Salesman Problem: a Computational Study*. Princeton University Press.

Russell, S. J., Norvig, P. (2010). *Artificial Intelligence: a Modern Approach*. Prentice Hall.

Talbi, E. G. (2009). *Metaheuristics: from Design to Implementation*. Wiley.

Vazirani, V. V. (2004). *Approximation Algorithms*. Springer.

Weihe, K. (2001). On the differences between "practical" and "applied". In *Algorithm Engineering* (pp. 1–10). Springer.

16 Large Numbers

Need large numbers when precision of built-in types isn't enough—mostly in cryptography and scientific computation. Most algorithms are a formalization of high school math. Operation complexity is usually measured in terms of the number of digits of the inputs.

16.1 Representation

A number consists of a sign and a vector of digits in some base. For unambiguous, simple, and efficient representation:

- The least significant digit is at index 0.
- Let w be the largest available word size, assumed to be `unsigned long long`. The base = $2^{w/2}$ because the product of two $w/2$ bit numbers fits into a w-bit word. Algorithms assume that the base is a power of two.
- !∃leading *0*'s, except when the number = 0.
- −0 and 0 are allowed—simpler than correcting −0 after every operation.

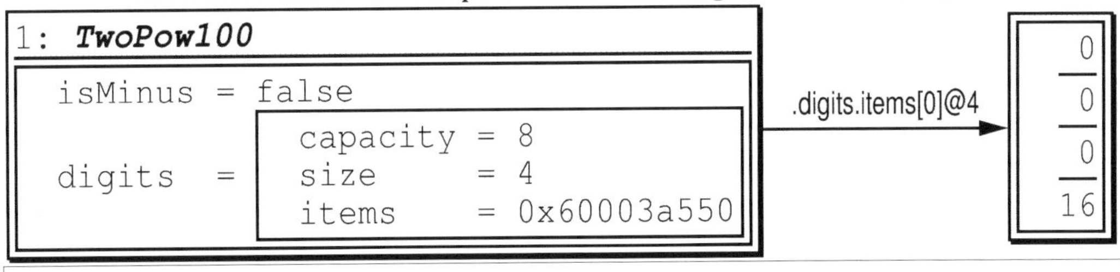

```
1: TwoPow100
isMinus = false
digits  = capacity = 8
          size     = 4
          items    = 0x60003a550
```

.digits.items[0]@4

```
0
0
0
16
```

```
class Number
{
    bool isMinus;
    typedef unsigned int DIGIT;
    typedef unsigned long long LARGE_DIGIT;
    enum{BASE_RADIX = numeric_limits<DIGIT>::digits};
    Vector<DIGIT> digits;
public:
    typedef DIGIT DIGIT_TYPE;
    DIGIT getDigit(int i)const{return i < nDigits() ? digits[i] : 0;}
    bool isZero()const{return digits.lastItem() == 0;}
    bool isPositive()const{return !isMinus && !isZero();}
    bool isNegative()const{return isMinus && !isZero();}
    int nDigits()const{return digits.getSize();}
    DIGIT& operator[](unsigned int i){return digits[i];}
    DIGIT const& operator[](unsigned int i)const{return digits[i];}
    void trim(){while(nDigits() > 1 && isZero()) digits.removeLast();}
    void negate(){isMinus = !isMinus;}
    Number operator-()const
    {
        Number result = *this;
        result.negate();
        return result;
    }
    Number abs()const{return isMinus ? -*this : *this;}
    bool isOdd()const{return digits[0] % 2;}
    bool isEven()const{return !isOdd();}
    Number(): isMinus(false) {digits.append(0);}
    void appendDigit(DIGIT const& digit){digits.append(digit);}
    void constructFrom(LARGE_DIGIT digit, bool theIsNegative)
```

```
    {
        assert(BASE_RADIX * 2 <= numeric_limits<LARGE_DIGIT>::digits);
        isMinus = theIsNegative;
        digits.append(digit);
        DIGIT first = digit >> BASE_RADIX;
        if(first != 0) digits.append(first);
    }
    Number(unsigned int x){constructFrom(x, false);}
    Number(unsigned long long x){constructFrom(x, false);}
    Number(int x){constructFrom(x < 0 ? -x : x, x < 0);}
    Number(long long x){constructFrom(x < 0 ? -x : x, x < 0);}
    Number(int size, unsigned long long fill): digits(size, fill),
        isMinus(false) {}
};
```

Comparisons handle −0:

```
    bool absLess(Number const& rhs)const
    {
        if(nDigits() != rhs.nDigits()) return nDigits() < rhs.nDigits();
        for(int i = nDigits() - 1; i >= 0; --i)
            if(digits[i] != rhs[i]) return digits[i] < rhs[i];
        return false;
    }
    bool absEqual(Number const& rhs)const
    {
        if(nDigits() != rhs.nDigits()) return false;
        for(int i = 0; i < nDigits(); ++i)
            if(digits[i] != rhs[i]) return false;
        return true;
    }
    bool operator<(Number const& rhs)const
        {return (isMinus && !rhs.isMinus && !isZero()) || absLess(rhs);}
    bool operator==(Number const& rhs)const
        {return (isMinus == rhs.isMinus || isZero()) && absEqual(rhs);}
```

16.2 Addition and Subtraction

A **full adder** adds digits *a*, *b*, and *carry* and returns the sum and the new carry. Using it, add two positive digit vectors digit by digit, propagating the carry. The result is at most one digit longer than either addend and trimmed if that digit = 0.

```
    static DIGIT fullAdder(DIGIT a, DIGIT b, DIGIT& carry)
    {
        LARGE_DIGIT sum = LARGE_DIGIT(a) + b + carry;
        carry = sum >> BASE_RADIX;
        return sum;
    }
    static Number add(Number const& a, Number const& b)
    {//O(|a|+|b|)
        int n = max(a.nDigits(), b.nDigits());
        Number result(n + 1, 0);
        DIGIT carry = 0;
        for(int i = 0; i < n; ++i)
            result[i] = fullAdder(a.getDigit(i), b.getDigit(i), carry);
        result[n] = carry;
        result.trim();
        return result;
    }
```

Subtraction of two positive numbers assumes that the first is greater and places the result in it. It propagates the carry like addition.

```
static void sub(Number& a, Number const& b)
{//O(|a| + |b|)
    bool carry = 0;
    for(int i = 0; i < a.nDigits(); ++i)
    {
        LARGE_DIGIT digit = LARGE_DIGIT(b.getDigit(i)) + carry;
        a[i] -= 0;
        carry = a[i] < digit;
    }
    a.trim();
}
```

Operators "+" and "–" are implemented on top of these functions and look at the sign:

```
friend Number operator+(Number const& a, Number const& b)
{
    if(a.isMinus == b.isMinus)
    {
        Number result = add(a, b);
        result.isMinus = a.isMinus;
        return result;
    }
    else return a - -b;
}
Number& operator+=(Number const&rhs){return *this = *this + rhs;}
Number& operator++(){return *this += 1;}
Number operator++(int)
{
    Number result = *this;
    ++*this;
    return result;
}
friend Number operator-(Number const& a, Number const& b)
{
    if(a.isMinus == b.isMinus)
    {
        bool less = a.absLess(b);
        Number larger = less ? b : a;
        sub(larger, less ? a : b);
        if(less) larger.isMinus = !larger.isMinus;
        larger.trim();
        return larger;
    }
    else return a + -b;
}
Number& operator-=(Number const& rhs){return *this = *this - rhs;}
Number& operator--(){return *this -= 1;}
Number operator--(int)
{
    Number result = *this;
    --*this;
    return result;
}
```

16.3 Shifts

Shifts multiply or divide by a power of two, shifting words and bits separately for efficiency, like for bitset. The runtime is $O(n)$.

```
Number& operator>>=(unsigned int k)
{
```

```
        int skipCells = k/BASE_RADIX, last = nDigits() - skipCells,
            skipBits = k % BASE_RADIX;
        if(skipCells > 0) for(int i = 0; i < nDigits(); ++i)
            digits[i] = i < last ? digits[i + skipCells] : 0;
        if(skipBits > 0)
        {
            DIGIT carry = 0, tempCarry;
            for(int i = last - 1; i >= 0; --i)
            {
                tempCarry = digits[i] << (BASE_RADIX - skipBits);
                digits[i] = (digits[i] >> skipBits) | carry;
                carry = tempCarry;
            }
        }
        trim();
        return *this;
    }
    Number operator>>(unsigned int k)const{return Number(*this) >>= k;}
    Number operator<<(unsigned int k)const
    {
        int skipCells = k/BASE_RADIX, skipBits = k % BASE_RADIX;
        Number result(nDigits() + 1 + skipCells, 0);
        result.isMinus = isMinus;
        for(int i = 0; i < result.nDigits(); ++i) result[i] = getDigit(i);
        if(skipCells > 0) for(int i = result.nDigits() - 1; i >= 0; --i)
            result[i] = i < skipCells ? 0 : result[i - skipCells];
        if(skipBits > 0)
        {
            DIGIT carry = 0;
            for(int i = skipCells; i < result.nDigits(); ++i)
            {
                DIGIT tempCarry = result[i] >> (BASE_RADIX - skipBits);
                result[i] = (result[i] << skipBits) | carry;
                carry = tempCarry;
            }
        }
        result.trim();
        return result;
    }
    Number& operator<<=(unsigned int k){return *this = *this << k;}
```

16.4 Multiplication

Use the $O(|a||b|)$ high school method. The result of multiplying a number by a digit is at most one digit larger than the number.

```
    static DIGIT digitMult(DIGIT a, DIGIT b, DIGIT& carry)
    {
        LARGE_DIGIT prod = LARGE_DIGIT(a) * b;
        carry = prod >> BASE_RADIX;
        return prod;
    }
    static Number mult(Number const& a, DIGIT const& b)
    {
        Number result(a.nDigits() + 1, 0);
        DIGIT carry = 0, multCarry = 0, temp;
        for(int i = 0; i < a.nDigits(); ++i)
        {
            result[i] = fullAdder(digitMult(a[i], b, temp), multCarry,
                carry);
```

```
            multCarry = temp;
        }
        result[a.nDigits()] = fullAdder(0, multCarry, carry);
        result.trim();
        return result;
    }
    friend Number operator*(Number const& a, Number const& b)
    {//O(|a| * |b|)
        Number product(a.nDigits()+b.nDigits(), 0);
        for(int j = 0; j < b.nDigits(); ++j)
            product += mult(a, b[j]) << BASE_RADIX * j;
        product.isMinus = a.isMinus != b.isMinus;
        product.trim();
        return product;
    }
    Number& operator*=(Number const& rhs){return *this = *this * rhs;}
```

16.5 Division

Division a/b computes the quotient and the remainder r using long division. Assuming positive numbers:

1. **Set $r = a$**
2. **Normalize r and b as discussed below**
3. **While $r < b$**
4. **Multiply b by the largest power of base B such that the result $s \leq r$**
5. **Subtract from r max k such that $ks \leq r$**
6. **Renormalize r**

Let $z \geq B/2$ be the most significant digit of s, x and y the two most significant digits of r, and $g = 1$ if r and normalized b have the same number of digits and $(xB + y)/z$ otherwise. Then $k \leq g \leq k + 2$.

Proof: When the number of digits is the same, $k = 1$ because $z \geq B/2$ and $z \leq x \leq B - 1$. Otherwise, $g - k$ is smallest or largest if the remaining digits of a are largest and of b smallest in the first case, vice verse in the second, and z is smallest. In the first case, due to the extra digits of a, $g - k \leq 1/z = 0$. In the second, $k = (xB + y)/(z + 1)$, $gz + r_1 = k(z + 1) + r_2$, and $g = k + (k + r_2 - r_1)/z \leq k + 2$ because $k/z < 2$ and $r_2 - r_1 < z$.

So division first shifts r and b to make $z \geq B/2$ and shifts back r after it's calculated.

```
    static DIGIT findK(Number const& a, Number const& b)
    {//O(|a|), find k such that 0 <= k < BASE and kb <= a < (k + 1)b;
        DIGIT guess = a.digits.lastItem()/b.digits.lastItem();
        if(a.nDigits() > b.nDigits())
            guess = (a.digits.lastItem() * (1ull << BASE_RADIX) +
                a[a.nDigits() - 2])/b.digits.lastItem();
        while(mult(b, guess) > a) --guess;//executes <= 2 times
        return guess;
    }
    static Number divide(Number const& a, Number const& b1, Number& q)
    {//O(|a| * |b|)
        assert(!b1.isZero());
        q = 0;
        Number b = b1.abs(), r = a.abs();
        int norm = BASE_RADIX - lgFloor(b.digits.lastItem()) - 1;
        r <<= norm;
        b <<= norm;
        for(int i = r.nDigits() - b.nDigits(); i >= 0; --i)
        {
            int shift = i * BASE_RADIX;
            DIGIT k = findK(r >> shift, b);
            q += mult(Number(1) << shift, k);
            r -= mult(b << shift, k);
        }
```

```
        q.isMinus = r.isMinus = a.isMinus != b1.isMinus;
        return r >>= norm;
    }
    friend Number operator%(Number const& a, Number const& b)
    {
        Number quotient(0);
        return divide(a, b, quotient);
    }
    Number& operator/=(Number const&rhs){return *this = *this/rhs;}
    friend Number operator/(Number const& a, Number const& b)
    {
        Number quotient(0);
        divide(a, b, quotient);
        return quotient;
    }
    Number& operator%=(Number const&rhs){return *this = *this % rhs;}
```

Need $O(|a||b|)$ time, as for multiplication.

16.6 Conversion to Decimal

Conversion to another base reduces to division and has the same complexity:

```
    Vector<unsigned char> toDigitVector()const
    {
        Vector<unsigned char> result;
        Number r = *this;
        while(!r.isZero())
        {
            Number q(0);
            result.append(divide(r, 10, q)[0]);
            r = q;
        }
        result.reverse();
        return result;
    }
    Number(Vector<unsigned char> const& digitVector,
       bool theIsNegative = false): isMinus(theIsNegative)
    {
        Number result(0);
        for(int i = digitVector.getSize() - 1; i >= 0; --i)
        {
            result *= Number(10);
            result += Number(digitVector[i]);
        }
        result.trim();
        digits = result.digits;
    }
```

16.7 Exponentiation

E.g., $x \times x \times x \times x \times x \times x \times x$ contains reusable square subproducts. When i is even, $x^i = x((x^2)^{i/2})$. This leads to an efficient algorithm with lg(i) multiplications. Modular exponentiation reduces by the modulus after every multiplication to avoid large subproducts.

```
    Number power(Number const& p)const
    {
        Number x = *this, y = 1, n = p;
        for(;;)
        {
            if(n.isOdd()) y *= x;
```

```
            n >>= 1;
            if(n.isZero()) break;
            x *= x;
        }
        return y;
    }
    Number modPower(Number const& p, Number const& modulus)const
    {
        assert(!modulus.isZero());
        Number x = *this, y = 1, n = p;
        for(;;)
        {
            if(n.isOdd())
            {
                y *= x;
                y %= modulus;
            }
            n >>= 1;
            if(n.isZero()) break;
            x *= x;
            x %= modulus;
        }
        return y;
    }
```

16.8 Lg

This takes O(1) time.

```
    long long lg()const
        {return BASE_RADIX * (nDigits() - 1) + lgFloor(digits.lastItem());}
```

16.9 Integer Square Root

Newton's method (see the "Numerical Algorithms" chapter) is correct for integer square root. For efficiency, it starts with log-based upper bound:

```
    Number sqrt()const
    {
        Number x(Number(1) << 1 + lg()/2);
        for(;;)
        {
            Number y = (x + *this/x)/2;
            if(y < x) x = y;
            else return x;
        }
    }
```

Usually need a few iterations to converge, so the runtime is effectively O(division).

16.10 Greatest Common Divisor

Euclidean algorithm subtracts the smaller number from the larger until the smaller = 0. For efficiency, the process uses division with remainder instead of repeated subtraction. The extended version computes x, y such that $\gcd(a, b) = ax + by$ by retaining all quotients. Because after each iteration the gcd remains the same when a becomes r, $\gcd(r, b) = rx + by = (a - bq)x + by = ax + b(y - qx)$, and when b becomes 0, $\gcd(r, b) = r \times 1 + b \times 0$. The runtime is $O(|a||b|)$ (Cormen et al. 2009).

```
Number extendedGcdR(Number const& a, Number const& b, Number& x, Number& y)
{
    if(!b.isPositive())
    {
```

```
        x = Number(1);
        y = Number(0);
        return a;
    }
    Number q, r = Number::divide(a, b, q), gcd = extendedGcdR(b, r, y, x);
    y -= q * x;
    return gcd;
}
Number extendedGcd(Number const& a, Number const& b, Number& x, Number& y)
{
    assert(a.isPositive() && b.isPositive());
    return a < b ? extendedGcdR(b, a, y, x) : extendedGcdR(a, b, x, y);
}
Number gcd(Number const& a, Number const& b)
{
    Number x, y;
    return extendedGcd(a, b, x, y);
}
```

16.11 Modular Inverse

The inverse of a % n exists only if $1 = \gcd(a, n) = ax + ny$—x is the inverse because $(ax + ny)$ % $n = ax$ % n.

```
Number modInverse(Number const& a, Number const& n)
{
    assert(a.isPositive() && a < n);
    Number x, y;
    extendedGcd(a, n, x, y);
    if(x.isNegative()) x += n;
    return x;
}
```

The runtime is $O(|a||n|)$.

16.12 Primality Testing

Fermat's theorem: if n is prime, $\forall a$ such that $1 < a < n$ and $\gcd(a, n) = 1$, a^{n-1} % $n = 1$. Using its converse with various a as a test fails for **Carmichel numbers** such as 561. **Miller-Rabin algorithm** factors $n - 1$ as $2^c d$ such that d is odd and calculates $x = b^d$ % n. Then it iteratively squares x mod n c times and checks that if the square = 1 then $x = 1$ or $n - 1$. If not, n is composite because for a prime p $x^2 = 1 \pmod{p} \leftrightarrow (x + 1)(x - 1) = 0 \pmod{p}$ and implies that $x = 1 \pmod{p}$ or $x = -1 \pmod{p}$. It's proven (Welschenbach 2005) that the answer:

- *composite* is correct.
- *not composite* is wrong with probability < ¼ when $1 < a < n$ is chosen randomly. This probability decreases with the size of n, as does the number of tests to make it $\approx 2^{-100}$.

```
bool provenComposite(Number const& a, Number const& n)
{
    Number ONE = Number(1), oddPart = n - ONE;
    int nSquares = 0;
    while(oddPart.isEven())
    {
        oddPart >>= 1;
        ++nSquares;
    }
    Number x = a.modPower(oddPart, n);
    for(int i = 0; i < nSquares; ++i)
    {//if x2 is 1 x must have been 1 or -1 if n is prime
        Number x2 = x.modPower(2, n);
        if(x2 == ONE && x != ONE && x != n - ONE) return true;
        x = x2;
```

```
    }
    return x != ONE;
}
```

Each test needs $\leq \lg(n)$ squarings of a, with the total cost $O(\lg(n)y^2)$ for random $a \in [1, n]$ and y digits. The algorithm first does trial division by small primes < 50. Doing so until ≈ 2000 is optimal experimentally but complicates the code. For efficiency, the implementation chooses $a \in [2, \min(n, B - 1)]$.

```
bool isPrime(Number const& n)
{
    if(n.isEven() || n < Number(2)) return false;
    int smallPrimes[] = {3,5,7,11,13,17,19,23,29,31,37,41,43,47};
    for(int i = 0; i < sizeof(smallPrimes)/sizeof(int); ++i)
    {
        Number p = Number(smallPrimes[i]);
        if(n != p && (n % p).isZero()) return false;
    }//Miller-Rabin if trial division was inconclusive
    int nTrials = 1;
    int sizes[] = {73,105,132,198,223,242,253,265,335,480,543,627,747,927,
        1233,1854,4096}, nTests[] = {47,42,35,29,23,20,18,17,16,12,8,7,6,5,4,
        3,2};
    for(int i = 0; i < sizeof(sizes)/sizeof(*sizes); ++i)
        if(n.lg() < sizes[i])
        {
            nTrials = nTests[i];
            break;
        }
    while(nTrials--)
    {//use single digit exponents for efficiency
        Number::DIGIT_TYPE max = numeric_limits<Number::DIGIT_TYPE>::max();
        if(provenComposite(GlobalRNG.inRange(2, (n > Number(max) ?
            max : int(n[0])) - 1), n)) return false;
    }
    return true;
}
```

To generate a random n-bit prime, until the result is prime, generate a random n-bit number, and set its highest and lowest bits. By the Riemann's hypothesis, $\forall n$ $O(1/n)$ numbers are prime, so E[the number of primality tests] = $O(n)$. The result isn't cryptographically secure if the random generator isn't.

16.13 Rationals

Can portably extract the integer base and the exponent out of a double:

```
long long rationalize(double x, int& e)
{
    for(x = frexp(x, &e); x != (long long)x; x *= 2) --e;
    return x;
}
```

A rational consists of a large number numerator and denominator and reduces them by their gcd after every operation:

```
struct Rational
{
    Number numerator, denominator;
    Rational(Number const& theNumerator = Number(0),
        Number const& theDenominator = Number(1)): numerator(theNumerator),
        denominator(theDenominator)
    {
        assert(!denominator.isZero());
        reduce();
    }
    Rational(double x): denominator(1), numerator(1)
```

```
    {
        long long n;
        int e;
        rationalize(x, n, e);
        numerator = Number(n);
        if(e < 0) denominator <<= -e;
        else numerator <<= e;
    }
    void reduce()
    {
        Number g = gcd(numerator, denominator);
        numerator /= g;
        denominator /= g;
    }
    bool isZero()const{return numerator.isZero();}
    bool isMinus()const
        {return numerator.isNegative() != denominator.isNegative();}
};
```

Addition and subtraction are $O(n^2)$ due to gcd. Arguably, don't need gcd for cheap operations.

```
    Rational operator-()const
    {
        Rational result = *this;
        result.numerator.negate();
        return result;
    }
    friend Rational operator+(Rational const& a, Rational const& b)
    {
        Rational result(a.numerator * b.denominator + b.numerator *
            a.denominator,a.denominator * b.denominator);
        result.reduce();
        return result;
    }
    friend Rational operator-(Rational const& a, Rational const& b)
    {return a + -b;}
    Rational& operator+=(Rational const&rhs){return *this = *this + rhs;}
    Rational& operator-=(Rational const&rhs){return *this = *this - rhs;}
```

Multiplication and division are $O(n^2)$.

```
    friend Rational operator*(Rational const& a, Rational const& b)
    {
        Rational result(a.numerator * b.numerator,
            a.denominator * b.denominator);
        result.reduce();
        return result;
    }
    friend Rational operator/(Rational const& a, Rational const& b)
    {
        assert(!b.isZero());
        Rational result(a.numerator * b.denominator,
            a.denominator * b.numerator);
        result.reduce();
        return result;
    }
    Rational& operator*=(Rational const&rhs){return *this = *this * rhs;}
    Rational& operator/=(Rational const&rhs){return *this = *this / rhs;}
```

Other useful operations are lg and evaluation to some precision:

```
    unsigned long long lg()const{return numerator.lg() - denominator.lg();}
    Number evaluate(Number const& scale = Number(1))
        {return numerator * scale/denominator;}
```

In many computations, can simulate rationals because a fixed-precision real number is an integer divided by a normalizing factor. This allows, e.g., to calculate π to n digits as floor($10^n\pi$), using power series for arctan and giving the integer several extra digits to avoid round-off errors.

16.14 Comments

For multiplication, after $\approx$ 100 digits Karatsuba multiplication is the fastest up to some value. The asymptotically best known method uses the **fast Fourier transform** (FFT) and is very complicated. Computations with millions of digits use it, but for such sizes few algorithms are feasible.

16.15 References

Brent, R. P., & Zimmermann, P. (2010). *Modern Computer Arithmetic*. Cambridge University Press.
Cormen, T. H., Leiserson, C. E., Rivest, R. L., & Stein, C. (2009). *Introduction to Algorithms*. MIT Press.
St Denis, T. (2006). *BigNum Math: Implementing Cryptographic Multiple Precision Arithmetic*. Syngress.
Welschenbach, M. (2005). *Cryptography in C and C++*. Apress.

17 Computational Geometry

17.1 Points

Computation geometry is about algorithms for points and other geometric objects in many dimensions. Can represent a **multidimensional point** as a vector, but usually know dimension D at compile time, so it's more efficient to use an array. The resulting point implements several arithmetic operators for convenience, using the usual vector space arithmetic:

```
template<typename KEY, int D = 2> class Point
{
    KEY x[D];
public:
    KEY& operator[](int i){assert(i >= 0 && i < D); return x[i];}
    KEY const& operator[](int i)const{assert(i >= 0 && i < D); return x[i];}
    int getSize()const{return D;}
    Point(){for(int i = 0; i < D; ++i) x[i] = 0;}
    Point(KEY const& x0, KEY const& x1)
    {
        assert(D > 1);
        x[0] = x0;
        x[1] = x1;
    }
    bool operator==(Point const& rhs)const
    {
        for(int i = 0; i < D; ++i) if(x[i] != rhs.x[i]) return false;
        return true;
    }
    Point& operator+=(Point const& rhs)
    {
        for(int i = 0; i < D; ++i) x[i] += rhs.x[i];
        return *this;
    }
    friend Point& operator+(Point const& lhs, Point const& rhs)
    {
        Point result = lhs;
        return result += rhs;
    }
    Point& operator*=(double scalar)
    {
        for(int i = 0; i < D; ++i) x[i] *= scalar;
        return *this;
    }
    friend Point operator*(Point const& point, double scalar)
    {
        Point result = point;
        return result *= scalar;
    }
};
typedef Point<double> Point2;
```

Most algorithms assume metric distances between points. **Euclidean distance** is the most useful and, when squared, = $\sum$individual dimension component distances, which is **computable incrementally** in $O(1)$ time per component. To compare two distances, compute the square of one, and stop computing the square of the other if the incremental result is larger.

```
template<typename VECTOR> struct EuclideanDistance
{
    static double iDistanceIncremental(VECTOR const& lhs, VECTOR const& rhs,
        int i)
    {
        double x = lhs[i] - rhs[i];
        return x * x;
    }
    static double distanceIncremental(VECTOR const& lhs, VECTOR const& rhs,
        double bound = numeric_limits<double>::max())
    {
        assert(lhs.getSize() == rhs.getSize());
        double sum = 0;
        for(int i = 0; i < lhs.getSize() && sum < bound; ++i)
            sum += iDistanceIncremental(lhs, rhs, i);
        return sum;
    }
    struct Distance
    {
        double operator()(VECTOR const& lhs, VECTOR const& rhs)
            {return sqrt(distanceIncremental(lhs, rhs));}
    };
    struct DistanceIncremental
    {
        double operator()(VECTOR const& lhs, VECTOR const& rhs)const
            {return distanceIncremental(lhs, rhs);}
        double operator()(VECTOR const& lhs, VECTOR const& rhs, int i)const
            {return iDistanceIncremental(lhs, rhs, i);}
        double operator()(double bound, VECTOR const& lhs, VECTOR const& rhs)
            const{return distanceIncremental(lhs, rhs, bound);}
    };
};
```

Efficient point data structures are hierarchies represented as trees where each subtree covers a part of the volume, with the root covering the whole. Given a distance function, the **hierarchy distance** is the closest distance between a query point and any point in the subtree.

17.2 VP Tree

Given a function that computes a metric distance between keys, can implement:

- Map operations
- ***k*-nearest neighbor query** (*k*-NN)— find *k* closest elements of a given key *x*
- **Distance query**—find all elements within a specified distance from *x*

These enable e.g., finding all strings within edit distance 2 from a given string. Also, can inefficiently implement distance and *k*-NN queries in terms of each other.

A VP tree picks an object as the root and some radius *r* for it. All objects at distance $\leq r$ go in the left subtree and $> r$ in the right. Use r = the distance to the first object inserted into the subtree of the root, making it a left child. To improve pruning during search, every node stores its max distance to any node in the subtree.

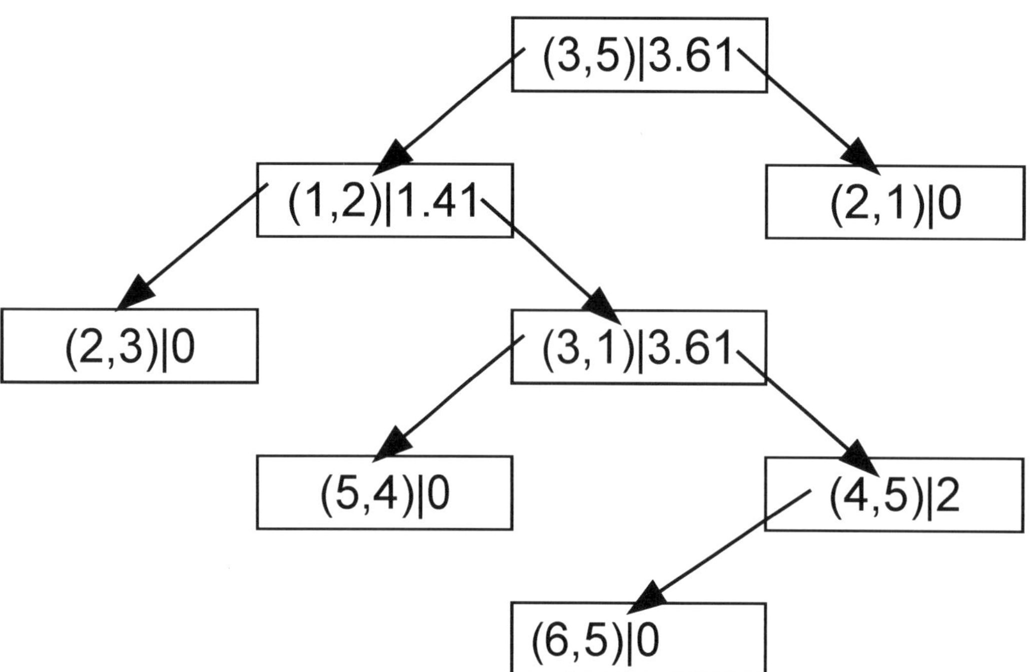

Theorem: Given a, b, c in a metric space, where $r_1 \le d(a, b) \le r_2$, and $d(a, c) = k$, $\max(0,\ k - r_2, r_1 - k) \le d(b, c)$. This bounds child distances when a is the key of the current node, b of the child, and c of the query.

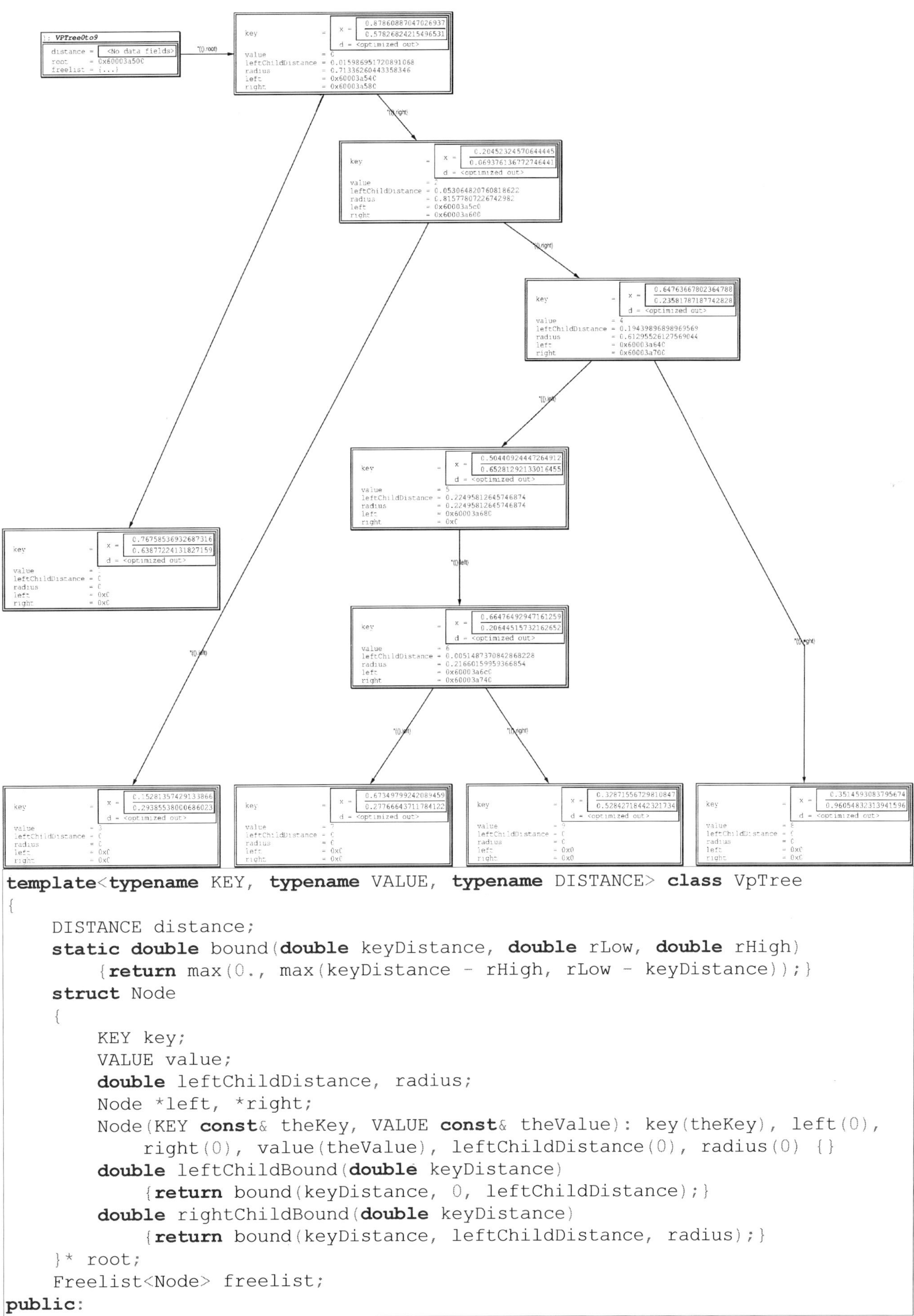

```
template<typename KEY, typename VALUE, typename DISTANCE> class VpTree
{
    DISTANCE distance;
    static double bound(double keyDistance, double rLow, double rHigh)
        {return max(0., max(keyDistance - rHigh, rLow - keyDistance));}
    struct Node
    {
        KEY key;
        VALUE value;
        double leftChildDistance, radius;
        Node *left, *right;
        Node(KEY const& theKey, VALUE const& theValue): key(theKey), left(0),
            right(0), value(theValue), leftChildDistance(0), radius(0) {}
        double leftChildBound(double keyDistance)
            {return bound(keyDistance, 0, leftChildDistance);}
        double rightChildBound(double keyDistance)
            {return bound(keyDistance, leftChildDistance, radius);}
    }* root;
    Freelist<Node> freelist;
public:
```

```
    typedef Node NodeType;
    bool isEmpty(){return !root;}
};
```

Constructors are similar to those of other binary trees, except for needing a distance functor instead of a comparator:

```
    VpTree(DISTANCE const& theDistance = DISTANCE()): root(0),
        distance(theDistance) {}
    Node* constructFrom(Node* node)
    {
        Node* tree = 0;
        if(node)
        {
            tree = new(freelist.allocate())Node(node->key, node->value);
            tree->leftChildDistance = node->leftChildDistance;
            tree->radius = node->radius;
            tree->left = constructFrom(node->left);
            tree->right = constructFrom(node->right);
        }
        return tree;
    }
    VpTree(VpTree const& other): distance(other.distance)
        {root = constructFrom(other.root);}
    VpTree& operator=(VpTree const& rhs){return genericAssign(*this, rhs);}
```

Find follows the tree definition:

```
    VALUE* find(KEY const& key)
    {
        Node* node = root;
        while(node && key != node->key)
            node = distance(key, node->key) <= node->leftChildDistance ?
                node->left : node->right;
        return node ? &node->value : 0;
    }
```

Insert maintains distance information in the resulting parent node if the new node becomes a left child:

```
    void insert(KEY const& key, VALUE const& value)
    {
        Node **pointer = &root, *node;
        while((node = *pointer) && key != node->key)
        {
            double d = distance(key, node->key);
            node->radius = max(node->radius, d);
            if(!node->left) node->leftChildDistance = d;
            pointer = &(d <= node->leftChildDistance ?
                node->left : node->right);
        }
        if(node) node->value = value;
        else *pointer = new(freelist.allocate())Node(key, value);
    }
};
```

The height isn't controlled because !∃a good way to balance, other than partial rebuilding. So the tree can be unbalanced, but, as with binary trees, random order insertion leads to good expected performance. Due to the hierarchies defined by parents, can use only weak deletion. Distance query uses the child bounds to prune subtrees further than a specified radius:

```
    void distanceQuery(KEY const& key, double radius, Vector<Node*>& result,
        Node* node)
    {
        if(!node) return;
        double d = distance(node->key, key);
```

```
        if(d <= radius) result.append(node);
        if(node->leftChildBound(d) <= radius)
            distanceQuery(key, radius, result, node->left);
        if(node->rightChildBound(d) <= radius)
            distanceQuery(key, radius, result, node->right);
    }
    Vector<NodeType*> distanceQuery(KEY const& key, double radius)
    {
        Vector<NodeType*> result;
        distanceQuery(key, radius, result, root);
        return result;
    }
```

The % of nodes are checked that don't need to be depends on the quality of the bounds. In the worst case, such queries check all nodes in O(n) time. k-NN query uses a max heap of k closest nodes and a generic helper function that finds the distance of the kth closest element, which is the heap's minimum:

```
template<typename NODE> struct QNode
{
    NODE* node;
    double d;
    bool operator<(QNode const& rhs)const{return d > rhs.d;}
    static double dh(Heap<QNode>& heap, int k)
    {
        return heap.getSize() < k ?
            numeric_limits<double>::max() : heap.getMin().d;
    }
};
```

k-NN query does branch and bound of the tree, using the heap to keep k closest found neighbors. Pruning and child selection use bounds of the currently furthest node. After being retrieved, the found neighbors are heap-sorted in order of closeness.

```
    typedef QNode<Node> HEAP_ITEM;
    void kNN(Node* node, KEY const& key, Heap<HEAP_ITEM>& heap, int k)
    {
        if(!node) return;
        //replace furthest node in heap with the current node if it's closer
        HEAP_ITEM x = {node, distance(key, node->key)};
        if(heap.getSize() < k) heap.insert(x);
        else if(x.d < HEAP_ITEM::dh(heap, k)) heap.changeKey(0, x);
        //expand closer child first
        double lb = node->leftChildBound(x.d),
            rb = node->rightChildBound(x.d);
        Node* l = node->left, *r = node->right;
        if(lb > rb)
        {
            swap(lb, rb);
            swap(l, r);
        }
        if(lb <= HEAP_ITEM::dh(heap, k)) kNN(l, key, heap, k);
        if(rb <= HEAP_ITEM::dh(heap, k)) kNN(r, key, heap, k);
    }
    Vector<NodeType*> kNN(KEY const& key, int k)
    {
        Heap<HEAP_ITEM> heap;
        kNN(root, key, heap, k);
        Vector<Node*> result(k);
        while(!heap.isEmpty()) result.append(heap.deleteMin().node);
        result.reverse();
        return result;
    }
```

```
    NodeType* nearestNeighbor(KEY const& key)
    {
        assert(!isEmpty());
        return kNN(key, 1)[0];
    }
```

To extend a VP tree for external memory, put more keys and pointers in each node, sorted by distances to the parent node.

17.3 *k*-d Tree

Multidimensional point items comparable in each dimension support **range query**—find all items whose the keys for the specified dimensions are in a given range. A *k*-d tree is a binary tree that branches on each dimension in turn. Some but not all dimension keys may be equal.

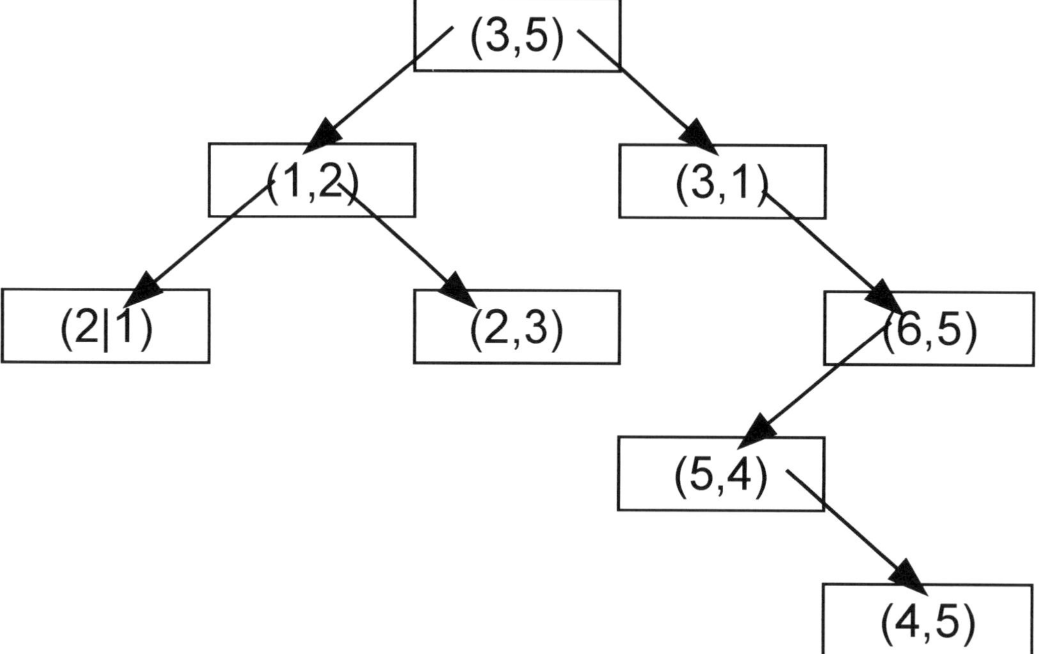

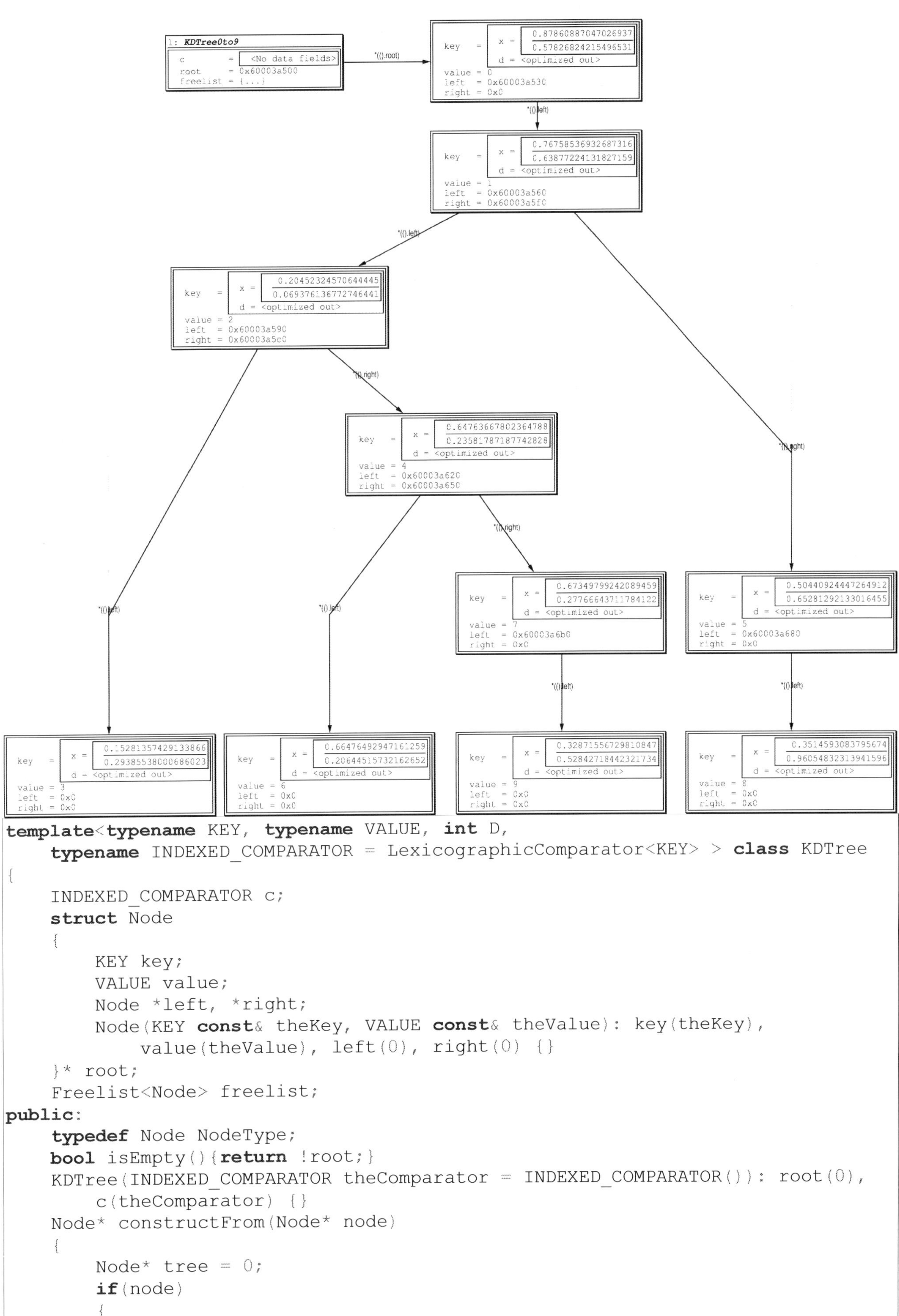


```
template<typename KEY, typename VALUE, int D,
    typename INDEXED_COMPARATOR = LexicographicComparator<KEY> > class KDTree
{
    INDEXED_COMPARATOR c;
    struct Node
    {
        KEY key;
        VALUE value;
        Node *left, *right;
        Node(KEY const& theKey, VALUE const& theValue): key(theKey),
            value(theValue), left(0), right(0) {}
    }* root;
    Freelist<Node> freelist;
public:
    typedef Node NodeType;
    bool isEmpty(){return !root;}
    KDTree(INDEXED_COMPARATOR theComparator = INDEXED_COMPARATOR()): root(0),
        c(theComparator) {}
    Node* constructFrom(Node* node)
    {
        Node* tree = 0;
        if(node)
        {
```

```
            tree = new(freelist.allocate())Node(node->key, node->value);
            tree->left = constructFrom(node->left);
            tree->right = constructFrom(node->right);
        }
        return tree;
    }
    KDTree(KDTree const& other): c(other.c)
        {root = constructFrom(other.root);}
    KDTree& operator=(KDTree const& rhs){return genericAssign(*this, rhs);}
```

Find and insert are like the unbalanced binary tree ones, except for the dimension cycling. The reusable `findPointer` also computes the parent of the found node for nearest neighbor query.

```
    Node** findPointer(KEY const& key, Node*& parent)
    {
        Node* node, **pointer = &root;
        parent = 0;
        for(int i = 0; (node = *pointer) && !c.isEqual(key, node->key);
            i = (i + 1) % D)
        {
            parent = node;
            pointer = &(c.isLess(key, node->key, i) ?
                node->left : node->right);
        }
        return pointer;
    }
    VALUE* find(KEY const& key)
    {
        Node *node = *findPointer(key, node);
        return node ? &node->value : 0;
    }
    void insert(KEY const& key, VALUE const& value)
    {
        Node *dummy, **pointer = findPointer(key, dummy);
        if(*pointer) (*pointer)->value  = value;
        else *pointer = new(freelist.allocate())Node(key, value);
    }
```

For VP and *k*-d trees with items inserted in random order, E[the height] = O(lg(n)), though the height is O(n). Usually this isn't a problem because if a single dimension is in random order, E[the height] = O(lg(n)). A better measure of performance is how effective a query is along every dimension it specifies. E.g., in a *k*-d tree balanced on the x-coordinate and not on the y-coordinate, a range query on (x, y) is the same as linear scan for y on the result of a range query on x. Rotations aren't supported, but insertion can partially rebuild to maintain balance using amortized or expected O(lg(n)^2) time (see the "Algorithmic Techniques" chapter). Can support deletions, but inefficiently; use weak deletions if needed.

Range query does depth-first search that checks if nodes are inside the specified box. If a node isn't, one of its children isn't, which allows pruning.

```
    void rangeQuery(KEY const& l, KEY const& u, bool* dimensions,
        Vector<Node*>& result, Node* node, int i)
    {
        if(!node) return;
        bool inRange = true;
        for(int j = 0; j < D; ++j)
            if(dimensions[j] && (c.isLess(node->key, l, j) ||
                c.isLess(u, node->key, i))) inRange = false;
        if(inRange) result.append(node);
        int j = (i + 1) % D;
        if(!(dimensions[i] && c.isLess(node->key, l, i)))
            rangeQuery(l, u, dimensions, result, node->left, j);
        if(!(dimensions[i] && c.isLess(u, node->key, i)))
```

```
            rangeQuery(l, u, dimensions, result, node->right, j);
    }
    void rangeQuery(KEY const& l, KEY const& u, bool* dimensions,
        Vector<Node*>& result)
        {rangeQuery(l, u, dimensions, result, root, 0);}
```

The runtime is $O(n^{(d-1)/d})$ for a balanced tree and a special type of query regardless of the data, which is optimal for $O(n)$ space. On average, for small D the runtime is $O(\lg(n))$ (Samet 2006). Intuitively, a k-d tree is most useful for small D because for large have many variables to partition on, and use each only a few times, which is what makes range query slow.

Implement **partial match query**, which finds all items with only the specified dimensions, as a range query where $l = u$, and **interval query**, which finds all intervals that contain a given point, as a 2D range query $[x, max] \times [min, x]$, where min/max are maintained explicitly or replaced by a suitable $-\infty$ and ∞. This generalizes to rectangles, cubes, etc.

Distance query is similar to range query and works with a metric distance:

```
    template<typename DISTANCE> void distanceQuery(KEY const& x,
        double radius, Vector<Node*>& result, Node* node, int i,
        DISTANCE const& distance, bool cut)
    {
        if(!node) return;
        if(distance(node->key, x) <= radius) result.append(node);
        else if(cut) return;
        else cut = true;
        i = (i + 1) % D;
        Node* nodes[] = {node->left, node->right};
        for(int j = 0; j < 2; ++j)
            distanceQuery(x, radius, result, nodes[j], i, distance, cut);
    }
```

k-NN query works with a metric distance, but for efficiency assumes an incrementally computable distance, which forces the distance function to have the form $f(d(x, y))$, where $d(x, y) = \sum_{0 \le i < d} g(h(x[i]) - h(y[i]))$ and f, g, and h are monotonically nondecreasing functions. The algorithm is a B&B, similar to that of the VP tree, but uses unnormalized distances of the form $d(x, y)$ and updates them incrementally on the search path. Initially, the partial key = x, corresponding to the 0 distance to the tree. When the search goes left, the partial key of the left node doesn't change, and of the right node sets its current coordinate to that of the current node. Symmetrically, for going right, the partial key of the right node doesn't change, and of the left node sets its current coordinate to that of the current node. So distance(x, the partial key) is the best possible lower bound on the hierarchy distance. It's nondecreasing on the search path. Distance comparison is incremental.

```
    typedef QNode<Node> HEAP_ITEM;
    template<typename DISTANCE> void kNN(Node* node, KEY const& key,
        Heap<HEAP_ITEM>& heap, int k, int i, KEY& partial,
        double partialDistance, DISTANCE const& distance)
    {
        double best = HEAP_ITEM::dh(heap, k);
        if(node && partialDistance < best)
        {//update partial distance
            double newPartialDistance = distance(key, node->key, i) -
                distance(key, partial, i);
            if(heap.getSize() < k)
            {
                HEAP_ITEM x = {node, distance(key, node->key)};
                heap.insert(x);
            }
            //use new partial distance to check for a cut again
            else if(newPartialDistance < best)
            {//incremental calculate-compare
                double d = distance(best, key, node->key);
                if(d < best)
```

```
                {
                    HEAP_ITEM x = {node, d};
                    heap.changeKey(0, x);
                }
            }
            int j = (i + 1) % D;
            //swap children for best order
            Node *l = node->left, *r = node->right;
            if(!c.isLess(key, node->key, i)) swap(l, r);
            kNN(l, key, heap, k, j, partial, partialDistance, distance);
            //set partial component to the node component, use the node
            //as temporary storage
            swap(partial[i], node->key[i]);
            kNN(r, key, heap, k, j, partial, newPartialDistance, distance);
            swap(partial[i], node->key[i]);
        }
    }
```

For $k = 1$, putting on the queue the parent of where the query would be inserted improves pruning, but for $k > 1$ could reinsert the parent into the heap when its size $< k$.

```
    template<typename DISTANCE> Vector<NodeType*> kNN(KEY const& key, int k,
     DISTANCE const& distance)
    {
        Heap<HEAP_ITEM> heap;
        KEY partial = key;
        kNN(root, key, heap, k, 0, partial, 0, distance);
        Vector<Node*> result(k);
        while(!heap.isEmpty()) result.append(heap.deleteMin().node);
        result.reverse();
        return result;
    }
    template<typename DISTANCE>
    NodeType* nearestNeighbor(KEY const& key, DISTANCE const& distance)
    {
        assert(!IsEmpty());
        Node* parent, *result = *findPointer(key, parent);
        if(result) return result;
        Heap<HEAP_ITEM> heap;
        HEAP_ITEM x = {parent, distance(key, parent->key)};
        heap.insert(x);
        KEY partial = key;
        kNN(root, key, heap, 1, 0, partial, 0, distance);
        return heap.getMin().node;
    }
```

For external memory, have nodes of size B with $k - 1$ keys and k pointers, fill them to capacity, and insert any new node between the appropriate keys.

17.4 Problems in High Dimensions

Range and k-NN queries are slower for large D because ∀ metric distance, as the dimension $\to \infty$, the difference between the distances to any object's nearest and furthest neighbors $\to 0$, so bounds become ineffective for pruning, forcing distance queries to look at almost every node.

Can reduce runtime if willing to get approximate answers:

- Multiply the lower bounds by $(1 + c)$ for some small constant c before a pruning check. This ensures that the found neighbors are at most a factor of $(1 + c)$ away from the nearest.
- Randomly project from to dimension $k < D$, by considering points as D-dimensional vectors and multiplying them by a $k \times D$ projection matrix, whose entries = −1 or 1 with probability 0.5. This transformation preserves Euclidean distances well on average (Fradkin & Madigan 2003).

17.5 Data Structures for Geometric Objects

The simplest solution is to have a bounding box around an object, and store its endpoints in a *k*-d tree. E.g., represent intervals or rectangles as multidimensional points.

Also can represent the box by its centroid, and store the endpoints in the node. This makes queries such as *k*-NN more efficient.

Alternatively, represent objects as images with each cell containing a list of pointers to objects that touch it and having at most one pointer per cell if objects don't overlap.

17.6 Geometric Primitives

The sign of the area of a triangle, given by three 2D points, tells if the points turn left, i.e., are in counter-clockwise (**CCW**) order. When the area = 0, the points don't turn, but usually consider this a left turn. The area of the triangle (a, b, c) in CCW order is the determinant

|1 a.x a.y|
|1 b.x b.y|
|1 c.x c.y|

```
double triangleArea(Point2 const& a, Point2 const& b, Point2 const& c)
    {return (b[0] - a[0]) * (c[1] - a[1]) - (b[1] - a[1]) * (c[0] - a[0]);}
bool ccw(Point2 const& a, Point2 const& b, Point2 const& c)
    {return triangleArea(a, b, c) >= 0;}//true if the points turn left
```

The result can be wrong for very thin triangles due to numerical cancellation in the subtraction. A `double` has 52 bits of precision, the subtraction doesn't change the required precision, and the multiplication doubles it, so if every term has ≤ 26 bits, the result is correct. Otherwise, avoiding numerical errors needs extended precision:

```
Rational robustTriangleArea(Point2 const& a, Point2 const& b, Point2 const& c)
{
    return (Rational(b[0]) - Rational(a[0])) * (Rational(c[1]) -
        Rational(a[1])) - (Rational(b[1]) - Rational(a[1])) * (Rational(c[0])
        - Rational(a[0]));
}
bool robustCcw(Point2 const& a, Point2 const& b, Point2 const& c)
    {return !robustTriangleArea(a, b, c).isMinus();}
```

17.7 Convex Hull

Given a set of 2D points, a convex hull is a subset of them such that a "rubber band" put over it encloses the set:

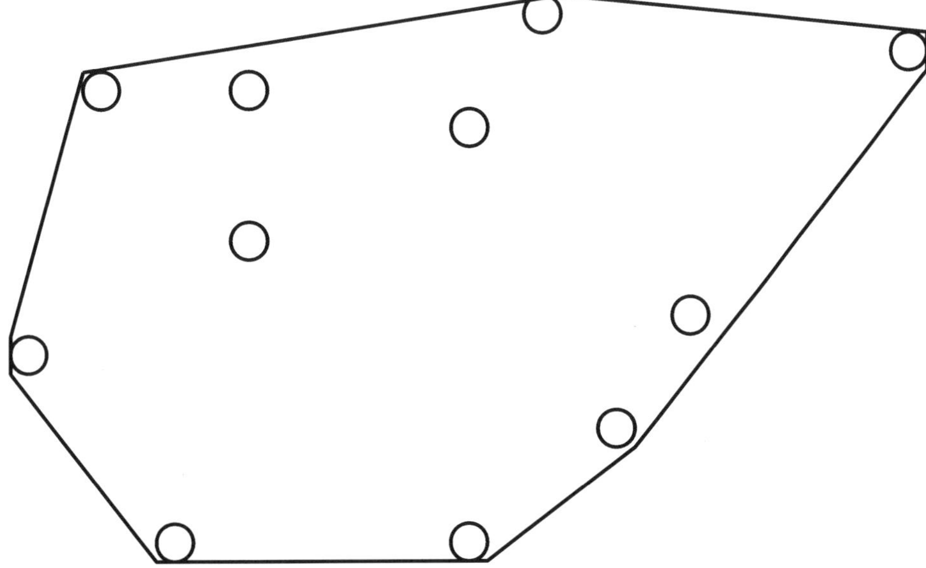

To compute it:

1. **Sort the points by the *x*-coordinate, breaking ties by the *y*-coordinate**

2. **Put the first two points on the hull**
3. **∀other point, put it on the hull, and, if the last three points make a left turn, remove the second last point—computes the upper hull**
4. **From the one before last to the first point, do the same, and remove the duplicate last added point—computes the lower hull**

```
void actOn(Vector<Point2>& hull, Point2 const& point)
{
    hull.append(point);
    while(hull.getSize() > 2 && ccw(hull[hull.getSize() - 3],
        hull[hull.getSize() - 2], hull[hull.getSize() - 1]))
    {
        hull[hull.getSize() - 2] = hull[hull.getSize() - 1];
        hull.removeLast();
    }
}
Vector<Point2> convexHull(Vector<Point2>& points)
{
    assert(points.getSize() > 2);
    quickSort(points.getArray(), 0, points.getSize() - 1,
        LexicographicComparator<Point2>());
    //upper Hull
    Vector<Point2> result;
    result.append(points[0]);
    result.append(points[1]);
    for(int i = 2; i < points.getSize(); ++i) actOn(result, points[i]);
    //lower hull, remove leftmost point which is added 2x
    for(int i = points.getSize() - 2; i >= 0; --i) actOn(result, points[i]);
    result.removeLast();
    return result;
}
```

With floating point arithmetic, points on a line may end up on the wrong side, or a too sharp left turn may become a right turn, destroying the topological structure. The runtime is O($n$lg(n)), but the bottleneck is the O(n) turn tests. For random points, E[the hull size] = O(lg(n)) (De Berg et al. 2008).

17.8 Plane Sweep

The plane sweep technique solves many problems. E.g., the convex hull calculation sorts the points on the x-coordinate, processes them from left to right, and then from right to left. Each point is an **event**, processing which puts some invariant on the space until the next event.

E.g., consider finding the area of possibly overlapping buildings on a picture, each represented by its two upper coordinates. A simple solution is to sort on the x-coordinate and process from left to right, maintaining the current height, and, when processing an event point, increment the total volume by the current height × the distance to the previous event. To keep track of the current max height, use a map of "open" buildings. A building opens when its left coordinate is an event and closes when the right one is.

17.9 Comments

Multidimensional data structures and computational geometry in general are large fields. The main problems with the former are lack of balancing ability and problems with large D. So many algorithms have been proposed (Samet 2006).

For the latter, the main issue is robust and efficient computation. Using large number arithmetic is the simplest solution, but an inefficient one. A more efficient but much more complicated one is using floating point filters (Mehlhorn & Näher 1999). The main idea is to do floating point computation with error bounds, and switch to large number arithmetic only if can't rule out errors.

17.10 References

De Berg, M., Cheong, O., & Van Kreveld, M., Overmars, M. (2008). *Computational Geometry: Algorithms and Applications*. Springer.

Fradkin, D., & Madigan, D. (2003). Experiments with random projections for machine learning. In *Proceedings of the Ninth ACM SIGKDD International Conference on Knowledge Discovery and Data Mining* (pp. 517–522). ACM.

Mehlhorn, K., & Näher, S. (1999). *LEDA: a Platform for Combinatorial and Geometric Computing*. Cambridge University Press.

Samet, H. (2006). *Foundations of Multidimensional and Metric Data Structures*. Morgan Kaufmann.

18 Numerical Algorithms

18.1 Floating Point Arithmetic

Hardware floating point arithmetic has limited precision. This is necessary because exact arithmetic suffers from combinatorial explosion—e.g., need 64 bits to exactly represent the product of two 32-bits numbers. Floating point always fixes precision, so in the above multiplication keep only the 32 most significant bits and discard the rest by rounding. `T = numeric_limits<double>` contains several important numbers:

Number	Accessor	Approximate Standard Value
Min x such that $1 + x \neq 1$	`T::epsilon()`	2.2E−16'
Min positive x	`T::min()`	1.8E−308'
Min positive x	`T::max()`	2.2E+308'
Infinity	`T::infinity()`	∞
NaN	N/A	N/A, anything = NaN is false

For these x, the corresponding negative numbers are $-x$. Use `isfinite` from `<cmath>` to check if a value is ∞ or NaN (also can use `isnan` for NaN). The infinities and NaN behave as expected—e.g., 2 × `T::max()` $= \infty$, $1/0 = \infty$, $0/0$ is NaN, and $-\infty < x < \infty$ if `isfinite`(x).

Four types of errors can happen:

- **Overflow**—e.g., $10!! = \infty$
- **Underflow**—e.g., $2^{-10000} = 3^{-10000} = 0$
- **Relative underflow**—e.g., evaluating the power series for π
- **Round-off accumulation**—Vandermonde system (google it)

Floating point registers have more precision than an in-memory `double`—e.g., $f(x) = f(x)$ may be false if the result of the first call is stored in memory, of the second isn't, and the difference is too small. To compare two numbers correctly to some both relative and absolute precision, use:

```
bool isELess(double a, double b,
    double eRelAbs = numeric_limits<double>::epsilon())
    {return a < b && b - a >= eRelAbs * (abs(a) + abs(b) + 1);}
```

Common operations introduce round-off errors, which may accumulate. E.g., numerically $\sum_{0 \le i \le \infty} 1/i$ is finite because eventually $1/i <$ the sum × `T::epsilon()`. So implementations of many algorithms fail despite correctness in the real RAM. Most algorithms need properly scaled inputs.

Some problems don't have consistent solutions. E.g., the best possible hardware solution of min of $|x|$ is ±`T::min()`, but of min of $1 + |x|$ it's $1 \pm$ `T::epsilon()`.

The real RAM (see the "Background" chapter) is useful for reasoning about correctness of many numerical algorithms. E.g., any iterative algorithm that gets more accuracy with each iteration can't find the exact solution because doing so requires infinitely many iterations. Also, without making further assumptions, such as boundedness of derivatives, algorithms that sample a function at a finite number of points can't bound their error.

A function f is **Lipschitz continuous** on an interval I if $\forall x_1, x_2$ $\exists$ a constant L such that $||f(x_1) - f(x_2)|| < L|| x_1 - x_2||$. Lipschitz continuity is important because it ensures that a function that is sampled at some points can't have arbitrarily different behavior between the samples, as it could, e.g., given only continuity. Numerical algorithms usually work with black-box functions, evaluating which gives finite precision after finitely many evaluations, unlike an analytic description of a function, which specifies it completely.

For analysis, usually make the **general position assumption** that have no equality in inputs. While this is helpful, must expect the equality cases in the code.

Without the real RAM, the next best thing is **stability**, in particular **backward stability**—a small change in input doesn't lead to a large change in output. Hardware operations "+", "−", "×", and "/" are stable, though "−" is the least so due to eating up more significant digits than the others (Corless & Fillion 2013).

18.2 Accuracy

Precision of an answer can be:

- **Absolute**—to how many decimal places the result is correct—meaningless for large numbers
- **Relative**—abs(the error/the magnitude of the result)—meaningless for numbers ≈ 0, unless the error is much smaller
- **Cauchy**—abs(the difference between two consecutive terms of a decreasing sequence)

Absolute precision is usually what matters to the user. Cauchy precision is very robust. The floating pointer representation maintains relative precision. Algorithms rarely compute to full precision for efficiency and let the caller specify wanted precision.

The **rate of convergence** is the number of correct digits gained per iteration. Linear convergence is usually fast enough.

!∃ a reasonable answer to problems with bad properties, such as minimizing a function with a −∞ spike. Here, a minimization algorithm's answer "10.02 with precision 0.001" isn't wrong when $f(10.02) = -100000$ and $f(10.0207) = -10^{100}$. This is the nature of ill-posed problems in general.

18.3 Interpolation

For an expensive-to-evaluate function, its approximation can use values at the evaluated points to evaluate others. **Linear interpolation** creates a line between two closest points enclosing the input x and gets its value as if it's on that line.

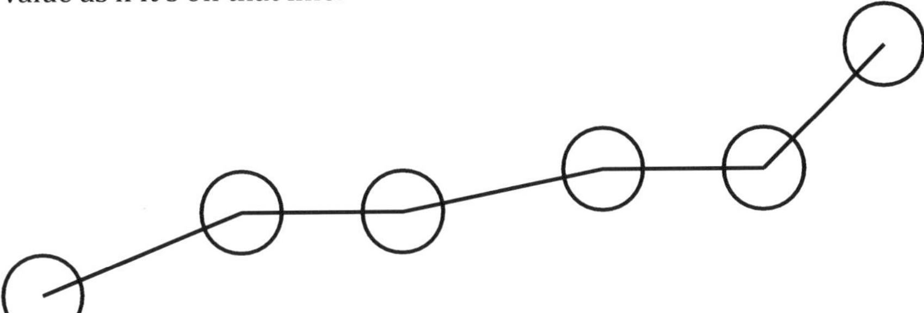

The implementation handles points dynamically using a dynamic sorted sequence. To interpolate at x, find its predecessor and successor, and use their values. This takes O(lg(n)) time.

```
class DynamicLinearInterpolation
{
    Treap<double, double> values;
public:
    double findMin()
    {
        assert(!values.isEmpty());
        return values.findMin()->key;
    }
    double findMax()
    {
        assert(!values.isEmpty());
        return values.findMax()->key;
    }
    double evaluate(double x)
    {
        assert(x >= findMin() && x <= findMax());
        double *y = values.find(x);
        if(y) return *y;
        Treap<double, double>::NodeType* left = values.predecessor(x),
            *right = values.successor(x);
        return left->value + (right->value - left->value) *
```

```
            (x - left->key)/(right->key - left->key);
    }
    void remove(double x){values.remove(x);}
    bool contains(double x){return values.find(x);}
    void insert(double x, double y){values.insert(x, y);}
};
```

18.4 Integration

The definite integral of a function over a range = the volume of the range × the average function value in the range. Want to find it with only the ability to evaluate the function at any point in the range.

For 1D, the simplest method is the **trapezoid rule**—linearly interpolate the function at equally spaced intervals, and integrate the interpolation. It starts with one interval and doubles the number of intervals until convergence, reusing the previous function evaluations. The user specifies the min and the max number of doublings because convergence isn't guaranteed or may be premature to a wrong value. Evaluation reuse works because after doubling all previous evaluations fall on some current grid points. The runtime is O(the total number of intervals).

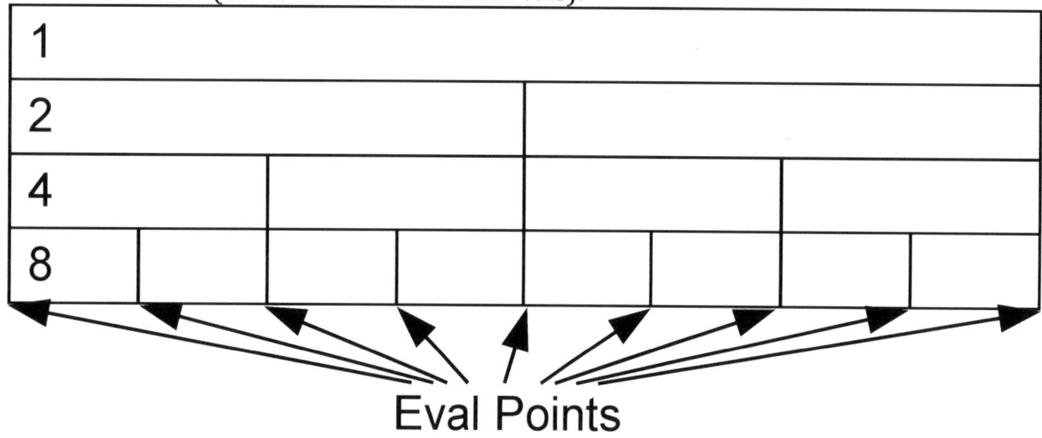


```
template<typename FUNCTION> class Trapezoid
{
    double sum;
    int nIntervals;
public:
    Trapezoid(): nIntervals(1) {}
    double addLevel(FUNCTION const& f, double xLeft, double xRight)
    {
        double dX = (xRight - xLeft)/nIntervals;
        if(nIntervals == 1) sum = (f(xLeft) + f(xRight))/2;
        else
        {//nIntervals/2 is the number of added points spaced 2 * dX apart
            double x = xLeft + dX;
            for(int i = 0; i < nIntervals/2; ++i, x += 2 * dX) sum += f(x);
        }
        nIntervals *= 2;
        return dX * sum;
    }
    static double integrate(FUNCTION const& f, double xLeft, double xRight,
        double maxXError = 0, int maxIterations = 10, int minIterations = 5)
    {
        Trapezoid t;
        double result = t.addLevel(f, xLeft, xRight), oldResult = 0;
        while(--maxIterations > 0 && (--minIterations > 0 ||
            abs(result - oldResult) >= maxXError))
        {
            oldResult = result;
```

```
            result = t.addLevel(f, xLeft, xRight);
        }
        return result;
    }
};
```

For $D > 1$, deterministic methods have $O(1/n^{1/D})$ convergence, and the integration range needn't be simple. By the CLT, **Monte Carlo integration** has $O(1/\sqrt{n})$ convergence. Maintaining incremental statistics on the integral to show the error isn't useful because waiting until it's very small takes too long. To calculate the integral given a membership tester:

1. **Find a bounding hyperrectangle and calculate its volume *v***
2. **Generate *n* random points uniformly inside the hyperrectangle**
3. **Let $s = \sum$function values of points $\in$range**
4. **Return sv/n**

Using $f = 1$ computes the range's volume. For m points $\in$ range, the average function value = s/m and the volume = vm/n.

```
template<typename POINT> double boxVolume(pair<POINT, POINT>const& box)
{
    double result = 1;
    for(int i = 0; i < box.first.getSize(); ++i)
        result *= box.second[i] - box.first[i];
    return result;
}
template<typename POINT, typename TEST, typename FUNCTION>
double MonteCarloIntegrate(pair<POINT, POINT> const& box, int n,
    TEST const& isInside = TEST(), FUNCTION const& f = FUNCTION())
{
    double sum = 0;
    for(int i = 0; i < n; ++i)
    {
        POINT point;
        for(int j = 0; j < point.getSize(); ++j)
            point[j] = GlobalRNG.uniform(box.first[j], box.second[j]);
        if(isInside(point)) sum += f(point);
    }
    return boxVolume(box) * sum/n;
}
```

No algorithm can accurately integrate a function with a concentrated spike. Known good ones are only successful heuristics that work well in most practical cases.

18.5 Function Evaluation

Functions such as sin and cos are usually evaluated by (Muller 2006):

1. **Partitioning the domain into suitable regions**
2. **Creating $\forall$region a specific approximation model, usually based on Taylor series, Chebyshev polynomials, or equation solving**
3. **To evaluate *f*(*x*), find its region, and use the region's model**

The performance generally depends on x, but is effectively $O(1)$ with a large constant. But some functions are evaluated by simulations that run for hours. In all cases, evaluating a function of D variables takes $O(D + F(D))$ time for some F.

Evaluating **elementary functions** such as cos by library routines generally gives the correctly rounded answer to full precision. For general functions, this is impossible due to the **table maker's dilemma**—deciding which way to round may need evaluation to an arbitrary precision.

18.6 Estimating Derivatives

It's usually easy to calculate the analytical derivative of a function represented by a syntax tree and impossible for a function given as a black box. The limit definition gives the forward difference formula $f'(x)$

= $(f(x + h) - f(x))/h$, which suffers from several problems, even for differentiable functions:

- The analytical error is $O(h^2 f''(x))$, which is too large if need high precision
- The numerical error caused by cancellation in the subtraction and the division is very large if $h \approx$ machine precision and f isn't evaluated to high precision

In the worst case, can't overcome these issues, but for a properly scaled f using $h = \sqrt{\text{machine precision}}$ with the **high-order central difference formula** $f'(x) = (f(x - 2h) + 8f(x + h) - 8f(x - h) - f(x + 2h))/(12h)$, which by Taylor series has analytical error $O(h^4 f^{(5)}(x))$, usually gives a good enough estimate.

```
double globalSafeDelta = sqrt(numeric_limits<double>::epsilon());
template<typename FUNCTION> double estimateDerivativeCD(double x,
    FUNCTION const& f, double relAbsDelta = globalSafeDelta)
{
    double h = globalSafeDelta * max(1.0, abs(x));
    return (-f(x + 2 * h) + 8 * f(x + h) - 8 * f(x - h) + f(x - 2 * h))/h/12;
}
```

Such methods use O(1) evaluations but are at best successful heuristics. Derivative estimation isn't backward stable (Corless & Fillion 2013), making it an ill-posed problem, so no algorithm can do well in the worst case. It's simply impossible to pick the right h.

To estimate the gradient of a D-variable function, estimate all the partial derivatives. This takes $O(D^2 + DF(D))$ time. Evaluating the analytical gradient takes $O(D + G(D))$ time, and $G(D) = O(D)$ if ∀ variable the partial derivative depends on O(1) other variables. The above central difference formula uses $4D$ evaluations to compute the gradient, but simpler, less accurate finite difference uses $D + 1$ evaluations and is enough for many applications:

```
template<typename FUNCTION, typename POINT> POINT estimateGradientFD(POINT x,
    FUNCTION const& f, double relAbsDelta = globalSafeDelta)
{
    POINT result = x;
    double y = f(x);
    for(int i = 0; i < x.getSize(); ++i)
    {
        double h = relAbsDelta * max(1.0, abs(x[i]));
        x[i] += h;
        result[i] = (f(x) - y)/h;
        x[i] -= h;
    }
    return result;
}
```

18.7 Single-variable Equation Solving

An equation in the most general form is $f(x) = 0$. The **bisection method** assumes an interval containing the solution where f(one endpoint) < 0 and f(the other endpoint) > 0. While the current interval < the previous one, the algorithm replaces *right*/*left* with middle if f(*middle*) and f(*left*) have different/same signs. The convergence is linear even with precision loss and stochastic discontinuous functions. For illustration, the implementation solves to full precision using Cauchy convergence. In practice, have a precision limit.

```
bool haveDifferentSign(double a, double b){return (a < 0) != (b < 0);}
template<typename FUNCTION> double solveFor0(FUNCTION const& f, double xLeft,
    double xRight)
{
    double yLeft = f(xLeft), xMiddle;
    assert(xRight >= xLeft && haveDifferentSign(yLeft, f(xRight)));
    for(;;)
    {
        xMiddle = (xLeft + xRight)/2;
        double yMiddle = f(xMiddle), prevDiff = xRight - xLeft;
        if(haveDifferentSign(yLeft, yMiddle)) xRight = xMiddle;
        else
        {
```

```
            xLeft = xMiddle;
            yLeft = yMiddle;
        }
        if(xRight - xLeft >= prevDiff) break;
    }
    return xMiddle;
}
```

Newton's method, derivable from Taylor series:

1. **Start with a guess *x***
2. **Until convergence**
3. **$x = x - f(x)/f'(x)$**

It converges quadratically but sometimes not at all, making it useful only for specific tasks such as root finding, where it's proven to converge and the formulas are simplified for the particular function and its derivative.

```
template<typename FUNCTION, typename DERIVATIVE> double solveFor0Newton(
    FUNCTION const& f, DERIVATIVE const& derivative, double x)
{
    for(double prevDiff = numeric_limits<double>::max();;)
    {
        double y = f(x), oldX = x;
        x -= y/derivative(x);
        double diff = abs(x - oldX);
        if(diff >= prevDiff) break;
        prevDiff = diff;
    }
    return x;
}
```

18.8 Single-variable Function Minimization

Assume a quasi-convex function on $[a, b]$. **Golden section search** maintains (a, b, c) such that $f(a) \leq f(b) \leq f(c)$:

1. **Until convergence**
2. **Pick $x \in$ the larger of $[a, b]$, $[b, c]$**
3. **If $a \leq x \leq b \leq c$ then (a, x, b) is the new triple**
4. **Else $a \leq b \leq x \leq c$ and (b, x, c) is**

The optimal x isn't in the middle, but 1 – the golden ratio into the larger interval from b. The algorithm converges linearly even with precision loss and stochastic discontinuous functions.

```
template<typename FUNCTION> pair<double, double> minimizeGS(
    FUNCTION const& f, double xLeft, double xRight,
    double relAbsXPrecision = numeric_limits<double>::epsilon())
{
    assert(isfinite(xLeft) && isfinite(xRight) && xLeft <= xRight &&
        relAbsXPrecision >= numeric_limits<double>::epsilon());
    double GR = 0.618, xMiddle = xLeft * GR + xRight * (1 - GR),
        yMiddle = f(xMiddle);
    while(isELess(xLeft, xRight, relAbsXPrecision))
    {
        bool chooseR = xRight - xMiddle > xMiddle - xLeft;
        double prevDiff = xRight - xLeft, xNew = GR * xMiddle + (1 - GR) *
            (chooseR ? xRight : xLeft), yNew = f(xNew);
        if(yNew < yMiddle)
        {
            (chooseR ? xLeft : xRight) = xMiddle;
            xMiddle = xNew;
            yMiddle = yNew;
        }
```

```
        else (chooseR ? xRight : xLeft) = xNew;
    }
    return make_pair(xMiddle, yMiddle);
}
```

Suppose $x > b$ without loss of generality, and let $w = (b - a)/(c - a)$ = the fraction of the way b is in $[a, c]$ and $z = (x - b)/(c - a)$ = the fraction of the way x is in $[a, x]$ after b. The next interval is $[a, x]$ of relative length $w + z$ or $[b, c]$ of relative length $1 - w$. The worst case is smallest when they are equal $\leftrightarrow z = 1 - 2w$. Assuming optimal choices in the past, x is the same fraction of the way in $[b, c]$ as b is in $[a, c]$, so $(x - b)/(c - b) = (b - a)/(c - a) \leftrightarrow z/(1 - w) = w$. So $w = 1$ – golden ratio. At the start, $b = c$ isn't optimal, but the intervals quickly become optimal. Due to geometrically shrinking intervals, the convergence is linear—i.e., need O(lg(1/precision)) evaluations.

To minimize stochastic functions, can get reasonably accurate averages, and minimize the resulting deterministic function, though this is a heuristic.

If know a starting point and not a containing interval, use **bracketing**—exponential search with initial distance large enough to exceed possible noise:

```
template<typename FUNCTION> double findIntervalBound(FUNCTION const& f,
    double guess, double d)
{//run with d < 0 for the left bound and d > 0 for the right bound
    for(double yBest = f(guess); d * 2 != d; d *= 2)//handle d = 0 and inf
    {
        double yNext = f(guess + d);
        if(yNext >= yBest) break;
        yBest = yNext;
    }
    return guess + d;
}
```

When the sought bound is b, need O(lg(b/d)) evaluations.

18.9 Multidimensional Function Minimization

For $D > 1$, the optimal move direction is unknown because $!\exists$a shrinking solution interval. All methods start with an initial guess, and guess the direction based on the values of nearby points or gradient information. No algorithm converges to a local optimum in predictably many iterations, even for sufficiently smooth functions. Because can partition the optimization landscape into local minimum regions, a minimum within such a region is what such local search finds.

A simple algorithm is **coordinate descent**:

1. **Start with dimension $i = 0$ and a user-given starting point**
2. **Until converge or exceed the specified number of iterations, do 1D optimization on $x[i]$:**
3.   **Find a bounding interval**
4.   **Do golden section search**
5.   **Set $i = (i + 1)$ % D**

This is robust and applicable to all cases with O(Dlg(1/the golden section precision)) time per iteration. But convergence to a local minimum isn't guaranteed or can be very slow, unless f is convex or other special cases apply because the function value can improve in mixed but not coordinate directions. Without such conditions, other algorithms could guarantee converge and be more efficient. Coordinate descent is more efficient if can update f incrementally from only $x[i]$. Also, may be able to replace bounding and golden section by the analytic solution in some cases such as lasso regression (see the "Machine Learning—Regression" chapter).

If f is differentiable, at a local minimum $\nabla f = 0$, and any direction d such that $d\nabla f < 0$ is a descent direction, moving into which by some step reduces the value of f. Gradient-based algorithms repeatedly do 1D search in a picked descent direction until convergence, i.e., $\nabla f < c$ for some tiny c. But this can fail if ∇f is estimated by finite differences, so it's more robust to stop when no progress in the value of f is made.

This **line search** either finds the exact minimizer on the line or an approximate one that gives **sufficient decrease**.

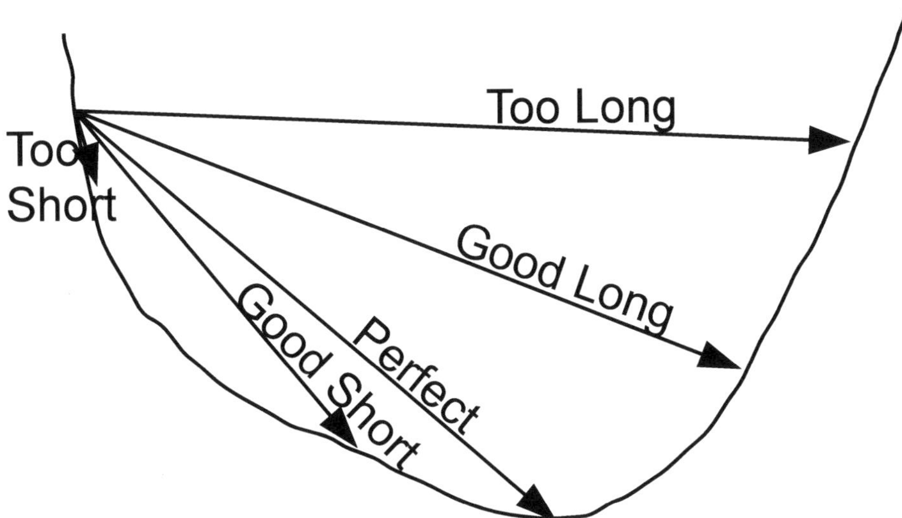

Wolfe conditions for convergent line search in a descent direction *d* require that for step *s* and some constants $0 < c_1 < c_2 < 1$, the step isn't too:

- Long—$f(x + sd) \leq f(x) + c_1 sd\nabla f(x)$
- Short—$\nabla f(x + sd) \geq c_2 d\nabla f(x)$

Exact search satisfies Wolfe conditions for properly chosen c_1 and c_2. **Zoutendijk's theorem**: line search converges to a local minimum if:

- *f* is continuously differentiable, bounded below, and ∇f is Lipschitz continuous
- Descent directions are picked
- Line searches satisfy Wolfe conditions

A simple algorithm that finds *s* satisfying Wolfe conditions is **backtracking**. It starts with an initial step large enough to satisfy the second condition and halves it until the first one is satisfied. Experimentally, a good choice of c_1 is 0.0001, and for algorithms that produce well-scaled directions such as Newton's and L-BFGS (covered later in this chapter), the initial step must be 1 to have superlinear local convergence (Nocedal & Wright 2006).

```
template<typename FUNCTION, typename POINT> pair<POINT, double>
backtrackLineSearch(POINT const& x, POINT const& direction,
    POINT const& gradient, FUNCTION const& f, double y,
    double yPrecision = numeric_limits<double>::epsilon(), double c = 0.0001)
{//dy = step * direction * gradient + O(step * step)`
    double dd = -(direction * gradient), minDecrease = dd * c, yNew;
    if(minDecrease > 0)//ensure decrease
        for(double step = 1; step * (dd + step) >= yPrecision; step /= 2)
        {
            POINT xNew = x + direction * step;
            if(y - (yNew = f(xNew)) >= minDecrease * step)
                return pair<POINT, double>(xNew, yNew);
        }
    return pair<POINT, double>(x, y);
}
```

Exact search reduces to 1D minimization. It usually needs many more function evaluations to get high precision, but is useful when gradient evaluation is the bottleneck, particularly when using a finite difference gradient for $D > \approx 100$.

```
template<typename POINT, typename FUNCTION> struct LineFunction
{
    FUNCTION f;
    POINT x, direction;
    LineFunction(POINT const& theX, POINT const& theDirection,
        FUNCTION const& theF = FUNCTION()): x(theX),
        direction(theDirection), f(theF) {}
    double operator()(double step)const
        {return f(x + direction * step);}
```

```
};
template<typename POINT, typename FUNCTION> pair<POINT, double> lineMinimize(
    POINT const& x, POINT const& direction, FUNCTION const& f = FUNCTION(),
double d = 1)
{
    LineFunction<POINT, FUNCTION> lf(x, direction, f);
    pair<double, double> result =
        minimizeGS(lf, 0, findIntervalBound(lf, 0, d));
    return pair<POINT, double>(x + direction * result.first, result.second);
}
```

The simplest line search algorithm is **gradient descent**. Given a stating point *x*, until convergence it performs a line search in the direction $-\nabla f$. By Zoutendijk's theorem, it converges. The convergence is linear, with *s* a constant that depends on the condition number of $\nabla^2 f$, and is very slow if this number is large (Nocedal & Wright 2006).

Newton's method uses directions $-(\nabla^2 f)^{-1}\nabla f$ with step = 1. The convergence is quadratic in the neighborhood of the solution, but it may not converge, and each iteration takes $O(n^3)$ time. Theorem (Nocedal & Wright 2006): Let *B* be a positive definite matrix and $\exists M > 0$ such that $||B||||B^{-1}|| < M$. Then $-B^{-1}\nabla f$ is a descent direction. So line search using Newton directions converges if $B = \nabla^2 f$ satisfies the conditions. But for an arbitrary *f* it may not.

L-BFGS evolved from attempts to make Newton's method convergent and reduce its iteration cost. It uses directions $-B^{-1}\nabla f$, updating *B* to approximate $\nabla^2 f$. Forcing *B* to satisfy certain criteria results in a mathematical model, solving which gives the update equation $H_{k+1} = V_k H_k V_k + p_k s_k^2$, where (Nocedal & Wright 2006):

- $H = B^{-1}$
- $p_k = 1/(y_k s_k)$
- $V_k = I - p_k \times \text{outerProduct}(y_k, s_k)$
- $s_k = x_{k+1} - x_k$
- $y_k = \nabla f_{k+1} - \nabla f_k$

L-BFGS stores $j \le m$ last s_i and y_i in a queue and uses them to compute H_k recursively by starting with $H_{k-j} = 1/(p_{k-1}y_{k-1}^2)I$ if $j > 0$ and $H_0 = I$ otherwise, and applying the update equation *j* times. Compared to the simpler $H_{k-j} = I$, this choice of H_{k-j} accelerates convergence theoretically and experimentally, and experimentally $m \in [3, 20]$, particularly $m = 8$, is a good choice (Nocedal & Wright 2006). Because queue uses a vector for storage, to avoid waste make *m* a power of two, so 4, 8, and 16 are good values.

Can compute $d = H_k\nabla f$ without explicitly forming *H* because H_{k-j} is a diagonal matrix, and can expand the update formula to calculate $H_k\nabla f$ directly from H_{k-j} and the stored s_i and y_i, so that each iteration uses $O(nm)$ time and space (Nocedal & Wright 2006):

1. $d \leftarrow \nabla f$
2. $\forall i \in [k-1, k-j]$
3. Store $a_i = p_i s_i d$
4. d -= $a_i y_i$
5. d *= H_{k-j}
6. $\forall i \in [k-j, k-1]$
7. d += $s_i(a_i - p_i y_i d)$

As Newton's method, L-BFGS produces well-scaled directions, so line search starts with step = 1. Need this to ensure superlinear convergence (Nocedal & Wright 2006).

```
template<typename POINT, typename FUNCTION, typename GRADIENT>
    pair<POINT, double> LBFGSMinimize(POINT const& initialGuess,
    FUNCTION const& f, GRADIENT const& g, int maxIterations = 10000,
    double yPrecision = numeric_limits<double>::epsilon(),
    bool useExactSearch = false, int historySize = 8)
{
    Queue<pair<POINT, POINT> > history;
    pair<POINT, double> xy(initialGuess, f(initialGuess));
    POINT grad = g(xy.first), d = -grad;
    while(maxIterations-- > 0)
```

```
    {
        double yLast = xy.second;
        pair<POINT, double> xyNew = useExactSearch ?
            lineMinimize(xy.first, d, f) : backtrackLineSearch(xy.first, d,
            grad, f, xy.second, yPrecision);
        if(!isfinite(xyNew.second) ||
            !isELess(xyNew.second, xy.second, yPrecision)) break;
        POINT newGrad = g(xyNew.first);
        if(history.getSize() >= historySize) history.pop();
        history.push(make_pair(xyNew.first - xy.first, newGrad - grad));
        xy = xyNew;
        d = grad = newGrad;//"double recursion" algorithm to update d
        Vector<double> a, p;
        int last = history.getSize() - 1;
        for(int i = last; i >= 0; --i)
        {
            double pi = 1/(history[i].first * history[i].second),
                ai = history[i].first * d * pi;
            d -= history[i].second * ai;
            a.append(ai);
            p.append(pi);
        }//initial Hessian is scaled diagonal
        d *= 1/(history[last].second * history[last].second * p[last]);
        for(int i = 0; i < history.getSize(); ++i)
        {
            double bi = history[i].second * d * p[last - i];
            d += history[i].first * (a[last - i] - bi);
        }
        d *= -1;
    }
    return xy;
}
```

L-BFGS converges superlinearly to a local minimum if (Nocedal & Liu 1989):

- f is convex and twice continuously differentiable
- $\forall z \in \mathbb{R}^n\ \exists m, M > 0$ such that $m||z||^2 \le z\nabla^2 fz \le M||z||^2$
- $||H_0||$ and $||H_0^{-1}|| < \infty$
- The line search satisfies the Wolfe conditions

The algorithm is very robust and usually converges even if f doesn't satisfy the conditions at every point. But even if it does, !∃ a useful bound on the number of iterations. It's possible, though unlikely, that the algorithm won't find a local minimum with wanted precision within the allowed number of iterations. Practically the number of iterations is a large constant, and theoretically O(lg(1/precision)), so setting the limit to ≈10000 is likely to work well for many functions. Few need more, most need less.

If gradient is unavailable, compute it by finite differences. Experimentally, L-BFGS still performs well as long as the estimation isn't too inaccurate, but !∃ supporting theory.

```
template<typename FUNCTION, typename POINT> struct GradientFunctor
{
    FUNCTION f;
    double delta;
    GradientFunctor(FUNCTION const& theF,
        double relAbsDelta = globalSafeDelta): f(theF), delta(relAbsDelta) {}
    POINT operator()(POINT const& p)const
        {return estimateGradientFD(p, f, delta);}
};
```

For a differentiable function, picking a descent direction is easy even without knowing ∇f because as long as $d\nabla f \neq 0$, $-d$ or d is a descent direction. For a nondifferentiable function, any d for which $d\nabla f < 0$ needn't be descent. E.g., in 2D, $f(x) = \max(||x—c||, ||x + c||)$ for $c = (-1, 1)$ isn't differentiable along $x = y$ and has the minimum at (0, 0). All directional derivatives exist, but at (−1, −1) neither $-\nabla f$ nor coordinate directions give descent, and at (0, 0) $\nabla f \neq 0$. ∃ f and x where only directions in an extremely small angular range give descent. If such range for a particular x is small enough, x is effectively optimal because finding a descent direction is infeasible.

∃ many methods for nondifferentiable functions. **Nelder-Mead heuristic** is among the most successful, particularly for $D < \sim 10$, where it's very efficient experimentally. It works from an initial **simplex**, which is a hyper-triangle of $D + 1$ points and consists of a guess point and its *uniform01* × the initial step displacements into each orthogonal direction. The initial step is user-defined and for well-scaled functions should be set to D. The important points are those with the best, the worst, and the second worst values. At every iteration, the algorithm pulls the simplex from the worst to the best using:

- **Scaling**—replace the worst by a convex combination of itself and the centroid of the other points. When the scale factor = −1, the result is a **reflection**.
- **Shrinking**—move all points ½ way toward the best.

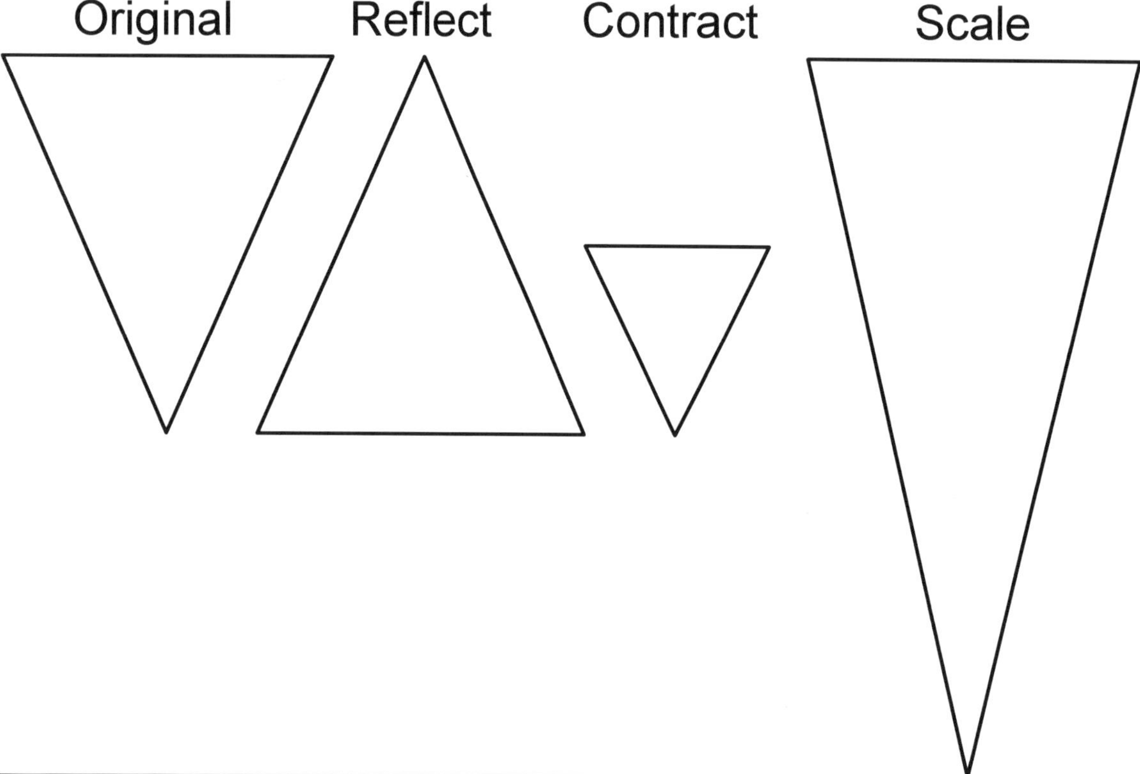


```
template<typename POINT, typename FUNCTION> class NelderMead
{
    FUNCTION f;
    int D;
    POINT vertexSum;//incremental centroid
    typedef pair<POINT, double> P;
    Vector<P> simplex;
    double scale(P& high, double factor)
    {
        P result = high;
        //affine combination of the high point and the
        //centroid of the remaining vertices
        //centroid = (vertexSum - high)/D and
        //result = centroid * (1 - factor) + high * factor
        double centroidFactor = (1 - factor)/D;
        result.first = vertexSum * centroidFactor +
            high.first * (factor - centroidFactor);
        result.second = f(result.first);
        if(result.second < high.second)
        {//accept scaling if improving
            vertexSum += result.first - high.first;
```

```
            high = result;
        }
        return result.second;
    }
public:
    NelderMead(int theD, FUNCTION const& theFunction = FUNCTION()):
        D(theD), f(theFunction), simplex(D + 1, D + 1){}
};
```

The main logic:

1. **Until convergence**
2. **Find the best, the 2nd best, and the worst**
3. **Converged if the best ≈ the worst**
4. **Try to reflect**
5. **If the reflected point is better than the best, try to scale the new best by 2**
6. **Else try to scale by ½**
7. **If the result is worse than the next worst, shrink all points toward the best**

```
    P minimize(POINT const& initialGuess, int maxIterations = 10000,
        double yPrecision = globalSafeDelta, double step = 1)
    {
        vertexSum = initialGuess;
        for(int i = 0; i < D; ++i) vertexSum[i] = 0;
        for(int i = 0; i <= D; ++i)
        {
            simplex[i].first = initialGuess;
            if(i > 0)simplex[i].first[i - 1] += GlobalRNG.uniform01() * step;
            simplex[i].second = f(simplex[i].first);
            vertexSum += simplex[i].first;
        }
        for(;;)
        {//calculate high, low, and nextHigh, which must be all different
            int high = 0, nextHigh = 1, low = 2;
            if(simplex[high].second < simplex[nextHigh].second)
                swap(high, nextHigh);
            if(simplex[nextHigh].second < simplex[low].second)
            {
                swap(low, nextHigh);
                if(simplex[high].second < simplex[nextHigh].second)
                    swap(high, nextHigh);
            }
            for(int i = 3; i <= D; ++i)
            {
                if(simplex[i].second < simplex[low].second) low = i;
                else if(simplex[i].second > simplex[high].second)
                {
                    nextHigh = high;
                    high = i;
                }
                else if(simplex[i].second > simplex[nextHigh].second)
                    nextHigh = i;
            }
            if(!maxIterations-- || !isELess(simplex[low].second,
                simplex[high].second, yPrecision)) return simplex[low];
            //try to reflect
            double value = scale(simplex[high], -1);
            //try to double if better than low
            if(value <= simplex[low].second) scale(simplex[high], 2);
            else if(value >= simplex[nextHigh].second)
            {//try reflected/unrefrected halving if accepted/rejected value
```

```
                double yHi = simplex[high].second;
                if(scale(simplex[high], 0.5) >= yHi)
                {//contract all to get rid of the high point
                    vertexSum = simplex[low].first;
                    for(int i = 0; i <= D; ++i) if(i != low)
                    {
                        vertexSum += simplex[i].first = (simplex[i].first +
                            simplex[low].first) * 0.5;
                        simplex[i].second = f(simplex[i].first);
                    }
                }
            }
        }
    }
```

For most functions, $\sqrt{\text{machine precision}}$ is a good choice of function value precision ϵ. For efficiency, if don't need high accuracy, use $\epsilon = 0.001$ with a properly scaled function. If the best point converges linearly and gets updated every D iterations, need $O(D\log(1/\epsilon))$ evaluations. Experimentally, a good choice of the max number of iterations is $\approx 50D\log(1/\epsilon) \approx 1000D$ for the default $\epsilon = 0.001$. Because usually $D < 10$, use 10000 for simplicity.

Nelder-Mead picks good directions for typical functions and always converges to something that needn't be a local minimum. For certain functions, it can stall because the simplex volume becomes too small and can't recover, particularly for $D > 10$. The simplest way to handle this is by restarting at the result until stop making progress. The max number of restarts should be set to ≈ 10 by default. If convergence needs more, Nelder-Mead isn't effective for the problem. But even if unable to converge, it usually gives substantial function value gain after few evaluations of f.

```
    P restartedMinimize(POINT const& initialGuess, int maxIterations = 10000,
        double yPrecision = numeric_limits<double>::epsilon(),
        int maxRepeats = 10, double step = 1)
    {
        P result(initialGuess, numeric_limits<double>::infinity());
        while(maxRepeats--)
        {
            double yOld = result.second;
            result = minimize(result.first, maxIterations, yPrecision, step);
            if(!isELess(result.second, yOld, yPrecision)) break;
        }
        return result;
    }
```

For functions where both L-BFGS with finite differences and restarted Nelder-Mead fail, **decreasing step random search** (DSRS) heuristic can be effective with $O(D)$ evaluations per iteration:

1. Start from some initial step size s, usually 1
2. Until convergence when s becomes too small based on ϵ
3. Generate a random unit direction
4. Move into s × the direction if doing so decreases f
5. If successful, double s
6. Else shrink by some factor $\in [0.5, 1]$, usually 0.8

The effect of s is estimated from Taylor series of f as $s(s + dd)$, where dd = the directional derivative estimated from the last move. This termination strategy is useful because, if a bad direction is picked, have many chances to recover before s is too small.

```
template<typename POINT, typename FUNCTION> pair<POINT, double>
    DSRS(POINT const& initialGuess, FUNCTION const& f,
    double step = 1, double factor = 0.8, int maxFEvals = 10000000,
    double yPrecision = numeric_limits<double>::epsilon())
{
    pair<POINT, double> xy(initialGuess, f(initialGuess));
    for(double dd = 0; --maxFEvals && step * (dd + step) > yPrecision;)
```

```
    {
        POINT direction = initialGuess;//ensure nonzero direction
        for(int j = 0; j < direction.getSize(); ++j) direction[j] =
            GlobalRNG.uniform01() * (GlobalRNG.next() % 2 ? 1 : -1);
        direction *= 1/sqrt(direction * direction);
        double yNew = f(xy.first + direction * step);
        if(isELess(yNew, xy.second, yPrecision))
        {
            dd = (xy.second - yNew)/step;
            xy.first += direction * step;
            xy.second = yNew;
            step *= 2;
        }
        else step *= factor;
    }
    return xy;
}
```

For an unknown *f*, apply L-BFGS, Nelder-Mead, and DSRS, in this order. If *f* is sufficiently smooth, L-BFGS will quickly find the optimum, if it fails, Nelder-Mead will at least improve the function value, and finally DSRS will find and improve in a rare descent direction. Specific functions from important problems are usually minimized using customized methods such as back-propagation for neural networks (see the "Machine Learning—Classification" chapter).

18.10 Global Minimization

The algorithms of the previous sections find local and not global minimums. **Grid search** is effective at finding an approximate region of the global minimum for small *D*. The idea is to create a uniform grid and try every point. This effectively turns the problem into discrete set optimization, covered later in this chapter. The benefit of a uniform grid is that can cover the entire optimization region up to ϵ, though this can be very inefficient.

To turn Nelder-Mead into a global optimization method, use iterated local search with the jump to a new random point or in a random direction decided by *cauchy01* variates:

```
template<int D, typename FUNCTION> struct ILSNelderMead
{
    typedef NelderMead<D, FUNCTION> NM;
    typedef typename NM::P P;
    struct Move
    {
        NM &nm;
        P current, best;
        int maxIterations;
        double precision;
        void localSearchBest()
            {current = nm.minimize(current.first, maxIterations, precision);}
        void bigMove()
        {
            for(int i = 0; i < D; ++i)
                current.first[i] = GlobalRNG.cauchy01();
        }
        void updateBest()
            {if(best.second > current.second) best = current;}
    };
    NM nelderMead;
    ILSNelderMead(FUNCTION const& theFunction = FUNCTION()):
        nelderMead(theFunction) {}
    P minimize(typename NM::Vertex const& initialGuess, int maxJumps = 1000,
        int maxIterations = 1000, double precision = 0.001)
    {
```

```
        P initial(initialGuess, numeric_limits<double>::max());
        Move move = {nelderMead, initial, initial, maxJumps, precision};
        iteratedLocalSearch(move, maxJumps);
        return move.best;
    }
};
```

18.11 Discrete Set Optimization

The goal is to optimize over values of a discrete set. Can generate such set even from a continuous range, particularly the exponential range 2^i, with $i \in$ some discrete interval, works well in many cases. It's a good heuristic preferred in practice, but doesn't have the uniform grid coverage described previously. The assumption is that solutions within a small multiplicative factor are indifferent, whereas uniform grid assumes an additive factor.

Grid search is the simplest such method, which tries all possibilities. Though it's infeasible with many dimensions, due to finding the optimal solution it's very useful for small *D*, particularly for parameter optimization. The main task is generating all value selections. The solution idea is to order variables, keep current indices ∀ variable, and:

- After advancing any variable, move to the next one. When have no variable to move to, a selection is complete.
- When the current variable loop ends, reset all higher variables. When variable 0 loop ends, the generation went through all selections.

```
template<typename FUNCTION> Vector<double> gridMinimize(
    Vector<Vector<double> > const& sets, FUNCTION const& f = FUNCTION())
{
    assert(sets.getSize() > 0);
    Vector<double> best;
    for(int i = 0; i < sets.getSize(); ++i)
    {
        assert(sets[i].getSize() > 0);
        best.append(sets[i][0]);
    }
    double bestScore = f(best);
    Vector<int> current(sets.getSize(), -1);
    current.lastItem() = 0;
    for(int level = 0; level > -1;)
    {
        if(level < sets.getSize())
        {
            if(++current[level] < sets[level].getSize()) ++level;
            else current[level--] = -1;
        }
        else
        {//process value selection
            Vector<double> values;
            for(int i = 0; i < sets.getSize(); ++i)
                values.append(sets[i][current[i]]);
            double score = f(values);
            if(score < bestScore)
            {
                bestScore = score;
                best = values;
            }
            --level;
        }
    }
    return best;
}
```

Another strategy is something similar to the classic compass search and tries to reduce the number of evaluations as much as possible but doesn't guarantee optimality.

1. Assume sorted values ∀variable
2. ∀variable initialize the last successful direction to +1
3. Until converge or reach the iteration limit
4. Select a variable
5. Try to move into its last successful direction once
6. If unsuccessful, try the reverse direction

This is also similar to coordinate descent, except making only 1 move and not complete optimization for 1D subproblems.

```
//assumes set values are in sorted (or reverse sorted) order!
template<typename FUNCTION> pair<Vector<double>, pair<double, int> >
    compassDiscreteMinimizeHelper(Vector<Vector<double> > const& sets,
    Vector<int> current, FUNCTION const& f = FUNCTION(),
    int remainingEvals = 100)
{//start with medians
    Vector<double> best;
    for(int i = 0; i < sets.getSize(); ++i)
    {
        assert(0 <= current[i] && current[i] < sets[i].getSize());
        best.append(sets[i][current.lastItem()]);
    }
    double bestScore = f(best);
    Vector<int> preferredSign(sets.getSize(), 1);
    for(bool done = false; !done;)
    {
        done = true;
        for(int i = 0; i < sets.getSize(); ++i)
            for(int j = 0; j < 2; ++j)
            {
                int sign = preferredSign[i];
                if(j == 1) sign = -sign;
                int next = current[i] + sign;
                if(0 <= next && next < sets[i].getSize())
                {
                    if(remainingEvals-- < 1)
                        return make_pair(best, make_pair(bestScore, 0));
                    best[i] = sets[i][next];
                    double score = f(best);
                    if(score < bestScore)
                    {
                        current[i] = next;
                        bestScore = score;
                        done = false;
                        preferredSign[i] = sign;
                        j = 2;
                    }
                    else best[i] = sets[i][current[i]];
                }
            }
    }
    return make_pair(best, make_pair(bestScore, remainingEvals));
}
```

A simple good starting point is consists of the median over each variable, which is reasonable assuming the ranges are chosen properly:

```
template<typename FUNCTION> Vector<double> compassDiscreteMinimize(
    Vector<Vector<double> > const& sets, FUNCTION const& f = FUNCTION(),
    int remainingEvals = 100)
```

```
{
    Vector<int> current;
    for(int i = 0; i < sets.getSize(); ++i)
    {
        assert(sets[i].getSize() > 0);
        current.append(sets[i].getSize()/2);
    }
    return compassDiscreteMinimizeHelper(sets, current, f,
        remainingEvals).first;
}
```

Can get stuck in a local minimum, so have ILS with random restart. As with pure random search, the optimal solution is found almost surely with enough restarts.

```
template<typename FUNCTION> Vector<double> ILSCompassDiscreteMinimize(
    Vector<Vector<double> > const& sets, FUNCTION const& f = FUNCTION(),
    int remainingEvals = 100)
{
    assert(remainingEvals > 0);
    double bestScore;
    Vector<double> best;
    while(remainingEvals > 0)
    {
        Vector<int> current;
        for(int i = 0; i < sets.getSize(); ++i)
        {
            assert(sets[i].getSize() > 0);
            current.append(sets[i][GlobalRNG.mod(sets[i].getSize())]);
        }
        pair<Vector<double>, pair<double, int> > state =
            compassDiscreteMinimizeHelper(sets, current, f, remainingEvals);
        remainingEvals = state.second.second;
        if(state.second.first < bestScore)
        {
            best = state.first;
            bestScore = state.second.first;
        }
    }
    return best;
}
```

18.12 Stochastic Optimization

For noisy f, want to minimize $E[f(x)]$. The expecation isn't the only way to specify qualities of a desired minimum—e.g., usually prefer x_2 with slightly larger $E[f(x_2)]$ but much smaller variance, but such formulations lead to much harder multiobjective optimization.

Can convert a stochastic problem into a deterministic one using **sample average approximation** (SAA), i.e., minimize $g(x)$ = the average of evaluating $f(x)$ n times for some n. For $n \to \infty$, $g(x) \to E[f(x)]$. This works with discrete, constrained, and global minimization. But it's unclear how to select n. **Sample path approximation** first solves the problem with small n and then many times with doubled n, using the solution of the previous round as the starting solution of the next. So heuristically, in the later rounds, though more simulations are used per evaluation, the algorithm solving the deterministic problem should converge quickly. Have convergence when averages and found solutions stop changing.

But for small n, g can have small jump discontinuities everywhere, and can't apply many deterministic optimization algorithms as is. E.g., the finite difference derivative will be garbage for the default choice of h, so need to make h large enough to overcome noise, but doing so gives only approximate gradients for high levels of noise and is likely to fail. Can apply Nelder-Mead and DSRS as is. With a large enough initial step, they are likely to find a solution as close to the optimum as the noise allows.

While this is a major use case for Nelder-Mead, it's wasteful to evaluate f many times at the same x for noise reduction. More efficient algorithms optimize and reduce noise simultaneously, avoiding bad solutions without needing their accurate value.

18.13 Stochastic Approximation Algorithms

Robbins-Munro algorithm (RM) solves a system of stochastic equations $f(x) = 0$ given observations $m(x)$ of $f(x)$ such that $E[m(x)] = f(x)$:

1. **Pick the starting x_0**
2. **For some large n and step sizes s_i, while $i < n$**
3. **$x_{i+1} = x_i - s_i m(x_i)$**

Let $e_i = f(x) - m(x)$ and H = the set of all roots. RM converges almost surely to $x \in H$ for $n \to \infty$ if (Bhatnagar et al. 2013):

- $\sum_{0 \le i \le \infty} s_i = \infty$, and $\sum_{0 \le i \le \infty} s_i^2 < \infty$
- $\sup_i ||x_i|| < \infty$ almost surely
- e_i form a martingale difference sequence, are square integrable, and $\exists k > 0$ such that $E[||e_i||^2] < k(1 + ||x_i||^2)$
- f is Lipschitz continuous, and the ODE $dx(t)/dt = f(x(t))$ has H as its set of globally asymptotically stable equilibria

Only the first condition is important. The others are impossible to verify in practice and are usually ignored because the algorithm tends to produce reasonable answers even if they aren't satisfied.

Under further conditions, using $s_i = 1/i$ is asymptotically optimal and leads to $O(1/\sqrt{n})$ convergence (Spall 2003). Because any algorithm, even if starting from a root x, needs to at least verify that $f(x) = 0$ using Monte Carlo, whose convergence is also $O(1/\sqrt{n})$, RM is asymptotically optimal. But with finite n, finding a root is more important than estimating its value, and slower-decreasing $s_i = 1/i^{0.501}$ usually leads to faster search, despite worse asymptotic convergence. In some sense, asymptotic convergence matters only for polishing the precision because it kicks in after already got some precision. Constant s_i is also used often, but doesn't satisfy the conditions. RM is very sensitive to s_0 because too large values diverge and too small ones converge too slowly. As for SPSA (described later), can use grid search to find a suitable value.

Stochastic gradient descent (SGD) uses RM to solve $\nabla f = 0$. Though don't know f, can come up with an unbiased estimator of ∇f with enough knowledge of m. Let ϵ_i come from a probability distribution with PDF p. Then $\nabla f(x) = \partial/\partial x \int_{-\infty < t < \infty} m(x, \epsilon(t, x)) p(\epsilon(t, x)) dt$. If ϵ doesn't depend on x, and can interchange the derivative and the integral, this simplifies to $\nabla f(x) = E[\partial m(x, \epsilon)/\partial x]$. In many cases, can compute $\partial m(x, \epsilon)/\partial x$ analytically, e.g., for neural network training (see the "Machine Learning—Classification" chapter).

E.g., linear regression, given a set of points (x_i, y_i), computes a hyperplane $y(x) = wx$ such that $\sum(y(x_i) - y_i)^2$ is minimal. When points arrive online, $m(w, \epsilon_i) = (y(x_i) - y_i)^2$ is an unbiased estimator of the true error on point i, and $\partial m(w, \epsilon_i)/\partial w = x_i(y(x_i) - y_i)/2$. So the RM iteration is w -= $s_i \partial m(w, \epsilon_i)/\partial w$.

Though RM easily converges for finding roots, SGD can swing into ∞ quickly if steps are too large, because don't check for decrease in f.

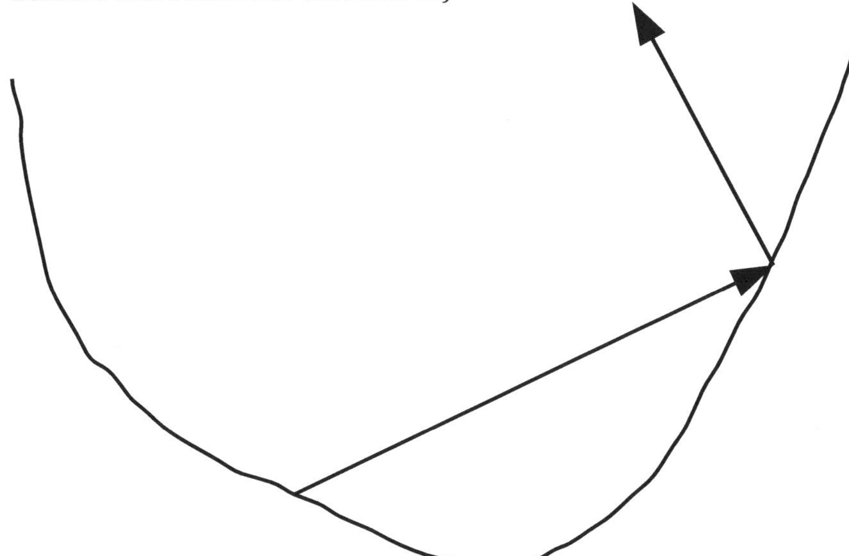

SGD works with nondifferentiable functions—gradient generalizes to **subgradient**, which in 2D is any tangent line to the function:

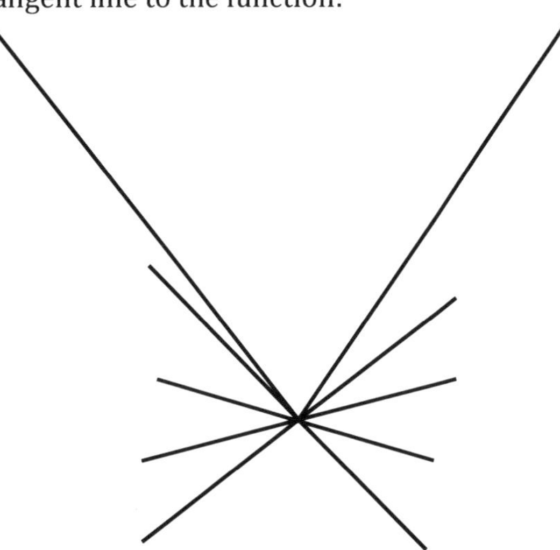

From possible subgradients, it seems best for stability to take the one with smallest norm, though all work well.

When don't have an analytical unbiased gradient estimate, **stochastic perturbation stochastic approximation algorithm** (SPSA) efficiently computes one numerically using only values of m, but modifies RM:

1. **Pick the starting point x_0**
2. **Pick gradient step sizes h_i and displacement vectors v_i**
3. **While $i < n$**
4. **For $0 < j < D$**
5. **$x_{i+1}[j] = x_i[j] - s_i(m(x_i + h_i v_i) - m(x_i - h_i v_i))/(2h_i v_i[j])$**

Let v_i be vectors of Bernoulli random variables that are 1 or −1 with probability ½. Other choices are possible but introduce extra complications (Spall 2003). Let $\epsilon_i(x) = f(x) - m(x)$ and H = the set of all ∇f roots. SPSA converges almost surely to $x \in H$ for $n \to \infty$ if (Bhatnagar et al. 2013):

- $\sum_{0 \le i \le \infty} s_i = \infty$, and $\sum_{0 \le i \le \infty}(s_i/h_i)^2 < \infty$
- $\sup_i ||x_i|| < \infty$ almost surely
- $\epsilon_i(x_i + h_i v_i) - \epsilon(x_i - h_i v_i)$ are independent random vectors with a common distribution and finite second moments
- f is Lipschitz continuous and has bounded second derivatives
- ∇f and m are Lipschitz continuous
- The ODE $dx(t)/dt = f(x(t))$ has H as its set of globally asymptotically stable equilibria

As with RM, only the first condition matters in practice. Need the continuity and differentiability assumptions only to ensure that the ODE is well-defined and the gradient estimate bias is provably small. The asymptotically optimal choices are $s_i = 1/i$ and $h_i = 1/i^{1/6}$, leading to $O(n^{-1/3})$ convergence (Spall 2003), which is worse than that of RM. As for RM, with finite n finding a root is more important than estimating its value and slow-decreasing $s_i = 1/i^{0.602}$ and $h_i = 1/i^{0.101}$ usually lead to faster search. The bias of an SPSA gradient is $O(h_i^2)$, which is the same of that of the finite difference estimate, but needs 2 and not D evaluations of m (Spall 2003). Using it for deterministic optimization, where each step must give improvement, doesn't work because it's usually far from the true gradient despite being almost unbiased.

SPSA is very sensitive to s_i and h_i, particularly the initial values. Because it doesn't ensure descent, for rapidly changing f a few wrong steps can throw x into ∞ if s_0 is too large, and x will negligibly crawl to an optimum if too small. Want the largest s_0 that won't result in a very distant jump. Another problem is that h_i effectively don't change.

A practical approach is to use the same initial step for both s_i and h_i to cut the number of parameters and make the search more stable. Then use grid search with a range of exponentially decreasing step sizes, by default from 2^{10} to 2^{-20}, accepting only runs that give improvement. This finds a suitable initial step because too large steps will diverge to ∞ and polishes the precision because restarting the search with a smaller initial step from the found solution will overcome the effects of $s_i \to 0$ too quickly.

```
template<typename POINT, typename FUNCTION> POINT SPSA(POINT x,
    FUNCTION const& f, int maxEvals = 10000, double initialStep = 1)
{
    POINT direction = x;
    for(int i = 0, D = x.getSize(); i < maxEvals/2; ++i)
    {
        for(int j = 0; j < D; ++j) direction[j] =
            GlobalRNG.next() % 2 ? 1 : -1;
        double step = initialStep/pow(i + 1, 0.101), temp =
            (f(x + direction * step) - f(x - direction * step))/
            (2 * pow(i + 1, 0.501));
        if(!isfinite(temp)) break;
        for(int j = 0; j < D; ++j) x[j] -= temp/direction[j];
    }
    return x;
}
template<typename POINT, typename FUNCTION> pair<POINT, double> metaSPSA(
    POINT x, FUNCTION const& f, int spsaEvals = 100000, int estimateEvals =
    100, double step = pow(2, 10), double minStep = pow(2, -20))
{
    pair<POINT, double> xy(x, numeric_limits<double>::infinity());
    for(; step > minStep; step /= 2)
    {
        if(isfinite(xy.second)) x = SPSA(xy.first, f, spsaEvals, step);
        double sum = 0;
        for(int i = 0; i < estimateEvals; ++i) sum += f(x);
        if(sum/estimateEvals < xy.second)
        {
            xy.first = x;
            xy.second = sum/estimateEvals;
        }
    }
    return xy;
}
```

If control the noise, evaluate $m(x_i + h_i v_i)$ and $m(x_i - h_i v_i)$ using common random numbers to reduce the noise in the gradient estimate.

18.14 Matrix Algebra

A vector and a mapping from 2D coordinates to its indices represent a matrix. Most algorithms are specifications of linear algebra methods. The complexities are for square matrices with n rows.

```
template<typename ITEM> struct Matrix
{
    int rows, columns;
    int index(int row, int column)const
    {
        assert(row >= 0 && row < rows && column >= 0 && column < columns);
        return row + column * rows;
    }
    Vector<ITEM> items;
public:
    ITEM& operator()(int row, int column){return items[index(row, column)];}
    ITEM const& operator()(int row, int column)const
        {return items[index(row, column)];}
    Matrix(int theRows, int theColumns): rows(theRows), columns(theColumns),
        items(rows * columns) {}
};
```

Multiplication by a scalar is $O(n)$

```
    Matrix operator*=(ITEM const& scalar)
    {
        for(int i = 0; i < rows; ++i)
            for(int j = 0; j < columns; ++j) (*this)(i, j) *= scalar;
        return *this;
    }
    friend Matrix operator*(ITEM const& scalar, Matrix const& a)
    {
        Matrix result(a);
        return result *= scalar;
    }
    friend Matrix operator*(Matrix const& a, ITEM const& scalar)
        {return scalar * a;}
```

Addition and subtraction are O(n)

```
    Matrix& operator+=(Matrix const& rhs)
    {
        assert(rows == rhs.rows && columns == rhs.columns);
        for(int i = 0; i < rows; ++i)
            for(int j = 0; j < columns; ++j) (*this)(i, j) += rhs(i, j);
        return *this;
    }
    friend Matrix operator+(Matrix const& a, Matrix const& b)
    {
        Matrix result(a);
        return result += b;
    }
    Matrix& operator-=(Matrix const& rhs)
    {
        (*this) *= -1;
        (*this) += rhs;
        (*this) *= -1;
    }
    friend Matrix operator-(Matrix const& a, Matrix const& b)
    {
        Matrix result(a);
        return result -= b;
    }
```

Multiplication is O(n^2).

```
    friend Matrix operator*(Matrix const& a, Matrix const& b)
    {
        assert(a.columns == b.rows);
        Matrix result(a.rows, b.columns);
        for(int i = 0; i < a.rows; ++i)
            for(int j = 0; j < b.columns; ++j)
            {
                ITEM sum(0);
                for(int k = 0; k < b.rows; ++k) sum += a(i, k) * b(k, j);
                result(i, j) += sum;
            }
        return result;
    }
    Matrix operator*=(Matrix const& rhs){return *this = *this * rhs;}
    Vector<ITEM> operator*(Vector<ITEM> const& v)
    {
        assert(columns == v.getSize());
        Vector<ITEM> result(rows, rows);
        for(int i = 0; i < rows; ++i)
            for(int j = 0; j < columns; ++j)
```

```
            result[i] += (*this)(i, j) * v[j];
        return result;
    }
    friend Vector<ITEM> operator*(Vector<ITEM> const& v, Matrix const& m)
        {return m.transpose() * v;}
```

Identity and transpose are O(n).

```
    static Matrix identity(int n)
    {
        Matrix result(n, n);
        for(int i = 0; i < n; ++i) result(i, i) = ITEM(1);
        return result;
    }
    Matrix transpose()const
    {
        Matrix result(columns, rows);
        for(int i = 0; i < rows; ++i)
            for(int j = 0; j < columns; ++j) result(j, i) = (*this)(i, j);
        return result;
    }
```

18.15 LUP Decomposition

LU decomposition is breaking up a square matrix M into L and U such that $LU = M$; L is lower-triangular with 0 entries on and above the diagonal, and U upper-triangular with 0 entries below the diagonal. Gaussian elimination computes this in O(n^3) time.

Transposing a row in an augmented matrix doesn't change the matrix equation solution. P is a permutation obtained by transposing rows. The algorithm permutes the matrix to pick pivots with the largest absolute value to avoid 0 pivots and improve numerical accuracy. A single matrix packs L and U.

```
template<typename ITEM> struct LUP
{
    Matrix<ITEM> d;
    Vector<int> permutation;
    bool isSingular;
    LUP(Matrix<ITEM> const& a): d(a), isSingular(false)
    {
        assert(d.rows = d.columns);
        for(int i = 0; i < d.rows; ++i) permutation.append(i);
        for(int i = 0; i < d.rows; ++i)
        {
            ITEM p = 0;
            int entering = -1;
            for(int j = i; j < d.rows; ++j)
                if(abs(d(i, j)) > p)
                {
                    p = abs(d(i, j));
                    entering = i;
                }
            if(entering == -1){isSingular = true; return;}
            swap(permutation[i], permutation[entering]);
            for(int j = 0; j < d.rows; ++j) swap(d(i, j), d(entering, j));
            for(int j = i + 1; j < d.rows; ++j)
            {
                d(j, i) /= d(i, i);
                for(int k = i + 1; k < d.rows; ++k)
                    d(j, k) -= d(j, i) * d(i, k);
            }
        }
    }
```

```
};
```

The determinant = ∏diagonal entries of U. Its sign changes when the permutation maps an even entry to an odd one or vice versa:

```
ITEM determinant()
{
    if(isSingular) return 0;
    ITEM result(1);
    for(int i = 0; i < d.rows; ++i)
    {
        result *= d(i, i);
        if(permutation[i] % 2 != i % 2) result *= -1;
    }
    return result;
}
```

Forward substitution solves matrix-vector equations using U as for Gaussian elimination in $O(n^2)$ time.

```
Vector<ITEM> solve(Vector<ITEM> const& b)
{
    assert(!isSingular);
    Vector<ITEM> result(d.rows, d.rows), y(result);
    for(int i = 0; i < d.rows; ++i)
    {
        y[i] = b[permutation[i]];
        for(int j = 0; j < i; ++j) y[i] -= y[j] * d(i, j);
    }
    for(int i = d.rows - 1; i >= 0; --i)
    {
        result[i] = y[i];
        for(int j = i + 1; j < d.rows; ++j)
            result[i] -= result[j] * d(i, j);
        result[i] /= d(i, i);
    }
    return result;
}
```

Augmenting the matrix with the identity of the same size and solving computes the inverse in $O(n^3)$ time. ∀ identity column the computation solves a matrix-vector equation:

```
Matrix<ITEM> inverse()
{
    assert(!isSingular);
    Vector<ITEM> identityRow(d.rows, 0);
    Matrix<ITEM> result(d.rows, d.rows);
    for(int i = 0; i < d.columns; ++i)
    {
        identityRow[i] = 1;
        Vector<ITEM> column = solve(identityRow);
        identityRow[i] = 0;
        for(int j = 0; j < d.rows; ++j) result(j, i) = column[j];
    }
    return result;
}
```

18.16 Cholesky Decomposition

If a matrix A is symmetric and positive definite, Cholesky decomposition computes a lower-triangular matrix L such that $A = LL^T$. This is useful for multidimensional covariance matrices.

Computating L proceeds column by column, using the following (derived by expanding $A = LL^T$):

- $s(r, c) = A(c, c) - \sum_{0 \leq k \leq} cL(r, k)L(c, k)$
- $L(c, c) = \sqrt{s(c, c)}$

- $L(r, c) = s(r, c)/L(c, c)$

```
template<typename ITEM> struct Cholesky
{
    Matrix<ITEM> l;
    bool failed;
    Cholesky(Matrix<ITEM> const& a): l(a.rows, a.columns), failed(false)
    {//a must be symmetric and positive definite
        for(int c = 0; c < l.columns; ++c)
            for(int r = c; r < l.rows; ++r)
            {
                ITEM sum = a(r, c);
                for(int k = 0; k < c; ++k) sum -= l(r, k) * l(c, k);
                if(r == c)
                {
                    if(sum <= 0){failed = true; return;}
                    l(c, c) = sqrt(sum);
                }
                else l(r, c) = sum/l(c, c);
            }
    }
};
```

Need $O(n^3)$ time.

18.17 Linear Programming

Optimize a linear function given linear constraints. For simplicity, vector transpose notation is omitted. The **simplex method** solves a linear programming problem

- min cx subject to
- $Ax = b$
- $x \geq 0$

where A is a $n \times m$ matrix with $n \geq m$, c and x vectors of size n, and b of size m.

The x are ordered so that $x = (x_b, x_n)$, where x_b is vector of m nonzero **basic variables**, and x_n of $n - m$ **zero variables**. Likewise, $C = (c_b, c_n)$ and $A = (A_b, A_n)$:

- min $z = c_b x_b + c_n x_n$ subject to
- $A_b x_b + A_n x_n = b$
- $x \geq 0$

Can get all solutions by solving $Ax = b$ $\forall$ combination of basic variable choices. A more efficient process:

1. **Start with an initial feasible basis**
2. **Until the solution is optimal**
3. **Improve the current basis by swapping a basic variable with a nonbasic one**

Let $y = c_b(A_b)^{-1}$. Then $z = yb + (c_n - yA_n)x_n$. So if $c_n - yA_n > 0$, can't decrease z by increasing any x_n, so can't improve the current basis by variable swapping. Linear programming is a **convex optimization problem**, so this local optimality test is global (Griva et al. 2008) and allows to select the entering nonbasic variable as the one with smallest $c_n - yA_n$.

The **leaving variable** can be the one which allows the entering variable to take on the max positive value while keeping other variables ≥ 0. Let vector a be the column of A_n corresponding to the entering variable and $v = (A_b)^{-1}sa$. Because all components of x_n except for the selected s remain 0, $b = A_b(x_b + v)$. For b to remain the same, s increase, and the basis be valid, one component of x_b needs to decrease to 0, and the rest change value but remain ≥ 0. If $v \leq 0$, the problem allows an infinitely large solution because an arbitrarily large s is possible when one of the basis variables increases. Variable i, decreasing which to 0 gives max s, is the one minimizing $x_b(i)/v(i)$ with $v(i) > 0$, where $x_b = (A_b)^{-1}b$.

```
struct LinearProgrammingSimplex
{
    Matrix<double> B, N;
    Vector<double> b, cB, cN, x;
    Vector<int> p;
```

```
    bool isUnbounded;
    bool performIteration()
    {
        Matrix<double> InvB = LUP<double>(B).inverse();
        x = InvB * b;
        //check if x is optimal or find entering variable
        Vector<double> y = cN - cB * InvB * N;
        int entering = 0;
        double bestValue = y[0];
        for(int i = 1; i < y.getSize(); ++i) if(y[i] < bestValue)
            {
                bestValue = y[i];
                entering = i;
            }
        if(bestValue >= 0) return false;
        //find leaving variable
        Vector<double> a;
        for(int i = 0; i < N.rows; ++i) a.append(N(i, entering));
        a = InvB * a;
        int leaving = -1;
        double minRatio, maxA = -1;
        for(int i = 0; i < x.getSize(); ++i) if(a[i] > 0)
            {
                double newRatio = x[i]/a[i];
                if(leaving == -1 || minRatio > newRatio)
                {
                    leaving = i;
                    maxA = max(maxA, a[i]);
                    minRatio = newRatio;
                }
            }
        if(maxA <= 0){isUnbounded = true; return false;}
        //swap variables
        for(int i = 0; i < N.rows; ++i){swap(B(i, leaving), N(i, entering));}
        swap(p[leaving], p[entering]);
        swap(cB[leaving], cN[entering]);
        return true;
    }
    LinearProgrammingSimplex(Matrix<double>const&B0, Matrix<double>
        const& N0, Vector<double>const& cB0, Vector<double>const& cN0,
        Vector<double> const& b0): isUnbounded(false), B(B0), N(N0), cB(cB0),
        cN(cN0), b(b0), x(b)
        {for(int i = 0; i < cB.getSize() + cN.getSize(); ++i) p.append(i);}
    Vector<pair<int, double> > solve()
    {
        while(performIteration());
        Vector<pair<int, double> > result;
        if(!isUnbounded)
            for(int i = 0; i < x.getSize(); ++i)
                result.append(make_pair(p[i], x[i]));
        return result;
    }
};
```

Simplex fails if A_b is singular, the problem is unbounded, or the problem is degenerate, cycling between two basis of equal value. More complicated variable selection rules avoid degeneracy, but in practice round-off errors are enough. The number of iterations is O(exponential) but linear in practice. Each takes $O(m^3)$ time due to matrix inversion (but see the comments).

General linear programming minimizes a linear combination of n variables, subject to m inequality constraints on different linear combinations of the variables:

- min cx subject to
- $Ax \geq b$
- $x \geq 0$

The **feasible region** consists of values of x that satisfy the constraints. Redundant constraints don't affect it. The optimal solution is a point in the feasible region where the objective is minimal. To make inequalities equalities, add a **slack variable** vector, and augment A with the $m \times m$ identity:

- min cx subject to
- $Ax + Is = b$
- $x \geq 0$ and $s \geq 0$

Other transformations allow further generalizations:

- If the problem is maximization, negate the objective
- If $x(i) < 0$ for some i, replace x with $x_1, x_2 \geq 0$ such that $x_1 - x_2 \geq 0$
- Replace any constraint equality $\sum A_{ji}x_i = b_j$ by both $\sum A_{ji}x_i \geq b_j$ and $-\sum A_{ji}x_i \geq -b_j$ to allow a simple initial feasible basis

Slack variables = 0 forms the initial basis. If it's infeasible, expand the feasible region to include the origin by adding to each violated constraint an **artificial variable** with the initial value > 0, and changing the cost of each variable to 1 if artificial and to 0 if not. Solving makes artificial variables 0 and succeeds if the program has at least one feasible solution. Then, the current values of nonartificial variables are feasible for the original program.

18.18 General Constrained Optimization

The most general constrained optimization problem called **nonlinear programming** is:

- min $f(x)$ subject to
- $g_i(x) \leq 0$
- $h_i(x) = 0$

If f, g_i are convex and h_i are linear, the problem is **convex**. If the feasible region defined by g_i and h_i is convex but they aren't, can create an equivalent problem where they are.

The **Lagrangian of the problem** is $L(x, l, v) = f(x) + \sum l_i g_i(x) + \sum v_i h_i(x)$. Let x^* be the optimal solution. The **dual problem** $g(l, v) = \min_{x \in \text{feasible region}} L(x, l, v)$ is provably concave and $< x^* \ \forall\, l, v$. The dual problem asks for the max feasible lower bound on the solution:

- min $-g(l, v)$ subject to
- $l_i \geq 0$

It's convex. E.g., for linear program:

- min cx subject to
- $Ax = b$
- $x \geq 0$

$g(a, b) = -bv$ if $Av - 1 + c = 0$ and $-\infty$ otherwise. So the dual problem is:

- min bv subject to
- $-Av \leq c$

Replacing "$Ax = b$" by "$Ax \leq b$" replaces "$-Av \leq c$" by "$-Av = c$".

If d^* is the optimal solution to the dual problem, $d^* \leq x^*$. This is called **weak duality**. **Strong duality** $d^* = x^*$ holds if a constraint qualification holds. Some are:

- $g_i(x^*)$ and $h_i(x^*)$ are linearly independent
- g_i and h_i are linear
- The problem is convex and $\exists$ a feasible solution

If strong duality holds, $\forall$ optimum x^*, l^*, v^* Karush-Kuhn-Tucker (KKT) conditions hold:

- $g(x^*) \leq 0$
- $h(x^*) = 0$
- $l^* \geq 0$
- $l^* g(x^*) = 0$
- $\nabla L(x^*, l^* v^*) = 0$

They have a unique solution if the problem is convex. Duality and KKT conditions transform problems into possibly easier ones. E.g., the linear programming dual is easier if the problem has fewer variables than constraints because the dual has the reverse.

18.19 Comments

Stability of many algorithms has been analyzed. See Corless & Fillion (2013) for a summary of many results.

Though golden section search is worst-case optimal, a heuristic improvement **Brent search** (which is much more complicated; Press et al. 2007) may be faster for smooth functions.

Conjugate gradient (Nocedal & Wright 2006) is a slightly simpler alternative to L-BFGS but generally performs worse. It's also difficult to give it a good starting scale, unlike for L-BFGS.

For the simplex method, using sparse matrix algebra and maintaining LUP decomposition dynamically is very complicated, but substantially speeds up the calculations (Griva et al. 2008). **Interior point methods** are an alternative to simplex for solving linear programs. Simplex traverses edges of the constraint simplex, but interior point methods go through the interior. They take much more time per iteration, but converge in O(polynomial) number of iterations, usually constant. Also, can extend them to solve convex nonlinear programs efficiently (Boyd & Vandenberghe 2004). Convexity seems crucial in the ability to solve efficiently, i.e., currently don't know efficient methods for nonconvex programs.

Numerical methods are a vast field, and this chapter is only a sampler of the main ideas, focused mostly on function minimization. A major topic omitted from this chapter is solving ordinary and partial differential equations. Classic algorithms such as **Rung-Kutta formulas** and the **finite difference method** have their flaws, and volumes have been written about alternative methods, with each having a niche in a particular set of problems (Press et al. 2007).

18.20 References

Bhatnagar, S., Prasad, H., & Prashanth, L. A. (2013). *Stochastic Recursive Algorithms for Optimization: Simultaneous Perturbation Methods*. Springer.

Boyd, S., & Vandenberghe, L. (2004). *Convex Optimization*. Cambridge University Press.

Corless, R. M., & Fillion, N. (2013). *A Graduate Introduction to Numerical Methods*. Springer.

Cormen, T. H., Leiserson, C. E., Rivest, R. L., & Stein, C. (2009). *Introduction to Algorithms*. MIT Press.

Griva, I., Nash, S. G., & Sofer, A. (2009). *Linear and Nonlinear Optimization*. SIAM.

Liu, D. C., & Nocedal, J. (1989). On the limited memory BFGS method for large scale optimization. *Mathematical programming*, *45*(1-3), 503–528.

Muller, J. M. (2006). *Elementary Functions*. Birkhũser.

Nocedal, J., Wright, S. (2006). *Numerical Optimization*, 3rd ed. Springer.

Press, W.H. et al. (2007). *Numerical Recipes: The Art of Scientific Computing*, 3rd ed. Cambridge University Press.

Spall, J. C. (2003). *Introduction to Stochastic Search and Optimization: Estimation, Simulation, and Control*. Wiley.

Wikipedia (2013). Stochastic approximation. http://en.wikipedia.org/wiki/Stochastic_approximation. Accessed May 18, 2013.

19 Cryptography

Want to secure various **communication protocols** such as two parties exchanging secret messages. Protocols are usually modeled by interactions between several parties. The conventional ones are:

- **Alice**, **Bob**, **Carol**, **David**, etc.—communicating parties.
- **Eve**—can see all messages.
- **Mallory**—can see and modify all messages. Though Mallory can drop all messages, want to ensure that Mallory can't profit from using them.
- **Trent**—a trusted authority able to confirm a party's identity.

Every party is assumed to know the protocol, and security relies on a **password key** that is known only to the authorized parties, and without which it's infeasible to get any useful information about the communication. E.g., someone wanting to read your email may know your service provider and username but not the password.

19.1 File Encryption

Many unsecure methods were used to **encrypt** a file so that can't **decrypt** it without the key. Julius Caesar rotated the alphabet by 3 so that *a* became *d*, *x a*, etc. In "The Dancing Men", letters corresponded to dancing figures, and Sherlock Holmes used the *etnorias* heuristic to break the code, substituting most likely letters for most repeated figures assuming the most common is *e*, the second most common *t*, etc., and backtracking wrong guesses.

Let *r* be a random bit string of size *n*. Given an *n*-bit message *m*, let code(m) = m ^ r and message(code c) = c ^ r. Can't decode *c* without *r* because every *n*-bit *m* is equally likely. This **one-time pad** is impractical because if use *r* for another message, c_1 ^ c_2 = m_1 ^ m_2, which leaks information.

A **stream cipher** initializes a secure random number generator with a sufficiently random seed and produces a stream of random bytes to form *r*. Guessing the future bytes from the past ones is infeasible if the encryption doesn't reuse the same seed. Using a checksum before encryption allows detecting bit errors in the encrypted file with high probability. To encrypt using RC4 and CRC:

1. **Create RC4 from a key and a Xorshift-transformed sequence from the current time**
2. **Calculate and append a CRC to the file**
3. **Encrypt the result with the stream**
4. **Append the time to it**

It's safe to use time as seed if not reusing time–key combinations.

```
void applyARC4(unsigned int seed, Vector<unsigned char> temp,
    Vector<unsigned char>& data)
{
    for(int i = 0; i < temp.getSize(); ++i)
        temp[i] ^= (seed = Xorshift::transform(seed));
    ARC4 arc4(temp.getArray(), temp.getSize());
    for(int i = 0; i < data.getSize(); ++i) data[i] ^= arc4.nextByte();
}
Vector<unsigned char> simpleEncrypt(Vector<unsigned char> data,
    Vector<unsigned char> const& key)
{
    unsigned int seed = time(0), s = sizeof(int);
    CRC32 crc32;
    Vector<unsigned char> theSeed = ReinterpretEncode(seed, s, crc =
        ReinterpretEncode(crc32.hash(data.getArray(), data.getSize()), s);
    for(int i = 0; i < s; ++i) data.append(crc[i]);
    applyARC4(seed, key, data);
    for(int i = 0; i < s; ++i) data.append(theSeed[i]);
```

```
    return data;
}
```

Decryption:

1. **Read the seed**
2. **Remove its bytes**
3. **Read and decrypt the rest using the seed**
4. **Read the CRC**
5. **Remove its bytes**
6. **Make sure the file matches the CRC**

```
Vector<unsigned char> simpleDecrypt(Vector<unsigned char> code,
    Vector<unsigned char> const& key)
{
    assert(code.getSize() >= 8);
    enum{s = sizeof(int)};
    Vector<unsigned char> seed, crc;
    for(int i = 0; i < s; ++i) seed.append(code[code.getSize() + i - 4]);
    for(int i = 0; i < s; ++i) code.removeLast();
    applyARC4(ReinterpretDecode(seed), key, code);
    for(int i = 0; i < s; ++i) crc.append(code[code.getSize() + i - 4]);
    for(int i = 0; i < s; ++i) code.removeLast();
    CRC32 crc32;
    assert(crc32.hash(code.getArray(), code.getSize()) ==
        ReinterpretDecode(crc));
    return code;
}
```

Both need O(n) time.

19.2 Key Length

A key should have a negligible probability of being guessed or enumerated. E.g., it's feasible for a massively parallel system to check all 64-bit keys if test each quickly. As a rule of thumb, a key needs to be such that the most efficient attack needs equivalent of brute force enumeration of 128-bit keys, which is infeasible even in future. Beware:

- Using shorter keys is more efficient, but handling the data is usually the bottleneck.
- Every year hardware gets faster and research produces more efficient attacks.
- Some data must be secure for many years, so a key length chosen now must be secure in future.
- The value of the data and who wants it matter. E.g., protecting your credit card from small criminals needs less security than protecting top secret information from other governments with code breakers and supercomputers working for years.

Can easily enumerate typical 8-character passwords, even if all letters are equally likely:

Character type	Number of possible passwords	Bits of security	Time to break at 10^9 passwords per second	Length needed for 128 bit security
Digits	10^8	27	0.13 seconds	39
Lowercase letters	26^8	38	275 seconds	27
Mixed case + digits	62^8	48	3.26 days	21
Keyboard characters excluding space, tab, and newline	94^8	52	52.1 days	20
Bytes	256^8	64	585 years	16

Users tend to pick passwords consisting of concatenations of dictionary words, each with < 16 bits of security. Rules like *must contain at least one nonletter* don't increase the bits per character by much because users will enter exactly one, and it's much more efficient to enumerate 6-letter-and-1-digit tuples than 7-letter-or-digit tuples.

A secure and easy-to-remember password is a memorable or a shocking phrase, e.g., *When_Under_a_Gun_Say_Merry_Christmas_To_911*. A secure random number generator with a high-entropy seed generates the most secure keys.

19.3 Key Storage

Need to store or remember a key. If it's lost, the encrypted data is unrecoverable. Might find a key with access to the decryption device because running it in a debugger may show the key. E.g., keys have been recovered from hardware devices by measuring heat emissions or freezing RAM chips. An application can't prevent such attacks.

The easiest way to get a key is to bribe someone or use **social engineering**. E.g., (Mitnick & Simon 2002): You get a traffic ticket, and in your city police officers attend training, that takes priority over ticket court appearance. You call the precinct and pretend to be a lawyer needing to subpoena the officer who gave you the ticket and ask when he is unavailable. The helpful clerk gives you the dates. You ask for a hearing on one of them. The fair judge agrees. You show up and the officer doesn't—ticket canceled.

19.4 Cryptographic Hashing

Hash function h is **cryptographically secure** if computing:

- $h(x)$ from x is easy
- Any bits of x from $h(x)$ is hard
- y such that $h(y) = h(x)$ is hard
- y and z such that $h(y) = h(z)$ is hard

These force h to output $\leq$ 128-bit results and be much less efficient than a universal hash function. **SHA3 algorithm** is the recommended choice.

19.5 Key Exchange

Two parties who don't know each other don't have a common key. A common model is that Alice and Bob exchange messages, and Eve reads them. In another model, Mallory intercepts messages and pretends to be Bob when talking to Alice and Alice when talking to Bob, exchanging keys with each.

RSA algorithm gives every party a **private key**, known only to the party, and a **public key**. A message is encrypted using the public key and decrypted using the private key. RSA doesn't suffer from the man-in-the-middle attack if Trent publishes the public key. E.g., web browsers have lists of trusted authorities such as Verisign. "Authority not recognized, do you want to proceed?" means fraud or that the website doesn't want to pay Verisign and acts as its own authority.

When designing a dedicated client and server, give the server a single private key and hard-code the public key into the client.

19.6 Other Protocols

Assume that every party wants to not be cheated and cheat every other party.

Protocol	Goal	Algorithm idea
Authentication	Verify user identity and protect stored passwords.	1. ∀account store the username, a long random string, and hash of the password concatenated with a random string. 2. To authenticate, retrieve the user's random string, calculate the password hash, and check if it matches the stored result.
Commitment	Alice wants to commit a decision	1. Bob sends Alice a long random

	without revealing it to Bob, and Bob doesn't want Alice to change it after committing.	string. 2. Alice appends her decision to it, encrypts the result with a random key, and sends it to Bob. 3. When it's time to reveal the decision, Alice sends Bob her key. Bob decrypts and verifies his random string.
Secret sharing	Give a secret to m parties, so that any k can determine it.	1. Pick a prime $p >$ max(k, the largest possible secret). 2. Generate a random polynomial of degree $k - 1$. The coefficient of the 0th term is the message. 3. Give party i the polynomial % p, evaluated at i. 4. To construct the secret, k parties solve the corresponding k equations for the coefficients.

19.7 Comments

Cryptography is a wide field. Due to existence of special cases and efficient hard problem solvers, must take great care to make sure that a randomly generated seed or other information doesn't fall into those by accident. For well-established protocols such as RSA, the easy cases are well-known, though ignored by many sources.

Can't rule out ∀protocol that special cases don't exist because they may be discovered in future. Security mostly relies on the belief that such cases are unlikely. Also, many protocols use extra scrambling, just in case some issues will be discovered. E.g., for hashing, older **MD5** and **SHA1** algorithms are considered broken despite strong beliefs in their security years ago. SHA3 was developed because currently safe **SHA2** seemed likely to be broken soon.

The quality of the random generator and the seed is very important for security. Using password + time as a seed is a good heuristic, but ideally have OS or special device random source. The latter can be the only choice because many algorithms such as secure hash functions work without needing a password.

The ability to update a protocol is very important. Germany might as well have lost WW2 because the British where able to break their Enigma. It was an improvement of the dancing men cipher that wouldn't yield to brute force human attacks but yielded to one of the first computers. Even experts in the field don't know for sure if the existing protocols are safe. At best can create libraries of robust implementations, and actively seek to replace those with known attacks. A good protocol must resist attacks by the white hat community for years to be considered usable. ∃many individuals who are motivated to spend time breaking proposed protocols because success gives minor fame and good job opportunities.

Trying to break a key using brute force is hard even for small keys. Need to be able to recognize properly decrypted data from garbage. E.g., the data may be in an unknown language.

19.8 References

Mitnick, K. D., & Simon, W. L. (2001). *The Art of Deception: Controlling the Human Element of Security*. Wiley.
Schneier, B. (1995). *Applied Cryptography: Protocols, Algorithms, and Source Code in C*. Wiley.
St Denis, T. (2006). *Cryptography for Developers*. Syngress.

20 General Machine Learning

20.1 Mathematical Learning

Want a predictor f that decides correctly in specific situations, represented as objects in some **feature space** X. X is usually a vector space but doesn't have to be—e.g., a metric space that gives distances between objects is enough for effective learning. In a vector space, every object is a vector of **features**, selected based on domain knowledge. Learning finds f that **partitions** X into possibly uncountably many pieces, assigning $\forall x \in X$ a partition label $ID \in \{ID\}$. x is assumed to represent all useful information about an object. E.g., to detect free riders in a team shooter game, can use the number of met enemies and the explored % of game space as features, and consider a player who met 0 enemies and explored < 5% of the space a free rider. Assume x follows distribution P and ID conditional distribution $P|x$. Depending on the task, the latter may be continuous, discrete, or Dirac delta. Only the last describes deterministic learning, where $\forall x\ \exists$ a unique ID. $\forall A$ need to understand it's partitioning strategy.

Instead of explicitly defining f (which might be practically impossible, e.g., how to locate a face in a photo?), an algorithm A sees a finite set S of n examples z_i, from which it hopefully learns f that **generalizes** to unseen z. $\forall z_i$ have x_i and **hint information** $y_i \in Y$.

For **prediction** tasks, $ID_i = y_i$ = a sample from $P|x_i$, but in general y_i can be arbitrary or not exist for some or all i. Generally, y is a function of x, sampled ID, and possibly other information. Humans learn from patterns, i.e., subsets of X, which this definition allows.

Would like to measure learning performance in terms of x and ID, but in general have only x and y. A **loss function** $L_f(z) = L_f(x, y)$ measures errors of f on z. For perfect performance, L must return the minimum possible finite value, usually 0. **Risk** $R_f(P) = E_z[L_f(z)]$ measures generalization error of f. Usually assume that all z are equally important, but can weigh by some $a \in (0, \infty)$. Z and L determine a **learning task**, and P a problem within it. A is usually designed to minimize risk for a specific task, doing which is the goal of learning. Typical tasks:

- **Classification**—$ID = y$ = **class label** $\in [0, k - 1]$. Assuming right decisions have profit 0 and wrong ones cost 1, $L_f(x, y) = (f(x) \neq y)$, with R_f = E[the % of misclassified z].
- **Regression**—ID = y are real-valued. Usually assume quadratic cost of errors, i.e., $L_f(x, y) = (f(x) - y)^2$.
- **Clustering**—same as classification, but don't have hint information, i.e., $y = x$. Usually use $L_f(x, y)$ = distance($f(x)$, x) to group similar x.
- **Semi-supervised learning**—same as classification, but have additional examples with no hint information, which somewhat helps improve the learned partition. L is conditional on whether have a hint.
- **Value function reinforcement learning**—classification or regression where a hint is assigned to a sequence of decisions. E.g., for games like chess some logic tells what is a good move, after a game such logic wins or loses, and this is the hint $\forall$ move, along with extra info such as how far the move was from the end.

E.g., for handwritten digit recognition, want to recognize a handwritten digit from its image, represented by an 8 × 8 array of cells with gray-scale colors $\in [0, 16]$:

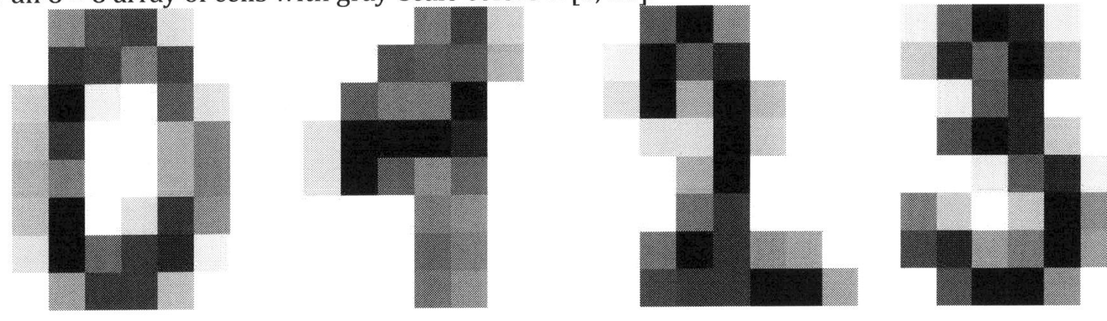

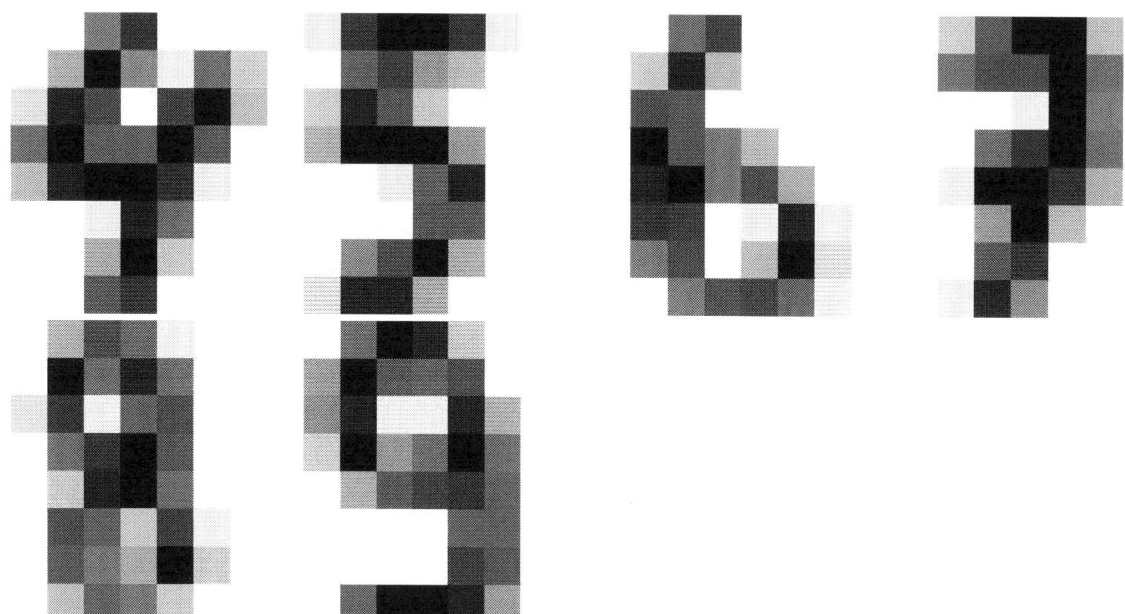

The iris flower data set gives measurements of iris leaves and asks to decide what type of iris it is. Some sample data (a sepal is similar to a petal, but supports it and is usually green):

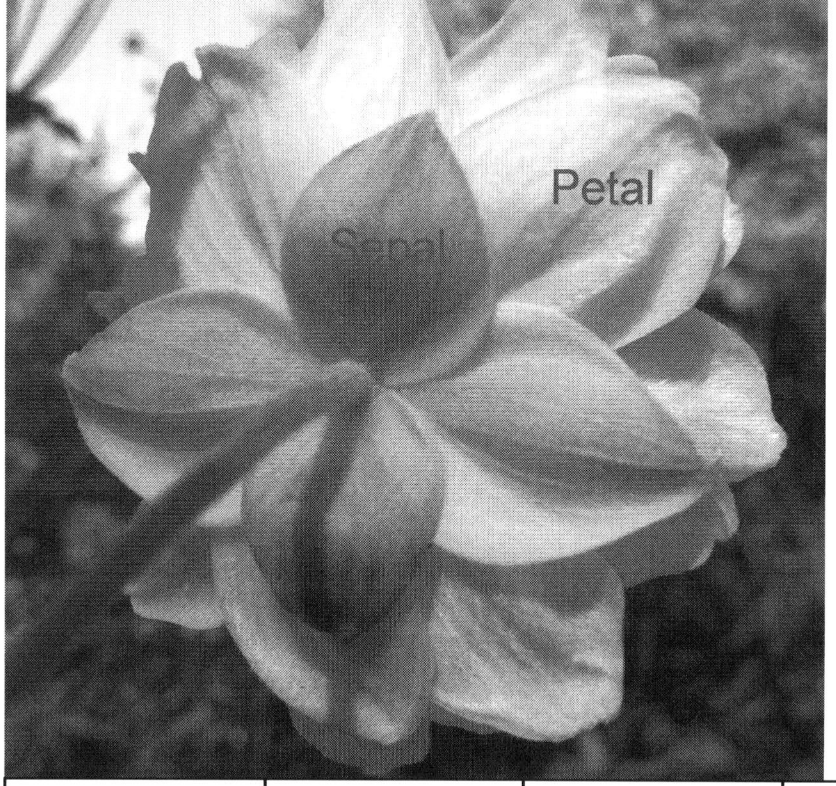

Type	Sepal Length	Sepal Width	Petal Length	Petal Width
Setosa	5.1	3.5	1.4	0.2
Setosa	5.4	3.9	1.7	0.4
Versicolor	6.4	3.2	4.5	1.5
Versicolor	5.6	2.9	3.6	1.3
Virginica	6.2	3.4	5.4	2.3
Virginica	7.2	3.6	6.1	2.5

Predicting resource use of *A* based on its explicit and implicit inputs is a typical regression problem. An industrial problem is predicting energy efficiency heating load:

Relative Compactness	Surface Area	Wall Area	Roof Area	Overall Height	Orientation	Glazing Area	Glazing Area Distribution	Heating Load
0.98	514.5	294	110.25	7	2	0	0	15.55
0.9	563.5	318.5	122.5	7	2	0.1	1	29.03
0.86	588	294	147	7	3	0.1	2	27.02
0.79	637	343	147	7	4	0.1	3	36.97
0.76	661.5	416.5	122.5	7	5	0.1	4	32.31
0.69	735	294	220.5	3.5	2	0.1	5	11.21

The UCI repository (Bache & Lichman 2013) contains these and many other data sets in an easy-to-read format. In the real world, collection and organization of data is usually unique to each task and done by parsing various log files and/or querying databases. Such data usually needs thoughtful cleaning such as removing useless features and examples.

The data is best represented with an accessor interface, which allows creating a data transformation pipeline to avoid excessive copying with argument passing.

```
template<typename X, typename Y> struct InMemoryData
{
    Vector<pair<X, Y> > data;
    typedef X X_TYPE;
    typedef Y Y_TYPE;
    typedef X const& X_RET;
    InMemoryData(){}
    template<typename DATA> InMemoryData(DATA const& theData):
        data(theData.getSize())
    {
        for(int i = 0; i < data.getSize(); ++i)
        {
            data[i].first = theData.getX(i);
            data[i].second = theData.getY(i);
        }
    }
    void addZ(X const& x, Y const& y){data.append(make_pair(x, y));}
    X_RET getX(int i)const
    {
        assert(i >= 0 && i < data.getSize());
        return data[i].first;
    }
    double getX(int i, int feature)const
    {
        assert(i >= 0 && i < data.getSize() && feature >= 0 &&
            feature < data[i].first.getSize());
        return data[i].first[feature];
    }
    Y_TYPE const& getY(int i)const
    {
        assert(i >= 0 && i < data.getSize());
        return data[i].second;
    }
    int getSize()const{return data.getSize();}
};
```

The pipeline can get deep sometimes, making access inefficient:

Storage → Train/Test Permutation → Scale → Other Permutations

So can buffer it before applying *A*. A buffer is most justified for *A* that already use much memory, so the extra due to a buffer doesn't change their use cases.

```
template<typename LEARNER, typename BUFFER, typename PARAMS =
    EMPTY> class BufferLearner
{
    LEARNER model;
public:
    template<typename DATA> BufferLearner(DATA const& data,
        PARAMS const& p = PARAMS()): model(data, p) {}
    typename BUFFER::Y_TYPE predict(typename BUFFER::X_TYPE const& x)const
        {return model.predict(x);}
};
```

Though machine learning isn't useful ∀real world problem, for many it's very successful, in particular (Witten et al. 2011):

- Face detection—implemented in most smart phones and identifies faces quickly and sufficiently reliably.
- Re-identification—recovering redacted personal information in published records. E.g., can uniquely identify most people by zip code, birth date, and gender. Famously, a governor who published anonymized health records, received his own by mail.

Learning aims to discover knowledge. Given a problem:

1. Get the data
2. Clean it if needed
3. Run *A* on it to get *f*
4. Deploy/use *f*

20.2 Risk Estimation of a Predictor

F, the space of functions that map *X* to task-dependent *ID*s, defines all possible *f* (technically only consider the measurable part of *F* to allow calculating risk). This ignores representation, i.e., two differently represented *f* such that ∀*x* their outputs agree are equivalent. $\forall f \in F$ R_f is well-defined but unknown due to not knowing *P*. Because randomly sampled *S* is the only information, at best can know that ∃ error ϵ and probability *p* such that with probability $\geq 1 - p$ have one of:

- $R_f \leq \epsilon$: f is **probably approximately correct** (PAC(ϵ, *p*))
- $R_f \in [\epsilon_-, \epsilon_+]$: have two-sided confidence

If know such bound and ϵ is small enough, with $1 - p \approx 95\%$ **learning succeeded**. But can't guarantee $p = \epsilon = 0$ unless *X* is finite and see all of *Z* instead of *S*, in which case don't need learning as memorization will do. So must be careful when deploying *f* as part of a critical system. E.g., can't know what a trained self-driving car will do when an animal suddenly jumps in front of it, and there is a motorcycle behind—such case was certainly not part of training. In many cases need human judgment, e.g., an obsolete work zone sign can cause a car to reduce speed and upset the drivers behind it. Conflicting lane marks, when one is clearly faded to a human, could be another problem.

Inferring general from particular is **induction**, which isn't as well understood as **deduction**, i.e., inferring particular from general. The problem is that a true particular doesn't imply true general, i.e., !∃ reverse modus ponens, and PAC is the next best thing. Can have rare events which are genuinely unpredictable, such as a chance of network failure due to malicious activity. So !∃ the true right *f*, only good enough ones. In a quantum-mechanical world, almost all natural phenomena have some noise. Not being able to get 0 or almost 0 (e.g., 10^{-4}) risk is a problem for many tasks because in many cases otherwise good accuracy (assuming classification) such as 95 or 99% isn't enough, and this hinders application to many domains.

If have access to all examples at once, can define **empirical risk** $R_{f,n} = (\sum L_f(z_i))/n$. Computing it needs $O(n)$ calls to *f*.

```
template<typename Y, typename DATA, typename LEARNER> Vector<pair<Y, Y> >
```

```
    evaluateLearner(LEARNER const& l, DATA const& test)
{
    Vector<pair<Y, Y> > result;
    for(int i = 0; i < test.getSize(); ++i)
        result.append(pair<Y, Y>(test.getY(i), l.predict(test.getX(i))));
    return result;
}
```

Assume $L_f(z_i)$ are iid when z_i are. Can use the CLT to get two-sided confidence. The result is valid only asymptotically and doesn't give a proper PAC bound, but is often used in practice anyway. If $L \in [0, 1]$, can use Hoeffding or empirical Bernstein to get PAC finite sample bounds. For other cases need more info such as a guarantee of thin tails of the distribution of values of L or its Lipschitz continuity is enough for other types of bounds. Upper bounds are enough for a PAC guarantee and are tighter than confidence intervals due to giving less information.

Unless found f by a lucky guess without looking at S, $L_f(z_i)$ aren't iid and the resulting bounds are overly optimistic due to multiple testing. The problem is that $\exists f$ that learn S well but have poor performance on other examples, which is called **overfitting**. E.g., given n phone numbers and credit cards, can fit a polynomial to come up with f that predicts the credit card number from a phone number and works $\forall z_i$. Also, polynomials are only a tiny subset of all possible functions, and $\exists$ uncountably many f with 0 risk on any finite data set. Overfitting happens with humans too—e.g., given a set of input-output examples, occasionally programming job interviewees write code that works only for the examples and not in general. Generalization is what matters, because f will be used on new unseen data.

To solve the problem can use the **holdout method**—reserve part of the data for risk estimation, and get a PAC bound from it using Hoeffding or the CLT. Typically use 80% for learning and the other 20% for testing. The implementation uses a permutation to index into the data and deterministically permute it to break any possible sort order, which can happen because, e.g., a sql query can sort by some database key.

```
template<typename DATA> struct PermutedData
{
    DATA const& data;
    Vector<int> permutation;
    typedef typename DATA::X_TYPE X_TYPE;
    typedef typename DATA::Y_TYPE Y_TYPE;
    typedef typename DATA::X_RET X_RET;
    PermutedData(DATA const& theData): data(theData) {}
    int getSize()const{return permutation.getSize();}
    void addIndex(int i){permutation.append(i);}
    void checkI(int i)const
    {
        assert(i >= 0 && i < permutation.getSize() &&
            permutation[i] >= 0 && permutation[i] < data.getSize());
    }
    X_RET getX(int i)const
    {
        checkI(i);
        return data.getX(permutation[i]);
    }
    double getX(int i, int feature)const
    {
        checkI(i);
        return data.getX(permutation[i], feature);
    }
    Y_TYPE const& getY(int i)const
    {
        checkI(i);
        return data.getY(permutation[i]);
    }
};
template<typename DATA> pair<PermutedData<DATA>, PermutedData<DATA> >
```

```
    createTrainingTestSetsDetPerm(DATA const& data,
    double relativeTestSize = 0.8)
{
    int n = data.getSize(), m = n * relativeTestSize;
    assert(m > 0 && m < n);
    pair<PermutedData<DATA>, PermutedData<DATA> > result(data, data);
    Vector<int> perm(n);
    for(int i = 0; i < n; ++i) perm[i] = i;
    permuteDeterministically(perm.getArray(), n);
    for(int i = 0; i < n; ++i)
    {
        if(i < m) result.first.addIndex(perm[i]);
        else result.second.addIndex(perm[i]);
    }
    return result;
}
```

Any tweak to a mathematical model, however minor, can invalidate its assumptions and any dependent analysis. This is particularly problematic for machine learning, where simplified models are analyzed due to the infeasibility of analyzing the actual ones. The conclusions are unlikely to be affected much by minor changes, but rigourous validity disappears. Violation of the iid assumption is probably the most common issue, as data is almost always not completely dependent. But it's okay to rely on heuristics when the alternative is to have almost nothing useful. In many cases, A is designed assuming such assumptions hold, but then it's informally assumed that have some kind of stability, i.e., the results with mildly violated assumptions are at most negligibly different.

20.3 Sources of Risk

Picking L allows defining an **optimal Bayes learner** that knows P and $\forall x$ picks $ID = \text{argmax}_z(\Pr(y(ID)|x))$. This decision is optimal based on available information, thus $R_{\text{oB}} = \text{E}_z[\min_f L_f(z)]$. Because P is usually unknown, it's useful only theoretically. $\forall f\ R_{\text{oB}} \leq R_f$, and in artificial cases where it's known, it provides insight into behavior of other A. E.g., for predicting a biased coin flip with 60% chance of heads and $L = 1$ if mistake else 0, $R_{\text{oB}} = 0.4$.

Theorem: For non-overlapping problems where $\forall x$ (excluding subsets of X of measure 0) have a single corresponding ID, so that $P|x$ puts all probability on a single point or discrete interval, $R_{\text{oB}} = 0$. Proof: Because it's decision function makes no mistakes, $\forall x\ \min_f L_f((x, y(x)) = 0$, and $R_{\text{oB}} = \text{E}_x[0] = 0$. An overlapping problem has a random component, thus chosen features don't give enough information to always make correct decisions. Need better features or !∃ more informative ones.

Existence of an optimal Bayes doesn't help find good A. A general idea for doing so is to reduce the search for f to optimization, i.e., optimize over some **search space** or **model class** $G \subseteq F$. Usually G is much smaller than F because F is uncountable but can only consider $G = \{f$ that don't take too much memory to represent$\}$. Limiting precision of numbers almost never causes problems because f different only at precision limits tend to be indistinguishable. $A = G +$ a strategy for picking $f \in G$. Can pick G based on data, but it's fixed after searching.

Want to minimize R_f based on S. $R_f \leq$ the sum of:

- **Feature informativeness error** $R_{\text{oB}} - 0$—due to not having informative features
- **Approximation error** $\min_{h \in G} R_h - R_{\text{oB}}$—due to not using G with best h
- **Estimation error** $R_f - \min_{h \in G} R_h$, for $f = \text{argmin}_{h \in G}\text{SearchObjective}(h, n)$—due to not knowing Z
- **Optimization error** $R_g - R_f$, for $g =$ approx $\text{argmin}_{h \in G}\text{SearchObjective}(h, n)$—due to optimizing approximately (exact optimization is usually hard)

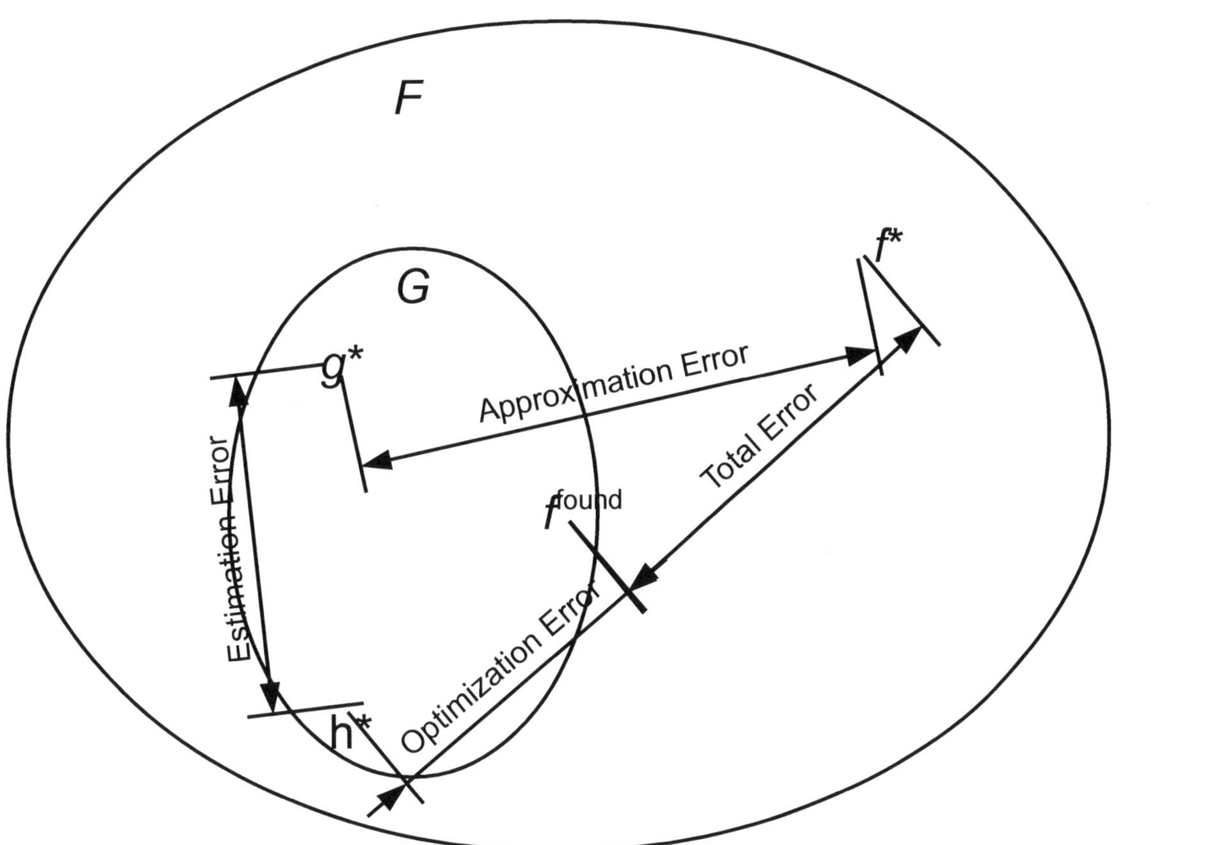

Assuming perfect features and optimization error = 0, approximation and estimation errors are what matters. Perfect optimization is a big assumption, i.e., essentially having a Turing machine, but it still doesn't help completely. To control estimation error, need a bound on it in terms of n. For some G, have a finite sample estimator of R_f, i.e., $\forall f \in G\ |R_f - R_{f,n}| \leq B(n, f, p)$ with probability $\geq 1 - p$ such that $\forall \epsilon > 0$ and $p > 0\ \exists n(\epsilon, f, p)$ such that $B \leq \epsilon$; B is independent of P. If B is the same $\forall f$, G has **uniform convergence**, and $B(n, f, p) = B(n, C(G), p)$, where C measures G's **capacity to overfit**. Finite sample bounds hold simultaneously over $\forall f \in G$, in particular, over any f returned by A. It's unclear exactly why overfitting happens, but restricting capacity prevents it by excluding f capable of accurately modeling noise in S and unable to generalize effectively, as in the credit card example.

A heuristic C is number of parameters to be estimated. It doesn't lead to general bounds, but is usually close to a C that does. E.g., the credit card example doesn't work if S = polynomials of degree $< n$. Hoeffding gives uniform convergence for singleton $S = \{f\}$ for tasks with bounded L.

Vapnik's principle suggests solving a simpler problem directly instead of first solving a more difficult intermediate problem. The idea is precisely about minimizing estimation error.

20.4 Complexity Control

Using $R_{f,n}$ as search objective is **empirical risk minimization** (ERM). If G has uniform convergence, B is the same $\forall f \in G$, and the found one will have a finite sample bound. ERM is only useful for a few special cases such as linear regression due to needing small C or very large n to come up with small B. Uniform convergence defines sufficient **sample complexity** of S, i.e., $\forall \epsilon > 0$ and $p > 0$ can solve for n such that the estimation error $< \epsilon$. To allow efficient learning, need $n = O(\text{polynomial})$. For a nonuniform finite sample bound this doesn't work because don't know G, so use of sample complexity is essentially restricted to linear regression.

Can construct G with a finite sample bound. Consider $G = \cup H_i$ and the corresponding $w_i \in (0, 1)$, picked before seeing the data so that $\sum w_i \leq 1$ and $\forall H_i$ have uniform convergence with bound B. Due to multiple testing, $R_f \leq B$ doesn't hold, but by Bonferroni correction $\forall f \in S\ |R_f - R_{f,n}| \leq B(n, C(H_i(h)), w_i(f)p)$ with probability $\geq 1 - p$ (Shalev-Shwartz & Ben-David 2014).

For G with a finite sample bound, using search objective = $R_{f,n} + B(n, f, p)$ is **structural risk minimization** (SRM). Usually it starts by looking at simpler models first and stops when for the best found f and all h not yet considered $R_{f,n} + B(n, f, p) \leq B(n, h, p)$. Let $g = \min_{h \in S} R_h$; because the search picked f and not g, $R_{f,n} + B(n, f, p) \le R_{g,n} + B(n, g, p)$, and thus $R_{f,n} - R_{g,n} \le B(n, g, p) - B(n, f, p)$. Then the estimation error = $R_f - R_g \le (R_{f,n} + B(n, f, p)) - (R_{g,n} - B(n, g, p)) = R_{f,n} - R_{g,n} + B(n, f, p) + B(n, g, p) \le 2B(n, g, p)$, which is a finite sample bound. From the proof see that need a two-sided bound because if only have an upper bound, $R_{h,n}$ can be bounded away from R_h and give no information about g. In SRM, the distinction between finding model structure and optimizing for parameters is lost. A conclusion is that even if the true model is known to be complex, due to not having enough data to estimate it, may need to settle for a simpler model.

The choice of w_i represents prior information but isn't very significant—e.g., can for H_i in increasing $C(H_i(h))$ order use $w_i = 6/(\pi(i+1))^2$, which decline slowly and sum to 1 in the limit. Can use whatever p is wanted for the final answer, such as 0.05 or 0.01, in all cases, and stop searching after the bounds prevent a better f from existing in H_i with of higher capacity. Must pick p, S, and w_i before seeing the data. But usually pick at least some of the above after seeing data, in which case the result is only a heuristic guidance.

Assume H_i consists of a single hypothesis h and $L \in [0, M]$. Plugging $w_i p$ into the two-sided Hoeffding bound, $|R_f - R_{f,n}| \le M\sqrt{(\ln(1/w_i) + \ln(2/p))/(2n)}$ with probability $\ge 1 - p$. So can do SRM over any countable set of hypothesis after assigning them weights. In particular, let every h be represented in binary using some prefix-free universal code such as gamma (see the "Compression Algorithms" chapter). Then for $w_i = 2^{-|h|}$, by Kraft inequality $\sum w_i \le 1$. This leads to **Occam risk minimization** (ORM) of finding $f = \text{argmin}_{h \in G}(R_{h,n} + M\sqrt{(|h|\ln(2) + \ln(2/p))/(2n)})$. For encoding a real number, use ad hoc "enough" or systematic $1/\sqrt{n}$ precision. The latter is more reasonable because even in the best case of taking an average have an estimate accurate to about that precision. The more economical the code, the better the bound.

A minor issue for ORM is that scaling y to change M doesn't affect the code for the model by much. Needing to define G before seeing the data isn't a problem because even defining a data structure able to represent f defines a prefix-free code. ORM is very general—it applies ∀task with bounded L, and it's usually easy to define and search a suitable G. It seems to be the ultimate induction principle, but using problem-specific information can give much better bounds for a complex enough h—ORM (usually very loose) lower bounds don't prevent this. So in practice, ORM's value is mostly conceptual; particularly, don't need the best code as a good enough one will do. Nevertheless, even with loose bounds, ORM can show design flaws that prevent generalization. Immediate application—for best generalization don't specify unnecessary precision for parameters.

In philosophy, **Occam razor** advises to not make things more complex than needed—i.e., a simple explanation is more likely to be right than a complex one, and ORM follows this. Benefits:

- Simplicity is useful in itself—e.g., a human can readily understand and inspect a simple model
- ∃ many more complex models than simple ones, so finding a complex one that fits the data by chance is more likely. I.e., picking a simple G limits overfitting by reducing "number" of f that can be tried.

Once find a good f for a problem, for solving the same problem in future might want to restrict G to whichever H_i f came from. But for SRM this is dangerous because having more or less data may produce more complex or simpler f, so this needn't give useful domain knowledge.

20.5 Approximation Error

Approximation error comes from the inability of any G to always compute the oB partition, which for a particular problem may be **arbitrarily complex**, as defined by its Kolmogorov complexity, i.e., the uncomputable smallest number of bits that can represent it (see the "Compression Algorithms" chapter), or a heuristic measure such as size in some simple encoding. So a partition may need arbitrarily many examples to express. Some complexities:

- Some $z_i \in S$ can appear to be **outliers** when it's hard to distinguish **hint noise** (some y_i are wrong) from valid information. Complex models should be able to handle local patches of X with different behavior, especially if such patches are supported by enough examples. Noise is problematic in case of nearby examples with different hints. Usually, if have enough **example support**, a patch is assumed to be locally different, else it's an outlier. Noise is more problematic in smaller local patches than in larger ones because the latter compensate for it more.

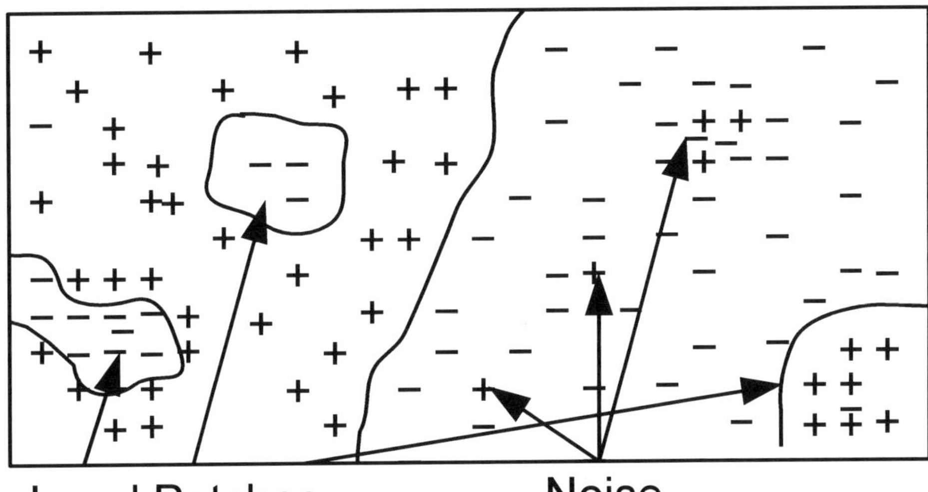

- **Curse of dimensionality**—for vector space data, learning gets harder as D increases. Even if x is a vector of binary variables, all 2^D possibilities are equally likely, so even getting enough data for estimation is a problem because a particular x say nothing about the others, e.g., for the multidimensional xor problem. More generally, a function can consist of many local regions, each behaving differently, and their number usually increases with D. Perhaps the best explanation for why theoretical bounds don't cause problems is the **manifold hypothesis** that for practical data sets the Z part with nonnegligible support is much smaller than Z. This helps control estimation error by focusing the data on regions that matter and ignoring unlikely regions, which is often enough for satisfactory performance.

So in general it's hopeless to try to discover the exact best partition, at least better than asymptotically. At best can approximate it using results such as Weierstrass theorem, which allows to approximate any continuous function arbitrarily well by a polynomial. Many other model types have the same effect, and the more expressive G is, the smaller is the approximation error. So usually pick the most expressive G where have satisfactory control of estimation error. Heuristically, $\forall f$ with low risk, $|f|$ is a good measure of data complexity, perhaps more so if tried to minimize $|f|$. Ultimately this can consider all f representable on a computer, which is the best that can be done. But doing so will result in too much estimation error.

!∃ finite sample bounds on approximation error, at least without some assumptions such as bounded range or that the partition has Lipschitz continuity or other exploitable regularity (i.e., similar x lead to similar y). E.g., ∃ a shape that most closely resembles both *1* and *7*, but which one is genuinely unclear, so in practice assume that such shape is unlikely appear. A human would say “don't know because this doesn't conclusively look like either one”. Also in games like chess human grandmasters only have intuition about a tiny subset of all possible positions. Partition complexity is the main cause of approximation error. One way to measure it for a problem is to see how complex is the partition logic of a particular sufficiently low risk A.

As $n \to \infty$, the sample distribution → true distribution, estimation error disappears, and $R_{f,n}$ effectively measures approximation error. A is **consistent** for a problem if $R_{f(A,n)} \to R_{\text{oB}}$ as $n \to \infty$, and **universally consistent** if it's consistent ∀ problem within a task (Devroye et al. 1996). For a given problem $\forall \epsilon > 0$ and $p > 0$, a consistent A finds f with a PAC(ϵ, p) bound after seeing enough samples. This needs asymptotic and not finite sample bounds on estimation and approximation errors. Some implications:

- Many A are universally consistent.
- For problems where simple partitions do poorly, a universally consistent A needs arbitrarily large n and memory to represent f.
- Strengthening the definition by requiring finite sample bounds leads to an impossible request because some problems need arbitrarily complex partitions. For specific problems, **no free lunch** (NFL) theorems prove this (e.g., see the “Machine Learning—Classification” chapter).

Because any training data is contained in a hypersphere of finite radius, making predictions on anything outside is extrapolation and essentially gives no guarantees. But encountering such x is exponentially unlikely in n.

The intuition behind other (more popularly known) NFL theorems for prediction tasks is that ∃ problems where finite training data is harmful and not helpful, so that over all problems no A wins. The basic proof idea (Lattimore & Hutter 2013) is that if learning is deterministic and X and Y are bounded, can put a uniform distribution on possible P so that every P is equally likely. Then $\forall A$ and finite training, if the training data is excluded from risk calculation, $E_P R_f(A, \text{data}) = E_{x \notin \text{data}} E_P L(f(x), y)$. Because under a uniform distribution of P, given x, all y are equally likely, and $E_P L(f(x), y) = E_P L(f(x), \text{uniformly random } y)$. For classification, the latter = $1/k$, i.e., the expected risk of a random guess. So:

- Over all problems, learning is impossible
- Because some A do better than others on some problems, they must do worse on other problems

More general NFL theorems (Wolpert 2002) lead to the same conclusions. Classification is the easiest learning problem both in terms of hint information and the range of y. So NFL theorems hold for more general tasks as well (Steinwart & Christmann 2008). This logic should apply to other impossibility or computational hardness results.

NFL doesn't contradict universal consistency, which allows arbitrarily much training data. The most problematic NFL assumption is that want to solve all possible problems. Some interpretations:

- It's pointless to compare different A assuming that some are better. Only particular assumptions distinguish them on various problems. Experimentally, different types of problems prefer different learners, so some partial NFL must be true in that the assumptions of a particular A are more appropriate for certain problems than for others. E.g., a linear function can do better than a piece-wise one on some problems and worse on others. But some A consistently do better on most tested problems, though it's conceivable that on other practical problems they will do poorly.
- Must supply domain knowledge about the particular problem to avoid the NFL. Experimentally, domain knowledge helps substantially in many cases, e.g., for image and natural language processing. But until a domain is mature enough to develop useful knowledge, generic methods usually do well. Because must select at least a model class from which to do model selection, how to do so is generic domain knowledge. In practice, should always include as much domain knowledge as possible.
- No one expects to solve problems where training data is harmful, i.e., hint info for S isn't related to that of $z \notin S$. The NFL doesn't work if only want to solve some P, so can ignore it. I.e., must assume something, at least “nice” distributions only. E.g., most A have a bias by assuming that nearby-in-some-way z are related. The above interpretations can hold only partially.

A particular A needn't be consistent, even if it's underlying knowledge representation allows consistency. At least want a knowledge representation that allows consistency, because more data can fix estimation error, but not approximation error. If can't have consistency, high approximation power is the next best thing.

Finite sample bounds on estimation error can be too large with small fixed n when G is expressive enough to have small approximation error and not consistent. E.g., G = polynomials of degree 1000 has finitely many parameters and should have uniform convergence for many problems, but n must be very large for useful bounds. So SRM and ORM are preferred over ERM.

Choosing a knowledge representation data structure usually determines G and suggests a search strategy. E.g., using a hyperplane means G = sets of all hyperplanes and a natural search is optimization of parameters. **Because must choose knowledge representation, must make at least some assumptions**. No clever induction principle can avoid this. Consistency remains the only theoretical guiding principle in the choice of knowledge representation and control of approximation error.

No induction principle can automatically come up with a good A. Theoretical training set bounds only offer guidance, and not useful error estimates. Even if bounds are tight for their corresponding worst cases, they could be very loose for practical data. Most A have been created ad hoc, though a commonality is design for consistency. Typical process:

1. Pick a knowledge representation that doesn't prevent consistency and is economical for simplicity and estimation error reduction
2. Control estimation error in some way, either through simplicity, stability, lack of multiple testing, or a combination of these
3. Respect other constraints, e.g., might need human-friendliness or scalability, to get which may need to give up some risk

No top-performing A in their exact implemented form give rigorous finite sample bounds, and known except-for-minor-violation bounds are loose. Given a good A, it's unclear if $\exists$ a better one for the problem.

E.g., ellipses must be complex to human intuition because it took centuries before Kepler discovered elliptical orbits. Every 10 years or so at least one very good A has been discovered. More often than not, in practice the choice of A is arbitrary and doesn't involve careful logic, despite what one is tempted to believe from successful applications. All computer information is binary, so can represent f as a Boolean function, but it's hard to optimize efficiently in this representation.

20.6 Stability

Intuitively, stability for A means producing similar f from different data sets (Mohri et al. 2012). Let training sets T_1 and T_2 with n iid examples differ in only one example. A is **uniformly *b*-stable** if given f from training on T_1 and h on T_2, $\forall z\ |L_f(z) - L_h(z)| \leq b$.

Theorem (Mohri et al. 2012): If $L \leq M$ and A is b-stable, $\forall T$ consisting of n iid samples, if A trained on T produces f, then $R_f \leq R_{f,n} + b + (2nb + M)\sqrt{\ln(1/p)/(2n)}$ with probability $\geq 1 - p$.

So if $b = O(1/n)$, as is the case for several algorithms (some discussed in the later chapters), the estimation error is $O(1/\sqrt{n})$. This is a very strong result, given its generality. Unfortunately, currently know b only for a few useful A. Nevertheless, this underscores the importance of stability—in particular, unstable A can't estimate their parameters to a reasonable accuracy, and are expected to have a high estimation error.

20.7 Risk Estimation of a Learning Strategy

Can estimate risk of f using theoretical bounds or holdout. But in many cases want to estimate risk of A (Vanwinckelen & Blockeel 2014; Dietterich 1998) on:

1. P when using only a specific S—for certain data-based decisions during training such as tuning parameters
2. P—for comparing several A independently of S but on fixed n—because typically will train on some data set of size n and use f thereafter
3. Several P—for comparing many A in general—for deciding which A to use for a new data set.

Will address (3) later, and (1) is a special case of (2). For (2), it's important to understand what must be independent and the sources of variance:

- A itself may be randomized
- The training data must be independent
- The test data must be independent among itself, and from the training data

Ideally, know P, and can m times train on a random sample of size n and test the resulting f on a randomly sampled example. This creates m iid unbiased performance estimates for statistical inference. To do this in practice, need a data set of size $m(n + 1)$, which isn't efficient use of data, but it's hard to do better without introducing bias.

Can run each training several times with random example order and average the test results, which reduces the variance due to A's own randomization and dependence on example order, but still gives an iid sample of size m. But this may be inefficient because more careful reruns can reduce variance more, and inconvenient because for some metrics it's hard to use averages.

Though this gives m iid estimates, they are likely to have a high variance. Can use maybe $0.2n$ examples to test instead of one, and average the scores (which are dependent due to same f). This reduces n, but also reduces variance as the averages are much more stable. So for the same n, slightly reducing m to allocate more examples for testing gives a more efficient experiment.

For (1), need an additional independent data set of size m. Then m times train A on original data in random order of examples and evaluate on a single example, getting m iid unbiased estimates. This is very similar to holdout, except training is redone $\forall$ test example. If A has no own randomization and doesn't depend on the example order, both will give the same result, with holdout being substantially more efficient and, in this case, the method of choice with a lot of data.

The outputs form matched tuples and can be fed into bootstrap or appropriate statistical comparison tests. Because m must be large enough to make the tests powerful enough, for both (2) and (1) must have enough data to study performance on training sets of the wanted size. But rigorous statistical testing usually isn't the goal, and want a procedure that doesn't need a separate data set and is more efficient in data and time use.

Cross-validation partitions the data into k equal subsets, and k times trains A on $k - 1$ subsets and tests on the remaining one, returning the average risk as the performance estimate:

Fold	Data Use				
1	Train	Train	Train	Train	Test
2	Train	Train	Train	Test	Train
3	Train	Train	Test	Train	Train
4	Train	Test	Train	Train	Train
5	Test	Train	Train	Train	Train

Then train f on all data. This way each example is tested once (upto round-off when k isn't a factor of n, but this doesn't matter for a typical small k). Experimentally, in typical cases $k = 10$ gives the best estimate, but 5 or 20 should be just as good (Kohavi 1995). The best value depends on the application (Arlot & Celisse 2010), but for efficiency the default $k = 5$.

```
template<typename LEARNER, typename Y, typename DATA, typename PARAM>
    Vector<pair<Y, Y> > crossValidateGeneral(PARAM const& p,
    DATA const& data, int nFolds = 5)
{
    assert(nFolds > 1 && nFolds <= data.getSize());
    Vector<pair<Y, Y> > result;
    int testSize = data.getSize()/nFolds;//roundoff goes to training
    for(int i = 0; i < nFolds; ++i)
    {
        PermutedData<DATA> trainData(data), testData(data);
        int testStart = i * testSize, testStop = (i + 1) * testSize;
        for(int j = 0; j < data.getSize(); ++j)
        {
            if(testStart <= j && j < testStop) testData.addIndex(j);
            else trainData.addIndex(j);
        }
        LEARNER l(trainData, p);
        result.appendVector(evaluateLearner<Y>(l, testData));
    }
    return result;
}
```

Understanding many aspects of cross-validation is still an open problem due to lack of independence:

- The training sets overlap in 60% or 80% of the data, depending on k
- If any two folds contain very different data from A's point of view, in all runs the training and the testing data can be very different

Other and related problems:

- k repetitions may not be enough to remove variance due to randomness in A.
- The estimate is for A trained on $n(k - 1)/k$ examples and is usually pessimistic for A trained on n examples as more data usually helps A.
- $!\exists$ an unbiased estimate of the variance of cross-validation's risk estimate (Bengio & Grandvalet 2004). Also, though not proven, it's likely that $!\exists$ a useful upper bound on it, so don't even have the asymptotic CLT error bound.

Some ways to improve cross-validation:

- Stratify by y—simple for discrete Y (for continuous Y discretize use quantiles?). This gives better estimates where applicable (Kohavi 1995).
- Deterministically scramble data order using a random generator with a fixed seed—generally makes different folds more similar, e.g., when the data is sorted by some property, and is probably

sufficient when stratification isn't applicable.

- Repeat cross-validation many times, maybe 10 or 20, with random permutations of data, average the test scores of each instance, and use the batch averages as samples for heuristic variance calculation. The repetition will remove variance due to randomness of *A* and, more importantly, the particular selection of the train sets from the data. For memory efficiency, use a data analysis functor to do incremental calculation.

```
template<typename PARAM, typename Y, typename DATA, typename LEARNER>
    Vector<pair<Y, Y> > repeatedCVGeneral(PARAM const& p, DATA const& data,
    int nFolds = 5, int nRepeats = 5)
{
    Vector<pair<Y, Y> > result;
    PermutedData<DATA> pData(data);
    for(int i = 0; i < data.getSize(); ++i) pData.addIndex(i);
    for(int i = 0; i < nRepeats; ++i)
    {
        GlobalRNG.randomPermutation(pData.permutation.getArray(),
            data.getSize());
        result.appendVector(crossValidateGeneral<PARAM, Y>(p, data, nFolds));
    }
    return result;
}
```

- Consider switching to holdout when *n* is large (>10^4 maybe). With large *n*, as long as *A* is reasonably stable, the results will be similar and will save considerable time. Also, can gradually reduce *k* to 2 before switching to holdout.

For (1), cross-validation and it's improved versions effectively give an almost iid sample, which can heuristically consider iid in many cases. For efficiency, usually use stratification or deterministic scrambling, even though repetition is likely to be more accurate. Also, averaging in the repetition may be inconvenient for computing some nonrisk metrics. So repeat only if need a much more accurate estimate, or *A* is known to be randomized.

It's very easy to get a biased estimate even in nonobvious ways. E.g., if *f* is the best on a test set, its estimate on the same test set is too optimistic because part of its best performance is by chance and favored by that test set. Even for validation (covered later in this chapter), overfitting can lead to selecting suboptimal parameters.

f trained using *A* with a given estimated risk may not have the same risk. If *A* has large variance, R_f will vary accordingly. An accurate estimate of $R_{f(A,\, n)}$ is all that can hope for. For online learning, need somewhat different algorithms.

For (3):

- Beware that comparisons may be flawed in that by NFL the overall best *A* needn't be best ∀ data set. Specific types of *A* do best on specific types of problems, and which does well where is often useful domain knowledge. E.g., digit and iris recognition are very different. Using domain knowledge often gives much better results. E.g., for digit recognition, including rotations of images gives extra useful data. For general conclusions, comparisons with domain knowledge vs without are meaningless.
- Pick a metric and calculate it ∀problem and *A*. The metric is usually $R_{f,\, n}$, a theoretical upper bound, or something else. If *A* is randomized, run it several times, and take the average to reduce the variance due to random seed choice.
- Because different problems can have different difficulty, to make them comparable, transform the metrics into curved grades or ranks (see the "Monte Carlo Algorithms" chapter). When the metric is risk, curved grades are particularly suitable because $R \geq 0$. This assumes that the transformed scores are iid and unbiased.
- ∀*A* calculate the average transformed metric and use that for comparison.

Can do this for several metrics such as risk and resource use and both curved grades and the rank transformation. Significant conclusions should apply to both. But for metrics such as runtime, the rank transformation is probably the only reasonable solution because the slowest *A* can be much slower than the fastest ones, and scaling makes little sense. Also *D* and *n* matter, but it's unclear how to take them into account by scaling, and runtimes from various domains aren't iid.

But any confidence bounds on the metrics are lost and small data sets count as much as large ones. Data set choice matters too because it's easy to find data sets where a particular A does well. To avoid biases, it's best to use different data sets, preferably from different domains and with different level of difficulty. Also, need enough data sets for statistical significance. Technically, (3) is more general than (2) because can reduce (2) to (3) by splitting the data set into m parts and considering them as independent data sets.

To compare independent samples for (1), (2), and (3), can use (see the "Monte Carlo Algorithms" chapter):

- Hypothesis tests:
  - Wilcoxon signed rank for two A.
  - Friedman for more. If it detects a difference, Nemenyi test can compare all pairs and Holm procedure the best A against the rest.
- Permutation tests for equality testing
- Bootstrap—effective for all types of comparisons and doesn't need applying the pessimistic Bonferroni correction. It's also more flexible, e.g., by allowing comparison of multiple metrics simultaneously in the wanted way. In case of binary loss, must handle ties correctly. But hypothesis tests (excluding permutation) are more efficient and directly control the type I error. For efficiency, instead of resampling can heuristically assume that the L_i come from some distribution and sample it instead. E.g., for binary loss, can use Bernoulli. Otherwise, the normal may be a good enough approximation, but, if not, need to resample.

When evaluating f and A using well-known data sets such as those from the UCI, beware that many A have been designed and tuned on them in the first place. It's likely that many algorithm and parameter configurations were tried and the unsuccessful ones were discarded. Comparisons of A tuned on mostly the same data are biased. A reasonable but imperfect solution is to use more data sets, particularly the newer ones in the UCI. Still, it's hard to correctly update existing studies with new data sets or A because some multiple testing usually occurs.

20.8 Making Choices and Model Selection

For A that have tunable parameters, need to reserve part of the training data for **validation** to properly optimize these. A parameter here is anything that restricts the considered set of predictors, such as a choice of strategy. In statistics, a **model** is a set of predictors—e.g., linear model is the set of all hyperplanes and is fit to the data to create a **predictor**. Don't confuse with the common use, where intuitively *model* = *predictor* (many sources do though, so these are effectively synonyms). A **model class** is a set of models such as the set of polynomials ≤ degree 3. Can also think of submodels, and often the difference is blurred.

The idea is the same as for risk estimation—to have good generalization, parameter optimization needs to look at different data. The simplest effective strategy for a few parameters is exponential range grid search (see the "Numerical Algorithms" chapter) with 5-fold cross-validation risk estimate as score. Cross-validation is particularly suitable because errors in estimates of differences between A are usually much smaller than errors in performance estimates (Kohavi 1995). Model selection is easier than performance estimation, because can reduce the former to the latter. Can also use n test results as iid samples and calculate their variance for use in rules such as selecting the simplest A with performance within one standard deviation of the best A, even though accuracy of such variance calculation is heuristic. For this rule and cross-validation, the standard error is calculated based on a sample of size k, i.e., assuming independent folds (Hastie et al. 2009). This assumption is questionable, but suffices for heuristic use. After picking parameters, retrain on all data.

If with probability $\geq 1 - p$ have bound $B(p)$ on the expected performance of f with arbitrary parameters, when picked by optimization out of m parameters on the same data set using methods such as cross-validation, the bound becomes $B(p/m)$, so should minimize m to reduce estimation error. So for parameters to which A isn't very sensitive, it's usually better to have reasonable defaults, which also saves runtime.

Using a separate validation set retains the original bounds on the training sets, but prevents the validation set's use in subsequent relearning. In some cases this may be useful. If train k functions, test them on a holdout of size m, and select the best f; then by Hoeffding $|R_f - R_{f,n}| \leq M\sqrt{(\ln(k) + \ln(2/p))/(2m)}$.

Because of multiple testing, even in presence of other overfitting control, restricting m reduces overfitting. So when possible, should use logic (i.e., prior knowledge) and not search over many possibilities to select structure and parameters. E.g., generating parameter sets by reducing bounds and increasing exponential increments between successive choices usually needs little prior knowledge. Still, need it for parameter ranges that work for most domains. Typically, make such ranges a little wider than needed because missing a good value for some problem is worse than minor estimation error and inefficiency in most problems. Can use custom ranges for particular domains.

Even when other methods such as complexity control bound estimation error, limiting optimization tends to reduce estimation error further. Complexity control, stability, and multiple testing avoidance are the main tools for estimation error control. For supervised learning, have move direct methods, covered in the later chapters.

Due to multiple testing, if want an accurate risk estimate after parameter selection, instead of using the risk of the best parameter set from selection data, need to evaluate that choice again on new data, used only when final predictor is computed. Nevertheless, though the risk estimate of a chosen parameter configuration on selection data is biased, the differences should be much less so, so the selection itself should be valid.

Can generalize to **nested model selection**, which applies when selecting multiple parameter sets. E.g., can use cross-validation to select a model, but *A* can do it's own cross-validation with the data it has for whatever internal parameters it needs. Nested selection generally overfits less than selection out of a multidimensional set but requires enough data.

Sometimes want to pass no parameters:

```
template<typename LEARNER, typename Y, typename X = NUMERIC_X>
struct NoParamsLearner
{
    LEARNER model;
    template<typename DATA> NoParamsLearner(DATA const& data,
        EMPTY const& p): model(data) {}
    Y predict(X const& x)const{return model.predict(x);}
    double evaluate(X const& x)const{return model.evaluate(x);}
};
```

20.9 Alternative Induction Principles

Many heuristic induction principles have been proposed. Some are consistent, i.e., capable of producing consistent *A* in general cases, but this is only a sign of good design. Most formalize Occam's razor in some way.

- Model selection based on hypothesis testing—same as validation-based selection, but instead of validating on separate data use pairwise hypothesis tests. I.e., assume the simplest model as the null and use something like the sign test to move on to more complex models. This is usually much faster than validation, but suffers from multiple testing due to making many inferences from the same data. Multiple testing isn't a problem only in specific cases such as pruning decision trees (covered in the "Machine Learning—Classification" chapter). Only in those cases hypothesis testing is useful.
- **Regularization**—"fix" SRM by using aB instead of B, for $a \in [0, 1]$ and determined by cross-validation. This way the data decides how much to penalize complexity. A further relaxation is using the search objective = $R_{h,n} + aC(h)$, for some heuristic C such as $|h|$ or the number of parameters, and $a \in [0, \infty)$. Many *A* have some form of regularization, whereas use of SRM/ORM is purely conceptual. Regularization affects both complexity and stability (i.e., it originates from methods for solving ill-posed problems, which are effectively unstable to begin with).
- Bayesian model selection—$\Pr(h|y) = O(\Pr(h) \times \Pr(y|h))$. $\Pr(h)$ is the **prior likelihood** that model h explains the data before seeing it and $\Pr(y|h))$ is the likelihood of seeing the data if it were perfectly explained by h, i.e., any errors are considered to be noise. E.g., for real y usually put a normal distribution on the residuals. Then $f = \text{argmax}_h\text{Prob}(h|y)$ is a **maximum a posteriori** (MAP) model. Usually the only prior knowledge is preference for simpler models, but this is automatic because a proper prior distribution can't be uniform over an unbounded range, and thus must make some assumptions, which tend to favor simplicity. I.e., without enough data, might as well assume that a parameter ≈ 0. While selecting a prior out of the blue might seem wrong, it has a stabilizing effect by reducing variance. Interpreting the prior is somewhat tricky, because usually the true function $\notin G$ and by the direct interpretation Pr(it's the right one) = 0. MDL reasoning (discussed later) shows

this to be false because a noise generator is implicitly added and can result in the model's predicting any output with small probability, so prior belief in G has no problems. So the prior = Pr(the structure) × Pr(the parameters). The biggest problem with MAP is that need to decide how much to believe in the prior, i.e., pick initial variances of the parameters. Regularization handles this using cross-validation and is thus preferred. Most forms of regularization are equivalent to some form of MAP, e.g., L_2 penalty on coefficients means Gaussian prior, and L_1 Laplace.

- Bayesian **posterior inference** without picking a model—similar to MAP, except $f = E[h] = \int_h \text{Prob}(h|y)$. The idea is to avoid committing to a particular h, which by itself is usually highly unlikely, and do inference directly. This follows the **Epicurus principle** of keeping all good explanations. The integral is usually approximated by MCMC, which is particularly suitable because know the posterior upto a constant (see the "Monte Carlo Algorithms" chapter). Regularization is implicit in that all models have probability > 0, but with a simple model nonnegligible probability is put on fewer data than with a more complex one. So the most likely model depends on data, enough data means that a not-too-complex and not-too-simple model is preferred, and the more data there is, the more complex model can be preferred. But complexity doesn't always correspond to what model is chosen by data (Murray & Ghahramani 2015).
- **Minimum description length** (MDL) principle— reduce learning to compression, i.e., pick $f = \text{argmin}_h(|h| + |(y|h)|)$ using some code for both (Grunwald 2007). The assumption is that being able to compress the data means having learned something about it, i.e., need less information to correct mistakes of h than to come up with the data. !∃ a known finite sample inequality to justify this, though how useful for a distribution is a code learned from samples surely depends on n. It seems as valid as wanting simplicity and is consistent in some cases (Grunwald 2007). Unlike ORM, MDL applies even if L is unbounded. **Crude MDL** is using an ad hoc code for $|h|$ and $|(y|h)|$. Can code $|h|$ as for ORM. For $|(y|h)|$, only code the differences between predicted and actual values, which is enough to reconstruct the latter. The math simplifies in some cases because constant-in-model-choice additive terms don't matter. Crude MDL is similar to MAP, because $\text{argmax}_h\text{Prob}(y|h) = \text{argmin}_h(-\lg(\Pr(h)) - \lg(\Pr(y|h)))$, but only works for countable models, so need to discretize reals, as for ORM. But, as for ORM, can use universal codes, for which !∃ equivalent in MAP. Picking a distribution = picking a code and "most likely" = "shortest". The shortest codeword length of a symbol ≈ −lg(Pr(symbol), so this measures the surprise of h's predicting the data, and "$\lfloor y|h|$" how much of data isn't predicted by h. These are the same thing, because ∀code ∃ a distribution for which it's the shortest. E.g., for real labels need to encode errors and their signs. The signs take 1 bit each and drop out as constants. When assuming that labels follow a distribution with PDF p and that errors are discretized to some tiny interval d, need about $-\lg(dp(\text{error}))$ bits to encode, so d drops as a constant additive term, and $-\lg(p)$ remains. E.g., for normal p with mean 0, after some further simplifications |y|h| is just the L_2 error. For classification, coding is more complicated—with k classes, prediction is either wrong or makes one of the $k(k-1)$ mistakes. Using a uniform code for these and counting the number of possibilities gives a multinomial, so with m correct answers and e_i wrong ones, for mistake i need $\lg(n!/(m!\prod(e_i!))$ bits to correct mistakes. This is a little clumsy, so with bounded L ORM wins over MDL. Usually, counting the number of possibilities and using universal codes on the result is optimal for MDL. Though crude MDL is intuitively appealing, designing codes for general A is messy, and the complexity penalty seems too strong, so it's practical use is essentially limited to suggesting penalty terms for regularization. Doing so is perhaps conceptually simpler than with MAP because it's easier to think about codes than distributions.
- **Greedy space partitioning**—mirror some multidimensional data structure and split X recursively using a simple h for each split. Greed considers only a small part of f at every step, which reduces the number of considered h and therefore overfitting.

20.10 Bias, Variance, and Bagging

Approximation–estimation–optimization isn't the only useful decomposition. Intuitively, A can err due to:

- **Bias**—preference for certain functional relationships over others due to prior knowledge. Unlike approximation error, bias takes into account all decisions such as optimization error in using local search.
- **Variance**—producing different f from different random S of the same size due to not being able to

estimate parameters effectively, mostly due to overfitting. Unlike estimation error, it takes part of optimization error and other randomness in decisions into account.

Intuitively, bias is like blindness, and variance like hallucination. For a clear view, want to minimize both. Ideologically, bias and variance exist, but to measure them need to use L for the problem. Let p be a random predictor variable and it's **optimal combination** $C(p) = \text{argmin}_m \text{E}_p[L(p, m)]$. E.g., for L being L_2 regression loss, $C(r)$ = the mean, for L_1 loss the median, and for classification loss the mode. The optimal combination gives another way of defining $\text{oB}(x) = C(y|x)$, i.e., oB can generate arbitrarily many samples from $y|x$ and combine them.

Because can only sample S of size n, the next best thing is the **main predictor** $M(x) = C(f_S(x))$, i.e., combining predictions of trained f on a randomly sampled S. Beyond the optimality of the optimal combination, the main predictor has no direct ideological meaning, but it is a good anchor point, around which variance is small due to in some sense being what is expected to be learned. To compare, uniform stability doesn't use an anchor point. Then define (Domingos 2000):

- $\text{Bias}(x) = L(\text{oB}(x), M(x))$—the main predictor performance relative to oB
- $\text{Variance}(x) = \text{E}_S[L(f_S(x), M(x))]$—the cost of performance differences from the main predictor
- $\text{Noise}(x) = \text{E}_S[L(\text{oB}(x), y(x))]$—can't avoid noise, i.e., $\text{E}_x[\text{noise}(x)] = R_{\text{oB}}$

Theorem (Domingos 2000): $\forall x$ and metric L, $L(x, y) \le \text{noise}(x) + \text{bias}(x) + \text{variance}(x)$. For L_2 loss for regression, have equality. This justifies the definitions of bias and variance. Want A with both of them small. Can estimate variance using bagging, which simulates the main predictor using bootstrap:

1. *T* times for some *T* such as 300
2. Create a resample of *S* of size *n*
3. Train *A* on it to get *f*
4. To predict x, form the main predictor out of all the *f* and return it's answer

To estimate the expected-over-x bias and variance, use **out-of-bag** samples, obtained by running the main predictor on S and, for a particular example, using only f in training which it wasn't included. For bias estimation, because don't know oB, use the loss of the main predictor as a combined bias + noise measure. Because a problem has fixed noise $\forall A$, this still allows detecting bias differences among various A.

Bagging is a useful estimator, but it too has inaccuracies. It injects randomness by using bootstrap samples for training and out-of-bag samples for evaluation. Both are different from using true random samples.

A with a high enough variance is deemed **unstable**. Many A have been studied using bagging and similar methods, with some interesting conclusions (Domingos 2000; Valentini & Dietterich 2004). E.g., bias and variance vary for different parameter choices and other decisions. Usually have a trade-off in that must lose one to gain the other, and sometimes only gain or lose.

Due to excellent performance, bagging with A = decision tree (see the "Machine Learning—Classification" chapter) is itself a good A for classification, though it's use is restricted to special cases due to being superseded by better random forest. In some sense, due to bootstrap samples, bagging increases bias of A a little and reduces variance by much, so using it usually improves A that have high variance. The ability to form the main predictor $\forall$ task makes bagging and improvements very extendable.

An interesting property of such **randomization ensemble** is that combining more base learners doesn't overfit more, contrary to complexity-based reasoning. Though formally proven for a special case (Breiman 2001; the idea is that for classification $\forall$ class the proportion of votes converges to a fixed value), this holds generally in most cases. The main idea of the semiformal reasoning is that specific m leads to specific unknown general risk, and for continuous m nearby m should lead to similar values of risk. Consider the risk of the optimal combination $R(p) = \min_m \text{E}_p[L(p, m)]$ for an ensemble. Assume L is bounded. Then given T base learners, making any one of them give an arbitrary prediction will only change R by $\le L/T$, regardless of whether the current min m changes or not. By McDiarmid inequality (Mohri et al. 2012), R converges to its expected value exponentially fast in T. This R value corresponds to a possibly infinite set of m. As more base learners are added, R stops changing, but the set shrinks. For discrete m, it converges to one or more values which equal R. More generally, for continuous m it converges to a countable set of neighborhoods of equal R minima. After some t, the neighborhood count becomes fixed, and the size of each is small enough to not matter for which m is eventually selected out of each.

So in both cases after a finite T, the set of materially distinct considered m stops changing, and adding arbitrarily more base learners, the effect of which is more than that of the first T ones, makes no difference.

So ensembles do not have any kind of drift behavior where adding more base learners overfits more. Intuitively, this is no multiple testing is done by combining and because stability is controlled indirectly to some degree. ∃ some technical issues here—e.g., for some L the limits may not exist, but for bounded L they do and, due to taking resamples from the same data and only considering reasonable m, for reasonable L always have the limits.

An important conclusion is that decision tree tends to be unbiased and unstable. Technically the former is a lie, because A is **unbiased** iff $\forall x$ bias(x) = 0, but for decision tree bias is very low.

Keep in mind that bias and variance depend on n and aren't asymptotic, though noise is. The variance part due to n will decrease as n increases. But bias and variance comparisons are still meaningful for particular data sets because reached conclusions are likely to hold for a variety of n, though maybe not for the asymptotic case.

It's not a contradiction for A to be both biased and consistent because as in general statistics can have bias and variance → 0. This is the case for k-NN (see the "Machine Learning—Classification" chapter; Domingos 2000). Many consistency proofs actually show that bias → 0 by slowly enlarging G so that also variance → 0.

For losses other than L_2, variance can cancel out part of the bias. An alternative decomposition is into the effects of bias and variance (James 2003), which together with noise exactly account for all loss instead of just bounding it. But bagging doesn't work for estimating effects, and by trying to explain interaction of bias and variance they lose simple intuitive meaning. Be sure to distinguish between variance, its measure, its effect, and the variance of its bagging estimator.

Structural bias and variance are an interesting ideological concept. Combining predictors combines and smooths out their partitions. But this is only relevant in as much as L can measure. E.g., even with full knowledge of the distribution on Z, can have lack of example support in certain areas, meaning that distinct partitions would be indistinguishable. Also certain partition differences lead to the same outcomes, e.g., for classification, so L can't make accurate distinctions even with needed example support. This suggests that in general, the partition of oB isn't unique. Also, different partitions may have different variance but the same variance effect.

Using ensembles, might reduce (Dietterich 2000):

- Approximation error—combining base learners widens G by including functions $\notin G$
- Estimation error—combining poorly estimated base learners can produce well-estimated averages
- Optimization error—reduce the risk that a single unlucky poor optimization by a local search method will produce a bad result

20.11 Design Patterns

Can observe certain recurring solutions to common problems, including:

- **Bet on sparsity**—a complex model with many parameters is unlikely to be effective, so set as many as possible to an ineffective value, usually 0, so that they have no influence, reducing complexity (Hastie et al. 2009).
- Optimize approximately—due to estimation error, there is usually very little difference between approximate and optimal solutions. **Early stopping** strategy is stopping optimization when the monitored validation set error starts increasing; a potential problem is when the increase is premature.
- **Convexification**—if optimization for certain L is hard because it's not convex, find a **surrogate loss function** that bounds L and leads to a convex optimization problem. Because of the bound the risk of the solution may be very close to the risk of the original problem's optimal solution. Using a function that approximates but not bounds L can also be useful.
- **Get more data**—this is usually the simplest and most effective way to reduce risk. A mediocre model with a lot of data outperforms great models with little data (Domingos 2012). Learning has been observed to fail particularly for x that are very different from all seen examples. Any learned f is practically incomplete, i.e., doesn't apply to $\forall x \in X$, in the same way that numerical interpolation is very different from extrapolation.
- Use domain knowledge—any information A doesn't have to learn can be very helpful. E.g., in image processing, neighboring pixels are related and rotations usually don't matter.
- Use SGD (see the "Numerical Algorithms" chapter) with a regularization penalty—convenient for

models that have subgradients because training is online, efficient, and under-optimization tends to keep estimation error small.

- Trust only validated *A*—for many tasks far too many *A* have been and keep being proposed, and it's practically impossible to conclusively compare more that a reasonable number of the most promising ones. It's a form of estimation error that qualities of each *A* aren't known completely, and finding them out is costly in terms of researcher time. A prudent strategy is to consider only *A* experimentally shown to have top performance on a variety of problems by someone other than the creators or with other desirable qualities such as interpretability, ease of use and parameter setting, efficiency, and a good design that justifies performance. Though other *A* may get better R_f, at least for particular problems, researching them is usually an undue effort from the problem solver, which instead should be focused on data preparation. Nevertheless, for problems of high economic significance, want to do extensive research. An interesting question is which *A* to try next if any when all the tried ones weren't satisfactory.

All known *A* have issues, but it's hard to fix them without breaking something else. The end goal is to deploy *f* as part of a decision making system. Commodity reasoning applies as usual, so want *A* with:

- A track record of getting low-risk *f* on common data sets, particularly the ones similar to the problem being solved
- Reasonable efficiency—ideally training takes at most a few days and making a decision is instant
- The ability to work as a black box, with at most minor help from the user—any parameters should be tuned automatically, but it's reasonable to have users give domain-specific information such as approximate parameter ranges or customized features
- Simplicity—e.g., Netflix chose not to deploy the overly complex winner of its recommendation competition (http://techblog.netflix.com/2012/04/netflix-recommendations-beyond-5-stars.html)
- Interpretability—a learned partition should be understandable by a human, and often prefer *f* with simple knowledge representation over slightly more accurate complicated *f*

20.12 Data Preparation

Feature selection is the most important step in the learning process. Uninformative or random features like record id (an easy mistake to make when the data is automatically read from some database) may influence *f* by appearing to have predictive power by chance. Though certain domains have natural features, for best results should do feature engineering based on domain knowledge as much as possible. E.g., for trying to predict a person's level of health, it's better to include body mass index instead of height and weight because, given the latter, the model won't necessarily learn that the former is useful. Also, for games like chess, humans decide the quality of a position using piece count, mobility, pawn structure, etc., and it's impractical to learn these from piece locations.

Falsely informative features are even more dangerous. E.g., a well-known case is when a military organization tried to train a tank recognizer and, to save costs, used photos taken over only two days for training—one with tanks and one without. It happened to be cloudy on one of the days, and the algorithm learned to predict from photo brightness.

It's usually easy to apply one of several good *A* to any data in a supported format. The hard part is collecting data from various often poorly maintained sources such as free-format logs or databases with data that needs cleaning, i.e., removing common-sense-encoded invalid values such as age = 0, gender = "N/A", etc. Given such noisy sources and a large *n*, coming up with derived features may be practically impossible without at least domain knowledge for cleaning. A simple heuristic to detect bad data is to check frequently occurring values because those are likely to be the invalid ones.

Generally, *x* is **numeric** (continuous or **discrete**), **ordinal**, **categorical**, mixed, or arbitrary but with a distance or a kernel function (discussed later). The difference between ordinal and categorical is that the latter gives no order relation.

```
typedef Vector<double> NUMERIC_X;
typedef Vector<int> CATEGORICAL_X;
template<typename DATA> int getD(DATA const& data)
{
    assert(data.getSize() > 0);
    return data.getX(0).getSize();
```

```
}
```

Can convert between categorical and numeric features. For categorical → numeric, define a binary 0/1 variable ∀ category value. This transformation gives the necessary gradient or linear separability for many algorithms.

For numeric → categorical, define subranges called **bins**, and for a given feature value return the corresponding bin number. Usually assume that a feature has bounded range, and put $z \notin S$ and outside this range in the end-of-interval bins. A simple binning strategy is **equal width**, with maybe lg(n) bins of the same size:

```
class DiscretizerEqualWidth
{
    ScalerMinMax s;
    int nBins;
    int discretize(double x, int i)const
    {
        x = s.scaleI(x, i);
        if(x < 0) return 0;
        if(x >= 1) return nBins - 1;
        return nBins * x;
    }
public:
    template<typename DATA> DiscretizerEqualWidth(DATA const& data,
        int theNBins = -1): s(data), nBins(theNBins)
    {
        assert(data.getSize() > 1);
        if(nBins == -1) nBins = lgCeiling(data.getSize());
    }
    CATEGORICAL_X operator()(NUMERIC_X const& x)const
    {
        CATEGORICAL_X result;
        for(int i = 0; i < x.getSize(); ++i)
            result.append(discretize(x[i], i));
        return result;
    }
};
```

For online learning, can use constant 5–10 bins. But binning loses information and is best avoided by picking A that doesn't need discretization. To minimize estimation error, each bin must be supported by enough examples, but even if that is the case, still have approximation error by putting dissimilar examples in the same bin.

If have a mix of numeric and categorical features, it's usually best to convert the latter into the former because this doesn't lose information.

20.13 Scaling

For numeric data, scaling can be an issue because many algorithms give equal priority to features when combining them, so those with large scale can have more influence. Only some A are scale-oblivious. One way to scale is mapping all feature values into the same range, usually [0, 1], using $scaledX = (x - xMin)/(xMax - xMin)$. $xMax$ and $xMin$ are computed from the training data.

```
class ScalerMinMax
{
    NUMERIC_X minX, maxX;
public:
    ScalerMinMax(int D): minX(D, numeric_limits<double>::infinity()),
        maxX(D, -numeric_limits<double>::infinity()){}
    template<typename DATA> ScalerMinMax(DATA const& data)
    {
        assert(data.getSize() > 0);
        minX = maxX = data.getX(0);
```

```
        for(int i = 1; i < data.getSize(); ++i) addSample(data.getX(i));
    }
    void addSample(NUMERIC_X const& x)
    {
        assert(minX.getSize() == x.getSize());
        for(int j = 0; j < x.getSize(); ++j)
        {
            minX[j] = min(minX[j], x[j]);
            maxX[j] = max(maxX[j], x[j]);
        }
    }
    double scaleI(double xi, int i)const
    {
        double delta = maxX[i] - minX[i];
        return delta > 0 ? (xi - minX[i])/delta : 0;
    }
    NUMERIC_X scale(NUMERIC_X x)const
    {
        for(int i = 0; i < x.getSize(); ++i) x[i] = scaleI(x[i], i);
        return x;
    }
};
```

Only training data is normalized into [0, 1], so test data may be mapped outside this range, but this shouldn't cause problems.

Another popular way to scale to studentization, i.e., ∀ feature making the mean 0 and the variance 1. It appears to perform worse overall, probably because variance as a measure of scale is meaningful only for normally distributed data, but better for A that need mean 0 (usually for SGD to help convergence).

```
class ScalerMQ
{
    Vector<IncrementalStatistics> ic;
public:
    ScalerMQ(int D): ic(D) {}
    template<typename DATA> ScalerMQ(DATA const& data): ic(getD(data))
        {for(int i = 0; i < data.getSize(); ++i) addSample(data.getX(i));}
    void addSample(NUMERIC_X const& x)
        {for(int j = 0; j < x.getSize(); ++j) ic[j].addValue(x[j]);}
    double scaleI(double xi, int i)const
    {
        double q = ic[i].stdev();
        return q > 0 ? (xi - ic[i].getMean())/q : 0;
    }
    NUMERIC_X scale(NUMERIC_X x)const
    {
        for(int i = 0; i < x.getSize(); ++i) x[i] = scaleI(x[i], i);
        return x;
    }
};
```

Can scale online by dynamically updating the relevant parameters. Though scales will adjust with data, and a first few $z_i \in S$ may be poorly scaled, this shouldn't cause problems.

Scaling isn't free lunch either. It usually improves performance but loses information when scales between features are dependent. E.g., neighboring pixels in images are related and having a light pixel next to a dark one signals contrast, which can be erased by scaling. Computationally, need $O(nD)$ time to scale S.

20.14 Handling Missing Values

Collected vector data can be incomplete if some x contain null values—e.g., survey respondents can fail to fill in some items. Despite not bothering oB, this is an issue for practical A. Can discard samples with missing values if n is large. But dropping missing value examples may introduce bias when values aren't

missing at random and follow a pattern (Garcia et al. 2014).

Another option is discarding features with missing values. This is particularly effective if mostly values of several specific features are missing—e.g., if respondents don't want to admit something.

But with small n it makes sense to use the information from incomplete examples. Some solutions:

- Use the mean or the median of values of other examples—the simplest option, but can introduce bias.
- Use the value of x's nearest neighbor, calculated using a distance that uses only nonmissing value features—probably the most practical replacement strategy.
- Do preliminary learning to guess missing values—more complex to setup, but probably the least biased replacement strategy.
- Use A that can handle missing features—doesn't lose information, but such A aren't necessarily good choices. For when dropping missing value examples removes too many, this seems to be the best solution.

That a value is missing can be useful information. E.g., might be able to make an accurate diagnosis based on only the names of tests requested by a doctor.

A different issue is predicting based on a sample with missing values. Even though f that work with missing values can give an answer, their performance estimates lose accuracy. May need to maintain replacement logic based on training data.

20.15 Feature Selection

Creating a useful feature needs human insight, but may be able to remove useless features automatically and keep the best subset. This has several goals:

- Gain simplicity—and the corresponding benefits. May even want to simplify at expense of slightly increased risk
- Reduce the cost of data collection—no need to measure removed features, e.g., by giving patients extra medical tests
- Improve time and memory efficiency—fewer features = less computation

Noisy features are a problem because A will try to use of the noise. E.g., if have many coin flips as features, some of them may seem useful for S and will be kept, resulting in a more complex model. Depending on A and the amount of noise, f may be ineffective because it would essentially try to solve problems different from the ones it was trained for.

Adding a feature can't reduce R_{oB}. A feature is (Kohavi & John 1997):

- **Strongly relevant** if removing it from any subset reduces R_{oB}
- **Weakly relevant** if not removing it from some but not all subsets reduces R_{oB}
- **Irrelevant** if removing it from any subset doesn't reduce R_{oB}

Optimal subsets consists of all strongly relevant, possibly some weakly relevant, and no irrelevant features. E.g., for the iris data, every variable allows reasonably accurate classification on its own, so chances are that for perfect classification don't need all four. Need weakly relevant features because any one of several can give the needed info. E.g., for learning the xor function, neither variable alone is helpful, but knowing both makes a difference.

Reducing risk by feature selection is usually hopeless. ∃ 2^D feature subsets, and each could be best. Attempting to discover which one needs reserving some validation data and increases estimation error because the subset found on reduced data needn't be the best for all data, because both useful and useless features may not appear so. Also, to claim that a subset of k features is best, must consider all subsets of 2^k features (Devroye et al. 1996).

On the other hand, reducing the number of features can improve estimation error by reducing model complexity, even if strongly relevant features are removed. But this is generally not the case because good A have built-in overfitting control, which benefits little from separate feature selection. Also, with large D it's hard to find the optimal subset because subsets that differ in a relatively few features should be similar. **A realistic goal is to reduce the number of used features with minimal risk increase**. So usually use all features included by a domain expert, and try to select only if efficiency and data collection cost are a problem. A good success metric is the % of retained features.

Embedded methods use A with built-in feature selection. Some A are usually very efficient and don't use some features, attach importance to features, or explicitly try to not use some features. These are task-specific. Typical examples (covered later in the corresponding chapters) are decision/regression trees and methods based in L_1 regularization. Embedded methods don't need a validation set as they train and select features simultaneously, avoiding estimation error and search inefficiency for free. But such A aren't typically the best performing (otherwise feature selection would be solved). Chose embedded methods when n is too small to use a validation set or too large for other methods to be efficient.

In some cases, a feature definitely isn't useful:

- If a subset of features is perfectly linearly correlated, none of them can be strongly relevant, and can remove all except one. In practice, perfect correlation is unlikely, but can use maybe |correlation| ≥ 0.95. Can compute the correlation matrix, single out sufficiently correlated entries, and greedily select variables correlated with most other variables to minimize the total number of them, though this is expensive computationally.
- If a feature has ≈0 variance, it's irrelevant, and can remove it.

Generally these aren't worth doing because computing the correlation matrix needs $O(D^2)$ time and space, and features rarely have ≈0 variance. Also have some estimation error—e.g., highly correlated features in S needn't be so in general. This is magnified by multiple testing because some features can be highly correlated by chance. Other methods are based on search.

```
class FeatureSelector
{
public:
    Vector<int> fMap;
public:
    FeatureSelector(Bitset<> const& selection)
    {
        for(int i = 0; i < selection.getSize(); ++i)
            if(selection[i]) fMap.append(i);
    }
    NUMERIC_X select(NUMERIC_X const& x)const
    {
        NUMERIC_X result;
        for(int i = 0; i < fMap.getSize(); ++i) result.append(x[fMap[i]]);
        return result;
    }
    double select(NUMERIC_X const& x, int feature)const
    {
        assert(feature >= 0 && feature < fMap.getSize());
        return x[fMap[feature]];
    }
};
template<typename DATA> struct FSData
{
    DATA const& data;
    FeatureSelector const & f;
    typedef typename DATA::X_TYPE X_TYPE;
    typedef typename DATA::Y_TYPE Y_TYPE;
    typedef X_TYPE X_RET;
    FSData(DATA const& theData, FeatureSelector const & theF): data(theData),
        f(theF) {}
    int getSize()const{return data.getSize();}
    X_RET getX(int i)const{return f.select(data.getX(i));}
    double getX(int i, int feature)const
        {return f.select(data.getX(i), feature);}
    Y_TYPE const& getY(int i)const{return data.getY(i);}
};
template<typename LEARNER> struct FeatureSubsetLearner
{
    FeatureSelector f;
    LEARNER l;
public:
```

```
    template<typename DATA> FeatureSubsetLearner(DATA const& data,
        Bitset<>const& selection): f(selection), l(FSData<DATA>(data, f)) {}
    int predict(NUMERIC_X const& x)const{return l.predict(f.select(x));}
};
```

For implementation, it's convenient to use one algorithm to find a number of good subsets and order them by the number of used features, and another to select the lowest risk one. A typical validation search picks the best-performing subset, resolving ties in favor of smaller ones. But because the realistic goal is to reduce the number of used features and not improve performance, instead can pick the smallest subsets with risk ≤ risk of the full subset. In case of some variance in the base *A*, the resulting multiple testing prefers much simpler subsets, offsetting estimation error and gaining some efficiency.

```
template<typename RISK_FUNCTOR> Bitset<> pickBestSubset(
    RISK_FUNCTOR const &r, Vector<Bitset<> >const& subsets)
    {return valMinFunc(subsets.getArray(), subsets.getSize(), r);}
template<typename RISK_FUNCTOR> Bitset<> pickBestSubsetGreedy(
    RISK_FUNCTOR const &r, Vector<Bitset<> >const& subsets)
{
    int best = subsets.getSize() - 1;
    double fullRisk = r(subsets[best]);
    for(int i = 0; i < best; ++i) if(r(subsets[i]) <= fullRisk) best = i;
    return subsets[best];
}
```

The subset with all features is the benchmark, included by the subset-creation algorithm, and is often selected. E.g., for digit recognition, though some image areas are more important, each pixel carries similar info, so only a few may be unneeded, but not being able to remove any isn't a failure—probably all are useful. But if the base *A* has high variance, the risk of the full subset may not be estimated well, leading to selection of an overly simple subsets. Consider repeated cross-validation for only the full subset.

With many subsets, to reduce computation time and estimation error can subsample the ranked subsets using grid search:

```
Vector<Bitset<> > subSampleSubsets(Vector<Bitset<> >const& subsets,
    int limit)
{
    assert(subsets.getSize() > 0 && limit > 0);
    Vector<Bitset<> > result;
    int skip = ceiling(subsets.getSize(), limit);
    for(int i = subsets.getSize() - 1; i >= 0; i -= skip)
        result.append(subsets[i]);
    result.reverse();
    return result;
}
```

∃ several useful strategies for generating and ranking subsets. **Wrapper methods** use one or more *A* to search through some subsets, using a validation set to estimate their risk. A minor problem with wrappers is that they tend to pick features that are good only for the used base *A* (Guyon 2008). But because usually use the same *A* to relearn on all data and the found subset, this doesn't matter. Due to estimation error, can't select best subsets to satisfy all possible learners because each can make use of different features and be confused by others, etc.

Complete enumeration is feasible upto maybe $D \leq 12$, depending on *n* and the base *A*.

```
struct SubsetLengthComparator
{
    bool isLess(Bitset<> const& lhs, Bitset<> const& rhs)const
        {return lhs.popCount() < rhs.popCount();}
    bool isEqual(Bitset<> const& lhs, Bitset<> const& rhs)const
        {return lhs.popCount() == rhs.popCount();}
};
Vector<Bitset<> > selectFeaturesAllSubsets(int D)
{
    assert(D <= 20);//computational safety
```

```
    int n = pow(2, D) - 1;
    Vector<Bitset<> > result(n, Bitset<>(D));
    for(int i = 0; i < n; ++i)
    {
        int rank = i + 1;
        for(int j = 0; rank > 0; ++j, rank /= 2)
            if(rank % 2) result[i].set(j);
    }
    quickSort(result.getArray(), 0, result.getSize() - 1,
        SubsetLengthComparator());
    return result;
}
```

Because look at every subset, can afford to find the best one, and should use the best search.

Forward search starts with no features and greedily adds the most useful one at a time until meeting the full subset's performance. It needs $O(D^2)$ evaluations, so is useful for maybe $D \leq 40$.

```
template<typename RISK_FUNCTOR>
Bitset<> selectFeaturesForwardGreedy(RISK_FUNCTOR const &r, int D)
{
    Bitset<> resultI(D);
    resultI.setAll();
    double fullRisk = r(resultI);
    resultI.setAll(0);
    for(int i = 0; i < D; ++i)
    {
        double bestRisk;
        int bestJ = -1;
        for(int j = 0; j < D; ++j) if(!resultI[j])
        {
            if(i == D - 1)
            {
                bestJ = j;
                break;
            }
            resultI.set(j, true);
            double risk = r(resultI);
            resultI.set(j, false);
            if(bestJ == -1 || risk < bestRisk)
            {
                bestRisk = risk;
                bestJ = j;
            }
        }
        resultI.set(bestJ, true);
        if(r(resultI) <= fullRisk) return resultI;
    }
    resultI.setAll();
    return resultI;
}
```

Used with oB, it finds a maximal subset that can't be increased to improve performance. But it can't find xor-like subsets, where single features don't appear useful. Nevertheless, this is usually not a problem for practical data, particularly, because useful subsets are discovered eventually.

A much more scalable approach is to consider the prediction ability of each feature individually, hoping that with large D this heuristic will at least give an approximate ranking of subsets. This is combined with subsampling for efficiency.

```
template<typename RISK_FUNCTOR> Vector<Bitset<> > selectFeatures1F(
    RISK_FUNCTOR const &r, int D)
{
    Vector<Bitset<> > selections;
```

```
    Vector<double> risks(D);
    for(int i = 0; i < D; ++i)
    {
        Bitset<> temp(D);
        temp.set(i);
        risks[i] = r(temp);
    }
    Vector<int> indices(D);
    for(int i = 0; i < D; ++i) indices[i] = i;
    IndexComparator<double> c(risks.getArray());
    quickSort(indices.getArray(), 0, D - 1, c);
    Bitset<> resultI(D);
    for(int i = 0; i < D; ++i)
    {
        resultI.set(indices[i]);
        selections.append(resultI);
    }
    return selections;
}
```

This ignores interactions between features and does poorly on xor-type problems. In general, can't tell whether a feature is useful based on a simple test. E.g., Zodiac sign may be useful in making predictions about a person if the person tries to live up to it. The xor problem leads to many counter-examples. Nevertheless, most problems are very different from xor, and efficiency makes single feature search useful. It's usually good at removing irrelevant features but not weakly relevant ones (Guyon 2008), which is still useful.

For wrappers, the overall strategy is to use:

- Complete enumeration if $D \leq 12$
- Greedy forward search if $D \leq 40$
- Single feature search with subsampling otherwise

A rough justification for 12 and 40 is runtime control. Assuming the base A runs in $O(D)$ time with respect to D, complete enumeration and forward search respectively take $O(D2^D)$ and $O(D^3)$ time, which are close for the selected numbers.

```
template<typename RISK_FUNCTOR> Bitset<> selectFeaturesSmart(
    RISK_FUNCTOR const& r, int D, int subsampleLimit = 20)
{
    if(D <= 12) return pickBestSubset(r, selectFeaturesAllSubsets(D));
    else if(D <= 40) return selectFeaturesForwardGreedy(r, D);
    else return pickBestSubsetGreedy(r, subSampleSubsets(
        selectFeatures1F(r, D), subsampleLimit));
}
```

20.16 Kernels

Kernels allow efficiently adding features that are combinations of other features. This is done by some feature-mapping function F. E.g., F = identity corresponds to no mapping, and a simple F can include all pairs of feature products.

Such mapping can drastically increase D and make learning computationally infeasible, so is usually done only when the **kernel trick** applies, i.e., when A only uses a dot product. E.g., for linear regression wx for some weight vector w becomes $F(w)F(x) = K(w, x)$, where K is a **kernel** function specific to F. K is computable directly, usually in $O(D)$ time, without mapping to the enhanced space first. This allows the dimension of the enhanced space to be very high, even ∞.

By definition, any function corresponding to a dot product in the enhanced space is a valid K, but not every function K is valid kernel. Theorem: (Aggarwal 2014), K is valid iff the all example $n \times n$ matrix M such that $M[i][j] = K_{ij}$ is **symmetric and positive definite** (SPSD), i.e., $M[i][j] = M[j][i]$, and $\forall u \in \mathbb{R}^n$ $uMu \geq 0$. Proof: M is SPSD $\rightarrow \exists$ matrix B such that $M = B^T B \rightarrow F(x_i)$ = the ith column of B is a feature map $\rightarrow K$ is valid. Also $K_{ij} = F(x_i)F(x_j) \rightarrow K_{ij} = F(x_j)F(x_i)$, and $uMu = \sum u_i u_j F(x_i)F(x_j) = ||\sum u_i F(x_i)||^2 \geq 0 \rightarrow M$ is SPSD.

So every valid K generates a numeric feature vector of some dimension $\forall x$, which itself needn't be a numeric vector. But this feature space on it's own is usually very high dimensional and useless. Because K is an inner product of such vectors, it's a Hilbert space functional—e.g., it's bi-linear. Intuitively, K measures similarity. In particular, the L_2 distance in the enhanced space is well-defined because using bi-linearity to get distance^2 = $||F(x_i) - F(x_j)||^2 = K_{ii} - 2K_{ij} + K_{jj}$.

M represents all available information about the training data. Conversion to M loses some information —e.g., because a dot product measures the cosine of an example to the origin, so any rotation information is lost.

A valid K isn't necessarily useful. Specific choice of K represents prior domain knowledge about the data, and no specific K and parameter choices for it work for all types of data. For numeric vector data, useful K are **linear** (plain dot product) and **Gaussian** (also called radial basis), defined by $K(x_1, x_2) = \exp(-||x_1 - x_2||/\sigma)$, where σ is the width parameter, similar to standard deviation. The latter can represent any continuous partition boundary and is usually the method of choice due to good experimental performance for classification with SVM (covered in the "Machine Learning—Classification" chapter; Bottou et al. 2007):

```
struct GaussianKernel
{
    double a;
    GaussianKernel(double theA): a(theA) {}
    double operator()(NUMERIC_X const& x, NUMERIC_X const& y)const
    {//beware - if x - y is too large, result = 0
        NUMERIC_X temp = x - y;
        return exp(-a * (temp * temp));
    }
};
```

∃ useful K for other types of data such as strings and graphs. Using kernels allows learning nonvector data directly if the chosen K is SPSD, and it's faster to compute the dot product as a kernel than in the enhanced space.

The **representer theorem** makes using kernels easier (Mohri et al. 2012): Let g be a nondecreasing function, H a Hilbert space corresponding to any K, and R any risk function. Then ∃ reals a_i such that $f(x) = \sum a_i K(x_i, x)$ is a solution of $\min_{h \in H} g(||h||) + R(h(x_0), ..., h(x_n - 1))$.

20.17 Online Training

Many top-performing A need too much time or memory for large n. Want online A that don't need all data before training and learn one example at a time. ∃ substantial difference between online training and online operation. Only the former is discussed here.

SGD is often the optimization algorithm of choice because it works online and usually finds low-precision solutions that are little improved by getting more precision due to estimation error. Beware that in most cases need to cross-validate the initial starting rate of SGD, otherwise it can quickly swing into ∞. Gradients are scale-sensitive, and using the same initial rate such as 1 only works in special cases, mostly for classification, where gradients can't get too large. SGD comes with some automatic stability by starting from parameters at 0 or some other low-complexity initial solution.

Estimation error is much less of a problem because seeing an example once usually isn't enough to overfit.

Can tune parameters in several ways:

- Buffer some initial data and use it for offline tuning; then use the results for online learning. This is simple, but the optimal values for all the data may be very different from those on the initial data.
- Racing—works for parameters that can be tuned offline by grid search. ∀ considered parameter combination, it creates an online A. After learning is almost complete, the remaining data is used for validation to pick the best f. In a fully online case where learning never ends, first evaluate on an example and then learn from it, keeping the running average. Prediction uses the best f so far, and can discard or discount earlier evaluations for estimating R_f. Such simple estimates are probably not accurate enough, but they are to pick the best or near-best parameters. Also, ∃ various strategies for dropping poorly performing racers after some time.

```
struct BinaryLoss
{
```

```
    double operator()(int predicted, int actual)const
        {return predicted != actual;}
};
template<typename LEARNER, typename PARAMS = EMPTY, typename Y = int,
    typename LOSS = BinaryLoss, typename X = NUMERIC_X> class RaceLearner
{
    Vector<LEARNER> learners;
    Vector<double> losses;
    LOSS l;
public:
    RaceLearner(Vector<PARAMS> const& p): losses(p.getSize(), 0)
        {for(int i = 0; i < p.getSize(); ++i)learners.append(LEARNER(p[i]));}
    void learn(X const& x, Y y)
    {
        for(int i = 0; i < learners.getSize(); ++i)
        {
            losses[i] += l(learners[i].predict(x), y);
            learners[i].learn(x, y);
        }
    }
    Y predict(NUMERIC_X const& x)const
    {
        return learners[argMin(losses.getArray(), losses.getSize())].
            predict(x);
    }
};
```

20.18 Dealing with Nonvector Data

Converting some types of data into vector form is common in many domains, but can be clumsy. E.g., for

- Text—try a **bag of words model**, where have a universe of D words and represent a document by D counts of occurred words
- Audio—typically use Fourier transform frequencies as features
- Image—use pixels, possibly reducing the color range

For text, the vector conversion loses information such as relationships between word positions. Generally, nonvector data is intuitively any data that isn't easily converted into vector form.

For most domains, need to do some knowledge engineering, i.e., describe the domain knowledge formally by means of an **ontology**, i.e., an object model that describes what is happening. E.g., can formalize geography by defining regions, countries, cities, etc., along with the appropriate containment relationships. Once a domain is formalized, it becomes easier to define features using common patterns. E.g., for chess, a game state is usually represented by a combination of:

- The difference in material from assigning a value to each piece type
- Positional factors such as king safety, mobility, center control, pawn structure, etc.

Without domain knowledge, the only features would be piece locations, which aren't as useful.

Instead of vector conversion, can use distance and kernel functions. Doing so for various A is discussed in the later chapters. The former is usually simpler, but, given distance d, something like e^{-d} or $1/(d + 1)$ is usually a good kernel.

20.19 Large-scale Learning

The primary challenge is efficiency—it usually takes too long to apply the common good A. Some general solutions:

- Use an online A—works, but these are usually not the most accurate.
- Sample the data to create a smaller but still representative S, and use the rest for validation and evaluation—usually a good strategy because most A are efficient at evaluation and can use all remaining data for evaluation. But training with all data should produce more accurate models. Sampling can work cleanly with ensembles (see the "Machine Learning—Classification" chapter).

E.g., can change random forest to use $\leq m$ (for some reasonable m such as 10^4) examples for bags.

- Keep the data on disk—works only with *A* that scale in *n* and access data cache-efficiently. Others are slow because of random access and/or superlinear runtime. Still, using a buffer can help. E.g., using permuted data directly causes I/Os—to avoid them, use external memory sorting to compute a buffer from the permutation. Random or deterministic permutation can also be done efficiently this way.

```
template<typename X, typename Y> struct DiskData
{
    EMVector<pair<X, Y> > data;
    DiskData(string const& filename): data(filename) {}
    template<typename DATA> DiskData(DATA const& theData,
        string const& filename): data(filename)
    {
        for(int i = 0; i < theData.getSize(); ++i)
            addZ(theData.getX(i), theData.getY(i));
    }
    void addZ(X const& x, Y const& y){data.append(make_pair(x, y));}
    typedef X X_TYPE;
    typedef Y Y_TYPE;
    typedef X const& X_RET;
    X_RET getX(int i)const
    {
        assert(i >= 0 && i < data.getSize());
        return data[i].first;
    }
    double getX(int i, int feature)const
    {
        assert(i >= 0 && i < data.getSize() &&
            feature >= 0 && feature < data[i].first.getSize());
        return data[i].first[feature];
    }
    Y_TYPE const& getY(int i)const
    {
        assert(i >= 0 && i < data.getSize());
        return data[i].second;
    }
    int getSize()const{return data.getSize();}
};
```

- Explicitly handle sparse feature vectors with many 0's. E.g., linear SVM SGD can handle sparse models such as bag of words using maps instead of vectors. This leads to a substantial efficiency gain.

"**Big data**" and related appealing terms are given by the media to large-scale learning. $\exists$ nothing magic about it because the best known approach is using online *A* and clusters of parallel computers. A challenge is that the standard data decomposition technique is usually impossible, because most *A*, even paralellizable ones, need to have access to all data, unless small subsamples suffice. Currently, big data research concerns mostly:

- Efficient storage systems such as Hadoop and Spark—these have already allowed working with much larger data sets
- Scalable algorithms that compute acceptable approximate answers
- Methods for large *D*—big data is still isn't enough to overcome the curse of dimensionality and the resulting estimation errors

20.20 Conclusions

Every *A* has some problems. If have the computation time, usually use several *A*, and have cross-validation select the best one.

20.21 Comments

The hint information concept is new but useful because in practice A must take x as input and return some ID as output.

Can use a nonlinear loss, but doing so doesn't seem preferable.

The name *ORM* is new. Somewhat misleadingly, it has also been called MDL (Shalev-Shwartz & Ben-David 2014), though it doesn't minimize the data description. The bound itself is Occam razor bound and is similar to PAC-Bayesian bounds with $\Pr(h) = 2^{-|h|}$ (Langford 2002).

Beware of terminology—in classical mathematics have uniform convergence for a sequence, uniform convergence in probability for an estimator, and here uniform convergence for G.

Using Bernstein or empirical Bernstein instead of Hoeffding may give slightly better bounds. But they would still be too loose for practical use, and lose intuitive informativeness in proof of concept and intuitive guidance.

G is **agnostic PAC learnable** (Shalev-Schwatz & Ben-David 2014) if $\exists A$ such that $\forall \epsilon > 0$ and $p > 0$ $\exists n$ such that A returns a PAC($R_{oB} + \epsilon, p$) f. Though this defines an appealing complexity class, it's not useful. The original **PAC learnability** is less general, and assumes binary classification and that $R_{oB} = 0$. Class label 1 forms a **concept** $\subset X$, and the task is to identify it. This is less general than imposing a distribution on X and Y. A further assumption is that, because all computer information is binary with limited memory, G consists of a finite number of Boolean functions. This allows proving that certain Boolean learning tasks are learnable in polynomial time and certain others aren't. PAC is important only for historical reasons because it's creation developed significant interest in statistical learning theory.

But the "concept" concept is intuitively useful for classification because this is how humans learn. A don't benefit from the idea because estimating a partition is a less general problem than estimating concepts $\forall$ class. But concepts have an advantage in deciding that, e.g., a certain digit image isn't a digit at all and doesn't belong to any class. Technically, can handle this by creating a "don't know" class, but this is rarely done. To compare, regular classification requires a complete partition of X, though some parts of it won't correspond to x with nonnegligible probability or to x valid for the domain. Knowing the number of classes k is also useful domain knowledge.

$\exists$ several similar definitions stability, i.e., can bound $E[R_f - R_{f,n}]$, and use the Markov inequality to derive a tail bound from this (Shalev-Schwatz & Ben-David 2014).

Classical statistical rules for model selection such as AIC and variants (Burham & Anderson 2002) are effective for some statistical models. A model with the minimum AIC = (the number of parameters – the log-likelihood) is considered best. Flaws:

- Only applies to models with a clearly defined number of parameters and log-likelihood
- Use with small n needs corrections such as AICc
- Assumes that all considered models are reasonably effective
- The rules are asymptotic, often needing specific conditions for theoretical effectiveness

MDL doesn't have these problems and is more intuitive.

Around 2000, much progress has been made in learning theory due to applications of **concentration inequalities** and **Rademacher complexity** (Mohri et al 2012), which give useful finite sample bounds when used together.

Many things are known about cross-validation, and many aren't (Arlot & Celisse 2010). The lack of fold independence hasn't prevented improper use in statistical tests. E.g., for comparing two A, an occasionally recommended solution is to average the results of each fold, obtaining k supposedly iid normal estimates, and apply the paired t-test. A heuristic estimate of variance (Nadeau & Bengio 2003) can be reasonably accurate, but comes with no guarantees and underestimates variance in a simple problem (Kuncheva 2014). Hidden dependencies cause problems in many ways; e.g., 2-fold cross-validation may appear independent, but have similarity dependence because instances in one fold are too similar or too dissimilar to those in another, relative to a random sample.

Repeated holdout is partitioning data randomly into test and train sets of the same size many times. Repeated cross-validation with the same number of trainings has less variance.

For cross-validation, the limiting case $k = n - 1$, called **leave-one-out cross-validation** (LOOCV), is appealing due to giving an estimate for training on almost all n examples and not needing repetition (except when A is randomized or depends on the example order), but usually ineffective:

- Need considerably more time than even repeated cross-validation.

- Due to using test examples from the same data set instead of independent ones, the held out instances are either very similar/dissimilar to the training set instances, resulting in high variance estimates for many A. For regular cross-validation, the test set is more likely to have balance between similar and dissimilar instances. Intuitively, smaller k is faster and gives smaller estimate variance, and larger reduces estimate bias. LOOCV has high variance with respect to small changes to S. Unless A is random or depends on example order, LOOCV is deterministic by producing the same result on the same data, but the choice of S still gives it randomness.

For small data sets and very stable A, LOOCV can be the method of choice. But regular cross-validation does almost as well and is usually used regardless.

An interesting question for cross-validation is whether a deterministic permutation improves the stratified version. The logic is that despite stratification, the data may have some sort order.

A natural statistical alternative to cross-validation is using bootstrap to repeatedly train on n resamples and test on the whole data. But about 63.2% of the training data would be in the test set, leading to a too optimistic risk estimate. Testing only on data not picked for training removes this bias but overestimates risk because the training set has about 0.632 of the data. Intuitively, bootstrap isn't appropriate because its assumption that the distribution of the functional of the sample $\approx$ the distribution of the resamples is questionable due to strong influence of repeated data.

Many bias-variance decompositions have been proposed and used to make various conclusions (James 2003). Despite technical differences, all of them are similar enough so that general conclusions made by one carry out to another, particularly about stability and low bias.

For parameter selection, a theoretical question is whether using a selection strategy is consistent (Devroye et al. 1996). In practice, this tends to not matter because consistency applies in the limit, and many biases are negligible with large enough n.

A classic induction rule is **maximum likelihood**—assuming some probability model, pick the most likely parameters. It's similar to Bayesian MAP but only used for fitting parameters and not model selection. The reason is that the use of a prior in MAP has a stabilizing effect, while maximum likelihood overfits for model selection.

For crude MDL, using Cauchy PDF for errors will give logarithmic error, but more in spirit of compression because the latter is similar to universal gamma code. Also, for real labels can discretize error as $\lceil error/d \rceil$ for small discretization interval d, and encode with gamma directly, but this is clumsy. **Refined MDL**, a supposedly improved version of MDL, particularly in using optimal codes (Grunwald 2007), is complicated, and deriving its codes is nontrivial even for simple parametric models such as linear regression (with the result being similar to BIC) and doesn't work for nonparametric ones.

A more robust scaling can replace min and max by respectively maybe 5th and 95th percentiles, but this is probably unnecessary. A more expensive but interesting way to scale is to remember S and use it to transform values into ranks, which are truly scale-invariant. Also, it's interesting to investigate a hybrid of mean-variance and range scaling by centering the means at 0 and using a robust measure of scale instead of standard deviation.

Another main binning method is **equal frequency**, with bin ranges defined so that the number of data points in each bin is about the same. This way, every interval is supported by some examples. Want the number of bins such that each has enough examples for accurate estimation, so use $\sqrt{n}$, which presumably gives a good balance between approximation and estimation errors. This seems to slightly outperform other binning methods (Garcia et al. 2014). An interesting idea is to make each bin have maybe ≥ 30 items.

$\exists$ many other solutions to filling in missing values (Garcia et al. 2014), but all of them are questionable due to introducing bias. Another preprocessing method that isn't worth it is instance selection, either for efficiency or noise removal, because $!\exists$ nonheuristic ways to identify bad instances, and good A are good at taking the right info from each instance.

For small D, it's feasible to use human insight to improve learning. One technique is to plot all pairs of variables, including the hint, and see if $\exists$ a visual pattern. Also, can plot each feature individually and see its distribution.

For feature selection, **backward search** starts with a subset containing all features and greedily removes the least useful feature at a time. Used with oB, it finds a minimal subset that can't be further reduced without increasing risk. But with many weakly relevant features in the initial stages, it can easily remove some very good ones due to their seemingly small marginal benefit. Nevertheless, on typical data sets this doesn't seem to be a problem and "improvements" such as using single feature scores to resolve ties give worse results. Still, greedy forward search results in similar risk, is much faster, and finds smaller subsets. **Bidirectional search** combines results of both backward and forward searches but is slower than both and seems to result in similar risk.

Can try to improve single feature search by taking feature interactions into account. Evaluate A ∀ pairs of features, and, starting from an empty subset B, greedily add feature $\text{argmin}_i(R_i - \sum_{j \in B} R_{ij}/|B|)$ to it. The idea is that this should select a next feature as the most useful and least redundant one. But need $O(D^2)$ time and space, and experimentally this doesn't pay off in terms of the number of selected features or risk.

A frequently mentioned class of feature selection algorithms is **filter methods**, which quickly heuristically evaluate importance of a feature to eliminate or rank it. Those that look at one variable at a time usually aren't useful because single feature search is more general, can use a good A, and has similar efficiency with many decent A. Nevertheless, some are interesting.

Classical statistics suggests single variable tests which consider one feature at a time. Assuming numeric vector x, can use for:

- Numeric y—rank correlation—detects monotonic relationships.
- Categorical y—ANOVA—checks if the differences between category-specific means of continuous variables are significant. Can't use a more robust Friedman test because usually don't have equal number of z_i ∀ category.

Can use the results to directly remove insignificant features or create a sequence of subsets by greedily ranking them by significance, as in single feature search. Despite somewhat appealing nature of this:

- Neither a difference between means nor rank correlation imply that a feature is useful for the used A if they are significant and not if not
- The tests make assumptions that may not hold and pay no attention to multiple testing

It's also tempting to generate a feature report for the user, containing maybe range, mean, and median ∀ feature, along with some test results, but this isn't scalable, and wrappers do the job faster and better than the user, though occasionally a human can notice something useful.

A more advanced and perhaps the best-known filter is **mRMR** (Garcia at et. 2014). Similarly to all pairs wrapper search, it computes mutual information MI between all pairs of features and all features and y, and computes a collection of subsets by greedily adding feature $\text{argmin}_i(MI(x[i], y) - \sum_{j \in S} MI(x[i], x[j])/|B|)$. It performs similarly too, with an additional problem that currently the best practical way to estimate MI (Kraskov et al. 2004) needs using a 2D k-NN query, which can be made efficient in time but still needs $O(n)$ extra space.

Relief (Garcia at et. 2014) is similar, but also needs a k-NN query, suffers from similar flaws as mRMR, and is less general. With filters, an occasionally suggested alternative to subset selection is keeping some % of the best features, hoping they contain the best subset. This is dangerous because can easily select a subset that's too small due to not having feedback from A because filters don't know how the features will be used.

Due to lack of published experimental comparisons, many other feature selection algorithms have been proposed (Garcia et al. 2014; Bolon-Canedo 2014) but aren't practically useful.

Feature extraction (Garcia et al. 2014) maps all features into a presumably more informative feature space and uses some or all features in that space. Usually scale first. The quality usually depends on how well can reconstruct the original features or how well properties such as relative distances are preserved. Potential benefits:

- Smaller D and increased efficiency
- Smaller estimation error due to approximate representation of data, which averages out noise

But it's unclear how to do this well. Popular techniques have flaws:

- **Principal component analysis** (PCA) retains only $k < D$ vectors responsible for at least 95% of the variance in X. This needs computing a $D \times k$ transformation matrix in $O(nD^2)$ time and is reasonable for upto a medium D. But using variance directions effectively assumes a multivariate normal distribution of the data, so the result isn't effective for multipeak or other nonnormal distributions because PCA effectively loses info that a good A can use. Techniques such as **kernel PCA** (Hastie et al. 2009) and sparse PCA variants (Hastie et al. 2015) try to improve it, but the former has $O(n^3)$ runtime and the latter still don't help intelligent A.
- The **random projection method** computes a random projection matrix (Witten et al. 2011), which tends to preserve distances between x. But most A lose more from information loss than gain from

reduction in *D*, so don't have good use cases.

Feature transformations can hide irrelevant variables. Need extensive experimental evidence to justify general use of feature extraction.

An interesting model for online learning allows **drift**, i.e., changes of the distribution on *Z* (Gama 2010). This is complex to handle both theoretically and computationally.

20.22 References

Anguita, D., Ghelardoni, L., Ghio, A., & Ridella, S. (2013). A survey of old and new results for the test error estimation of a classifier. *Journal of Artificial Intelligence and Soft Computing Research*, *3*(4), 229–242.

Arlot, S., & Celisse, A. (2010). A survey of cross-validation procedures for model selection. *Statistics Surveys*, *4*, 40–79.

Bache, K. & Lichman, M. (2013). *UCI Machine Learning Repository* [http://archive.ics.uci.edu/ml]. University of California. Accessed 10/19/2014.

Bengio, Y., & Grandvalet, Y. (2004). No unbiased estimator of the variance of k-fold cross-validation. *The Journal of Machine Learning Research*, *5*, 1089–1105.

Bolón-Canedo, V. (2014). *Novel Feature Selection Methods for High Dimensional Data*. PhD Thesis.

Blum, A., Kalai, A., & Langford, J. (1999). Beating the hold-out: Bounds for k-fold and progressive cross-validation. In *Proceedings of the Twelfth Annual Conference on Computational Learning Theory* (pp. 203–208). ACM.

Breiman, L. (2001). Random forests. *Machine learning*, *45*(1), 5–32.

Devroye, L., Gyorfi, L., & Lugosi, G. (1996). *A Probabilistic Theory of Pattern Recognition*. Springer.

Dietterich, T. G. (1998). Approximate statistical tests for comparing supervised classification learning algorithms. *Neural computation*, *10*(7), 1895–1923.

Domingos, P. (1999). The role of Occam's razor in knowledge discovery. *Data Mining and Knowledge Discovery*, *3*(4), 409–425.

Domingos, P. (2000). A unified bias-variance decomposition. In *Proceedings of 17th International Conference on Machine Learning*. Morgan Kaufmann (pp. 231–238).

———. (2012). A few useful things to know about machine learning. *Communications of the ACM*, *55*(10), 78–87.

Gama, J. (2010). *Knowledge Discovery from Data Streams*. CRC Press.

García, S., Luengo, J., & Herrera, F. (2014). *Data Preprocessing in Data Mining*. Springer.

Grünwald, P. D. (2007). *The Minimum Description Length Principle*. MIT Press.

Guyon, I. (2008). Practical feature selection: from correlation to causality. *NATO Science for Peace and Security*, *19*, 27–43.

Hastie, T., Tibshirani, R., & Friedman, J. (2009). *The Elements of Statistical Learning*. Springer.

James, G. M. (2003). Variance and bias for general loss functions. *Machine Learning*, *51*(2), 115–135.

Kohavi, R. (1995). A study of cross-validation and bootstrap for accuracy estimation and model selection. In *IJCAI* (Vol. 14, No. 2, pp. 1137–1145).

———, & John, G. H. (1997). Wrappers for feature subset selection. *Artificial intelligence*, *97*(1), 273–324.

Kraskov, A., Stögbauer, H., & Grassberger, P. (2004). Estimating mutual information. *Physical Review E*, *69*(6), 066138.

Lattimore, T., & Hutter, M. (2013). No free lunch versus Occam's razor in supervised learning. In *Algorithmic Probability and Friends. Bayesian Prediction and Artificial Intelligence* (pp. 223–235). Springer.

Langford, J. (2002). *Quantitatively Tight Sample Complexity Bounds*. PhD thesis, Carnegie Mellon.

Mohri, M., Rostamizadeh, A., & Talwalkar, A. (2012). *Foundations of Machine Learning*. MIT Press.

Murray, I., & Ghahramani, Z. (2005). A note on the evidence and Bayesian Occam's razor.

Nadeau, C., & Bengio, Y. (2003). Inference for the generalization error. *Machine Learning*, *52*(3), 239–281.

Rissanen, J. (2008). Minimum description length. *Scholarpedia*, *3*(8), 6727.

Shalev-Shwartz, S., & Ben-David, S. (2014). *Understanding Machine Learning: From Theory to Algorithms*. Cambridge University Press.

Steinwart, I., & Christmann, A. (2008). *Support Vector Machines*. Springer.

Valentini, G., & Dietterich, T. G. (2004). Bias-variance analysis of support vector machines for the development of SVM-based ensemble methods. *The Journal of Machine Learning Research*, *5*, 725–775.

Vanwinckelen, G., & Blockeel, H. (2014). Look before you leap: some insights into learner evaluation with

cross-validation. In *JMLR: Workshop and Conference Proceedings* (pp. 1–17).
Witten, I. H., Frank, E., & Hall, M.A. (2011). *Data Mining: Practical Machine Learning Tools and Techniques*. Morgan Kaufmann.
Wolpert, D. H. (2002). The supervised learning no-free-lunch theorems. In *Soft Computing and Industry* (pp. 25–42). Springer.

21 Machine Learning—Classification

For some A, with $k = 2$ it's more convenient to have labels $\in \{-1, 1\}$. Many algorithms and theoretical results are for binary classifiers, but such results might apply to $k > 2$ at least heuristically because $\exists$ simple methods to reduce such problems to a collection of binary ones.

In many cases, need to count the number of distinct classes:

```
template<typename DATA> int findNClasses(DATA const& data)
{
    int maxClass = -1;
    for(int i = 0; i < data.getSize(); ++i)
        maxClass = max(maxClass, data.getY(i));
    return maxClass + 1;
}
```

21.1 Stratification by Class Label

Some algorithms are sensitive to the order of examples; particularly, want to prevent sorting by label. Randomizing data before partitioning and/or using stratified sampling usually corrects this. The latter usually suffices and gives repeatable partitioning by being deterministic.

```
template<typename DATA> pair<PermutedData<DATA>, PermutedData<DATA> >
    createTrainingTestSetsStatified(DATA const& data,
    double relativeTestSize = 0.8)
{
    int n = data.getSize(), m = n * relativeTestSize;
    assert(m > 0 && m < n);
    pair<PermutedData<DATA>, PermutedData<DATA> > result(data, data);
    Vector<int> counts(findNClasses(data)), p(n);//need p for legacy only
    for(int i = 0; i < n; ++i){++counts[data.getY(i)]; p[i] = i;}
    for(int i = 0; i < counts.getSize(); ++i) counts[i] *= relativeTestSize;
    for(int i = 0; i < p.getSize(); ++i)
    {
        int label = data.getY(p[i]);
        if(counts[label]){--counts[label]; result.first.addIndex(p[i]);}
        else
        {
            result.second.addIndex(p[i]);
            p[i--] = p.lastItem();
            p.removeLast();
        }
    }
    return result;
}
```

For cross-validation without stratification, need to randomize data in case the examples are sorted by class because breaking them up in folds naively creates substantial class imbalance. The implementation is tricky. It computes class sizes and, keeping track of the last used example $\forall$class, $\forall$fold marks examples to be used. Then the test set is created from the marked examples and used, and the original data is restored. For splitting and restoration to work, the included example numbers are sorted.

```
template<typename LEARNER, typename DATA, typename PARAMS>
    Vector<pair<int, int> > crossValidationStratified(PARAMS const& p,
    DATA const& data, int nFolds = 5)
{
    assert(nFolds > 1 && nFolds <= data.getSize());
    int nClasses = findNClasses(data), testSize = 0;
```

```
    Vector<int> counts(nClasses, 0), starts(nClasses, 0);
    PermutedData<DATA> pData(data);
    for(int i = 0; i < data.getSize(); ++i)
    {
        pData.addIndex(i);
        ++counts[data.getY(i)];
    }
    for(int i = 0; i < counts.getSize(); ++i)
        counts[i] /= nFolds;//roundoff goes to training
    for(int i = 0; i < counts.getSize(); ++i) testSize += counts[i];
    Vector<pair<int, int> > result;
    for(int i = 0;; ++i)
    {//create list of included test examples in increasing order
        Vector<int> includedCounts(nClasses, 0), includedIndices;
        for(int j = valMin(starts.getArray(), starts.getSize());
            includedIndices.getSize() < testSize; ++j)
        {
            int label = data.getY(j);
            if(starts[label] <= j && includedCounts[label] < counts[label])
            {
                ++includedCounts[label];
                includedIndices.append(j);
                starts[label] = j + 1;
            }
        }
        PermutedData<DATA> testData(data);
        for(int j = testSize - 1; j >= 0; --j)
        {
            testData.addIndex(includedIndices[j]);
            pData.permutation[includedIndices[j]] =
                pData.permutation.lastItem();
            pData.permutation.removeLast();
        }
        result.appendVector(evaluateLearner<int>(LEARNER(pData, p),
            testData));
        //put test data back into data in correct places
        if(i == nFolds - 1) break;
        for(int j = 0; j < testSize; ++j)
        {
            pData.addIndex(includedIndices[j]);
            pData.permutation[includedIndices[j]] =
                testData.permutation[testSize - 1 - j];
        }
    }
    return result;
}
```

21.2 Risk Estimation

The most common R_f is expected error = E[the % of misclassified examples]. It has a binomial distribution with some unknown mean, so using the Bernstein inequality for test set bounds is particularly suitable (see the "Monte Carlo Algorithms" chapter). **Empirical accuracy** = $1 - R_{f,n}$. For equally likely classes, the random f has expected $1/k$ accuracy.

Accuracy is sensitive to **class imbalance**, i.e., the data needn't come from a random sample that represents all classes well, which can easily happen due to human error or unequal costs of getting the data. E.g., if the digit data test set only had 90 *0* and 10 *1* digits, f that always returns 0 has 90% accuracy despite being useless. **Balanced error rate** (and correspondingly **balanced accuracy**) weighs each class equally. Bernstein applies to it too because, by a few algebraic manipulations, equal class weights are equivalent to using a generalized version of the inequality on the average of the example results, with class "counts" for class i ranging from 0 to $w_i = n/(n_i k)$. E.g., $0.75a + 0.25b = 0.5(1.5a + 0.5b)$. With these weights, use range $[0, M]$ for $M = \sqrt{(\sum w_i^2)/n}$, and apply the usual inequality.

Also, have limited knowledge about how much to trust each prediction. E.g., for the iris data, because seposa is linearly separable from others, predicting *seposa* is less likely to be wrong than *versicolor* or *virginica*. No R can account for this confidence. Think of it as conditional accuracy, i.e., accuracy on the predicted class. Models with very high confidences for some classes are useful—can trust confident enough decisions and send the rest to humans for review. E.g., if a system's performance is insufficient, a partially automated system with high performance is better than nothing. E.g., for credit card fraud detection, should be able to automatically flag most transactions as not suspicious, and use human labor only for investigating what is marked suspicious.

Some A can give reliable probability estimates for individual examples, though most don't because estimating probabilities is a more general problem, and the results tend to be less accurate than label predictions.

For f that only returns labels, the **confusion matrix** M gives complete information about the performance, containing the number of assigned examples ∀ predicted and actual label pair. A predicted label is a row coordinate, and an actual one a column one. Need $O(k^2)$ space to represent M and $O(n + k^2)$ time to compute it.

```
Matrix<int> evaluateConfusion(Vector<pair<int, int> >const& testResult,
    int nClasses = -1)
{
    if(nClasses == -1)
    {
        int maxClass = 0;
        for(int i = 0; i < testResult.getSize(); ++i) maxClass =
            max(maxClass, max(testResult[i].first, testResult[i].second));
        nClasses = maxClass + 1;
    }
    Matrix<int> result(nClasses, nClasses);
    for(int i = 0; i < testResult.getSize(); ++i)
        ++result(testResult[i].first, testResult[i].second);
    return result;
}
```

From M can compute many useful metrics by summing over its rows and columns:

- $t = \sum M[r, c]$ = the total number of examples in the test set
- $a = (\sum_{r \neq c} M[r, c])/t$ = accuracy
- $t_l = \sum M[r, l]$ = the number of examples with label l
- $a_l = (\sum_{r \neq l} M[r, l])/t_l$ = accuracy on examples with label l, also called **recall**
- $p_l = \sum M[l, c]$ = the number of examples with predicted label l
- $c_l = (\sum_{r \neq l} M[r, l])/p_l$ = confidence in prediction of label l, also called **precision**

These allow defining derived metrics, such as **balanced accuracy** = $(\sum a_l)/k$. E.g., consider a single-feature binary data set with decision boundary 00100|111. Here, precision(0) < recall(0) but precision(1) > precision(1). For the averages, the 0/0 NaNs are skipped. But when c_l = NaN, it makes sense to have $f_l = a_l$ but not the other way around because a label should always be represented unless the data set is incomplete, though a classifier might not assign any examples to it.

Bernstein bounds are used for all of these. They apply to both accuracies and precisions because applicable data points are independent given an actual or a decided label.

```
struct ClassifierStats
{
    struct Bound
    {
        double mean, lower, upper;
        Bound(): mean(0), lower(0), upper(0) {}
        Bound(double theMean, pair<double, double> const& bounds):
            mean(theMean), lower(bounds.first), upper(bounds.second) {}
        Bound operator+=(Bound const& rhs)
```

```
        {
            mean += rhs.mean;
            lower += rhs.lower;
            upper += rhs.upper;
        }
        Bound operator*=(double a)
        {
            mean *= a;
            lower *= a;
            upper *= a;
        }
    };
    Bound acc, bac;
    Vector<Bound> accByClass, confByClass;
    int total;
    static Bound getBound(IncrementalStatistics s)
    {
        double inf = numeric_limits<double>::infinity();
        pair<double, double> bound(-inf, inf);
        double mean = inf;
        if(s.n > 0)
        {
            mean = s.getMean();
            bound = s.bernBounds(0.95);
        }
        return Bound(mean, bound);
    }
    ClassifierStats(Matrix<int>const& confusion): total(0)
    {//same row = same label, same column = same prediction
        Vector<int> confTotal, accTotal;
        int k = confusion.getRows(), nBac = 0, actualK = 0;
        IncrementalStatistics accS, basSW;
        Vector<IncrementalStatistics> precS(k);
        Vector<double> weights(k);
        for(int r = 0; r < k; ++r)
        {
            int totalR = 0;
            for(int c = 0; c < k; ++c)
            {
                totalR += confusion(r, c);
                weights[r] += confusion(r, c);
                total += confusion(r, c);
            }
            accTotal.append(totalR);
            actualK += (totalR > 0);
        }
        double M = 0;
        for(int r = 0; r < k; ++r)
        {
            weights[r] = total/weights[r]/actualK;
            IncrementalStatistics bacS;
            for(int c = 0; c < k; ++c)
            {
                int count = confusion(r, c);
                bool correct = r == c;
                while(count--)
                {
                    accS.addValue(correct);
                    basSW.addValue(correct * weights[r]);
```

```
                    M += weights[r] * weights[r];
                    bacS.addValue(correct);
                    precS[c].addValue(correct);
                }
            }
            accByClass.append(getBound(bacS));
        }
        M = sqrt(M/total);
        for(int c = 0; c < k; ++c)
        {
            int totalC = 0;
            for(int r = 0; r < k; ++r) totalC += confusion(r, c);
            confTotal.append(totalC);
            confByClass.append(getBound(precS[c]));
        }
        acc = getBound(accS);
        bac = getBound(basSW);
        bac.lower *= M;
        bac.upper *= M;
    }
};
```

Random forest (discussed later in this chapter) results for the digits data:

```
acc.mean * total 1749
total 1798
Accuracy: 0.97274749721913234 95% Bernstein range: 0.9594249042106171 0.98195767
205284434
Balanced Accuracy: 0.97270040745096531 95% Bernstein range: 0.95945573317337196
0.98200763962286763
Accuracy by class and 95% range:
0.99438202247191O1 0.93860022778231333 1
0.99450549450549453 0.93989491350553755 1
0.98870056497175141 0.92948549076491593 0.99962107534647271
0.95081967213114749 0.87850212432285202 0.98328226194444546
1 0.94864386376293519 1
0.97252747252747251 0.90741271249304201 0.99436062668930714
0.98342541436464093 0.92271875110723123 0.99836810928949227
0.93296089385474856 0.85450788038747305 0.97283426310194276
0.94857142857142862 0.87323004997885156 0.98251206328016949
0.96111111111111114 0.89125115081927508 0.98903015527237759
Confidence by class and 95% range:
0.98333333333333328 0.92230794372861469 0.99835903257744307
0.96276595744680848 0.89566829178234331 0.98949939877632798
1 0.94695552926728999 1
0.98305084745762716 0.92104889735403872 0.99833118633475804
0.98369565217391308 0.92392551868986350 0.99839474678494455
0.97790055248618779 0.91471789374552614 0.99654341794807821
0.98888888888888893 0.93061128037750407 0.99962739273497692
0.98235294117647054 0.91794622745839183 0.99826238497361208
0.94318181818181823 0.86657671488121391 0.97931126443590866
0.92513368983957223 0.84706727570717977 0.96712601669207O1
```

Probably all of them are useful for describing f's performance on a particular task. The difficult question is which single one or combination to use for optimizing parameters and comparing A. Currently, $!\exists$ the best answer, but balanced accuracy is probably the safest bet for most cases because it:

- Forces f to treat all cases equally, which may be a priority even if the examples represent a true biased distribution.
- Is equal to overall accuracy with perfectly balanced classes.
- Is a special case of risk over an input distribution that expects all labels to occur equally.
- Not always $\leq$ accuracy. When performance on minority classes is better, have average accuracy > accuracy.

A small flaw of balanced accuracy is that it has higher variance than accuracy in case of strong class imbalance because a few examples have large impact on it. So accuracy has slightly more accurate confidence due to better binomial approximation and average precision has slightly worse confidence because class preferences may be very uneven, resulting in less accurate binomial conversion.

Accuracy is preferred in many cases because it's built into many algorithms and allows influencing the input distribution by assuming S is representative or resampling. In particular, the implementation of cross-validation uses accuracy as a single metric to pick parameters. Intuitively, using accuracy moves margins (discussed later in this chapter) further from the majority and using average accuracy from the minority, but with no class imbalance both give the same result.

```
template<typename LEARNER, typename DATA, typename PARAMS> double
    crossValidation(PARAMS const& p, DATA const& data, int nFolds = 5)
{
    return ClassifierStats(evaluateConfusion(
        crossValidationStratified<LEARNER>(p, data, nFolds))).acc.mean;
}
template<typename LEARNER, typename PARAM, typename DATA>
struct SCVRiskFunctor
{
    DATA const& data;
    SCVRiskFunctor(DATA const& theData): data(theData) {}
    double operator()(PARAM const& p)const
        {return 1 - crossValidation<LEARNER>(p, data);}
};
```

One problem with accuracy and balanced accuracy is not distinguishing predictors that have mediocre confidence ∀ label and high confidence on some labels and poor on others. Accuracy and other binomial measures tend to have high variance for small n because need many 0/1 observations to express risk with reasonable precision. The overall recommendation is using balanced accuracy for the final evaluation and accuracy for creating f.

21.3 Reducing Multiclass to Binary

∃two simple ways to extend binary learners for $k > 2$. **One vs all** (OVA) works for f that output probabilities. It trains k binary learners which aim to output *1* if $y = k$, and the result is the largest output label.

One vs one (OVO) trains $O(k^2)$ learners for all combinations of binary classifiers and chooses the class with most votes. It's usually better:

- If the actual class wins all the time and the rest are arbitrary, the result is always correct and fairly robust if the rest are random. E.g., for digits, *2* vs *3* wouldn't know what to do with a *7* and make a somewhat random choice.
- Asymptotic efficiency—though need more trainings, each is much faster due to solving a smaller problem; thus faster overall as most A are superlinear.
- Decision boundaries between any two classes are simpler, and class imbalance is less of a problem. E.g., for the iris data, versicolor, which is between seposa and verginica, can't be separated by a single line with OVA, but can be with OVO. Theoretically, OVO leads to a smaller worst case approximation error than other methods (Daniely et al. 2012).
- The implementation stratifies two-class data to improve learning for many online algorithms such as SGD.

```
template<typename DATA> struct RelabeledData
{
    DATA const& data;
    typedef typename DATA::X_TYPE X_TYPE;
    typedef typename DATA::Y_TYPE Y_TYPE;
    typedef typename DATA::X_RET X_RET;
    Vector<Y_TYPE> labels;
    RelabeledData(DATA const& theData): data(theData) {}
    int getSize()const{return data.getSize();}
    void addLabel(Y_TYPE y){labels.append(y);}
    void checkI(int i)const
    {
        assert(i >= 0 && i < data.getSize() &&
            labels.getSize() == data.getSize());
    }
    X_RET getX(int i)const
    {
```

```
        checkI(i);
        return data.getX(i);
    }
    double getX(int i, int feature)const
    {
        checkI(i);
        return data.getX(i, feature);
    }
    Y_TYPE const& getY(int i)const
    {
        checkI(i);
        return labels[i];
    }
};
template<typename LEARNER, typename PARAMS = EMPTY, typename X = NUMERIC_X>
class MulticlassLearner
{//if params not passed, uses default value!
    mutable ChainingHashTable<int, LEARNER> binaryLearners;
    int nClasses;
public:
    Vector<LEARNER const*> getLearners()const
    {
        Vector<LEARNER const*> result;
        for(typename ChainingHashTable<int, LEARNER>::Iterator i =
            binaryLearners.begin(); i != binaryLearners.end(); ++i)
            result.append(&i->value);
        return result;
    };
    template<typename DATA> MulticlassLearner(DATA const& data,
        PARAMS const&p = PARAMS()): nClasses(findNClasses(data))
    {
        Vector<Vector<int> > labelIndex(nClasses);
        for(int i = 0; i < data.getSize(); ++i)
            labelIndex[data.getY(i)].append(i);
        for(int j = 0; j < nClasses; ++j) if(labelIndex[j].getSize() > 0)
            for(int k = j + 1; k < nClasses; ++k)
                if(labelIndex[k].getSize() > 0)
                {
                    PermutedData<DATA> twoClassData(data);
                    RelabeledData<PermutedData<DATA> >
                        binaryData(twoClassData);
                    for(int l = 0, m = 0; l < labelIndex[j].getSize() ||
                        m < labelIndex[k].getSize(); ++l, ++m)
                    {
                        if(l < labelIndex[j].getSize())
                        {
                            twoClassData.addIndex(labelIndex[j][l]);
                            binaryData.addLabel(0);
                        }
                        if(m < labelIndex[k].getSize())
                        {
                            twoClassData.addIndex(labelIndex[k][m]);
                            binaryData.addLabel(1);
                        }
                    }
                    binaryLearners.insert(j * nClasses + k,
                        LEARNER(binaryData, p));
                }
    }
```

```
    int predict(X const& x)const
    {
        Vector<int> votes(nClasses, 0);
        for(int j = 0; j < nClasses; ++j)
            for(int k = j + 1; k < nClasses; ++k)
            {
                LEARNER* s = binaryLearners.find(j * nClasses + k);
                if(s) ++votes[s->predict(x) ? k : j];
            }
        return argMax(votes.getArray(), votes.getSize());
    }
    int classifyByProbs(X const& x)const
    {
        Vector<double> votes(nClasses, 0);
        for(int j = 0; j < nClasses; ++j)
            for(int k = j + 1; k < nClasses; ++k)
            {
                LEARNER* s = binaryLearners.find(j * nClasses + k);
                if(s)
                {
                    double p = s->evaluate(x);
                    votes[k] += p;
                    votes[j] += 1 - p;
                }
            }
        return argMax(votes.getArray(), votes.getSize());
    }
};
```

21.4 Complexity Control

A good measure of complexity C of G, consisting of binary classifiers for vector data, is **VC-dimension** = max d such that $\exists d$ x, arranged so that $\forall$ assignment of binary labels to them, $\exists f \in G$ that can separate (**shatter**) them. E.g., a line can separate three points in 2D, but not four (e.g., the xor problem).

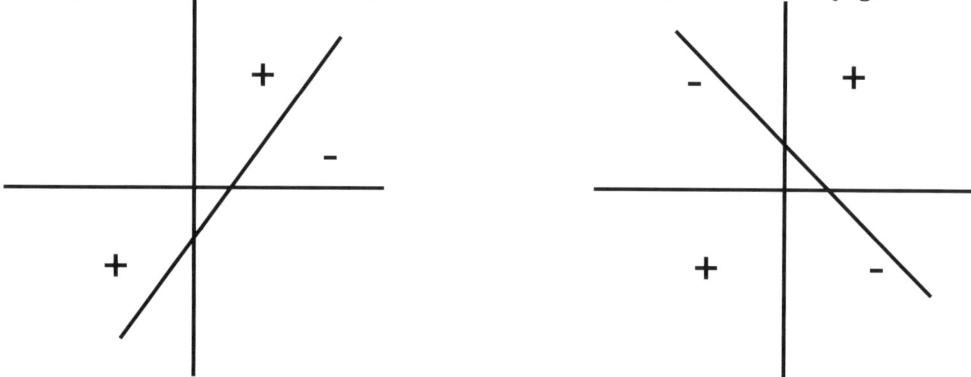

So for 2D lines, $d = 3$. For D-dimensional hyperplanes, $d = D + 1$. E.g., can solve the xor problem by a split along the z-coordinate.

Can bound generalization error by a function of $R_{f,n}$, n, and d. Theorem (Mohri et al. 2012): Let G have VC-dimension d. Then with probability $\geq 1 - p$, $R_f \leq R_{f,n} + \sqrt{2d\ln(en/d)/n} + \sqrt{-\ln(p)/(2n)}$. So if $n/d \to \infty$ as $n \to \infty$, $R_{f,n} \to R_f$. E.g., even hyperplanes can overfit for $D \approx n$. The intuition is that though can have uncountably many $f \in G$, each can classify n examples in finitely many ways. Occam bounds are usually, but not always, worse than VC-dimension ones—e.g., for G = {sine functions}, VC-dimension = ∞, but the description is quite small.

For SRM, can consider H_i with $i + 1 = d$; thus $w_i = 6/(\pi d)^2$. Then the search objective = $R_{h,n} + \sqrt{2d\ln(en/d)/n} + \sqrt{(2\ln(\pi d) - \ln(6p))/(2n)}$; the 3rd term is tiny relative to the 2nd for reasonable p. If know d, this is easy to calculate but applies only to $k = 2$, and the bound is loose unless n is large enough to counter the pessimism of d. In particular, model selection using theoretical upper bounds based on VC-dimension is less effective than cross-validation (Hastie et al. 2009).

Margin is distance of a patch of examples of a particular class to partition boundaries. E.g., in case of 2D data and a line that splits it, the margin = the smallest distance of any example to the line. Intuitively, the larger the margin, the more certain is the partition, so in some cases can bound risk as a function of the margin, which usually gives much better bounds than using d or ORM. A very complex f can have small margins and much smaller risk bounds than suggested by complexity bounds. Many successful algorithms implicitly or explicitly maximize margins in some way. Still, for known A, margins don't fully explain R_f. They are equivalent to more general bias-variance decomposition (Domingos 2000), but more intuitive in most cases.

Borderline examples are close to partition boundaries and involved in forming the margins. Label noise in these is more problematic than in interior examples due to affecting margins (Garcia et al. 2014). Can't detect noise without enough support from correct examples.

Class boundary complexity is the source of approximation error. It can have arbitrarily large Kolmogorov complexity. ∃ some metrics of data complexity (Orriols-Puig et al. 2010), but they don't seem effective. E.g., the number of support vectors in a SVM or the size of an unpruned decision tree (both covered later in this chapter) seem more informative and are simpler. Also, the amount of SVM margin violation in is a good measure of linear separability of classes.

21.5 Impossibility Results

Theorem (Devroye et al. 1996): ∀A that uses n examples for learning f and $\epsilon > 0$ ∃ a problem with $R_{oB} = 0$ such that $R_f \geq ½ + \epsilon$. This **no free lunch** (NFL) theorem confirms that some problems need arbitrarily many examples. Also it suggests that no particular A is best in all cases because for one that is bad for some problem another may do well. Some A are better than others in most practical cases, which this NFL allows.

Theorem (Mohri et al. 2012; Anthory & Bartlett 1999): Let G have VC-dimension $d > 1$. Then ∀n such that $\epsilon = \sqrt{d/(320n)} \leq 1/64$, ∀$A$ that returns $f \in G$, ∃ a problem such that $\Pr(R_h - \min_{f \in G} R_f > \epsilon) \geq 1/64$. This holds even for finite G and A that remember all examples because examples are sampled and ∃ a problem that withholds enough examples from A during training to meet the bound. This doesn't contradict the upper bound on risk—can make probability of a larger ϵ (which can be made arbitrarily small) arbitrarily small.

The general problem with lower bounds is that they apply only to the restricted model considered. E.g., radix sort still works in $O(n)$ time, despite the comparison model's $n\lg(n)$ lower bound. Likewise, this bound assumes that know d for the problem exactly, which usually isn't true. E.g., for G = {sine functions}, $d = \infty$ because it can shatter any number of points, but if frequency and amplitude take $O(1)$ bits to represent, this is no longer true. In general, considering numerical restrictions and X boundaries gives lower d. No bounds are preventing estimation error from being 0 for most problems, but the lower bound is conceptually interesting because always $d > 0$, even if data that invokes it is unlikely practice.

21.6 Naive Bayes

Assume x consist of independent categorical features (equivalently discrete features with bounded range). By the independence, $\Pr(x|y) = \prod_j \Pr(\text{the value of feature } j|y)$, which is called **likelihood**. Estimate Pr(value| y) by (the number of examples with the value ∈ class/the number of examples ∈ class). These counts start from 1 to not divide by 0 and as prior info to stabilize probabilities. To avoid underflow, compute likelihood as **log likelihood**. This doesn't change comparison results because log is monotonically increasing.

1. **∀class and feature value initialize the count to 1**
2. **∀example**
3. **∀feature value increment the count associated with it and *y***
4. **At prediction ∀class *i***
5. **Find $ll_i = \sum_j \ln$(estimated Pr(the value of feature *j*|class *i*)) using counts for class *i***
6. **Return $\text{argmin}_i(ll_i)$**

```
class NaiveBayes
{
    struct Feature
    {
        int count;
        LinearProbingHashTable<int, int> valueCounts;
```

```
        Feature(): count(0) {}
        void add(int value)
        {
            ++count;
            int* valueCount = valueCounts.find(value);
            if(valueCount) ++*valueCount;
            else valueCounts.insert(value, 1);
        }
        double prob(int value)
        {
            int* valueCount = valueCounts.find(value);
            return (valueCount ? 1 + *valueCount : 1)/(1.0 + count);
        }
    };
    typedef ChainingHashTable<int, Feature> FEATURE_COUNTS;
    typedef ChainingHashTable<int, FEATURE_COUNTS> CLASS_COUNTS;
    mutable CLASS_COUNTS counts;
public:
    typedef Vector<pair<int, int> > SPARSE_CATEGORICAL_X;
    static SPARSE_CATEGORICAL_X convertToSparse(CATEGORICAL_X const& x)
    {
        SPARSE_CATEGORICAL_X result;
        for(int i = 0 ; i < x.getSize(); ++i)
            result.append(make_pair(i, x[i]));
        return result;
    }
    void learn(SPARSE_CATEGORICAL_X const& x, int label)
    {
        for(int i = 0; i < x.getSize(); ++i)
        {
            FEATURE_COUNTS* classCounts = counts.find(label);
            if(!classCounts) classCounts = &counts.insert(label,
                FEATURE_COUNTS())->value;
            Feature* f = classCounts->find(x[i].first);
            if(!f) f = &classCounts->insert(x[i].first, Feature())->value;
            f->add(x[i].second);
        }
    }
    int predict(SPARSE_CATEGORICAL_X const& x)const
    {
        double maxLL;
        int bestClass = -1;
        for(CLASS_COUNTS::Iterator i = counts.begin(); i != counts.end();
            ++i)
        {
            double ll = 0;
            for(int j = 0; j < x.getSize(); j++)
            {
                Feature* f = i->value.find(x[j].first);
                if(f) ll += log(f->prob(x[j].second));
            }
            if(bestClass == -1 || maxLL < ll)
            {
                maxLL = ll;
                bestClass = i->key;
            }
        }
        return bestClass;
    }
```

```
};
```

Features are rarely independent and need a lot of data to sufficiently cover every feature–class–value combination, so on most tasks naive Bayes isn't competitive with the best methods, but for some it is. But it has many advantages:

- Learning n examples with D features, k classes, and v values takes $O(nD)$ time and $O(Dkv)$ space, and classifying takes $O(kD)$ time.
- Very reliable by ORM because the complexity term $O(\sqrt{Dkv/n})$ is very small for large n.
- Learning is online, allowing appearance of new classes, features, and feature values.
- Natural handling of sparse features and missing values. E.g., this makes naive Bayes the method of choice for e-mail spam classification.

Can handle numeric data using equal-width binning:

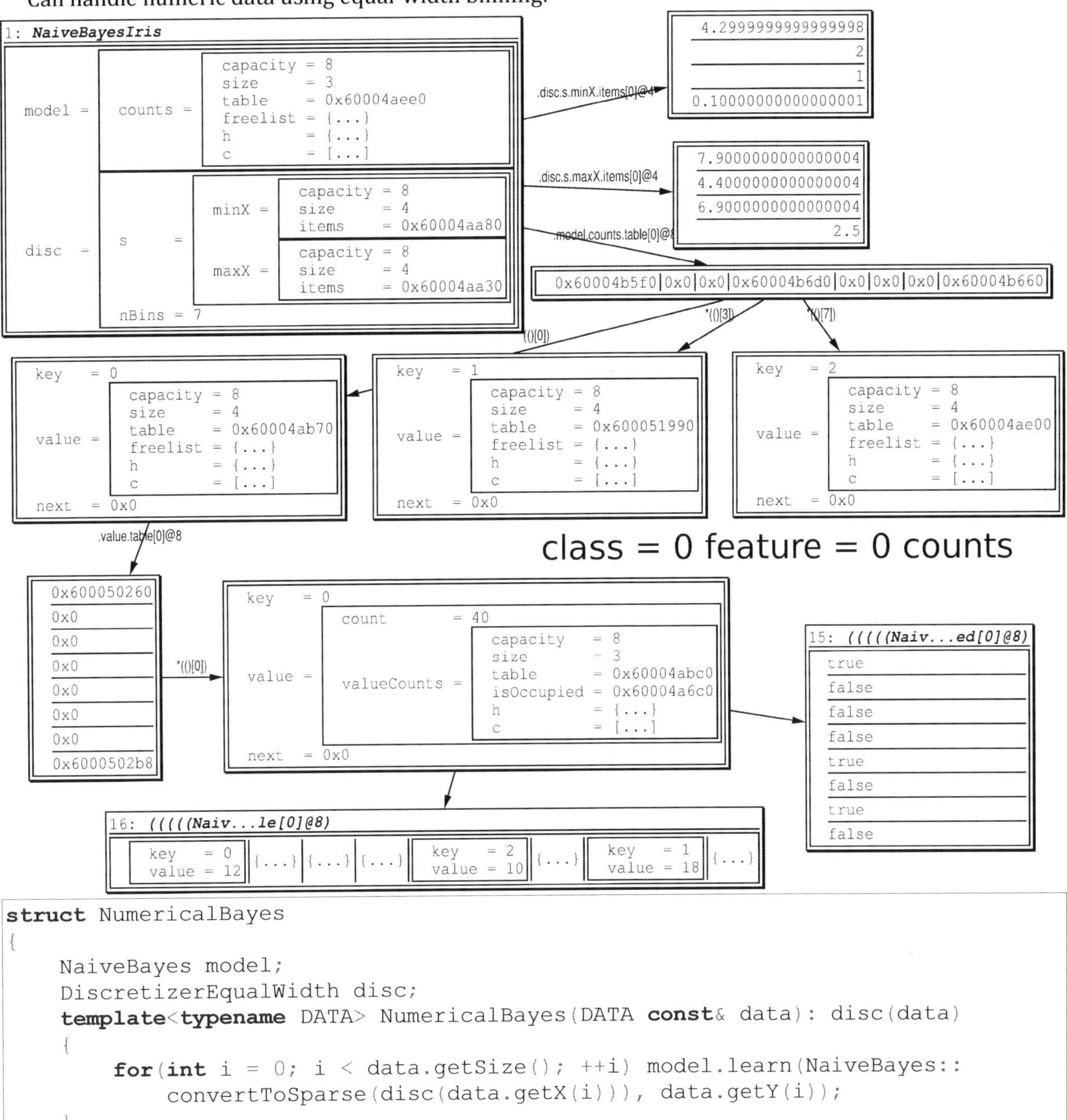


```
struct NumericalBayes
{
    NaiveBayes model;
    DiscretizerEqualWidth disc;
    template<typename DATA> NumericalBayes(DATA const& data): disc(data)
    {
        for(int i = 0; i < data.getSize(); ++i) model.learn(NaiveBayes::
            convertToSparse(disc(data.getX(i))), data.getY(i));
    }
    int predict(NUMERIC_X const& x)const
        {return model.predict(NaiveBayes::convertToSparse(disc(x)));}
};
```

But this needn't work well and isn't online; naive Bayes is useful only for discrete or easily discretized data.

21.7 Nearest Neighbor

When X has a distance function, remembering S and classifying by returning the class of the nearest example reduces to the nearest neighbor problem (see the "Computational Geometry" chapter):

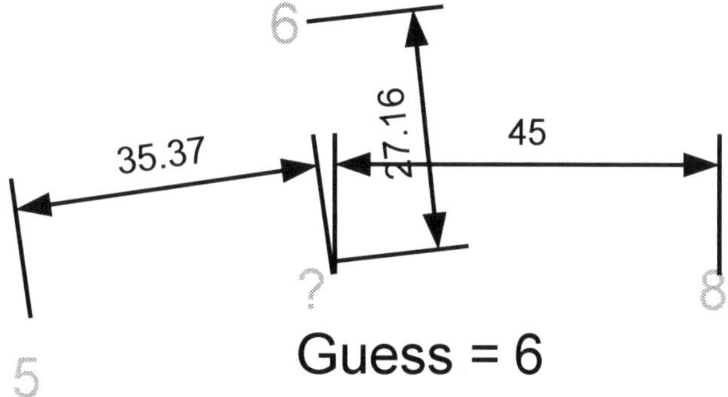

Distances must be meaningful and properly scaled. E.g., Euclidean distance in age-height space doesn't mean much. Equivalently, can have the distance function do the scaling.

More generally, can use majority class of k (don't confuse with the number of classes) nearest neighbors (k-NN) for $k > 1$. If X is a vector space with $D < \infty$, as $n \to \infty$ (Devroye et al. 1996):

- If $k \to \infty$ and $k/n \to 0$, k-NN is universally consistent
- $R_{1\text{-NN}} \leq R_{oB}(1 - R_{oB}) \leq 2R_{oB}$
- For odd k, $R_{(k+1)\text{-NN}} = R_{k\text{-NN}} \leq R_{oB} + (ke)^{-½}$

These don't hold if $D = \infty$ or for general metric spaces (Cerou & Guyader 2006). Scaling is irrelevant because change of scale is equivalent to change of P. Because want odd k, $k = 2\lfloor \lg(n)/2 + 1\rfloor$ seems to be a good default. It satisfies consistency, agrees with typical recommendation $k = 3$ or 5 to avoid high variance of using $k = 1$, and on my tests performs as well as k selected by cross-validation (all performance measures use curved balanced accuracy, averaged across several data sets; "S" notation means default [0, 1] range scaling):

SKNN_oddlg	MQKNN_oddlg	S1NN
0.910	0.900	0.900

Bias-variance analysis suggests that for fixed n, as k increases, bias increases and variance decreases (Domingos 2000), which also supports increasing k with n. The runtime of a k-NN query also increases with k due to less effective bounds.

```
template<typename X = NUMERIC_X, typename INDEX = VpTree<X, int, typename
    EuclideanDistance<X>::Distance> > class KNNClassifier
{
    mutable INDEX instances;
    int n, nClasses;
public:
    KNNClassifier(int theNClasses): nClasses(theNClasses), n(0) {}
    template<typename DATA> KNNClassifier(DATA const& data): n(0),
        nClasses(findNClasses(data))
    {
        for(int i = 0; i < data.getSize(); ++i)
            learn(data.getY(i), data.getX(i));
    }
    void learn(int label, X const& x){instances.insert(x, label); ++n;}
    int predict(X const& x)const
    {
        Vector<typename INDEX::NodeType*> neighbors =
            instances.kNN(x, 2 * int(log(n))/2 + 1);
        Vector<int> votes(nClasses);
        for(int i = 0; i < neighbors.getSize(); ++i)
```

```
            ++votes[neighbors[i]->value];
        return argMax(votes.getArray(), votes.getSize());
    }
};
```

On training data, 1-NN has perfect accuracy, but it's VC-dimension is n, and $|h|$ is O(n), so neither VC-dimension nor ORM bounds guarantee generalization. But further assumptions give a finite sample bound. Theorem (Shalev-Schwartz & Ben-David 2014): Let $P(y|x)$ be Lipschitz continuous with constant c, X a vector space, and $k > 1$. Then for Euclidean distance $R_{k\text{-NN}} \leq (1 + \sqrt{8/k})R_{\text{oB}} + (6c\sqrt{D} + k)/n^{1/(D+1)}$. Because c is usually unknown, this doesn't even help select k.

But it illustrates the curse of dimensionality—learning becomes more difficult with large D. For points distributed uniformly $\in [0, 1]^D$, the distribution of distances is highly skewed to the maximum distance, so it's easier to pick a wrong neighbor due to noisy features instead of true closeness. But for typical practical data the performance is usually good because the underlying dimension of that data is much smaller, and the distances in its feature space don't have the same problem because the distribution in X is far from uniform.

Don't need to know the number of classes if use a hash table instead on the votes array. In practice, k-NN has high accuracy even with little training data, but uses too much memory and can be slow for large D, perhaps even enough to not quality for real time applications. So it doesn't scale beyond medium n. Overall, k-NN is useful only for nonvector data, where can come up with a good distance function such as edit distance between strings, and for vector data only as a simple second-opinion method.

A somewhat different approach is **nearest mean**—compute centroids of each class and assign x to the class of the nearest centroid. It's not competitive (being a simplification of LDA; discussed in the comments) but interesting because it corresponds to ***k*-means** for clustering (see the "Machine Learning—Other Tasks" chapter), and it's mediocre performance (≈84%) suggests a similar problem for k-means.

21.8 Decision Tree

Create a binary tree where nodes look at specific feature values to decide which branch to take, and leaves give the resulting class. This is very similar to what k-d tree (see the "Computational Geometry Algorithms" chapter) does. The latter typically uses the next-in-order feature with the value of a random example as split, while the former greedily picks the best feature and value. **Decision trees are easily interpretable by a human**, thus with unknown data they are the first A to use for getting some intuition about the data.

Creating an optimal tree using any reasonable error measure is NP-complete (Hyafil & Rivest 1976). Practical construction greedily proceeds top-down, picking the best feature and its value as the split point for the root, and recursively constructing its children.

A good split criteria is entropy = $\sum \text{H}(p_i)$, with p_i = the % of examples of class i ($\text{H}(p) = p\text{lg}(p)$; see the "Compression" chapter). Want a split that minimizes the total entropy after split = the number of left child examples × entropy(left child examples) + the number of right child examples × entropy(right child examples). With equally accurate splits, entropy favors those where in the resulting nodes some classes are more concentrated than others, so prefer it over accuracy. Intuitively, with every split, entropy gains more information about the labels by being able to compress them better. Eventually, all examples in a leaf have the same label, entropy = 0, and splitting stops.

For a numerical feature, have $n - 1$ possible splits at the root. An efficient way to pick the best one is sorting the values and considering all splits one by one from left to right, updating after each split the left and the right count tables ∀ class, and recomputing entropy from these. Considering all splits at the root takes O($n$lg(n)D) time.

The worst case depth is n, and a tree that reaches it would overfit and take much longer to build, so need to restrict the depth. The best case depth = lg($nClasses$) due to similarity of examples. Typical depth for a modestly effective tree is probably based on the fact that most data remains in a single large chunk, and every split peels off a small fraction a of it. Here depth = lg(n)/lg($1/a$) and, because max depth mostly controls runtime and not complexity, the default max depth = 50 seems robust for most data sets of different sizes and difficulty because smaller values wouldn't improve runtime by much and larger values won't improve generalization. Depth restriction makes it unnecessary to use a stack instead of recursion. Some problems need greater depth, i.e., D-dimensional xor needs a complete binary tree of depth D, but meaningful data usually doesn't have such complexity. Using a larger number such as 100 buys a little safety at the expense of efficiency loss when for difficult tasks deep nodes are created and later pruned (pruning is explained later).

Decision trees have no error on the training set (unless depth restriction stops growth), and thus overfit. ∀ function ∃ a decision tree that represents it arbitrarily well. For $k = 2$, VC-dimension of a tree = the number of leaves (Shalev-Schwartz & Ben-David 2014), which is not a specific function of depth but is bounded by depth restriction. A common solution to overfitting is **pruning**, i.e., replacing a subtree by a majority leaf. This loses accuracy on the training data, but usually improves generalization because decisions not justified enough by data are replaced by the safer majority ones. E.g., for $k = 2$, a subtree created by a split using purely random, falsely appealing feature that results in two leaves will have 50% accuracy, but majority vote is better or equal if correctly picked the majority class.

A simple way to decide if to prune a subtree is by using the sign test (see the "Monte Carlo Algorithms" chapter). A correctly/incorrectly classified example by both the tree and the node is a draw, otherwise it's a win for whoever got it right. Because the subtree isn't worse than the node, the number of wins for the node and the subtree is respectively *nDraws*/2 and (*nDraws*/2 + the difference in correctly classified examples). By default, pruning uses *z*-score = 1, which overprunes a little but gives a much simpler tree. Experimentally, 0.5 and 0.25 give the best results, and values > 1 do poorly for most tested data sets. Selecting *z*-score using cross-validation doesn't improve and is slower.

DT_zcv_50	DT-z0_50	DT-z0.25_50	DT-z0.5_50	DT-z1_50	DT-z2_50
0.899	0.907	0.910	0.901	0.871	0.783

Pruning is done recursively, on the way back after a tree is constructed and not before to avoid a situation like the xor problem, where any first feature isn't effective and any second one is. Multiple testing due to applying the sign test many times isn't a problem because, assuming balanced splits, only ≈50% of the data are the same for two different tests, which appears to be sufficient. The overall algorithm:

1. **Find the best split using incremental calculation**
2. **Split the data based on it into left and right parts**
3. **Recurse on the parts until get a pure node or exceed some depth *m***
4. **Try to prune**

The implementation assumes numerical *x* and has several safeguards to avoid issues with bad data. Also, it support random forest mode (discussed later in this chapter), which is implemented simply, but can avoid memory use through online reservoir sampling.

```
struct DecisionTree
{
    struct Node
    {
        union
        {
            int feature;//for internal nodes
            int label;//for leaf nodes
        };
        double split;
        Node *left, *right;
        bool isLeaf(){return !left;}
        Node(int theFeature, double theSplit): feature(theFeature),
            split(theSplit), left(0), right(0) {}
    }*root;
    Freelist<Node> f;
    double H(double p){return p > 0 ? p * log(1/p) : 0;}
    template<typename DATA> struct Comparator
    {
        int feature;
        DATA const& data;
        double v(int i)const{return data.data.getX(i, feature);}
        bool isLess(int lhs, int rhs)const{return v(lhs) < v(rhs);}
        bool isEqual(int lhs, int rhs)const{return v(lhs) == v(rhs);}
    };
    void rDelete(Node* node)
```

```
{
    if(node)
    {
        rDelete(node->left);
        f.remove(node->left);
        rDelete(node->right);
        f.remove(node->right);
    }
}
typedef pair<Node*, int> RTYPE;
template<typename DATA> RTYPE rHelper(DATA& data, int left, int right,
    int nClasses, double pruneZ, int depth, bool rfMode)
{
    int D = data.getX(left).getSize(), bestFeature = -1,
        n = right - left + 1;
    double bestSplit, bestRem, h = 0;
    Comparator<DATA> co = {-1, data};
    Vector<int> counts(nClasses, 0);
    for(int j = left; j <= right; ++j) ++counts[data.getY(j)];
    for(int j = 0; j < nClasses; ++j) h += H(counts[j] * 1.0/n);
    int majority = argMax(counts.getArray(), nClasses),
        nodeAccuracy = counts[majority];
    Bitset<> allowedFeatures;
    if(rfMode)
    {//sample features for random forest
        allowedFeatures = Bitset<>(D);
        allowedFeatures.setAll(0);
        Vector<int> p = GlobalRNG.sortedSample(sqrt(D), D);
        for(int j = 0; j < p.getSize(); ++j)allowedFeatures.set(p[j], 1);
    }
    if(h > 0) for(int i = 0; i < D; ++i)//find best feature and split
        if(allowedFeatures.getSize() == 0 || allowedFeatures[i])
        {
            co.feature = i;
            quickSort(data.permutation.getArray(), left, right, co);
            int nRight = n, nLeft = 0;
            Vector<int> countsLeft(nClasses, 0), countsRight = counts;
            for(int j = left; j < right; ++j)
            {//incrementally roll counts
                int label = data.getY(j);
                ++nLeft;
                ++countsLeft[label];
                --nRight;
                --countsRight[label];
                double fLeft = data.getX(j, i), hLeft = 0,
                    fRight = data.getX(j + 1, i), hRight = 0;
                if(fLeft != fRight)
                {//don't split equal values
                    for(int l = 0; l < nClasses; ++l)
                    {
                        hLeft += H(countsLeft[l] * 1.0/nLeft);
                        hRight += H(countsRight[l] * 1.0/nRight);
                    }
                    double rem = hLeft * nLeft + hRight * nRight;
                    if(bestFeature == -1 || rem < bestRem)
                    {
                        bestRem = rem;
                        bestSplit = (fLeft + fRight)/2;
                        bestFeature = i;
```

```
                    }
                }
            }
        }
        if(depth <= 1 || h == 0 || bestFeature == -1)
            return RTYPE(new(f.allocate())Node(majority, 0), nodeAccuracy);
        //split examples into left and right
        int i = left - 1;
        for(int j = left; j <= right; ++j)
            if(data.getX(j, bestFeature) < bestSplit)
                swap(data.permutation[j], data.permutation[++i]);
        if(i < left || i > right)
            return RTYPE(new(f.allocate())Node(majority, 0), nodeAccuracy);
        Node* node = new(f.allocate())Node(bestFeature, bestSplit);
        //recursively compute children
        RTYPE lData = rHelper(data, left, i, nClasses, pruneZ, depth - 1,
            rfMode), rData = rHelper(data, i + 1, right, nClasses, pruneZ,
            depth - 1, rfMode);
        node->left = lData.first;
        node->right = rData.first;
        //try to prune
        int treeAccuracy = lData.second + rData.second,
            nTreeWins = treeAccuracy - nodeAccuracy, nDraws = n - nTreeWins;
        if(signTestAreEqual(nDraws/2.0, nDraws/2.0 + nTreeWins, pruneZ))
        {
            rDelete(node);
            node->left = node->right = 0;
            node->label = majority;
            node->split = 0;
            treeAccuracy = nodeAccuracy;
        }
        return RTYPE(node, treeAccuracy);
    }
    Node* constructFrom(Node* node)
    {
        Node* tree = 0;
        if(node)
        {
            tree = new(f.allocate())Node(*node);
            tree->left = constructFrom(node->left);
            tree->right = constructFrom(node->right);
        }
        return tree;
    }
public:
    template<typename DATA> DecisionTree(DATA const& data, double pruneZ = 1,
        bool rfMode = false, int maxDepth = 50): root(0)
    {
        assert(data.getSize() > 0);
        int left = 0, right = data.getSize() - 1;
        PermutedData<DATA> pData(data);
        for(int i = 0; i < data.getSize(); ++i) pData.addIndex(i);
        root = rHelper(pData, left, right, findNClasses(
            data), pruneZ, maxDepth, rfMode).first;
    }
    DecisionTree(DecisionTree const& other)
        {root = constructFrom(other.root);}
    DecisionTree& operator=(DecisionTree const& rhs)
        {return genericAssign(*this, rhs);}
```

```
    int predict(NUMERIC_X const& x)const
    {
        if(!root) return 0;
        Node* current = root;
        while(!current->isLeaf()) current = x[current->feature] <
            current->split ? current->left : current->right;
        return current->label;
    }
};
```

The resulting tree for the iris data uses only petal length (feature *2*) and gets 100% accuracy on seposa (label *0*) and versicolor (label *1*), but only 60% on virginica (label *2*):

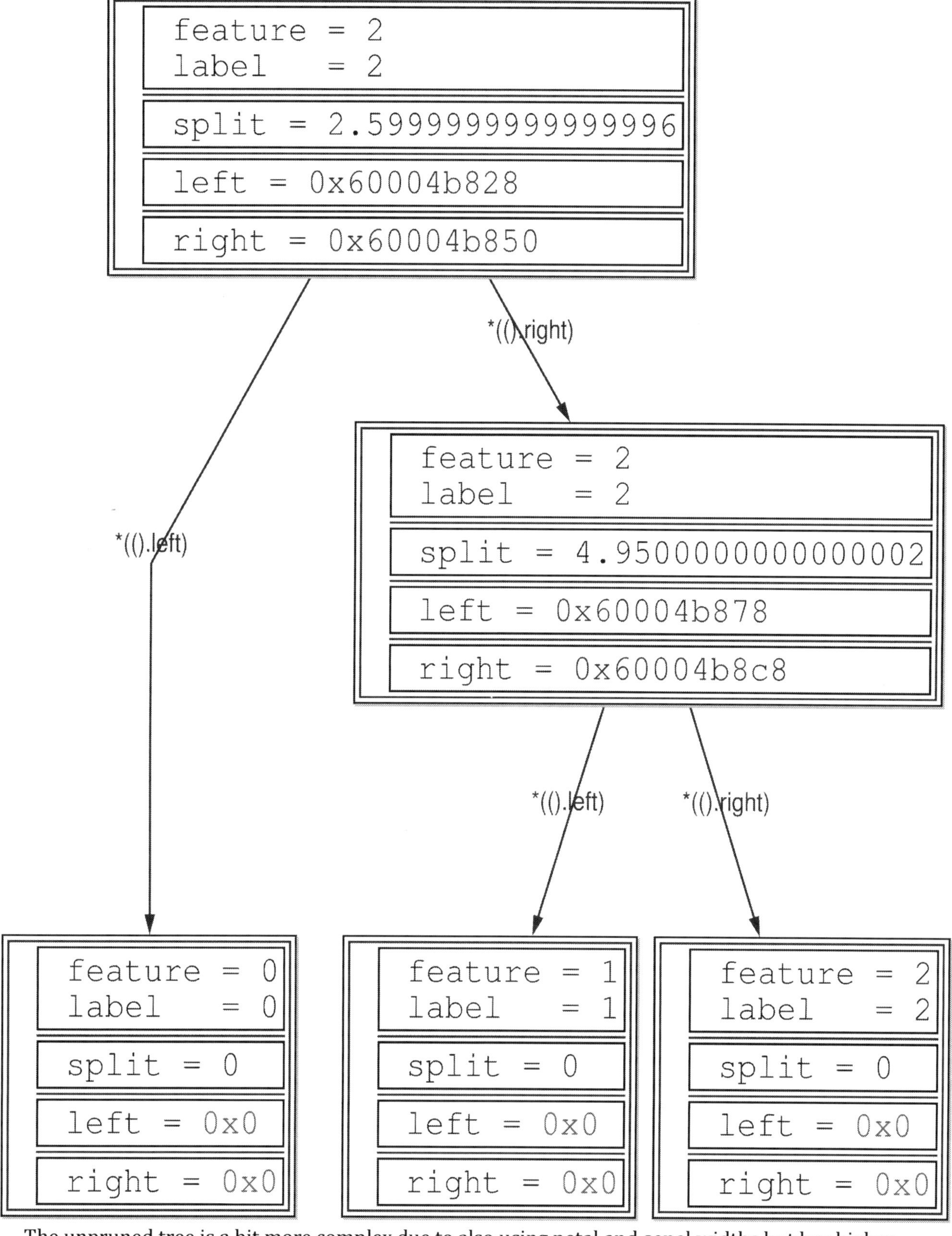

The unpruned tree is a bit more complex due to also using petal and sepal widths but has higher accuracy:

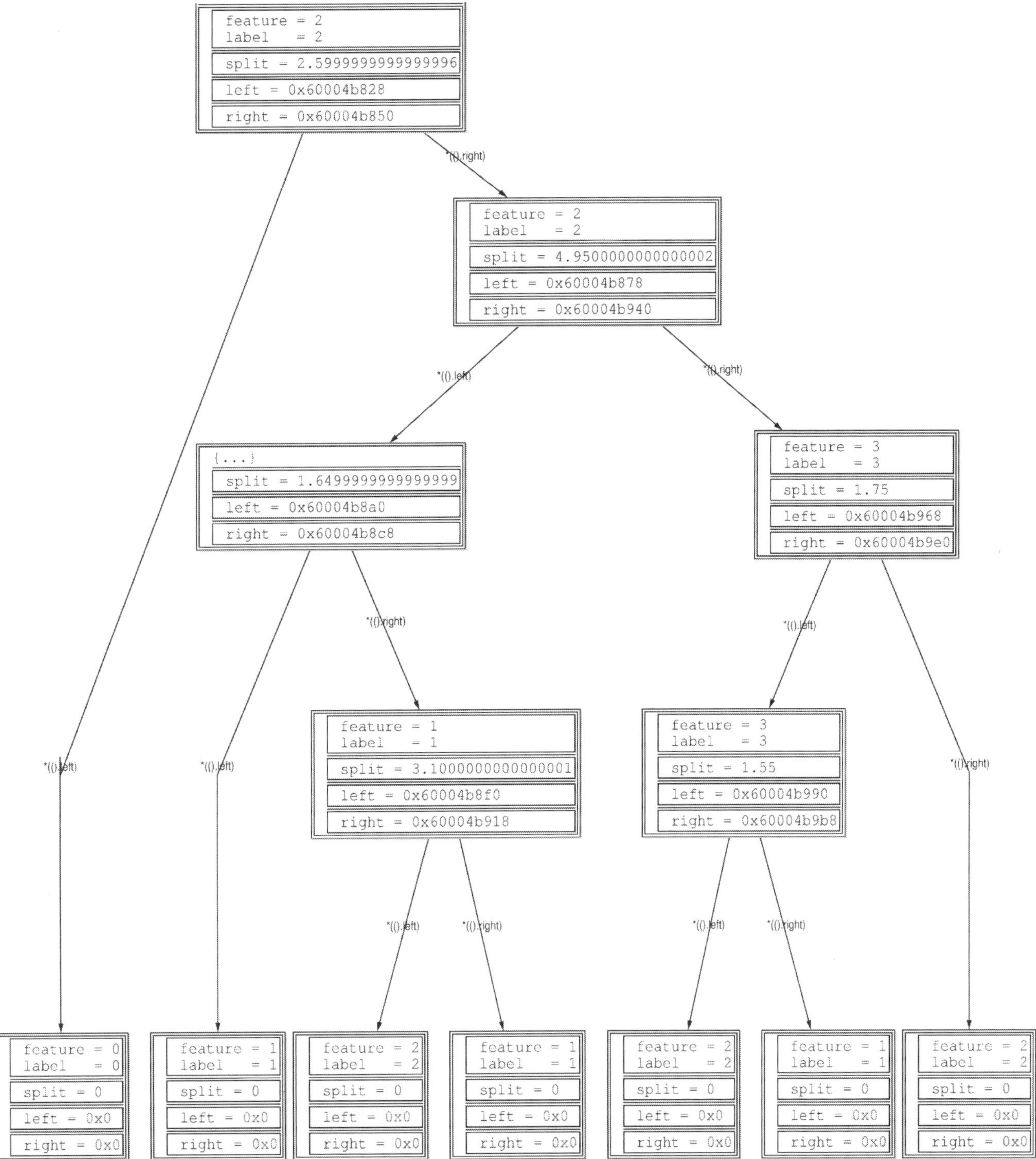

Assuming balanced splits, because for the root (and recursively ∀ node with n examples) picking the split takes $O(n\lg(n)Dk)$ time, the total work for the root $C(n) = 2C(n/2) + O(n\lg(n)Dk)$, so by the master theorem $C(n) = O(n\lg(n)^2Dk)$. Because max depth is m, the worst case is $O(mn\lg(n)Dk)$. Pruning doesn't affect this.

Applying ORM is interesting. The set of decision trees is easily encoded with an ad hoc code. Because `sizeof(Node)` = 16, with m nodes and $p = 0.05$, the complexity term = $\sqrt{120m\ln(2) + \ln(40))/m}$, which leads to useless bounds. To optimize, can encode tree structure using 2 bits per node, i.e., using depth first traversal to write a node, then 1 bit for the left child, and 1 bit for the right. Feature id needs $\lceil\lg(D)\rceil$ bits and label $\lceil\lg(k)\rceil$. For a split, can scale the data into [0, 1] and represent to precision 0.001, so about 10 bits should be enough; scaling has no influence on the logic because decision trees are scale-invariant. Have $m/2$ internal nodes and $m/2 + 1$ leaves, so $|h| \approx m(10 + \lg(kD)/2)$, which is much better but still not good enough.

For $k = 2$, getting a tree with d leaves means (by the VC-dimension bound) that with $p = 0.05$ have the complexity term $\approx \sqrt{d\ln(2en/d)/n} + \sqrt{1.5/n}$. This is slightly better than the ORM bound.

The number of used features $\leq 2^{\text{max depth}} \leq n$ because each branch can use different features and having a leaf at depth m means that the examples getting to it must pass m checks. This makes overfitting exponentially more likely in depth, though usually the same features are selected, making decision tree a good embedded feature selector.

Flaws of decision tree:

- Not universally consistent because ∃ distributions where splitting based on entropy fails to make progress on S of size ∞ (Devroye et al. 1996). In practice, this isn't a problem because data sets tend not to have such structure.
- Decision boundaries tend to be very coarse, consisting of piecewise functions. If the data is linearly separable, this doesn't matter if the margin is wider than coarseness. Random forests and boosting (covered later in this chapter) smooth out the boundary, usually increasing accuracy.
- Instability (Breiman 1996). Small changes in the data lead to large changes in the structure, but little change in overall accuracy. With heavy pruning, this is less of a problem but still can be.

21.9 Support Vector Machine

SVM is a theoretically good classifier with very good practical performance on many types of data. The basic version works with $k = 2$. If the data is linearly separable, ∃a set of hyperplanes $f(x) = wx + b$ such that $\forall x_i \in$ data $f(x_i) < 0$ when $y_i = -1$ and > 0 when $y_i = 1$. SVM computes a hyperplane separating the two classes, with w and b such that the margin = min distance(x_i, hyperplane) is maximal, i.e., the x_i closest to the hyperplane are equidistant to it. Intuitively, when walking in a minefield, it's best to walk between the mines.

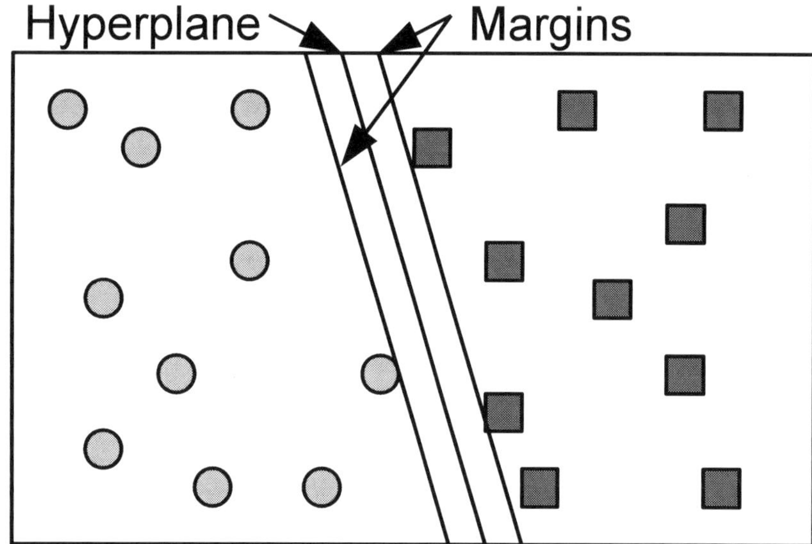

Distance(x, hyperplane) = $f(x)/||w||$. Because can scale f to produce arbitrary margins, normalize to get a canonical hyperplane where $\min|f(x)| = 1$. So for support vectors, $|f(x)| = 1$, and the margin = $1/||w||$—maximizing it is equivalent to minimizing w^2. General SVM works linearly nonseparable data by:

- Mapping x to a higher dimensional enhanced feature space using function F. The hyperplane becomes $f(x) = wF(x) + b$.
- Allowing some x_i to be outside the margins. Though a properly chosen F can make linearly nonseparable data separable, this handles noise better (Bottou et al. 2007). Use slack variables ϵ_i to decide to what degree x_i can be outside.

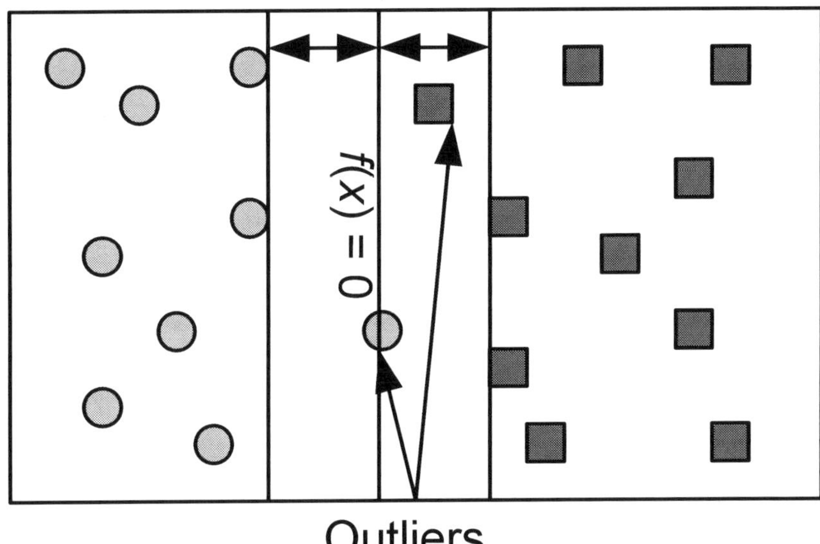

So have constrained optimization problem (Bottou et al. 2007):

- min ½w^2 + $C\sum\epsilon_i$ subject to
- $y_i f(x_i) \geq 1 - \epsilon_i$
- $\epsilon_i \geq 0$

A constant $C > 0$ defines the trade-off between margin size and accuracy; $C = 0$ means no x_i can be outside. The cases, depending on $y_i f(x_i)$:

- > 1—correctly classified and away from but on the right side of the margin
- = 1—correctly classified and on the margin
- > 0 and < 1—correctly classified and inside the margin
- < 0—incorrectly classified and on the wrong side of the margin

Though can plug in VC-dimension d of a hyperplane to bound risk, better analysis is possible. The simplest case is when the data is linearly separable. Theorem (Mohri et al. 2012): Assume that the coordinate plane is shifted so that the optimal $b = 0$. Let r be the radius of the smallest hypersphere containing the data in the enhanced space and Q such that $\min_i|f(x_i)| = 1$ and $1/||w|| \leq Q$ size of the margin. Then $\forall$ hyperplane with such w, $d \leq (rQ)^2$. So parameter values and not just their number bound d, and maximizing the margins is a legitimate goal.

21.10 Linear SVM

Using the identity feature map results in linear SVM, which is restricted to linear class boundaries but much is faster to train and works online. SVM constrains imply that $\epsilon_i = \max(0, 1 - y_i f(x_i))$, leading to an equivalent unconstrained problem min ½$lw^2 + \sum\max(0, 1 - y_i f(x_i))$, with $l = 1/C$. Prefer penalty $l|w|$ because using L_1 regularization of the weights (also called **lasso**) tends to produce a **sparse solution**, with many $w_i = 0$ (Hastie et al. 2015). This is because in the equivalent constrained problem the feasible region contains cusps corresponding to some variables set to 0, and one of them is likely to attain the best feasible level set:

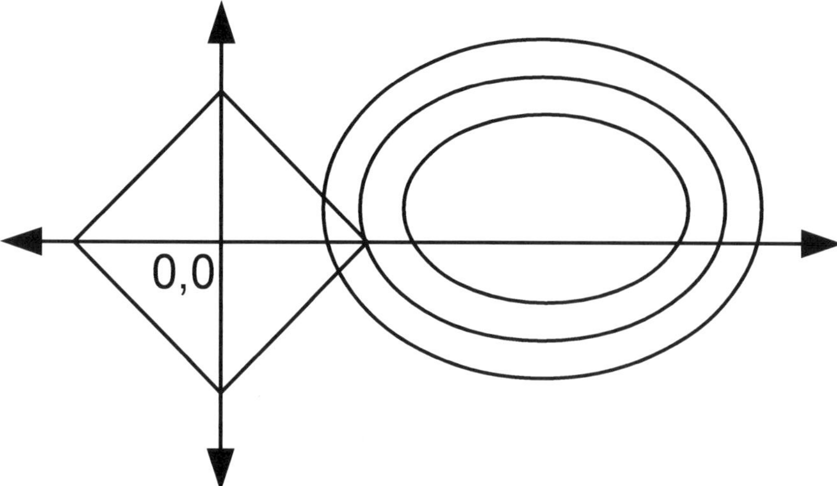

This problem is convex, but not differentiable. Using SGD gives a good approximate solution (Montavon et al. 2012; Sra et al. 2011) and allows online learning. For a nondifferentiable function, need an expression whose expected value is a subgradient of the function. Here, the subgradient is the sum, and use $n \times$ the value of example i, for random i. The update equations for observing example i:

- $\forall\ 0 \le j \le D$, w_{ij} $-=$ $r_i(w_{ij} > 0\ ?\ 1 : -1)l - n(y_i f(x_i) > 1\ ?\ 0 : y_i x_i))$
- b $+=$ $r_i(y_i f(x_i) > 1\ ?\ 0 : y_i)$

These make intuitive sense—examples outside the margin increase it, and examples on the correct side shrink it. Presenting close to margin examples first or last gives a different answer, so order matter. For parameters:

- The initial learning rate = 1, which seems to work well for many problems, without divergence.
- The number of passes over the data = $\lceil 10^5/n \rceil$ because SGD convergence asymptotically is $O(\sqrt{n})$. This reaches relative precision O(0.003), which seems reasonable and performs well in my experiments. For very large n, only do a single pass, and it may not be necessary to go through all data. For small n, a single pass isn't enough.
- Order = stratified by class or random. The default order can have examples sorted by class, so stratified is usually the best, but random may be simpler and has known theoretical performance.

Though SGD is good for generalization, it's not for deciding which coefficients are 0 to get a sparse solution, due to slow convergence. Doing the latter is an active research topic (Hastie et al. 2015), but coordinate descent (see the "Numerical Algorithms" chapter) usually does well in batch mode. To optimize one weight at a time efficiently, use $f(x_i) = \text{sum}_i + w_{ij}x_{ij}$ or $\text{sum}_i + b$, with sum_i being the sum of the untouched weights. So can evaluate the impact of variable j in O(n) time, independently of D. The 1D optimizations are solved using bracketing and golden section (see the "Numerical Algorithms" chapter).

Coordinate descent isn't guaranteed to converge or be fast, but usually no problems happen. For the implementation:

- Max iterations = 100.
- Termination precision $\epsilon = 10^{-6}\ \forall$ coordinate, and single variable search precision = $\epsilon/10$. This allows not doing golden section when the bracket interval is within the termination precision.
- For bracket search, the initial step size = 1 and is adjusted to the distance moved in previous iteration for the same coordinate.
- Because SGD is good at initial convergence and for robustness when coordinate descent gets stuck, do it first.

1. **$\forall$ pass process every example with SGD**
2. **Run coordinate descent to get better precision**
3. **For prediction, given *x*, compute the hyperplane margin and classify accordingly**

```
class BinaryLSVM
{
    Vector<double> w;
    double b, l;
    int learnedCount;
```

```
    static int y(bool label){return label * 2 - 1;}
    static double loss(double fxi, double yi){return max(0.0, 1 - fxi * yi);}
    double f(NUMERIC_X const& x)const{return w * x + b;}
    template<typename DATA> struct GSL1Functor
    {
        DATA const& data;
        Vector<double> sums;
        double l;
        int j;
        double operator()(double wj)const
        {
            double result = j < 0 ? 0 : l * abs(wj);
            for(int i = 0; i < data.getSize(); ++i) result += loss(sums[i] +
                (j < 0 ? 1 : data.getX(i, j)) * wj, y(data.getY(i)));
            return result/data.getSize();
        }
    };
    template<typename DATA>void coordinateDescent(DATA const& data, double l,
        int maxIterations, double eps)
    {
        int D = getD(data);
        GSL1Functor<DATA> f =
            {data, Vector<double>(data.getSize(), b), l, -1};
        for(int i = 0; i < data.getSize(); ++i)
            for(int j = 0; j < D; ++j)
                f.sums[i] += w[j] * data.getX(i, j);
        bool done = false;
        Vector<double> prevDiffs(D + 1, 1);
        while(!done && maxIterations--)
        {
            done = true;
            for(int j = -1; j < D; ++j)
            {
                double &wj = (j < 0 ? b : w[j]);
                for(int i = 0; i < data.getSize(); ++i)
                    f.sums[i] -= j < 0 ? b : w[j] * data.getX(i, j);
                f.j = j;
                double& pd = prevDiffs[j < 0 ? D : j];
                double left = findIntervalBound(f, wj, -pd),
                    right = findIntervalBound(f, wj, pd);
                if(right - left > eps)
                {
                    double wjNew = minimizeGS(f, left, right, eps/10).first;
                    pd = abs(wj - wjNew);
                    if(pd > eps) done = false;
                    wj = wjNew;
                }
                for(int i = 0; i < data.getSize(); ++i)
                    f.sums[i] += j < 0 ? b : w[j] * data.getX(i, j);
            }
        }
    }
public:
    BinaryLSVM(pair<int, double> const& p): w(p.first), l(p.second), b(0),
        learnedCount(0) {}
    template<typename DATA> BinaryLSVM(DATA const& data, double theL,
        int nGoal = 100000, int nCoord = 100): l(theL), b(0),
        w(getD(data)), learnedCount(0)
    {
```

```
        for(int j = 0; j < ceiling(nGoal, data.getSize()); ++j)
            for(int i = 0; i < data.getSize(); ++i)
                learn(data.getX(i), data.getY(i), data.getSize());
        coordinateDescent(data, l, nCoord, pow(10, -6));
    }
    int getLearnedCount(){return learnedCount;}
    void learn(NUMERIC_X const& x, int label, int n = -1)
    {
        if(n == -1) n = learnedCount + 1;
        double rate = RMRate(learnedCount++), yl = y(label);
        for(int i = 0; i < w.getSize(); ++i)
            w[i] -= rate * (w[i] > 0 ? 1 : -1) * l/n;
        if(yl * f(x) < 1)
        {
            w -= x * (-yl * rate);
            b += rate * yl;
        }
    }
    int predict(NUMERIC_X const& x)const{return f(x) >= 0;}
};
```

For many problems, even coordinate descent doesn't get wanted precision, but currently !∃ known better methods. Coordinate descent is slow when the data is stored on disk example by example because of noncontiguous access. To apply it, store the data in D contiguous pieces, each containing all examples from single feature. Even in memory, if have extra, should use a buffer to remove the slowdown due to repeated data pipeline evaluation, particularly scaling.

SLSVM100k	SLSVMcd100	mqLSVMsgd100kcd100	SLSVMsgd100kcd100
0.880	0.772	0.915	0.918

LSVM can't solve the xor problem with $k = 2$ because !∃ a line that can. Despite such lack of modeling power, it's a useful method for many problems where D is high or the classes are mostly separable.

For $k > 2$ use OVO. For better estimation, it's best to use a single l for all binary learners. Pick C using grid search with cross-validation among values 2^i, with odd $i \in [-15, 5]$. For best generalization, start with large l first.

```
    template<typename MODEL, typename DATA>
    static double findL(DATA const& data)
    {
        int lLow = -15, lHigh = 5;
        Vector<double> regs;
        for(double j = lHigh; j > lLow; j -= 2) regs.append(pow(2, j));
        return valMinFunc(regs.getArray(), regs.getSize(),
            SCVRiskFunctor<MODEL, double, DATA>(data));
    }
struct NoParamsLSVM
{
    typedef MulticlassLearner<BinaryLSVM, double> MODEL;
    MODEL model;
    template<typename DATA> NoParamsLSVM(DATA const& data): model(data,
        BinaryLSVM::findL<MODEL, DATA>(data)) {}
    int predict(NUMERIC_X const& x)const{return model.predict(x);}
};
typedef ScaledLearner<NoParamsLearner<NoParamsLSVM, int>, int> SLSVM;
```

21.11 Kernel SVM

For problems like xor, !∃ linear separators but ∃ nonlinear ones. The simplest way to introduce nonlinearity is to include artificial features that are nonlinear functions of the original features. Kernels are good at this. It doesn't make sense to use L_1 regularization with kernels because removing features in the enhanced space doesn't affect features in the original space, so directly minimize margins.

With kernels, the problem is still convex because both the objective and the constraints are convex, so strong duality holds (Mohri et al. 2012). The Lagrangian $L = ½w^2 + C\sum\epsilon_i - \sum a_i(y_if(x_i) - 1 + \epsilon_i) - \sum c_i\epsilon_i$. The KKT conditions at the optimum (see the "Numerical Algorithms" chapter) are:

1. $0 = \nabla_w L = w - \sum a_iy_if(x_i) \rightarrow w = \sum a_iy_if(x_i)$
2. $0 = \nabla_b L = -\sum a_iy_i \rightarrow \sum a_iy_i = 0$
3. $0 = \nabla_{\epsilon i} L = C - a_i - c_i$
4. $0 = a_i(y_if(x_i) - 1 + \epsilon_i)$
5. $0 = c_i\epsilon_i$
6. $a_i, c_i \geq 0$

(3) and (6) imply $0 \leq a_i \leq C$. The cases:

- $a_i = C \rightarrow 0 < \epsilon_i = 1 - y_if(x_i) \rightarrow$ inside or on the wrong side of the margin
- $a_i = 0 \rightarrow \epsilon_i = 0 \rightarrow$ correctly classified and beyond the margin
- $0 < a_i < C \rightarrow 0 = \epsilon_i = 1 - y_if(x_i) \rightarrow$ correctly classified and on the margin, can compute b from these

Plugging in the dual values for w leads to $L = ½(\sum a_iy_if(x_i))^2 - \sum a_iy_if(x_i)(\sum a_iy_if(x_i)) + \sum a_i - b\sum a_iy_i + \sum\epsilon_i(C - a_i - c_i)$. The first two parts combine and last two are 0, so $L = \sum a_i - ½\sum a_iy_ia_jy_jK_{ij}$. $\forall i$ such that $0 < a_i < C$, $b = y_i - \sum a_jy_jK_{ij}$. Directly using K and simplifying, get:

- max $V(a) = \sum a_i - ½\sum a_iy_ia_jy_jK_{ij}$ subject to
- $0 \leq a_i \leq C$
- $\sum a_iy_i = 0$

Can solve this standard SVM formulation using a quadratic programming library for the optimal a_i^*; then $f(x) = \sum a_iy_i^*K(x_i, x) + b$. **Support vectors** are x_i for which $a_i^* > 0$. Numerically, use the typical precision $\sqrt{\text{machine epsilon}}$ (such small value may seem surprising, but most examples are never touched during optimization). The solution stores them with the corresponding x_i and y_i.

The special structure of the problem allows a simpler and more efficient solution than by quadratic programming. Let $d_i = y_ia_i$ (also $a_i = y_id_i$) and $[L_i, H_i] = [0, C]$ if $y_i = 1$ and $[-C, 0]$ otherwise, so get:

- max $\sum y_id_i - ½\sum d_id_jK_{ij}$ subject to
- $L_i \leq d_i \leq H_i$
- $\sum d_i = 0$

By Osuma decomposition theorem (Bottou et al. 2007), iteratively optimizing over any subset of two or more variables converges to the solution. In particular, $\forall$ two variables i and j, d_i and d_j are in a box defined by the constraints:

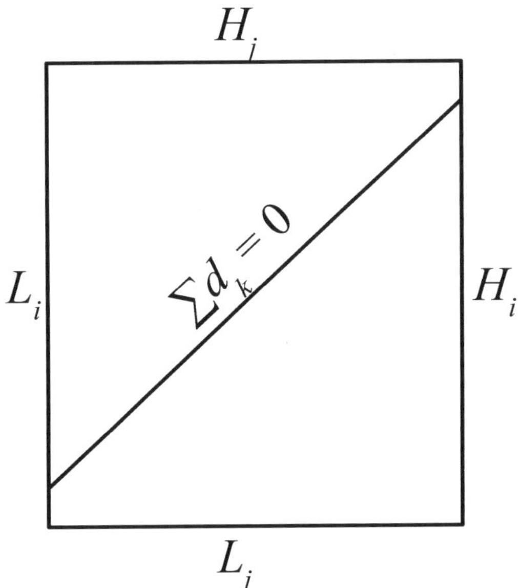

Let $g_k = \nabla V(d_k)[k] = y_k - \sum d_lK_{kl}$ (the "½" disappears due to symmetry). If the solution isn't optimal, $\exists$ i such that $d_i < H_i$ and j such that $d_j > L_j$, so that can increase V by increasing d_i and decreasing d_j by some step s. Temporarily ignoring the box constrains, $d_k(s) = d_k + (s_k = s$ if $k = i$, $-s$ if $k = j$, and 0 otherwise). Then $V(s) = C_1 + \sum_{k \in \{i,j\}} d_k(s)(y_k - \sum_{l \notin \{i,j\}} d_l(s)K_{kl}) - ½\sum_{k,l \in \{i,j\}} d_k(s)d_l(s)K_{kl} = C_2 + \sum_{k \in \{i,j\}} s_k(y_k - \sum_{l \notin \{i,j\}} d_lK_{kl}) - ½\sum_{k,l \in \{i,j\}}(s_kd_l + s_ld_k)K_{kl} - ½\sum_{k,l \in \{i,j\}} s_ks_lK_{kl}$. The symmetric $½\sum_{k,l \in \{i,j\}}(s_kd_l + s_ld_k)K_{kl} = \sum_{k \in \{i,j\}} s_k(\sum_{l \in \{i,j\}} d_lK_{kl})$, so can combine the l partitions to get $V(s) = C_2 + \sum_{k \in \{i,j\}} s_kg_k - ½\sum_{k,l \in \{i,j\}} s_ks_lK_{kl}$. $V(s)$ is maximized when $0 = \partial V/\partial s = g_i - g_j - s(K_{ii} - 2K_{ij} + K_{jj})$. So $s_{\text{opt}} = (g_i - g_j)/(K_{ii} - 2K_{ij} + K_{jj})$.

This formula is the basis of the **SMO algorithm**:

1. **Use the dual representation**
2. **Initialize the support coefficients to 0 and their gradients to 1**
3. **For some number of iterations**
4. **Pick two variables to optimize, using greedy selection**
5. **Check for convergence**
6. **Solve the resulting optimization problem analytically**
7. **Update the gradients**
8. **Store the nonzero support coefficients and the corresponding vectors**
9. **To predict *x*, compute the margins and choose the max margin class**

By positive definiteness of the kernel matrix, the denominator > 0 (it's actually the squared L_2 distance between the examples in the enhanced space) unless K is invalid, numerical cancellation is strong enough, or examples with the same x have different y. So for robustness, use dummy $s_{\text{opt}} = \infty$, which will make one such example a support vector (an clumsy alternative is to remove both). Taking the box constraints into account, $s = \min(H_i - d_i, d_j - L_j, s_{\text{opt}})$. To update g, use $\partial g_k/\partial s = -(K_{ik} - K_{jk})$. The simplest choice of i and j is such that the gap $= g_i - g_j$ is maximal (this is called the **maximal violating pair heuristic**). So the solution is optimal if the gap = 0, but for numerical reasons use some small precision, usually 0.001 (Chang & Lin 2011). Because $b = g_k$, $\forall k$ such that $L_k < d_k < H_k$, $g_j < g_k < g_i$. So can set b to g_i or g_j (or for numerical stability to $(g_i + g_j)/2$) at termination. Can't find proper i and j only if all y are the same, in which case $w = 0$, and $\forall k$ $b = y_k$ is a solution because $\forall k$ $\epsilon_k = 0$.

In practice, the runtime bottleneck is computing K, values of which are cached for efficiency. LRU cache with a memory limit is good for this, but for simplicity the implementation caches all values. Asymptotically, the number of support vector is $O(n)$ with a properly scaled C (Bottou et al. 2007). SMO converges to any precision in finite number of iterations (Bottou et al. 2007), but for safety the implementation uses $\max(10n, 10000)$. The idea is that each iteration updates two (usually) support vectors, so small data sets get more precision, and larger ones have $O(n)$ support vectors, though typically much less than n.

```
template<typename KERNEL = GaussianKernel, typename X = NUMERIC_X> struct SVM
{
    Vector<X> supportVectors;
    Vector<double> supportCoefficients;
    double bias;
    KERNEL K;
    template<typename DATA> double evalK(LinearProbingHashTable<long long,
        double>& cache, long long i, long long j, DATA const& data)
    {
        long long key = i * data.getSize() + j;
        double* result = cache.find(key);
        if(result) return *result;
        else
        {
            double value = K(data.getX(i), data.getX(j));
            cache.insert(key, value);
            return value;
        }
    }
    int makeY(bool label){return label * 2 - 1;}
    double lowDiff(bool label, double C, double d){return label ? d : d + C;}
    double highDiff(bool label, double C, double d){return label ? C - d: d;}
public:
    template<typename DATA> SVM(DATA const& data, pair<KERNEL, double> const&
        params, int maxRepeats = 10, int maxConst = 10000): K(params.first)
    {
        double C = params.second;
        assert(data.getSize() > 0 && C > 0);
        bias = makeY(data.getY(0));//just in case have 1 class only
        LinearProbingHashTable<long long, double> cache;
        int n = data.getSize(), maxIters = max(maxConst, n * maxRepeats);
```

```
        Vector<double> d(n, 0), g(n);
        for(int k = 0; k < n; ++k) g[k] = makeY(data.getY(k));
        while(maxIters--)
        {//select directions using max violating pair
            int i = -1, j = -1;//i can increase, j can decrease
            for(int k = 0; k < n; ++k)
            {//find max gi and min gj
                if(highDiff(data.getY(k), C, d[k]) > 0 && (i == -1 ||
                    g[k] > g[i])) i = k;
                if(lowDiff(data.getY(k), C, d[k]) > 0 && (j == -1 ||
                    g[k] < g[j])) j = k;
            }
            if(i == -1 || j == -1) break;
            bias = (g[i] + g[j])/2;//ave for stability
            //check optimality condition
            double optGap = g[i] - g[j];
            if(optGap < 0.001) break;
            //compute direction-based minimum and box bounds
            double denom = evalK(cache, i, i, data) -
                2 * evalK(cache, i, j, data) + evalK(cache, j, j, data),
                step = min(highDiff(data.getY(i), C, d[i]),
                lowDiff(data.getY(j), C, d[j]));
            //shorten step to box bounds if needed, check for numerical
            //error in kernel calculation or duplicate data, if error
            //move points to box bounds
            if(denom > 0) step = min(step, optGap/denom);
            //update support vector coefficients and gradient
            d[i] += step;
            d[j] -= step;
            for(int k = 0; k < n; ++k) g[k] += step *
                (evalK(cache, j, k, data) - evalK(cache, i, k, data));
        }//determine support vectors
        for(int k = 0; k < n; ++k) if(abs(d[k]) > globalSafeDelta)
            {
                supportCoefficients.append(d[k]);
                supportVectors.append(data.getX(k));
            }
    }
    int predict(X const& x)const
    {
        double sum = bias;
        for(int i = 0; i < supportVectors.getSize(); ++i)
            sum += supportCoefficients[i] * K(supportVectors[i], x);
        return sum >= 0;
    }
};
```

The runtime is O(the number of iterations × n). The solution is similar to k-NN because the radial basis kernel effectively averages only nearby (due to exponential weight decrease in distance) margin examples. A small C results in fewer support vectors because the margin is less accommodating to isolated examples.

For nonlinearly separable data, can't bound the VC-dimension as a function of the margin, but customized analysis produces a similar bound (Mohri et al. 2012). Let the p-margin loss be $L_p(x) = 1$ if $x < 0$, 0 if $x < p$, and $1 - x/p$ otherwise. Then have an empirical p-risk R_p on the training data. Theorem (Mohri et al. 2012): Let $b = 0$ and Tr(G) be the trace of the kernel matrix. Then $\forall p, q > 0$ with probability $\geq 1 - q$, $R(h) \leq R_p + 2\sqrt{\mathrm{Tr}(G)/mQ}/p + 3\sqrt{\ln(2/q)/(2m)}$.

In particular, $p = 1$ is useful because hinge loss bounds p-loss, and $R_1 \leq \sum\epsilon_i$. This justifies SVM design as trying to both minimize the sum of margin violations and maximize the margin. Making $b = 0$ makes the analysis much easier, and $b \neq 0$ is only a minor assumption violation in practice (Yuan et al. 2012) and theory because other parameters should make up for it.

In some sense, using kernels is optimal because it allows to express any boundary shape and do so only with enough example support, exploiting the manifold assumption.

21.12 Multiclass Nonlinear SVM

Use OVO for its general advantages and because it needs less memory for the kernel cache:

```
template<typename KERNEL = GaussianKernel, typename X = NUMERIC_X>
class MulticlassSVM
{//need buffer for speed
    typedef pair<KERNEL, double> P;
    MulticlassLearner<BufferLearner<SVM<KERNEL, X>,
        InMemoryData<X, int>, P>, P> mcl;
public:
    template<typename DATA> MulticlassSVM(DATA const& data,
        pair<KERNEL, double> const& params): mcl(data, params) {}
    int predict(X const& x)const{return mcl.predict(x);}
};
```

A good but slow approach to picking y and C is exponential range grid search (see the "Numerical Algorithms" chapter) with cross-validation. All else equal, want small C and large y. Grid points used by LIBSVM are 2^i with odd $i \in [-15, 3]$ for y and $[-5, 15]$ for C, with 110 values to try (Bottou et al. 2007). This works well in practice, but assumes the data is scaled in a way that this range is reasonable. But simple discrete compass search with max = 10 evaluations (see the "Numerical Algorithms" chapter) gives similar accuracy and is several times faster based on my experiments.

```
struct NoParamsSVM
{
    MulticlassSVM<> model;
    struct CVSVMFunctor
    {
        typedef Vector<double> PARAMS;
        MulticlassSVM<> model;
        template<typename DATA> CVSVMFunctor(DATA const& data,
            PARAMS const& p):
            model(data, make_pair(GaussianKernel(p[0]), p[1])) {}
        int predict(NUMERIC_X const& x)const{return model.predict(x);}
    };
    template<typename DATA> static pair<GaussianKernel, double>
        gaussianMultiClassSVM(DATA const& data, int CLow = -5,
        int CHigh = 15, int yLow = -15, int yHi = 3)
    {
        Vector<Vector<double> > sets(2);
        for(int i = yLow; i <= yHi; i += 2) sets[0].append(pow(2, i));
        for(int i = CLow; i <= CHigh; i += 2) sets[1].append(pow(2, i));
        Vector<double> best = compassDiscreteMinimize(sets,
            SCVRiskFunctor<CVSVMFunctor, Vector<double>, DATA>(data),
            10);
        return make_pair(GaussianKernel(best[0]), best[1]);
    }
    template<typename DATA> NoParamsSVM(DATA const& data): model(data,
        gaussianMultiClassSVM(data)) {}
    int predict(NUMERIC_X const& x)const{return model.predict(x);}
};
typedef ScaledLearner<NoParamsLearner<NoParamsSVM, int>, int> SSVM;
```

The authors of LIBSVM recommend scaling features into [0, 1] (Hsu et al. 2010).

SSVM_10n10k_001_seps_c10	SSVM_10n10k_001_seps_r20	SSVM_10n10k_001_seps_g	MQSVM_10n10k_001_seps_c10
0.95	0.92	0.95	0.96

Kernel SVM is slow with parameter selection, and scales poorly for large n. So its use is restricted to small or medium n.

21.13 Neural Network

A neural network is designed for regression. For classification, predict $\Pr(f(x) = y)$. A **neuron** has an **activation function** $g(x)$ such as the logistic $1/(1 + e^{-x})$, which normalizes x into a simple range such as (0, 1), a list of weights w $\forall$ feature f, and a **bias feature** with constant value 1. w form a hyperplane $\sum w_i x_i = 0$ in X. A neuron computes a given point's distance to that hyperplane as $g(\sum w_i f_i)$, which is a distance because $\sum w_i x_i = a$ $\forall a$ is a set of hyperplanes. So a neuron splits X into $a \geq 0$ and $a < 0$.

A network is a DAG of neurons, arranged in layers so that inputs to the first layer are features, but to any other outputs of the previous layer. The last layer is the **output layer**. A network is usually fully connected, but doesn't have to be.

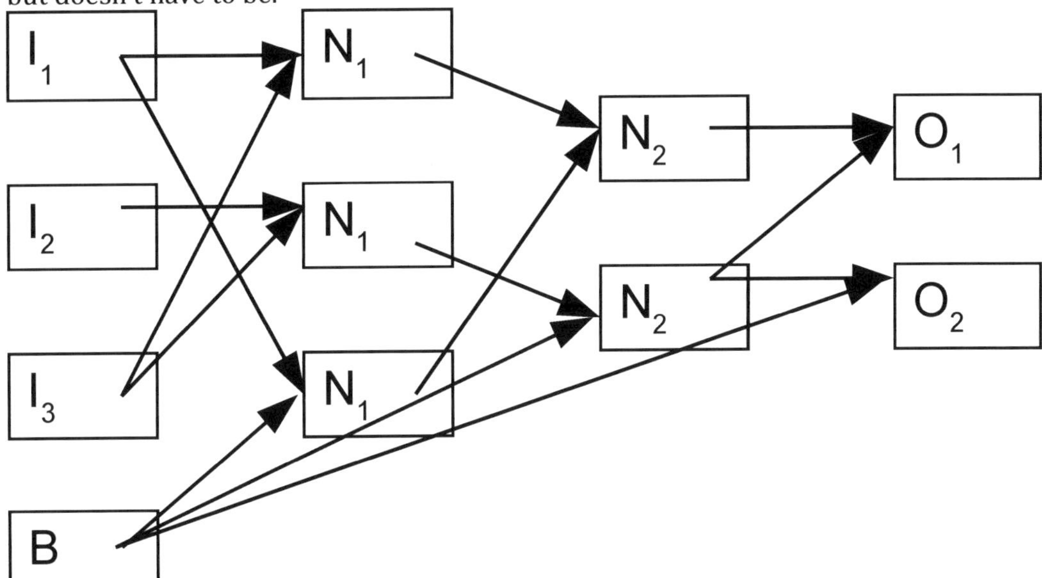

A **feed-forward network** with L layers is a function defined recursively by $f(x) = f_{k,L-1}, f_{k,j+1} = \sum g(w_{kj} f_{kj})$, $f_{k,0} = x[k]$. It usually has a different g, depending on the task:

- Output layer, regression—identity.
- Output layer, classification—logistic. It's symmetric about (0, 0.5).
- Hidden layer—tanh.

Intuitively, each subsequent layer is a transformed feature space that is closer to Y. Effectively, the nonoutput layers find an arrangement of X (in 2D, it's a set of possibly intersecting lines that splits 2D into regions), a particular value of which defines a specific region for x, which is then used by the output layer to make a decision. Typically, but not always, every neuron connects to every neuron of the previous layer and the bias.

Theorem (Hornik 1991; Leshno et al. 1993): A network with a single identity g output and one hidden layer with bounded and nonconstant activation function can approximate arbitrarily well with enough hidden neurons in:

- L_∞ norm—any continuous function on a compact domain, if g is also continuous
- L_p norm—$\forall p$ any function whose L_p distance to the 0 function $< \infty$

To be useful for training, g must be also differentiable. Common sigmoids such as logistic or tanh satisfy this. On the other hand, the theorem technically doesn't apply to classification because, even with $k = 2$, the wanted function isn't continuous and usually not finitely close to 0, so neither condition applies. But in practice this doesn't seem to cause problems. The number of hidden neurons needed for getting a specific approximation error is unknown and depends the problem.

```
class NeuralNetwork
{
    struct Neuron
    {
        Vector<int> sources;
        Vector<double> weights;
        double output, error;
    };
```

```
    mutable NUMERIC_X inputs;
    bool isContinuousOutput;
    mutable Vector<Vector<Neuron> > layers;
    double actOutput(double x)const
        {return isContinuousOutput ? x : 1/(1 + exp(-x));}
    double actInner(double x)const{return tanh(x);}

public:
    NeuralNetwork(int D, bool theIsContinuousOutput = false,
        double theInitialLearningRate = 1): inputs(D), learnedCount(1),
        initialLearningRate(theInitialLearningRate),
        isContinuousOutput(theIsContinuousOutput) {}
    void addLayer(int nNeurons){layers.append(Vector<Neuron>(nNeurons));}
    void addConnection(int layer, int from, int to, double weight)
    {
        Vector<Neuron>& last = layers[layer];
        last[from].sources.append(to);
        last[from].weights.append(weight);
    }
};
```

Inputs are propagated to next layers, and outputs of the last layer have the result:

```
    void propagateInputs(NUMERIC_X const& x)const
    {
        inputs = x;
        for(int i = 0; i < layers.getSize(); ++i)
            for(int j = 0; j < layers[i].getSize(); ++j)
            {
                Neuron& n = layers[i][j];
                double sum = n.error = 0;
                for(int k = 0; k < n.sources.getSize(); ++k)
                    sum += n.weights[k] * getInput(i, n.sources[k]);
                n.output = i == layers.getSize() - 1 ?
                    actOutput(sum) : actInner(sum);
            }
    }
    double getInput(int layer, int source)const
    {
        return source == -1 ? 1 : layer == 0 ?
            inputs[source] : layers[layer - 1][source].output;
    }
    Vector<double> evaluate(NUMERIC_X const& x)const
    {
        propagateInputs(x);
        Vector<double> result;
        for(int i = 0; i < layers.lastItem().getSize(); ++i)
            result.append(layers.lastItem()[i].output);
        return result;
    }
```

Learning adjusts weights to minimize L_2 error = $\sum$((the actual − the correct result of output neuron $i)^2)/2$, from evaluating every training example. This isn't convex, so use local optimization. The simplest, scalable, and effective training method is SGD, with derivatives calculated using **back-propagation**. ∀ neuron only its weights contribute to the error, so can use gradient descent. ∀ output neuron, error $\epsilon = (g(wf) - y)^2/2$. With respect to w, $\epsilon' = tf$ for $t = og'(w, f)$ and output error $o = g(wf) - y$. For neuron j in the layer feeding the output layer, $\epsilon_j = \sum$errors of neurons that use its output as feature $= \sum(g(w_k f_k) - y_k)^2/2$. With respect to w_j, $\epsilon_j' = \sum(g(w_k f_k) - y_k)g'(w_k f_k)w_k[j]g'(w_j f_j)f_j = t_j f_j$ for $o_j = \sum t_k w_k[j]$. Inductively, this works ∀ nonoutput neuron, leading to gradient descent update $w_{i+1} = w_i - s_i tf$, where s_i is some step size that satisfies Robbins-Munro (see the "Numerical Algorithms" chapter). SGD converges slowly, so usually don't need explicit regularization. Use $\lceil 10^5/n \rceil$ or $\lceil 10^6/n \rceil$ passes over the data to get reasonable accuracy (about

10^{-3} to 10^{-2} asymptotically).

For $g(x) = 1/(1 + e^{-x})$, $g'(x) = g(x)(1 - g(x))$; for tanh, $g'(x) = 1 - g(x)^2$. These relations allow computing the derivatives directly from neuron outputs, avoiding the extra storage needed otherwise.

```
    long long learnedCount;
    double initialLearningRate;
    double learningRate()
        {return initialLearningRate/pow(learnedCount++, 0.501);}
    double actOutputDeriv(double fx)const
        {return isContinuousOutput ? 1 : fx * (1 - fx);}
    double actInnerDeriv(double fx)const{return 1 - fx * fx;}
    void learn(NUMERIC_X const& x, Vector<double> const& results)
    {
        assert(results.getSize() == layers.lastItem().getSize());
        propagateInputs(x);
        Vector<Neuron>& last = layers.lastItem();
        for(int j = 0; j < last.getSize(); ++j) last[j].error =
            last[j].output - results[j];
        double r = learningRate();
        for(int i = layers.getSize() - 1; i >= 0; --i)
            for(int j = 0; j < layers[i].getSize(); ++j)
            {
                Neuron& n = layers[i][j];
                double temp = n.error * (i == layers.getSize() - 1 ?
                    actOutputDeriv(n.output) : actInnerDeriv(n.output));
                for(int k = 0; k < n.sources.getSize(); ++k)
                {//update weights and prev layer output errors
                    int source = n.sources[k];
                    if(i > 0 && source != -1)
                        layers[i - 1][source].error += n.weights[k] * temp;
                    n.weights[k] -= r * temp * getInput(i, source);
                }
            }
    }
```

For $k = 2$, only know VC-dimension d bounds for networks with particular g. Let W = the number of weights in a network with sigmoid hidden layer activations and threshold output activation. Then (Shalev-Schwatz & Ben-David 2014; Anthony & Bartlett 1999) $O(W^2) < d < O(W^4)$. But these don't consider weight and data sizes and make assumptions on activations. Assuming that each weight takes $O(1)$ bits to represent, a network needs $O(W)$ bits, leading to a better ORM upper bound. Probably ∃ better, currently unknown bounds that consider data and weight sizes. Nevertheless, these show that every weight matters. Learning from a single example takes $O(W)$ time.

Applying SGD needs some care (Montavon et al. 2012). A problem is **saturation**, i.e., when $\forall x$ the sums at one or more neurons are too small/large, and $g'(x) \approx 0$. Nevertheless, though for some examples the sums can be huge, resulting in negligible updates, for others they should lead to reasonably large $g'(x)$. A typical classification recipe for structure and parameters:

- For $k > 2$, use OVO; binary problems have a 0/1 output neuron. A neural network is better at discriminating between two classes than between many. Count the output layer outputs as fractions for the OVO voting, without rounding to 0 or 1. (Alternatively, for OVA ∀ class use a 0/1 output neuron with logistic activation, and pick the class corresponding to the highest value neuron. Unlike for SVM, OVO is less efficient by a factor of $O(k)$, but the decision boundaries are simpler and a few hidden neurons suffice.)
- Use one hidden layer with 5 neurons. This tends to work well experimentally (my tests and Fernández-Delgado et al. 2014) and allows online operation. For 5, the nonlinearity is more than with logistic regression and not too much to overfit. Other $2i + 1$ numbers such as 3 or 9 or cross-validation give similar results.
- Scale inputs to mean 0 and standard deviation 1. This helps keep the sums small.
- Initialize all output neuron and bias weights to 0, and the rest to uniform$(-a, a)$ samples for $a = \sqrt{3/D}$. Then the latter weights have mean 0 and standard deviation $1/\sqrt{D}$, and the sum mean 0 and

standard deviation 1. This makes saturation unlikely and gives different hidden neurons different weights, so that they don't learn the same thing (using 0 for everything causes this because of symmetry). Each hidden unit essentially does a random projection at initialization.

- For hidden layers, use g symmetric around 0. Most sources recommend g = tanh—the same logic as for scaling inputs to 0—e.g., with logistic $g(0) = 0.5$, so the sums at the next layer neurons will be 0.5 × the number of inputs, which could saturate immediately.
- The initial learning rate = 1 seems to work well.
- Use 5 networks, differing only in initial weights, and average their outputs. This is to remove variance and tends to work well experimentally (my tests and Fernández-Delgado et al. 2014).

mqk2nn_b	mqk2nn	mqk2nn3	mqk2nn9	mqk2nn17	mqk2nncv	ave100kmq_5
0.946	0.946	0.948	0.943	0.938	0.944	0.931

```
class BinaryNN
{
    Vector<NeuralNetwork> nns;
    void setupStructure(int D, int nHidden)
    {
        double a = sqrt(3.0/D);
        for(int l = 0; l < nns.getSize(); ++l)
        {
            NeuralNetwork& nn = nns[l];
            nn.addLayer(nHidden);
            for(int j = 0; j < nHidden; ++j)
                for(int k = -1; k < D; ++k) nn.addConnection(0, j, k,
                    k == -1 ? 0 : GlobalRNG.uniform(-a, a));
            nn.addLayer(1);
            for(int k = -1; k < nHidden; ++k) nn.addConnection(1, 0, k, 0);
        }
    }
public:
    BinaryNN(int D, int nHidden = 5, int nNns = 5):
        nns(nNns, NeuralNetwork(D)){setupStructure(D, nHidden);}
    template<typename DATA> BinaryNN(DATA const& data, int nHidden = 5, int
        nGoal = 100000, int nNns = 5): nns(nNns, NeuralNetwork(getD(data)))
    {
        int D = getD(data), nRepeats = ceiling(nGoal, data.getSize());
        setupStructure(D, nHidden);
        for(int j = 0; j < nRepeats; ++j)
            for(int i = 0; i < data.getSize(); ++i)
                learn(data.getX(i), data.getY(i));
    }
    void learn(NUMERIC_X const& x, int label)
    {
        for(int l = 0; l < nns.getSize(); ++l)
            nns[l].learn(x, Vector<double>(1, label));
    }
    double evaluate(NUMERIC_X const& x)const
    {
        double result = 0;
        for(int l = 0; l < nns.getSize(); ++l)
            result += nns[l].evaluate(x)[0];
        return result/nns.getSize();
    }
    int predict(NUMERIC_X const& x)const{return evaluate(x) > 0.5;}
};
class MulticlassNN
{
    MulticlassLearner<NoParamsLearner<BinaryNN, int>, EMPTY> model;
public:
```

```
    template<typename DATA> MulticlassNN(DATA const& data): model(data) {}
    int predict(NUMERIC_X const& x)const {return model.classifyByProbs(x);}
};
typedef ScaledLearner<NoParamsLearner<MulticlassNN, int>, int, EMPTY,
    ScalerMQ> SNN;
```

Neural networks have many problems, which haven't been solved by years of research:

- Search (SGD or other methods) easily gets trapped in local minima of arbitrary quality. Averaging several randomly trained networks essentially gives in to the central limit catastrophe (see the "Optimization" chapter), but don't have better alternatives. Can try global optimization methods, but need explicit regularization for them not to overfit—can use the L_2 penalty, which for neural networks is called **weight decay**. Still, this takes too long, and the results are unlikely to be reproducible. So kernel SVM mostly replaced neural network as the black box method when need nonlinearity. But in some applications such as game playing, a globally trained neural network can give good results (Mandziuk 2010); nevertheless, other methods might have given better results if used instead.
- Training is slow even with SGD—about $O(k^2D$ × the number of examples × the number of hidden neurons). Essentially don't have room for parameter selection. Some implementations cross-validate decay (Fernández-Delgado et al. 2014; Caruana & Niculescu-Mizil 2006; Caruana et al. 2008), but in my experiments this doesn't improve performance, probably because low-precision SGD gives automatic regularization.

Black-box single hidden layer networks generally do worse than top-performing *A* such as SVM or random forest (discussed later), but are useful in specific cases such as online learning. **Top-performing networks use domain knowledge**. E.g., the famous convolution network for digit recognition (Hastie et al. 2009) groups neighboring pixels (more generally, highly correlated features), and years of design went into it. Some form of grouping correlated features may get close to this, but it's unclear how to do so effectively. Another domain-specific information is training on slightly rotated images, which improved performance substantially (Montavon et al. 2012).

Deep learning is an advance in neural networks, with two fundamental changes, by the use of (Montavon et al. 2012):

- More than one hidden layer (deep architecture). A single hidden layer may need exponentially many neurons to learn some functions. Having more layers avoids this.
- Unsupervised pre-training, which makes deep architecture training feasible. For a standard network with more than one hidden layer, have **vanishing gradient** (errors sent to lower layers ≈ 0) and too many local minimums problems.

A simple to use unsupervised data is auto-encoding:

- ∀ hidden layer attach an extra decoder layer, which tries to reconstruct the input. Can use standard SGD with back-propagation.

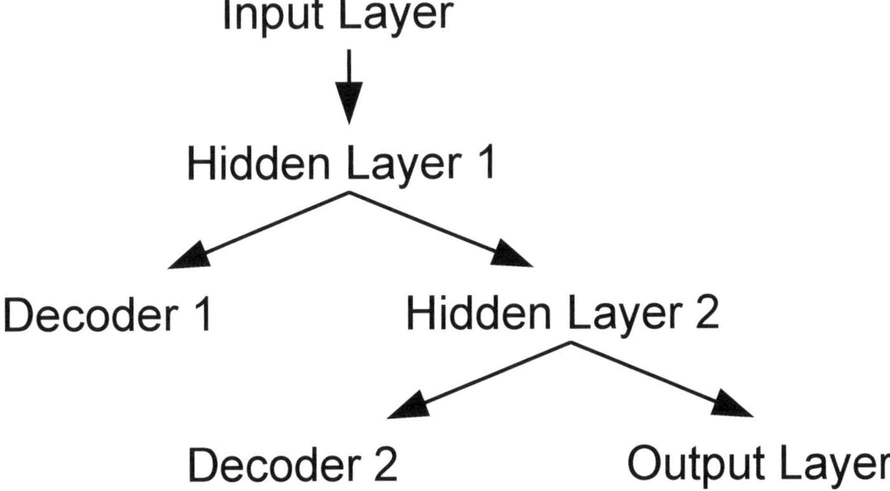

- Starting from the first layer, train each layer using a decoder as last layer, but without modifying already trained layers. Need to cross-validate the initial learning rate for the decoder units because activation derivatives are no longer bounded.

- Finally, use y to back-propagate as usual.
- A simple architecture is using the same number of hidden neurons (cross-validated, or maybe $D^{0.75}$) ∀ layer, and maybe 5 layers. This is to avoid overfitting, but have many probably better choices (Bengio et al. 2015).
- Due to using unsupervised data, can't decompose into binary problems, so use k output units with OVA. This requires learning more complex boundaries but is faster, and a deep architecture supposedly makes up for this by giving better features.

These instructions are only a proof of concept. Deep learning is an active research field and hasn't produced a competitive black box A yet (this is debatable and remains to be experimentally validated), though some application-specific results are very impressive.

21.14 Randomization Ensembles

Combining multiple f may do better than using a single one. The simplest way to do so is by using majority vote, i.e., the most popular class is the answer. **Jury theorem**: if T combined f are independent and for each Pr(the chosen class is right > 0.5), as $T \to \infty$, Pr(the majority is wrong) → 0. Actually, with $k > 2$, only need correctness > $1/k$, assuming no wrong answer is more likely then the correct one. This is because the probability of the correct answer will increase much faster than that of another answer, which can only increase by chance.

But a set of f can't be fully independent because all are trained on the same data. Also, if many f are uninformative due to excessive randomization, performance will suffer because variance of the noninformative f will bring significant noise to close decisions by the informative f; so it's important to make sure that f stay informative.

Bagged decision tree is an application of bagging (see the "General Machine Learning" chapter) to get the benefits of randomization. Trees aren't pruned to reduce bias. **Random forest** improves bagged decision tree by reducing bias at the expense of higher variance by reducing correlation between trees. Specifically, it makes each tree more random by disallowing a random subset of features from being used for splits; a different subset is sampled ∀ node. Generally, f with little correlation to each other have little in common, meaning that A that produced them has little bias. Despite not using pruning, depth should remain at 50, as for regular decision tree.

The number of allowed features a should be small enough to decorrelate the trees but large enough to not weaken each one. The original paper default choice $a = \sqrt{D}$ seems robust. An alternative frequent suggestion $a = \lfloor \lg(D) \rfloor$ gets less correlation, and logical $a = D^{3/4}$ (8 out of 16, 27 out of 81, etc.) more strength. According to my tests the former is worse, and the latter about the same, so no reason to prefer either. Generally, to improve:

- Diversity of trees—want smaller a
- Strength of each tree—want larger a
- Efficiency—want smaller a and T

Choosing T depends on the problem and is difficult:

- Too large is inefficient in time and memory use
- Too small isn't enough to stabilize predictions and results in a randomized algorithm with high variance

$T = 1000$ is suggested in the original paper and frequently used. It's reasonable to do grid search from this number using approximately factor $\sqrt{10}$ step. Based on the results, 300 seems to be better:

- Prior knowledge in favor of 1000 due to use; experimentally, using more than some number stops making a difference (Breiman 2001)
- 100 is smallest with good enough performance
- 100 is close to mediocre performance, and 1000 to unnecessary inefficiency
- Relative standard deviations of all three are close and slightly favor more trees
- Prediction needs $O(T)$ base learner predictions
- Random forest is useful as a black box and, in several cases, with augmentations, so neither efficiency nor variance should be a problem with its default choice
- Using cross-validation on doubling numbers is slow, variance in performance can lead to bad

selection, and T, as long as large enough, makes little difference

Bag_1k	RF_05_1k	RF_075_1k	RF_075_100	RF_075_200	RF_075_1k
0.941	0.970	0.974	0.967	0.972	0.973

Random forest estimates probabilities reasonably well using count proportions. Bagging does too, but only with unstable base A.

1. **Pick T**
2. **$\forall$tree**
3. **Create a resample of size n from S**
4. **Learn a decision tree from the resample, randomly selecting features $\forall$node and not pruning**
5. **To predict x, classify it using every tree, and find the majority class, or use count proportions to get probabilities**

```
class RandomForest
{
    Vector<DecisionTree> forest;
    int nClasses;
public:
    template<typename DATA> RandomForest(DATA const& data, int nTrees = 300):
        nClasses(findNClasses(data))
    {
        assert(data.getSize() > 1);
        for(int i = 0; i < nTrees; ++i)
        {
            PermutedData<DATA> resample(data);
            for(int j = 0; j < data.getSize(); ++j)
                resample.addIndex(GlobalRNG.mod(data.getSize()));
            forest.append(DecisionTree(resample, 0, true));
        }
    }
    template <typename ENSEMBLE> static int classifyWork(NUMERIC_X const& x,
        ENSEMBLE const& e, int nClasses)
    {
        Vector<int> counts(nClasses, 0);
        for(int i = 0; i < e.getSize(); ++i) ++counts[e[i].predict(x)];
        return argMax(counts.getArray(), counts.getSize());
    }
    int predict(NUMERIC_X const& x)const
        {return classifyWork(x, forest, nClasses);}
    Vector<double> classifyProbs(NUMERIC_X const& x)const
    {
        Vector<double> counts(nClasses, 0);
        for(int i = 0; i < forest.getSize(); ++i)
            ++counts[forest[i].predict(x)];
        normalizeProbs(counts);
        return counts;
    }
};
```

Random forest has several extra features. One is **out-of-bag** risk estimate, i.e., $\forall z_i \in S$ compute y based on the subforest consisting of trees not trained on z_i. This create a risk estimate, which is as accurate as the one on an independent test set (Breiman 2001), removing the need for an extra test set. Because about $1/e$ trees don't include a particular example, and ≈200 trees gives good performance, this is best done with > 600 trees.

A theoretical problem is that, as decision tree, random forest based on greedily trained decision tree isn't consistent (Biau et al. 2008). This doesn't seem to cause problems in practice.

21.15 Boosting

Boosting tries to create a set of f such that each next one tries to improve the performance on the examples misclassified by the ensemble so far by giving them more weight. Assuming $k = 2$ with $y \in \{-1, 1\}$, want to find base classifiers h_i and weights a_i, such that the combined classifier sign($F = \sum a_i h_i$) has the minimum risk = $\sum L(F_j, y_j)$, where L is some loss function and F_j is the sum for the example j.

The optimization is NP-hard when L is binary loss, so instead must use a **surrogate loss function** L that:

- ≥ binary loss—boosting reduces the latter using an upper bound
- Is convex—then $\sum L_j$ is convex an easy to optimize
- Is monotonically decreasing—F effectively determines the confidence of a correct decision, so examples with large F are safer to ignore

Finding F that minimizes L is numerical minimization in the space of functions, and can be done using gradient descent. Starting from no information $F = 0$, each next h is a step toward the minimum:

1. **$F_j = 0$ ∀example j**
2. ***T* times**
3. **Find the h closest to $d = -dL/dF$**
4. **Pick a_j analytically or numerically**
5. **F_j += $a_j h_j$ ∀example j**

To find h, minimize one of:

- **AnyBoost**—dot product $h \times d$—convenient for classification and needs weighing of examples. For L such that $d \ge 0$, which holds for all popular L, this is equivalent to weighing each example j by d_j. To avoid training base A on weighed examples, resample using the distribution specified by the weights. Usually, the resample size = n.
- **Gradient boosting**—L_2 norm $||h - d||$—convenient for regression with L_2 loss and doesn't need weighing. Need to train a regression algorithm to predict real-valued y to minimize L. For $L \neq L_2$ loss, regression may be inefficient because most algorithms were developed for L_2 loss. E.g., computing the optimal split in a regression tree (see the "Machine Learning—Regression" chapter) updates loss incrementally, which is efficient only for some L.

AdaBoost is derived by using exponential loss $L(F, y) = e^{-yF}$. If $r = \sum(h \neq y)d$ is the weighted error of h, the optimal $a = \ln((1 - r)/r)/2$ (Schapire & Freund 2012).

Theoretically need a **weak learner** base A (Schapire & Freund 2012), which has error $\epsilon < 0.5$ with probability $\ge 1 - p$ ∀ $p > 0$ and large enough (depending on p) n. For the implementation to work, only need $\epsilon < 0.5$ ∀ resample. Theorem (Mohri et al. 2012): Assume:

- The base A is weak, and it's G has VC-dimension d
- a_i are normalized such that $\sum a_j = 1$
- L_1 margin $m = \min_i y_i(ah(x_i)) > 0$
- Each h_j achieves $\epsilon_j < ½$

Then after T rounds and any fixed achieved m, with probability $\ge 1 - p$ $R_f \le 2^T \prod \sqrt{\epsilon_j^{1-m}(1-\epsilon_j)^{1+m}} + \sqrt{8d\ln(en/d)/n}/m + \sqrt{-\ln(p)/(2n)}$.

In particular, for a fixed p and enough rounds, the generalization error is $O(1/\sqrt{n})$ and → 0. This is impossible for $R_{oB} > 0$—the weak A assumption is too strong, so it's more intuitive to assume that the distribution on Z is trimmed so that any undecided label examples have 0 support. Then, observing a noisy example from the real distribution in the:

- Testing data leads to a single error
- Training data leads to a margin-based "error hole" around the example

The second problem is much worse—experiments with AdaBoost show that generalization error ≈ 0.5 for training on very noisy-label data (Schapire & Freund 2012). More generally (Long & Servedio 2010), any boosting algorithm with any convex loss, under the assumption of constant fraction of noisy examples in training data, can be made to perform almost randomly. But most practical data sets aren't such worst case, and AdaBoost performs well (Schapire & Freund 2012). Still, theoretically !∃ any middle ground between great performance for $R_{oB} = 0$ and poor for $R_{oB} > 0$.

An important conclusion is that the base A should balance having low complexity and strength to get good margins. A heavily pruned decision tree is a natural base A. For base A, generalization and training errors should be close, and performance maximally better than random. The former is more important—

e.g., an unpruned decision tree is highly likely to have training error 0 even with resampling. It may seem that decision stumps, used in face recognition, are the best A. But experimentally (Caruana & Mizil 2006) and theoretically (Schapire & Freund 2012), in general stumps perform poorly. Also, for something like the xor problem, stumps aren't weak learners. Finally, stumps put more margin around noisy-label examples, leading to larger holes. Ideally, base A should be strong enough to isolate the holes as much as possible. Face recognition uses very specifically engineered stumps, with which boosting happened to work well due to its bias-decreasing property. For vector x, !∃ a reason to not use decision trees as base A.

SAMME extends AdaBoost for $k > 2$, needing base learner accuracy $> 1/k$ (Zhu et al. 2009). As for random forest, use $T = 300$. A smaller T is less likely to overfit, which isn't a problem for random forest. The implementation follows gradient descent with exponential loss but makes simplifications:

- Negative gradients d are maintained directly, and data weights and sums F aren't.
- The weights are $\log((1 - r)/r) + \log(k - 1)$, as for AdaBoost for $k = 2$ (constant factors don't matter), and the weight update formula uses $y \in \{0, 1\}$ to simplify algebra.

If any accuracy $< 1/k$, for robustness the ineffective h is removed. If error = 0, $\log(1)/0$ = NaN, and resampling will fail ∀ subsequent round. A robust solution is to replace the ensemble by h (removing it may remove all effective h for very easy problems).

```
template<typename LEARNER = NoParamsLearner<DecisionTree, int>,
    typename PARAMS = EMPTY, typename X = NUMERIC_X> class AdaBoostSamme
{
    Vector<LEARNER> classifiers;
    Vector<double> weights;
    int nClasses;
public:
    template<typename DATA> AdaBoostSamme(DATA const& data, PARAMS const&
        p = PARAMS(), int nClassifiers = 300): nClasses(findNClasses(data))
    {
        int n = data.getSize();
        assert(n > 0 && nClassifiers > 0 && nClasses > 0);
        Vector<double> dataWeights(n, 1.0/n);
        for(int i = 0; i < nClassifiers; ++i)
        {
            AliasMethod sampler(dataWeights);
            PermutedData<DATA> resample(data);
            for(int j = 0; j < n; ++j) resample.addIndex(sampler.next());
            classifiers.append(LEARNER(resample, p));
            double error = 0;
            Bitset<> isWrong(n);
            for(int j = 0; j < n; ++j) if(classifiers.lastItem().predict(
                data.getX(j)) != data.getY(j))
                {
                    isWrong.set(j);
                    error += dataWeights[j];
                }
            if(error >= 1 - 1.0/nClasses) classifiers.removeLast();
            else if(error == 0)
            {//replace ensemble by classifier
                Vector<LEARNER> temp;
                temp.append(classifiers.lastItem());
                classifiers = temp;
                weights = Vector<double>(1, 1);
                break;
            }
            else
            {
                double expWeight = (nClasses - 1) * (1 - error)/error;
                weights.append(log(expWeight));
                for(int j = 0; j < n; ++j)
                    if(isWrong[j]) dataWeights[j] *= expWeight;
```

```
                normalizePobs(dataWeights);
            }
        }
    }
    int predict(X const& x)const
    {
        Vector<double> counts(nClasses, 0);
        for(int i = 0; i < classifiers.getSize(); ++i)
            counts[classifiers[i].predict(x)] += weights[i];
        return argMax(counts.getArray(), counts.getSize());
    }
};
```

Certain modifications make sense and improve extendability, but not performance in general:

- Use L that put less weight on misclassified examples—in particular, due to it's probabilistic interpretation, many variants use **binomial deviance** (also called **logistic**) loss = lg(1 + $e^{-\text{margin}}$)/lg(2), scaled to bound binary loss (constant factors don't matter though). Because it's almost linear on the left, the worst case weight ≈ 1 ∀ misclassified example. But experimentally this doesn't help with either noise or overfitting (Schapire & Freund 2012). Deriving analytic weights works only with exponential and logistic losses (Schapire & Freund 2012)—for many others, the only choice is numerical optimization, which is hard to analyze and needs robust implementation. Hinge loss doesn't work because correctly classified examples over margin = 1 have weight 0, and too many examples are ignored in subsequent rounds.

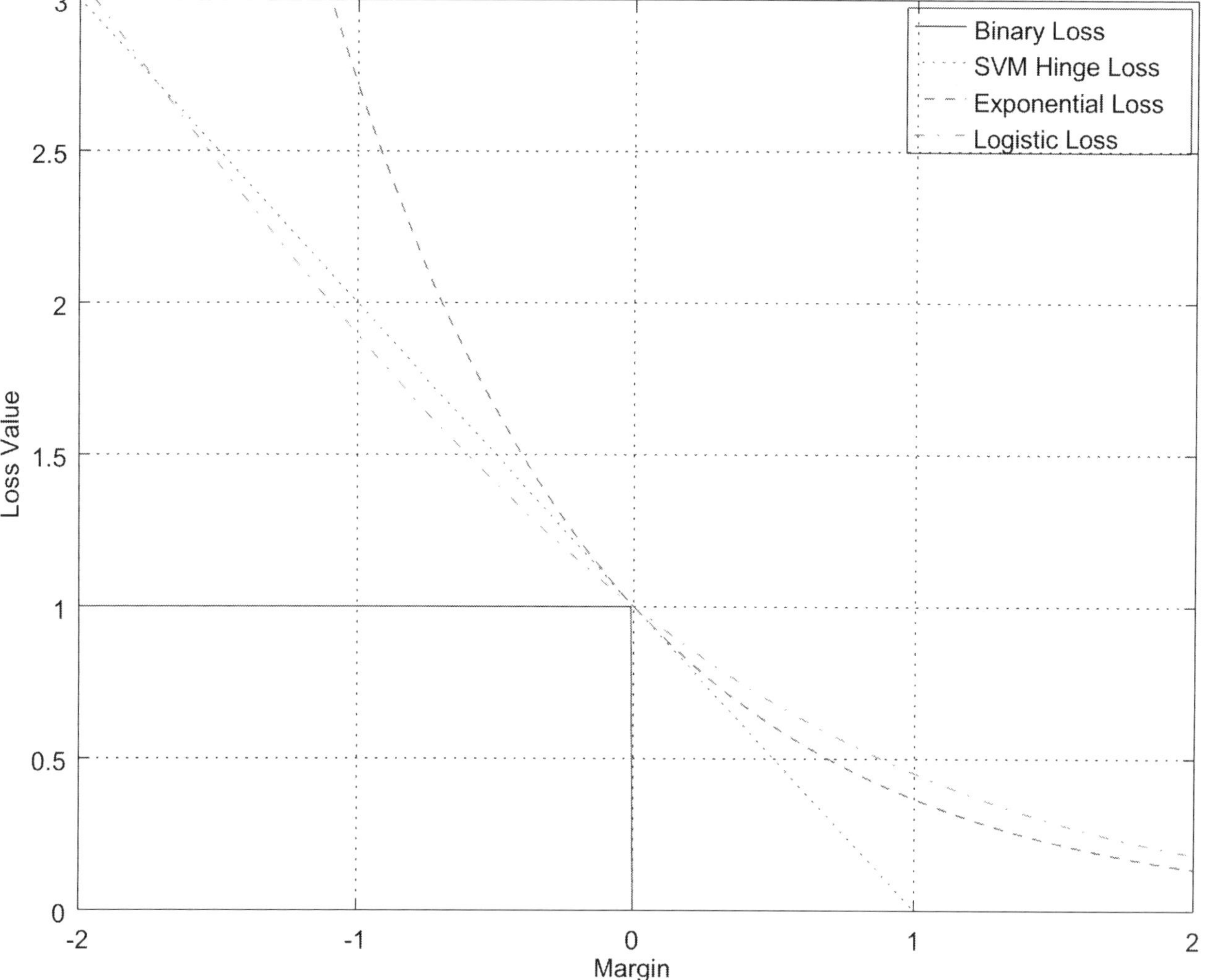

- For $k > 2$, the proper margin to use is F(the label) – F(the best false label) because this is what classification uses. But many variants use F(the label) – $\sum_{i \neq \text{the label}} F(i)$, which is too pessimistic (majority instead of plurality) but bounds the proper margin and is easier to analyze.

- Analytic weights may overfit. Small constant weights are suggested instead (Hastie et al. 2009), and Robbins-Munro weights seem better still, guaranteeing convergence of the gradient descent. But such uninformed choice may underfit by over-weighing learners with poor performance.

The resulting algorithm is **RMBoost**. $T = 1000$ by default, based on experimental comparisons; 100 performs slightly worse. In general, use SAMME for boosting, but RMBoost is easily extended to cost-sensitive classification. This is useful because for boosting count proportions don't give accurate probabilities in my experiments, probably because of stronger dependence between base f. The code is presented in the cost learning section later in the chapter.

SAMME100	SAMME300	SAMME1k	RMB100	RMB300	RMB1k
0.926	0.937	0.941	0.929	0.932	0.933

It's best to treat boosting as a method that performs well in general, superbly on some data, and poorly on some others. As random forest, boosting has high variance: about 0.02 for 100 boosts, and 0.01 for 1000. Unlike with random forest, using large T can overfit, so don't have a good solution to high variance and must accept that another run may give slightly better or worse combined f. Another minor problem is needing extra $O(n)$ memory for alias sampling.

Intuitively, while random forest decreases variance, boosting decreases both, mostly bias in the first few iterations and mostly variance in the latter ones (Schapire et al. 2012).

21.16 Online Training

Naive Bayes, nearest neighbor, linear SVM, and neural network are online A. But the performance of naive Bayes is usually poor for numeric data, nearest neighbor takes too much memory, and linear SVM and neural network don't have the top performance. Also, from consistency point of view, all except nearest neighbor keep a model of constant complexity with respect to the number of learned examples, whereas top offline algorithms adapt their models. Technically, it's possible to increase model complexity dynamically for some A, but such approaches don't seem to have been investigated, probably because the data used for training the old model is lost in online training.

Online A that need $k = 2$ can also work with $k > 2$. After seeing a new example, k is adjusted if necessary, and new binary learners are created. If some classes are unknown for a long time, the new learners will have less data to train on. E.g., if 0 and 1 appeared first and 2 later, 0 vs 2 and 1 vs 2 would have missed out examples with $y = 0$ and 1. This isn't a problem as long as data isn't sorted by class.

```
template<typename LEARNER, typename PARAMS = EMPTY, typename X = NUMERIC_X>
class OnlineMulticlassLearner
{
    mutable Treap<int, LEARNER> binaryLearners;
    int nClasses;
    PARAMS p;
    int makeKey(short label1, short label2) const
        {return label1 * numeric_limits<short>::max() + label2;}
public:
    OnlineMulticlassLearner(PARAMS const& theP = PARAMS(),
        int initialNClasses = 0): nClasses(initialNClasses), p(theP) {}
    void learn(X const& x, int label)
    {
        nClasses = max(nClasses, label + 1);
        for(int j = 0; j < nClasses; ++j) if(j != label)
        {
            int key = j < label ? makeKey(j, label) : makeKey(label, j);
            LEARNER* s = binaryLearners.find(key);
            if(!s)
            {
                binaryLearners.insert(key, LEARNER(p));
                s = binaryLearners.find(key);
            }
            s->learn(x, j < label);
        }
    }
```

```
    int classify(X const& x)const
    {
        assert(nClasses > 0);
        Vector<int> votes(nClasses, 0);
        for(int j = 0; j < nClasses; ++j)
            for(int k = j + 1; k < nClasses; ++k)
            {
                LEARNER* s = binaryLearners.find(makeKey(j, k));
                if(s) ++votes[s->classify(x) ? k : j];
            }
        return argMax(votes.getArray(), votes.getSize());
    }
};
```

This framework enables simple implementation of online linear SVM. Though don't know *n*, using the number of processed examples instead works well. Effectively, this increases *l* by a factor of 2. For scaling, studentization tends to work better than range. For testing on offline data, sample from *S* 10^6 examples and learn them online. Random sampling gives much better performance than using the original order for most data sets because it improves balance. Ensuring balance is a critical problem in online learning because *A* estimates partition boundaries, for which a learnable unit is a strata of examples with different labels.

```
class SRaceLSVM
{
    ScalerMQ s;
    typedef pair<int, double> P;
    RaceLearner<OnlineMulticlassLearner<BinaryLSVM, P>, P> model;
    static Vector<P> makeParams(int D)
    {
        Vector<P> result;
        int lLow = -15, lHigh = 5;
        for(int j = lHigh; j > lLow; j -= 2)
        {
            double l = pow(2, j);
            result.append(P(D, l));
        }
        return result;
    }
public:
    template<typename DATA> SRaceLSVM(DATA const& data):
        model(makeParams(getD(data))), s(getD(data))
    {
        for(int j = 0; j < 1000000; ++j)
        {
            int i = GlobalRNG.mod(data.getSize());
            learn(data.getX(i), data.getY(i));
        }
    }
    SRaceLSVM(int D): model(makeParams(D)), s(D){}
    void learn(NUMERIC_X const& x, int label)
    {
        s.addSample(x);
        model.learn(s.scale(x), label);
    }
    int predict(NUMERIC_X const& x)const{return model.predict(s.scale(x));}
};
```

The performance strongly depends on having enough examples (≥ 10000) in balanced order. This allows SGD to find margins quickly, and not find distant illusory margins and adjust them back too far or too little. Neural network extends similarly:

```
class SOnlineNN
{
```

```
    ScalerMQ s;
    OnlineMulticlassLearner<BinaryNN, int> model;
public:
    template<typename DATA> SOnlineNN(DATA const& data): model(getD(data)),
        s(getD(data))
    {
        for(int j = 0; j < 1000000; ++j)
        {
            int i = GlobalRNG.mod(data.getSize());
            learn(data.getX(i), data.getY(i));
        }
    }
    SOnlineNN(int D): model(D), s(D) {}
    void learn(NUMERIC_X const& x, int label)
    {
        s.addSample(x);
        model.learn(s.scale(x), label);
    }
    int predict(NUMERIC_X const& x)const{return model.predict(s.scale(x));}
};
```

SraceLSVM_10r6	MqraceLSVM_10r6	SonlineNNr_10r6
0.906	0.920	0.933

21.17 Large-scale Learning

Many algorithms are naturally paralellizable, e.g.:

- Cross-validation—folds and tested parameters are independent
- Nearest neighbor—keep several indices and combine the answers
- Random forest—trees are independent
- Multiclass transform—binary learners are independent

But many aren't:

- Boosted learners depend on each other
- Can't train binary SVM trained in parallel

21.18 Cost-sensitive Learning

A general problem is considering costs of errors. E.g., for weather prediction, the loss of carrying an umbrella < the loss of not having one during a storm, but *f* can say *no umbrella needed* if its Pr(rain) = 49%. Also, for a secure facility, incorrectly denying entry is much cheaper than letting in someone who should be denied entry.

With costs, right decisions have cost 0 or some negative cost profit value, and wrong ones cost *C*(the predicted class, the actual class) for some cost matrix *C*, which assigns a cost ∀ confusion matrix cell. If every error is equally costly, all costs = 1. Usually *C* is normalized:

- The diagonal = 0, i.e., a correct answer costs nothing.
- All other entries ∈ (0, 1]. Having costs ≤ 1 isn't necessary but ensures no range effect for algorithms that are affected by it. Multiplying *C* by a scalar leads to an equivalent problem

```
void scaleCostMatrix(Matrix<double>& cost)
{
    double maxCost = 0;
    for(int r = 0; r < cost.getRows(); ++r)
        for(int c = 0; c < cost.getRows(); ++c)
            maxCost = max(maxCost, cost(r, c));
    cost *= 1/maxCost;
}
```

Theorem (Margineantu 2001): Adding a constant to any column of *C* leads to an equivalent problem. This makes normalization simple for a typical case of negative cost diagonals—add −the diagonal value to every corresponding column.

Can calculate cost risk for a model using cost and confusion matrices. Usually use **cost risk**, but as for equal costs, can calculate **balanced cost risk**, cost risk by class, and cost confidence by class, with the corresponding Bernstein bounds.

```
double evalConfusionCost(Matrix<int> const& confusion,
    Matrix<double> const& cost)
{
    int k = confusion.rows, total = 0;
    assert(k == confusion.columns && k == cost.rows && k == cost.columns);
    double sum = 0;
    for(int r = 0; r < k; ++r)
        for(int c = 0; c < k; ++c)
        {
            total += confusion(r, c);
            sum += confusion(r, c) * cost(r, c);
        }
    return sum/total;
}
```

Some solutions for minimizing cost risk:

- Ignore costs—acceptable for highly accurate A and without huge cost differences, because mistakes are rare and, due to normalization, cost risk ≤ binary risk × max cost of any mistake.
- Use A that output probabilities. This is particularly convenient with random forest, where probability estimates are reasonably accurate. The idea of other methods is to reduce estimation error by adjusting margins to respect costs.

```
template<typename LEARNER = RandomForest> class CostLearner
{
    Matrix<double> cost;
    LEARNER model;
public:
    template<typename DATA> CostLearner(DATA const& data,
        Matrix<double>const& costMatrix): model(data), cost(costMatrix) {}
    int predict(NUMERIC_X const& x)const
        {return costClassify(model.classifyProbs(x), cost);}
};
```

- Change A individually to take costs into account. Want to replace binary risk by cost risk in all decisions, including parameter choice by cross-validation and internal objective optimization or greedy decision making. This is sometimes clumsy—e.g., for decision tree !∃ cost-weighted entropy.
- Use generic methods to make any A take costs into account. A simple solution is resampling, e.g., picking an example with weight proportional to it's expected cost. This works well for $k = 2$. **Cost folk theorem** (Zadrozny et al. 2003): For $k = 2$, $\forall f$ the expected risk from classifying with costs is equivalent to the expected risk from classifying without costs on samples from the cost-proportional distribution. So can run A on samples from the latter, obtained by resampling. For $k > 2$ this breaks down because costs depends on unknown predicted labels. A heuristic trick is using the average cost (Margineantu 2001).

```
template<typename LEARNER, typename PARAMS = EMPTY,
    typename X = NUMERIC_X> class AveCostLearner
{
    LEARNER model;
    template<typename DATA> static Vector<double> findWeights(
        DATA const& data, Matrix<double> const& costMatrix)
    {//init with average weights
        int k = costMatrix.getRows(), n = data.getSize();
        assert(k > 1 && k == findNClasses(data));
        Vector<double> classWeights(k), result(n);
        for(int i = 0; i < k; ++i)
            for(int j = 0; j < k; ++j)
                classWeights[i] += costMatrix(i, j);
        for(int i = 0; i < n; ++i) result[i] = classWeights[data.getY(i)];
```

```
        normalizeProbs(result);
        return result;
    }
public:
    template<typename DATA> AveCostLearner(DATA const& data,
        Matrix<double>const& costMatrix, PARAMS const& p = PARAMS()):
        model(data, findWeights(data, costMatrix), p) {}
    int predict(X const& x)const{return model.predict(x);}
};
```

A simple way to create a weighted *A* is using a small weight-based bagging ensemble of size 5–15. Base *A* need no changes because ensembles are easily tweaked to support weights directly. Bagging-based resampling is better than classical over-sampling, which generates too much data.

```
template<typename LEARNER, typename PARAMS = EMPTY>
    class WeightedBaggedLearner
{
    Vector<LEARNER> models;
    int nClasses;
public:
    template<typename DATA> WeightedBaggedLearner(DATA const& data,
        Vector<double> weights, PARAMS const& p = PARAMS(), int nBags = 15):
        nClasses(findNClasses(data))
    {
        assert(data.getSize() > 1);
        AliasMethod sampler(weights);
        for(int i = 0; i < nBags; ++i)
        {
            PermutedData<DATA> resample(data);
            for(int j = 0; j < data.getSize(); ++j)
                resample.addIndex(sampler.next());
            models.append(LEARNER(resample, p));
        }
    }
    int predict(NUMERIC_X const& x)const
        {return RandomForest::classifyWork(x, models, nClasses);}
};
```

Boosting is naturally adapted to handle costs because it uses feedback in subsequent rounds. SAMME and other analytic solvers don't apply because the formulas don't extend to costs, but can modify numerical solvers such as RMBoost. Instead of bounding binary loss by logistic, bound cost-adjusted loss by cost-adjusted logistic. E.g., for RMBoost, the adjusted gradient = the logistic gradient × *C*(the actual class, the best wrong class).

```
Matrix<double> getEqualCostMatrix(int nClasses)
{
    Matrix<double> result(nClasses, nClasses);
    for(int i = 0; i < nClasses; ++i)
        for(int j = 0; j < nClasses; ++j) if(i != j) result(i, j) = 1;
    return result;
}
template<typename LEARNER = NoParamsLearner<DecisionTree, int>,
    typename PARAMS = EMPTY, typename X = NUMERIC_X> class RMBoost
{
    Vector<LEARNER> classifiers;
    int nClasses;
    struct BinomialLoss
    {
        Vector<Vector<double> > F;
        BinomialLoss(int n, int nClasses): F(n, Vector<double>(nClasses, 0))
            {}
        int findBestFalse(int i, int label)
```

```
        {
            double temp = F[i][label];
            F[i][label] = -numeric_limits<double>::infinity();
            double result = argMax(F[i].getArray(), F[i].getSize());
            F[i][label] = temp;
            return result;
        }
        double getNegGrad(int i, int label, Matrix<double>const& costMatrix)
        {
            int bestFalseLabel = findBestFalse(i, label);
            double margin = F[i][label] - F[i][bestFalseLabel];
            return costMatrix(label, bestFalseLabel)/(exp(margin) + 1);
        }
    };
public:
    template<typename DATA> RMBoost(DATA const& data, Matrix<double>
        costMatrix = Matrix<double>(1, 1), PARAMS const& p = PARAMS(),
        int nClassifiers = 100): nClasses(findNClasses(data))
    {//initial weights are based on ave cost
        if(costMatrix.getRows() != nClasses)
            costMatrix = getEqualCostMatrix(nClasses);
        int n = data.getSize();
        assert(n > 0 && nClassifiers > 0);
        BinomialLoss l(n, nClasses);
        Vector<double> dataWeights(n), classWeights(nClasses);
        for(int i = 0; i < nClasses; ++i)
            for(int j = 0; j < nClasses; ++j)
                classWeights[i] += costMatrix(i, j);
        for(int i = 0; i < n; ++i)
            dataWeights[i] = classWeights[data.getY(i)];
        for(int i = 0; i < nClassifiers; ++i)
        {
            normalizeProbs(dataWeights);
            AliasMethod sampler(dataWeights);
            PermutedData<DATA> resample(data);
            for(int j = 0; j < n; ++j) resample.addIndex(sampler.next());
            classifiers.append(LEARNER(resample, p));
            for(int j = 0; j < n; ++j)
            {
                l.F[j][classifiers.lastItem().predict(data.getX(j))] +=
                    RMRate(i);
                dataWeights[j] = l.getNegGrad(j, data.getY(j), costMatrix);
            }
        }
    }
    int predict(X const& x)const
    {
        Vector<double> counts(nClasses, 0);
        for(int i = 0; i < classifiers.getSize(); ++i)
            counts[classifiers[i].predict(x)] += RMRate(i);
        return argMax(counts.getArray(), counts.getSize());
    }
};
```

Since costs ∈ (0, 1], can define **cost accuracy** = 1 − cost risk. These are curved and averaged across several data sets as regular accuracies. On C generated deterministically by making every non-diagonal entry either 0.01 or 1, this gives:

RF	AveCRF	RFProbC	RMB	RMBC	SVM	SVMAve15	SVM_RMB15
0.963	0.985	0.999	0.955	0.969	0.964	0.981	0.990

So random forest, RMBoost and SVM do reasonably well as is, but using the average cost heuristic improves random forest and SVM, and extensions specific to individual A do even better. So for vector X, random forest with probability output seems to be the method of choice. Otherwise, boosted SVM ensemble of small size 15 does well. The implementation is for vector X for simplicity.

```
class BoostedCostSVM
{
    RMBoost<MulticlassSVM<>, pair<GaussianKernel, double> > model;
public:
    template<typename DATA> BoostedCostSVM(DATA const& data,
        Matrix<double> const& cost = Matrix<double>(1, 1)):
        model(data, cost, NoParamsSVM::gaussianMultiClassSVM(data), 15) {}
    int predict(NUMERIC_X const& x)const{return model.predict(x);}
};
typedef ScaledLearner<BoostedCostSVM, int, Matrix<double> > SBoostedCostSVM;
```

Boosted SVM doesn't do better than SVM for noncost learning though. For $k = 2$, an alternative to cost boosting is the average cost method, which performs well with re-sampling:

```
class AveCostSVM
{
    typedef pair<GaussianKernel, double> P;
    AveCostLearner<WeightedBaggedLearner<MulticlassSVM<>, P>, P> model;
public:
    template<typename DATA> AveCostSVM(DATA const& data,
        Matrix<double> const & cost = Matrix<double>(1, 1)):
        model(data, cost, NoParamsSVM::gaussianMultiClassSVM(data)) {}
    int predict(NUMERIC_X const& x)const{return model.predict(x);}
};
typedef ScaledLearner<AveCostSVM, int, Matrix<double> > SAveCostSVM;
```

Despite appeal, generic methods change the data in some way, which can be problematic. E.g., re-sampling duplicates examples and increases the chance of overfitting. Estimation error is magnified because the particular instances selected for replication may not be representative, and A can pay too much attention to them. On the other hand, using probabilities as in random forest can be problematic if they are inaccurate. So A-specific modifications will have the advantage of least estimation error, but changing each A to handle costs is time-consuming.

An interesting possibility is to introduce a *don't know* class. The idea is that not knowing is usually much cheaper than making a wrong decision. This can help reduce E[the cost risk], but need A-specific modifications to handle a *don't know*. A generic approach is to modify RMBoost to return *don't know* if the overall margin is small enough, using maybe some cross-validated constant or Hoeffding bound.

An interesting idea is to relabel examples on which mistakes are costly. This is implemented by **Metacost** (Witten et al. 2011). Relabeling data may seem problematic because it introduces extra label noise, but nothing wrong with this. A more fundamental problem is using bagging to estimate probabilities. The estimates are accurate only for unstable A, which are few, and for decision trees random forest is much better. If the goal is to produce an understandable decision tree, using Metacost with random forest instead of bagging is a good solution.

21.19 Imbalanced Learning

In a given data set, some classes may appear more often than others. This can be by natural data distribution or bias in selection because rare class instances are more costly to get. E.g., for weather prediction, on most days it doesn't rain, so always predicting no rain is quite accurate.

Can have two main types of imbalance:

- Global—the iid example assumption is violated, causing unnatural imbalance.
- Local—X has many patches of few examples, which are surrounded by more numerous examples of different classes. This can happen even if examples are iid and for the majority class, just need a complex enough distribution.

In either case, classification will have estimation error by pushing the margins toward the smaller group, increasing generalization error. The best solution to both problems is getting more iid data if possible.

Can remedy global imbalance to some degree. Want to recover as much as possible of the risk due to imbalance (Prati et al. 2014). Ignoring imbalance during training is reasonable for mildly imbalanced data sets, i.e., when the example ratio is on the order of 2-to-1. It's usually hard to tell exactly when imbalance is mild. Also, it's the difference between *S* and the actual data distribution that counts, not between *S* and all-equal-class-distribution. E.g., postal envelop digits come from zip codes, where some digits are less likely than others due to population and zip code distribution, even though the data set is reasonably balanced. Global imbalance is usually a problem only if it causes local imbalance. E.g., if have 1000 or so examples in the minority class, even 1000-to-1 imbalance might not affect good *A* because for a simple enough distribution all patches will have enough support. For intuition about this, consider *k*-NN consistency requirements. Can at first ignore imbalance, and check the difference between accuracy and balanced accuracy. Need to consider correcting only if they are sufficiently different. It may also be helpful to compare class counts before learning to decide if to try correction. Some *A* such as boosting and SVM seem naturally resistant to local imbalance by trying to impose margins around all small-example groups.

A simple solution seems to be reduction to cost-sensitive learning. By the cost folk theorem, the risk on samples from a balanced distribution = the risk learning from the original one with cost(predicted, actual) = (the number of instances of the predicted class/the number of instances of the actual class). But, though costs are known without estimation error, costs from class proportions are likely to not be reflective of the distribution from which they were sampled, unless *n* is large. Reduction to cost learning tends to do poorly (Prati et al. 2014). By the same reasoning, changing *A* individually to take class distribution into account can put too much emphasis on it, though this should improve performance on balanced accuracy if the test data has similar imbalance proportions.

Direct resampling is more robust in a sense that various *A* don't blindly trust the resample proportions but learn as much as needed from them. Want to have each class is equally represented, i.e., with equal total weight ∀class.

```
template<typename DATA>
Vector<double> findImbalanceWeights(DATA const& data)
{
    int n = data.getSize(), properK = 0, nClasses = findNClasses(data);
    Vector<double> counts(nClasses);
    for(int i = 0; i < n; ++i) ++counts[data.getY(i)];
    for(int i = 0; i < nClasses; ++i) if(counts[i] > 0) ++properK;
    Vector<double> dataWeights(n, 0);
    for(int i = 0; i < data.getSize(); ++i)
        dataWeights[i] = 1.0/properK/counts[data.getY(i)];
    return dataWeights;
}
```

Weighted bagging allows this for other base learners such as SVM:

```
class ImbalanceSVM
{
    WeightedBaggedLearner<MulticlassSVM<>,
        pair<GaussianKernel, double> > model;
public:
    template<typename DATA> ImbalanceSVM(DATA const& data): model(data,
        findImbalanceWeights(data), NoParamsSVM::gaussianMultiClassSVM(data)){}
    int predict(NUMERIC_X const& x)const{return model.predict(x);}
};
typedef ScaledLearner<NoParamsLearner<ImbalanceSVM, int>, int> SImbSVM;
```

Random forest extends directly—change its bootstrap to use the alias method, and sample as in boosting:

```
class WeightedRF
{
    Vector<DecisionTree> forest;
    int nClasses;
public:
    template<typename DATA> WeightedRF(DATA const& data, Vector<double> const
        & weights, int nTrees = 300): nClasses(findNClasses(data))
    {
```

```
        assert(data.getSize() > 1);
        AliasMethod sampler(weights);
        for(int i = 0; i < nTrees; ++i)
        {
            PermutedData<DATA> resample(data);
            for(int j = 0; j < data.getSize(); ++j)
                resample.addIndex(sampler.next());
            forest.append(DecisionTree(resample, 0, true));
        }
    }
    int predict(NUMERIC_X const& x)const
        {return RandomForest::classifyWork(x, forest, nClasses);}
};
class ImbalanceRF
{
    WeightedRF model;
public:
    template<typename DATA> ImbalanceRF(DATA const& data, int nTrees = 300):
        model(data, findImbalanceWeights(data), nTrees) {}
    int predict(NUMERIC_X const& x)const{return model.predict(x);}
};
```

Resampling can introduce estimation error through duplication of examples, so it's not perfect but arguably the best available solution for strong imbalance:

RF_05_300	SSVM_10n10k_001_seps_c10	ImbRF_300	ImbSVM
0.964	0.940	0.971	0.946

Ideally, would like A that automatically addresses imbalance. This is hard because even NFL thinking shows that can't address all cases. Also, the discussed methods don't offer any theoretical guarantees. Solving local imbalance is essentially hopeless—at best, a clever A can put reasonable margins around small groups, but need enough examples to do so, otherwise it's best to consider small groups as noise. For online A, resampling for imbalance is problematic because can't even reasonably estimate class proportions.

21.20 Feature Selection

For the first attempt, a convenient strategy is using wrapper search with decision trees because this may simplify the model substantially. Otherwise, random forest is probably the best base A due its high accuracy and speed. It has some variance in performance, but this shouldn't be a problem.

```
template<typename SUBSET_LEARNER = RandomForest> struct SmartFSLearner
{
    typedef FeatureSubsetLearner<SUBSET_LEARNER> MODEL;
    MODEL model;
public:
    template<typename DATA> SmartFSLearner(DATA const& data, int limit = 20):
        model(data, selectFeaturesSmart(SCVRiskFunctor<MODEL, Bitset<>,DATA>(
        data), getD(data), limit)) {}
    int predict(NUMERIC_X const& x)const{return model.predict(x);}
};
```

The percentage of feature selected and balanced accuracy, are on average:

0.44	0.938

, which is reasonable. For the iris data, only feature 3 is selected.

For small D and n, SVM can also be useful because is too gets high accuracy and doesn't have variance, though is slower. Can try to speed it up by selecting parameters once ∀ runs, but this can spoil search if different subsets need different parameters.

Among embedded methods, decision tree and linear SVM are the most useful. E.g., linear SVM weights, perhaps multiplied by the average feature value, decide relative influence of features on the result of the linear combination; thus features with larger influence should be more important. Also, because adding features to a linearly separable problem doesn't improve accuracy, for data perfectly classified by linear SVM, can take out features until no longer linearly separable.

21.21 Handwritten Digit Recognition Performance

For the digit data, nearest neighbor is one of the most accurate methods, getting 97.96% accuracy in very little time. Some of its errors:

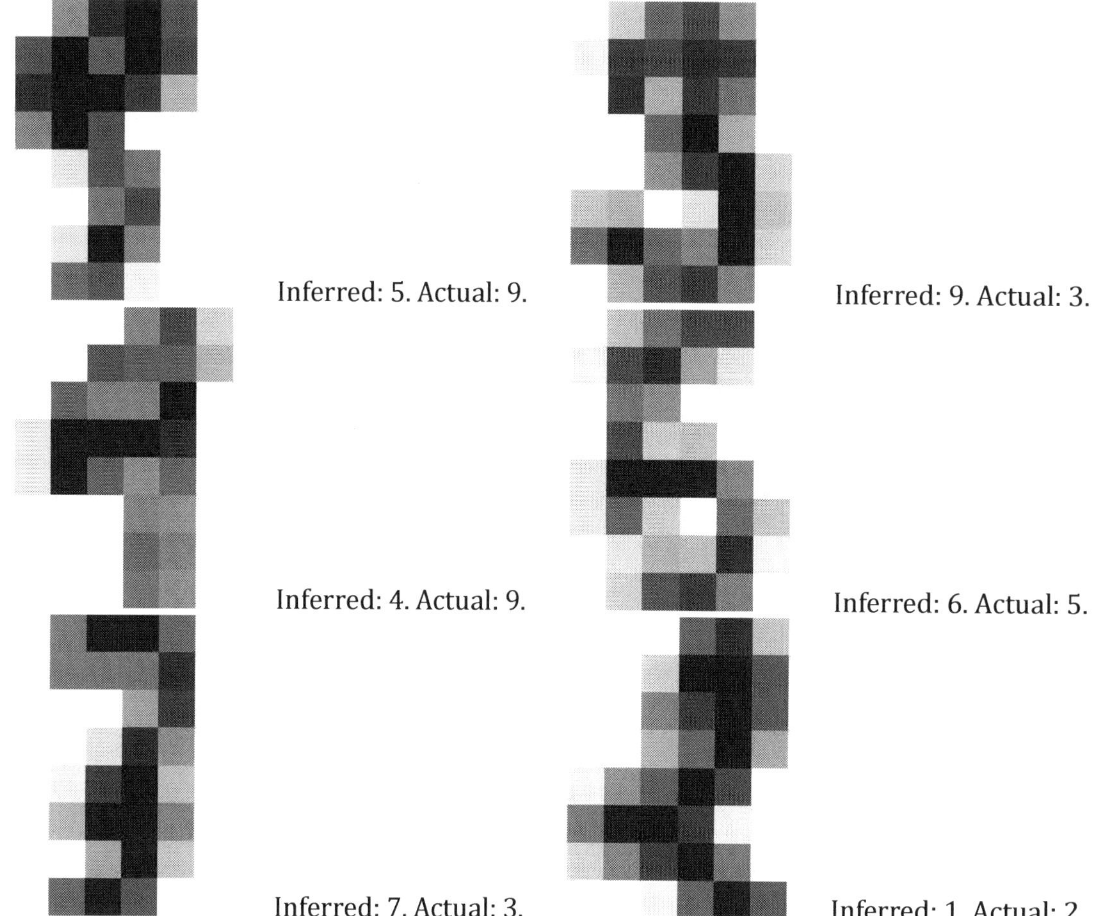

Inferred: 5. Actual: 9.

Inferred: 9. Actual: 3.

Inferred: 4. Actual: 9.

Inferred: 6. Actual: 5.

Inferred: 7. Actual: 3.

Inferred: 1. Actual: 2.

21.22 Comparing Classifiers

Experimentally (Caruana & Niculescu-Mizil 2006), boosted decision tree, random forest, and SVM, in this order, are best overall. Decision trees, nearest neighbor, and naive Bayes do poorly, and neural networks okay. On a specific problem, any of them can be best. Boosted SVM is also a possible choice. Random forest overtakes boosting in large *D* (Caruana et al. 2008) and is the best black-box *A*. It also performs best in another study (Fernández-Delgado et al. 2014), followed by SVM and neural network. This study compares hundreds of *A* on many data sets, suggesting that only a handful are useful for getting top accuracy. Others, which also have no desirable special properties, have no use cases.

Below is a simpler comparison on several UCI data sets. Some are already partitioned into training and testing. Those that aren't have been partitioned using stratified 20% holdout.

sMeanNN	NumericalBayesE	SAMME300	SSVM_10n10k_001_seps_c10
0.842	0.820	0.937	0.940
SLSVMsgd100kcd100	mqk2nn	DT-z1_50	RF_05_300
0.917	0.927	0.871	0.964
SKNN_oddlg	B_RF_SAM_SVM_NN		
0.910	0.969		

The results suggest to expect best performance from random forest, SVM, random forest, boosted decision tree, and neural network. Choosing the best of them gives even better performance:

```
template<typename X, typename Y> struct LearnerInterface
{
    virtual Y predict(X const& x)const = 0;
    virtual LearnerInterface* clone()const = 0;
```

```
};
template<typename LEARNER, typename X, typename Y>
struct TypeFreeLearner: public LearnerInterface<X, Y>
{
    LEARNER model;
    template<typename DATA> TypeFreeLearner(DATA const& data): model(data) {}
    Y predict(X const& x)const{return model.predict(x);}
    LearnerInterface<X, Y>* clone()const{return new TypeFreeLearner(*this);}
};
template<typename Y, typename X = NUMERIC_X>
class BestCombiner
{
    LearnerInterface<X, Y>* model;
    double risk;
public:
    BestCombiner(): model(0) {}
    BestCombiner(BestCombiner const& rhs): model(rhs.model->clone()) {}
    BestCombiner& operator=(BestCombiner const& rhs)
        {return genericAssign(*this, rhs);}
    template<typename LEARNER, typename DATA, typename RISK_FUNCTOR>
        void addNoParamsClassifier(DATA const& data, RISK_FUNCTOR const& r)
    {
        double riskNew = r(EMPTY());
        if(!model || riskNew < risk)
        {
            delete model;
            model = new TypeFreeLearner<LEARNER, X, Y>(data);
            risk = riskNew;
        }
    }
    Y predict(X const& x)const{assert(model); return model->predict(x);}
    ~BestCombiner(){delete model;}
};
class SimpleBestCombiner
{
    BestCombiner<int> c;
public:
    template<typename DATA> SimpleBestCombiner(DATA const& data)
    {
        c.addNoParamsClassifier<RandomForest>(data, SCVRiskFunctor<
            NoParamsLearner<RandomForest, int>, EMPTY, DATA>(data));
        c.addNoParamsClassifier<AdaBoostSamme<> >(data, SCVRiskFunctor<
            NoParamsLearner<AdaBoostSamme<>, int>, EMPTY, DATA>(data));
        c.addNoParamsClassifier<SSVM>(data, SCVRiskFunctor<
            NoParamsLearner<SSVM, int>, EMPTY, DATA>(data));
        c.addNoParamsClassifier<SNN>(data, SCVRiskFunctor<
            NoParamsLearner<SNN, int>, EMPTY, DATA>(data));
    }
    int predict(NUMERIC_X const& x)const{return c.predict(x);}
};
```

An interesting result is that combining only random forest and SVM gave better average curved balanced accuracy of 0.971, but it seems more prudent to compare more models for a new task. Could include LSVM and remove boosted tree and neural network to keep only A with well-justified generalization ability, but for general use the best selection policy needs an extensive study with many data sets, and is somewhat NFL-questionable.

Other A are generally useful only for special cases, even though ∃ data sets for which they have top performance:

- Nearest neighbor—for unusual distance functions

- Naive Bayes—for large-scale categorical data
- Linear SVM—for large-scale data

One dilemma is whether to try to make sense of the data by learning understandable patterns, or deploy classifiers that "magically" do well. Performance can be acceptable/unacceptable and understanding good/bad. A problematic outcome is bad understanding of unacceptable performance. Usually, understandable models such as small decision trees or linear SVM are so only for very small *D*, which is the case for many applications where need understandably, such as deciding to grant a loan. A reasonable strategy for a new data set:

1. If *X* isn't vector, use nearest neighbor with a specialized distance function or SVM with a specialized kernel. Boosting may improve performance. Prefer SVM over *k*-NN due to its sparser model, but *k*-NN is often the first quick-to-setup *A* to run.
2. If *n* is too large, use LSVM for numeric data and naive Bayes for categorical.
3. Try a highly pruned decision tree, then LSVM. Don't need others if the performance of either is good enough because the results give insight into the data. Decision tree is essentially the only fast *A* with $o(n^2)$ resource use, so for exploratory analysis it's the best method.
4. Try effective black-box learners: the best among random forest, SVM, boosted decision tree, and neural network, or just random forest due to its speed. The latter is preferable due to efficiency and may work better when *n* is too small (<100 maybe) to pick the best out of several *A*. Trying a few simpler things first on the same data set is technically multiple testing, but with a reduced effect because predictor clarity is the main rejection criteria.
5. If performance isn't good enough, look at the data and try to find out why learning fails. Probably need to help *A* by doing feature engineering, or augment it with domain-specific logic such as a known good neural network structure.
6. If the above still isn't good enough, research domain-specific methods for the considered domain and related ones. ∃ many other specialized *A*, useful for specific domains but not in general, that aren't covered in this chapter. But it's likely that the data doesn't have any useful information about the labels.

21.23 Comments

Traditionally, recall and precision have been used for $k = 2$ and computed only for examples with $y = 1$, which presumably is the class of interest. So these metrics may be thought of as losing too much information if both classes are important, but this is false if they are computed for all classes. Perhaps the best combined metric is something like the average of accuracy and balanced accuracy, but don't want to make this complicated.

Other somewhat popular performance metrics are application-specific (Witten et al. 2011):

- ***F*-measure**—defined for a class as the harmonic mean of precision and recall, out of which it attempts to produce a single combined metric. But it makes sense only for problems with $k = 2$ where one class is important and the other one isn't. E.g., for online search, only the relevant results matter and want to neither miss some nor get irrelevant ones. But in general treat all classes equally unless costs are specified.
- **Area under an ROC curve** (**AUC**)—applies to binary classifiers. Tries to capture performance over all possible cost matrices (Witten et al. 2011) and is sometimes popular among researchers, but for a single cost matrix reduces to something like *F*-measure, but less intuitive. Calculating it directly makes sense only for probabilistic binary classifiers. For others can use simulation to learn with costs with randomly picked cost matrices, which works well for $k = 2$. Toolkits such as Weka compute AUC automatically, but it's irrelevant for classifiers trained for a specific cost matrix. Its advantage, if any, over balanced accuracy in unclear, and the calculation complexity is substantial. Also unclear how to extend to $k > 2$.
- **Kappa** is technically a measure of agreement giving values $\in [-1, 1]$ but in this context measures adjusted accuracy by not counting accuracy on examples expected to be correctly classified by chance. E.g., any *f* with preference for more represented classes will have artificially high accuracy by chance, and kappa can detect this. Comparison on kappa is similar to that on accuracy, except kappa penalizes preference for more represented classes. Generally, performance over a baseline method is useful because it determines if a model is useful; e.g., any weather prediction model

should outperform the historical average and yesterday's weather. Kappa isn't performance over an uninformed A that always returns the majority class, but over an uninformed specific A, making it similar to balanced accuracy, but much less intuitive. It's also hard to extend to learning with costs, but balanced accuracy is easy.

For kappa and other metrics that don't come with confidence, the only way to get it is by resampling test set results, creating the corresponding confidence matrices, and using bootstrap on the resulting metrics.

Many methods can give heuristic probabilities, but with issues. E.g., naive Bayes needs to normalize, but the model itself is usually simplistic. Logistic regression (discussed in later comments) also naturally outputs probabilities, but those are accurate only assuming its model is correct and no weight penalty is used. For a decision tree, a common solution is to report leaf counts and not majorities, but the resulting probabilities aren't accurate because leaves are small.

The analog of VC-dimension for $k > 2$ is **Natarajan dimension** (Shalev-Schwartz & Ben-David 2014). But concentration bounds based on Rademacher complexity haven't yet been developed for it, and doing so will bring little improvement in conceptual understanding.

Another version of SRM doesn't depend on the confidence term but needs VC-dimensions of the considered classes to satisfy $\sum\exp(-d_i) < \infty$ (Devroye et al. 1996).

For naive Bayes, instead of binning, can use the prior-posterior methods of Bayesian statistics to model numeric data, but simple distributions such as normal are specified by few parameters and can't model multipeak distributions. Counts of categorical features with enough categories can, so binning tends to work better (Witten et al. 2011).

For k-NN, other natural extensions aren't useful:

- Weighing found neighbors by a function of distance—intuitively, should weigh closer neighbors more, maybe using $\text{weight}_i = 1/(1 + \text{distance}(x, \text{neighbor}_i))$, but in practice this partially cancels out the smoothing effect of $k > 1$. Asymptotically, not weighing is optimal (Devroye et al. 1996). Related **Kriging** for regression takes the average of all neighbors weighed by distance, and is successful, but apparently only for regression in small D, e.g., for spatial statistics.
- Removing some instances—this seems to potentially cure the memory problem. But !∃ a good way to do this because only instances well inside the margins and noisy mislabeled ones aren't useful. Asymptotically, instance selection can't lower risk (Devroye et al. 1996). One reasonable method, **IB3**, does poorly on tests (Fernández-Delgado et al. 2014). Other heuristics are better in accuracy, memory saving, or performance (Garcia et al. 2014), but not enough to justify use, mostly due to inefficiency—usually $O(n^2)$ runtime. Theoretically useful results (Gottlieb et al. 2014) aren't practical. It appears that only SVM does instance selection properly when selecting support vectors.

Locality-sensitive hashing (LSH) (for details see Andoni & Indyk 2008) allows finding nearest neighbors within a fixed distance R with high probability and more efficiently than by using exact search data structures by calculating hashes that are likely to map close x to the same bucket. Though very successful in some applications (most not related to classification, and using specialized hash functions), a generally useful implementation with Euclidean distance is problematic. A basic attempt is saving memory by storing only y and hashes, and returning the majority of found labels or defaulting to nearest mean if none is found. R and parameter "k" are found by cross-validation, and "l" set to 10. In my tests, this is only slightly more accurate than nearest mean. Any improvement will need much more memory and isn't much better than the usual k-NN query, for which VP or k-d tree are very fast on typical data despite the poor worst case.

For decision trees, **Gini index** (Aggarwal 2014) is an alternative to entropy. Intuitively, it represents probability that an example will be misclassified and has similar performance.

Can cut a $\lg(n)$ factor in decision tree construction runtime by presorting the examples by each attribute (Witten et al. 2011), but the extra memory use and code complexity aren't worth it. Some decision tree variants allow multiway trees, where a feature is split only once and not considered again. But have estimation problem in that split points may be hard to determine because election based on information gain becomes biased in favor of features with a larger number of splits. Corrections such as **gain ratio** (Aggarwal 2014) address this somewhat, but not completely. Also, the implementation is more complicated.

Many decision tree pruning methods have been proposed. Experimentally, none of several major ones is best in all cases (Aggarwal 2014). Most need a separate validation set, which can't be reused in creating the final tree, resulting in a weaker overall model. The best-known is **cost complexity pruning**—generate a number of increasingly simpler trees by pruning the "least useful" node at a time, and pick the simplest tree whose performance is at least within one standard deviation of the most accurate tree's performance. Because VC-dimension of a tree is the number of leaves, this makes sense. The main method that uses the same data set is **pessimistic error pruning**. Implemented in C4.5, it uses binomial confidence limits from table interpolation. It would be interesting to try pessimistic pruning with Bernstein bounds. Also, chi-squared test (Russell & Norvig 2010) can decide if a split is ineffective. There seem to be no published experimental comparisons between it and other methods. Based on my tests, using the sign test is simple and works better than chi-squared and pessimistic pruning by loosing less accuracy with more pruning, but !∃ published extensive studies. Also, obvious testing based on difference of normals fails because if a subtree is perfect, due to poor normal approximation of the binomial error rate, it will be deemed to perform better if the node makes $\geq 1/(1/n + 1/z^2)$ mistakes, which is a small constant ∀ reasonable z, whereas the sign test allows more reasonable $O(\sqrt{n})$ mistakes.

A possible extension (called **model tree**) is replacing majority leafs by smarter models such as logistic regression (Rusch 2012). Despite intuitive appeal, model trees don't seem to be extensively experimentally investigated. Some apparent design flaws:

- Lost interpretability
- Leaves need to have a lot of data to avoid estimation error, which isn't a much of problem for majority
- Splitting is much less efficient because need to build leaf models ∀ split, instead of quickly incrementally updating entropy

Another possibility (called **oblique tree**) is splitting on a linear combination of several variables. This is generally difficult, and tested approaches don't perform better than a regular decision tree (Fernández-Delgado et al. 2014). The main goal is producing trees with fewer nodes, which presumably makes the tree more interpretable, but this is subjective because need more estimation for complex splits. Useful algorithms for multivariate splits rely on heuristics and can be slow for large k (Truong 2009).

A logical attempt is having oblique tree nodes separate space using LSVM. The intuition is to mimic something like a BSP tree (google it), so that when linear separation is problematic, further separation should improve performance. But this fails because, due to linear SVM's own usually high accuracy, the split data will have strong class imbalance; so 2nd- and higher-level LSVMs are likely to learn to pick the majority class, mostly because SGD is very sensitive to class imbalance, and fixing it by oversampling doesn't help.

A somewhat silly extension of trees is **rules** (Witten et al. 2011). The idea is that rules are easier to understand, so try to flatten a tree into a list of rules. But a compact tree can bloat into many rules, trees are easy to understand when small, and rules are never smaller than trees.

Due to simplicity of linear separators like linear SVM, ∃ many varieties:

- **Logistic regression**—equivalent to both neural network without hidden layers and linear regression which attempts to predict $\Pr(y_i = 1|x_i)$. After a few decades of use, it's popular in statistics and very similar to linear SVM. The optimization problem of both more generally minimizes penalty(w) + $\sum L(y_i, f(x_i))$. Using $L = \ln(1 + \exp(y_i f(x_i)))$ gives logistic regression. Both usually perform similarly in terms of generalization error. SVM is preferred theoretically because it doesn't estimate probabilities, ignoring examples outside the margins and thus being more robust. On the other hand, solving logistic regression to high precision is easier because it's objective = convex function + differentiable function, for which currently ∃ more efficient solvers (Lee et al. 2014). Also, coordinate descent for logistic regression is guaranteed to converge, unlike for SVM (Hastie et al. 2015).
- **Linear discriminant analysis** (LDA)—assumes that the examples with different labels come from multivariate normal distributions with same covariance. It works well for many problems, is very efficient, online, and not affected by the order of examples, unlike SGD. But normality and same covariance assumptions are rarely satisfied in practice, and logistic regression is more robust by making strictly fewer assumptions because linearity of log odds is implied by normality (Hastie et al. 2009). Also, need $n \geq D$ for LDA to work as is. For large D, even with modifications to the algorithm, covariance matrix estimation is difficult. Nevertheless, LDA may have an advantage for online learning due to not caring about example order.
- Linear SVM/linear SVM with squared hinge loss/logistic regression, all based on L_2 regularization. This leads to easier optimization problems because of extra differentiability, but no advantages otherwise. Despite much more efficient algorithms for solving to high precision in some cases (Yuan

et al. 2012), in terms of generalization error, simple SGD is hard to improve enough to prefer a more complex approach.

Beware that some sources use the formulation "penalty + sum/n". This and a few other variants are a somewhat different problem with different properties, and !∃ need to prefer them over the standard SVM. Intuitively, with L_1 penalty and logistic regression loss, in Bayesian terms it corresponds to using a Laplace prior.

Some sources mention the outdated **perceptron algorithm**. It's designed for training neural networks without hidden layers, uses user-specified small constant learning rate and, unlike SGD, doesn't converge if the examples aren't linearly separable.

For SMO, values of the termination precision, the maximum number of iterations, and the precision to select support vectors are heuristic but currently the best known and seem robust for properly scaled data and kernels. Termination precision 0.001 is particularly suspicious because it's absolute and fails to take relative C and b into account. Still, for efficiency the value should be the largest one such that decreasing it won't noticeably improve generalization for vast majority of problems, and it's hard to improve the tried-and-true LIBSVM strategy. Using $b = 0$ reportedly leads to smaller runtime and better termination criteria (Steinwart et al. 2011) but needs more research to be favored.

Another optimization, used by LIBSVM, is selecting i and j based on 2nd order information (Bottou et al. 2007). This is faster than maximal violating pair, but not substantially. Several other optimizations are useful (Chang & Lin 2011).

Kernel SVM can't work online properly because $O(n)$ memory use is unacceptable for large n. Need to maintain a set of examples and eventually discard those that allegedly can't be support vectors. If high memory use isn't an issue, among many algorithms (Shawe-Taylor & Sun 2011; Du & Swamy 2014) **LASVM** (Bordes et al. 2005) is currently the most efficient approach. Also, can solve SVM in the primal. In particular, the representer theorem directly applies to SVM with $b = 0$ (also indirectly to $b \neq 0$), because minimizing inverse margin + hinge risk has exactly this form. Then can use SGD or **kernel PEGASOS**, but unlike LASVM and SMO, because the primal isn't differentiable, these can't use gradient information to select variables to optimize. By leaving many support vectors at 0, LASVM finds a sparse solution unlike others.

Since larger C correspond to larger margins, it would be interesting to change parameter selection objective to give up some accuracy to favor larger C or at least resolve ties this way. This appears unexplored.

For both kernel and linear SVM and variants, when picking C or l, it seems better to start with the solution to a previously solved problem for efficiency. But starting will all 0's is better for regularization for many solvers because making a value 0 tends to be easier then setting it back to 0.

Though always using a good kernel such as Gaussian works well, can try to automatically pick the kernel from data (Gönen & Alpaydın 2011). But benefits of doing so in practice are unclear, mostly due to inefficiency of currently best known approaches.

Random forest is similar to bagging merged with **random subspace method**, which trains ensembles of classifiers on random subsets of features. The latter applies to any base A, and the former only to trees but gets much less correlation between trem. Because low bias and high variance of trees makes them ideal for random forests, there is little interest in extending to other A.

∃ several attempted improvements of random forests, but all have flaws. **Rotation forest** (Kuncheva 2014) uses a sparse matrix to rotate x and creates a decision tree of the result, making a forest of these. The idea is appealing, but rotating is slow, needs scaling of data, and generally doesn't improve on random forests (Fernández-Delgado et al. 2014). Another possibility is, when constructing a tree, to sample the next feature based on some function of how useful that feature is, but the result is similar to bagging.

More is known about the approximation power of neural networks (Scarselli & Tsoi 1998), but little of it is useful. Beware that some such results appear to not depend on D, but the constants in various bounds depend on D, and neural networks don't overcome the curse of dimensionality. ∃ asymptotic lower bounds on function approximation that depend on n and D (Ripley 1996).

SGD training is not an exact science. Another recommendation is to use initial learning rate $1/\sqrt{D}$ to make sure the sums don't swing by much, and give hidden layers a constant factor more weight to counter vanishing gradients (Montavon et al. 2012), but the two roughly cancel out for typical D.

For hidden neurons, it seems better to use an activation function with polynomial decrease, such as **Elliot's function** (Elliot 1993). But in my experiments tanh performs slightly better. Another interesting idea is to cap weight updates in the hidden layer (saturation in the output layer is unlikely due to only having 5 units). E.g., tanh(1.83) = 0.95, and to avoid saturation it seems that the sums for an example shouldn't be > 1.83 or so. But capping doesn't improve performance in my experiments. Perhaps examples are different enough to not cause saturation, or the exponential drop has a stabilizing effect by not letting weights get too large.

Instead of using OVO and 5 hidden neurons, can use a single OVA network with cross-validated number of neurons (Caruana & Niculescu-Mizil 2006). But in my experiments this tends to be much slower and performs worse. With a single network, hidden neurons may benefit from seeing all data, but the magnitude of this effect is unclear.

mqk2nn_l436	mqk2nn_el	mqk2nn_1m	mqk2nn_cap183_1m	mqk2nn_cap183	ave100kmq_5	mqk2nn
0.939	0.936	0.944	0.941	0.950	0.931	0.946

SGD isn't the only way to train neural networks. Batch methods compute gradients based on all examples and use general optimization methods such as L-BFGS, which converges superlinearly (see the "Numerical Algorithms" chapter), enabling high precision solutions. But for large n calculating gradients is expensive, and both high- and low-precision solutions have similar generalization, so prefer SGD. Contrary to intuition, many hidden neurons can work better than a few, maybe because due to random initialization have a higher chance of discovering a good pattern in some neurons, while the rest harmlessly remain ineffective without introducing extra estimation error.

Another approach to regularizing a network is early stopping. But risk can decrease even more after increasing (Montavon et al. 2012), so don't have a clear way to do this. Weight decay is safer.

Feed-forward network is the most used but not the only type. **Recurrent network** allows neurons to feed themselves with own outputs (i.e., self-criticism attempt), but suffer more from vanishing gradients. **RBF network** uses kernels in input layer, but also doesn't perform well (Fernández-Delgado et al. 2014), and kernel SVM is better at nonlinearity. **Bayesian neural network** got top performance on several high-dimensional data sets (Hastie et al. 2009). The idea is to have normal(0, σ) prior weights for some σ such as 1. Assume independent outputs, and calculate Pr(y_i | x_i, weights). This allows inference by MCMC sampling from the posterior. The method is very slow but seems suitable to the problems that were solved (Hastie et al. 2009). Complexity and slowness prevent its general use. Intuitively, should be able to get the same results from averaging several networks optimized using global search with weight decay, but this too would be very slow. Because MCMC is optimizing and averaging at the same time, maybe iterated local search can do the same, i.e., average all of its locally optimized results across the jumps, but unclear how to find a good jump step.

Another, more popular, way to do deep learning is **restricted Boltzmann machine** (RBM). But auto-encoder is simpler, and currently !∃ experimental comparisons preferring one over the other in general. See Montavon et al. (2012), Du & Swamy (2014), and Bengio et al. (2015) for further discussion of many complexities of neural networks. It's also interesting to use unsupervised output from a deep network as features to another A.

Many boosting variants have been proposed, but no extensive studies have yet established their merits. **AdaBoost.M1** uses AdaBoost for $k > 2$ as is, except for disallowing answer flipping, but needs base A accuracy > 0.5. **AdaBoost.MH** and others based on output codes (Schapire & Freund 2012) allow weaker learners but are more complex than SAMME and haven't been shown to perform better. **AdaBoost.L** (Schapire & Freund 2012) uses binomial loss with analytically derived optimal weights, improving earlier **LogitBoost**, but according to published (Schapire & Freund 2012) and my tests it performs similarly to AdaBoost.M1, and !∃ a reason to prefer it over SAMME. Intuitively, logistic loss isn't very different from exponential because in both correct example weights drop off exponentially fast. It would be interesting to investigate a polynomial drop loss and use of low-depth lightly pruned trees as base A.

Even though gradient boosting isn't suitable for classification, **gradient tree boosting** is claimed to perform well (Hastie et al. 2009). The idea is to do OVA and train k low-depth regression trees. Then ∀ example, their outputs are combined using multinomial loss into a single score = 1 − the estimated correct class probability. Multinomial loss also gives probabilities directly, but those have numeric problems without proper normalization. However:

- Inefficient—need k trees, training each to minimize multinomial loss gradient can't use increment computation, and finding multinomial loss minimizers needs numerical minimization. Using low depth doesn't help.
- Not statistically significantly better than that of substantially faster random forest.
- Small constant tree weights are recommended because the optimal weights can lead to substantial

overfitting, which is very suspicious.

- !∃ studies comparing it with other boosting variants on many data sets.

In practice, !∃ a reason to generally prefer boosting over random forest, which is robust to noise. More complex algorithms such as **BrownBoost** (Schapire & Freund 2012; Cheamanunkul et al. 2014) resist noise by eventually giving up on some examples (which loses convexity), but !∃ experimental evidence in their favor.

Can combine unrelated A using **weighted majority voting**, where base A with accuracy a have relative weight $\ln(a/(1-a))$ (Kuncheva 2014). This is less efficient than picking the best due to having to train all and use the results of all. Also, it's not better:

W_RF_SAM_SVM_NN	B_RF_SAM_SVM_NN
0.962	0.969

The reason for not improving performance probably is that, unlike in homogeneous combinations such as random forest, base learners aren't intended to have low correlation. In fact !∃ an optimal combination method due to NFL effects (Hu & Damper 2008).

Can adapt decision trees for online learning. A typical method is **VLDT** (Gama 2010). A simplified version of it, which also applies to continuous labels, recursively buffers examples in each leaf until have m (maybe 100), splits the leaf, and discards its examples. Discarding makes pruning unnecessary because don't have estimation error due to reusing examples for further splits. One problem is that can have a nonrandom stream with m examples of the same class, in which case must either increase m or drop the majority ones until meet some balance criteria. Memory can become an issue, and keeping leaf buffers on disk can incur 1 I/O per update in the worst case, though using a large LRU cache will help. This works for regression trees (see the "Machine Learning—Regression" chapter) as well.

Can also make bagging (and thus random forest) online by drawing the multiplicity of each example from an appropriate Poisson distribution (Gama 2010). But because decision tree buffers don't like multiplicity, this is probably a bad idea.

Cost-sensitive learning needs more experimental research and research for methods appropriate for various cases and supporting theory, all of which are currently lacking.

For imbalance correction, a classic solution is oversampling, i.e., randomly increasing the number of minority classes' examples by resampling. This can cause too much duplication and overfit and, unlike ensemble resampling, commits to a single resample. So it's not recommended, despite being faster. **SMOTE** (Lopez et al. 2013) attempts to solve overfitting by interpolating known examples, which seems silly regardless of its good performance and works only for vector x. Experimentally, studying the extra risk due to imbalance is difficult because have many possibilities to consider, such as n, imbalance ratio, specific local clusters, etc.

A class of algorithms generalizing naive Bayes is **graphical models** such as **Bayesian network**. They try to estimate probabilities more accurately by assuming dependencies among groups of features (Russell & Norvig 2010). E.g., in an image, neighboring pixels are dependent and distant pixels usually aren't. But finding out which features depend on which others is difficult. Though some graphical models are successful in certain application domains such as natural language processing, where substantial prior knowledge suggests structure, they aren't black-box because automatically and efficiently finding good structure from data is problematic. A typical approach is iteratively grouping correlated variables using some correlation measure such as mutual information, or doing iterated local search using MDL as the score function. These and others have numerous flaws, with both estimation and approximation errors. Also, estimating probabilities accurately solves a more general problem, increasing estimation error.

21.24 References

Andoni, A. & Indyk, P. (2008). Near-optimal hashing algorithms for approximate nearest neighbor in high dimensions. *Communications of the ACM*, *51*(1), 117–122.

Anthony, M., & Bartlett, P. L. (2009). *Neural Network Learning: Theoretical Foundations*. Cambridge University Press.

Aggarwal, C. C. (2014). *Data Classification: Algorithms and Applications*. CRC Press.

Bache, K. & Lichman, M. (2013). *UCI Machine Learning Repository* [http://archive.ics.uci.edu/ml]. University of California. Accessed 10/19/2014.

Bengio, Y., Goodfellow, I. J., & Courville, A. (2015). Deep Learning (Draft).

http://www.iro.umontreal.ca/~bengioy/dlbook/.

Biau, G., Devroye, L., & Lugosi, G. (2008). Consistency of random forests and other averaging classifiers. *The Journal of Machine Learning Research, 9*, 2015–2033.

Bordes, A., Ertekin, S., Weston, J., & Bottou, L. (2005). Fast kernel classifiers with online and active learning. *The Journal of Machine Learning Research, 6*, 1579–1619.

Bottou, L. (Ed.). (2007). *Large-scale Kernel Machines*. MIT Press.

Breiman, L. (1996). Heuristics of instability and stabilization in model selection. *The annals of statistics, 24*(6), 2350–2383.

———. (2001). Random forests. *Machine learning, 45*(1), 5–32.

Caruana, R., Karampatziakis, N., & Yessenalina, A. (2008). An empirical evaluation of supervised learning in high dimensions. In *Proceedings of the 25th international conference on Machine learning* (pp. 96–103). ACM.

Caruana, R., & Niculescu-Mizil, A. (2006). An empirical comparison of supervised learning algorithms. In *Proceedings of the 23rd international conference on Machine learning* (pp. 161–168). ACM.

Cérou, F., & Guyader, A. (2006). Nearest neighbor classification in infinite dimension. *ESAIM: Probability and Statistics, 10*, 340–355.

Chang, C. C., & Lin, C. J. (2011). LIBSVM: a library for support vector machines. *ACM Transactions on Intelligent Systems and Technology (TIST), 2*(3), 27.

Cheamanunkul, S., Ettinger, E., & Freund, Y. (2014). Non-convex boosting overcomes random label noise. *arXiv preprint arXiv:1409.2905*.

Daniely, A., Sabato, S., & Shwartz, S. S. (2012). Multiclass learning approaches: a theoretical comparison with implications. In *Advances in Neural Information Processing Systems* (pp. 485–493).

Devroye, L., Gyorfi, L., & Lugosi, G. (1996). *A Probabilistic Theory of Pattern Recognition*. Springer.

Domingos, P. (2000). A unified bias-variance decomposition. In *Proceedings of 17th International Conference on Machine Learning. Stanford CA Morgan Kaufmann* (pp. 231–238).

Du, K. L., & Swamy, M. N. S. (2014). *Neural Networks and Statistical Learning*. Springer.

Elliott, D. L. (1993). A better activation function for artificial neural networks.

Fernández-Delgado, M., Cernadas, E., Barro, S., & Amorim, D. (2014). Do we need hundreds of classifiers to solve real world classification problems?. *The Journal of Machine Learning Research, 15*(1), 3133–3181.

Gama, J. (2010). *Knowledge Discovery from Data Streams*. CRC Press.

García, S., Luengo, J., & Herrera, F. (2014). *Data Preprocessing in Data Mining*. Springer.

Gönen, M., & Alpaydın, E. (2011). Multiple kernel learning algorithms. *The Journal of Machine Learning Research, 12*, 2211–2268.

Gottlieb, L. A., Kontorovitch, A., & Nisnevitch, P. (2014). Near-optimal sample compression for nearest neighbors. In *Advances in Neural Information Processing Systems* (pp. 370–378).

Hastie, T., Tibshirani, R., & Friedman, J. (2009). *The Elements of Statistical Learning*. Springer.

Hastie, T., Tibshirani, R., & Wainwright, M. (2015). *Statistical Learning with Sparsity: The Lasso and Generalizations*. CRC Press.

Ho, T. K. (2002). Multiple classifier combination: Lessons and next steps. *Series in Machine Perception and Artificial Intelligence, 47*, 171–198.

Hornik, K. (1991). Approximation capabilities of multilayer feedforward networks. *Neural networks, 4*(2), 251–257.

Hsu, C. W., Chang, C. C., & Lin, C. J. (2010). A practical guide to support vector classification.

Hu, R., & Damper, R. I. (2008). A 'no panacea theorem' for classifier combination. *Pattern Recognition, 41*(8), 2665–2673.

Hyafil, L., & Rivest, R. L. (1976). Constructing optimal binary decision trees is NP-complete. *Information Processing Letters, 5*(1), 15–17.

Jeatrakul, P. (2012). *Enhancing Classification Performance over Noise and Imbalanced Data Problems*. Murdoch University.

Kohavi, R. (1995). A study of cross-validation and bootstrap for accuracy estimation and model selection. In *IJCAI* (Vol. 14, No. 2, pp. 1137–1145).

King, R. D., Feng, C., & Sutherland, A. (1995). Statlog: comparison of classification algorithms on large real-world problems. *Applied Artificial Intelligence an International Journal, 9*(3), 289–333.

Kuncheva, L. I. (2014). *Combining Pattern Classifiers: Methods and Algorithms*. Wiley.

Lee, J. D., Sun, Y., & Saunders, M. A. (2014). Proximal Newton-type methods for minimizing composite

functions. *SIAM Journal on Optimization, 24*(3), 1420–1443.
Leshno, M., Lin, V. Y., Pinkus, A., & Schocken, S. (1993). Multilayer feedforward networks with a nonpolynomial activation function can approximate any function. *Neural networks, 6*(6), 861–867.
Long, P. M., & Servedio, R. A. (2010). Random classification noise defeats all convex potential boosters. *Machine Learning, 78*(3), 287–304.
López, V., Fernández, A., García, S., Palade, V., & Herrera, F. (2013). An insight into classification with imbalanced data: Empirical results and current trends on using data intrinsic characteristics. *Information Sciences, 250*, 113–141.
Mandziuk, J. (2010). *Knowledge-Free and Learning-Based Methods in Intelligent Game Playing* (Vol. 276). Springer.
Margineantu, D. D. (2001). Methods for cost-sensitive learning. (Doctoral dissertation, Oregon State University).
Mohri, M., Rostamizadeh, A., & Talwalkar, A. (2012). *Foundations of Machine Learning*. MIT Press.
Montavon, G., Orr, G. B., & Müller, K. R. (2012). *Neural Networks: Tricks of the Trade*. Springer.
Orriols-Puig, A., Macia, N., & Ho, T. K. (2010). Documentation for the data complexity library in C++. *Universitat Ramon Llull, La Salle, 196.*
Prati, R. C., Batista, G. E., & Silva, D. F. (2014). Class imbalance revisited: a new experimental setup to assess the performance of treatment methods. *Knowledge and Information Systems*, 1–24.
Ripley, Brian D. (1996). *Pattern Recognition and Neural Networks*. Cambridge University Press.
Russell, S. J., Norvig, P. (2010). *Artificial Intelligence: a Modern Approach*. Prentice Hall.
Rusch, T. (2012). *Recursive Partitioning of Models of a Generalized Linear Model Type*. WU Vienna University of Economics and Business.
Scarselli, F., & Tsoi, A. C. (1998). Universal approximation using feedforward neural networks: A survey of some existing methods, and some new results. *Neural networks, 11*(1), 15–37.
Shalev-Shwartz, S., & Ben-David, S. (2014). *Understanding Machine Learning: From Theory to Algorithms*. Cambridge University Press.
Shawe-Taylor, J., & Sun, S. (2011). A review of optimization methodologies in support vector machines. *Neurocomputing, 74*(17), 3609–3618.
Sra, S., Nowozin, S., & Wright, S. J. (2012). *Optimization for Machine Learning*. MIT Press.
Steinwart, I., Hush, D., & Scovel, C. (2011). Training SVMs without offset. *The Journal of Machine Learning Research, 12*, 141–202.
Truong, A. K. Y. (2009). *Fast Growing and Interpretable Oblique Trees via Logistic Regression Models*. University of Oxford.
Witten, I. H., Frank, E., & Hall, M.A. (2011). *Data Mining: Practical Machine Learning Tools and Techniques*. Morgan Kaufmann.
Yuan, G. X., Ho, C. H., & Lin, C. J. (2012). Recent advances of large-scale linear classification. *Proceedings of the IEEE, 100*(9), 2584–2603.
Zadrozny, B., Langford, J., & Abe, N. (2003). Cost-sensitive learning by cost-proportionate example weighting. In *Data Mining, 2003. ICDM 2003. Third IEEE International Conference on* (pp. 435–442). IEEE.
Zhu, J., Zou, H., Rosset, S. & Hastie, T. (2009) Multi-class AdaBoost. *Statistics and Its Interface*. (Vol 2, pp. 349–360).

22 Machine Learning—Regression

22.1 Regression

Technically, regression is stochastic multidimensional function approximation (stochastic because of possible y noise), except that function approximation is a little easier because can query a function at any point, whereas for regression must use given points. Extrapolation is particularly difficult for regression because for regions far enough from those with available data, at best can assume that the unknown function has value = weighted average of known points.

22.2 Risk Estimation

The most natural error metric is by how much a prediction is expected to be wrong. This is L_1 loss. But many algorithms have difficulty minimizing it, and want to have larger penalty on larger errors. So differentiable L_2 loss, called **root-mean-squared error** (RMSE), is used instead as the main optimization criteria. Also, L_∞ loss makes sense because it's the worst-case error, at least on the test set.

RMSE is more difficult to interpret than the other two. Think of it as the standard deviation of y given f. This leads to **expStd** criteria—the % of explained standard deviation = 1 − RMSE/stdev(test data y). Think of expStd as how much f explains more over the simple average of test data labels. It seems to be the best criteria for comparing various A. Because −expStd is a monotonic function of RMSE, using either for comparison gives the same result, but the former is easy to turn into a curved grade for comparing many A on many data sets.

Cross-validation uses RMSE directly. Though it has no problem with minimizing the more intuitive and direct L_1 loss, it seems more appropriate to use RMSE because various A use it, and it puts larger penalty on larger errors. Not all applications have such preference, but it's hard to define a perfect error metric. In regression, what you need, want, and get can be all different, and L_2 loss tends to give what you need more than others. May think that need some kind of relative L_1 loss to measure precision of a prediction, but for applications such as air temperature prediction this makes no sense. Special applications must use customized error metrics that take costs into account.

```
struct RegressionStats{double expStd, rmse, l1Err, lInfErr;};
RegressionStats evaluateRegressor(
    Vector<pair<double, double> > const& testResult)
{
    IncrementalStatistics yStats, l2Stats, l1Stats;
    for(int i = 0; i < testResult.getSize(); ++i)
    {
        yStats.addValue(testResult[i].first);
        double diff = testResult[i].second - testResult[i].first;
        l1Stats.addValue(abs(diff));
        l2Stats.addValue(diff * diff);
    }
    RegressionStats result;
    result.lInfErr = l1Stats.maximum;
    result.l1Err = l1Stats.getMean();
    result.rmse = sqrt(l2Stats.getMean());
    result.expStd = 1 - result.rmse/yStats.stdev();
    return result;
}

template<typename LEARNER, typename DATA, typename PARAMS> double
    crossValidateReg(PARAMS const& p, DATA const& data, int nFolds = 5)
{
```

```
    return evaluateRegressor(crossValidateGeneral<LEARNER,
        typename DATA::Y_TYPE>(p, data, nFolds)).rmse;
}
template<typename LEARNER, typename PARAM, typename DATA>
struct RRiskFunctor
{
    DATA const& data;
    RRiskFunctor(DATA const& theData): data(theData) {}
    double operator()(PARAM const& p)const
        {return crossValidateReg<LEARNER>(p, data);}
};
```

Stratification isn't available unlike for classification, but repeated cross-validation is:

```
template<typename LEARNER, typename DATA, typename PARAMS> double
    repeatedCVReg(PARAMS const& p, DATA const& data, int nFolds = 5,
    int nRepeats = 5)
{
    return evaluateRegressor(repeatedCVGeneral<double>(
        LEARNER(data, p), data, nFolds, nRepeats)).rmse;
}

template<typename LEARNER, typename PARAM, typename DATA>
struct RRCVRiskFunctor
{
    DATA const& data;
    RRCVRiskFunctor(DATA const& theData): data(theData) {}
    double operator()(PARAM const& p)const
        {return repeatedCVReg<LEARNER>(p, data);}
};
```

22.3 Complexity Control

For a useful analysis of regression, must assume loss ≤ some large constant M. This isn't the case for L_2 loss, but intuitively can consider L_2 loss trimmed at M, or make M large enough. If don't have a bound on loss, a single very bad loss value's can skew the risk by an arbitrary amount, so can't give a probabilistic guarantee.

Similarly to classification, a good complexity measure of G is **pseudo-dimension** (Mohri et al. 2012):

- For n points, create a set of classifiers IG, given by picking constants t_i ∀ example and defining $ig(x_i) = \text{sign}(g(x_i) - t_i)$. Essentially, g are discretized around how much they oscillate around a particular set of control points.
- $\text{PDim}(G) = \text{VC-dim}(IG)$ under the worse-case choice of t_i.

Theorem (Mohri et al. 2012): For G consisting of linear predictors, $\text{PDim}(G) = D + 1$.

As for classification, can bound generalization error by a function of training error, n, and the complexity of G. Theorem (Mohri et al. 2012): Let G have pseudo-dimension d. Then, with probability $\geq 1 - p$, $R_f \leq R_{f,n} + M(\sqrt{2d\ln(en/d)/n} + \sqrt{-\ln(p)/(2n)})$.

22.4 Linear Regression

Regression finds the best fit linear combination of features $y = wx + b$, where the weight vector w and the bias term b minimize $\sum(y_i - f(x_i))^2$ for the training data. For simplicity, make b part of w by adding a constant feature to x with value 1. Then for X = the $n \times (D+1)$ matrix of feature values for all data and Y the vector of outputs, $w = (X^TX)^{-1}X^TY$. Assuming normally distributed $y_i - f(x_i)$, ∃ confidence intervals for the result.

The computation fails when $D > n$ or X is singular without additional logic such as computing a pseudo-inverse, or, in the latter case, remove redundant features or examples.

Computing the inverse needs $O(n^3)$ time and $O(n^2)$ space, which doesn't scale beyond medium size problems. A more efficient way to compute the solution is using an iterative process such as the one for lasso regression.

22.5 Lasso Regression

A good solution to the classical regression's problems is to use L_1 penalty on weights, getting minimization objective $l|w| + \sum(y_i - f(x_i))^2$, for small constant l. This is also called the **lasso**. As for LSVM, L_1 penalty leads to sparse solutions.

The problem is convex and of the form convex function + differentiable function. This means coordinate descent (see the "Numerical Algorithms" chapter) is globally convergent (Hastie et al. 2014). Also, 1D problems have analytic solutions.

For simplicity, add a ½ factor, and minimize $l|w| + ½\sum(y_i - f(x_i))^2$. When working with weight j, can aggregate the other components of $f(x_i)$ into $s_i = y_i - (b + \sum_{k \neq j} w_k x_{ik})$, getting the equivalent problem min $l|w_j| + ½\sum(s_i - w_j x_{ij})^2$ + constant. It's at the optimum when $0 \in$ subgradient set, i.e., $0 = lS(w) + \sum(s_i - w_j x_{ij})(-x_{ij})$, where S is the sign function. Solving, $w_j c = a + lS(w_j)$ for $a = \sum s_i x_{ij}$, and $c = \sum x_{ij}^2$. Because $c \geq 0$, $a \geq -l$ if $w_j \geq 0$ and $\leq l$ if $w_j \leq 0$. So considering intervals of a, $w_j < 0$ if $a < -l$, > 0 if $a > l$, and 0 otherwise. So $w_j = (a - l)/c$ if $a < -l$, $(a + l)/c$ if $a > l$, and 0 otherwise. The formula is numerically stable because very small c cause $w_j = 0$.

$b = \sum s_i/n$ because then $½\sum(s_i - b)^2$ is smallest. l is selected using cross-validation, from same range as for linear SVM. For energy data:

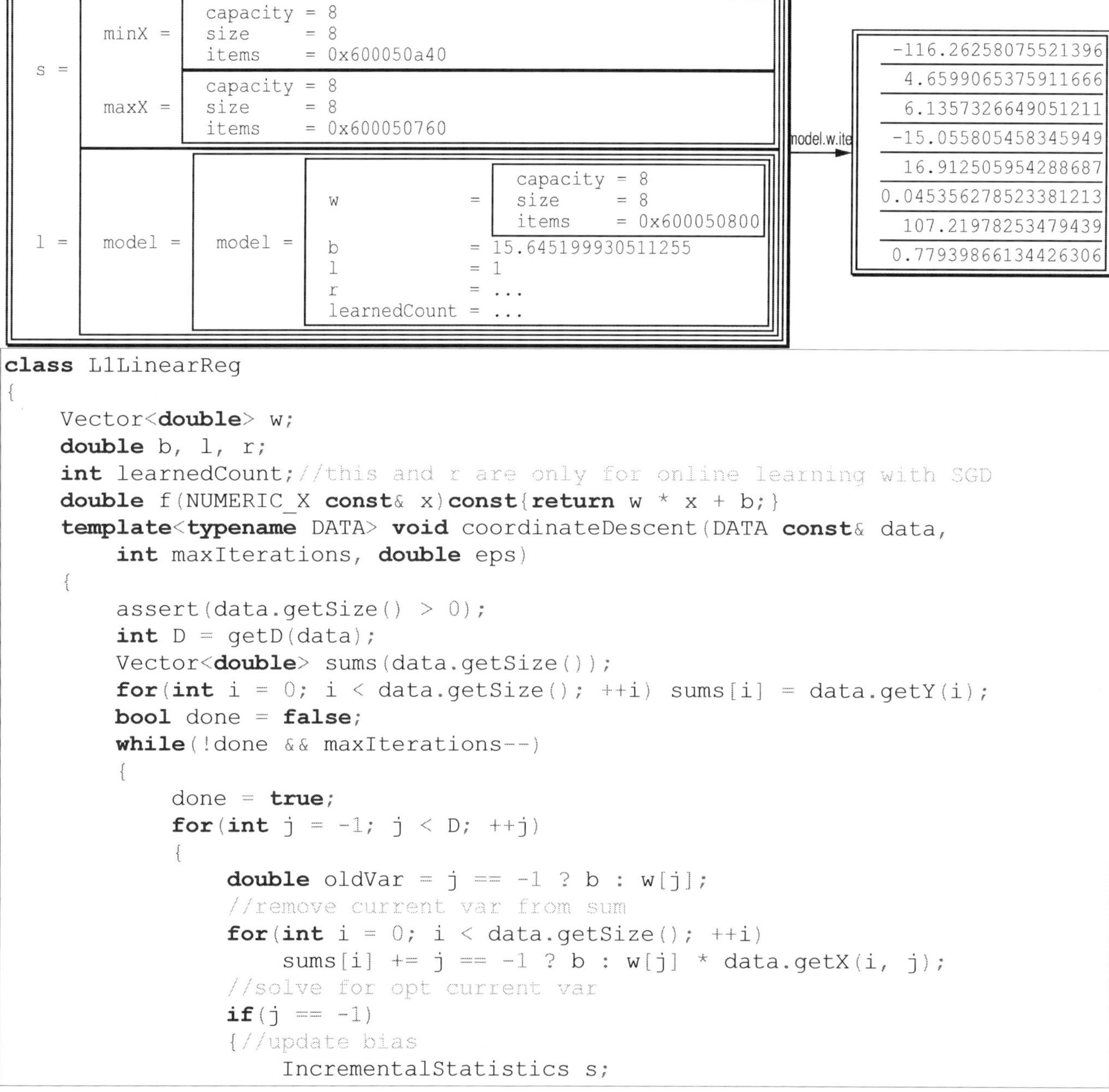


```
class L1LinearReg
{
    Vector<double> w;
    double b, l, r;
    int learnedCount;//this and r are only for online learning with SGD
    double f(NUMERIC_X const& x)const{return w * x + b;}
    template<typename DATA> void coordinateDescent(DATA const& data,
        int maxIterations, double eps)
    {
        assert(data.getSize() > 0);
        int D = getD(data);
        Vector<double> sums(data.getSize());
        for(int i = 0; i < data.getSize(); ++i) sums[i] = data.getY(i);
        bool done = false;
        while(!done && maxIterations--)
        {
            done = true;
            for(int j = -1; j < D; ++j)
            {
                double oldVar = j == -1 ? b : w[j];
                //remove current var from sum
                for(int i = 0; i < data.getSize(); ++i)
                    sums[i] += j == -1 ? b : w[j] * data.getX(i, j);
                //solve for opt current var
                if(j == -1)
                {//update bias
                    IncrementalStatistics s;
```

```
                for(int i = 0; i < data.getSize(); ++i)
                    s.addValue(sums[i]);
                b = s.getMean();
            }
            else
            {//update weight
                double a = 0, c = 0;
                for(int i = 0; i < data.getSize(); ++i)
                {
                    double xij = data.getX(i, j);
                    a += sums[i] * xij;
                    c += l * xij * xij;
                }
                if(a < -l) w[j] = (a - l)/c;
                else if(a > l) w[j] = (a + l)/c;
                else w[j] = 0;
            }
            //add back current var to up
            for(int i = 0; i < data.getSize(); ++i)
                sums[i] -= j == -1 ? b : w[j] * data.getX(i, j);
            if(abs((j == -1 ? b : w[j]) - oldVar) > eps) done = false;
        }
    }
}
public:
    template<typename DATA> L1LinearReg(DATA const& data, double theL,
        int nCoord = 1000): l(theL/2), b(0), w(getD(data)), learnedCount(-1)
        {coordinateDescent(data, nCoord, pow(10, -6));}
    double predict(NUMERIC_X const& x)const{return f(x);}
    template<typename MODEL, typename DATA>
    static double findL(DATA const& data)
    {
        int lLow = -15, lHigh = 5;
        Vector<double> regs;
        for(double j = lHigh; j > lLow; j -= 2) regs.append(pow(2, j));
        return valMinFunc(regs.getArray(), regs.getSize(),
            RRiskFunctor<MODEL, double, DATA>(data));
    }
};
struct NoParamsL1LinearReg
{
    L1LinearReg model;
    template<typename DATA> NoParamsL1LinearReg(DATA const& data):
        model(data, L1LinearReg::findL<L1LinearReg>(data)) {}
    double predict(NUMERIC_X const& x)const{return model.predict(x);}
};
typedef ScaledLearner<NoParamsLearner<NoParamsL1LinearReg, double>, double>
    SLasso;
```

Each iteration takes $O(n)$ time (see the "Machine Learning—Classification" chapter for when the data is on disk).

To solve online, can use SGD. Given rate r, differentiating the objective gives the update equations w_i += $r(x\epsilon - \text{sign}(w_i)l/n$ and b += $r\epsilon$, for $\epsilon = y - f(x)$. As for online LSVM, use the number of seen examples as n. Unlike for LSVM, need to race-tune the initial r because SGD steps can become too large. Also, SGD converges very slowly, so can't get sparsity because many eventual 0 components of w may not get close enough to 0. For racing, the initial r use the same range as for l, which is the same as for classification.

```
    typedef pair<int, pair<double, double> > PARAM;//D/l/r
    L1LinearReg(PARAM const& p): l(p.second.first/2), r(p.second.second),
        b(0), w(p.first), learnedCount(0) {}
```

```
    void learn(NUMERIC_X const& x, double y)
    {
        assert(learnedCount != -1);//can't mix batch and offline
        double rate = r * RMRate(learnedCount++), err = y - f(x);
        for(int i = 0; i < w.getSize(); ++i) w[i] +=
            rate * (x[i] * err - (w[i] > 0 ? 1 : -1) * l/learnedCount);
        b += rate * err;
    }
class SRaceLasso
{
    ScalerMQ s;
    RaceLearner<L1LinearReg, L1LinearReg::PARAM> model;
    static Vector<L1LinearReg::PARAM> makeParams(int D)
    {
        Vector<L1LinearReg::PARAM> result;
        int lLow = -15, lHigh = 5, rLow = -15, rHigh = 5;
        for(int j = lHigh; j > lLow; j -= 2)
        {
            double l = pow(2, j);
            for(int i = rHigh; i > rLow; i -= 2) result.append(
                L1LinearReg::PARAM(D, pair<double, double>(l, pow(2, i))));
        }
        return result;
    }
public:
    template<typename DATA> SRaceLasso(DATA const& data):
        model(makeParams(getD(data))), s(getD(data))
    {
        for(int j = 0; j < 1000000; ++j)
        {
            int i = GlobalRNG.mod(data.getSize());
            learn(data.getX(i), data.getY(i));
        }
    }
    SRaceLasso(int D): model(makeParams(D)), s(D) {}
    void learn(NUMERIC_X const& x, double y)
    {
        s.addSample(x);
        model.learn(s.scale(x), y);
    }
    double predict(NUMERIC_X const& x)const
        {return model.predict(s.scale(x));}
};
```

Lasso is the default approach, replacing linear regression as a black box due to favorable properties of the L_1 penalty. Using $l = 0$ and not scaling reduces to linear regression. The only conceivable benefit of doing so is to avoid scaling to get a slightly easier-to-explain model. But can reverse-scale w and b (which correspondingly absorb the multiplicative and the additive term of the scaling) of lasso to get the same result.

22.6 Nearest Neighbor Regression

Nearest neighbor works for regression as for classification, but uses average instead of majority:

```
template<typename X = NUMERIC_X, typename INDEX = VpTree<X, double, typename
    EuclideanDistance<X>::Distance> > class KNNReg
{
    mutable INDEX instances;
    int k;
public:
```

```
    template<typename DATA> KNNReg(DATA const& data, int theK = -1): k(theK)
    {
        assert(data.getSize() > 0);
        if(k == -1) k = 2 * int(log(data.getSize())/2) + 1;
        for(int i = 0; i < data.getSize(); ++i)
            learn(data.getY(i), data.getX(i));
    }
    void learn(double label, X const& x){instances.insert(x, label);}
    double predict(X const& x)const
    {
        Vector<typename INDEX::NodeType*> neighbors = instances.kNN(x, k);
        IncrementalStatistics s;
        for(int i = 0; i < neighbors.getSize(); ++i)
            s.addValue(neighbors[i]->value);
        return s.getMean();
    }
};
typedef ScaledLearner<NoParamsLearner<KNNReg<>, double>, double> SKNNReg;
```

As for classification, search can take ≈$O(n)$ time for large D. The algorithm is consistent for L_2 loss under the same conditions as for classification (Györfi et al. 2002). Same theoretical logic applies to selecting k. Kernels seem to be better at weighing neighbors (instead of using the average weights) because very distant examples take on ≈ the average value of all examples, not just the closest ones.

22.7 Regression Tree

A regression tree is like a decision tree, but tries to predict real-valued labels. This assumes that a piecewise constant function is a good approximation to the real function. A natural loss is the **sum of squared errors** (SSE), the minimizer of which is the average of y values. It's easy to update incrementally, which is essential for efficient split calculation.

As for classification, the idea behind pruning is that every subtree must be better than its root to not be pruned. This is checked by comparing squared errors using the sign test with the default z-score 0.25, which seems to be best experimentally.

```
struct RegressionTree
{
    struct Node
    {
        union
        {
            double split;//for internal nodes
            double label;//for leaf nodes
        };
        int feature;//for internal nodes
        Node *left, *right;
        bool isLeaf(){return !left;}
        Node(int theFeature, double theSplit): feature(theFeature),
            split(theSplit), left(0), right(0) {}
    }* root;
    Freelist<Node> f;
    double SSE(double sum, double sum2, int n)const
        {return sum2 - sum * sum/n;}
    template<typename DATA> struct Comparator
    {
        int feature;
        DATA const& data;
        double v(int i)const{return data.data.getX(i, feature);}
        bool isLess(int lhs, int rhs)const{return v(lhs) < v(rhs);}
        bool isEqual(int lhs, int rhs)const{return v(lhs) == v(rhs);}
    };
```

```
    void rDelete(Node* node)
    {
        if(node)
        {
            rDelete(node->left);
            f.remove(node->left);
            rDelete(node->right);
            f.remove(node->right);
        }
    }
    double classifyHelper(NUMERIC_X const& x, Node* current)const
    {
        while(!current->isLeaf()) current = x[current->feature] <
            current->split ? current->left : current->right;
        return current->label;
    }
    template<typename DATA> Node* rHelper(DATA& data, int left, int right,
        double pruneZ, int depth, bool rfMode)
    {
        int D = data.getX(left).getSize(), bestFeature = -1,
            n = right - left + 1;
        double bestSplit, bestScore, sumY = 0, sumY2 = 0;
        Comparator<DATA> co = {-1, data};
        for(int j = left; j <= right; ++j)
        {
            double y = data.getY(j);
            sumY += y;
            sumY2 += y * y;
        }
        double ave = sumY/n, sse = max(0.0, SSE(sumY, sumY2, n));
        Bitset<> allowedFeatures;
        if(rfMode)
        {//sample features for random forest
            allowedFeatures = Bitset<>(D);
            allowedFeatures.setAll(0);
            Vector<int> p = GlobalRNG.sortedSample(pow(D, 0.75), D);
            for(int j = 0; j < p.getSize(); ++j) allowedFeatures.set(p[j], 1);
        }
        if(sse > 0) for(int i = 0; i < D; ++i)//find best feature and split
            if(allowedFeatures.getSize() == 0 || allowedFeatures[i])
            {
                co.feature = i;
                quickSort(data.permutation.getArray(), left, right, co);
                double sumYLeft = 0, sumYRight = sumY, sumY2Left = 0,
                    sumY2Right = sumY2;
                int nRight = n, nLeft = 0;
                for(int j = left; j < right; ++j)
                {//incrementally roll counts
                    int y = data.getY(j);
                    ++nLeft;
                    sumYLeft += y;
                    sumY2Left += y * y;
                    --nRight;
                    sumYRight -= y;
                    sumY2Right -= y * y;
                    double fLeft = data.getX(j, i), score =
                        SSE(sumYLeft, sumY2Left, nLeft) +
                        SSE(sumYRight, sumY2Right, nRight),
                        fRight = data.getX(j + 1, i);
```

```
                    if(fLeft != fRight && //don't split equal values
                        (bestFeature == -1 || score < bestScore))
                    {
                        bestScore = score;
                        bestSplit = (fLeft + fRight)/2;
                        bestFeature = i;
                    }
                }
            }
        if(n < 3 || depth <= 1 || sse <= 0 || bestFeature == -1)
            return new(f.allocate())Node(-1, ave);
        //split examples into left and right
        int i = left - 1;
        for(int j = left; j <= right; ++j)
            if(data.getX(j, bestFeature) < bestSplit)
                swap(data.permutation[j], data.permutation[++i]);
        if(i < left || i > right) return new(f.allocate())Node(-1, ave);
        Node* node = new(f.allocate())Node(bestFeature, bestSplit);
        //recursively compute children
        node->left = rHelper(data, left, i, pruneZ, depth - 1, rfMode);
        node->right = rHelper(data, i + 1, right, pruneZ, depth - 1, rfMode);
        //try to prune
        double nodeWins = 0, treeWins = 0;
        for(int j = left; j <= right; ++j)
        {
            double y = data.getY(j), eNode = ave - y, eTree =
                classifyHelper(data.getX(j), node) - y;
            if(eNode * eNode == eTree * eTree)
            {
                nodeWins += 0.5;
                treeWins += 0.5;
            }
            else if(eNode * eNode < eTree * eTree) ++nodeWins;
            else ++treeWins;
        }
        if(signTestAreEqual(nodeWins, treeWins, pruneZ))
        {
            rDelete(node);
            node->left = node->right = 0;
            node->label = ave;
            node->feature = -1;
        }
        return node;
    }
    Node* constructFrom(Node* node)
    {
        Node* tree = 0;
        if(node)
        {
            tree = new(f.allocate())Node(*node);
            tree->left = constructFrom(node->left);
            tree->right = constructFrom(node->right);
        }
        return tree;
    }
public:
    template<typename DATA> RegressionTree(DATA const& data, double pruneZ =
        0.25, int maxDepth = 50, bool rfMode = false): root(0)
    {
```

```
        assert(data.getSize() > 0);
        int left = 0, right = data.getSize() - 1;
        PermutedData<DATA> pData(data);
        for(int i = 0; i < data.getSize(); ++i) pData.addIndex(i);
        root = rHelper(pData, left, right, pruneZ, maxDepth, rfMode);
    }
    RegressionTree(RegressionTree const& other)
        {root = constructFrom(other.root);}
    RegressionTree& operator=(RegressionTree const& rhs)
        {return genericAssign(*this, rhs);}
    double predict(NUMERIC_X const& x)const
        {return root ? classifyHelper(x, root) : 0;}
};
```

The runtime = that of decision tree.

22.8 Random Forest Regression

The only difference from classification is that use average instead of majority to combine:

```
class RandomForestReg
{
    Vector<RegressionTree> forest;
public:
    template<typename DATA> RandomForestReg(DATA const& data,
        int nTrees = 300){addTrees(data, nTrees);}
    template<typename DATA> void addTrees(DATA const& data, int nTrees)
    {
        assert(data.getSize() > 1);
        for(int i = 0, D = getD(data); i < nTrees; ++i)
        {
            PermutedData<DATA> resample(data);
            for(int j = 0; j < data.getSize(); ++j)
                resample.addIndex(GlobalRNG.mod(data.getSize()));
            forest.append(RegressionTree(resample, 0, 50, true));
        }
    }
    double predict(NUMERIC_X const& x)const
    {
        IncrementalStatistics s;
        for(int i = 0; i < forest.getSize(); ++i)
            s.addValue(forest[i].predict(x));
        return s.getMean();
    }
};
```

22.9 Boosting for Regression

As for classification, can use boosting to improve results, particularly of a regression tree. Use the gradient boosting version (see the "Machine Learning—Classification" chapter), so only change y, and don't need to resample. Given current F, want to find a for the last h such that $\sum(F(x_i) + ah(x_i)) - y_i)^2$ is minimal. The solution is $a = \sum(y_i - F(x_i))h(x_i)/\sum h(x_i)$ (Schapire & Freund 2012). For regression, boosting is intuitively similar to **Tukey twicing**, i.e., first do regression for y, then again for the errors.

```
template<typename LEARNER = NoParamsLearner<RegressionTree, double>,
    typename PARAMS = EMPTY, typename X = NUMERIC_X> class L2Boost
{
    Vector<LEARNER> classifiers;
    Vector<double> weights;
    double getWeight(int i)const{return 1/pow(i + 1, 0.501);}
    struct L2Loss
```

```
    {
        Vector<double> F;
        L2Loss(int n): F(n, 0) {}
        double getNegGrad(int i, double y){return 2 * (y - F[i]);}
        double loss(int i, double y){return (F[i] - y) * (F[i] - y);}
    };
public:
    template<typename DATA> L2Boost(DATA const& data,
        PARAMS const& p = PARAMS(), int nClassifiers = 300)
    {
        int n = data.getSize();
        assert(n > 0 && nClassifiers > 0);
        L2Loss l(n);
        RelabeledData<DATA> regData(data);
        for(int j = 0; j < n; ++j) regData.addLabel(data.getY(j));
        for(int i = 0; i < nClassifiers; ++i)
        {//find gradient, relabel data, fit learner, and update F
            for(int j = 0; j < n; ++j)
                regData.labels[j] = l.getNegGrad(j, data.getY(j));
            classifiers.append(LEARNER(regData, p));
            Vector<double> h;
            for(int j = 0; j < n; ++j)
                h.append(classifiers.lastItem().predict(data.getX(j)));
            double sumH2 = 0, weight = 0;
            for(int j = 0; j < n; ++j)
            {
                sumH2 += h[j] * h[j];
                weight += (data.getY(j) - l.F[j]) * h[j];
            }
            if(weight > 0 && isfinite(weight/sumH2))
            {
                weights.append(weight/sumH2);
                for(int j = 0; j < n; ++j)
                    l.F[j] += weights.lastItem() * h[j];
            }
            else
            {
                classifiers.removeLast();
                break;
            }
        }
    }
    double predict(X const& x)const
    {
        double sum = 0;
        for(int i = 0; i < classifiers.getSize(); ++i)
            sum += classifiers[i].predict(x) * weights[i];
        return sum;
    }
};
```

Can try RM weights instead of the optimal ones or RM fractions of optimal ones (instead of the implicit 1) if overfitting is a problem. Due to not resampling, an early termination due to 0 training error is likely and the default 300 trees may not be reached, which can give efficiency advantage over random forest.

22.10 Neural Network

The structure is similar to the one for classification, but with some changes:

- Cross-validate the number of hidden neurons. Quadrupling from 1 until 64 seems reasonable.
- Cross-validate the initial learning rate for SGD to not diverge. Use the same range as for online lasso.

- Don't use an activation function for the output unit.

```
class HiddenLayerNNReg
{
    Vector<NeuralNetwork> nns;
public:
    template<typename DATA> HiddenLayerNNReg(DATA const& data,
        Vector<double>const& p, int nGoal = 100000, int nNns = 5):
        nns(nNns, NeuralNetwork(getD(data), true, p[0]))
    {//structure
        int nHidden = p[1], D = getD(data),
            nRepeats = ceiling(nGoal, data.getSize());
        double a = sqrt(3.0/D);
        for(int l = 0; l < nns.getSize(); ++l)
        {
            NeuralNetwork& nn = nns[l];
            nn.addLayer(nHidden);
            for(int j = 0; j < nHidden; ++j)
                for(int k = -1; k < D; ++k)
                    nn.addConnection(0, j, k, k == -1 ? 0 :
                        GlobalRNG.uniform(-a, a));
            nn.addLayer(1);
            for(int k = -1; k < nHidden; ++k)
                nn.addConnection(1, 0, k, 0);
        }
        //training
        for(int j = 0; j < nRepeats; ++j)
            for(int i = 0; i < data.getSize(); ++i)
                learn(data.getX(i), data.getY(i));
    }
    void learn(NUMERIC_X const& x, double label)
    {
        for(int l = 0; l < nns.getSize(); ++l)
            nns[l].learn(x, Vector<double>(1, label));
    }
    double evaluate(NUMERIC_X const& x)const
    {
        double result = 0;
        for(int l = 0; l < nns.getSize(); ++l)
            result += nns[l].evaluate(x)[0];
        return result/nns.getSize();
    }
    int predict(NUMERIC_X const& x)const{return evaluate(x);}
};
struct NoParamsNNReg
{
    HiddenLayerNNReg model;
    template<typename DATA> static Vector<double> findParams(DATA const&
        data, int rLow = -15, int rHigh = 5, int hLow = 0, int hHigh = 6)
    {
        Vector<Vector<double> > sets(2);
        for(int i = rLow; i <= rHigh; i += 2) sets[0].append(pow(2, i));
        for(int i = hLow; i <= hHigh; i += 2) sets[1].append(pow(2, i));
        return gridMinimize(sets,
            RRiskFunctor<HiddenLayerNNReg, Vector<double>, DATA>(data));
    }
    template<typename DATA> NoParamsNNReg(DATA const& data):
        model(data, findParams(data)) {}
    double predict(NUMERIC_X const& x)const{return model.predict(x);}
};
```

```
typedef ScaledLearner<NoParamsLearner<NoParamsNNReg, double>, double, EMPTY,
    ScalerMQ> SNNReg;
```

As with classification, the runtime per example is O(W). With global optimization and properly chosen number of hidden units, neural network is consistent for L_2 loss (Györfi et al. 2002).

22.11 Feature Selection

As for classification, wrapper search with random forest is useful for selecting features:

```
template<typename SUBSET_LEARNER = RandomForestReg> struct SmartFSLearnerReg
{
    typedef FeatureSubsetLearner<SUBSET_LEARNER> MODEL;
    MODEL model;
public:
    template<typename DATA> SmartFSLearnerReg(DATA const& data,
        int subsampleLimit = 20): model(data, selectFeaturesSmart(
        RRiskFunctor<MODEL, Bitset<>, DATA>(data), getD(data),
        subsampleLimit)) {}
    double predict(NUMERIC_X const& x)const{return model.predict(x);}
};
```

22.12 Comparing Performance

When using average curved expStd, random forest seems to be the best A.

mqLasso	RegTree	RFRegTree	B_RF_Lasso	L2Boost	sKNNReg	mqNNcv
0.615	0.495	0.805	0.899	0.697	0.723	0.739

Combining it with lasso gives even better results at the cost of an extra cross-validation:

```
class SimpleBestCombinerReg
{
    BestCombiner<double> c;
public:
    template<typename DATA> SimpleBestCombinerReg(DATA const& data)
    {
        c.addNoParamsClassifier<RandomForestReg>(data, RRiskFunctor<
            NoParamsLearner<RandomForestReg, double>, EMPTY, DATA>(data));
        c.addNoParamsClassifier<SLasso>(data, RRiskFunctor<
            NoParamsLearner<SLasso, double>, EMPTY, DATA>(data));
    }
    double predict(NUMERIC_X const& x)const{return c.predict(x);}
};
```

22.13 Comments

For regression, costs matter too as an overestimate can be less or more expensive than an underestimate, but modeling this in a way that leads to efficient A is difficult.

Another interesting complexity measure is **fat-shattering dimension**, which, however, is more complicated and doesn't lead to a more useful upper bound (Mohri et al. 2012). It leads to a lower bound though, similar to the VC-dimension one (Anthory & Bartlett 1999). Nevertheless, that bound is also to be taken with a grain of salt because imposing extra conditions on G such as restricting number sizes usually automatically lowers any complexity measure.

Many classical methods such as polynomial and spline regression or wavelets don't scale beyond small D because the number of basis functions grows exponentially in D. See Hastie et al. (2009) and Györfi et al. (2002) for overview of such methods if curious. They have use cases for specialized domains, particularly for producing visualizations. Kernels are the only scalable way to use a rich basis set. Scalable methods essentially assume that the data lies on a small-D manifold and fit it adaptively.

Sparsity is an active research field (Hastie et al. 2015). Additional tricks for lasso include using a simpler formula for coordinate descent when features use mean-variance scale, and starting with the previous l solution to next problem when selecting l. But doing this with cross-validation is clumsy.

Ridge regression uses L_2 penalty, which also removes linear regression problems and has an analytic solution but doesn't lead to sparsity. Also, the analytic solution takes $O(\min(n, D)^3)$ time, which doesn't scale. Perhaps the biggest problem with lasso is that when have correlated variables it can select any of them. An interesting proposal to address this is **elastic net**, i.e., using a combination of L_1 and L_2 penalties. It also has an analytic solution, but have an extra combination weight parameter, and know less about it theoretically.

Kernel support vector regression (also called SVR) fits an ε-tube for some number ε in the enhanced feature space, instead of a line (Mohri et al. 2012). This gives sparseness in the number of support vectors because examples inside a tube can't be support vectors. But SMO-like solution is more complicated than the classification one (Liao et al. 2002), and cross-validation also needs to pick ε. All else equal, want small C, large y, and large ε.

Kernel ridge regression is a direct extension of ridge regression (Mohri et al. 2012). It also has an analytic solution, but again the $O(n^3)$ runtime doesn't scale. Also, unlike for ε-SVM, solutions aren't sparse in the number of support vectors. Likewise, using quadratic ε-loss gives less sparse solutions.

For a regression tree, many pruning criteria have been proposed, though fewer than for a decision tree. Cost complexity pruning also applies and is the main alternative. More powerful tests than the sign also apply but have some flaws—e.g., the normal difference assumes normality, and Wilcoxon signed rank symmetry around the median. The latter also needs extra $O(n)$ memory to rank the scores.

Can alternatively consider L_1 loss for the tree, whose minimizer is the median. It may be more robust than the average but not suitable for all cases, and its incremental calculation is a bit complicated. One way to do it efficiently is using a balanced search tree with subtree size augmentation, where the key is combination of absolute error and the number of the example (to allow nonunique items in the tree). For loss functions where calculation of the minimizer needs numerical minimization, efficient incremental calculation is impossible, and split calculation needs $O(n^2)$ time, which usually isn't worth any potential benefits.

An interesting alternative is a model tree with linear regression at the leaves that uses smoothing (Witten et al. 2011). But despite claims of outperforming a regular regression tree, it doesn't seem to have a use case:

- It's much less interpretable than a regular regression tree
- Random forest does smoothing better
- ∃some design flaws such as needing a smoothing degree parameter and to fit a linear model to leaves with few examples

For random forest, the original paper recommendation for the number of used features is $D/3$. But there seems to be no clear reason to prefer this over the more efficient $\sqrt{D}$, as for classification.

Currently !∃published comprehensive comparisons of modern regression methods based on many data sets.

An interesting application of regression is making very expensive simulations more efficient. E.g., consider designing a better car crash system, where a simulation is driving a car with dummy passengers into a wall. To save cars, create a regression model (called **surrogate model**), and optimize it to know which design parameter configuration to try next.

22.14 References

Györfi, L., Kohler, M., Krzyzak, A., & Walk, H. (2002). *A Distribution-Free Theory of Nonparametric Regression*. Springer.

Hastie, T., Tibshirani, R., & Wainwright, M. (2015). *Statistical Learning with Sparsity: The Lasso and Generalizations*. CRC Press.

Liao, S. P., Lin, H. T., & Lin, C. B. (2002). A note on the decomposition methods for support vector regression. *Neural Computation*, *14*(6), 1267–1281.

Mohri, M., Rostamizadeh, A., & Talwalkar, A. (2012). *Foundations of Machine Learning*. MIT Press.

Wikipedia (2013). Regression analysis. http://en.wikipedia.org/wiki/Regression_analysis. Accessed May 18, 2013.

Witten, I. H., Frank, E., & Hall, M.A. (2011). *Data Mining: Practical Machine Learning Tools and Techniques*. Morgan Kaufmann.

23 Machine Learning—Other Tasks

23.1 Clustering

Usually have a domain-specific distance function d to compare various x. Mathematically, clustering is an ill-posed problem with no clear:

- Guidance for selecting the number of classes k.
- Logical solution when user-specified k is too big/small; at best can split/join some groups.
- Choice between alternative groupings suggested by different features, even when k is correctly selected—e.g., group by height or by weight. Correct choice depends on domain knowledge. So feature selection is more important for clustering than for supervised tasks. Also, need to scale features to not give some an undue prior influence.

To humans, clustering in $D \leq 3$ tends to be easy visually. The process is all about picking out distinct shapes and concluding that some are similar. To A, even deciding if a set of examples forms one group or several is difficult without further info because, unlike a human, it can't use prior knowledge to decide the nature of the considered x and guess their relationship.

For $D > 3$, perhaps the only useful way to validate a cluster is to check how well-separated the groups are. But this too is ill-posed as need to define the exact criteria of how much distance is too much, or use some kind of relative distance of examples within groups vs distances of distinct groups, etc.

Despite these problems, some A can produce useful clusters from some data. Large amount of unlabeled data is cheaply and readily available, and discovering clusters in easily separable data automatically can be very valuable.

Clustering is very different from auto-encoding. Both are unsupervised, but the goal of clustering is not to reconstruct X but to group related x using reconstruction distance to do so in some cases. Also, for auto-encoding don't need to pick k.

Given k, d, and vector space X, ***k*-means** is simple and efficient:

```
1. To initialize, randomly assign points to clusters
2. Until converge or reach the iteration limit
3.     Calculate centroids of the current clusters
4.     Assign each point to the cluster of the closest centroid
```

For the iris data:

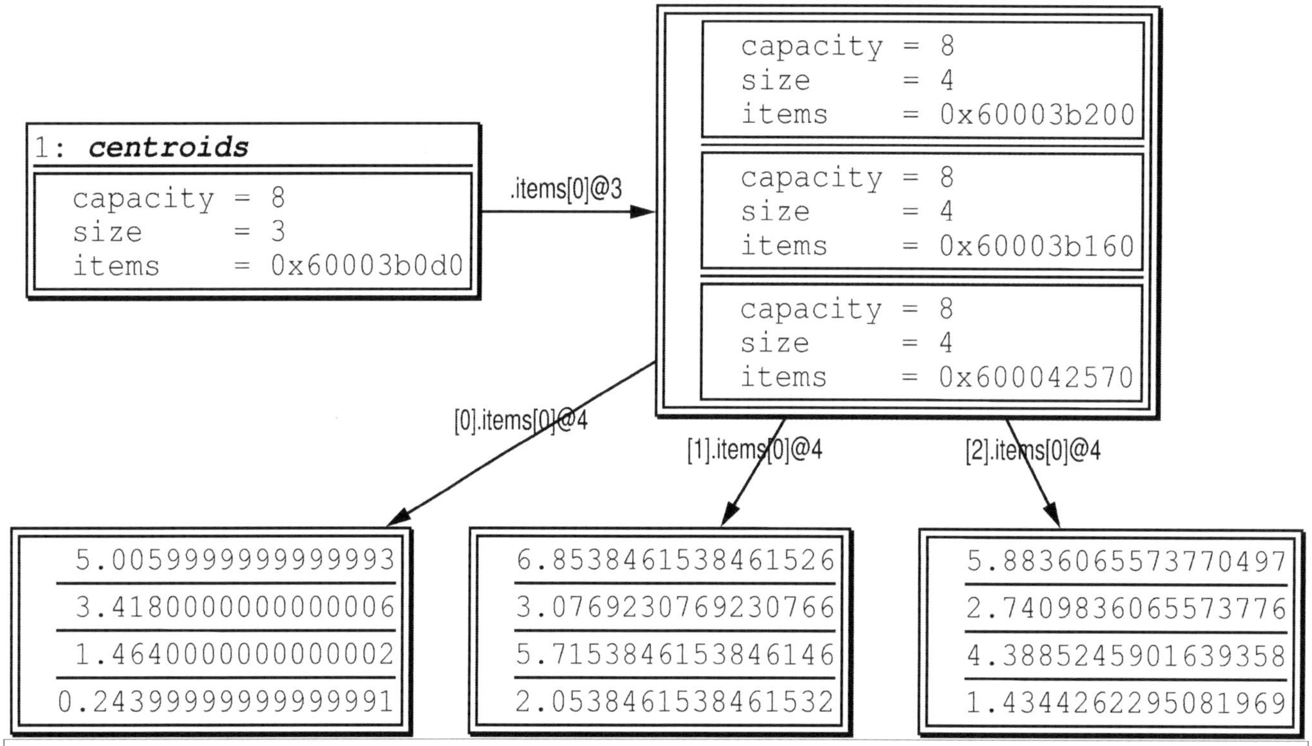

```
template<typename POINT, typename TREE = VpTree<POINT, int,
    typename EuclideanDistance<POINT>::Distance> > struct KMeans
{
    static Vector<int> findClusters(Vector<POINT>& points, int k,
        int maxIterations = 1000)
    {
        assert(k > 0 && k <= points.getSize() && points.getSize() > 0);
        //generate initial assignment
        Vector<int> assignments;
        //each cluster has at least 1 point, rest are random
        for(int i = 0; i < points.getSize(); ++i)
            assignments.append(i < k ? i : GlobalRNG.next() % k);
        bool converged = false;
        for(int m = 0; !converged && m < maxIterations; ++m)
        {//calculate centroids
            Vector<int> counts(k, 0);
            Vector<POINT> centroids(k, points[0] * 0);
            for(int i = 0; i < points.getSize(); ++i)
            {
                ++counts[assignments[i]];
                centroids[assignments[i]] += points[i];
            }
            for(int i = 0; i < k; ++i) centroids[i] *= 1.0/counts[i];
            TREE t;
            for(int i = 0; i < k; ++i) t.insert(centroids[i], i);
            //assign each point to the closest centroid
            converged = true;
            for(int i = 0; i < points.getSize(); ++i)
            {
                int best = t.nearestNeighbor(points[i])->value;
                if(best != assignments[i])
                {
                    converged = false;
                    assignments[i] = best;
                }
            }
```

```
        }
        return assignments;
    }
};
```

The most expensive operation is finding the closest centroids. This takes expected $O(nD\lg(k))$ time assuming efficient nearest neighbor search, but could be upto $O(nDk)$.

The greedy reassignment is a form of local search called **expectation maximization**, is guaranteed to converge to a local minimum, and usually does to quickly. But may need exponentially many iterations to converge (Russell & Norvig 2010). k-means suffers from high approximation error, in the same way as the nearest mean classifier. In particular, it can only distinguish well-separated shapes, but still not necessarily well because a small shape can take away support from a larger one:

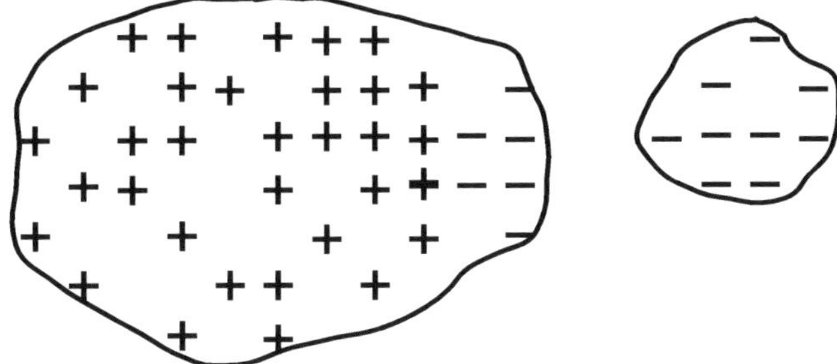

Finding optimal clustering in the same setup is equivalent to NP-complete facility location. It has an approximation algorithm, which can be used to replace random initialization, usually with more effective results (Arthur & Vassilvitskii 2007). But random initialization is simpler and allows checking stability by comparing results of various initializations.

Efficiency can too be improved in some ways (Drake 2013). E.g., one idea is that in later iterations few points change clusters, and it may be faster to maintain the centroids incrementally. Also, for larger k, better data structures can reduce the cost of centroid search, though k-d or VP tree are usually quite good.

Extension to nonvector X needs modifications such as ***k*-medoids** (Hastie et al. 2009), where the centroid is selected to be one of the points.

23.2 Reinforcement Learning

Want to find a **value-maximizing move picking policy** for an agent that moves in some **state space** and receives **reward**(state) on entering a state. The **value** of a state = E[the reward + the value of the state into which will move next] = E[$\sum$rewards over the picked sequence of states starting from the state]. An **episode** is sequence that leads to a terminal state. Rewards are **discounted**, so that reward r k states away is worth ry^k for $0 < y \leq 1$. For nonepisodic state spaces, $r < 1$ prevents $\sum$rewards $\to \infty$. This models many problems:

- Games like chess—any move sequence leads to checkmate or absence of material exchange for 50 moves. Also blackjack—take another card or not, given knowledge of played and held cards. A common r is 1 for a win, ½ for a draw, and −1 for a loss. An optimal reward-maximizing policy defines a perfect player.
- Control of complex systems such as autopilot. Possible settings of navigation and other controls define moves. !$\exists$terminal states, and rewards are danger and quality of performance signals.
- The **multi-armed bandit problem**. A bandit is a casino slot machine with many levers, each with unknown E[payout]. r is a payout after pulling a lever.
- Resource allocation. E.g., an investor perpetually chooses between cash and bonds with different interest rates, maturities, and default risks after every income event.

Simulation is the simplest and most general solution strategy. Given a state, from every next state generate many random episodes, and pick the state maximizing the average $\sum$sequence rewards. For nonepisodic tasks, run for a fixed number of moves or until r becomes too small.

For efficiency, give more simulations to promising moves based on the initial simulations. **UCB1 criteria**, after n simulations in a state, simulates move $i = \text{argmax}_i(\text{average}(i) + \sqrt{2\log(n)/n(i)})$ for rewards $\in [0, 1]$, where move i was simulated $n(i)$ times. For differently scaled rewards, the constant $\neq 2$. Any choice guarantees asymptotically optimal E[the loss of not making the best move discovered after n trials] $\forall n$ (Auer et al. 2000).

```
double UCB1(double averageValue, int nTries, int totalTries)
    {return averageValue + sqrt(2 * log(totalTries)/nTries);}
```

Applying UCB1 to more than one step doesn't change optimality (Kocsis & Szepesvari 2006), so after an episode, if have enough memory, store and update the averages and counts ∀visited state. Can discard saved information after committing a move.

23.3 Value Function Temporal Difference Learning

Another scalable approach is to create a function that assigns a value to every state and move to the max-value state. Value(current state) = reward(current state) + the average of observed value(next state) V_{next}. The incremental average update ave(n) = ave(n – 1) + (x_n – ave(n – 1))/n) gives $V_{current}$ += (reward + V_{next} – $V_{current}$)/n. The algorithm sets all V = 0 and repeatedly starts an episode from the initial state, picking the next state using current V and applying the update rule. It provably converges to values satisfying $V_{current}$ = reward + E[V_{next}] for the explored states (Russel & Norvig 2010). Changing the 1/n learning rate to slower-growing $n^{-0.501}$ or a constant such as 0.001 can converge faster. Making the initial values optimistic/pessimistic encourages exploration/exploitation and converges faster if the hint is useful. Converged values needn't be optimal if next state selection is greedy and doesn't explore. Using UCB1 or starting episodes from random states ensures convergence to optimal values.

```
template<typename PROBLEM> void TDLearning(PROBLEM& p)
{
    while(p.hasMoreEpisodes())
    {
        double valueCurrent = p.startEpisode();
        while(!p.isInFinalState())
        {
            double valueNext = p.pickNextState();
            p.updateCurrentStateValue(p.learningRate() * (p.reward() +
                p.discountRate() * valueNext - valueCurrent));
            p.goToNextState();
            valueCurrent = valueNext;
        }
        p.updateCurrentStateValue(p.learningRate() *
            (p.reward() - valueCurrent));
    }
}
```

For small state spaces, V is discrete and remembers the value of each state:

```
struct DiscreteValueFunction
{
    Vector<pair<double, int> > values;
    double learningRate(int state){return 1.0/values[state].second;}
    void updateValue(int state, double delta)
    {
        ++values[state].second;
        values[state].first += delta;
    }
    DiscreteValueFunction(int n): values(n, n, make_pair(0.0, 1)){}
};
```

For huge state spaces such as chess, V is an approximation. A linear combination of state features provably converges to the best possible linear approximation for a Robbins-Munro rate (Russell & Norvig 2010). Other representations such as a neural network can give better results, but may not converge.

```
struct LinearCombinationValueFunction
{
    Vector<double> weights;
    int n;
    double learningRate(){return 1.0/n;}
    void updateWeights(Vector<double> const& stateFeatures, double delta)
    {//set one of the state features to 1 to have a bias weight
```

```
        assert(stateFeatures.getSize() == weights.getSize());
        for(int i = 0; i < weights.getSize(); ++i)
            weights[i] += delta * stateFeatures[i];
        ++n;
    }
    LinearCombinationValueFunction(int theN): weights(theN, theN, 0), n(1) {}
};
```

Learning with a value function is similar to doing regression, but need a policy to assign the end goal value to intermediate states, and learn online for efficiency.

23.4 Finding Frequent Item Combinations

Recommendation systems such as Amazon show "customers who bought this also bought" items. A database records every purchase as a subset of **item ids**. Let n = max size of any **basket**. Any Choose(k, n) combination is **frequent** if it occurs in other baskets enough times.

Counting all combinations is a loop ∀ entry in the database ∀ combination. **Apriori algorithm** makes this feasible for large n by sorting items in a basket by id and including a combination if $k = 1$ or the last item and the combination of the $k - 1$ first items are frequent enough. It processes baskets in rounds, with round k considering k-combinations. Sorting ensures that combinations of $k - 1$ items are processed before combinations of k items.

```
struct APriori
{
    LcpTreap<Vector<int>, int> counts;
    void noCutProcess(Vector<Vector<int> >const& baskets, int nRounds)
    {
        for(int k = 1; k <= nRounds; ++k)
            for(int i = 0; i < baskets.getSize(); ++i)
                processBasket(baskets[i], k);
    }
};
```

Basket processing returns the number of added items so that the calling code can stop if nothing is added in the current round or adjust cutoffs.

```
    int processBasket(Vector<int> const& basket, int round,
        int rPrevMinCount = 0, int r1MinCount = 0)
    {
        int addedCount = 0;
        if(basket.getSize() > round)
        {
            Combinator c(round, basket.getSize());
            do//prepare current combination, needn't sort if each
            {//basket is already sorted
                Vector<int> key, single;
                for(int i = 0; i < round; ++i) key.append(basket[c.c[i]]);
                quickSort(key.getArray(), 0, key.getSize() - 1);
                int* count = counts.find(key);
                if(count) ++*count;//combination is frequent if already
                else if(round == 1)//frequent or round is 1
                {
                    counts.insert(key, 1);
                    ++addedCount;
                }
                else//combination is frequent if the last item and
                {//combination without the last item are both frequent
                    single.append(key.lastItem());
                    if(*counts.find(single) >= r1MinCount)
                    {
                        key.removeLast();
                        if(*counts.find(key) >= rPrevMinCount)
```

```
                        {
                            key.append(single[0]);
                            counts.insert(key, 1);
                            ++addedCount;
                        }
                    }
                }
            }while(!c.next());
        }
        return addedCount;
    }
```

23.5 Semi-supervised Learning

Want to classify using both labeled and unlabeled samples because labeling is usually expensive in human labor. So labeled data sets are almost never too large, unless some data is from labeling by an automatic source. But unlabeled data is usually plentiful. Though can train a predictor using labeled samples only, unlabeled samples might have useful information.

Unlabeled samples allow better estimation of the properties of the distribution on X. E.g., LDA estimates feature covariance matrix without using labels, so unlabeled samples improve it's estimate. But it's generally a poor classifier even with a good covariance matrix estimate. PCA dimension reduction also works without needing labels.

Another baseline approach is to cluster all samples and use a classifier trained on the labeled ones to classify them. This works well in many cases, but not when the clusters don't correspond to actual classes.

∃ several unsolved problems:

- Model selection is hard because it can base it's decision only on labeled samples.
- Experimentally, !∃ good black-box methods (Chapelle et al. 2006), unlike for supervised learning. Algorithm selection needs understanding the data.

23.6 Density Estimation

The task is to estimate a probability distribution, given samples from it. It's ill-posed in that $\Pr(x) = x \in$ data ? $1/n$: 0, so must give probability to $x \notin$ data, and at best can use something like ORM to find a simple way to do so.

Several algorithms have been useful for small D (Scott 2015):

- **Histogram**—partition X into a grid, and ∀ cell estimate its probability by the proportion of contained examples. To balance approximation and estimation errors, use o(n) cells. Can start the counts at 1 for smoothing. It's interesting to consider using a k-d or a VP tree to extend to large D by doing adaptive space partitioning. Then to estimate $\Pr(x)$, can walk the tree, and average the current node's example proportions.
- **Kernel density estimator** (KDE)—express the PDF as a sum of kernel functions, as for SVM. Typically use Gaussian kernel.

Without knowing the true density to be estimated, !∃ a good L for evaluation. So it's hard to compare estimates, even for picking parameters.

Taking into account how a density estimate will be used and solving that problem directly is better due to less estimation error and being less ill-posed. E.g., oB reduces classification to density estimation, but in practice solve the former directly. Theoretical aspects of density estimation are covered by Devroye & Lugosi (2001).

23.7 Comments

The iid assumption is very important for theoretical understanding of learning. Methods such as **active learning** (A learns online and picks the next example) violate it and thus weaken their theoretical guarantees considerably (at least with the current theoretical knowledge). Active learning must use a collection of unlabeled examples and ask one at a time to be labeled, and finding the best one may be inefficient. Simply generating examples has the problem that they needn't correspond to anything valid, e.g., an image that isn't a digit.

Transfer learning is another problematic model. The idea is that examples from one problem can help learning for another. This is true for humans, but hard to do efficiently and successfully for a computer.

Outlier detection is another difficult problem (Aggarwal 2013). It's very useful economically—e.g., any fraud activity such as with credit cards is an outlier relative to the usual transactions. A classic rule of thumb is to consider observations at more than 3 standard deviations from the mean outliers. This works only for normally distributed data, and even then using 3 is somewhat arbitrary. In general, at best can pick some small failure probability because it's hard to know without domain knowledge whether an example is an outlier or not.

Another model is **concept drift**, i.e., when the data distribution is changing—e.g., the chance of someone hitting a dart board in a correct place improves because the person is learning.

23.8 References

Aggarwal, C. C. (2013). *Outlier Analysis*. Springer.

Arthur, D., & Vassilvitskii, S. (2007). *k*-means++: The advantages of careful seeding. In *Proceedings of the Eighteenth Annual ACM-SIAM Symposium on Discrete Algorithms* (pp. 1027–1035). SIAM.

Chapelle, O., Schölkopf, B., Zien, A. (2006). *Semi-supervised Learning*. MIT Press.

Devroye, L. & Lugosi, G. (2001). *Combinatorial Methods in Density Estimation*. Springer.

Drake, J. (2013). *Faster k-means Clustering*. Baylor University.

Hastie, T., Tibshirani, R., & Friedman, J. (2009). *The Elements of Statistical Learning*. Springer.

Russell, S. J., Norvig, P. (2010). *Artificial Intelligence: a Modern Approach*. Prentice Hall.

Auer, P., Cesa-Bianchi, N., & Fischer, P. (2002). Finite-time analysis of the multiarmed bandit problem. *Machine Learning*, *47*(2–3), 235–256.

Kocsis, L., & Szepesvári, C. (2006). Bandit based Monte Carlo planning. In *Machine Learning: ECML 2006* (pp. 282–293). Springer.

Scott, D. W. (2015). *Multivariate Density Estimation: Theory, Practice, and Visualization*. Wiley.

Index

81805041R00230

Made in the USA
Middletown, DE
28 July 2018